14 *Iacobi Cornuti*
ORIGANVM FISTVLOSVM CAN.

American Gardens in the Eighteenth Century

"FOR USE OR FOR DELIGHT"

American Gardens in the Eighteenth Century

"For Use or for Delight"

BY

ANN LEIGHTON

with illustrations of the period

Houghton Mifflin Company

Boston   1976

Copyright © 1976 by Isadore Leighton Luce Smith

Library of Congress Cataloging in Publication Data

Smith, Isadore Leighton Luce.
    American gardens in the eighteenth century.

    Bibliography: p.
    Includes index.
    1. Gardening—United States—History.   I. Title.
SB451.S62   635'.0974   76–21621
ISBN 0–395–24764–0

Printed in the United States of America

A 10 9 8 7 6 5 4 3 2 1

DEDICATION

AS BEFORE, TO MY GRANDCHILDREN

Julia Herrick Macaulay Smith
Ann Leighton Macaulay Smith
Sarah Stuart Macaulay Smith
Patrick Eliot Macaulay Cain

AND NOW TO

Sarah Luce Smith
Jessica Chandlee Smith

Acknowledgments

THE LONGER A BOOK is in preparation, the more people there are to thank and the greater is the danger some may be overlooked. There is no true measure of one's indebtedness. A ready ear, a comforting laugh, children sorting file cards upon the floor, can rank with the most untiring zeal for unearthing references in rare book libraries and hours of retyping undecipherable notes. The chance gift of an invaluable book, a trip to a garden full of clues . . . what an abundance of friendly support appears from even unlikely sources. I am grateful for it all.

Most particularly, in this book's writing, am I grateful to my son Jim who, when a student, gave his father and me a handsome book for Christmas from that purveyor of all good books, Goodspeed's Book Shop. Twenty years later I based my research on this copy of Philip Miller's *Gardener's Dictionary,* edition of 1768, which exactly answers to all the allusions made by Lady Skipwith, Jefferson, Bartram and Washington, an inestimable aid in deciding what they meant in their garden lists.

And to my son Tom and his family for the traveling they have undertaken with and for me — Julia, Ann and Sarah always willing to look into yet one more bookshop or museum or garden, always good company. They welcomed me in London where my daughter-in-law Jane engineered innumerable trips to botanical parks and libraries. In Washington they hosted me while I took advantage of a Harvard Junior Fellowship at Dumbarton Oaks, which I owe to my most helpful and encouraging friend, Sidney Shurcliff's recommending me to the Dumbarton Oaks Garden Advisory Committee. I hope they will approve my use of their aid.

I am, as always, in debt to my horticulturally expert son-in-law, Tom Cain, for his advice and for his generosity in lending me my daughter, Emily, as a nurse as well as literary counselor. Their son, Patrick, has always added an encouraging note of his own. My daughter-in-law Kathy, eager gardener, brought Sarah Luce and Jessica, who made things gay.

Awards for total patience and encouragement go to the Goodales, Bob and Susie, the Fosters, Elizabeth and Max, the Pereiras, Marie and Felix, and to Sylvia Coolidge. Sigrid Hart and Margaret Austin contributed hours of gardening. To Elizabeth Newton I owe the list of Salem seeds.

Librarians in this country who helped beyond their duties are Muriel Cousins and Frances Dowd at the Massachusetts Horticultural Library; David McKibben at the Boston Athenaeum (where my record for keeping books out must exceed all others); Richard Wolfe at the Countway Library of Harvard Medical School, for Benjamin Franklin and Bartram; Stella Edwards of Allegheny College, for James Winthrop; Juanita Etter of the Ohio Historical Society, who sent me the requirements for settling Ohio; Anne Nuss of the Dumbarton Oaks Library, to whom I owe nearly all my illustrations and a great debt for assistance; Commander J. P. Dickson of both Dumbarton Oaks and the Library of Congress, who was able to produce books and answers to all my most urgent questions; and to the staff of the Rare Book Section of the New York Public Library and the staff of our Ipswich Public Library for producing a rare book each.

As for libraries abroad: I am totally indebted to the Botanical Library of the British Museum and the great Dr. W. T. Stearn for his many Open Sesames; to the Linnaean Society Library for Collinson's lists; to my friend Peter Green and the library at Kew for the little book where Furber explains his *Twelve Months of Flowers.*

I thank Vivian Endicott and the Danvers Historical Society for my introduction to the Endicott pear tree and its picture. And I am duly grateful to Bailey Bishop for coming through in the nick of time with a good copy of M'Mahon.

Here is the place to thank two indefatigable typists, Tiny Savory and Jane Langton, and all those anonymous myriad Xeroxers everywhere who have made it possible for me to have copies of the most remote books ready to hand.

I am glad to be indebted again to the Massachusetts Historical Society for help with the garden illustrations from Jefferson's letters. James M. Osborn has been most generous in allowing me to see and to use original material from his collection of the Spence papers in the Beinecke Library at Yale. Robert Fisher of Mount Vernon, who has made the restoration of the gardens there the best anywhere, was completely generous and helpful with his time and the records upon which he has based his restoration. William B. Hill, Director of the Roanoke River Museum at Prestwould House, was long my friend. To recreate Lady Skipwith's garden there with authentic material can be an important achievement horticulturally and historically.

I am particularly grateful to Professor and Mrs. Joseph Ewan for their friendly stimulation and especially for their masterful, entertaining and scholarly books, whose deep research and total accuracy restore confidence in one afraid to leave the path of primary research.

I am indebted to Caroline Sinkler Lockwood for information on Eliza Pinckney and Charleston generally; to John Bethell for information on his ancestor-in-law Manasseh Cutler; to Margaret Hopkins for the quote from "Mr. Addison" and for finding many missing links among the used books for the Yankee Bookstall sale for the Children's Medical Center in Boston; to Walter Edmonds for references to William Johnson in his part of the world in upper New York State; to Ruth Piwonka for the van Rensselaer garden; to my cousin-in-law Bernard Babington Smith for putting me on guard against careless errors and helping my discovery of Anne Grant by producing original letters and a portrait; to Charles van Ravenswaay for many assists, all welcome; to Homer White for Arabic medicine; to Rom Weatherman of Washington and Lee University for the portrait of John Custis with his tulip; to Louise Hodgkins for a hair-raising handbook on home and ship medicine; to Gordon de Wolf of the Arnold Arboretum for identifying two deep-southern plants by telephone (no mean feat); to my old schoolmate Tom Craig for helpful contributions of a medical-chemical nature; to Ralph and Gladys May, for the map — now the property of the Society for the Preservation of New England Antiquities — of the Rundlett-May garden I knew as a child and to Dr. William Wigglesworth and Dr. Francis Moore for skillfully hauling me over some major impediments to book-writing.

I thank my publishers, especially David Harris for cheerfully seeing me through yet one more book and Linda Glick for an attention to detail which affords an author undeserved credit.

And last of all, but actually first, I am grateful to those great American men who remain great: Washington, Adams, Jefferson, Franklin, all resourceful, wise, just and interesting, from whose accomplishments, even those so basic as the use of our natural resources, no one of even half their stature can detract.

Contents

Illustrations for American Gardens in the Eighteenth Century

FOR THOSE wishing to check the sources of the illustrations without consulting each one:

All the illustrations from Catesby, Curtis, Lettsom, Kaempfer, Parkinson, Furber, Bradley, Hills, Linnaeus, Mawe and Whately (except one) I owe to the Garden Library at Dumbarton Oaks. The Bartram and Prince Catalogues, the Oldmixon and Jefferson maps, the manuscript letters of John Clayton and some of John Custis I owe to the United States Congressional Library. For the portraits of Evelyn and Compton I am indebted to the National Portrait Gallery in London; for the portrait of John Custis, to Washington and Lee University; for the bust of Lady Skipwith and the little garden plans, to the archives of William and Mary College. The library of the Botanical section of the British Museum of Natural History provided me with Bartram and Collinson letters and lists and the slip from Dr. Fothergill. The Linnaean Society let me have Collinson lists and some letters to and from Collinson. The library at Kew Gardens provided me with the books by Furber and the Association of Gardeners, from which I took several frontispieces. Prestwould Foundation headquarters of the Roanoke River Historical Society let me have the Skipwith garden plan.

I owe to the American Antiquarian Society the reproduction of William Bartram's illustration for Dr. Schultz' essay on the Pokeweed, and the pictures of the Collinson-Custis correspondence.

The Massachusetts Historical Society, which many years ago let me have the Jefferson garden plan photographed from his letter, has kindly given me permission to use it now. The plan of the Rundlett-May House was furnished by the Society for the Preservation of New England Antiquities. The Rare Book Room of the Boston Public Library allowed me to have a photograph made of the page from Whately where Adams wrote the date of his visit with Jefferson. The three bees I use for the title page and for my bookplate are from an Italian seventeenth-century book in the library of McMaster University.

The Oxford Botanic Garden and the Chelsea Physic Garden kindly lent me plans and pictures of their layout. To the Jardin des Plantes in Paris I owe the picture of what was then the Jardin du Roi. Houghton Library at Harvard had pictures made for me of the Lawson map and beasts. The Danvers Archival Center gave me the picture of the Endicott pear tree. James M. Osborn allowed me to have the picture of the Spence garden plan from his collection of Spence papers in the Beinecke Library at Yale. The Boston Athenaeum allowed me to use the pictures from their copy of Watts' *Seats of the Nobility* to illustrate the garden tour made by Jefferson and Adams. The Rare Book Room of the New York Public Library furnished me with photographs of the Logan Garden Calendar. The firm of Shurcliff, Merrill and Footit professionally copied for me my sketches of the Skipwith flower bed plans. The Francis A. Countway Library of Medicine allowed me to take pictures of the Franklin edition of Short's *Materia Medica*. Friends who remain anonymous allowed me to use the plough design by Jefferson and the plans of the New Bern Governor's Palace Garden. The Ipswich Public Library produced a fine copy of Benson T. Lossing's illustrations of Mount Vernon in the nineteenth century. To Mount Vernon and Mr. Fisher I owe the plan of Mount Vernon in Washington's time. To the Massachusetts Horticultural Society I am indebted for the pictures of ploughs from Arthur Young's books on English farming.

As with *Early American Gardens* all the photographs made from my own material, and in many cases from the Boston libraries and societies, are the work of that expert photographer George Cushing.

List of Illustrations
in their Order of Appearance

xv

American Gardens in the Eighteenth Century
"FOR USE OR FOR DELIGHT"

Introduction:
Like Birds on a Gate

THE TURN of one century into the next is as arbitrary a way of marking time and defining history as the human mind can devise. Suddenly the flow of events, the change of seasons and fashions, the thinking, manners and motives of living creatures are cut, to go on again with a new label, a fresh beginning. To assume that each century will develop its own individuality, send out its own blooms and fruits, harbor its own blights and pests, cast its own shadows and patterns and colors upon all within its time-barriers compounds the falsity.

Yet, for the purposes of a history of gardening in a still New World, the division between seventeenth and eighteenth centuries falls as sharp and clear as any divider of time could desire. If we rotate our area for cultivation from a primitive New England in the seventeenth century to those still rather wild and disorganized colonies farther south on the Atlantic seaboard of eighteenth-century North America, the differences are nearly total.

We have seen New Englanders importing plants from the old country; adopting for their gardens what "Indian plants" they found useful, laying out their plots to furnish themselves and their neighbors with all possible household seasonings and medicinal aids and forgoing any postures of vanity or acquisitiveness or willful ostentation. We know their books and their backgrounds, their sages and advisers, their hopes and fears, their flowers and fruits.

From this rockbound society of determined saints and nation-build-ers in the north to the more heterogeneous colonists farther south, all so soon to be united by the end of the century, we find ourselves in a new and other world of landscapes, crops, gardens and people. Unlike each from each, these future states south of New England are more nearly alike than any one of them to New England. There, where the Puritan wave arrived with its charter, its minds, it souls and its seedlists all made up, the cord with the mother country was cut clean. Making their own remedies for everything from sins to sickness, New Englanders could afford to mark time, continuing in their own designs, until their fellow Americans had settled themselves in the ways of their individual origins and purposes and it became expedient to unite. We can leave New England to tend its gardens and await its future, and, with the same sorts of clues and probings, the same attention to stage backdrops and ornamental details, we can assemble quite new and different settings for the continuation of American garden history in the next century and farther south.

Quite naturally, at the beginning of the eighteenth century some of the seventeenth-century authorities are still very strong, notably John Parkinson and his two great books, *Paridisus in Sole, Paradisus Terres-tris* of 1629, and *Theatrum Botanicum,* of 1640. John Evelyn also still looms large, though this time we are less concerned with his dissertation on salads and more involved with *Sylva,* his great work on trees. The Old Testament is no longer the prime sounding board. John Locke surpasses John Milton as spokesman for the thoughts of those planning to shape their world. Writings of the time and place cease to be chiefly sermons and become lively contemporary accounts and histories, dia-tribes against commercial and agricultural matters, protests, pleas and proposals. Hebrew is forgotten as culturally useful, but Greek and Latin are still desired knowledge, although the purpose of familiarity with Greek and Latin is not theological but aesthetic and literary, especially useful to groping botanists seeking to communicate their dis-coveries.

Happily for us in our garden research, John Parkinson's listing of the Almighty's reasons for creating gardens for men embraces the two first centuries of gardening in the New World and divides neatly between the two. God, says Parkinson, when He created Adam, inspired him with the knowledge of all natural things: "What Herbes and Fruits were fit, eyther for Meate or Medicine, for Use or for Delight." The

first half of the phrase, "for Meate or Medicine," describes the gardening world of the seventeenth century in New England. "For Use or for
Delight" serves well for the gardens of the struggling settlements farther south as they develop and become colonies and, finally, states.

From the beginning, there lay the land in its great variety of contours,
qualities, conveniences and dangers. Unexplored, unplumbed, un-
ploughed, uncut, with areas and distances unguessed, it beckoned the
adventurous, the "curious," the landless, the persecuted and the greedy.
Belonging presumably to the Indians, it was graciously given away by
sovereigns in need of money, some parts of it over and over again. It
was taken up by nobles to whom the king was indebted, or hoped to be
so, or by small companies of financiers and overseers inspired by the
success of East Indian and Russian enterprises, or by undertakers of
settlements who proposed to put people on their own land for a small
annual tax or quitrent and then to sell to, and buy from, them. Some
nobles hardly knew what they had and forgot about it until others had
moved in and proved it practicable. Some companies sold out or failed,
and abandoned their plans and their people. Some individuals moved
in and onto land, taking it up obsessively at a rate far beyond their
powers to settle or to hold, gambling with it and losing it to other
equally land-mad individuals, who sought to consolidate their rights to
it with a little mill, a little mine, a small trading post in the wilderness.

Individual purposes in all this land-taking and land-holding differed
from grant to grant, from holding company to holding company.
Sometimes the land had already been settled: by Swedes used to lum-
bering, Dutch expert at trading, religious sects seeking only to live by
themselves. The tide of English migration rolled over them and assimi-
lated them into the new pattern, respecting them for what they could
contribute, disdaining them for their variety of nonconformities until
even that, too, could prove useful.

New England had stood firmly within itself and its self-conceived
rights. New York had been passed from hand to hand, from nation to
nation, always desirable, often fought for, secure in its natural advantages of a great navigable highway from its forests to its harbors. Finally it, too, became a gift from the king, this time to a brother who
presumably could be trusted to make it pay. Pennsylvania had been
graciously granted to William Penn collecting a debt owed his admiral
father. The Jerseys and Delaware were tokens of royal favor, as was
Maryland. It was only with reference to Virginia and the Carolinas that
the crown became finally and personally interested, eager to be directly
informed and as avid for returns as all the other owners, investors,
proprietors and exploiters. Farther south, Georgia represented a buffer

and was to receive its own commitments and purposes later and more slowly.

Whatever the settlements or agreements under which the tracts of land were given out or obtained or wrested from the previous owners, Indian or European, the first step for each and all was to get workers to start working. It was a seller's job and the selling had to be done in London, where there were the most people and available transportation. Each area, each arrangement, had its own promoters of varying degrees of fluency and rectitude. One who had never seen the place wrote two volumes. Others made quick visits, took up a bit of land or fastened onto a large landholder, and went home to promote their findings. Agents were sent over by powerful and monied interests to survey, map, advise, explore, spy and come home to write useful guides. Residents who had succeeded, loved the country, knew it well and wished to be heard above the tumult of false-findings wrote their own accounts. And some botanists, subsidized by "curious" stay-at-home scientists or by interested members of church, state or crown, came to collect specimens and record great quantities of plants and shells, beasts and birds never seen before.

Sometimes the entrepreneurs were hard put to decide whether to expand upon likenesses to the mother country, and similarities between all the plants and trees and ways of life, or to wax eloquent upon wonders never before imagined. Fortunately, a little of each was true. Those medicinally inclined found the New World plants had much the same effect upon "English bodies," as John Josselyn had said, as the plants they were accustomed to use at home. Whatever was most lacking at home, like pure water and fuel, was said here to be at their doors. One possible doorstep blessing, at least for those settling in Pennsylvania, was said to be a whale, useful indeed for keeping lamps alight, as the story of one washed ashore most graphically showed. What an opportunity to live where such a source of convenience could be deposited by tides running up from Chesapeake Bay. To one who had never seen a whale, the disposal problem would have seemed negligible, compared with the benefits.

The advancement of gardening in eighteenth-century North America began by being as indebted to religious principles, purposes and fervors as that of the seventeenth. Yet there was a basic difference. The gardens of seventeenth-century New England were the solution to living of settlers determined to set their holy city upon a hill in a wilderness. The gardens of eighteenth-century colonials had more worldly horizons. They were in closer communication with their patrons, forwarders and underwriters at "home." And they had an underlying consciousness that they were the outer rim of a westward expansion to which they could as yet detect no final boundaries. They had an exhilaration of imagination, geographically, that was lacking in the spiritual ambitions of their northern neighbors. New Englanders went as far north as would stop the French, as far south as would stop the Dutch and as far west as the White Mountains would stop them. And every one of their self-imposed boundaries was pricked with increasingly angry Indians. Farther south, in New York and Pennsylvania and Virginia, in the Carolinas and Georgia, the colonists' limits to expansion north and south were governed by negotiations with people not too unlike themselves. Expansion westward was a matter of defending what one believed to be, or hoped to make, one's own for future development. Here also, the danger was from hostile tribes of Indians, but here the burden was the greater since the Indians were openly supported and promoted by rival invaders of the New World, especially the French.

For the French had come early to the New World. As explorers to claim land for a New France, and as apostles to collect souls for Rome, they had suffered and surmounted great hardships, traveled far into the interior, descended great rivers and totally circumscribed later colonists by their command of the three great natural inner boundaries, the St. Lawrence, the Great Lakes and the Mississippi. Priests had moved in, planted their crosses, converted the Indians to at least an impressed respect for their symbols and their tenets and proceeded to organize the new lands for business. Living among the Indians, teaching them as much as would do them good in the world to come, both upon this earth and in the priests' heaven, these early missionaries were a wholly astounding group of dedicated, educated, capable men. Medicine, botany and warfare were side accomplishments to each individual's developing control of his particular bit of wilderness and the savages upon and about it. That they were fanatics, as easily carried away as their red neighbors, is provable; but that they were great men individually must not be denied. The Protestants, Dissenters, Puritans, Pilgrims, Quakers, Baptists, Church of England Conformists, German Lutherans and whatever nonreligious characters might be adhering to the above for personal gain were all alike to the priests. They were heretics, as depraved as the Indian savages and lacking the one literally saving grace that distinguished them from the Indians, of whom the French were able to make allies — the possibility of being converted.

It shocked the English settlers, whatever their religious backgrounds and impulses, to be confronted upon their troubled frontiers by hordes of Indians led by French priests in war paint. To the French priests this must have seemed a God-given opportunity to rid the land of infidels however directly encouraged, if not always protected, by a home government with no intention of yielding up one inch of soil to belligerents in the back-country, Indian or French.

While there was nothing quite like the migration wave of the early seventeenth century, which had deposited the Puritans to make a New England upon a very rocky coast, there were minor upheavals of similarly depressed and oppressed sects in a deeply disturbed homeland, which sent other groups looking for space in which they could be free from persecution by all except what they might consider natural enemies. And there was always the hope that perhaps the Indians did not necessarily have to be hostile, that fair-dealing might make them friendly, that perhaps the savage was basically truly noble and only mismanagement and misunderstanding had turned him against the white man, who was, after all, coming to educate him, to settle upon his land, develop his resources, improve his lot and push him farther back into the wilderness. Quakers, especially, saw themselves as exemplars of how to deal with the natives, and managed so well under the benign direction of William Penn at the end of the seventeenth century that well into the eighteenth century a Quaker in England who had never seen an Indian reproached a Philadelphia naturalist for being hesitant to ride into the back-country alone to collect seeds for English gardens.

Considering that the French had long held the northern waterways to the west and the great river complexes that joined all to the Gulf of Mexico, that the Dutch had built themselves into Chesapeake Bay and as far up the Hudson as they could profitably trade, and that the Spaniards were busily exploiting the warm everglades and jungles across the southern reaches, the English did well to squeeze in at all. And squeeze it was, however great the space and undignified the term. When William Penn asked for his grant from Charles II as payment of a debt owed his father for monies advanced the crown and services rendered, he had in mind a tract that should be heavily wooded, in recognition of the need for timber in a swiftly self-depleting island dependent upon ships. And with great, safe harbors. The intention was good on both sides, but due to other royal commitments, unfortunately to noblemen who had no intention of "going over" themselves, Penn found himself pushed up and inland. The Jerseys, East and West, with actual settlements of flourishing Swedes and good shipping, and Lord Baltimore's haven for *his* particular persecuted sect, made last-minute accommodations inevitable. William Penn finally laid out the city of Philadelphia, not upon the coast, but where two rivers joined to give him easy access to the sea. It was not quite what he had planned, but the splendid timbers of the upcountry forests and the beautiful shrubs and flowers abounding there, which he carefully noted, had to make up for no convenient sea-coast.

The more northern of the English colonies, whatever the terms of their inceptions, felt that close connections with the homeland were never primary concerns in their individual adventurings. Perhaps no one at home had expected any of them to be all that much of a success. Puritans and Quakers, Lutherans and Anabaptists, Dutch Reformers, Swedish freethinkers were all used to being laws unto themselves. Mutual love and understanding may have been sadly lacking, but cordiality between different persuasions was not then a way of the times. Even the great Lord Baltimore, seeking to find a refuge for Roman Catholics and going first to Virginia "to try how he liked the place," found "the people there looked upon him with an evil eye on account of his religion, for which alone he sought this retreat, and by their ill treatment discouraged him from settling in that county." From this on-the-spot account we learn that his lordship, "finding land enough up the Bay of Chesapeak," returned to England and "got a grant of the Proprietary of Maryland."

Of the many dividing lines between the northern and southern colonies, the most apparent division lay between those who were resolved never to look back and felt no pulls of indebtedness to the homeland and those less willfully prepared to be a law unto themselves, more consciously dependent upon their immediate origins and with every intention of maintaining close contacts with the mother country. These last were, in fact, true colonials.

Colonialism came late to the northern colonies and was not welcome. They had done well enough on their own. Even in Pennsylvania and New York they had little enough to thank the mother country for before it began demanding more from them than they felt was fair or proper. But farther south, in the great tidelands all the way to the Spanish borders, the people recognized themselves as colonials, happy to receive whatever succor was forthcoming from a rather harsh but ambitious mother, eager mainly for their successful exploitation.

One of the odder manifestations of the ability of Americans to make words mean what they want them to mean, or to attach themselves to a word used for convenience's sake and then to freight it with associations it does not bear outside this country, is our American use of the word "colonial" as pertaining to our own history. Hard as we all struggled not to be colonies, in spite of all the blood we shed to make us free of the colonial yoke, glorious as we have always felt that freedom to be, our use today of the word "colonial" in connection with our own past is somehow both glamorous and grateful. Today royal governors are reinstated in far greater than their original grandeur. More beautiful furniture than existed in an entire colony is imported and arranged in settings beyond any colonial governor's needs and dreams; indeed, well beyond limits that, if exceeded by himself, would have sent him home in disgrace. One of the worst criticisms of the royal governors at the time was that they had come primarily to make or recoup their own fortunes while making sure that the crown received all possible revenues for itself. Ostentation was chiefly prized by successful colonials. It shows, perhaps, republican zeal on our part to transfer possible reproaches for ostentatious overstrain to the governors, now so cordially celebrated.

From Maryland and Virginia through the Carolinas and down to the still unsettled Georgia, sleeping like a guardian alligator between the Carolinas and the Spaniards, the whole outlook and way of life was purely colonial. Georgia, teeming with creatures and plants later to be discovered by the Bartrams, festooned with trees and flowers of unbe-

Cartouche from Peter Jefferson's and Joshua Fry's map of Virginia, Maryland, Pennsylvania, New Jersey and North Carolina. 1775. Showing the Commissioners of Trade and Plantations the chief export from that part of the world.

lievable brilliance, its uplands covered with pine, its lowlands full of crawling bogs, was largely unknown at the end of the seventeenth century. South Carolina was still almost a colony of a colony, what was hoped to serve as a healthful retreat for the planters of Barbados, then England's largest and most prosperous colony on the eastern seaboard. North Carolina with its almost untouched uplands lay close to Virginia with overlapping boundaries and needs and urgencies. And overlooking them all was the greedy crown, needing revenue.

It may have been due to the comparative mildness of the Indians of these more southerly parts, to their being less warlike and more inclined to crop-growing than the warriors to the north. They may have looked with a more innocent hopefulness toward the taking over of their superfluous lands by white men, from whom, after all, they had already acquired, but not in great quantities, two of their mainstays to existence, peaches and pigs. In any case, it was from the Indians that these early southern settlers received the key crop that would unlock gold from the poor red soil. Tobacco.

But it was not from the Indians that the settlers would obtain the labor they needed to grow a paying crop, for which they had to give up all their small self-supporting farms and their hopes for being happily independent and free. Slaves were offered them, and they became themselves enslaved.

Furber's Flowers for the Month of January

1. Pellitory with daisy flowers S
2. **Winter Aconite F E**
3. Great Early Snow Drop B
4. Single Snow Drop F E
5. White edged Polyanthos B
6. Double Peach-coloured Hepatica F E
7. Double Blue Violet S E
8. Winter Blue Hyacinth B
9. Lesser black Hellebore B
10. Dwarf white Kingspear G
11. Ilex-leaved Jasmine S
12. Red Spring Cyclamen G
13. Acacia or sweet button tree S
14. White Cyclamen G
15. Creeping Borage or Bugloss S E
16. Striped Spurge B
17. Lisbon Lemon tree G
18. Canary Campanula S
19. Dwarf Tithymall G
20. Double Stock G
21. Filberd tree in flower T
22. True Venetian Vetch B
23. Seville Orange G
24. Grey Aloe
25. Winter white Hyacinth B
26. Spotted Aloe G
27. Narrow Curled-leaved Bay G
28. Tree Savory G
29. Triangle Yellow Ficoides
30. Striped Orange G
31. Striped Candy tuft G
32. Tree Sedum G
33. Single blue Anemone B

1 "All Was Virginia"

VIRGINIA was where everyone had always meant to go in the first place, Pilgrims and Puritans not excepted. The only early choices, as advertised by Sir Walter Raleigh, had been between Virginia and Guiana. And by "Virginia" Raleigh had meant more or less what we mean by Virginia today, William Byrd II notwithstanding. No one in his senses had ever wanted to go to New England. The fair promises of Virginia, however, had not worked out. They had not worked out because the people who first went there had not worked out. Time after time attempts were made to make a settlement that would really settle. Time after time it had proved not what the settlers were up to or looking for, and those who survived went home. And yet Virginia was the part of the New World that most closely held the attention of the Old, from the settlement of which much could be hoped, that seemed most deserving of royal promotion.

There were those who, by the end of the seventeenth century, had succeeded in managing both the country and the climate, small landholders who supported their families on their own acres by their own labors. There were also traders with the Indians who ran their boats and pack-horse trains up and back, to and from interiors of potential horticultural richness. The first Randolphs were independent small landholders come to support themselves and raise families in the New World. The first Byrd and the first Carter were traders, merchants of trifles to be traded for whatever they could get from the Indians. The independent early farmers settled as far apart, each from each, as was possible, needing to be separate from each other to make sure of having land to spread into when the first land "ran out." The soil was not naturally rich. Lacking manure, the farmers had not even supplies of fish to dig into the ground. The only profitable system was always to move out and on. Neighbors were near enough several miles away up or down the riverways, which served as roads. With every man on his own land near a river, there was no need for city settlement. Traders who dealt with contacts reaching far into the back-country, reaping rich rewards for their trinkets and pots, could see bright futures for themselves as landholders. Indentured servants brought from England realized hard-earned dreams of independent small farms and moved, for freeholdings, farther into the interior. The early traders began to take up large tracts of land, which they proposed to settle with their own people to create their own small profitable worlds, in touch with the mother country for all they might not be able to supply for themselves, and with something beyond furs and free land to make things attractive. What was needed was a marketable crop . . . a marketable crop and labor to till, sow and reap it. This was the problem upon the solution of which depended the futures of all the colonies to the south of those with natural deep harbors, great forests and hard-minded, hand-laboring settlers.

Travelers in, and reporters of, seventeenth-century Virginia had not been lacking before the eighteenth century. From glowing accounts written for Sir Walter Raleigh and the later, more realistic, comments of Captain John Smith, from simple diaries of simple seamen and less credible accounts of those who saw what they had come to see, monsters and all, English booksellers had put out rather a lot of material on Virginia.

For Virginia had figured largely even on the London stage. In 1691, in London, appeared a play by Mrs. Aphra Behn, noted playwright, born in Surinam of English parents, novelist, poet and spy in France for Charles II. Called *The Widow Ranter, or Bacon in Virginia,* Mrs. Behn's play had plenty of local color. Produced in Drury Lane after her death, it gave a popular picture of Virginia. It must, in fact, have given some Virginians quite a turn. One can imagine their leaving the theater determined to create on their own the stereotype of the Virginia gentleman, with which noble motive, after reading the play, one cannot sympathize too much.

Captain John Smith had gone on to do what he could for New England after Virginia had very nearly finished him. With that in mind, he made a moving plea to the English gentry to send their "spare kindred," a cry from the heart. But more and more graphic accounts

New Map of North America, 1708. From Oldmixon's *British Empire in America*

began to shoulder his book and each other off the shelves, each containing more or less of the supposed facts from all previous volumes.

Contemporary histories and accounts are often of most value because of imperfections and omissions. The space allotted to each subject shows its estimated importance. Denials and minimizations of drawbacks are revealing. Even an account by one who has never seen the place he is writing about shows the prejudices of the world from which he views his subject. As see *The British Empire in America,* a work in two volumes, by John Oldmixon, published in London in 1708.

The first volume gives us "Newfoundland, New-Scotland, New England, New York, New Jersey, Pennsylvania, Maryland, Virginia, Carolina and Hudson's Bay." There is a map that makes the area seem very busy — Florida enormous and full of rivers; Virginia, with only the James River, looking rather squeezed in with Carolina, between Lake Erie and the ocean. Maryland, Pennsylvania and New York are strung in a line up the coast to New England. The St. Lawrence and a tract of land called "Iroquois" mark the western boundaries. Above New England lie New Scotland and Newfoundland and, brooding largely over all, is a huge Hudson's Bay. The whole has a promising appearance. Indeed, Oldmixon felt very sanguine about it all, considering he had never seen the place. The second volume is about islands: Barbados, chiefly; Jamaica in part; and a few smaller islands and projects in the Caribbean.

He had, however, he says, read a great deal and talked with anyone who would talk to him, discounting, of course, any overenthusiastic accounts or the descriptions of those who appeared to wish to sell their province as superior. As half the first volume is devoted to Virginia, it is easy to see where his friends came from.

When he had to rely upon reading, he acknowledged his sources: Cotton Mather, for instance, is his authority for New England. The *Magnalia* had just been published and Oldmixon had obviously been put off by distaste for the style and personality of the author. Oldmixon took what history he could and was glad to be "leaving his Puns, Anagrams, Acrosticks, Miracles, Prodigies, Witches, Speeches, Epistles and other Incombrances to the original author and his admirers, among whom, as an Historian this writer is not so happy as to be ranked."

We may suspect Oldmixon gave as short shrift to accounts of other places until he let himself go, on and for Virginia. Here he borrowed lavishly from all accounts, written and spoken, and admittedly from writings shown him before publication by those to whom the manuscripts had been sent. (This made for later recriminations, when he described Indians at firsthand.) He claims to have known William Byrd II, and to have been shown by him the history in manuscript by Byrd's brother-in-law Robert Beverly. In London at the time and writing *his* firsthand history, Beverly was shown Oldmixon's manuscript by the publishers, for corrections, and disapproved of Oldmixon's inaccuracies. Oldmixon then added insult to Beverly by crediting Byrd with the information he had gained. Beverly's book came out ahead, in the end, with several editions in French and a second English edition.

We can be grateful to Oldmixon for showing us the relative importance of each American colony as seen from London in the beginning of the eighteenth century. Obviously the most favored points for fortune-making were Barbados and Virginia. South Carolina had her origins from Barbados. North Carolina, with no deep harbors of her own, and, shut off from the sea by her low-lying outer beaches, still awaited development from north and south rather than from the sea like the other colonies. Virginia loomed large. "In the beginning all was Virginia" is a sentence and sentiment used by both Oldmixon and William Byrd II, one likely to appeal to a good Virginian.

That epitome of all Virginia gentlemen, William Byrd II, gave his own view of the settling of Virginia. He introduced his personal version to "clear the way" for his account of surveying the dividing line between Virginia and North Carolina, which he was commissioned to do in 1727, a commission he much enjoyed. As well as the official *History of the Dividing Line,* Byrd wrote the *Secret History of the Dividing Line,* full of scurrilous observations about his fellow workers, both Virginian and North Carolinian. This "secret" he seems to have been happy to hand out among his friends, along with the official history, which is full of dignity and information. It is in the preface to the official document that he is impelled "to clear the way" by showing how all the other British colonies on the mainland had, one after the other, been carved out of Virginia "by grants from His Majesty's royal predecessors."

He begins sweepingly:

All that part of the northern American continent now under the dominion of the King of Great Britain and stretching as far as the Cape of Florida . . . went first under the general name of Virginia . . . the first settlement in this fine country . . . owing to that great Ornament to the British Nation, Sir Walter Raleigh . . . who invited sundry persons of distinction to share in his Charter and join their Purses with his in the laudable project of fitting out a Colony in Virginia.

When Raleigh's "good friends," Amidas and Barlow, dropped anchor and went ashore upon "an island now called Colleton . . . set up the arms of England . . . and kindly invited the neighboring Indians to trade with them," this voyage was such a success, with a thousand percent profit on the return cargo (which included "some of the bewitching Vegetable Tobacco"), that it created a "modish Frenzy" to take "a trip to America." Volunteers, however, were easier for the Company to collect than money. "Idle and extravagant," they were soon "starved or cut to pieces by the Indians." "The Itch of sailing to this New World" was thus allayed until, in 1606, the Company invited the Earl of Southampton, with several other "Persons eminent for their Quality and Estates," to join with them, and one hundred men embarked, "most of them Riprobates of good Familys" or relations of members of the Company.

This more promising group landed at the mouth of the James, where their settlement "stood its ground from that time forward," due to Captain John Smith's efforts to hold together those members who quarreled incessantly and those who "looked upon all Labour as a Curse."

They were reinforced the next year by "fewer gentlemen and more Labourers, who, however, took care not to kill themselves with over-work." Byrd introduces his possible solution: intermarriage with the Indians. Had the English not "disdained to intermarry," had they truly intended either to civilize or convert "these gentiles," they should have "brought their Stomachs to embrace this prudent Alliance . . . The poor Indians would have less reason to complain that the English took away their land had they received it by way of Portion with their daughters . . . A sprightly lover is the most prevailing Missionary that can be sent amongst these or any other, Infidels . . . If a Moor may be washt white in three Generations, Surely an Indian might have been blanched in two." These points had originally been made by Robert Beverly in 1705, though in a less sprightly manner.

Returning to clearing, Byrd says about this time New England was "pared off from Virginia" by a grant obtained by a group of gentlemen in Plymouth led by Lord Chief Justice Popham, and about the year 1620 "a large Swarm of Dissenters fled thither," founded a small town called New Plymouth and, though they had "many discouragements to Struggle with . . ." they "by Degrees Triumphed." Brethren flocked over so fast that the colony became thronged with large detachments of "Independents and Presbyterians who thought themselves persecuted at home." These, though, "ridiculed for some Pharisaical Particularities in their Worship and Behaviour . . . were very useful subjects, giving no Scandal or bad Example. By which excellent qualities they had much the Advantage of the Southern Colony . . . For this Reason, New England improved much faster than Virginia."

Byrd rushes on:

Another Limb lopt off from Virginia was New York . . . but what wounded Virginia deepest was the cutting of Maryland from it . . . Soon after the Reduction of New York the Duke was pleased to grant out of it all that Tract of land included between Hudson and Delaware Rivers to the Lord Berkeley and Sir George Carteret . . . So soon as the Bounds of New Jersey came to be distinctly laid off, it appeared there was still a Narrow Slip of a Land, lying between that Colony and Maryland. Of this, William Penn, a man of much worldly wisdom and some Eminence among the Quakers got early notice . . . The Quakers flocked over to this Country in shoals . . . not a few of good substance who went vigorously upon every kind of improvement . . . by Diligence and Frugality, for which this Harmless Sect is remarkable . . . they have in a few years made Pensilvania a very fine Country.

He skips over dismembered Virginia to describe its southern neighbors:

Both the French and the Spaniards had . . . long ago taken Possession of that Part of the Northern Continent that now goes by the Name of Carolina . . . Finding it produced neither Gold nor Silver . . . they totally abandonned it . . . King Charles the 2d finding it a Derelict, granted it away to the Earl of Clarendon and others . . . March the 24th, 1663.

The boundaries of his Virginia now having been drawn, Byrd launches into his concurrent accounts of his experiences with the maligned North Carolinians. This is obviously written for posterity, in the manner of many English letters of the period of his youthful upbringing in England. At the time of his expedition through "the Dismal" Byrd was fifty-four years old. We shall see more of him later. At the moment, his early history serves as a colorful and broadly brushed backdrop.

For us and everyone else, the most valuable and reliable mine for information on Virginia for the next hundred years — is Byrd's brother-in-law's book, *The History and Present State of Virginia . . . By a Native and Inhabitant of the Place,* published by R. Parker at the Unicorn under the Piazzas of the Royal Exchange in 1705. A handsome frontispiece showing the coat of arms of Virginia has a discreet little script at the base attributing the authorship to "R. B. Gent."

And obviously the coat of arms of Virginia set a seal upon the opinions of William Byrd II and many other Virginians. On a quartered shield are shown the four coats of arms of England, Ireland, Scotland and Wales. The Latin motto on a ribbon at the base of the shield reads, in translation, "And Virginia makes five."

Robert Beverly is a true Virginian, modest and industrious, devoted to the promotion of the country. He had married the elder sister of William Byrd II when she came home from her English upbringing in her mother's early home in England. She died in childbirth and Robert Beverly never married again. He brought up their son to be a Virginia planter, successful and exemplary, while he lived simply on a plantation furnished by his own workmen from his own lands.

Published in the year 1705, his is a careful analysis of the state of Virginia at the beginning of the eighteenth century. In four parts it deals with the history of the first settlements and their governments, the natural productions of the country with a view to trade, the native Indians and their customs and the present state of the country as governed and improved. We are greatly indebted to this modest "Native and Inhabitant of the Place, R. B. Gent."

In laying forth all its advantages and disadvantages, he would seem to have no motive beyond love of his country. Financially interested in bringing over indentured servants, he drew a picture of the other Virginians and their work habits that makes one consider this venture a

Catesby's Plate A-20, *"Pseudo Acacia hispida"* with the now extinct Woods Buffalo, a regular part of William Byrd's diet when he was laying out the Dividing
Line through the Great Dismal

charitable enterprise. For himself, he is a sincerely American citizen, long before there was an independent country to embrace him. He saw the relationship between himself, other ambitious Virginia planters and the greedy crown in a prophetic light. He recognized the concentration on growing tobacco as a "disease," and foresaw the dangers of reliance upon slave labor.

Beverly begins his book, however — lest we expect him to be beyond all human faults and prejudices — with a diatribe against all royal government, reserving praise only for Sir William Berkeley, with whom Beverly's father had been loyally associated. To Berkeley goes credit for trying "to set a useful example at home by the Essays he made of Pot-Ash, Flax, Hemp, Silk, etc." Berkeley had gone to England to wait upon Charles II and returned with "pressing instructions for encouraging the People in Husbandry and Manufactures, but more especially to promote Silk and Vineyards." Prizes were to be given for the best pieces of linen and woolen cloth, and "a Reward of Fifty Pounds of Tobacco . . . for each pound of Silk." All persons were enjoined to plant mulberry trees for "Food of the Silk-worm . . ." Suggestions for such industries as would benefit trades in England, such as salt-making and shipbuilding, wine-making and silk-weaving, were "kindly encouraged." Beverly resolved to illustrate the possibilities of home industry by forgoing English artifacts imported by his peers in payment for their tobacco and settled himself to make his own furniture on his own plantation.

Beverly, however, is always unforgiving of the spirit in which royal governors were visited upon the planters, and he ticks off each one with condemnatory phrases: "made use of," "as great an Affection for Money as his Predecessor," "without Respect either to the Laws of the Plantation, or the Dignity of his Office," "under his Despotick Administration." A New Englander can feel pleasure in hearing from Beverly that Andros, who had so irked the Puritans in New England that they turned him out, ran true to form in Virginia, where, "he was likewise frequently pleased to say, they had no Title to their Lands, for a Reason which neither himself, nor anybody else knew. These things caused great Heart-burnings." Andros did, however, encourage fulling-mills and the planting of cotton, and is also credited with good will toward the college proposed by the Reverend James Blair and approved as "a pious design of the Plantation" by their majesties, William and Mary. Also, as we know, encouraged by that great gardener, London's Bishop Compton.

Beverly ends his first section with an account of affairs under Francis Nicholson in 1689, upon whom Beverly shipwrecked his future as a public servant by stating flatly that it was "the constant Maxim of this Gentleman to set the People at Variance as much as possible amongst themselves." William Byrd II had been impressed to represent Virginia's case in England. Initially, the idea had been to protest having to send troops from Virginia to defend New York. Aided by Beverly, who turned up in London to help him, they also attacked, before the Board of Trade, the governor's policy of discouraging manufacture of cloth. Beverly claimed Nicholson apparently intended the colonists to "go naked," a point he considered telling, but as the merchants and clothiers in London felt the prohibition a good idea, Byrd and Beverly both lost their jobs in the colony.

Byrd recovered his career in Virginia politics, but Beverly returned to retirement and re-editing his history for a later edition, in which he modified his opinions of royal governors, took out his lyric description of the Byrd summerhouse at Westover, redid his thoughts about noble savages being quite so noble and in other ways spoiled the fine and, literally, careless rapture of the first edition.

Beverly had embellished his Indian section with illustrations drawn from those made by the artist John White for Sir Walter Raleigh and engraved by Theodore deBry of Frankfort for Hariot's *Briefe and True Report of the new found land of Virginia,* published in 1588. Beverly selected the pictures best illustrating his text, and explained each drawing with the Indian names. Sometimes he quotes Captain John Smith. Occasionally he corrects often-borrowed versions, as when Beverly says the Indian name for Indian medicine is "wisoccan," mistaken for the name of a particular root, an error handed on to and by the great John Parkinson.

Beverly's acknowedged authorities on the Indians, apart from his own firsthand observation, are the accounts of French priests and English explorers, taken from their books or records published by Purchas. Beverly feels the French accounts take great license, possibly because of "the strong Genius of that Nation to Hyperbole and Romance. They are fond of dressing up everything in their gay Fashion, from a happy Opinion that their own Fopperies make any subject more entertaining." The English, Beverly finds, "invest more within the Compass of Probability and are contented to be less Ornamental, while they are more Sincere."

There are only a few references in Beverly's Indian section that concern gardeners. "Puccoon" is a word we shall meet often, described by Beverly as "a kind of Anchuse or yellow Alkanet." Mixing it with the root of the wild angelica and bear's oil, the Indians made an ointment with which they anointed themselves, "capapee," after bathing. This

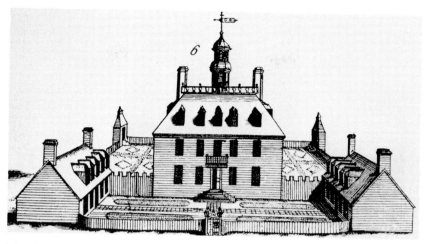

The Governor's Mansion, Williamsburg. About 1740. From Arthur A. Shurcliff's *Gardens of the Governor's Palace Williamsburg*

ointment also served as a protection against "all Lice, Flease, and other troublesome Vermine," with which "by reason of the nastiness of their Cabbins" they would otherwise be infested. Their priests refused to divulge any cures except those that must be immediately applied, far from a priest's help, such as "Rattle-Snake-Root."

"Their cookery has nothing commendable about it," says Beverly, "but that it is performed with little trouble. They have no other sauce but a good stomach . . . They boil, broil or toast all the meat they eat, and it is very common with them to boil Fish as well as Flesh with their Homony. This is Indian corn soaked, broken in a Mortar, husked and then boiled in water over a gentle fire for ten or twelve hours to the consistency of a Furmity. The thin of this is what my Lord Bacon calls Cream of Maise, and highly commends for an excellent sort of Nutriment." This, we can see, is the origin of many American dishes throughout the centuries. Other methods of cooking have also come down to us. "They have two ways of Broyling, viz. one by laying the Meat itself upon the Coals, the other by laying it upon Stocks raised upon Forks at some distance above the live Coals; which heats more gently and dries up the Gravy: this they, and we also from them, call Barbacueing."

Beverly's Indians, he says, do not know the "sweet juice of Maple," said to be drunk with water by Indians to the north. They bake bread in holes in the ground, and make it of Indian corn, wild oats and sunflower seeds. Their great treat is green Indian corn roasted on the ear, and to

Tradescantia virginica (Virginia Tradescantia or Spiderwort). One of the first flowers to be taken to English gardens. Curtis *Botanical Magazine*

prolong the corn season they collect varieties of "all the several sorts." Peaches, strawberries, "cushawes," melons, pompions and macocks they have growing near their towns. They "lay by" and preserve peaches by drying them. They grow several sorts of beans and eat all sorts of peas and other pulse. They cook the fruit of a kind of arum, which looks like boiled peas, and dig earthnuts. Onions and a tuberous root called "tuckahoe," of a "hot and virulent quality," grow "like Flagg in the Marshes." Nuts they gather and make a drink by pounding the nuts of the hickory "so that they call our milk Hickory." Apart from these vegetable matters, we are told, they skin and "paunch" all quadrupeds, pluck their fowl, but eat their fish without gutting and with the scales on, throwing away scales, entrails and bones afterward. Curiously enough, they eat no leaves or "any sorts of Herbs."

Beverly's section devoted to "The Natural Product and Conveniences of Virginia in its Unproved State before the English went thither" begins with the fact "heard before" that "Virginia was the Name first given, to all the Northern Part of the Continent of America." He does not, however, elaborate on its dismemberment, but launches directly on the benefits of its waters, soils, minerals, ores, contours and mineral springs. And then we come to the section, "The Wild Fruits of the Country," which can serve as reference for later requests for shipments to English gardens.

Of the better Sorts of the wild Fruits, that I have met with, I will barely give you the names, not Designing a Natural History . . .

Stoned Fruits

Of stoned Fruits, I have met with Three good sorts, *viz.* Cherries, Plums and Persimmons.

1. Of Cherries natural to the Country, and growing wild in the Woods, I have seen Three Sorts. Two of these grow upon Trees, as big as the common English White Oak, whereof one grows in Bunches like Grapes. Both of these Sorts are black without, but one of them red within; that which is red within, is more palatable than the English black Cherry, as being without its bitterness. The Other, which hangs on the Branch like Grapes, is Water-colour'd within, of a faintish Sweet. Third Sort is call'd the Indian Cherry, and grows higher up on the Country, than the Others do . . . This is certainly the most delicious Cherry in the World; it is of a dark Purple when ripe, and grows upon a single Stalk, like the English Cherry, but it is very small, though, I suppose, it may be made larger by Cultivation, if any Body would mind it.

2. The Plums which I have observ'd to grow wild there, are of Two Sorts, the Black and the Murrey Plum, both of which are small, and have much the same Relish with the Damasine.

A page from Parkinson's *Paradisus,* illustrating "The Orchard." The
Persimmon or Virginia Plum is in the lower left, already (1629) incor-
porated into the group of useful fruits with the Service Tree and the
Medlar

3. The Persimmon is by Hariot call'd the Indian Plum; and so Smith, Purchase, and DuLake call it after him . . . These Persimmons amongst them retain their Indian Name. They are of several Sizes, between the Bigness of a Damasine and a Burgamot Pear. The Taste of them is so very rough, it is not to be endured, till they are fully ripe, and then they are a pleasant Fruit. Of these some *Vertuosi* make an agreeable kind of Beer; to which Purpose they dry them in Cakes, and lay them up for Use.

Berries

Of Berries there is a great Variety, and all very good in their Kinds. Our Mulberries are of Three sorts, two Black and one White; the long Black sort are the best, being about the Bigness of a Boy's Thumb; the other Two sorts are of the Shape of the English Mulberry, short and thick, but their Taste does not so generally please, being of a faintish Sweet, without any Tartness. They grow upon well spread, large bodied Trees, which run up surprisingly fast. These are the proper Food of the Silk-Worm.

1. There grow naturally Two Sorts of Currants, one red, and the other black, far more pleasant than those of the same Colour in England. They grow upon small Bushes.

2. There are Three Sorts of Hurts, or Huckleberries, upon Bushes, from Two to Ten Foot high . . .

3. Cranberries grow in the low Lands, and barren sunken Grounds, upon low Bushes, like the Gooseberry, and are much of the same Size. They are of a lively Red, when ripe, and make very good Tarts . . .

4. The wild Raspberry is by some there, preferr'd to those, that were transplanted thither from England . . .

5. Strawberries they have, as delicious as any in the World, and growing almost every where in the Woods, and Fields. They are eaten almost by all Creatures; and yet are so plentiful, that very few Persons take care to transplant them, but can find enough to fill their Baskets, when they have a mind, in the deserted old Fields.

Nuts

There grow wild several Sorts of good Nuts, *viz.* Chesnuts, Chinkapins, Hasel-nuts, Hickories, Walnuts, etc.

1. Chesnuts are found upon very high Trees, growing in barren Ridges. They are something less than the French Chesnut; but, I think, not differing at all in Taste.

2. Chinkapins have a Taste something like a Chesnut, grow in a Husk or Bur, being of the same sort of Substance, but not so big as an Acorn . . .

3. Hasel-nuts are there in infinite Plenty in all the Swamps; and towards the Heads of the Rivers, whole Acres of them are found upon the high Land.

4. Hickory-nuts are of several Sorts, all growing upon great Trees, and in an Husk, like the French Walnut, except that the Husk is not so thick, and

more apt to open . . . There are also several Sorts of Hickories, call'd Pig-nuts, some of which have as thin a Shell as the best French Walnuts, and yield their Meat very easily.

5. They have a sort of Walnut they call, Black-Walnuts, which are as big again as any I ever saw in England, but are very rank and oily . . .

6. Their Woods likewise afford a vast Variety of Acorns, Seven Sorts of which have fallen under my Observation . . . But now they only serve as Maste for the Hogs, and other wild Creatures, as do all other Fruits afore-mention'ed; together with several other sorts of Maste growing upon the Beech, Pine, and other Trees. The same Use is made also of divers Sorts of Pulse, and other Fruits, growing upon wild Vines; such as Pease, Beans, Vetches, Squashes, Maycocks, Maracocks, Melons, Cucumbers, Lupines, and an Infinity of other sorts of Fruits, which I cannot name.

Grapes

Grapes grow wild there in an incredible Plenty, and Variety; some of which are very sweet, and pleasant, to the Taste, others rough and harsh, and, per-haps fitter for Wine or Brandy . . . I have observed Six very different Kinds, *viz.*

1. Two of these Sorts grow among the Sandbanks, upon the Edges of the low Grounds, and Islands next the Bay, and Sea. They grow thin in small Bunches, and upon very low Vines. These are noble Grapes . . . One species of them is white, the other purple, but both much alike in Flavour.

2. A Third Kind is produced throughout the whole Country, in the Swamps and Sides of Hills. These also grow upon small Vines, and in small Bunches; but are themselves as big as the English Bullace, and of a rank Taste when ripe, resembling the Smell of a Fox from whence they are called Fox-Grapes. All these Three Sorts, when ripe, make admirable Tarts . . .

3. There are Two Species more, that are common to the whole Country, some of which are black, and some blue on the Outside, but are both red within. They grow upon vast large Vines, and bear very plentifully . . . Of the former of these Two Sorts, the French Refugees at the Monacan Town have lately made a sort of Clarret, tho' they were gather'd off the wild Vines in the Woods. I was told by a very good Judge, who tasted it, that it was a pleasant, strong, and full body'd Wine . . .

4. The Sixth Sort is far more palatable than the rest, and of the Size of the white Muscadine in England; but these are peculiar to the Frontiers, on the Heads of the Rivers . . .

Honey and Sugar Trees

The Honey and Sugar-Trees are likewise spontaneous, near the Heads of the Rivers. The Honey-Tree bears a thick swelling Pod, full of Honey; ap-pearing at a Distance like the bending Pod of a Bean or Pea. The Sugar-Tree yields a kind of Sap or Juice, which by boiling is made into Sugar. This Juice is drawn out, by wounding the Trunk of the Tree, and placing a

Receiver under the Wound. The Indians make One Pound of Sugar out of Eight Pounds of the Liquor.

Candle Berries

At the Mouth of their Rivers, and all along upon the Sea and Bay, and near many of their Creeks and Swamps, grows the Myrtle, bearing a Berry, of which they make a hard brittle Wax, of a curious green Colour, which by refining becomes almost transparent. Of this they make Candles, which are never greasie to the Touch, nor melt with lying in the hottest Weather: Neither does the Snuff of these ever offend the Smell, like that of a Tallow-Candle; but, instead of being disagreeable, if an Accident puts a Candle out, it yields a pleasant Fragrancy to all that are in the Room; insomuch, that nice People often put them out, on purpose to have the Incense of the expiring Snuff.

Hops

There are also in the Planes, and rich Grounds of the Freshes, abundance of Hops, which yield their Product without any Labour of the Husbandman, in Weeding, Hilling, or Poling.

Curious Plants and Flowers

All over the Country, is interspers'd here and there, a surprizing Variety of curious Plants and Flowers. They have a sort of Brier, growing something like the Sarsaparilla. The Berry of this is as big as a Pea, and as round, being of a bright Crimson Colour. It is very hard, and finely polish'd by Nature; so that it might be put to divers Ornamental Uses.

There are several Woods, Plants and Earths, which have been fit for the Dying of curious Colours. They have the Puccoon and Musquaspen, Two Roots, with which the Indians use to paint themselves red: There's the Shumack and the Sassafras, which make a deep Yellow . . .

There's the Snake-Root, so much admired in England for a Cordial, and for being a great Antidote in all Pestilential Distempers.

There's the Rattle-Snake-Root, to which no Remedy was ever yet found comparable; for it effectually cures of the Bite of a Rattle-Snake, which sometimes has been mortal in Two Minutes. If this Medicine be early applied, it presently removes the Infection, and in Two or Three Hours, restores the Patient to as perfect Health, as if he had never been hurt. This operates by violent Vomit; and Sweat.

The James-Town Weed (which resembles the Thorny Apple of Peru, and I take to be the Plant so call'd) is supposed to be one of the greatest Coolers in the World. This being an early Plant, was gather'd very young for a boil'd Salad, by some of the Soldiers sent thither, to pacifie the Troubles of Bacon; and some of them eat plentifully of it, the Effect of which was a very pleasant Comedy; for they turn'd natural Fools upon it for several Days . . .

Of spontaneous Flowers they have an unknown Variety: the finest Crown

The Tulip Tree. An early sensation and long-time
favorite. *Liriodendron tulipifera.* Curtis *Botanical
Magazine*

Imperial in the World; the Cardinal-Flower, so much extoll'd for its Scarlet
Colour, is almost in every Branch; the Moccasin Flowers, and a Thousand
others, not yet known, to English Herbalists. Almost all the Year round, the
Levels and Vales are beautified with Flowers of one Kind or other, which
make their Woods as fragrant as a Garden. From these Materials their wild
Bees make vast Quantities of Honey, but their Magazines are very often
rifled, by Bears, Raccoons, and such like liquorish Vermine.

Flowering Trees

There is also found, the fine Tulip-bearing, Lawrel-Tree, which has the
pleasantest Smell in the World, and keeps Blossoming and Seeding several
Months together . . . So also the large Tulip-Tree, which we call a Poplar,
the Locust, which resembles much the Jasmine, and the Perfuming Crab-
Tree, during their Season. With one sort or other of these, as well as many

other Sweet-flowering Trees not named, the Woods are almost everywhere adorn'd, and yield a surprizing Variety to divert the Traveller.

Medicinal Plants

They find a World of Medicinal Plants likewise in that Country; and amongst the rest, the Planters pretend to have a Swamp-Root, which infallibly cures all Fevers, and Agues. The Bark of the Sassafrass-Trees has been experimented to partake very much of the Virtue of the Cortex Peruviana. The Bark of the Root of that which we call the Prickly Ash, being dried and powder'd, has been found to be a Specifick, in old Ulcers, and Long-running Sores . . .

Fruiting Vines

Several Kinds of the Creeping Vines bearing Fruit, the Indians planted in their Gardens or Fields, because they wou'd have Plenty of them always at hand; such as, Musk-melons, Water-melons, Pompions, Cushaws, Macocks, and Gourds.

1. Their Musk-melons resemble the large Italian Kind, and generally fill Four or Five Quarts.
2. Their Water-melons were much more large, and of several Kinds, distinguished by the Colour of their Meat and Seed; some are red, some yellow, and others white meated, and so of the Seed, some are yellow, some red, and some black; but these are never of different Colours in the same Melon . . . They are excellently good, and very pleasant to the Taste, as also to the Eye; having the Rind of a lively green Colour, streak'd and water'd, the Meat of a Carnation, and the Seed black, and shining, while it lies in the Melon.
3. Their Pompions I need not describe, but must say they are much larger and finer, than any I ever heard of in England.
4. Their *Cushaws* are a kind of Pompion, of a bluish green Colour, streaked with White, when they are fit for Use. They are larger than the Pompions, and have a long narroe Neck . . .
5. Their Macocks are a sort of Melopepones, or less sort of Pompion, of these they have great Variety, but the Indian Name Macock serves for all, which Name is still retain'd among them. Yet the Clypeata are sometimes call'd Cynmels . . . Squash, or Squanter-Squash, is their Name among the Northern Indians.
6. The Indians never eat the Gourds, but plant them for other Uses . . . When it is ripe the . . . Indians . . . use the Shells instead of Flagons and Cups; as is done also in several other Parts of the World.

The Maracock, which is the Fruit of what we call the Passion Flower, our Natives did not take the Pains to plant, having enough of it growing every where; tho' they eat it with a great deal of Pleasure; this Fruit is about the Size of a Pullet's Egg.

Other Vegetables and Tobacco

Besides all these, our Natives had originally amongst them, Indian Corn, Pease, Beans, Potatoes, and Tobacco.

This Indian Corn was the Staff of Food, upon which the Indians did ever depend . . .

There are Four Sorts of Indian Corn, Two of which are early ripe, and Two, late ripe; all growing in the same manner . . . Oftentimes the Increase of this Grain amounts to above a Thousand for one . . . All these Sorts are planted alike, in Rows, Three, Four or Five Grains in a Hill, the larger Sort at Four or Five Foot Distance, the lesser sort nearer. The Indians used to give it One or Two Weedings, and make a Hill about it, and so the Labour was done. They likewise plant a Bean in the same Hill with the Corn, upon whose stalk it sustains itself.

The Indians sow'd Peas sometimes in the Intervals of the Rows of Corn, but more generally in a Patch of Ground by themselves . . .

Their Potatoes are either red or white, about as long as a Boy's Leg, and sometimes as long and big as both the Leg and Thigh of a young Child, and very much resembling it in Shape . . . The Way of propagating Potatoes there, is by cutting the small ones to Pieces, and planting the Cuttings in Hills of loose Earth . . .

How the Indians order'd their Tobacco, I am not certain, they now depending chiefly upon the English, for what they smoak; But I am inform'd they used to let it all run to Seed, only succouring the Leaves, to keep the Sprouts from growing upon, and starving them; and when it was ripe, they pull'd off the Leaves, cured them in the Sun and laid them up for Use. But the Planters make a heavy Bustle with it now, and can't please the market neither.

Beverly's description of the Indians was copied and recopied from 1705. His descriptions of the wealth of horticultural material to be found in the country, and his dissertation on what English gardening can do — or could do were the inhabitants not so lazy — is less well known. For besides savaging the royal governors throughout his history, Beverly has it in for his contemporaries, the planters, who do not take advantage of their blessings and are content to sow and reap within the narrow compass of tobacco-growing. There is also his much-quoted slur against doctors, more complimentary to Virginia and more innocent than it is allowed to be. Speaking of the injustice of every newcomer's calling whatever his first sickness may be "a Seasoning," Beverly says the planters have "the Happiness to have very few Doctors, and those such as make use only of simple Remedies, of which their Woods afford great Plenty. And indeed, their Distempers are not many and their cures so generally known that there is not mystery enough to make a Trade of Physick here, as the Learned do in other Countries, to the great oppression of Mankind."

About his lazy fellow Virginians he is very caustic.

They have their Cloathing of all sorts from England, as Linen, Woollen, Silk, Hats and Leather. Yet Flax and Hemp grow no where in the World better than there; their Sheep yield a mighty increase and bear good Fleeces, but they shear them only to cool them. The mulberry tree, whose Leaf is the proper Food of the Silk-Worm, grows there like a Weed, and Silk-Worms have been observed to thrive extremely and without any hazard . . . Nay, they are such abominable Ill-husbands that tho' their Country be over-run with Wood, yet they have all their Wooden Ware from England; their cabinets, Chairs, Tables, Stools, Chests, Boxes, Cart-Wheels, and all other things, even so much as their Bowls and Birchen Brooms, to the Eternal Reproach of their Laziness.

Not all things English take precedence — some are too much trouble. While "English grain" will grow, Beverly says his fellow Virginians won't sow it because it has to be fenced. The bread in gentlemen's houses is generally made of wheat, but some of them and most of the poorer people choose "pone," made of Indian meal and so called from the Indians' name "oppone."

The only thing holding back Virginia is the tobacco-dependent planters, large and small, but all lazy. Beverly's chapter "The Natural Products of Virginia, and the Advantages of their Husbandry" is impassioned. The "extream fruitfulness" of the country has been shown. No seed is sown in Virginia "but it thrives, and most plants are improved by being transplanted thither." Yet little improvement is made and nothing is "us'd in Traffique, but Tobacco." Apples, when seeds are planted, produce better fruit than the mother tree. Improving his trees by grafting, in six or seven years a man may bring an orchard to bear, from which he may make a great store of cider or distill quantities of brandy, but those who have good orchards expose the trees to be torn and barked by cattle. Peaches, nectarines and apricots, as well as plums and cherries, grow upon standard trees. The best sorts cling to the stone and can reach twelve inches in girth. They are raised so easily that some husbandmen plant orchards of them for their hogs and others make a drink of them called "Mobby," either drunk like cider or distilled. Grapes bear abundantly, both English and native. A single tree left in a clearing with a vine upon it will produce enough to fill a London cart. The almond, pomegranate and fig will all grow. A garden is no sooner made anywhere than in Virginia. Even tulips from seed flower the second year. All sorts of English grains thrive: wheat, barley, oats, rye, peas, rape . . . Yet they make a trade of none of them.

Here even Beverly has to admit an excuse. The characteristic of Virginian development was the distances between holdings. There were no towns except Jamestown and the Middle-Plantation, now Williamsburg. The river was the road. Every place had to be self-contained. "It is thought too much for the same Man," says Beverly, "to make the Wheat and grind it, bolt it and bake it himself." The planter who is willing to sow barley finds it too great a charge to build a malt house and brew house, too. Rice, though successful in Carolina, suffers for "the want of a community to husk and clean it and after all to take it off the planters' hands." With "cohabitations" more would be worth attempting.

Flax, hemp, cotton, silkworms, silk grass, sheep, bees, beeves, hogs . . . the list of things not made proper use of is endless. Even naval stores are neglected. It is all due to "the unfortunate Method of the Settlement, and want of Cohabitation." He trusts his publishing an account of the slothful indolence of his countrymen will rouse them out of their lethargy.

Some of Beverly's diatribes against his fellow Virginians should be reckoned an inducement to hard-working settlers to "come over," on their own or as indentured servants, in the procurement of which Beverly was financially interested. Beverly spells out their conditions very carefully. Every settler receives fifty acres for himself and as much for every individual he brings with him. In return he pays twelve pence as quitrent on each fifty acres and has to "settle," — build and till land and keep some cattle, — within three years or forfeit the land to others. Men who have not got land for themselves, as, for instance, indentured servants who have worked off their indenture, may buy from him after this, if he pleases to sell. Depending upon their ages, they must work either for five years each, or until they are twenty-four. At the end of his time, each man is given fifteen bushels of corn (a year's supply) and two suits of clothes, one wool and one linen. Except that no white woman need work in the fields, no special provision seems made for maids brought over. With women at such a premium, one may assume they were snapped up in matrimony before their time was up (as in *The Widow Ranter*). Beverly, sometimes anxious to please his father-in-law, the first William Byrd, and also obviously desirous of attracting Huguenot refugees, deals at length with Colonel Byrd's kind provisions for those who have "come over" and settled on his land up the river by the falls, where he has a "Store."

As a major inducement to prospective Virginians, Beverly described kitchen gardens.

A Kitchin-Garden don't thrive better or faster in any part of the Universe than there. They have all the Culinary Plants that grow in England, and in far greater perfection, than in England: Besides these, they have several Roots, Herbs, Vine-fruits, and Salate-flowers peculiar to themselves, most of which will neither increase, nor grow to Perfection in England. These they dish up various ways, and find them very delicious Sauce to their Meats, both Roast and Boild, Fresh and Salt; such are the Red-Buds, Sassafras-Flowers, Cymnels, Melons, and Potatoes . . .

It is said of New England, that several Plants will not grow there, which

Parkinson's illustration of purslane, cresses, mustard and asparagus, from "The Kitchen Garden" in *Paradisus,* 1629

thrive well in England, such as Rue, Southernwood, Rosemary, Bays and Lavender: And that others degenerate, and will not continue above a year or two at the most; such are July-Flowers, Fennel Enula, Campana, Clary, and Bloodwort: But I don't know any English Plant, Grain or Fruit, that miscarries in Virginia; but most of them better their kinds very much, by being sowed or planted there . . .

The simplest household does not want for liquor.

Their Small-drink is either Wine and Water, Beer, Milk and Water, or Water alone. Their richer sort generally brew their Small-Beer with Malt, which they have from England, though they have as good Barley of their own, as any in the World; but for want of the convenience of Malt-Houses, the Inhabitants take no care to sow it. The poorer sort brew their Beer with Mollasses and Bran; with Indian Corn Malted by drying in a Stove; with Persimmons dried in Cakes, and baked; with Potatoes; with green stalks of Indian Corn cut small, and bruised; with Pompions; and with *Batates Canadensis,* or Jerusalem Artichoke, which some People plant purposely for that use, but this is the least esteem'd, of all the sorts before mention'd.

Their Strong Drink is Madera Wine, which is a Noble strong Wine; and Punch, made either of Rum from the Caribee Islands, or Brandy distilled from their Apples, and Peaches; besides French-Brandy, wine and strong Beer, which they have constantly from England.

It is only fair to allow a foreign visitor to comment upon Beverly's efforts in grape-growing. In 1715 he was visited by a Huguenot who knew the *History* and may indeed have been coaxed "over" by it. He comments:

After breakfast we went to see Mr. Beverly's vineyard. This Beverly is the same that made the history of Virginia. When we saw his vineyard we saw several sorts of vines which are natural and grow here in the woods. This vineyard is situated upon the side of a hill and consists of three hundred acres of land. He assures us that he made this year about four hundred gallons of wine. He hath been at great expense about this improvement. He hath also caves and a wine press; but according to the method that they use in Spain he hath not the right method for it, nor is his vineyard regularly managed. He hath several sorts of French vines among them . . . This man lives well . . . He lives upon the products of the land.

Besides pleasing French readers and promoters, Beverly left a legacy among English readers of the delights to be found in Virginia wildlife and in possible horticultural and botanical rewards. He immortalized two American birds, the mockingbird and the hummingbird, to such an extent that they were being asked for, even dead, for collections, throughout the next century.

In his final description of the delights of the country he begins to sound like the mockingbird himself:

I believe it is as healthy a Country as any under Heaven . . .

The clearness and brightness of the Sky add new vigour to their Spirits and perfectly remove all Splenetick and sullen Thoughts. Here they enjoy all the benefits of a warm Sun and by their shady Groves are protected from its Inconvenience. Here all their Senses are entertained with an endless Succession of Native Pleasures. Their Eyes are ravished with the Beauties of naked Nature. Their Ears are serenaded with the perpetual murmur of Brooks and the thorow-base which the Wind plays when it wantons through the Trees. The merry Birds, too, join their pleasing Notes to this rural Consort, especially the Mock-birds, who love Society so well that, whenever they see Mankind, they will perch upon a Twigg very near them, and sing the sweetest wild Airs in the World. But what is most remarkable in these Melodius Animals, they will frequently fly at small distances before a Traveller, warbling out their Notes several Miles on end, and by their Musick, make a Man forget the Fatigues of his Journey.

"Of the Recreations, and Pastimes used in Virginia" Beverly begins with a sentence that underlies the garden design of colonial Virginia and could have been written by William Byrd II as a *vade mecum* of life at Westover.

For their Recreation, the Plantations, Orchards, and Gardens constantly afford 'em fragrant and delightful Walks. In their Woods and fields, they have an unknown variety of Vegetables and other Rarities of Nature to discover and observe . . .

Their Taste is regaled with the most delicious Fruits, which without Art, they have in great Variety and Perfection. And then their smell is refreshed with an eternal fragrancy for Flowers and Sweets with which Nature perfumes and adorns the Woods almost the whole year round.

Have you pleasure in a Garden? All things thrive in it, most surprisingly; you can't walk by a Bed of Flowers, but besides the entertainment of their Beauty, your Eyes will be saluted with the charming colours of the Humming Bird, which revels among the Flowers and licks off the Dew and Honey from their tender Leaves on which it only feeds. Its size is not half so large as an English Wren, and its colour is a glorious shining mixture of Scarlet, Green and Gold. Colonel Byrd in his garden which is the finest in that Country has a Summer House set round with the Indian Honey-Suckle which all the summer is continually full of sweet Flowers, in which these Birds delight exceedingly. Upon these Flowers I have seen ten or a dozen of these Beautiful Creatures together, which sported about me so familiarly, that with their little Wings they often fanned my Face.

Furber's Flowers for the Month of February

1. Duke Vantol Tulip B C
2. Silver Edged Alaternus
3. Yellow bloach Alater- nus B T
4. Cornelian Cherry L T
5. White Mezereon B T
6. Red Mezereon B T
7. Double Narcissus of Constantinople B C
8. Single Anemone Purple & White B
9. Venetian Vetch B
10. Double blue Hepatica F E
11. Early white Hyacinth B
12. Blush red Dens Caninus B
13. Spring Cyclamen white Edged G

14. Striped & Edged Poly- anthos B
15. Single white Hepatica F E
16. Single blue Hepatica F E
17. White Dens Caninus B
18. Double Peach-coloured Hepatica F E
19. The greater Snow-drop B
20. White Crocus F E
21. Double Snow-drop F E
22. Small yellow Crocus F E
23. Great blue Crocus F E
24. Small blue Crocus F E

25. Single dark red Ane- mone B
26. Pantaloon Striped Poly- anthos F E
27. Persian Iris B
28. Yellow Dutch Crocus F E
29. Scotch white striped Crocus F E
30. Blue Hyacinth Pas- toute B C
31. Fruit-bearing Almond L T
32. Single Persian blue Anemone B
33. Yellow Colutea G
34. Peach-coloured single Hepatica F E
35. Double Pilewort F E

2 "Seed of a Nation"

AMONG THE VARIED URGENCIES that sparked the origins of the mutually so dissimilar colonies on the North Atlantic seaboard, the inception of Pennsylvania was the most nobly conceived. Georgia may run it a close second a hundred years later, but in the seventeenth century not even the Puritan leader, John Winthrop, with the charter under his arm, had so carefully planned, spiritually, economically and horticulturally, the future of his followers.

Credit for the conception of a place anywhere on the late seventeenth-century earth where every man would be free to worship, or even not to worship, as he saw fit, could have come only from a totally original character, a man ahead of his own time and yet able to survive it, capable of planning the government of such a future state, of finding a place and a way to secure it and of settling it with people of like mind with his own. Too much credit can never be given to William Penn for the fruition of his plan to rescue the persecuted Quakers, friends in the Society to which he had become a convert, and to bring them to a land where they could be free and successful.

It is unfair to the Puritans who settled early New England to chide them for seeking religious toleration and then becoming intolerant themselves. They had no intention of forming a City upon a Hill in which everyone was to pursue his own religious beliefs. They would sooner have stayed at home. Having made the great experiment of creating a Puritan stronghold and free-hold, they felt they could not

37

afford to see it eroded by other sects and nonsects. From the Massachusetts Bay Colony blew seeds of other than purely Puritan inspiration to form governments with less rigorous exclusions, but all New England by the end of the seventeenth century had nowhere near approached the studied liberalism of the new settlements beyond their borders in East and West New Jersey and in Pennsylvania.

Those who saw William Penn grow up in the disturbed England of Cromwell and Charles II would have held it most unlikely that this troublesome and original young man would accomplish anything except the death in sorrow of his famous father. Pepys, the diarist, who knew them both, had few good words for either, though he admitted that the boy, constantly and industriously publishing "tracts," wrote well. When the younger Penn returned from exposure to the manners of the French court, an experiment in reform made by his father probably on Pepys' advice, Pepys laughed at the boy's acquired affectations in speech and dress. What neither of the older men realized was that Penn, repelled by the frivolity of the French court, had spent most of his two years abroad studying under the friendly tutelage of Moses Amyraut at Saumur, a Protestant stronghold. Amyraut, author of *La Morale Chrétienne,* preached that supreme good could be achieved by man's moving closer to God through piety, charity and responsibility for his fellow men, a far cry from beliefs held by either the elder Penn or Samuel Pepys, his fellow at the Admiralty.

Ever a trimmer, the elder Penn had managed early on to serve Cromwell and acquire vast holdings of land in Ireland, to which he judiciously retired with his wife and young children during the turmoil preceding the return of Charles II. Here the young Penn learned estate management, how to bear arms (see his portrait as a very young man in armor) and, through his father's kindness to an itinerant Quaker preacher, the tenets of the Quaker faith.

The elder Penn managed to be back in England in time to wait to welcome the king and be knighted on the deck of his ship. He was given a place on the council for administration of naval affairs, working under the Duke of York as Lord High Admiral and with Sir George Carteret as Treasurer. Lord Berkeley was a fellow commissioner; Samuel Pepys a young clerk. It was to the Duke of York that vast territory in the New World would be granted. Berkeley and Carteret would receive the Jerseys, East and West. The son of commissioner Penn would later be able to realize his dream of a perfect state and refuge for Quakers by adapting his boundaries to fit in with these previous grants and by collecting on his father's earlier financial assistance to the king to pay for it.

In the beginning, however, the younger Penn, sent to Oxford with his father's high hopes for his future, was expelled within two years for refusing to conform. He was then sent to France, and on his return from that experiment toward what his father intended as worldly living, he entered Lincoln's Inn. Again his hopeful father exposed his son to the world for which he hoped to train him by taking him to sea aboard the *Royal Charles,* training him in naval matters and sending him to the king with a personal message. The king knew who Penn was and asked after his father, an incident later of value to the young reformer. Back in London at Lincoln's Inn, the younger Penn was witness, when the plague struck, to the extraordinary work of the Quakers among the terrified inhabitants, whose leaders had left town. The elder Penn, beginning to consider his heretofore troublesome son as an able family agent, sent him to Ireland to secure properties there, and was devastated to hear he had become involved in a meeting to protest the Quaker Act, a law prohibiting Quakers from meeting together. The young Penn had been willingly thrown into jail, and then released, to his regret, because his sword and clothing showed him to be a Cavalier. This exhilarating experience confirmed him in his allegiance to the Quakers. Pepys wrote, "Mr. William Penn lately come over from Ireland is a Quaker again, or some very melancholy thing," a fact Pepys found very "pleasant," the father being "such a hypocritical rogue."

His father's discomfort was now complete. Between the return from Ireland and his father's death, when a certain reconciliation was said to have been effected, the younger Penn's career was entirely devoted to writing and preaching his faith, and to being punished for so doing. He traveled on the continent to preach in France and in Germany (from where some of his later colonists were to come). He was arrested in London for preaching in Gracechurch Street (where we shall later meet Peter Collinson) and thrown again into jail. This last episode produced yet another of those valuable pieces to be fitted into the future colony of Pennsylvania. Penn at his trial personally addressed the jury to point out to them that they were all free men and need not vote to find him guilty as instructed by the judge. To a man they followed Penn's legal advice, found him not guilty and they all went to jail together. Penn's own offense, after the judgment against them, was his refusal to pay a fine for keeping his hat on in the courtroom. This entire incident not only marked a step forward in British justice, but aided Penn later in setting up a judicial system in his colony. It would seem to have finished off the elder Penn, who secured his son's release from jail, as he had done many times, and died.

Penn was left an income of fifteen hundred pounds a year, a great amount in those days, and learned of the king's debt to his father of sixteen thousand pounds, which he later turned into the grant allowed him as Pennsylvania. But not immediately. Marriage, further tracts, more jails, friendship with Fox and other Quaker leaders intervened. The "holy experiment" was to proceed at a deliberate speed.

Penn's father had died in 1670 when Penn was twenty-six years old and had already led a life full enough for many. In 1672 he married a Quaker heiress, Gulielma Springett, who had waited for him while he served a six-month jail term and traveled in Holland and Germany with his friend George Fox. For four years Penn and his wife lived at Rickmansworth, with Penn constantly writing and preaching, and then moved to an estate in Sussex, Wormingshurst, which Penn loved but from which again he was constantly absent. This patient first wife is commemorated in the name of his first dwelling in Pennsylvania, Springettsbury. The stately home later built upon the banks of the Delaware River, to which he took his second wife, was named Pennsbury.

Persecution of Quakers in England was increasing. The Conventicle Act, passed when Penn was at Lincoln's Inn, forbade any gathering for worship except under the auspices of the Anglican Church. Punishment was confiscation of property and imprisonment. Many prominent Quakers suffered. Those fleeing to the New World were considering purchasing land from the Susquehanna Indians, who apparently felt they still had some left to offer, when, by one of those fortuitous incidents seemingly foreordained to assist with the founding of Pennsylvania, Penn was called in to arbitrate a geographically related property dispute. In 1674, with eleven other Quaker worthies, he was able to purchase part of West New Jersey and to open it to Quaker settlement.

For the new colony of West New Jersey a constitution called "Concessions" was drawn up by a group of Quakers, including Penn. Founding it "as nearly as may be conveniently to the primitive ancient and fundamental laws of the nation of England," the first provision was for religious freedom. No one could be condemned in life, liberty or estate except by a jury of twelve, with the right of challenging. Imprisonment for debt was reduced to a minimum. Punishment for theft was twofold restitution, in value or in labor. Three justices, elected by the people, were to preside over the twelve jurors, "in whom only the judgement resides." Questions between settlers and Indians were to be arranged by a mixed jury. An assembly once a year was to consist of one hundred elected representatives, chosen by the inhabitants, both free-holders and proprietors, each representative to receive a shilling a day to signify him as a "servant of the people." Executive power was to rest in ten commissioners chosen by the assembly. The then inhabitants assented to this document.

Even this refuge, however, lost its security when an agent for the Duke of York, feeling West New Jersey was still a part of the Duke of York's grant, moved to tax all imports and exports on the Delaware River. Although it was finally decided that the Quakers had, indeed, bought their land, the disturbance left them longing for land more certainly beyond conflicting boundaries. It was then that Penn decided to collect his father's old debt. Mindful also of a need of which he had been made increasingly conscious by his family's early obsession with ships, he agreed to accept great forest tracts far inland, providing there was access to good harbors and the sea. With the trees in mind, he wished to call the land Sylvania. The king, in memory of the admiral, affixed the Penn. With the agreement of the Duke of York and Lord Baltimore, the Royal Charter was finally dated March 4, 1681, making Penn sole proprietor of a tract north of Maryland, west of the Delaware and as far north as "plantable." Beholden only to the King of England, empowered to make laws and establish justice with the assent of free men, Penn was to divide the land and keep the remainder. All trade in raw materials and finished goods was to be with England. And, as decided in West New Jersey, no taxes were to be levied without the consent of the proprietor. For all this, the proprietor was required to keep an agent always in London to represent the colony in the courts; he was to pay annually two beaver skins every January at Windsor, and yield to the crown a fifth of all gold and silver ore discovered.

It was from all this that William Penn wrote a friend on March 5, 1681, that he believed God would make "the seed of a nation."

Pennsylvania needed no whales upon its doorsteps to get off to a good start. Industry and skill, frugality and selflessness, lack of affectation and ostentation, charity toward neighbors, a fondness for tending land, an instinct for conserving resources, respect for learning and a will to educate their children were all ingrained in the members of the Society of Friends. All they lacked as pioneers was the determination to defend their boundaries against any who might trouble them. While this firmly held resolution did not bother them or their neighbors until later in the century, when Indians began marauding their colony, it was something for their neighbors to reckon with in times of stress.

While Penn had paid for the grant, the idea was still to purchase the land from the Indians. Information about the colony and how to arrive there was published, including the cost of the ocean passage and the rights of the settlers. Shares of land were five thousand acres each and cost one hundred pounds, but land could be rented in lots of two hundred acres at the rate of one penny per acre. Ocean passage would cost approximately six pounds a head for masters and mistresses, five pounds for servants and two and a half pounds for children. Penn sent a cousin, Captain Markham, to America to act as governor and to deal with some land problems, chiefly Lord Baltimore's objections. In 1681 one hundred families sailed for the new land.

In October, 1682, the sole proprietor of Pennsylvania arrived off Newcastle, that much-to-be-desired port lately ceded by the Duke of York, later to be claimed for the colony of Lord de la Warr. A motley crowd greeted him: Dutch who had built the courthouse in which the ceremonies would take place; Indians in full regalia; Swedish lumbermen; German farmers; English Quakers and his cousin and appointed steward, Captain Markham, who had already established friendly relations with the Indians.

A month later Penn had laid out the City of Philadelphia on inspired lines. On ten thousand acres at the junction of two rivers he placed a checkerboard plan with four one-hundred-foot-wide streets intersected at right angles by twenty-eight cross streets each fifty feet wide. A public square or park of ten acres was designated centrally with four others, of eight acres each, in the four quarters "for the comfort and recreation of

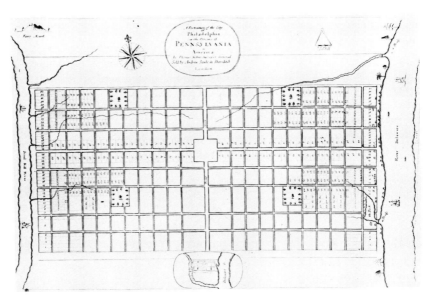

Plan of the City of Philadelphia by Thomas Holme, 1682

all forever." Within a year he had laid out the province into counties, and six on the banks of the river were "begun to be seated."

In two years there were six hundred houses, some of brick, a printing press, a school. A postal system followed. Five hundred farmers settled in villages and divided the land according to their ability to plant it. Penn purchased land for himself from the Indians, over six thousand acres, and began to build Pennsbury Manor. For the sole proprietor of Pennsylvania would need a good house and land to serve as an example to those he was urging to build and cultivate his colony. In Philadelphia he especially recommended: "Let every house be placed, if the person pleases, in the middle of its plat as to the breadth way of it, that so there be ground on each side for gardens, or orchards, or fields, that it may be a green country town which will never be burnt and will always be wholesome."

The "accounts" and "letters" Penn wrote to set forth the securities and amenities to be found within the folds of his colony are among the best of the colonial presentations urging settlers to make their homes on the North Atlantic seaboard. There are no promises of gold or easy fortunes; only every assurance of plenty of land and work. Laws and rights and privileges are set forth. Prospects advanced are circumscribed only by the powers of the individuals undertaking them. Everyone will have land and freedom. Some may take up more land than others but no one shall be less bound than anyone else to the common success of the "holy experiment." By the time any man has made up his mind to "come over" he knows exactly where he will stand and what his rights will be. It is only after all this is set forth that Penn permits himself to wax lyrical about horticultural resources.

These are set forth in his last promotion plan offered in his *Letter to the Committee of the Free Society of Traders of that Province residing in London . . . from William Penn, Proprietary and governor of Pennsylvania in America,* written in 1683 and published in the same year in London with an added "Account of the City of Philadelphia Newly Laid Out."

For patient gardeners waiting for a little greenery to show itself among structural details, here is their reward. For William Penn was at heart a country man and "curious," like so many of his Quaker brethren. His great friend George Fox had early urged that all schools established by the Society of Friends should teach "the nature of herbs, roots, plants and trees." Plant exchange was a foregone principle among settlers under Quaker guidance. Thomas Lawson, a Westmoreland school-master and botanist, wrote in 1691 that Fox and Penn had planned to purchase land near London to plant it with "many English and outlandish plants." Penn himself had spoken of the desirability of "studying and following nature and endeavouring to become good naturalists" and had written to his first wife, "Let my children be husbandmen and housewives." That he himself was the first real conservationist to arrive in this country and to lay down rules for developing lands for both crops and forests, is evident in all his plans. In a document of 1681, he urged that "in clearing the ground, care be taken to leave one acre of trees for every five cleared, especially to preserve oak and mulberries for silk and shipping."

Penn was determined to make his colony productive of all the crops known in England needed for subsistence, and to adopt the native crops as introduced to the settlers by friendly Indians. The Indians' corn was called "maize" until the settlers gave over calling their field crops of barley and wheat "corn" and let the Indian crop take precedence with the ancient name.

Penn brought into his garden native plants and fruits, studying what the Indians had produced from earlier European introductions, like peaches, and comparing them with the English variety. His hopes were set upon making wine and silk, encouraged by the quantities of native grapes and the indigenous American mulberry trees.

To the Free Society, Penn wrote at length, enthusiastic but cautious.

The country itself in its Soil, Air, Water, Seasons and Produce, both natural and artificial, is not to be despised. The land containeth divers sorts of Earth, as sand, yellow and black, poor and rich. Also gravel both loamy and dusty, and in some places a fast fat earth, like to our best vales in England, especially by inland brooks and rivers, God in his wisdom having ordered so, that the advantages of the country are divided . . .

He had far-reaching plans for ground-improvement, not to be equaled until late in the next century by Eliot and Washington, Adams and Jefferson. He wrote to his steward, James Harrison:

I recommend to thee for the gardens and improvement of the lands, that ashes and soot are excellent for the ground, grass and corn. Soot may be got at Philadelphia, I suppose, for the fetching. I suppose it should be sewed pretty thick . . . Let me desire thee to lay down as much as thou canst with English grass and plow up new Indian fields and after a crop to two they must be laid down so too; for that feeds sheep, and that feeds the ground, as well as they feed and clothe us.

For a society where even one physician or surgeon would be unusual and nearly every housewife or interested husbandman could be expected to produce cures for prevalent distempers and afflictions, Penn is careful to note to the Free Society of Traders:

Catesby's Plate A-8 *Lilium angustifolium* (Pennsylvania Lily)

There are divers Plants that not only the Indians tell us but we have had occasion to prove by Swellings, Burnings, Cuts, etc. that they are of great Virtue, suddenly curing the patient.

Aesthetically the country is not lacking and may prove rewarding to the horticulturally minded noblemen at home.

The Woods are adorned with lovely Flowers for Colour, Greatness, Figure and Variety: I have seen the Gardens of London best stored with that sort of Beauty, but think they may be improved by our Woods. I have sent a few to a Person of Quality this year for a Tryal.

But for the ordinary farmer the important news was what he might be able to grow, to live on and even to sell, to support himself and his family in the new land.

The artificial produce of the Country is Wheat, Barley, Oats, Rye, Peases, Beans, Squashes, Water-melons, Musk-melons, and all Herbs and Roots that our Gardens in England usually bring forth . . .

The Natural Produce of the Country of Vegetables is Trees, Fruits, Plants, Flowers. The Trees of most note are the Black Walnut, Cedar, Cyprus,

Chestnut, Poplar, Gumwood, Hickery, Sassafras, Ash, Beech, and Oak of divers Sorts as Red, White, and Black, Spanish Chestnut and Swamp, the most durable of all, of all which there is plenty for the Use of Man.

And there are the native fruits to be found in the woods:

White and Black Mulberry, Chestnut, Wallnut, Plumbs, Strawberries, Cranberries, Hurtleberries, and Grapes of divers Sorts . . .

Of which last Penn had great hopes:

The Great Red Grape (now ripe) called by Ignorance the Fox Grape (because of the Relish it hath with unskilful palates) is in itself an extraordinary Grape, and by Art, doubtles may be cultivated to an excellent Wine, if not so sweet, yet little inferior to the Frontenack, as it is not much unlike in taste, ruddiness set aside, which in such things, as well as mankind, differs the case much. There is a white kind of Muskadel and a little black grape like the cluster grape of England, not yet so ripe as the other, but they tell me when ripe, sweeter, and that they only want skilful vinerons to make good use of them. I intent to venture on it with my Frenchman this season, who shews some knowledge of these things.

Peach brandy was one of the first drinks made by all the colonies where the Indian's random-sown peaches flourished and made mast for the pigs and a drink for their owners.

Penn writes:

Here are also peaches and very good and in great quantities. Not an Indian plantation without them, but whether naturally here at first I know not. However, one may have them by the bushels for little. They make a pleasant drink, and I think not inferiour to any peach you have in England, except the true Newington. It is disputable with me whether it be best to fall to fining the fruits of the country, especially the grape, by the care and skill of art, or send for foreign stems and sets already good and approved. It seems most reasonable to believe that not only a thing groweth best where it naturally grows but will hardly be equalled by another species of the same kind that doth naturally grow there. But to solve the doubt I intend, if God give me life, to try both and hope the consequence will be as good wine as any European countries of the same latitude do yield.

This was in 1683, cautious and honest.

In 1685 one Thomas Budd felt moved (or was moved, perhaps by investors in Pennsylvania), to publish a "small treatise" with a title claiming to be *A True Account of the Country . . . Pennsilvania and New Jersey: in which there was Good Order Established."* He waxed warm upon his title page about the

great improvements that may be made by means of Publick Stone Houses

Two early bulb importations were the *Narcissus biflorus* and the *Narcissus jonquilla,* like these from Curtis *Botanical Magazine.* Collinson sent some to Bartram who reported them already here and in quantities

for Hemp, Flax and Linen Cloth, also the Advantages of a Publick School, the Profits of the Publick Bank, and the Probability of its arising, if those directions laid down are followed. With the advantages of publick Granaries . . . Likewise several other things needful to be understood by those that are or do intend to be concerned in planting in the said Countries. All of which is laid down very plain in this small Treatise; it being easie to be understood by any ordinary Capacity To which the Reader is referred for his further Satisfaction.

On the sixth page, indeed, Mr. Budd gives free rein to his fancies, once he has dismissed the pests:

. . . very little troubled with *Musketoes;* and if Cattel did commonly feed on this Ground, and tread it as in England, I suppose it would not be inferior to the rich Meadows on the River of *Thames;* and were quantities of this land laid dry, and brought to Tillage, I suppose it would bear great Crops of *Wheat, Pease,* and *Barley, Hemp,* and *Flax,* and it would be very fit for *Hop-Gardens,* and for *English Grass,* which might serve for rich pastures or Meadow. Also these Marshes are fit for *Rape* and were *Rape*-Mills built, and the design managed, so as it would if it were in *England* or *Holland,* a great Trade might be carried on, and many hundred Tuns of *Rape*-Oyl might be made Yearly, and sent to *England,* to the Planters inrichment; and not only so, but would be for Merchants advantage, they thereby having Goods to freight their Ships, which would tend to the benefit of the Inhabitants in general . . .

The *Land* is in Veins, some good, and some bad, but the greatest part *will* bear good Corn, as *Wheat, Rye, Barley, Oats, Indian Corn, Buck-Wheat, Pease* and *Indian Beans,* &c.

Fruits that grow naturall in the Countries are *Strawberries, Cranberries, Huckleberries, Blackberries, Medlars, Grapes, Plums, Hickery-Nuts, Walnuts, Mulberies, Chestnuts, Hazle nuts, &c.*

Garden Fruits groweth well, as Cabbage, Colvoris, Colliflowers, Sparagras, Carrots, Parsnips, Turnups, Oynions, Comcumers, Pumkins, Water-Mellons, Musk-Mellons, Squashes, Potatoes, Currants, Gooseberries, Roses, Cornations, Tulips, Garden-Herbes, Flowers, Seeds, Fruits, &c. for such as grow in England certainly will grow here.

Orchards of Apples, Pears, Quinces, Peaches, Aprecocks, Plums, Cheries, and other sorts of the usual Fruits of England may be soon raised to good advantage, the Trees growing faster than in England, whereof great quantities of Sider may be made.

It is supposed that we may make as good Wines as in France (if Vineyards were planted on the sides of Hills or Banks, which are defended from the cold North-West Winds) with such Vines as the French-men commonly make those Wines of; for the Climate is as proper as any part of France, therefore it is rational to believe, that the Wines will be as rich and good as in France. There are some Vine-yards already planted in Pennsylvania, and more intended to be planted by some French-Protestants, and others, that are gone to settle there.

Several other Commodities will be raised here, as Rice, which is known to have been sown for a tryal, and it grew very well, and yielded good increase . . . Also Annis-Seeds I have been informed groweth well, and might be a profitable Commodity, there being great Quantities used in England by Distillers . . . Liquorice doubtless would grow very well. And I question not but that Madder, Woad, and other Plants and Roots for Dyers use might be raised. Shamuck groweth naturally. Also several useful Drugs grow naturally, as Sassafras, Sassaparella, Callumus Aromaticus, Snake-Root, Fallsopa, &c.

The Pine-Tree groweth here, out of which is made Pitch, Tar, Rosin and Turpentine. In New England some make quantities of Tar out of the knots of Pine Trees, with which they supply themselves and others . . . There are many other forms of Plants, Roots and Herbs of great Virtue, which grow here, which are found to cure such Distempers as the People are insident to

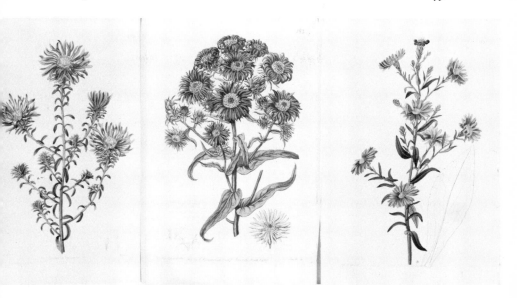

Three North American asters sent to English gardens. Curtis *Botanical Magazine*

. . . Hops in some places grow naturally, but were Hop-Gardens planted in low rich Land, quantities might be raised to good advantage.

In the Woods groweth plentifully a course sort of Grass, which is so proving that it soon makes the Cattel and Horses fat in the Summer, but the Hay being course, which is chiefly gotten on the fresh Marshes, the Cattel loseth their Flesh in the Winter, and become very poor, except we give them Corn: But this may be remydied in time, by draining of low rich Land and by plowing of it, and sowing it with English-Grass-Feed, which here thrives very well.

The Hogs are fat in the Woods when it is a good Mast-Year . . .

The Woods are furnished with store of Wild Fowl, as Turkeys, Phesants, Heath-Cocks, Partridges, Pidgeons, Blackbirds, &c. And People that will take the pains to raise the various sorts of tame Fowl, may do it with as little trouble, and less charge, than they can in England, by reason of what they find in the Woods . . . Bees are found by the experiance of several that keep them, to thrive very well.

Compared with Budd's promises, Penn's comments are subdued. Besides sending unusual plants to be tried out in English gardens, Penn ordered one of his gardeners "to have . . . roots and flowers next spring by transplanting them out of the woods." And, probably in

1 *Rosa alba.*
The white Rose.

Rosa alba From Gerard's *Herbal.* One of the earliest roses brought to the settlers'
gardens

reference to the same operation, he wrote to Robert Boyle in England
". . . of flowers, I may say, I never saw larger, more varity, or brighter
colours, in the curious gardens of England. Of them I have ordered my
gardener to make a collection against them next year."

And again: "Our gardens supply us with all sorts of herbs and even
some which are not in England. Here are roses, currants, gooseberries . . ."

Pennsbury Manor was designed by William Penn on his first visit,
and work was started on the great brick house with rooms big enough
for meetings, terraces dropping gradually down to the river and a parklike surround of many acres setting off the house with its "upper" and
"lower" gardens, its courtyards and many outbuildings. A poplar-
planted avenue ran from the front door to the barge landing. The place
occupied Penn's thoughts long after his first visit ended in an unexpectedly hurried departure for England to settle boundary disputes, wait
upon his ill wife and try to make order out of his financial affairs,
snarled by a dishonest steward. Not for fifteen years would he see his
plans completed and be able to live in his house up the river, on his
second visit and with his second wife.

A broad walk led down to the river where lay his barge, one of his greatest treasures and a source of one of his great pleasures. Rides ran through the surrounding forests. Walks were graveled from pits nearby. He brought roses and fruit and nut trees from England, and hawthorne, probably for hedging.

Not the least wonder in Pennsylvania's becoming one of the most prosperous and rewarding of the colonies horticulturally is the fact that its moving spirit, whose impact was so strong and lasting, actually made only two "visits" to the colony, each of those for only about two years. Events in the troubled world from which he had created this refuge tore him from it. A jealous sovereign, quarrelsome fellow proprietors of neighboring grants, bitterly contending later settlers, less regenerate and loyal than the first families, all compelled Penn twice to leave his own promised land. First he had had to hasten also to the deathbed of his first wife left in England. The second departure was shadowed by the lack of enjoyment his second wife and daughter found in beautiful Pennsbury, elegant but too remote for their tastes. That Penn was determined to return to his life's project in spite of all obstacles, foreign and domestic, is implicit in letters he wrote from England to those he had left in charge of state and house and gardens.

But where his first leave-taking had been to ensure the continuance of his proprietorship, which was threatened by the crown, his second was to land him in the grasp of his dishonest steward, who had been plotting, notes in hand, to ruin his master and take over his Pennsylvania holdings. As Penn's troubles worsened and he fell ill, in spite of the rallying of his friends, one can imagine that what he had accomplished in Pennsylvania was his mainstay and that he knew he had successfully completed his "holy experiment."

Furber's Flowers for the Month of March

1. Royal Widow Auricula P
2. Dwarf white starry Hyacinth B
3. White Bazleman Narciss B E
4. High Admiral Anemone B C
5. Rhyven Narciss B C
6. White passe flower B
7. White Grape Flower B
8. The lesser black Hellebore B
9. Danae Auricula P
10. White flowering Almond
11. Dwarf blue starry Hyacinth B
12. American flowering Maple L T
13. Goldfinch Polyanthos B
14. Larger blue starry Hyacinth B
15. Virginian flowering Maple L T
16. Narciss of Naples B
17. Best Claremon Tulip B C
18. The checkered Fritillaria B
19. Large-leaved Norway Maple L T
20. Double Pulchra Hyacinth B C
21. Queen of France Narcissus B
22. Palto Auriflame Tulip B C
23. Blue Oriental Hyacinth B C
24. Single bloody Wall B
25. Admiral blue Anemone B C
26. Bell Baptice Anemone B C
27. Monument Anemone B C
28. Red Flowering Larch tree L T
29. Blue Passe Flower B
30. Rose Tonker Anemone B C
31. White flowering Larch-Tree L T
32. Purple striped Anemone B
33. The Velvet Iris B
34. Jerusalem Cowslip B

3   *Voyages to Carolina*

W H E N the Reverend Andrew Burnaby, Vicar of Greenwich, arrived from England to dock in New York and begin his *Travels through the Middle Settlements of North America,* he realized that conditions between the colonies and the mother country were "worsening." Indeed, that may have been the reason for his visit. In the years 1759 and 1760 he traveled about, giving succinct and exact reports of rivers and harbors, crops and industries and his own opinions of the inhabitants of each colony he visited. He admired the tobacco fields on the way to Williamsburg but found the town "far from being a place of any consequence," though it had a "handsome appearance" and no mosquitoes. The governor's palace was "tolerably good, one of the best on the continent." As a general observation he noticed the prevalence of lightning rods. In fact, he believed "no country has more certainly proved the efficiency of electrical rods." He admired George Washington, a hero for undertaking the trip through the wilderness in 1753 to warn the French to withdraw from a fort upon the Ohio, and he felt Mount Vernon was "most beautifully situated . . . truly deserving of its owner." Philadelphia and its surrounding "villas, gardens and luxuriant orchards" he considered remarkable especially when one realized that "not eighty years ago the place where it now stands was a wild and uncultivated desert inhabited by nothing but ravenous wild beasts and a savage people." He commiserated with the inhabitants of New York for their lack of freshwater springs. He found Boston more receptive to the arts and sciences than any other city, but the women stiff. Portsmouth, New Hampshire, was not worthy of notice except for the great white pine trees, reserved for masts for the Royal Navy, which had to be cut when there was snow on the ground and then started on a non-stop slide toward the water's edge. Of Rhode Islanders, he had a very low opinion as traders, with their three-point traffic in sugar, slaves and rum. The women of Brunswick were most comely, the institutions of Philadelphia most advanced, with three libraries, many houses of worship and an insane asylum. All in all, he does justice to Philadelphia and rather less to all else. His conclusions, however, after he had rated all the places and their inhabitants, must have been of comfort to the Crown. He "firmly believed . . . a permanent union or alliance of all the colonies" would never take place because "such is the difference of character, of manners, of religion, of interest of the different colonies that I think, if I am not wholly ignorant of the human mind, were they left to themselves, there would be a civil war from one end of the continent to the other, while the Indians and Negroes would, with better reason, impatiently watch the opportunity of exterminating them altogether."

The inhabitants of the southern colonies, he said, by which he meant Virginia and Maryland, as he never went south of Virginia, "sooner than apply to laborious occupations" would eventually filter westward to richer lands requiring less dependence upon slavery, "an unsurmountable cause of weakness." The northern colonies, he felt, would become more populous, but were so composed of people of "different nations, different manners, different religions, and different languages . . . They have a mutual jealousy of each other . . ."

Perhaps it is as well the reverend visitor did not travel farther south and have to consider the differences among the Carolinas and, by this time, Georgia. Three more utterly diverse colonies and their inhabitants might, indeed, have finished off one so truly "ignorant of the human mind."

The initial impulse for settling Carolina, southernmost colony until Georgia joined the line in 1733, came from the West Indies. Southern Carolina had seemed a healthful refuge from the malaria-infested "Sugar Islands" of the seventeenth century. Some of the traders and planters on the islands invested in real estate on the mainland and ran additional enterprises there under overseers. We know that Eliza Lucas, for instance, was brought by her father to the Carolina country and settled with her mother on a place her father had bought to be run by an inefficient and dishonest overseer. Eliza as a teen-age girl took over the management and made a success of growing indigo. She was able so to bolster the economy of the south, that Washington, a keen observer of agricultural economy, asked to be a pallbearer at her funeral.

But this was long after the early efforts to organize a colony. The pull-

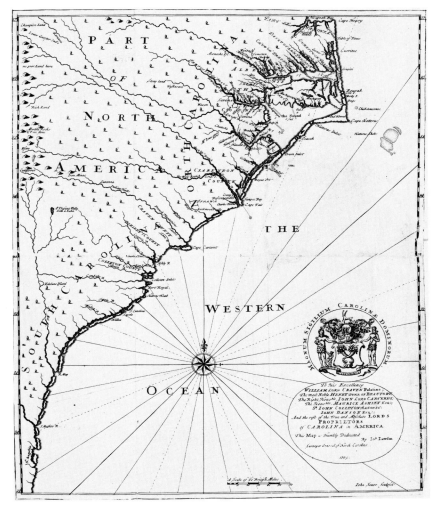

Map for the Proprietors of Carolina. From Lawson's *Two Voyages to Carolina*

together of Carolina as a colony began to be effected with a second charter granted by Charles II in 1663 to a group of proprietors, some of whom had had experience in Virginia, one of whom had known problems of overcrowding in Barbados, and several of whom were merely ambitious stay-at-homes. All were noblemen.

For South Carolina was aristocratic from the start, both because of its founding fathers' sonorous titles and their inclinations as to the form approved for its government. The charter was granted to "Edward Earl of Clarendon, George Duke of Albermarle, William Earl of Craven, John Lord Berkeley, Anthony Lord Ashley, Sir George Carterett, Sir John Colleton, and Sir William Berkeley." After no one did much about it, young Ashley came to the fore and drew up a form of government that has amazed, amused and puzzled many ever since.

"The Fundamental Constitution of Carolina" has been attributed to John Locke, soon to become the most influential philosopher for eighteenth-century Americans, but it is so foreign to any of his writings it is impossible to forgo ferreting out the origins of these landgraves of the rice fields. And it is rewarding. In 1667, when Locke went to live with Ashley as his private secretary and become his intimate friend for many years, he had just returned from a trip to visit Frederick William, the Great Elector of Brandenburg. Frederick William had inherited the margraviate as a bankrupt constitutional government. He left it a thriving monarchy, germ of the Prussia it was to become. Land was the source of both power and nobility. Taxation of the peasantry was the source of funds, formerly raised only by donations from the nobles. In Carolina the adaptation of this demonstrated success must have held charm for both nonresident and resident nobility. The purchase of three thousand acres ensured the rank of cassique, a Caribbean Island name for both a native chief and the mockingbird. Twenty thousand acres made the owner a landgrave. We must remember that Locke had become an empiricist through his friendship with Robert Boyle, the physicist, and Sydenham, the physician with whom he "rode out" when he had considered becoming a doctor. No one can deny the landgrave system had worked with the infant Prussia. It did not, however, work with Carolina, though echoes and vestiges of it are still with us.

The fate of the future colony was happily settled by the arrival in 1680 of a group of Huguenots. A substantial group of these industrious French Protestants was transported by proprietors eager to make silk and wine. The result, again, was not quite what was intended. Rice proved a more rewarding crop than either wine or silk, and slaves were welcomed to tend yet another tropical crop beyond the white man's powers of endurance, or supposed to be so.

The settlement of Georgia in 1733 finishes our southern boundary line of colonies, sitting all in a row like birds on a gate. It took place with, declaredly, the very highest motives — to rescue those in prison for minor offenses such as debt, and it had the greatest advance notices of all the colonies. After all, by this time the writers commissioned to persuade settlers to leave home and risk all had plenty of material to

Dodecatheon meadia (American Cowslip). Catesby's "Meadia." From Curtis *Botanical Magazine*

copy and hardly needed to stir from their desks to give "true and fair" accounts. Again, as with South Carolina, we shall have glowing specific references to Georgia throughout the text.

The two colonies of South Carolina and Georgia seem diverse enough in their inception to suit even the Reverend Burnaby, but there is a third colony that he also neglected to visit and that is, again, unlike any one of the others in its colonizing, although we shall depend upon it to represent the others in its fruits.

Although for long referred to as "Carolina" and then as "the Carolinas," North Carolina was totally unlike South Carolina as well as all the other colonies, first in having no coastline where ships could land readily. In *her* promotion pieces this was represented as a blessing and a safeguard, but it was a deterrent to easy settling. And to trading. Whoever or whatever came into North Carolina had to come by land from the north or the south. Poor though the geographical circumstances were, word of horticultural and agricultural riches seeped out from the highland; wine and silk again titillated the colonizers, merchants and gamblers in London, and the countryside was deemed worth looking into. To which budding concern we owe one of the best early surveys of this country, John Lawson's *A New Voyage to Carolina,* published in 1709, the source, like Beverly's *Virginia,* of all subsequent accounts.

As in the case of the other colonies, previous descriptions had not been lacking. Natural blessings to be found, as in all others, had included "stately woods, groves, marshes and meadows." There were the usual wild fruits: grapes, medlars, cherries . . . The plants were "odoriferous" and green all the year. Pine, cedar, cypress, oak, elm, ash and walnut trees were everywhere. Unlike the come-ons for the other colonies, however, here oranges and lemons grew in the same orchards as apples, pears, plums, peaches, apricots and nectarines.

In South Carolina there had even been a sort of model farm started by the proprietors at their own expense to be managed for them by Joseph West, later to be governor and landgrave. He was to furnish himself with seeds and roots for planting cotton, indigo, ginger, sugar cane, grapes and olives. As soon as he had arrived and built housing for himself and his people, he was to clear land and plant "Indian corne, beanes, peases, turnipps, carretts and potatoes for provisions . . . for experience sake" and "as foundation for your plantation." The proprietors were to send cattle from Virginia. If this can be called an experimental farm, it would seem to have been of short duration and not to have afforded a very stimulating example. In 1675 the Earl of Shaftesbury, the erstwhile Lord Ashley, was trying without success to unload it on the settlement generally, apparently to pay the proprietors' debts to Mr. West. But the site chosen later for Charleston was not profitably near the proprietors' model plantation, and the center of the settlement shifted, as well as, apparently, did Mr. West. He at least got to be a landgrave.

In 1700 a young man, from nowhere in particular and with no urge to explain himself, arrived in Carolina because, he said, when he was in London with an intention "to travel" he "accidentally met with a Gentleman who had been abroad and was very well acquainted with the ways of living in both Indies." Having inquired of him concerning them, John Lawson was assured that Carolina was the best country he could go to and that there was then a ship in the Thames upon which he could have passage. And that is all we know from John Lawson of his reasons for turning up in Carolina to spend the next eight years there, exploring, surveying, laying out two cities and writing a history dedicated to the proprietors. Accident or not, the result was most beneficial to the settling of Carolina and the book is one of the soundest descriptions of any of the accounts of the early eighteenth century in the colonies. It was published in London in 1709, and not for another generation, until the travels of John and William Bartram, was Carolina so to stir the imagination of the Old World. Lawson's book is called *A New Voyage to Carolina, containing the Exact Description and Natural History of that Country, together with the Present State thereof, and a Journal of a Thousand Miles Travel'd thro' Several Nations of Indians. Giving a particular Account of their Customs, Manners, etc.*

Besides the perennial fascination of the Indians and the practical interest in the state of the settlement generally, Lawson introduced a new note in accounts of the New World — its natural history. John Josselyn had attempted to describe such matters in his *New England Rarities* in 1672, but Lawson's is a more thorough account and the author is far better informed. Later Mark Catesby will bring out his great folios, and William Bartram will write his masterpiece, but Lawson is to lay the groundwork of fact and legend for them both and for many other chroniclers, who needed to do no more than copy him to sell their wares.

Whereas in the seventeenth century "truthful accounts" of the New World held the Christianizing of the Indians as the shining motive before all crass incentives, in eighteenth-century accounts the attention-winning prod was more likely to be getting ahead of the French or the Spanish and a tempting account of natural wonders calculated to persuade "curious" noblemen and collectors to invest their capital.

In the preface to his *New Voyage to Carolina,* John Lawson puts it very clearly.

'Tis a great Misfortune, that most of our travellers who go to this vast Continent in America, are persons of the Meaner Sort, and generally of a very slender Education; who, being hired by the Merchants to trade amongst the Indians, in which Voyages they often spend several years, are yet, at their Return, uncapable of giving any reasonable Account of What they met withal in those remote Parts, tho' the Country abounds with Curiosities worthy of a nice Observation. In this Point, I think, the French outstrip us . . . First, By their numerous Clergy . . . Secondly They always send abroad some of their Gentlemen in Company of the Missionaries, who upon their arrival, are ordered into the Wilderness, to make Discoveries . . . to

Lawson's description of the animals to be found in the Carolinas awakened great interest especially about the opossum

keep a strict Journal . . . which is industriously spread about the Kingdom to their Advantage . . . their Monarch being a very good Judge of Mens Deserts . . .

He goes on to say that he has spent eight years in Carolina "travelling." He surveyed the seacoast, which is inhabited by Christians, and then made discovery of a tract of land between the seacoast, with its inhabitants, and the "Ledges of Mountains, from when our noblest Rivers have their Rise . . . inhabited by none but Savages who covet a Christian Neighborhood for the Advantage of Trade."

How much Lawson was obliged to others than himself for the idea of his journey, for the means to make it, for the requirements he set for his reports on all vegetable and animal matters, and for his thorough study of the topography of the country and its Indians we cannot guess. He had recorded indebtedness to James Petiver, naturalist and apothecary of London. Petiver, said by John Ray to have "the greatest correspondence both in the East and West Indies of any man in Europe," was an ardent collector and had been made a member of the Royal Society in 1695. It would be of the greatest interest to him to have an able man, indebted to him, exploring the Carolinas and sending him specimens. That Lawson undertook this mission seriously is seen in his surviving letters to Petiver, the first dated April in 1701, promising shells and butterflies with assurances to be "very industrious to that Imploy." The other letters are dated after Lawson's return to England with his book and during his second trip to the Carolinas in 1709, by which time his involvement with Petiver is on a more businesslike basis.

Lawson was to die before he could perform much of his grand design as written to Petiver:

A complete history of these parts . . . To make a strict collection of all plants, animal, vegetable and mineral I can and also: meet with all in Carolina always keeping one of a sort by me giving an account of ye time and day they were gotten, when they first appearing, what soil of ground, when they flower seed and disappear and what individuall uses the Indians or English make thereof . . . Besides I would send seeds of all the physicall plants and flower to be planted in England. As for the trees the time they bred flowers bring their ripe fruit and soil. I hope to comply with most of them this year 1711.

We are the losers today, as was the Royal Society then, that Lawson, like his predecessor Banister in Virginia, never lived to finish his mission.

Lawson has, however, left us in his debt for descriptions of Carolina as he found it. His book opens with a "Journal of a Thousand Miles Travel among the Indians, from South to North Carolina," followed by

"A Description of North Carolina," beginning with the history of the earliest adventurers, confirmed, says Lawson, by the Hatteras Indians, who, he says interestedly, are frequently gray-eyed. He quotes an early account of the inlets and waterways made by three adventurers from Barbados in 1664 and then gives his own account of the crops in the country: wheat, rye, barley, oats, Indian corn and rice, "the Rice of Carolina being esteemed the best . . ." There grows also: Guinea corn, buckwheat "to feed hogs and poultry"; the "Bushel-bean," a "spontaneous product" so called because for every bean that is planted "they bring a Bushel"; kidney beans "here before the English came" and "Indian or Rounceval or Miraculous Pease."

We quote verbatim the end of Lawson's chapter "A Description . . ."

The Garden-Roots that thrive well in Carolina, are Carrotts, Leeks, Parsnips, Turneps, Potatoes, of several delicate sorts, Ground Artichokes, Radishes, Horse-Radish, Beets, both sorts, Onions, Shallot, Garlick, Cives, and the Wild Onions.

The Sallads are the Lettice, Curl'd, Red, Cabbage and Savoy. The Spinage round and prickly, Fennel, sweet and the common Sort, Samphire in the Marshes excellent, so is the Dock or Wild-Rhubarb, Rocket, Sorrel, French and English, Cresses of several Sorts, Purslain wild, and that of a larger Size which grows in the Gardens; for this Plant is never met withal in the Indian Plantation, and is, therefore, suppos'd to proceed from Cow-Dung, which Beast they keep not. Parsley two Sorts; Asparagus thrives to a Miracle, without hot Beds or dunging the Land, White-Cabbage from European or New England Seed, for the People are negligent and unskilful, and don't take care to provide Seed of their own. The Colly-Flower we have not yet had an Opportunity to make Tryal of, nor has the Artichoke ever appeared amongst us, that I can learn. Coleworts plain and curl'd, Savoys; Besides the Water-Melons of several Sorts, very good, which should have gone amongst the Fruits. Of Musk-Melons we have very large and good, and several Sorts, as the Golden, Green, Guinea, and Orange. Cucumbers long, short, and prickly, all these from the Natural Ground, and great Increase, without any Helps of Dung or Reflection. Pompions yellow and very large, Burmillions, Cashaws, an excellent Fruit boil'd; Squashes, Simnals, Horns, and Gourds; besides many other Species, of less Value, too tedious to name.

Our Pot-herbs and others of use, which we already possess, are Angelica wild and tame, Balm, Bugloss, Borage, Burnet, Clary, Marigold, Pot-Marjoram, and other Marjorams, Summer and Winter Savory, Columbines, Tansey, Wormwood, Nep, Mallows several Sorts, Drage red and white, Lambs Quarters, Thyme, Hyssop of a very large Growth, sweet Basil, Rosemary, Lavender: The more Physical are *Carduus Benedictus,* the Scurvy-grass of America, I never here met any of the European sort; Tobacco of many sorts, Dill, Carawa, Cummin, Anise, Coriander, all sorts of Plantain of England, and two sorts spontaneous, good Vulneraries; Elecampane, Comfrey, Nettle, the Seed from England, none Native; Monks Rhubarb, Burdock, Asarum wild in the Woods, reckon'd one of the Snake-Roots; Poppies in the Garden, none wild yet discover'd; Wormseed, Fever-few, Rue, Ground-Ivy spontaneous, but very small and scarce, *Aurea virga,* four sorts of Snake-Roots, besides the common species, which are great Antidotes against the Serpent's Bite, and are easily raised in the Garden; Mint; James-Town-Weed, so-called from Virginia, the Seed it bears is very like that of an Onion, it is excellent for curing Burns, and aswaging Inflammations, but taken inwardly brings on a sort of drunken Madness. One of our Marsh-Weeds, like a Dock, has the same Effect, and possesses the Party with Fear and Watchings. The Red-Root whose Leaf is like Spearmint, is good for Thrushes, and sore Mouths; Camomil, but it must be kept in the Shade, otherwise it will not thrive; Houseleek first from England; Vervin, Night-Shade, several kinds, Harts-Tongue; Yarrow abundance, Mullein the same, both of the Country; Sarsaparilla, and abundance more I could name, yet not the hundredth part of what remains, a Catalogue of which is a Work of many Years, and without any other Subject, would swell to a large Volume, and requires the Abilities of a skilful Botanist: Had not the ingenious Mr. Banister (the greatest *Virtuoso* we have ever had on the Continent) been unfortunately taken out of this World, he would have given the best Account of the Plants of America, of any that ever yet made such an Attempt in these Parts . . .

The Flower-Garden in Carolina is as yet arriv'd, but to a very poor and jejune Perfection. We have only two sorts of Roses; the Clove-July-Flowers, Violets, Princes Feather, and *Tres Colores.* There has been nothing more cultivated in the Flower-Garden, which, at present, occurs to my Memory; but as for the wild spontaneous Flowers of this Country, Nature has been so liberal, that I cannot name one tenth part of the valuable ones . . .

Lawson's chapter on the "present State of Carolina" tells of cheap land; superior livestock; possible mineral deposits; industrious French refugees; beautiful, industrious, fruitful women; long-lived men; cheap provisions; friendly Indians; equable climate and things necessary for settling. On the way through all this he drops in a paragraph that must have electrified his audience in England, whether in the Royal Society or coffee houses where "curious" gentlemen met. After a prophecy about "Wine, Oil, Fruit and Silk" becoming as familiar as "Drugs and Dyes" he adds:

And at present the Curious may have a large field to satisfy and divert themselves in, as Collections of strange Beasts, Birds, Insects, Reptiles, Shells, Fishes, Minerals, Herbs, Flowers, Plants, Shrubs, Intricate Roots, Gums, Tears, Rozins, Dyes and Stones . . .

In his section "The Natural History of Carolina," he discusses "Vegetables," "Timber" and "Beasts," which will not, unfortunately, detain us here although they very likely caused the craze in London for specimens of the opossum, the hummingbird and assorted snakes. The book ends with a masterful "Account of the Indians."

His description of the "Vegetables" is enthusiastic:

The spontaneous Shrubs of this Country are, the Larkheel-Tree; three sorts of Hony-Suckle-Tree, the first of which grows in Branches, as our Piemento-Tree does, that is, always in low, moist Ground; the other grows in clear, dry Land, the Flower more cut and lacerated; the third, which is the most beau-

The Upright Honeysuckle of Catesby, Plate 57, Vol. I. From his *Natural History*

tiful, and, I think, the most charming Flower of its Colour, I ever saw, grows betwixt two and three Foot high, and for the most part, by the side of a swampy Wood, or on the Banks of our Rivers, but never near the Salt-Water. All the Sorts are white; the last grows in a great Bunch of these small Hony-Suckles set upon one chief Stem, and is commonly the Bigness of a large Turnep. Nothing can appear more beautiful than these Bushes, when in their Splendour, which is April and May. The next is the Hony-Suckle of the Forest; it grows about a Foot high, bearing its Flowers on small Pedastals, several of them standing on the main Stock, which is the Thickness of a Wheat-Straw. We have also the Wood-bind, much the same as in England; Princes-feather, very large and beautiful in the Garden; *Tres-Colores,* branch'd Sun-flower, Double Poppies, Lupines, of several pretty sorts, spontaneous; and the Sensible Plant is said to be near the Mountains, which I have not yet seen. Saf-Flower; (and I believe, the Saffron of England would thrive here, if planted), the yellow Jassamin is wild in our Woods, of a pleasant Smell. Ever-Greens are here plentifully found, of a very quick Growth, and pleasant Shade; Cypress, or white Cedar, the Pitch Pine, the yellow Pine, the white Pine with long Leaves; and the small Almond-Pine which last bears Kernels in the Apple, tasting much like an Almond, and in some years there falls such plenty, as to make the Hogs fat. Horn-Beam; Cedar, two sorts; Holly, two sorts; Bay-Tree, two sorts; one the Dwarf-Bay, about twelve Foot high; the other the Bigness of a middling Pine-Tree, about two Foot and half Diameter; Laurel-Trees, in Height equalizing the lofty Oaks, the Berries and Leaves of this Tree dyes a Yellow; the Bay-Berries yield a Wax, which besides its use in Chirurgery, makes Candles that, in burning, give a fragrant Smell. The Cedar-Berries are infused, and made Beer of, by the Bermudians, they are Carminative and much of the Quality of Juniper-Berries; Yew and Box I never saw or heard of in this Country.

There are two sorts of Myrtles, different in Leaf and Berry; the Berry yields Wax that makes Candles, the most lasting, and of the sweetest Smell imaginable. Some mix half Tallow with this Wax, others use it without Mixture; and these are fit for a Lady's Chamber, and incomparable to pass the Line withal, and other hot Countries, because they will stand, when others will melt, by the excessive Heat, down in the Binnacles.

Ever-green Oak, two sorts; Gall-Berry-Tree, bearing a black Berry, with which the Women dye their Cloaths and Yarn black; 'tis a pretty Ever-Green, and very plentiful, growing always in low swampy Grounds, and amongst Ponds.

We have a Prim or Privet, which grows on the dry, barren, sandy Hills, by the Sound side; it bears a smaller sort than in England and grows into a round Bush, very beautiful.

Last of Bushes, (except Savine, which grows every where wild) is the famous Yaupon, call'd by the South-Carolina Indians, Cassena, is a Bush, that grows chiefly on the Sand-Banks and Island, bordering on the Sea of

Carolina; on this Coast it is plentifully found. It grows the most like Box, of any Vegetable that I know, being very like it in Leaf, only dented exactly like Tea, but the Leaf somewhat fatter. Some of these Bushes grow to be twelve Foot high, others are three or four. The Wood thereof is brittle as Myrtle, and affords a light ash-color'd Bark. There is sometimes found of it in Swamps and rich low Grounds which has the same figured Leaf, only it is larger, and of a deeper Green; This may be occasion'd by the Richness that attends the low Grounds thus situated. The third Sort has the same kind of Leaf, but never grows a Foot high, and is found both in rich, low Land, and on the Sand-Hills. I don't know that ever I found any Seed or Berries on the dwarfish Sort, yet I find no Difference in Taste, when Infusion is made; Cattle and Sheep delight in this Plant very much and so do the Deer, all which crop it very short, and browze thereon, wheresoever they meet with it. I have transplanted the Sand-Bank and dwarfish Yaupon, and find that the first Year, the Shrubs stood at a stand; but the second Year they throve as well as in their native Soil. This Plant is the Indian Tea, us'd and approved by all the Savages on the Coast of Carolina, and from them sent to the West-ward Indians, and sold at a considerable Price. All which they cure after the same way, as they do for themselves; this is thus: They take this Plant (Not only the Leaves, but the smaller Twigs along with them) and bruise it in a Mortar, till it becomes blackish, the Leaf being wholly defaced; Then they take it out, put it into one of their earthern Pots over the Fire, till it smoaks; stirring it all the time, till it is cur'd. Others take it, after it is bruis'd, and put it into a Bowl, to which they put live Coals, and cover them with the *Yaupon,* till they have done smoaking, often turning them over. After all, they spread it upon their Mats, and dry it in the Sun to keep for Use. The Spaniards in New-Spain have this Plant very plentiful on the Coast of Florida, and hold it in great Esteem. They prefer it above all Liquids, to drink with Physick, to carry the same safely and speedily thro' the Passages, for which it is admirable, as I myself have experimented.

Lawson's list of "Timber" is thorough and was much referred to. Regretfully, we merely sketch it in:

Chestnut Oak . . . a very lofty Tree, clear of Boughs and limbs, for fifty or 60 Foot . . . I have seen of them so high that a good Gun could not reach a Turkey, tho' loaded with Swan-Shot . . . call'd Chestnut, because of the Largeness and Sweetness of the Acorns.

White, Scaly-bark Oak . . . used, as the former . . . building Sloops and Ships . . .

Red Oak . . . large and lofty . . . used to rive into Rails for Fences . . . for Pipe and Barrel-Staves . . . makes good Clap-boards.

Spanish Oak . . . rives very well into Clap-boards . . . some use to build Vessels with it for the Sea . . . These all bear good Mast for the Swine.

Black Oak . . . a durable Wood, under Water . . . sometimes used in House-work.

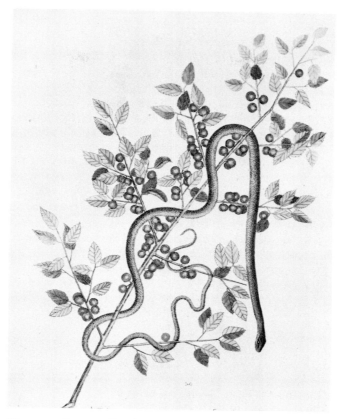

Yapon, or Cassena. Catesby's Plate 57, Vol. II. A much discussed remedy

White Iron, or Ring Oak . . . the best Oak for Shipwork . . . tho Live Oak be more lasting . . .

Live Oak . . . an evergreen, and the most durable Oak all America affords. The Shortness of this Wood's Trunk, makes it unfit for Plank . . . Limbs serve for excellent Timbers, Knees, etc. for Vessels . . . The Acorns . . . are as sweet as Chestnuts . . . Indians draw an Oil from them, as sweet as that from the Olive . . . With these Nuts, some have counterfeited the Cocoa, whereof they have made Chocolate, not to be distinguished by a good Palate. Window-Frames, Mallets, and Pins for Blocks, are made thereof.

Willow-Oak . . . a sort of Water Oak . . .

Ash . . . Of Ash we have two sorts, agreeing nearly with the English in the Grain . . .

Elm . . . two sorts of Elm; the first grown on our High-Land, and approaches our English. The Indians take the Bark of its Root . . . beat it, whilst green, to a Pulp . . . dry it in the Chimney . . . use as a Sovereign Remedy to heal a Cut or green Wound . . . The other Elm grows in low Ground, of whole Bark the English and Indians make Ropes . . .

The Tulip Trees . . . by the Planters, call'd Poplars . . . grow to a prodigious Bigness, some . . . One and twenty Foot in Circumference . . . another, where in a lusty Man had his Bed and Household Furniture . . . till his Labour got him a more fashionable mansion . . . The Wood makes very pretty Wainscot . . . The Buds, made into an Ointment, cure Scalds, Inflammations, and Burns . . .

Beech . . . here frequent, and very large . . . for Firewood.

Horn-Beam . . . grows, in some Places, very plentifully; yet the Plenty of other Woods makes it unregarded.

Sassafrass . . . The Vertues of Sassafras are well known in Europe . . . durable and lasting, used for Bowls, Timbers, Posts for Houses, and other Things that require standing in the Ground . . . It bears a white Flower . . . very cleansing to the Blood . . . eaten in the Spring . . . The Berry, when ripe, is black . . . oily, Carminative . . . prevalent in Clysters for the Colick. The Bark of the Root is a Specifick to those afflicted with the Gripes. The same in Powder, and a Lotion made thereof, is much used by the Savages, to mundify old Ulcers . . .

Dog-wood . . . is plentiful . . . It flowers the first in the Woods; its white Blossoms making the Forest very beautiful . . . a fine Grain . . . serves for several Uses within doors . . . The Bark of this Root is infused, is held as an infallible Remedy against the Worms.

Laurel . . . Bay and Laurel generally delight in the low, swampy Ground . . . no use but for Fire Wood . . .

Bay-Tulips . . . The Bay-Tulip-Tree is a fine Ever-green.

Sweet Gum . . . The sweet Gum-Tree . . . cures the Herpes and Inflammations; being apply'd to the Morphew and Tettars . . . an extraordinary Balsam . . .

Black-Gums . . . two sorts; both fit for Cart-Naves . . . one bears a black, well-tasted Berry, which the Indians mix with their Pulse and Soups, it giving 'em a pretty Flavour, and scarlet Colour. The Bears crop these Trees for the Berries, which they mightily covet, yet kill'd in that Season, they eat very unsavory . . . The other Gum bears a Berry . . . bitter and ill-tasted. This Tree (the Indians report) is never wounded by Lightning . . .

White Gum . . . bearing a sort of long bunch'd Flowers . . .

Red Cedar . . . an Ever-green . . . Of this Wood, Tables, Wainscot, and other Necessaries, are made, and esteemed for its sweet Smell . . . much used in Posts for Houses and Sills; likewise to build Sloops, Boats, etc. by reason the Worm will not touch it . . . so plentiful in this Settlement, that they have fenced in Plantations with it, and the Coffins of the Dead are generally made thereof.

White Cedar . . . nearly approaches the other Cedar, in Smell, Bark and Leaf; only this grows taller, being as strait as an Arrow . . . good for Yard, Top-Masts, Booms and Boltsprits . . . The best Shingles for Houses are made of this Wood . . . Good Pails and other Vessels, free from Leakage, are likewise made thereof. The Bark of this and the red Cedar, the Indians use to make their Cabins of . . .

Cypress . . . not an Ever-green with us, and is therefore call'd the bald Cypress . . . the largest for Height and Thickness, that we have in this Part of the World; some of them holding thirty-six Foot in Circumference . . . the Nuts . . . yield a most odoriferous Balsam, that infallibly cures all new and green Wounds . . . Of these great Trees the Pereaugers and Canoes are scoop'd and made . . . Some are so large, as to carry thirty Barrels . . . Others, that are split down the Bottom, and a piece added thereto, will carry eighty, or an hundred . . . a Chest made of this Wood, will suffer no Moth, or Vermine, to abide therein.

Two Sorts of Locust, white and Yellow . . . rare if varnished. The Locust, for its enduring the Weather, is chosen for . . . all sorts of Works that are exposed thereto. It bears a Leaf nearest the Liquorice-Plant. 'Tis a pretty tall Tree. Of this the Indians make their choicest Bows . . .

Honey Tree: a Locust. The Honey-Tree bears as great a Resemblance to the Locust, as a Shallot does to an Onion. It is of that Species, but more prickly . . . Of the Honey, very good Metheglin is made, there being Orchards planted in Virginia for that intent.

Sowr Wood. The Sorrel, or Sowr-Wood-Tree, is so call'd because the Leaves taste like Sorrel. Some are about a Foot or ten Inches Diameter . . .

Pine. Of Pines, there are, in Carolina, at least four sorts. The Pitch-Pine, growing to a great Bigness . . . but a short Leaf . . . so durable that it seems to suffer no Decay . . . used in several Domestic and Plantation Uses . . . afford the four great Necessaries, Pitch, Tar, Rozin, and Turpentine . . .

The white and yellow Pines are saw'd into Planks . . . Masts, Yards . . . the most useful Tree in the Woods.

The Almond-Pine serves for Masts . . . Dwarf-Pine, it is for Shew alone . . .

Hiccory . . . is of the Walnut-kind, and bears a Nut as they do, of which there are found three sorts. The first is . . . the common white Hiccory . . . not a durable Wood . . . another sort . . . we call Hiccory, the Heart thereof being very red, firm and durable; of which Walking-Sticks, Mortars, Pestils, and several other fine Turnery-wares are made. The third is call'd the Flying-bark'd Hiccory, from its brittle and scaly Bark . . . Of this Wood, Coggs for Mills are made, etc. The Leaves smell very fragrant.

Walnut. The Walnut-Tree of America is call'd Black Walnut to distinguish it from the Hiccories, it having a blacker Bark . . . The Wood is very firm and durable, of which Tables and Chests of Drawers are made . . .

to bottom Vessels for the Sea withal; and they say, that it is never eaten by the Worm. The Nuts have a large Kernel, which is very oily, except laid by, a long time to mellow. The Shell is very thick, as all the native Nuts of America are . . .

Maple . . . of which we have two sorts, is used to make Trenchers, Spinning-wheels, etc. . . .

Chinkapin . . . is a sort of Chesnut, whose Nuts are most commonly very plentiful; insomuch that the Hogs get fat with them . . . The Wood . . . is used to timber Boats, Shallops, &c. . . . It's good Fire Wood, but very sparkling as well as Sassafras.

Birch . . . grows on all the Banks of our Rivers . . . Its Buds in April are eaten by the Parrakeetos . . . as to the Wine, or other Profits it would yield we are, at present, Strangers to.

Willow. The Willow, here . . . differs both in Bark and Leaf . . .

Sycamore . . . grows in a low, swampy Land . . . Its Bark is quite different from the English and the most beautiful I ever saw, being mottled and clowded with several Colours, as white, blue, etc. It bears no Keys but a Bur like the sweet Gum . . .

Holly . . . we have two sorts; one having a large Leaf, the other a smaller. They grow very thick in our low Woods . . . They make good Trenchers, and other Turnery Ware.

Red-Bud. The Red-Bud-Tree bears a purple Lark-Heel, and is the best Sallad, of any Flower I ever saw . . .

Pelletory . . . grows on the Sand-Banks and Islands . . . used to cure the Tooth-ach . . . the Bark . . . being very hot, draws a Rhume from the Mouth and causes much Spittle . . .

Arrow-Wood . . . growing on the Banks, is used, by the Indians for Arrows and Gun-Sticks . . .

Chesnut . . . The Chesnut-Tree of Carolina, grows up towards the hilly Part thereof, is a very large and durable Wood, and fit for House-Frames, Palisado's, Sills, and many other Uses. The Nut is smaller than those from Portugal, but sweeter.

Persimmons . . . is a Tree, which agrees with all Lands and Soils. Their Fruit, when ripe, is nearest our Medlar; if eaten before, draws your Mouth up like a Purse, being the greatest Astringent I ever met withal, therefore very useful in some Cases . . . The Fruit is rotton, when ripe . . .

Mulberry. We have three sorts of Mulberries . . . The first is the common red Mulberry, whose Fruit is the earliest we have, (except the Strawberries) and very sweet. These Trees make a very fine Shade, to sit under in Summer-time . . . their Fruit . . . used instead of Raisins and Currants . . . The others are a smooth-leav'd Mulberry, fit for the Silk-Worm. One bears a white Fruit, which is common; the other bears a small black Berry, very sweet . . . This Tree grows extraordinary round and pleasant to the Eye.

Hazel-Nut . . . grows plentifully . . . especially towards the Mountains;

but ours are not so good as the English Nuts, having a much thicker Shell . . .

Black-Cherries . . . grow to be very large Trees. One sort, which is rarely found, is red . . . the common Cherry grows high, and in Bunches . . . of a bitterish sweet Relish . . . valuable with our small Black-Cherries, for an Infusion in Spirits . . .

Piemento. All-Spice-Tree, whose Berries differ in shapes from those in the West Indies, being Taper or Conic, yet not inferiour to any of that sort.

Damsons of America . . . both black and white . . . grow anywhere . . . I have planted several in my Orchard, that came from the Stone, which thrive well amongst the rest of my Trees.

Red-Haws. The Haw-thorn grows plentifully in some parts of this Country. The Haws are quite different from those in England, being four times as big, and of a very pleasant agreeable Taste. We make no use of this Plant, nor any other, for Hedges, because Timber is so plentiful at present. In my Judgment, the Honey-Locust would be the fittest for Hedges . . .

Black-Haws. The Black Haw grows on a slender Tree, about the Height of a Quince-Tree . . . and bears the black Haw, which People eat, and the Birds covet also . . .

Lawson's trees will serve us, as they did many others, as our basic list of American trees, many so soon to be demanded for English and French cultivation and for popularization in American gardens.

Lawson returned, after eight years in Carolina, to England and saw to the publication of his book. This must have put him in a new category for proprietors, underwriters and "curious" subscribers, for we find him embarking for a return to North Carolina in January, 1710, to conduct six hundred and fifty Palatine Germans with the assistance of the Chief Justice of North Carolina.

England had lately received an influx of thirteen thousand Palatinate refugees and Queen Anne was anxious to hand them on. Quite possibly the reported success of the French refugees helped. In any case, a Baron Christopher von Graffenried was intent upon a scheme for settling a group of the Germans and some Swiss, both deemed desirable tenants. He announced he would be selective and accept only "young people, healthy, laborious and of all kinds of avocations and handicrafts." His flamboyant portrait is enough to give pause to anyone considering anything to do with him, but perhaps prospective settlers were not favored with a sight of the company head. In any case, von Graffenried arranged to have the first lot conducted across the Atlantic by no less a leader than John Lawson, assisted by Christopher Gale, Chief Justice of North Carolina. Von Graffenried remained behind to await the Swiss group.

The voyage, according to Lawson, was a nightmare, half the people dying of "ship-fever." Far from being the enterprising spirits the Ger-

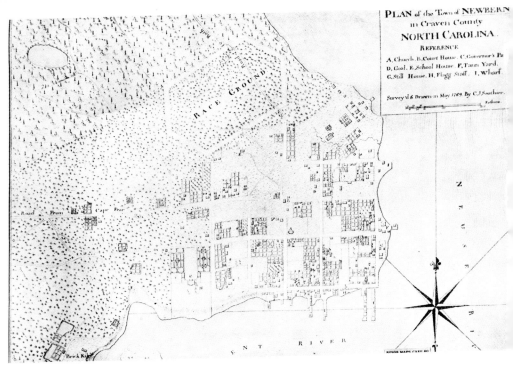

PLAN of the Town of NEWBERN in Craven County NORTH CAROLINA

REFERENCE
A, Church. B, Court House. C, Governor's Pa
D, Goal. E, School House. F, Tann Yard.
G, Still House. H, Flagg Staff. I, Wharf

Survey'd & Drawn in May 1769. By C.J.Sauthier.

Plan of New Bern, North Carolina, 1769, with a detail of the Governor's Palace and Garden on opposite page

mans were expected to be, they took to their bunks, Lawson reported, and lay there until they either died or recovered. When von Graffenried and the Swiss arrived in September, the colony was in a parlous state.

For what happened after that we have, unfortunately, to rely on the baron. Unfortunately, because there seems to have been bad feeling at the start, the baron having ordered Lawson to proceed to the future site of New Bern and there to lay out the new city as the baron had planned it, wide streets and three acres to each house site, all divided into a cross with a church at the center. Lawson, who owned part of the land, had already planned lots along the river. The baron later spoke bitterly of the land as "triple-purchased," feeling he had paid for it three times: to the proprietors, to Lawson and to the Indians. There was also some idea in his mind and memoirs that Lawson settled the workers on his own piece. By the baron's account, however, his settlers made better progress than "the English inhabitants in several years." This, at least for eighteen months, was the original founding and laying out of New Bern, of which now no records remain. The map of New Bern in 1769 owes nothing to either Lawson or the baron.

Whose relationship was to end very quickly. According to the baron, the "Surveyor General" was eager to go up the river Neuse on a fifteen-day trip to see how far the river could be navigated for a possible link

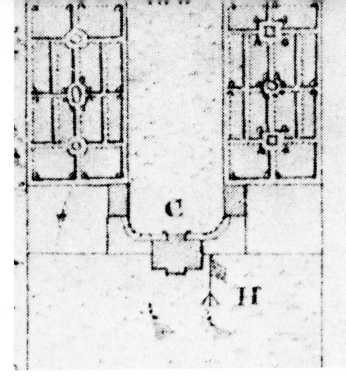

with Virginia by road. Questioned by the apprehensive baron, Lawson assured him he had made the trip before and that there were no savage Indians. They started out with two friendly Indian neighbors, one of whom spoke English, and two Negroes to row. They also had horses, for, when they got to the site of the intended road, Lawson borrowed the baron's horse and attracted the attention of an Indian town to the expedition. The horse was taken. The baron again wished to return. Lawson again reassured him. They proceded and were captured.

The baron's account now becomes less than clear. The Tuscarora Indians believed they had the governor in the baron, and held a trial that impressed the baron, he says, by its dignity. He and Lawson were acquitted, but new Indians arrived, complications arose and the two men were bound and condemned to die. The baron seems to have talked his way out, claiming the queen's protection for himself. He made no attempt to save Lawson, arousing contemporary suspicions that he was willing to be rid of him and escape his debt to him. The baron got back to New Bern and left at once for England, where he publicly printed recriminations of all concerned.

Some say Lawson had his throat cut with his own knife. Some say he was burned to death by being stuck full of splinters of torch wood, which were then set alight. However it happened and why, the Tuscaroras descended upon New Bern and nearly put an end to it. They had certainly deprived the world of a careful study of the *Complete History of Carolina*.

Furber's Flowers for the Month of April

1. Keysers Jewel Hyacinth B C
2. Diamond ditto B C
3. Double blossomed peach L T
4. Single Orange Narcissus B C
5. Double Endroit Tulip B C
6. Glory of the East Auricula P
7. Double Wall Flower P
8. Blush red Lilly of the Valley B
9. British King Anemone B C
10. Celestis Anemone B C
11. Amaranthus trache ditto B C
12. Single Jonquill F E
13. Loves Master Auricula P
14. Double painted Lady Auricula P
15. Palurus Christ's Thorn L T
16. White Lilly of the Valley B
17. Merveille du Monde Auricula P
18. Lady Margareta Anemone B C
19. Julian ditto B C
20. Double Jonquill F E
21. Duke of Beauford Auricula P
22. Lecreep No. 1 Tulip B C
23. Beau Regard Tulip B C
24. Dwarf Single-flowering Almond B T
25. Duke of St. Albans Auricula P
26. Turky Ranuncula's sweet scented B C
27. Double Cuckou Flower B
28. Grand Presence Auricula P
29. Sea Pink S E
30. Double flowering Almond B T

4 Naturalists and Botanists

To modern sentimental gardeners seeking to reconstruct an "old-fashioned garden" it seems axiomatic that American gardeners of the eighteenth century, so lately allied to origins in the Old World, would have confined themselves to nostalgic plantings in the New, with seeds and slips, bulbs and roots, brought from what many settlers continued for several generations to call "home."

This would be a reasonable assumption if the New World had proved devoid of the green and gay surroundings to which the adventuring settlers had become accustomed near their original homes. All over the world we see English garden flowers, transported to tropical islands and palm-fringed plains, and wherever a bare earth could be induced to give them asylum to comfort expatriate hearts. Prudent settlers anywhere would carefully transport plants, known and grown at home in orchards and fields, to a New World for certain support of man and beast. Such was the case along the Atlantic seaboard with fruits and grains and vegetables, and with field crops like clover and lucerne, which could be ploughed in to improve the soil. We read of vegetables growing to sizes unseen before and we know that orchard fruits, especially apples, took to the new land to become famous for their proliferating progeny. Time-honored herbs "for Meate or Medicine" we have seen established in every forethoughtful settler's plot. Many of these, their uses forgotten, now crowd our country roadsides. For purely ornamental plantings, we know that roses were tenderly transported, with pinks, peonies, white lilies and other favorites like hyacinths and daffodils.

75

But the fact is that the New World seems to have risen up in such a horticultural exuberance of flowers and blossoming shrubs and vines and trees as to quiet the fears of the doubtful and satisfy the most compulsive early American gardeners. And also to awaken the concupiscence of gardeners overseas, as witness lists given to westward-bound sea captains, and the sacks and boxes, tins and tubs of seeds, nuts and roots, that struggled to survive the return voyage.

There were five great and separate influences that sparked the interest in American horticulture. From the beginning there was the English government's need for wood for shipbuilding and stores and the universal interest in new medicinal plants. Credit for the second stimulus must go to the Royal Society, that august body of active minds formed in London and dedicated to further matters of scientific interest around the world. This was a group to which naturalists everywhere aspired to belong. The members were influential and affluent — some even individually able to fund investigations and explorations, to see works published and to encourage the adventurous. From its incorporation in 1662 as the "Royal Society of London for Improving Natural Knowledge," it played an important part in encouraging scholarship in the budding branches of science, and from its earliest days it attracted those searching out the treasures of the New World. Cotton Mather, for instance, among other seventeenth-century American aspirants to membership, initiated a correspondence from New England about natural phenomena, witchcraft and medicinal plants. It is safe to say that no advances were made in natural history throughout the eighteenth century that were not sieved through the Royal Society.

After the Royal Society, the next two stimuli to American horticulture and gardening in the eighteenth century were religious, not related, but each in a different way responsible for the flowering of the interest in American gardens and English horticultural gains from them. While the British colonies on the Atlantic seaboard were diversely conceived and constructed, they all had social origins based upon some religious belief, sect, persuasion, philanthropy or state church.

The first of these religious sparks, and the one deserving great credit, came from the Quakers. We have seen encouragement toward botany and horticulture in the very inception of Pennsylvania. In our next chapter we shall see more of this dedication to the study of nature and its invaluable contributions to American gardens at home and English gardens abroad.

The other religious impetus toward promoting American contributions to American and English gardens came, not directly from the Church of England, but from one of its bishops working through his church office. Its importance, also, like the influence of the Quakers, cannot be underrated.

The fifth and last influence, eventually underlying all others, rests with the invention and adoption of the Linnaean system of plant identification. A great piece of good fortune for world gardeners in the eighteenth century was the miracle of the emergence of Linnaeus with his binomial system of plant identification, which, by the middle of the century, enabled aspiring botanists, gardeners, explorers and nurserymen to communicate accurately with one another.

The first indication of a horticultural tide turning to run toward England from the New World began with trees, and rose from the government's real need, as we can see in the enthusiasm of early reports of American timber for ships. England and Europe had run heedlessly through their natural resources for building, much as we have run through our energy resources today. Denuded forests were badly in want of replenishing. England had been forced to turn to the Baltic and to become dependent upon Norway and Russia. The prospect of having colonies in America that could supply materials for shipbuilding was bright and should have induced a careful approach toward both the supplies and the colonies. But it was a rough age. New World forests loomed limitless and everyone knew colonies existed for the support and convenience of the mother country. The only precaution taken toward conservation of these giant trees was to reserve all the largest and best for the crown.

As early as 1662 John Evelyn, statesman, diarist, courtier, epicure, gardener and author, had sensed the emergency and read a paper before the newly formed Royal Society on the need for England to practice forestry. It purported to be an answer to "certain Queries propounded to that illustrious Assembly by the Honourable the Principal Officers and Commissioners of the Navy," whose anxiety was primarily for England's "wooden walls." Evelyn's "paper" became his great work *Sylva,* published in 1664, destined to go through many editions as an authoritative *Discourse on Forest Trees and the Propagation of Timber in His Majesty's Dominions.*

Evelyn was among the first to conceive of the usefulness of growing trees from abroad on home soil, especially trees that grew so tall as to yield masts all in one piece, like the New England white pine. Evelyn was an intimate friend of Samuel Pepys at the Admiralty. That Pepys valued both his friendship and his service to the nation is evidenced by Evelyn's sitting to Kneller for his portrait, at Pepys' request, his *Sylva* in his hand.

In 1686 Evelyn wrote to Pepys to request that he ask a captain, whom

Portrait of John Evelyn

Evelyn had met at dinner with Pepys the night before, to send from New England, where the captain was going "to command some forces," some "natural productions of the Vegetable Kingdome." The letter includes directions for transporting the material: seeds in papers, nuts in dry sand, trees in barrels with their roots wrapped in moss.

The list to be given to a "Captaine . . . going to . . . New England" is as follows:

New England

1. The White Cedar	The Seeds only
2. Cedar of New England	Seedes
3. Larch-tree	Seedes & plants
4. Lime-tree	Seedes & plants
5. Hemlock-tree	Seedes & plants
6. Poplar or Tulip tree	Seedes & plants
7. Filbert tree	Nutts & plants
8. Firrs of all kinds	Seedes
9. Pines of all kinds	Nutts
10. Wall Nutts of all kinds	Nutts
11. Plums of all sorts	Stones & plants
12. Sarsaparilla	plants
13. The Scarlet Nut which some call Wallnut	Nutts & plants

Virginia

14. Benjamin Tree	Seedes & plants
15. Gumme Tree	Seedes & plants
16. Sugargras Tree	Seedes & plants
17. Date Plum	Stones & plants
18. Pappaw-tree	Seedes & plants
19. Chinquapine	Nutts & plants
20. Piekhickeries	Nutts & plants
21. Sumac trees, 3 kinds	Plants
22. Cedar of Virginia	Seedes
23. Maple tree bearing keys of crimson colour	Seedes & plants
24. Peacock taile tree	Seedes & plants
25. Oakes, six kinds	Acorns and plants

This is quite an order for anyone at any time, let alone a captain going to command forces. The interesting thing about the list is the indicated provenances of the materials, although Evelyn added that it could be supposed that those plants noted as growing in Virginia might be found also in New England. The list embraces some forty different trees, counting "all kinds" and "all sorts."

It would be interesting to know the sources from which Evelyn made his list. William Wood had made trees into a poem in his *New England's Prospect,* published in 1634. Extracted from his rhymed comments, his order of trees is: oak, cypress, pine, chestnut, cedar, walnut, fir, ash, aspen, elm, alder, elder, maple, birch, hawthorne, hornbeam, cherry, plum, hazel, sassafras, sumac. John Josselyn had made notes of New England trees in his two little books, *New England's Rarities Discovered,* published in 1672, and *Two Voyages to New England,* published in 1674. Josselyn's order in *Rarities* runs: oak, juniper, willow, spurge laurel, gaul or myrtle, elder, dwarf elder, alder, hazel, filbert, walnut, chestnut, beech, ash, quick-beam or wild ash, birch, poplar, plum (several kinds: long, round, white, yellow, red and black). Elsewhere in his *Rarities* he mentions elm, lime tree ("the line-tree, both kinds . . . the line-tree with long nuts, the other kind I never could find") and maple. And in still another context: the fir tree or pitch-tree, larch, spruce, hemlock. In *Two Voyages* he lists oak, the red oak for wainscot; the pine tree or board pine; fir tree; spruce; hemlock; white cedar; sassafras; walnut; line-tree; maple; birch; alder.

These were the experts on New England.

For Virginia in the seventeenth century many lists were compounded since the first count made by Thomas Hariot in 1595 of oaks, walnuts, firs, cedar, cypress, maple, witch hazel, holly, willows, beech, ash, elm and two trees with Indian names, one with spicy bark, the other of "sweet wood," used for canoes. Seeds and plants had been brought from Virginia by the younger John Tradescant and others to be grown in the gardens of Bishop Compton at Fulham, the Chelsea Physic Garden and the Oxford Physic Garden. The younger Tradescant had introduced before 1660 such already known American trees and shrubs as the tulip tree, the occidental plane tree, witch hazel, staghorn sumac, the Virginian cypress, red-osiered dogwood, the red maple (so-called Virginian), Canadian and New England walnuts, the persimmon, the Virginian locust, the red cornel tree, the Virginian mulberry.

A prime source for the inspiration of Evelyn's list may be the early finds of the first scientific approach to recording the horticultural resources of the New World. John Banister had gone to Virginia in 1678 with the blessings of Bishop Compton to save souls and to collect plants. Evelyn's spelling of "piekhickeries" is the same as Banister's in his first letter from Virginia to Dr. Robert Morison of the Oxford Physic Garden in 1679. And Banister also refers to the "Maple bearing keys of crimson colour." Parkinson's name for the persimmon tree was "the Virginia Date Plum" in his *Theatrum.* The curly and knotted grain of bird's-eye maple gave it the name of "the Peacock Tail Tree."

Banister listed the oaks as dwarf, black, white, red, Spanish, chestnut, live or willow, shrubby. On sumac Banister reported to Morison that he had not yet seen the kind growing in Morison's garden, which Parkinson calls *Rhus Virginiana,* but he lists two others that are used to season meat and sometimes to make vinegar. Banister also listed *Styrax folio aceris:* "Here it is called the sweet gumme." Of Banister, more later.

Evelyn's request for "Sugargras Tree" is perhaps a request for sassafras, long *s*'s being often hard to read.

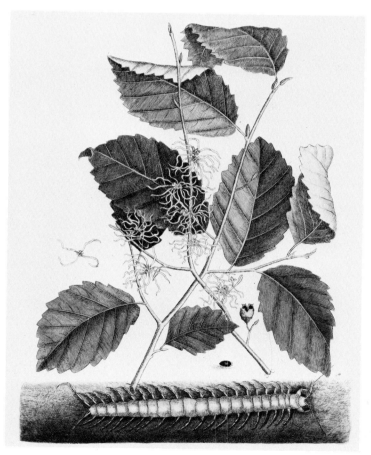

Catesby's *Hamamelis,* Plate A-2. Witch-hazel

Portrait of Bishop Compton

One of the earliest individuals, of even more importance to the colonies' contributions to the gardens of England than John Evelyn, was Henry Compton, Bishop of London. Born at Compton Wynyates, still an impressive example of all that was best in early English gardens, including topiary, he grew up in a tradition of rural beauty and public service. Of a soldierly inclination, like his father, he was politically ambitious, with the experience of serving in the army in Tangiers and traveling in France. Ordained after studying at Queens College, Oxford, he entered his career in the church with such an open mind, he became slightly suspect to his sovereign and fellow churchmen. He could see reason on the Puritan side; he voted against the Exclusion Bill; he refused to suppress afternoon lectures by the clergy in which honest doubts similar to his own were expressed. He ruined his ambitious pursuit of an archbishopric by being suspended in his office as Bishop of London and spending a period in exile in the Bishop's Palace and beautiful garden at Fulham. Called the "Puritan Bishop," he was regarded as a martyr to the Protestant cause. Finally, an alarmed James II, invited by his bishops, hastily restored Compton to active service in the church just before the arrival of William and Mary in 1688.

Compton is important to both American and English gardens because, after having had time to cultivate his thoughts as well as his trees, shrubs and flowers by the Thames, he took an active part in opening up the riches of the American forests with the highest, if mixed, motives. As a member, by right of his office, of the Commissioners of Trade and Plantations, he was responsible for the "spiritual jurisdiction" of the colonies. When the committee was reconstituted under William and Mary in 1689, Compton was the only churchman among a dozen members. He undertook his role with vigor. Though even his known Puritan sympathies did not open up New England to him, he managed to get Pennsylvania to permit a minister to be sent in, a deal somehow related to the granting by the Lords Commissioners of absolute proprietorship to William Penn and his heirs.

He was also able to further the foundation of William and Mary College at Williamsburg on the suggestion of the Reverend Mr. Blair at the end of the seventeenth century and to become a member of the governing board of the college. Mr. Blair had met a traditional rebuff when he feared for the souls of his parishioners unless a college was started. The report was that he had approached the agents for the colony and had been told, "Damn your souls. Grow tobacco," which, if not true, was certainly the spirit of the time. But the Bishop of London had lent a kindly ear to the Reverend Mr. Blair and the college was accomplished.

When even the "Puritan Bishop" could see it was only in Crown Colonies he would be able to exercise his duties, he applied himself to mainland Virginia and the West Indies, where the planters and settlers had suffered social neglect from greedy underwriters and agents. They had written for young men to come out as clergymen to take over duties in regions already marked out as "parishes." Bishop Compton saw the opportunity to sweeten the task for appointees who would have to live as planters and be paid in tobacco. As a great and well-known gardener, he had friends at the universities and among botanists, especially at Oxford, where Robert Morison was Professor of Botany. There Compton discovered a young man who, after taking Holy Orders, had stayed to work in the Herbarium. Familiar with specimens from the New World, he was a favorite with the authorities. Bishop Compton, with the approval and anticipation of his horticultural acquaintances, selected John Banister to go to Virginia and there, while saving souls, to observe the flora.

Banister left with high hopes and firm intent of writing a *Natural History of Virginia.* He began industriously and sent records, plants and seeds to Morison from the time of his arrival in 1678 until 1692, when he was accidentally shot by a soldier mistaking the botanizing figure for a wild beast. (He had accompanied a party to inspect land on the lower Roanoke River belonging to William Byrd I, who was considered Banister's "patron in Virginia" by his botanical friends in Oxford.)

The fittest memorial to Banister is our friend John Lawson's comment in 1709 saluting him as "the greatest *Virtuoso* we ever had on this Continent.

Evelyn could have seen some of Banister's reports sent to Morison or Bishop Compton, also an acquaintance of Evelyn's. A letter from Banister to Morison from The Falls, William Byrd I's place on the James River where there was a fort, is dated April 6, 1679, and gratefully mentions Bishop Compton as having recommended Banister to Lord Culpeper.

Both William Byrd I and William Byrd II had fostered John Banister throughout his fourteen-year stay in America and were the keepers of much of his library and papers after his tragic death. Banister had worked hard and well, striving to build up property for himself and his heirs, all with a view to his being independent and able to complete his natural history. He had sent plants and seeds, which had been successfully grown in London by Bishop Compton and his gardener, John London, and in Oxford by Robert Morison at the Physic Garden. With his death, his papers began to find their way into the histories and collections of others.

His library was similarly scattered, his copy of Parkinson's *Theatrum Botanicum* having only recently surfaced. A leading botanist, the great John Ray, used Banister's discoveries in his *Historia Plantarum* and ended the third and last volume with a copy of Banister's list. James Petiver, London apothecary and naturalist, friend to Lawson, published his *Museum Petiverianum,* from 1695 to 1703, mentioning Banister's plants. Petiver translated Banister's Latin names for sixty-five Virginian plants and trees, sent to the "Right Reverend Father in God, Henry, Lord Bishop of London," into their familiar names. Scholars refer to this as "popularizing" the names. These appeared in Petiver's little publication, justly called *Memoirs for the Curious,* published in December, 1707. William Sherard, called "the Consul" for his having served as such in Aleppo, had a traveling fellowship from Oxford, and went to study botany under Tournefort in Paris and Hermann in Leiden. He assisted Hermann with his *Paradisus Batavus* and added some of Banister's discoveries. Sherard also helped the younger Bobart, Morison's successor at Oxford, with finishing Morison's three-volume *Plantarum Historiae Universalis Oxoniensus* and included some of Banister's plants there. (We shall find ourselves indebted to Sherard again; he translated Catesby's English and Indian plant names into Latin.)

Leonard Plukenet, recommended to Queen Mary by Compton for a post at Hampton Court that Sherard coveted, used some of Banister's drawings in his *Pythographia.* Banister's observations on the Indians appeared in Beverly's and Oldmixon's books. Banister's shell collections were seized upon by experts. And, of course, Banister's trees were already flourishing in Fulham Palace and the Oxford Physic Garden. Linnaeus saw the Banister plants, both alive and dried, at Oxford in 1736 when he demonstrated to Dillenius his new system of classification. Sherard willed his collection of Banister manuscripts to Oxford, with three thousand pounds to establish a chair of botany, which he stipulated that Dillenius should occupy.

The value of American trees and plants collected by Banister had become apparent to English "collectors," especially to the Royal Society. Members realized that if a concerted effort were made to "send over" a skilled investigator, explorer, writer, artist and botanist, all combined in one man, the venture might pay richly.

William Byrd II had written as much to the members when he returned to Virginia on the sudden death of his planter-trader father. Byrd had been admitted to the Royal Society when he was only twenty-two, probably due to his patron, Sir Robert Southwell, mentioned with loyal affection on the obelisk erected in Byrd's garden at Westover. During years of cheerful dissipation while receiving his education in England and training to be a Virginia planter-trader, Byrd had been admitted to the bar and had had the opportunity of enlightening the Royal Society upon such subjects as the use of tobacco as a plague-preventive, the efficacy of ginseng as a preserver of youth and health, the virtues of snakeroot as a cure for gout and the charms of female opossums as pets. (Lady Wager later requested the gift of one, pregnant.)

When he returned home, the Society apparently pressed him to collect on their behalf. In reply, he wrote of the dearth of scientists in Virginia and the desirability of sending a "fitt person."

Perhaps because the Royal Society seemed slow to move, a group drawn from some of its members had started to meet as the "Temple Coffee House Botany Club." Later, after Banister's time, they began to finance traveling naturalists. Several members of the group, Compton and his gardener, John London, Plukenet, William Sherard, James Petiver and others, had been personal gainers from Banister's efforts to compose a *Natural History of Virginia.*

In the end, the entire Banister episode was a rehearsal for a more successful attempt to write and illustrate a natural history of the southern part of the New World colonies.

As the obvious value of Banister's interrupted work became apparent, so did the need to find a successor to continue it. Bishop Compton was again involved and the search began again for young churchmen with botanical inclinations who could build up their own fortunes while being paid in tobacco for work among the Indians and those outlying, lonely parishes requesting someone to take care of them.

Strangely, no one anticipated American talent. Early in the eighteenth century, probably as a result of Banister's stimulating if interrupted work, a native American plant collector appeared on Virginia's soil. Jefferson was later to refer to the younger John Clayton as the "first American botanist." Son of Attorney General John Clayton, an old schoolmate of William Byrd II, the younger John Clayton became Clerk of Gloucester County in 1722. Familiar with Banister's lists, he sent his own records of Virginia plants to Gronovius in Leiden, who published them without Clayton's permission or even knowledge. Clayton had given his work the title *A Catalogue of Plants, Fruits and Trees Native to Virginia.* It was accompanied by specimens and seeds. With the editing of Gronovius, it became *Flora Virginica,* appearing in two parts in 1739 and 1743. Gronovius' excuse for publishing it so hastily was to prevent its "being destroyed by envious fate at some time or other." And, actually, all Clayton's own records were indeed lost after the Revolution, when the Gloucester County Courthouse was burned to the ground. And at this same time, Dr. John Mitchell, author, physician, mapmaker, who was also collecting in Virginia, was also to lose the results of his efforts, this time to pirates at sea. So Gronovius had a point.

It seems curious that neither of these men, Clayton and Mitchell, was seriously taken up by the scientific searchers in London. It is even more curious when we realize that, with the advent of Linnaeus upon the botanical scene (an event comparable to the American Revolution in general shock and subsequent intellectual influence), the only resources available to him in cataloguing and naming American plants were the records of Banister and Clayton and some notes by John Mitchell. Recognition of the efforts of these early botanists lingers in the names of the little "spring beauty," *Claytonia virginica* L. and the "partridge berry," *Mitchella repens* L. The only North American commemoration of Banister in a plant name was awarded to an oak, *Quercus banisteri,* by Michaux, because, as his son François said, the "Bear Oak or Barren Oak was first introduced to notice by Banister, an English writer." It is now known as *Quercus ilicifolia.* The name of *Banisteria* now belongs to a West Indies plant.

However, in spite of what may seem missed opportunities, the writer of the first great natural history of the American colonies was on his way. Literally. When Mark Catesby decided to visit relatives in Williamsburg, Virginia, in 1712, he came, rather as Lawson had, because "Virginia was the place." Catesby's sister had married Dr. William Cocke, with a degree in medicine from Queens College, Cambridge, and had emigrated with him to Virginia, apparently to the dismay of her father. Dr. Cocke was, however, a popular and successful man when Mark Catesby, aged twenty-eight, elected to visit his sister.

For Mark Catesby Virginia was indeed "the place." He arrived in April, met William Byrd II within a week and within a month was visiting at Westover for three weeks where, Byrd told his diary, he "directed how I should mend my garden and put it into better fashion than it is at present." Mark Catesby must have been good company for he was back at Westover in September and accompanied Byrd to a Pamunkey Indian town on the Pamunkey River. Byrd had shown Catesby a hummingbird on his first visit. On this expedition, Byrd showed him an Indian who had recovered from a snakebite by taking snakeroot. As an additional historic experience, Catesby also came down with the ague when back at Westover, to cure which Byrd recommended a swim in the James.

Meantime, Catesby was beginning to collect and to sketch. In the spring of 1713 seeds were sent to Bishop Compton by Governor Spotswood as from "a gentleman now in this country . . . and one very curious in such things," but Compton had died before they arrived. More seeds went from Catesby direct to Samuel Dale, apothecary of Braintree, a collector and neighbor, friend to John Ray and, with Catesby and Dale, a native of East Anglia. Catesby sent seeds also to Thomas Fairchild, nurseryman of Hoxton, eager for American exotics, author of *The City Gardener,* and later one of the first to hybridize

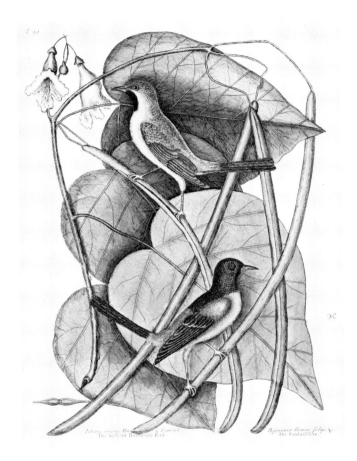

Catesby's Catalpa, Plate 49, Vol. I. A tree he introduced from the Carolina high-lands to lowland gardens. Shown with the bird that received its name from Lord Baltimore's armorial colors

garden flowers. (He combined a carnation and a sweet William as reported by Collinson, and named the sterile hybrid "mule.") Petiver heard of the shipments to Fairchild and spoke warmly of "that curious botanist Mr. Mark Catesby of Virginia." In 1714 Catesby managed a voyage to the West Indies and collected in Jamaica for Mr. Dale.

Seven years passed and, by Catesby's own account, he thought so little of "prosecuting a design" in the nature of a natural history, he gratified his inclination merely in observing and admiring, "only sending from thence some dried Specimens of Plants and some of the most Specious of them in Tubs of Earth, at the Request of some curious Friends, among whom was Mr. Dale of Braintree . . ." So passed Catesby's first visit to America. He returned to England in the autumn of 1719. Not, however, empty-handed or without plans for his future. He called upon Mr. Dale and was sent by him, with his paintings of birds, to William Sherard in the spring of 1720. By that autumn there appeared this note in the Council Minutes of the Royal Society:

Colonel Francis Nicholson going to South Carolina was pleased to declare that he would allow Mr. Catesby, recommended to him as a very proper person, to Observe the Rarities of that Country for the uses and purposes of the Society the pension of twenty pounds per Annum during his Government there . . .

The Royal Society was contributing nothing, apparently, beyond its seal of approval, but William Sherard undertook to raise funds. The Society's president, Sir Hans Sloane, was one of the first patrons, with Charles Dubois, Treasurer of the East India Company, and Sherard himself. Dr. Richard Mead was another patron who endeared himself to Catesby and had our "shooting star" or "bears-ear of Virginia" named Meadia for him. (Linnaeus, for a reason suited only to himself, renamed it after a plant in Dioscorides with a slightly similar description and it is now *Dodecatheon media* L.)

Sherard, realizing the temper of his times, secured the Duke of Chandos to head the list of sponsors arranged in a social sequence suitable for a diplomatic dinner. The first Duke de Chandos, very recently James Brydges, was enormously wealthy and supposed to be the original for the satirical picture of Timon and his grandiose gardens in Pope's biting lines directed to Lord Burlington about the uses of wealth. The duke had early on nearly wrecked the Carolina enterprise by persuading Catesby to go to Africa. Sherard wrote regretfully in 1721 of Catesby being "too far engaged with the Duke of Chandos" to think of "Carolina, which is better known to us" and was going to Africa, a "sickly place." Nicholson had to set sail without Catesby, but he left his contribution with the committee to be used toward another appointee.

Finally, however, Catesby did, indeed, arrive in "Charlestown, South Carolina," early in 1722 and within four years had completed the groundwork of collecting and recording for one of the most important works in the natural history of the North American settlements. While he had to spend the next twenty years of his life in its production and publication, the first quarter of the eighteenth century was the time of its inception.

During his earlier visit to Virginia, however carefree, his collecting for his project seems to have served him well. Perhaps the funds advanced gave him confidence. In any case, he went about his task in Carolina with great industry, reporting faithfully to his promoters, not hesitant on occasions to complain to and of some of them. His plan, which he faithfully carried out, was to visit both the lowlands and the highlands in the spring season and to return in the autumn to collect seeds from the places visited. He was constantly sketching birds, trees, shrubs, flowers, snakes, insects, animals and fish, and writing his own descriptions of them and where they were found. He devised a way of

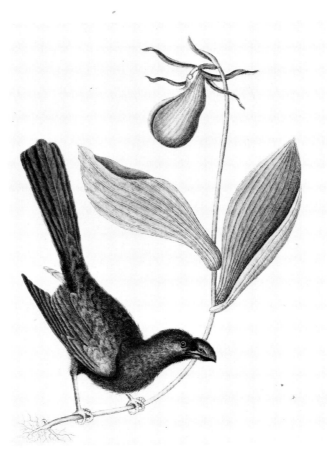

Catesby's Lady's-slipper, *Calceolus,* Plate A-3

grouping his subjects, arranging them naturally with their associates. The compositions of birds in rare and beautiful trees are inspired.

Other combinations seem a little contrived, like the blackbird on the stalk of a lady's-slipper and snakes wound about lily stems. The small buffalo (which furnished meat for Byrd's expedition to establish the dividing line but is now extinct) looks a little pathetic rubbing himself against a pseudo-acacia stump, with one beautiful and blooming sprig sticking out above his head. The chimney swift sitting on her eggs in a chimney on one half of a page with a wood lily suspended on the other half is obviously a crowding to save space, like the skunk and a very thin little fox parading past some of our prettier swamp flowers.

However, these groupings were well advised, as Catesby, back in England again, found himself having to learn engraving to be able to afford putting all his drawings into plates to be printed and then individually colored by himself. European publishing with more funds, which he had rather counted on and hoped for, beyond the original arrangements, were not forthcoming. The tedious business of learning to etch was also expensive. He supported himself in part by working in London nurseries, notably Thomas Fairchild's at Huxton and Gray's nursery at Fulham, where he could see actually growing some of the plants he was drawing. It would have been reciprocal as Gray got out a one-sheet catalogue in 1737, of *American Trees and Shrubs That Will Endure the Climate of England,* ten years before Catesby finished his second volume. So Catesby did not lack for models, although we shall see him sending to America for more. Literally, the saving grace was his being supported in and for his work by the generous Quaker merchant, patron of American horticulture, Peter Collinson.

It was Peter Collinson who wrote to Linnaeus in 1747, "Catesby's noble work is finished." Catesby had been enjoying a fellowship in the Royal Society since 1733, introduced by Collinson. He had been publishing his book in sections of twenty plates each since 1729.

Catesby dedicates his *Natural History of Carolina, Florida and the Bahama Island* "to the Queen. As these volumes contain an Essay towards the Natural History of that Part of your Majesty's Dominions which are particularly honored by bearing your august name CAROLINA." He implores her protection and favor for his "slender performance," and signs himself "M. Catesby." On his illustrations he left a minuscule monogram of *MC* made by letting the final flourish of the *M* enclose a *C*.

In his preface he states that "the early inclination to search after plants and other productions of Nature, much suppressed by my residing too remote from London, the Center of all Science . . ." brought him

Catesby's Plate 61, Vol. II, the Laurel Tree of Carolina. He appears to have felt the great Ehret could do it justice better than he

to the city, where he "soon imbibed a passionate desire for viewing as well the Animal as Vegetable Productions in their Native Countries . . ."

With "the assistance and encouragement" of his patrons (who included a duke; two earls; one lord; two baronets; Sir Hans Sloane, Bar., President of the Royal Society and of the College of Physicians; the Honorable Colonel Francis Nicholson, Governor of South Carolina; Dr. Richard Mead and three Fellows of the Royal Society, including William Sherard, L.L.D., F.R.S.) Catesby set out for Carolina. At Charleston, "inhabited by English above an age past . . . abounding in the blessings of Nature . . . little known except what related to commerce, such as Rice, Pitch, Tar . . ." he arrived the twenty-third of May, 1722.

He describes the inhabited parts of Carolina as extending "west from the sea about sixty miles . . . almost the whole length of the coast . . . being a level, low country." He spent his first year here and then went "to the upper uninhabited parts . . . and continued at about Fort Moore, a small fortress on the banks of the River Savanna . . . which runs three hundred miles to the sea and three hundred from its source in the mountains." He was so "delighted to see Nature differ in these parts" that he was "encouraged to take several journeys with the Indians higher up the rivers." To these "friendly Indians" he is much indebted. His "method" with plants he says was to have principally a "regard" to "Forest Trees and Shrubs, shewing their several mechanical and other uses, as in Building, Joynery, Agriculture, and others used for Food and Medicine." He also took "notice of those plants that will bear our English climate" and has them growing even as he writes at "Mr. Bacon's, successor of the late Mr. Fairchild at Hoxton." As for the animals "of the feathered kind," he shows them "having oftenest relation to the Plants on which they feed and frequent." The beasts do not differ much from Europe's. Few serpents escape his notice. His fish are mostly from the Bahamas. After three years in "Carolina and the adjacent parts (which the Spaniards call Florida, particularly that Province lately honored with the name of Georgia)" he went to Providence in Barbados and returned to England in 1726. "As to the Plants," he said, "I have given them the English and Indian names they are known by in these countries . . . For the Latin names I was beholden to the above-mentioned learned and accurate Botanist, Dr. Sherard."

To explore a new country, collect and study specimens of the trees, shrubs and flowers, observe the birds, animals, snakes, insects and fish, write about them, draw pictures of them and then go home to learn etching to be able to illustrate the resulting two-volume masterpiece, with an appendix to make sure of having missed nothing, is a staggering task, even as the occupation of a lifetime. We are forever indebted to those gentlemen, whether chosen for their titles and fortunes or their interest and knowledge, who underwrote the expedition, and to Peter Collinson, who saw the book through to completion with loans of money for which he asked no repayment. Considering the magnitude of the endeavor, the written sections have a disarming style, which endears the author to us. Illustrations are clear and decisive for trees, shrubs and flowers, although a little blurred for the birds where Catesby obviously had difficulty and let his tools follow "the humour of the feathers." Snakes and fish show he had no trouble with scales. For several of the grander blossoms he seems to have felt others could do better than he and there are a few very dramatic, page-filling illustrations for the magnolias by one of the greatest naturalists and artists of the time, George Dionysius Ehret.

London street trees, shrubberies at Mount Vernon, English parks in the landscape style, Philadelphia and Connecticut parkways, Charleston gardens, Boston "front yards" . . . wherever we go today in a temperate climate where "curious" gardeners abound we recognize debts to Catesby.

And here, with Catesby, our horticultural net begins to grow heavy. The first quarter of the eighteenth century served to show the wealth of material and the possibilities of a great deal more of interest "for Meate or Medicine, for Use or for Delight" in the American colonies. In England and France botanic and physic gardens were beginning to become the repositories for growing "exoticks," many purely ornamental. Patrons who were to guide the acquisition of all this horticultural treasure were beginning to appear and make themselves felt. And at exactly the right moment the genius for organization of the world's animals, vegetables and minerals appeared.

To imply that Linnaeus and his binomial system burst upon an astonished world, and that soon afterward far distant plantsmen were able to communicate, is to idealize garden history of the eighteenth century. Botany had come a long way since fifteenth-century Germans tried to identify the plants in Dioscorides among those in their own countrysides and to draw accurate representations of what they found to establish exactly which part of which plant was needed for medicine. We cherish their woodcuts and prints with the root system paramount, the stem often bent or truncated and the leaves and blossoms sideways to get them all on the block. They may have saved lives but they fell short of later illustrations, still carefully accurate but with greater regard to artistic composition. The long Latin descriptions of those early medicinal plants, especially those without pictures, must have baffled many ambitious plant collectors seeking for something similar, and so, possibly similarly healing, in their own meadows. Later herbals were content to use many of these earlier illustrations, some over and over again. This was not so much plagiarizing as perhaps playing safe in identifying helpful or even poisonous plants. After all, the beginnings of botany sprang from early medicine; the first botanists were apothecaries seeking their wares.

Gradually a great compendium of European plants had been achieved, with mixed histories and derivations, well or not well depicted, to which new plants came to be joined in the same sort of confused masquerade. Herbariums became of the greatest importance in helping to identify fresh plants from actual specimens. But an explorer in a new land must have been sorely perplexed to see how to describe his discoveries and then get them home to be officially identified, through all the perils waiting to beset him and them.

It was this confused agglomeration of records, specimens, identifications, illustrations and arguments that a young Swede, trained for medicine, but preferring to revert to his interim study of botany, suddenly determined to set in order. The magnitude of his commitment is staggering — to invent a system by which all the world's animals, vegetables and minerals could be docketed in such a manner as to be understandable to all those wishing to have their possessions and discoveries recognized and to be able to add others to them.

To call Linnaeus' system "binomial" rather than the former "polynomial," when the plant was described in toto, is to make it sound easier than it must have been for those who adopted it to tell what they had found to remote but eager experts. When Jane Colden, for instance, instructed by her eminent father, Cadwallader Colden, who himself longed for the company of men of his own intelligence, learned the Linnaean system in the wilds of upper New York, she had to establish, first of all, the orders and classes of her wildflowers before she could get to the genera and species, which were the "binomials" in the system. She was written about as one of the charming examples of what women in the New World could do. Linnaeus himself received approving reports of her efforts. In the end it may have appeared rather like the preaching woman and the dog on his hind legs. Still, the great thing is that her efforts can be appraised today as those of our first woman botanist, and the fact remains that she could have done little for and by herself in the wilds without Linnaeus' system.

Briefly, the idea that shook the horticultural world, roused the ire of

REGNUM
VEGETABILE

SECUNDUM

SYSTEMA SEXUALE.

Linnaeus' *Vegetable Kingdom,* introducing his Sexual System into Plant Identification

REGNUM VEGETABILE. 13

CLAVIS SYSTEMATIS SEXUALIS.

NUPTIÆ PLANTARUM.

Actus generationis incolarum Regni vegetabilis.

Florefcentia.

PUBLICÆ.

Nuptiæ, omnibus manifeſtæ, apertè celebrantur.

Flores unicuique viſibiles.

MONOCLINIA.

Mariti & uxores uno eodemque thalamo gaudent.

Flores omnes hermaphroditi ſunt, & ſtamina cum piſtillis in eodem flore.

DIFFINITAS.

Mariti inter ſe non cognati.

Stamina nulla ſuâ parte connata inter ſe ſunt.

INDIFFERENTISMUS.

Mariti nullam ſubordinationem inter ſe invicem ſervant.

Stamina nullam determinatam proportionem longitudinis inter ſe invicem habent.

1. MONANDRIA.   7. HEPTANDRIA.
2. DIANDRIA.   8. OCTANDRIA.
3. TRIANDRIA.   9. ENNEANDRIA.
4. TETRANDRIA.   10. DECANDRIA.
5. PENTANDRIA.   11. DODECANDRIA.
6. HEXANDRIA.   12. ICOSANDRIA.
           13. POLYANDRIA.

SUBORDINATIO.

Mariti certi reliquis præferuntur.

Stamina duo ſemper reliquis breviora ſunt.

14. DIDYNAMIA. 15. TETRADYNAMIA.

AFFINITAS.

Mariti propinqui & cognati ſunt

Stamina cohærent inter ſe invicem aliqua ſua parte vel cum piſtillo.

16. MONADELPHIA.   19. SYNGENESIA.
17. DIADELPHIA.   20. GYNANDRIA.
18. POLYADELPHIA.

DICLINIA à δίς bis & κλίνη thalamus ſ. duplex thalamus.

Mariti & fœminæ diſtinctis thalamis gaudent.

Flores Maſculi & feminei in eadem ſpecie.

21. MONOECIA. 23. POLYGAMIA.
22. DIOECIA.

CLANDESTINÆ

Nuptiæ clam inſtituuntur

Flores oculis noſtris nudis vix conſpiciuntur.

24. CRYPTOGAMIA.

CLAS-

such great men as Erasmus Darwin, shocked nongardening bishops, incited fears of ladies unable to survive the revelation, kindled wits and persuaded other groping systematists to allow its rule was — put very simply — that the vegetable world is governed by sex. Others had had the idea before Linnaeus, notably some of his scientific friends, but no one had applied it arbitrarily to the whole world of plants. Confusingly, this is considered an "artificial" classification as opposed to the "natural," which was espoused by some other botanists then, and has now taken over from Linnaeus' classification by sexual organs only. Linnaeus knew his system lacked flexibility and by-passed relationships other than those of the sexual organs, but he felt that a system recognizing natural relationships was in his time unattainable. He offered his "artificial system" and the eighteenth-century world accepted it, howbeit somewhat grudgingly.

Those who refused to consider the sexual system as a valid method of identification were the great Tournefort, considered by some the "founder of genera in the vegetable kingdom." (He preferred his own system founded on the outward form of the flower parts, and restricted his descriptive definitions to the genera.) Kasper Bauhin, on the contrary, put more emphasis into describing the species. His great work, *Pinas,* was influential in forming the system of Robert Morison of Oxford, who strove to perfect the classification of plants by special attention to the fruits. But these are the battles of giants, whose repercussions are faintly introduced here because they were known to horticulturally minded colonists whose libraries included their books.

By Linnaeus' "Systema Sexuale," all flowering plants are divided first into "classes," decided by the number of male organs or stamens. These are named from the Greek: Monandria, Diandria, Triandria and so on up to twenty-three. Each of these classes is in turn divided into "orders" decided by the number of female organs, or styles. Thus, in examples I gratefully quote from Dr. W. T. Stearn, "A lily (*Lillium*) and a snowdrop (*Galanthus*) both having six stamens and one style, would be placed in the class *Hexandria* order *Monogynia*." After the class and the order were established by counting, the next thing to be determined was the genus and after that the special characteristic that will set the plant apart from all others.

Begging mercy from botanists, let us pursue the problem of identification for ambitious collectors in "this wildernesse." To consider the genera, they would have to seek help from cherished herbals like Gerard's and Parkinson's or, if they could read Latin, from Ray or Morison. The names of the genera of those plants familiar to European botanists were often very ancient. Some went back to Dioscorides,

Theophrastus, Pliny and Galen. Obviously, with these origins, some were in Greek and some in Latin. *Chrysanthemum,* the generic name for the common field daisy (which John Bartram declared made him decide to study botany), is Greek, from *chrysos,* gold; *anthos,* flower. *Ranunculus* is a Latin name for the buttercup family, from *rana,* a little frog, because many species grow in damp places. Some plants, of course, had long ago received names to denote their appearance, as *Campanula* most fittingly means like a bell. And even before Linnaeus made a practice of it, some plants, and so genera, had been named for great men, like, for instance, *Lobelia,* named for Mathias de l'Obel, Flemish botanist and physician to James I of England. This is the genus to which our cardinal flower belongs.

After the genus of the plant had been determined, the specific character had to be described — just what in the appearance of the leaves, stem, root and flower seemed most worthy of recording to help define the whole.

Each herbal would have a botanical Latin index, an English index and, in most cases, an index of all the ills one could hope to be relieved of by studying the herbal and procuring the plants.

Jane Colden's work in manuscript is safe in the British Museum of Natural History, except for a recently selected publication of about fifty of her over three hundred plants. Jane, who was born in 1724, married in 1759 to Dr. Farquhar and who died in 1766, learned all she knew from her parents. Her father was especially distinguished, with a medical degree, a great interest in botany and a flair for dealing with Indians. An unfortunately insignificant plant, our "Missouri railroad weed," was named *Coldenia* for him by Linnaeus. Jane was never commemorated although there were suggestions she should be and Linnaeus heard of her from several mutual friends.

Jane sets up her studies by listing the Latin terms she will use and their English equivalents. These are her spellings. "*Radix,* the root; *Caules,* the stalk; *Folia,* the leaves; *Calix,* the general cup; *Corola,* the compound flower; *Stamina,* the chives; *Anthera,* the caps; *Pistillum,* the pestle or germen; *Stigma,* the tips; *Semen,* seed; *Flores,* flowers." She learned to make clear ink drawings of the leaves, which are less than masterful, but her lengthy descriptions in English more than make up for the limitations of her drawings. After counting the stamens and pistils and determining the *"Classis"* and the *"Div,"* she set her order of description as: Cup, Flower, Chives, Pestle, Seed, Stalk, Leaves.

Dr. Colden was greatly pleased by his daughter's interest in botany, since she lived in a countryside where that might easily become an absorbing occupation. He wrote to Peter Collinson in London to ask for books for her. "As she cannot have the opportunity of seeing plants in a Botanical Garden, I think the next best is to see the best cuts or pictures of them for which purpose I would buy for her Tournefort's *Institutiones Herbariae,* Morison's *Historia Plantarum,* or if you know any better books for this purpose as you are a better judge than I am will be obliged to you in making this choice."

Collinson answered, "I have at last been so lucky to get you a fine Tournefort's *Herbal* and the *History of Plants* and Martin in excellent preservation . . ." Collinson sent also two copies of the *Edinburgh Essays,* which contained a "Curious Botanical Dissertation" by Colden's "ingenious daughter being the only lady that I have yet heard of that is a professor of the Linnaean system of which he is not a little proud." (In case a little clarification is needed: Martin translated Tournefort into English, "Professor" here means "advocate of" and carried no academic sense, and Linnaeus is said to be proud of her.)

Jane Colden's "dissertation" was on the subject of a St. Johnswort, *Hypericum virginicum,* about which she and Dr. Garden of South Carolina had corresponded. They had both found it in New York State and she wished to name it for him — "Gardenia." However, John Ellis, also acquainted with Dr. Garden, had already decided to name the cape jasmine, *Gardenia jasminoides,* for him. In any case, Jane saw her dissertation printed.

John Clayton and John Bartram were both Jane Colden's contemporaries and acquaintances and their objectives were also to report on the plants of their own particular part of the New World in such a way that experts abroad would be able to identify them correctly, rename them if they pleased and make use of them as they saw fit.

We shall see John Bartram at work later. John Clayton, called by Jefferson "our first American botantist," deserves his moment here.

John Clayton's manuscript of his *Catalogue of Plants, Fruits and Trees Native to Virginia,* which he decided to compile after many years of sending seeds and plants to England is, unhappily, not to be seen as it was before it was gobbled up by Gronovius to make *Flora Virginia.* That this work is popularly attributed to Clayton does not make up for there being no separate representation of his own work, either before *Flora Virginica* was published in 1739, or afterward, when he planned to improve upon it. John Ellis, a botanist and member of the Royal Society, saw the original and wrote "notes," which are still preserved, on the "method used in *Flora Virginica Claytonii."* These differ enough from Gronovius' "editing" to seem to be the material that Clayton originally sent to Gronovius. That Clayton wrote easily in Latin we can see elsewhere, and we assume the descriptions in Latin are his. He is said to have used Ray's methods of determining the genera. The Linnaean system is the framework in Ellis' "Notes taken on Clayton's Flora." From Clayton's manuscript obviously came the familiar American names, standing out oddly in the Latin text. Gronovius combined Clayton's *Catalogue* with two books by Linnaeus, *Hortus Cliffortianus* and his book on the Lapland journey, *Flora Lapponica,* because many plants seemed to be the same in each. In *Flora Virginica* the order followed is to give a Linnaean entry first, followed by such authorities as Tournefort, Ray, Bauhin and Dodonaeus. Mentions of the plant by Catesby and Bartram are next with references to Petiver and Collinson. The entry ends with Clayton's identification of the plant with its description in Latin, and at the very end of this is its familiar name and the plant's number among the more than nine hundred plants Clayton catalogued.

On the whole, perhaps Clayton's true memorial is Jefferson's comment.

Furber's Flowers for the Month of May

1. Cinnamon Rose B T
2. Narrow Leaved Striped Flower de-luce B
3. Columbine Striped B
4. Bishop of Canterbury Tulip B C
5. Double Catchfly B
6. Late white Hyacinth B
7. Blue bell Hyacinth B
8. Mountain bulbed Crow foot B
9. Belsilvia Anemone B C
10. Venetian Vetch Major B
11. Blue Hyacinth of Peru S E

12. China Pink F E
13. Savoy Spiderwort B
14. Double Orange Lilly B
15. White Hyacinth of Peru B
16. Pheasants Eye B
17. Purple Mallou B
18. Arbor Judae L T
19. Embroidered Crane's Bill B
20. Dwarf Dutch Tulip B
21. Indian Queen Ranunculus B C
22. Yellow Austrian Rose B T
23. Double white Mountain Ranunculus B

24. Dutch yellow Ranunculus B C
25. Indian King Ranunculus B C
26. Yellow Globe Flower B
27. Red Austrian Rose
28. Cytissus Secundus Clusii B T
29. Lotus with yellow flowers G
30. Virginian Columbine B
31. White Asphodil B
32. Yellow Asphodil B
33. Princess's Pink B

5 Gardeners and Collectors

THE EIGHTEENTH CENTURY was an acquisitive one for gardeners on both sides of the Atlantic. Those with friends or business interests on the other side of the ocean were in enviable positions. Besides the avid interest in the home country in hardy "exoticks," unique trees and shrubs and vines and flowers unlike anything then grown by noble lord or humble — though no less keen, cottager — there was also a considerable effort among the "curious" to create a liaison with the New World and maintain a representative there.

American gardeners, who knew and grew their own American plants, were of particular interest to gardeners in England, aristocrats, collectors and nurserymen alike. The most acquisitive gardener among them, and friend to most, was the Quaker merchant Peter Collinson. Through this one man and his correspondence during his long lifetime, which ended in 1768, we see gardens on both sides of the Atlantic more clearly than in any other records. And we can feel our garden indebtedness to the Society of Friends.

Horticulturally, the eighteenth century was alert to discover new places and plants. Trade was in the ascendant, pulse of England's development. "Golden Lines" from "the late Mr. Addison, speaking of Commerce," quoted in *A History of the British Navy to the Year 1734,* by one Thomas Lediard, sum it up for us.

Nature seems to have taken a particular Care to disseminate her Blessings among the different regions of the World, with an Eye to mutual Intercourse and Traffick among Mankind, that the Natives of the several Parts of the Globe might have a Kind of Dependence upon one another, and be united together by their Common Interest. Almost every Degree produces something peculiar to it; the Food often grows in one Country, and the Sauce in another, etc. . . . Nor has Traffick more enriched our Vegetable World, than it has improved the whole Face of Nature among us. Our ships are laden with the Harvest of every Climate . . . Traffick . . . supplies us with every Thing that is Convenient and Ornamental . . .

Kipling's later "Dominion over palm and pine . . ." was a trumpet call that would have been recognized with joy by eighteenth-century English-speaking gardeners, eager to grow both.

Peter Collinson was the real spirit to preside over the growing horticultural exchanges across the Atlantic. Born into a London Quaker family, he was sent at the age of two in 1696 to be brought up by grandparents in Peckham with a garden "remarkable for fine cut greens, the fashion of those times and for curious flowers." He "often went with them to visit the few nursery gardens around London, to buy fruit and flowers and clipt yews in the shapes of birds, dogs, men and ships." He was an apprentice at an early age in his father's haberdashery firm and accustomed himself to study at nights after business. When he and his brother eventually took over the firm, he made it his special interest to improve trade with the American colonies and to combine gardening with business. He was living at Peckham with a large garden of his own when he married, in 1724, a young Quaker, Mary Russell, whose father owned a handsome piece of property at Mill Hill, a Quaker stronghold outside London. Collinson and his wife moved there in 1749, uprooting the Peckham garden to create another at Mill Hill in 1753. Peter Collinson continued to develop his "little Paradise" until he, too, died there in 1768.

It is hard for one age to judge the foibles of another, but it is absurd to say that Quakers, "prohibited from many occupations," resorted to gardening as a form of "freemasonry which enabled them to mix with people of all denominations and all classes." The opposite is more nearly true. By their inculcated interest and skill in gardening, they attracted all those likewise inclined. Two social quirks of the times did, however, augment their successful inspiriting of English horticulture. First, as they could not attend either Oxford or Cambridge because they were not prepared to take Holy Orders, they resorted to Scottish universities, especially the University of Edinburgh, where medical studies, with the concomitant study of botany, were particularly important. And, second, as they could not go into politics, they were able to maintain friendly relations with whatever government was in power.

Also, since they were known because of their religion to be scrupulously honest, they enjoyed the trust of all in business.

Collinson was elected a Fellow of the Royal Society in 1728, the year that Sir Hans Sloane became its president. While Collinson's written contributions were rather less than absorbing "observations" — on the sole-fish, Pennsylvania wasps' nests, distemper among cows, Cancer Major, migration of swallows, the American cicada and American fossil teeth — his more valuable contributions were the distinguished people he "introduced" to the Society.

A passionate gardener and collector by proxy of plants wherever he could get anyone to adventure for him, he moved within the rigidly striated social structure of early eighteenth-century London as one who

Portrait of Peter Collinson

recognized no barriers. He wrote to Thomas Storey, the Quaker preacher, from Peckham in 1731:

I have retreated from the hurrys of the town to breathe the air of content and quiet, being the centre of my humble wishes, a little cottage, a pretty garden well filled, a faithful loving partner, a little prattling boy, the pledge of mutual love, surrounded with these blessings I pronounce myself happy. I only desire their continuance and ask for no more, the gay appearance of the great don't disturb me, perhaps they'd be glad to exchange their gilded shows for my real enjoyment. I am of Horace's mind for every man to suit his pleasure to his abilities . . .

This was a popular attitude among gardeners in eighteenth-century England and with Americans like Jefferson and Washington, but it does not mean Collinson was not also constantly involved with his firm on Gracechurch Street. Protesting his occupation with business, however, he could still write to Linnaeus in 1749 about six pots of flowers blooming in January in his city window and, later, about peas and beans in blossom and a fig tree in leaf in his office garden. He included in his correspondence with business agents and friends discussions of botanical matters. He had correspondents in Russia, among them Dr. Mounsey, the Czarina's physician, who sent him hornbeam from Persia, and M. Demidoff, of the Siberian Iron Mines, who sent him Siberian martagon. He corresponded with two friends in China, Father D'Incarville, who sent him the *Ailanthus glandulosa,* and Father Herberstein, who sent a "bastard acacia." Collinson grew camellias from the Far East, "evergreen shrubs with red or white flowers," with which his friend, young Lord Petre, had "great success." On the return of Catesby from the Carolinas in about 1730, Collinson was able to interest himself in the importation of a great many American plants, which he grew with varying success in his own gardens and gave to friends and nurserymen. This grew into an industrious interchange of some proportions. With Collinson turning the wheel gently, belts joined remote gardeners and collectors and made them into friends: Charleston doctors and lady gardeners, explorers in wild hinterlands, aristocratic London collectors, compassionate Quaker philanthropists, Virginia slave-holders agitating against British exploitation, Pennsylvania visionaries of a new world in the making — all were linked together by this wise and kindly London haberdasher.

Since James II's Act of Indulgence, which, if we are to believe prejudiced historians like Macaulay, was promulgated to bring Roman Catholics and Dissenters together to destroy the Church of England, Quakers had made it a habit to call upon the King to thank him for not persecuting them. Collinson seems to have been a regular member of these delegations, and to have used his audiences to persuade his sovereigns of the beauties of horticulture. His reports of these occasions recount how he was remembered, and how much the conversation had dealt with his (Collinson's) favorite subject. Considering that the rule in court was to let the king and queen introduce a subject, they seem to have been more tactful and resourceful than many have given them credit for. Collinson always came away happy. It is charming to think of this grave Quaker, with business connections all over the then explored world sending him seeds, taking up the subject of horticulture with what must have been fairly apathetic royalty and leaving them indebted to him for seeds and roots and ideas for the royal gardens.

At an audience with the King and Queen arranged by Lord Bute, Collinson was pleased to have had a conversation on the subject of

One of the first camellias. From Engelbert Kaempfer's *Amoenitatum Exoticarum,* 1712. Lord Petre had one from Collinson

botany and to have received invitations to the royal gardens at Kew.
Lord Bute, whom Collinson called "the Maecenas of Gardening," had
been "improving" the gardens there, and Collinson requested him to be
his guide. Collinson had noted in his commonplace-book the happy
effect of Bute's "influence and example and advice" on the King's conduct while Prince of Wales. And added, "From his Lordship's great
knowledge of the science of Botany the gardens at Kew have been
furnished with all the rare exotick trees and flowers that could be procured."

When Catesby returned to England to write his book and found he
must work on his own, making his drawings into plates that could be
published and then colored by himself, he had to fill in the gaps by
drawing plants growing in England from specimens sent from Virginia
and Carolina to friends and nurserymen. Collinson "loaned" him
money and interested himself in the work. And in the plants. It became
apparent that Collinson needed an agent in the colonies to procure seeds
and plants for him and send them to England.

This man, of course, was John Bartram, to whom we shall be greatly
indebted later; but before, and even while, the business understanding
with Bartram was underway, Collinson had another very fruitful correspondence with John Custis of Williamsburg.

Even a brief glance through their twelve-year correspondence and
plant exchange across the Atlantic reveals the early arrivals of English
flowers and fruits, and patient answers to the demands for their American counterparts and for new, solely American plants.

Several paths must have led Peter Collinson in London to his friendship and correspondence with John Custis in Virginia. His friendship
with William Byrd II for whom he had great respect and Catesby's
needs for fresh models were probably foremost among them. John
Custis, future father-in-law of Martha Dandridge Custis, was a prominent and peppery planter, land-mad, encumbered by debts inherited by
his wife and her sister (married to Byrd) and a great gardener. Mes-
dames Custis and Byrd were daughters of Daniel Parke, a rich Virginian
landowner who achieved notoriety as a young member of the King's
Council by striking the Governor with a horse whip. He repaired to
England, served as Marlborough's aide-de-camp and carried the news of
Blenheim to Queen Anne. Rewarded with her miniature set in dia-
monds, one thousand pounds and governorship of the Leeward Islands,
he never returned to Virginia. When he was assassinated by a mob in
Antigua his will disclosed an illegitimate island family well provided
for. His two legitimate daughters were left considerable properties in
England and Virginia and his debts, also considerable, destined to plague

Portrait of John Custis

both Custis and Washington all their lives. When John Parke Custis married the dowerless but charming Martha Dandridge in 1749, the year his father died, he was a very rich man. He left her a rich widow with two children at the White House plantation on Pamunkey River when he died, intestate, in 1757. The Parke daughters would seem to have inherited also generous portions of their father's temper. John Custis retaliated when he had it carved on his tombstone that his last seven years as a bachelor were his happiest.

The portrait of John Custis shows him to be of a dignified and kindly appearance, his hand upon a book and a tulip. As he died the year his son married Martha, then eighteen years old, it cannot be assumed he was able to hand on much of his personal skill and taste in gardening to the future mistress of Mount Vernon. Martha was widowed at twenty-six and married George Washington two years later, in 1759.

John Custis would seem to have been a difficult enough man in all conscience, even his own; but it is sad to think of him with his joy wrapped up in his garden and his most receptive friend and fellow gardener an ocean away. The letters that passed between Custis and Collinson in the years between 1734 and 1746 have been arranged and annotated by a great scholar, E. G. Swem, under a title taken from one of Collinson's comments early in their correspondence. Collinson is requesting Custis to send him "Yoppon or Carolina Tea" seeds, as well as some seeds of trees Collinson has already growing in his Peckham garden but which do not seed with him: locust, redbud and persimmon. "For," he says, "tho I have enough already myself, yet I think there is no greater pleasure than to be communicative and oblige others. It is laying an obligation and I seldom fail of returns for we Brothers of the Spade find it very necessary to share among us the seeds that come annually from abroad. It not only preserves a Friendly Society, but secures our Collections."

Thus begins a long, sociable exchange of plants, seeds, bulbs and information. Collinson sends double Dutch tulips and Guernsey lilies, the double-blossomed peach, horse chestnuts, carnations and auriculas. Custis has already sent dogwoods (with catbirds) to Catesby (who, we remember, is working on his book, supported by Collinson) and sends Collinson mountain cowslip, more dogwoods, flowering bay, laurel and chinquapin nuts. Collinson asks for the fringe tree and sends yellow province roses and double honeysuckles. Custis is able to persuade a "particular friend," a captain, to take casks containing shrubs of the fringe tree, pearl tree, redbuds and laurels. Cypress and juniper seeds go also. Collinson is overcome with gratitude and sends more tulips and Italian tuberoses, which he knows "increase prodigiously" in South Carolina. He has received boxes of puccoon.

Regrettably, the "particular friend" had a "sad turbulent passage" and lost all the tubs. Hickories, honey locusts and laurel seed arrived, however, and Collinson sent pistachio nuts to be tried in Virginia, and dates. Mr. Catesby tells him of a very pretty tree called sorrel tree

Catesby's Dogwood, Plate 27, Vol. I

growing near Williamsburg. Seed will be acceptable and Collinson sends "half a cone of the Cedar of Lebanon." The other half goes to "a curious friend in Pensylvania." (Received, as we know, by John Bartram.) Collinson sends also double rocket seeds and Jerusalem cowslip. Custis writes that from one shipment, mostly dead, he has a yellow rose, the Chili strawberry, four altheas, laurels, of which he already had plenty, a red rose, a Guernsey lily and some striped box, for which he is grateful. Custis admits to being "a great admirer of all the tribe striped gilded and variegated plants, and especially trees. I am told those things are out of fashion, but . . . I always make my fancy my fashion." He is pleased in his turn to "gratify so curious a gentleman and so kind a friend."

Custis planted almonds and pistachios and dates and Cedar of Lebanon, laburnum, radishes and Spanish sage trees, but as for the "Italian beans" — he yearly raised hundreds of bushels as "black-eyed Indian peas" and ships them to the West Indies. Virginia is too hot for grapes and plums but dwarf apple trees are most acceptable. He sends yoppon, bayberries, white mulberry trees (they grow like weeds in Virginia) and some "Angola seeds" (he is told that when dried they make a rich chocolate). Collinson is glad the tuberoses bloomed, altheas survived and hopes to hear the China aster flowered. He is sending more Chili strawberries and "Houtboys" in pots. Autumn is the time to send rooted trees. "A long voyage and a small neglect" ruin herbaceous plants. The chinquapins are coming up and so is the toothache tree, a rarity. He sends seeds of melons, Spanish broom and Italian evergreen oaks. He longs for a fringe tree, a walking stick made from the sorrel tree, and cones of sweet white-flowering swamp bay, acorns of willow-leaved oaks, cones of the tulip tree, burrs of the sweet gum. It is now only two years since they began to correspond.

Mr. Catesby wants to know if Custis has a red flowering dogwood and Collinson would like the red or white moccasin flower and the white-flowering laurel or sweet bay. The oriental persicary, which he has sent, is a fine annual. Collinson prays to know if Custis has Mr. Miller's *Dictionary*, a "work of the greatest use." If he would like to buy it, Collinson will get him a copy. Custis writes at gloomy length in 1737 about a harsh spring ruining his Dutch box edgings, hardy though they be, and spoiling his tulips. He could not find the lilac seeds, regrettably, as he has only the pale blue, "the hardiest tree in the world." Mocassin flowers are scarce, but he will try. He is glad the fringe trees and mountain cowslips are doing well. The white hollow-blossomed plant sent by Collinson, whose name he forgets, is blooming. Collinson writes it is foxglove. By now they are able to correspond philosophically on many other matters, most of the things they have exchanged having finally done well.

In January, 1737, Collinson now wishes to bring his friends and sources together and tells Custis to write to Dr. Witt in Germantown or John Bartram on the "Skulkill," as they have received "a double flowering China or India Pink" and will send him seed if he mentions Collinson's name to either one. In December, 1737, Collinson sends Custis more crown imperial lilies, blue and white hyacinths, yellow asphodel, white moley and double yellow pilewort, all by Captain Friend, who will now be their intermediary. He advises planting European plants in Virginia between quick-growing hedges for protection, thanks Custis for the sorrel tree plants in tubs (please make holes in the bottoms for drainage) and requests Custis to start umbrella tree seeds for him. A noble plant. A friend has one and the tulip tree is successful in England.

Two weeks later, still in December, 1737, Collinson writes that he is sending to call upon Custis "a down right plain country man," a Quaker into the bargain. He has a credential from Collinson, who begs his friend Custis to look "not at the man but at his mind." "Imployed by a Sett of Noble Men" on Collinson's recommendation, he collects seeds and specimens of rare plants and "does not Value rideing 50 or 100 miles to see a New Plant . . . Pray direct him . . . The Umbrella Tree will make him think his journey worth comeing . . . The Gardens of Pensilvania are well furnished with European rarities. Possibly he may assist you with some plants that you want . . . His name is John Bartram."

In spite of Collinson's new business arrangement with Bartram, the pace of his correspondence with Custis quickens. Catesby needs "that curious peach-coloured dogwood." (This remained a problem. Was Custis' red dogwood only a faded white one or was there indeed a natural pink? Much was written, little settled.) John Clayton of Glouces-ter had sent London "seeds or tufts" of a beautiful scarlet sumac. Collin-son still wishes for more toothache tree, fringe tree, sassafras, umbrella tree and chinquapins. He identifies for Custis the "Virginia tree prim-rose." Wild larkspur seed is received, and are there *two* wild passion flowers? Custis writes he is sure Captain Friend is a fine man but he prefers to stick by his own agent, Mr. Cary. In fact, Friend was late and the stuff came through poorly, rotten and dead except for the strawberry tree, striped box and Persian lilac. Seeds of the India pink have come up. So has the globe thistle. Collinson writes in a philo-sophical vein and sends "some of our best peaches and nectarines." Custis is concerned with the demise of Lady Wager's possum, and goes on at length about how to grow seeds in Virginia and the infirmities of his age (sixty-two), which prevented his going about with Bartram on his welcome visit. The greatest pleasure Custis finds is in his garden "and sometimes even that is insipid." He has preserved the Persian lilac, Arabian jessamine, strawberry tree, imperial lily and some martagons.

In January, 1739, Collinson thanks Custis for his kind reception of Bartram and reports that Bartram was delighted with the Custis garden, the "best furnished" and nearest to John Clayton's of any gardens Bar-tram met with in that journey. Collinson thanks Custis for the seeds of the long cucumber he requested and the black haws, "an Indian sweet-meat." He has sent more of everything, with some spring aconite and cyclamens. Collinson has had to keep fires in his stove and greenhouses. In 1740 Custis complains that, due to Captain Friend's having to take a load of "vile convicts" to Rappahannock to be sold, Custis was late in receiving rose trees and other splendid plants, all dead in powdery earth. Only the Catherine peach, the nutmeg peach and some white currants survived the neglect. Colonel Byrd's trees are all alive, "the more lucky man." In 1741 Collinson explains that "deers' eyes" is the common name for some horse chestnuts a friend brought Custis, and the tree from them (which grows in the gardens of the "curious" in England) is

Catesby's Fringe Tree with a letter from Collinson to Custis saying it is coming up
in his garden

Lond.: March 21: 1736/7

D. M. Curtis

I have the pleasure to tell you
that the Seed of the fringe Tree is now
comeing Up & your Mountain Cowslip
is now in flower —— these are
Living Memorials with many others
of your great Kindness —— the Cinquapin
you sent Last year by the help of a Little
Art (are a finger high), & yet I beg your further assistance
this year for it is a Tree Wee are in great
Want off amongst our Curious Planters
and you above all others are So very happy
In Packing them up & Sending So Early that
Wee never had Such Luck before —— for by
Long Experience I know this to be the most
Ticklish Seed (to bring) from your part of the World
& pray some Acorns of your Narrow Leafed
Ones, Cypress Cones —— &c

It is a Detriment to the Cargo
of Strawberries (there is a pott of Chilli &
one of Hautboys) Going So late; the
Captain is very Anctious to Carry them
Safe I have given Directions to Water
them Once or Twice a Week which if he
does & gives them Air, I am in hopes
they will Come Safe, if not Wee will
have be other Try all Next year ——
I am Truly your Affectionate fr.
C. Collinson

(left margin:) a few Days agoe I rec.d the pot of Mellon Seed from Africa if I recollect this year it will bring fole next ——

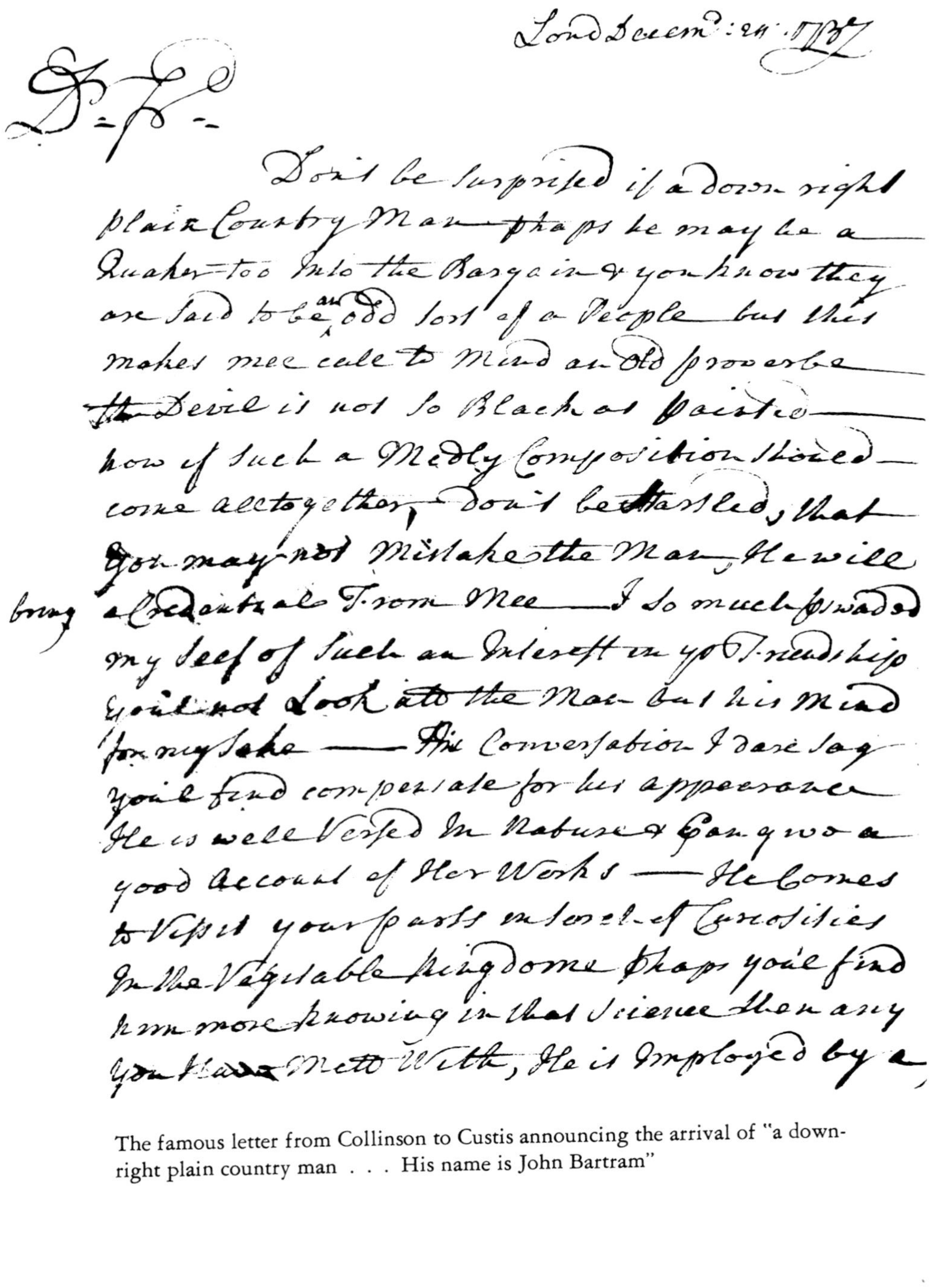

Lond Decemb: 24 1737

Sir—

Don't be surprised if a down right
plain Country Man—phaps he may be a
Quaker—too Into the Bargain & you know they
are said to be an odd sort of a People—but this
makes mee call to Mind an Old proverbe
the Devil is not so Black as Painted—
how if such a Medly Composition should—
come alltogether—don't be startled, that
you may not Mistake the Man, He will
bring a Credentials From Mee——I so much perswaded
my self of such an Interest in yo Friendship
you'd not Look into the Man but his Mind
for my sake——His Conversation I dare say
you'l find compensate for his appearance
He is well Versed In Nature & Can give a
good Account of Her Works——He Comes
to Visit your parts in search of Curiosities
In the Vegitable Kingdome phaps you'l find
him more knowing in that Science then any
you have Mett With, He is Imployed by a,

The famous letter from Collinson to Custis announcing the arrival of "a down-right plain country man . . . His name is John Bartram"

Sett of Noble Men (⅌ my Recommendation) to
Collect Seeds & Specimen of Rare plants, and
He has been very successfull in this affair
wch proceeds from His Thorough knowledge in those
Matters, be so kind to give him a little entertainm^t
& recommend Him to a Fr^d or Two of yours in
the Country, for He does not Value riding 50 or
100 Miles to see a New plant —— pray direct
Him to the Umbrella Tree, this plant or tree
will make Him think his Journey worth
persuing, I have a further Designe in his
waiting On you, the Gardens of pensilvania
are well furnish'd with Europian Rarities
possibly He may assist you with some plants
that you Want & you may assist Them ——
for I presume you have a Vessells passing
too & fro often from one province to the other
His Name Is John Bartram ——

    Your Friendship to Him will
    a singular favour to y^r
    affect^te friend
    Collinson

not to be compared to the eastern kind, but Custis must pardon "a Cockney who lives in a wilderness of chimneys" for pretending to tell "the nature of trees growing in yours."

After this the lists of plants sent and received is mainly repetitive. The cassena nut is requested by Collinson. The loss of his "philereas" lamented by Custis and gilded firs and alpine larches requested. Custis has complained of his debt troubles and failing health. Collinson agrees it is unfair he should be sued for debts not his own, and consults Dr. Fothergill about Custis' health, as we see in another chapter. Custis sends seeds of fringe trees he came upon on his own lands "fully blowd." Collinson sends instructions on pruning and rejoices that Custis has the amaranthoides, which do so well dried. Apples of love are called "tamiata" and put into soups in Italy. Collinson sends a quantity of roses, and some red and white fraxinellas and other repeated plants, the box to be returned, please, full of sweet flowering bay, tulip tree, cassena, pellitory, papaw and umbrella. He wishes John Clayton and Dr. Mitchell would annually sow the umbrella tree lest it be lost. In 1746 the sight of a letter from Custis gladdens Collinson as he had feared Custis to be "among the happy." The correspondence ends.

Peter Kalm, pupil of and friend to Linnaeus, was one of the living links between Bartram and Collinson and has left an account of his visits to each one. He first visited Peter Collinson at Peckham in 1748, the year before Collinson moved to Mill House. Kalm was then on his way to America. He writes:

June 10, in the afternoon, I went to Peckham, a pretty village which lies 3 miles from London in Surrey, where Mr. Peter Collinson has a beautiful little garden, full of all kinds of the rarest plants, especially American ones, which can endure the English climate and stand out the whole winter. However neat and small it is, there is scarcely a garden where so many kinds of trees and plants, especially the rarest, are to be found. Peter Collinson uses knucklebones for his borders and he explained to me his method of sowing mistletoe and also experiments he had made with cranberries. He thinks it is best for a garden to have the morning sun so that it may help to dry up the vapours. Quadrilateral is the best shape and is the one which he had adopted, whereas the gardens of the Duke of Richmond are round. The sun is not so effective . . . I saw a tree clipped to form the roof of a summer-house and also a chestnut cut so as to make a shelter over a bench . . .

Collinson, described to Kalm as "the great patron of Natural History and lover of learned men," took Kalm to the Royal Society, where he met Mark Catesby, and gave him letters of introduction to friends in the colonies, among them Benjamin Franklin.

Franklin had visited England as a young man seeking his future career, possibly in printing. He had been misled by the fair promises of

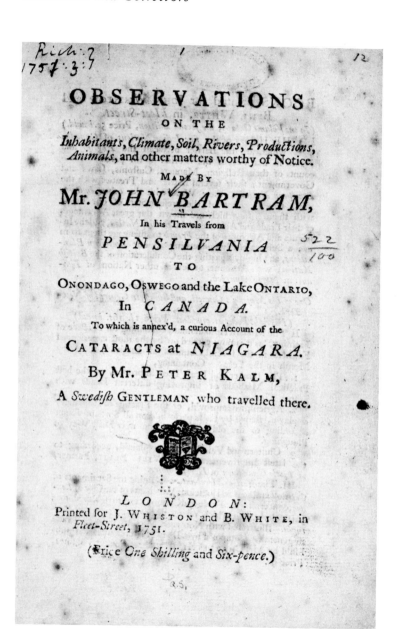

OBSERVATIONS

ON THE

Inhabitants, Climate, Soil, Rivers, Productions, Animals, and other matters worthy of Notice.

MADE BY

Mr. JOHN BARTRAM,

In his Travels from

PENSILVANIA

TO

ONONDAGO, OSWEGO and the Lake ONTARIO,

In CANADA.

To which is annex'd, a curious Account of the

CATARACTS at NIAGARA.

By Mr. PETER KALM,

A *Swedish* GENTLEMAN who travelled there.

LONDON:
Printed for J. WHISTON and B. WHITE, in
Fleet-Street, 1751.

(*Price One Shilling* and *Six-pence.*)

The little book Peter Collinson had published without Bartram's knowledge or permission, combining his account of his travels with that of Peter Kalm

the English governor, who had given him cause to expect financial support for his trip. His disappointment, however, pure dross, turned to gold in the acquaintances he made while he worked briefly in printing offices and explored London. Peter Collinson knew of him as an inventive genius and, on Franklin's return home, sent him some "observations" on electricity that had come before the Royal Society. Franklin was spurred on with his own experiments and sent his observations to Collinson, which Collinson instantly published. It was an age when it seems not to have been required to have an author's permission to make a book of a private communication. Collinson did the same thing with Bartram's report on his trip into Indian country and to the conference called by Cadwallader Colden. It was bound up with Kalm's account of his journey into much the same territory when he saw Niagara Falls. Kalm had visited Collinson at Peckham, and Collinson had sent him to visit Bartram at Kingsessing.

Kalm, commissioned by Linnaeus to travel in the American colonies and bring back what he could find in new plants for Linnaeus to classify, arrived in Philadelphia from London and went immediately to call upon Benjamin Franklin. He was given permission to borrow books from the "Library which was first begun in the year 1742 on a public spirited plan formed and put into execution by the learned Mr. Franklin." Kalm began instantly to observe and comment on the city, on the people, on the diseases, trade and shipping, population growth, a few snakes and, within a week of his arrival, upon American trees, fifty-eight of which he lists by their botanical names. He also touches upon shrubs, plants, a few birds, petrified wood and the premature aging of Americans, and calls upon John Bartram before he has been ten days in the country.

This is his account:

Mr. *John Bartram* is an Englishman, who lives in the country about four miles from Philadelphia. He has acquired a great knowledge of natural philosophy and history, and seems to be born with a peculiar genius for these sciences. In his youth he had no opportunity of going to school, but by his own diligence and indefatigable application he got, without instruction, so far in Latin as to understand all books in that language and even those which were filled with botanical terms. He has in several successive years made frequent excursions into different distant parts of North America with an intention of gathering all sorts of plants which are scarce and little known. Those which he found he has planted in his own botanical garden and likewise sent over their seeds or fresh roots to England. We owe to him the knowledge of many rare plants which he first found and which were never known before. He has shown great judgment and an attention which lets nothing escape unnoticed. Yet with all these qualities he is to be blamed for his negligence, for he did not care to write down his numerous and useful observations. His friends in London once induced him to send them a short account of one of his travels, and they were ready, with a good intention though not with sufficient judgment, to get this account printed. As he is rather backward in writing down what he knows, this publication was . . . not filled with a thousandth part of the great knowledge which he has acquired in natural philosophy and history, especially in regard to North America. I have often been at a loss to think of the sources whence he obtained many things which came to his knowledge. I, also, owe him much, for he possessed that great quality of communicating everything he knew. I shall therefore in this work frequently mention this gentleman. I should never forgive myself if I were to omit the name of a discovery and claim that as my contribution which I had learned from another person.

The Collinson-Custis communication extended from 1734 to 1746. The correspondence between Collinson and John Bartram extended from early in the 1730's to Collinson's death in 1768.

Collinson had been directed toward Bartram by Joseph Breintnall of Philadelphia, a letter from whom describing Braddock's defeat in exactly the light we see it in today is in the Collinson letter books. Bartram was a successful and inquiring farmer with a large family and a natural interest in all plants.

Bartram and Collinson from the beginning had a staunch mutual friend in Benjamin Franklin, whom Collinson had encouraged in his electrical experiments. Franklin had founded the Philosophical Society of Philadelphia, with John Bartram as a charter member. Other Philadelphia worthies known to both men were the eccentric Dr. Witt, James Logan of the maize-propagation experiment, and Bartram's tree-collecting cousin, Humphry Marshall. Through Collinson's introductions, Bartram became a correspondent of English horticulturists and collectors like Dr. John Fothergill, who wished to have the greatest collection of North American plants in England; Gronovius, who sent him *Flora Virginica;* Catesby; Linnaeus, busy identifying specimens sent by Bartram; and lesser worthies no less anxious to make Bartram's acquaintance. Collinson (first aware of Bartram in 1730–1731) entered into a business agreement with him before 1735. Collinson died in 1768. Bartram survived him by only nine years, howbeit very active ones.

Customs and reticences change. Records are lost or destroyed and years later copies turn up from somewhere far away. Credits are lost and regained. One of the more regrettable instances of lost credit is the expurgation of John Bartram's experiments with hybridization in 1739 from the *Memorial* of his letters, collected and edited by William Darlington, M.D., LL.D., in 1849.

"Fairchild's Mule," an artificial cross between a carnation and a sweet William in 1717, was a famous curiosity of the eighteenth-century gardener. But credit for early artificial hybridization also belongs to John

Bartram, who experimented with *Lychnis* and in 1739 wrote to William Byrd II of having achieved a peach-colored bloom from a cross of red and white. He made other experiments with other plants as well and told Byrd that he had "made several microscopical observations upon the male and female parts in vegetables to oblige some ingenious botanists in Leyden, who requested that favour of me, which I hope I have performed to their satisfaction, and as a mechanical demonstration of the certainty of this hypothesis, of the different sex in all plants that have come under my notice . . ." Here Dr. Darlington left out some details that I am unable to replace. Bartram continued, "I have made several succesful experiments of joining several species of the same genus whereby I have obtained curious mixed colours in flowers never known before; but this requires an accurate observation and judgement to know the precise time . . ." Here Dr. Darlington steps in again, but we here are able to continue: "when the female organ is disposed to receive the masculine seed and likewise when it is by the masculine organs fully perfected for ejection." Dr. Darlington lets Bartram in again to say "I hope by these practical observations to open a gate into a very large field of experimental knowledge which if judiciously improved may be a considerable addition to the beauty of the florist's garden."

What other details have been denied us by editing and loss of letters we can only guess until full justice is done John Bartram by scholars who can patch together all he wrote to Byrd, Collinson, the "ingenious botanists in Leyden" and probably others, as he was justly gratified to prove that "the male parts of vegetables" are "necessary to vegetation." This had been surmised by Bradley in 1714, observing the spontaneous hybridization in *Auricula,* and illustrated by Fairchild, fertilizing the carnation with the pollen from the sweet William; but Bartram was the first American to practice and to prove the possibilities of artificial hybridization of garden flowers. In 1740 he wrote proudly to Collinson that "the flesh coloured Lychnis was Bartram's hybrid."

The tone of the Collinson-Bartram correspondence is quite different from the gentlemanly give-and-take of the Custis-Collinson letters. There we could see Collinson's instincts to instruct and improve somewhat curbed by good manners and Custis' testiness tempered by his passion for his garden, until his health is touched upon and an overseas diagnosis rendered. With the Bartram-Collinson letters we sense Collinson's insistence on shaping the usefulness of his new acquaintance to his own ends and Bartram's freedom from any inhibitions to resist all influence other than horticultural. Quaker stands up to Quaker and in the end they become staunch and understanding friends for over thirty years. Although all these letters are well worth quoting at length, it must serve us here to be brief to the point of showing only the trends of the plant exchanges. Custis-Collinson exchanges alone would furnish a charming Virginia garden today; the Bartram-Collinson trafficking, undertaken at much the same time, would furnish also great English parks and shrubberies, apothecaries' gardens and wild gardens in woods and glades.

Sometime before 1735, suggestions were made that Bartram receive an allowance of about twenty pounds a year, for which he would collect seeds and plants, with dried specimens of the leaves and flowers to be described by their familiar names or, later, by using the Linnaean system. These were to be packed in several boxes, which Collinson would then be able to pass on to "noble friends" who are very "curious" and might be moved to subscribe financially. Live specimens can be sent if kept under the captain's bed. Collinson felt justified in urging Bartram to procure all sorts of plants only heard of or still unknown in England, obviously with no conception of the hardships or dangers of the terrain.

The arrangement would seem to have started slowly, with Bartram considering he was doing a favor and asking for "some botanical books" in return. Collinson's reply was a suggestion that he repair to the "gentlemen of the Library Company" in Philadelphia who, at Collinson's request, will indulge him "the liberty to peruse their botanical books," especially Miller's *Dictionary.* This must have been rather dampening. Especially when in this same letter of January, 1734, Collinson asks for Solomon's seals, hellebores, all sorts of lilies, especially small martagons, devil's bit or blazing star, lady's slippers, the *Aristolochia,* recommended for sore breasts, the *Euonymous* or spindle tree, wild senna, mountain goat's rue, snakeroot, ground cypress, seed of birch or black beech, swallowwort or *Apocinon,* red root, cottonweed or life everlasting, the "perannual Pea," a walking cane of canewood and "the woody vine with variegated leaves." Collinson does not expect all these at once; a year or more will do.

By 1735 Collinson is thanking Bartram for "two choice cargoes of plants . . . very curious and rare, and well worth my acceptance." He sends calico for Bartram's wife and some things that may be "of use amongst the children," and a box of books for Joseph Breintnall. With these come a large bundle of waste paper for wrapping up the seeds and a quire of white paper for dried specimens.

Once a year Bartram will send dried specimens with duplicates of the same to be "named by our most knowing botanists" and returned to him, "which will improve thee more than books." Collinson thanks Bartram for the laurel and shrub honeysuckle, skunk cabbage, a sedum and the canewood, which he says is the Virginia guelder rose. And please to send a box of laurel and honeysuckle started in earth and also other "odd and uncommon" plants from the woods. Collinson "designs to make a present . . . to a very curious person" and hopes to procure in return some present for Bartram . . ."

After this the momentum and the general temperature pick up a little. Collinson sends almonds and grapes and the Neapolitan medlar to be grafted on to white thorn. Bartram sends berries and cherry stones, sassafras and scented goldenrod. "Our noble friend" is sent the lot. Bartram "discharged that affair very elegantly." More paper is on the way, chestnuts, Spanish nuts and Katherine peach stones, seeds of the China aster "sent per the Jesuits from China to France," and the "Lebanon cone." Bartram has asked for seeds of English wildflowers. Seeds are being sent from the Chelsea Physic Garden, sixty-nine sorts, from Collinson's "knowing friend Philip Miller."

By this time the "noble friend, a universal lover of plants," wants to collect seeds of American forest trees, and Collinson sends Bartram stuff for a suit to be made up as compensation "for thy loss of time." And please to call upon one John White for buds or scions of some of the collection of pears he had brought to Philadelphia from England. It is now 1736 and the noble friend is revealed as Lord Petre, who orders Collinson to give Bartram credit for eighteen pounds. Bartram has suggested an annual allowance and Lord Petre will contribute ten guineas. Perhaps another may be induced to give as much to "enable thee to prosecute further discoveries . . . to set apart a month, two or three to make an excursion on the banks of the Schuylkill . . ." They will send him paper for an exact journal and a pocket compass. They "apprehend" it will be necessary to take a servant, two horses and a spare horse "to carry linen, provisions and other necessaries." They need no more tulip, swamp laurel, hickory, black walnut, sassafras, dogwood, sweet gum, white oak, swamp oak, Spanish oak or red cedar, but they do want all other oaks, firs, pines, black gum or haw, Judas tree, persimmon, cherries, plums, services, hop tree, benjamin or allspice, all sorts of ash, sugar tree, wild roses, black beech or hornbeam, all sorts of flowering and berry-bearing shrubs, honey locust, lime tree, arrow-wood, a particular locust, and guelder rose. In fact, "not anything can come amiss." Noble friends will pay shipping charges. Lord Petre will contribute ten guineas and they are in hopes to raise ten more.

By 1737 Bartram has been given Parkinson's *Herbal* (probably the *Theatrum Botanicum*) by James Logan and Miller's *Dictionary* by Collinson, who has also requested Thomas Penn to show Bartram the first eight of Catesby's sections of his *Natural History*. Collinson has referred to Lawson's *Voyages* only with reference to the animals, however. Lord Petre would like some wild fowl. Bartram is busy.

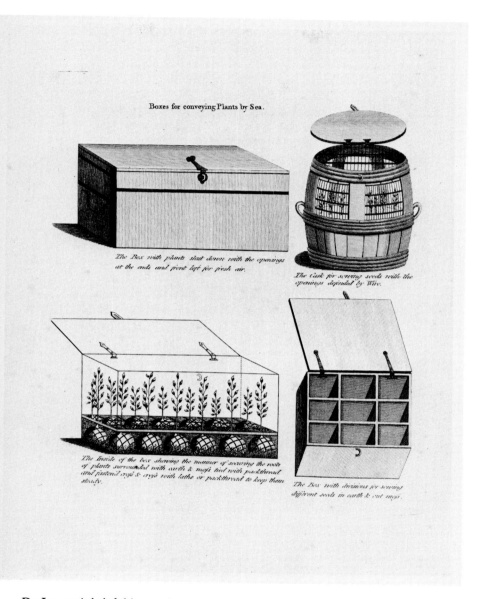

Boxes for conveying Plants by Sea.

The Box with plants shut down with the openings at the ends and front left for fresh air.

The Cask for sowing seeds with the openings defended by Wire.

The Inside of the box shewing the manner of securing the roots of plants surrounded with earth & mefs tied with packthread and fastened crofs & crofs with laths or packthread to keep them steady.

The Box with divisions for sowing different seeds in earth & cut mofs.

Dr. Lettsom's helpful instructions on how to send plants by sea

From Collinson's little account book, recording "the first introduction of American seeds into Great Britain," we see that by 1740 they have raised ten guineas more from the Duke of Norfolk and in return he and Lord Petre each received two boxes of seeds. In 1741 Collinson again records two boxes each from Bartram to these same two underwriters. In 1742 the two originals (again with two boxes each) are joined by the Duke of Richmond and the Duke of Bedford with one box each. In 1743 Lord Petre's name has disappeared, though the others remained as before and Peter Collinson laments the death of his friend, his "young brother," the "man who was dearer . . . than all men . . . carried off by the small pox in the thirtieth year of his age." Petre's share of Bartram's seeds will be offered to the Duke of Norfolk "and P. Miller." In 1744 the list has three dukes, Norfolk, Richmond and Bedford, and a man named Blackbourne. In 1745 it has only a gentleman named Fenwick. But in 1746 the list is headed by Lord Bute, the dukes of Norfolk and Richmond, Messrs. Fenwick, Blackbourne, Miller and a new one, Mr. Williamson. No shipments are shown for 1747; 1748 gives only two, to the Duke of Argyle and a gentleman named Hamilton. But 1749 and 1750 are banner years. The first begins with the Duke of Argyle, Lord Leicester, Lord Lincoln, Lord Deckford, Lord Hopton, Sir Hugh Smithson, and three gentlemen, James West, and Williamson and Dobbs of Ireland, the last in for two boxes as opposed to all the others' one each. In 1750 the Duke of Argyle leads off, followed by the Duke of Marlborough, Lord Larchmont, Lord Deckford, Sir Hugh Smithson, Thomas Penn, and Messrs. Nugent, Jackson, Powell, Williamson and Dobbs of Ireland in for three boxes. The year 1751 sees the Prince of Wales subscribing for one box and, in 1752, for four. There is also a large order from Dr. Mitchell "for some nobility in Scotland."

If one synchronizes these charges with the letters between Bartram and Collinson one can see what went into the shipments. Unhappily for Peter Collinson, who cared deeply for his friends, he lost the Duke of Richmond in 1751 and the Prince of Wales soon after. But John Bartram has a quarter of a century still ahead of him.

While this traffic may seem one-sided, Bartram had, in fact, received many plants from Collinson and, as time went on, all the books he asked for. Among much else, Collinson sent lilacs and Bartram took pains to assure him he was well stocked, which shocked Collinson (who could never let Bartram's surprised resentments go unreplied to) as, he said, Custis had "the best collection of lilacs" in the country and was still glad to receive them. (This we suspect, knowing Custis' own reply.) Again, Collinson sent some "double white daffodils" and re-

In the Year - - - 1763

Lord Willoughby de Broak . . . 1 Box . . . 5 5
Lord Montfort . . . 1 Do . . . 5 5
Lord Orre . . . 1 Do . . . 5 5
Sr Geo: Colebrook . . . 1 Do . . . 5 5
Mr Orwell . . . 2 Do . . . 10 10
Mr Tom . . . 2 Do . . . 10 10
Mr Dobson . . . 4 . . . 25 s
Mr Milion . . . 1 . . . 5 5
Germany Mr Bush . . . 3 . . . 15 15
Poland Marquis Wildare . . . 3 . . . 15 15
Order of Prussia . . . 1 . . . 5 5

In the Year - - - 1751

H.R. Prince of Wales . . . 1 Box 5 Bx5 — 5 5
Duke of Cumberland . . 2 D° — 7½ 7½
Duke of Marlbrough . . 1 D° — 5 5
Earl of Northumberland . 1 — 8 8
L. Comery Jr — 5 5
Lord Leicester Bqt — 5 5
Duke of Bedford Esqr — 5 5
Mr Ward Esqr — 5 5
Mr Gregson Jr — 5 5
Tabitt Esqr — 5 5
Eliott Esqr — 5 5
Mr Breed — 8 8
Lord Germaine — 5 5
Mr Wilkinson — 7 7
Fra C Bds sqr — 5 5

Two of Collinson's records of plants received from Bartram

sented Bartram's saying his countryside was overrun with them, the early settlers having brought them years before. Collinson replies they are rare in England and, again, that Custis wanted them. Collinson sent the stones of peaches, plum, apricots and nectarines; seeds of the annual "oriental *Persicaria,*" China aster and, apparently, a collection of pears, which he fears were "little regarded." Seeds of the stone pine were to be procured from "my friend T. Penn." Please go to him for them.

Tulips were sent and a box of bulbs: twenty sorts of crocuses, narcissus, all the available martagons and lilies, gladiolus and ornithogalums, moleys, irises. A box of seeds of "our finest wild flowers" and some Larix and evergreen seeds.

As Collinson and Bartram became steadily better acquainted throughout their years of corresponding, they dealt with many subjects beyond plants: treatment of Indians, slavery, wars, family matters, mutual friends, biblical references, government. Bartram was always able to give as well as he got, sometimes better. When Collinson urged him not to give up collecting in the wild interior of the country for fear of Indians, who, Collinson felt, would respond in kind to kindness shown them, Bartram replied tartly with the story of his riding down a trail and meeting an Indian who snatched the hat from Bartram's head, chewed the brim fiercely as if he wished to show what he would like to do to Bartram and then flung it on the ground. When Collinson, who occasionally sent presents of clothes for Bartram and lengths of cloth for his wife, sent a cap with a hole in it, Bartram discarded it and prompted the reproaches of Collinson, who claimed he had planned to wear it longer himself. They were both Quakers and not above instructing each other.

By 1761 Bartram writes of the "glorious appearance of Carnations from thy seed" and that he can "challenge any garden in America for variety." The correspondence blooms with successful reports from both sides.

These two elderly gentlemen were also not above a few little jokes about ladies who appeared so eager to give plants to Bartram — two ladies of Charleston whose acquaintance and generosity made Collinson declare his jealousy. Bartram protested that he did indeed know only one of them, having visited her garden. This last is Martha Logan, who, at the age of seventy, wrote the garden "treatise" that we consider under vegetables. In 1760 she sent to Bartram seeds of "Virginia stock . . . you so much admired in my garden," some seeds of striped stock gillyflowers, and, all in one bag, a middle division full of the seeds of flowering shrubs, trees and vines, which they esteem and wish may be new to Bartram. The next year she sent a tub and some roots of the "Indian or Worm Pink" to Mrs. Bartram, as requested. Mrs. Logan also sent "Padus, the lovely tree growing in Governor Glenn's garden among others," and a "Golden Lily," different in bud from the atamasco. From the other lady, Mrs. Lamboll, Bartram wrote Collinson he had received "two nobel cargoes" unspecified. Collinson said he yearned for the lily and some widows to indulge him.

In 1763, with fifty or more other Quakers, Collinson was chosen to represent the Friends with a loyal address to King George III congratulating him upon the Peace of Paris. The address, read by Dr. Fothergill, was graciously received and the king took particular notice of Collinson. At the levee, he reported, the king spoke graciously about a box of specimens sent him by John Bartram from Pennsylvania.

Probably as a result of this kindly condescension on the part of the king, Collinson approached him on Bartram's behalf to ask he be appointed Botanizer Royal for America. Bartram had complained to Collinson that a brash Philadelphian named Young was going about airing an official appointment and had "got more honour by a few miles' travelling to pick up a few common plants" than Bartram had "by near thirty years' travel with great danger and peril."

In 1765 Collinson reported to Bartram that "Our Gracious King . . . had appointed thee his botanist with a salary of £50 a year . . . Now dear John thy wishes are in some degree accomplished to range over Georgia and Florida . . . It must be left to thine own judgement how to proceed."

This last comes nearly at the end of their correspondence, the whole of which makes wonderful reading — two good and great men who never met but loved each other for years across the wide Atlantic, which they literally ploughed with their plants and seeds.

William, John Bartram's third son, who grew to be an explorer and plant collector, was an artist and naturalist born. In 1755 he was seventeen and traveled up the Delaware to Goshen to call on Cadwallader Colden. In 1755 he visited with his father at the home of Reverend Jared Eliot. With his living to make, after attending the Old College in Philadelphia for a time, he tried, or was pushed into trying, business ventures, each unsuccessful to a degree that would drain creativity from a lesser soul. It seems as if his father had not dared resign himself to fostering his son's talent for sketching all he found on his explorations. John Bartram took William on long trips, valued him as a companion, sent his sketches abroad, urged him to paint turtles and birds for London scientists and yet pressed him into whatever depressing apprenticeships he could find. Finally, at twenty-two, William was sent to an uncle in North Carolina to help run a store, as unsuccessfully as ever; but he was always studying and drawing and when his father came through on his way to Florida as the Royal Botanist to George III,

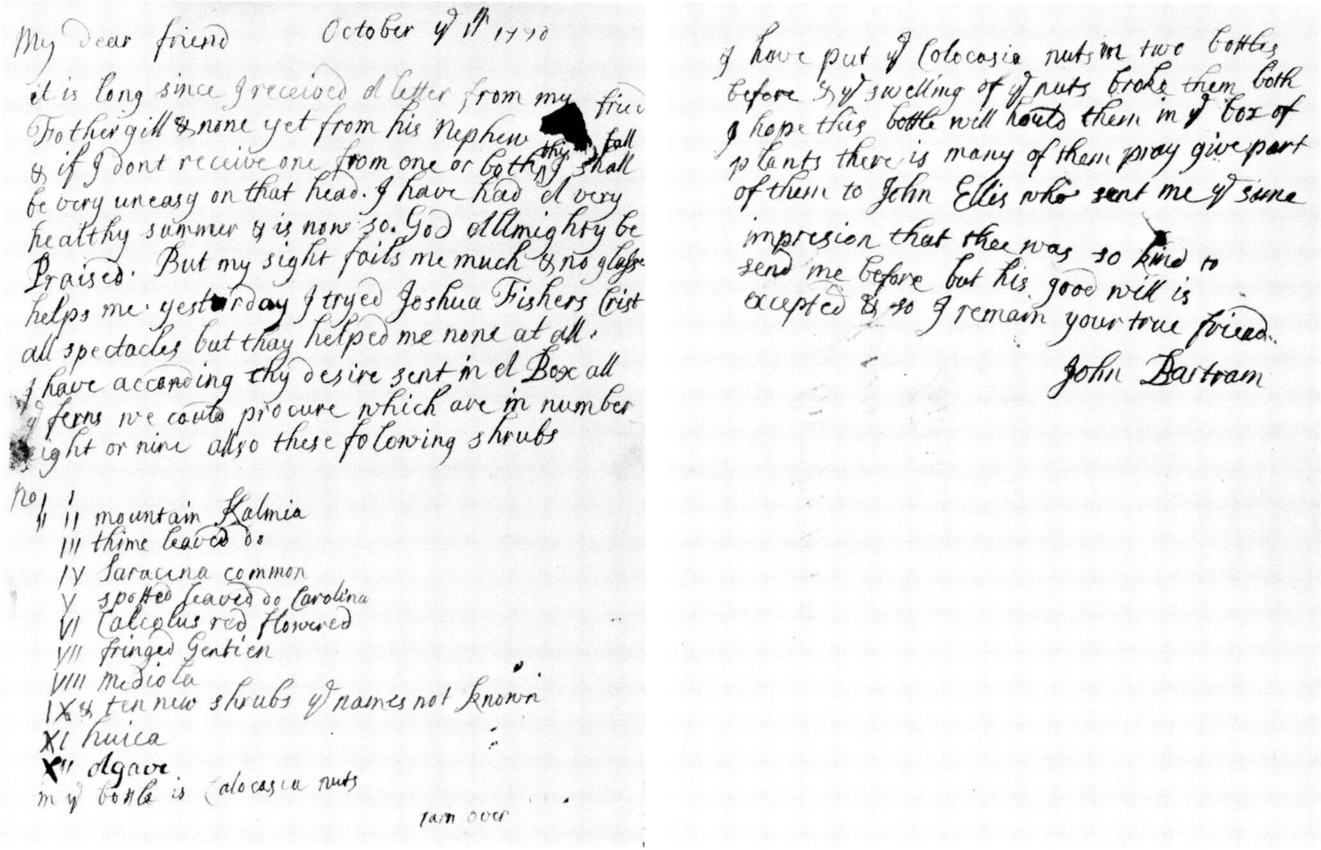

My Dear friend   October 9th 1770

it is long since I received A letter from my friend
Gothergill & none yet from his nephew the fall
or if I dont receive one from one or both y[e] I shall
be very uneasy on that head. I have had a very
healthy summer & is now 70. God allmighty be
praised. But my sight fails me much & no glasses
helps me yet now I try[e]d Joshua Fishers (first
all spectacles but they helped me none at all).
I have according they desire sent in el Box all
ferns we could procure which are in number
y[e] yt or nine also these following shrubs

no I. mountain Kalmia
   II thime leaved [Laurel] &c
   III Saracena common
   IV spotted leaved Carolina
   V Calicobus red flowered
   VI fringe gentian
   VII Medeola
   VIII ten new shrubs of names not known
   XI Yucca
   XII Agave
my Colocasia is Colocasia nuts

I have put of Colocasia nuts in two bottles
before by y[e] swelling of y[e] nuts broke them both
before this bottle will reach them in y[e] Box of
plants there is many of them pray give part
of them to John Ellis who sent me y[e] some
impression that the way to sow is
sow me before but this you will is
accepted & so I remain your true friend
         John Bartram

Letter from the aged Bartram to Collinson

William was taken along as an assistant in 1765. At the end of this trip William again essayed business, this time to raise rice and indigo. The wretched state into which this reduced him prompted Henry Laurens of Charleston to appeal to John Bartram to rescue his son. Back in Philadelphia again, William was still supposed to make money in either business or agriculture, but his persistence in studying natural history and in drawing was beginning to pay off. In 1768 he was elected to the Philadelphia Society for Promoting Useful Knowledge, of which his father and Benjamin Franklin were both members. And in the same year, Peter Collinson, near the end of his long and beneficent life, procured a commission for William to draw mollusks and turtles for the Duchess of Portland and Dr. Fothergill, and made arrangements for Dr. Fothergill to become the patron of William. In 1772 Dr. Fothergill wrote to John Bartram that it seems "a pity that such a genius should sink under distress," and Dr. Lionel Chalmers of Charleston was appointed fiscal agent for Dr. Fothergill's support of William as a naturalist with an allowance of fifty pounds a year. William immediately began to make preparations for his expedition, which lasted from 1773 to 1774 and resulted in one of the world's great books.

That one of William Bartram's gifts was for dramatic writing becomes apparent on any and every page of his *Travels Through North and South Carolina, Georgia, East and West Florida,* finally published, after years of neglect, in Philadelphia in 1791. It received "mixed" and astonished reviews and was criticized for its emotional style, but the facts remain that it had great vogue abroad, was much imitated by writers of the day like Coleridge, Wordsworth and Châteaubriand, and very nearly precipitated the founding of several adventurous groups desiring to live with nature in the beautiful raw, alligators and all. Bartram's description of bull alligators fighting can rank with Mrs. Anne Grant's description of the ice going out in Albany among the best descriptions of American natural phenomena before Thoreau. Bartram's description of the baby bear bereft of its mother does not bear quoting by the kindly disposed. However firmly based upon a profound faith in a divine Creator who orders all, however embellished with classical and biblical references, however overenthusiastic about the wonders of the wilds and the roles of the simplest flowers and creatures, it is a great book.

In Collinson's letter books in the Linnaean Society Library in London is a list in his hand of "Seeds and Forest Trees and Flowering Shrubs gathered in Pensilvania, the Jerseys and New York by John and William Bartram and sent over the last years of their correspondence, being the largest collection that had ever before been imported into this Kingdom." They number over one hundred. (See the list on page 490.)

Furber's Flowers for the Month of June

1. Perennial dwarf Sun flower G
2. Ultramarine & Persian blue Iris Major B C
3. Blue Nigella or Fennel Flower B
4. Moon Trefoile G
5. Upright Sweet William P
6. Saxifrage B
7. Cinque Foile B T
8. Pansies, or Hearts-ease B
9. Maidens-blush Rose
10. Yellow Jasmine B T
11. Blue Corn-flower B
12. Blush Belgick Rose B T
13. The Franckfort Rose B T
14. Double Martagon B
15. Orchis or Bee flower G
16. Scarlet Colutea G
17. Fraxinella B
18. Moss Province Rose B T
19. Double Virginian Silk Grass B
20. White Rose B T
21. Dutch Hundred Leaved Rose B T
22. White Bachelor Button B
23. Rosa Mundi B T
24. Mountain Lychnis B
25. Dwarf Iris Striped B
26. White Jasmine B T
27. Scarlet Geranium G
28. Yellow Martagon B
29. Red Martagon B
30. Teucrium or Germander G
31. Mountain dwarf Pink E S
32. Yellow Corn-Marygold G
33. Purple Sweet Pea B
34. Greek Valerian B

6 *American Husbandry*

Since AMERICAN HUSBANDRY was of foremost importance to all settlers and their supporters, we here "take a view" of what went on with the land at large while relatively small fractions of it were concentrated in gardens for pleasure and for the kitchen. Information abounds. Advice runs high. Experience is at a premium. Fortunately for us, George Washington, one of the leading farmers, kept careful records, and Thomas Jefferson, also "curious," was equally given to noting everything down on paper.

There are two American classics upon the subject of American husbandry, one mid-eighteenth-century and one later, the first being Jared Eliot's *Essays upon Field Husbandry in New England,* published in Boston in 1760, and the other J. Hector St. John de Crèvecoeur's *Letters from an American Farmer,* published in England in 1782.

Jared Eliot's essays, six in all, are valuable to us for his character, a typical New England farmer-doctor-minister-philosopher figure, a man of parts and great good will, corresponding with the outstanding men of his time, like John Bartram and Benjamin Franklin and Peter Collinson. He writes a measured and scholarly prose and is also proficient with his hands, and inventive. Just as Washington and Jefferson were always striving to make a plough more fit for our "new" American land than the heavy, deep-ploughing machines from England, Eliot is occupied with improving upon Mr. Jethro Tull's English drill plough with his own, which makes a "channel," sows seed and fertilizer and closes over

J.W. Jefferson presents his compliments   , and incloses him the drawings of the mouldboard. being done by the eye merely and without measuring the parts, there is a sensible disparity, in the dimensions of the several figures, which should have been avoided. but they will suffice for the references in the Description given in the Philosophical transactions till the plate is published, which it is said will be ready a fortnight.

Apr. 29. 1800.

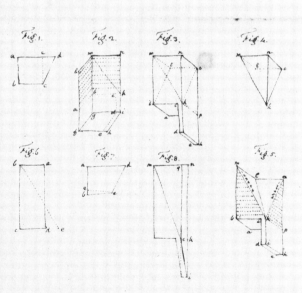

Jefferson's sketch for a "mould board" for a plough, 1800

the top of the trench as it moves along. Tull's machine is heavy and too much for our shallow soil. The needs and lacks in our agricultural situation are apparent to Eliot and it is to correct these and redirect individual efforts that he writes six papers "to be of service, not an history of our practice, nor an account of what we do in our present husbandry, but rather what we do, to our advantage." Land reclamation, increase of food production, crop rotation and diversification, improvement of our stock of sheep, the mechanics of tilling and encouragements for new ventures like silk manufacture and the manufacture of oil from colewort seeds to enable us to export our flax to Ireland are his subjects, more or less in that order. That these essays were infinitely stimulating to farmers working the land wherever their lots had fallen we know from their popularity.

Our other American farming classic is nearly all fiction. Except for the account of his interview with John Bartram and his description of the summerhouse from which he wrote one of his letters, de Crèvecoeur writes of our rural economy with all the charm and philosophical inflorescence of a French romanticist. He develops characters that have been picked up and perpetuated, like those whom William Byrd II immortalized on the North Carolina border. Here, in de Crèvecoeur, for instance, we have the gently teasing American wife, underestimating her husband's powers, whom we encounter in Mrs. John Bartram, who, in all kindness, like de Crèvecoeur's wife, felt more secure to see her husband behind a plough than with a pen or a Latin dictionary in his hand.

Both Eliot's *Essays* and de Crèvecoeur's *Letters* give us a sense of their writers' bucolic joys, unusual for their hard times and not seen again until the signs of contentment in the correspondence of Washington and Jefferson writing from their hearts and their homes.

For an overall picture of the eighteenth-century American rural and agricultural economy one cannot do better than a book, purportedly written by "An American," called *American Husbandry,* published in London in 1775. Its chief authorship remains in doubt although it is obviously a compilation of the comments of several different observers. Some editors have considered it the work of Arthur Young, the English agriculturist with whom Washington corresponded and who printed the correspondence. Others see Dr. John Mitchell, eminent botanist and physician of Urbanna upon the Rappahannock, as the compiler, quoting both his own observations and those of Arthur Young. But neither of these two men quite accounts for the entire work, which includes quotations at length from Governor Glen of Charleston, those from an anonymous Georgia planter and lyric descriptions of the promise of new lands opened up by recently completed treaties with the Indians.

A

SURVEY

Of the Ancient

Huſbandry and *Gardening,*

Collected from

CATO, VARRO, COLUMELLA,
VIRGIL, and others the moſt eminent
Writers among the

Greeks and *Romans :*

Wherein many of the moſt difficult Paſ-
ſages in thoſe Authors are explain'd, and the
whole render'd familiar to our Climate; with
Variety of new Experiments.

Adorn'd with CUTS.

With a PREFACE, ſhewing the Uſe of
Huſbandry, and the Neceſſity of erecting Publick Gardens.

By R. BRADLEY, *Profeſſor of Botany in the
Univerſity of* Cambridge, *and* F. R. S.

L O N D O N :

Printed for B. MOTTE, at the *Middle Temple
Gate, Fleet-Street.* M.DCC.XXV.

Bradley was a popular author in many American eighteenth-
century farmers' libraries
Title page of Bradley's book of instructions, adapting the
wisdom of the ancients for eighteenth-century English
husbandry

The whole is a fast-moving account of conditions in the British colonies from Nova Scotia to the Floridas, with particular reports on each of the thirteen colonies, so soon and so unexpectedly to declare themselves free. Nowhere else can we get such accurate pictures of the crops and produce of the individual colonies in 1775. We summarize them here, in the order, from north to south, in which they were given by this "American," so anxious to encourage both efficiency and cooperation, and only a little too late.

New England is treated all of a piece, "the oldest of our American colonies," so that "the best parts of it may be supposed to be granted away or purchased, which is the case." In Maine, where many Germans have settled "since the war," maize is "the grand product of the country," a crop well suited to being cultivated between the hills in which it is planted by Mr. Tull's recently invented horse-hoe.

"Even common farmers in some parts of New England" now practice ploughing between the rows of this grain, "so that it is now no longer an unusual method." The rest of the book deplores the lack of this procedure in other states. Unfortunately New England has to raise so much maize and wheat for its own consumption that it is unable to raise sufficient hemp or flax for rigging or clothing or export. Some of the "more intelligent gentlemen farmers" sow clover between crops of wheat. Turnips are introduced into field culture. Pease, beans and tares are sown and every farmer grows enough for fattening hogs, "in great plenty and very large."

Apples are the "prime article of culture," each "farmer or even cottager" having a large orchard and making hundreds of hogsheads of cider. "The orchards in New England are reckoned as profitable as any other part of the plantation," not forgetting the "noble woods," oak for shipbuilding and fir for masts for the Royal Navy and lumber of the West Indies. A fresh note is the presence in New England of grassland for cattle, in rich meadows and fields sown with "a grass which has made much noise in England under the name Timothy grass." Discovered growing wild in New Hampshire by one John Herd in 1700, who started to cultivate it, it was honored by the name of Timothy Hanson, who introduced it into Virginia twenty years later.

Fittingly, after this last entry, New England horses are "the most hardy in the world," the cattle fat, the sheep produce long wool, the dairies succeed "as well as in Old England," fish, tar and pitch abound, and by means of all this "the farmers and country gentlemen are enabled very amply to purchase whatever they want from abroad." Since New England cannot be impressed to raise anything solely for the Crown, it is of interest only as a market.

New York, surprisingly more lightly settled than New England, considering that its winter is shorter, has superior wheat, splendid "shell marle" on Long Island, maize for the cattle in winter, barley for beer sufficient to export, pease (whose straw makes winter food for the cattle), potatoes, though not as many as in New England, two hay crops a summer and timber comparable to that in New England. Here hemp is grown (our author or compiler is plagued by the fact that England has to go to the Baltic for both hemp and timber), grapes grow wild, flax is exported and fruits are superior. Peaches, nectarines (impossible to grow in New England), melons and watermelons are as good as those in Spain and Italy, and, of course, there are turnips and clover and all kitchen garden stuffs.

In New Jersey the milder winters allow the cattle to be left out all year (whereby manure is lost). Maize grows to eight feet, asparagus is a weed, buckwheat is for cakes and for fattening poultry and hogs. Bread, whether of maize, wheat or rye, is of the finest sort. The "great white winter cabbage" is cultivated in gardens and fields. Hemp does well (not even sugar is more valuable) and saffron is planted. Careless husbandmen, they plant no clovers or artificial grasses, relying instead upon their marshy meadowlands. Orchards abound. Shiploads of apples go to the West Indies. The climate is so "favourable to fruit" that even the poor have plenty of apples, peaches, cherries, gourds and watermelons. The white cedar is the most useful of all their trees, but they are deficient in their care of it. Sassafras, scarcely less valuable, is left standing about in their cleared fields.

In Pennsylvania the climate is ideal and "the productions," in corn, timber and fruits, are nearly the same as those of the Jerseys, exceeding them in quality and plenty. Vines are in abundance; mulberry trees are common. Hogs are fattened on peaches. Wool is scarce; wheat the "grand article" of the province. Firewood is dear because of building and ironworks. Sowing wheat on clover lays is practiced as in England, and Mr. Tull's drill plough has been introduced. Rye is grown and so is barley, but not to the extent it is in England, where it "yields the universal drink of all ranks of people." In Pennsylvania, although hops are cultivated and beer is drunk, the farmers make quantities of cider, and rum is consumed in great quantities. Hemp and flax are raised for home consumption. "Indian hemp," "dog's bane" (*Acopynum cannabinum* L.), which country people have learned from the Indians to use instead of flax, "promises to be a treasure." Cabbages and turnips are commonly cultivated, "partly for the table and partly for cattle." Meadow irrigation is understood and helps get three crops a year but "successive crops of corn are crowded upon their land in much too quick succession." Great stocks of cattle are let run through the woods in summer and winter. Wool might be a valuable article of export "unwrought." Fencing is scarce and "live hedges" of privet are used instead, as they have "not yet sagacity" to use the native hawthorn.

The compiler now deals with labor for the first time, having mentioned only the high wages paid in New England. In Pennsylvania, he says, there are some Negro slaves but not many compared to white servants. These are of two sorts, the first the same as in England, hired by the year, washed, lodged and boarded, but finding their own clothes. The second sort, unknown in Britain, are the new settlers, who are very poor and agree with the captain of the ship that he shall sell them to be servants for a certain number of years. There are laws in the province to regulate this kind of servitude. Some Germans with money enough will not pay and choose to work out while learning about the country. Both these sorts are preferred to those procured by the common hiring method.

Much is to be improved in Pennsylvania, where lucerne sowing is advisable. By broadcasting it and confining their cattle for the summer upon it, they could raise enough dung, if they used litter plentifully, to increase their yields of corn. From now on we are going to hear much about litter made of straw or the stalks of harvested vegetables called "haulm," and marle or clay, all mixed and made into compost. Besides lucerne planting, silk culture could be introduced, as it is succeeding in Georgia, and cultivation of "native flax . . . by sensible planters."

The meals served in country gentlemen's families in Pennsylvania are described: three a day and nearly like those in England. Coffee, tea and chocolate of the best sorts; sugar (cheaper than in England), with bread and butter make a superior breakfast. For dinner and supper one can consider the quantities of game that abound, fish, poultry, meat, venison. Fruits are in a plenty surpassing anything known in the best climates in Europe: melons, cucumbers (grown in the open fields), apples, cherries, peaches, nectarines, gooseberries, currants, strawberries and raspberries. (The grapes are inferior.) Obviously, it is "neither difficult nor expensive to keep an excellent table."

The wine is commonly Madeira at not more than half the price of England. French and Spanish wines are also drunk; rum, and good beer, "brewed by those who are attentive to the operation."

There follows a prolonged accounting to show that an income, which in Britain "will hardly give a man the appearance of a gentleman," will in Pennsylvania enable a man to live well and, eventually, make a fortune. Even the poor, facing up to "poisonous serpents" to escape starving, will do well to cross the "immense ocean and live in another hemisphere — after all, these are done by others even in wealthy situations at home . . . There is nothing terrible in it to people of sense."

With which bright note we come to Virginia and Maryland, treated as one since their climates and their dedication to tobacco are similar. All fruits thrive and are fed to hogs here also. Wheat and other grains and pulse do well. No part of America does better with all sorts of garden vegetables. But tobacco is, uniquely in these provinces, an object of exportation of immense consequence. A description follows of the two main sorts: Oronooke, grown chiefly in Chesapeake Bay, strong and hot, sold in Germany and the north; and "sweet scented," of the finest flavor and most valued, grown chiefly in the lower parts of Virginia, on the James and York rivers, on the Rappahannock and the south side of the Potomac.

Tobacco planters live more like country gentlemen of fortune than any other settlers in America . . . spread about the country, their labour being mostly by slaves who are left to overseers and the masters live in a state of emulation with one another . . . Buildings, furniture, wines, dress, diversions . . . Such a country life as they lead . . . with little to do themselves in a climate that seems to create rather than check pleasure . . . bringing them to be just such planters as foxhunters in England make farmers.

The writer points out that the settler who goes north (and this would seem the main point he wishes to make in all his descriptions of the colonies) "can raise no commodities that are of consequence to Britain." It is to the tobacco colonies only, in the central country, free of the intense cold of the north and the oppressive heats of the south, with a staple crop of value to Britain, that settlers should come, where the culture supports luxury and pays eight percent interest on their debts. "What," he asks, "common culture in Europe will do this?" What, indeed.

He ends his dissertation upon the central colonies with an accounting to show how important tobacco is in their exports. In thousands of pounds: tobacco brings seven hundred and sixty-eight; Indian corn, beans, pease etc., thirty; wheat, forty; deer and other skins, twenty-five; sassafras, ginseng and snakeroot, seven; masts, plank, staves, turpentine and tar, fifty-five; flaxseed, fourteen; pickled pork, beef, hams, bacon, fifteen; ships built for sale, thirty; and hemp, twenty-one. Even the most cursory glance will show that tobacco brings in nearly three times all the other exports put together.

And now the future possibilities in the rich Ohio lands, recently purchased from the Six Nations and declared beyond the Virginian's rights to settle, can be hinted at. The writer again brings in his dreams of cultivated grapes and silkworms and wild hemp. He reports that Dr. Mitchell was employed to make a map to accompany his treatise upon *The Contest in America between Britain and France,* in which he stressed the importance of getting the French out of this country abounding in "deer, wild cows and wild oxen . . ." In another book, *The Present State,* published in 1767, "Doctor Mitchell stresses the fresh land, so much wanted in the tobacco colonies." Whoever commands these rich lands on the Mississippi and the Ohio "must soon command the tobacco trade," since "that exhausting weed" has already worn out so much land. There is a future as well for hemp, oil (olive), silk and wine, cotton, madder, indigo . . . The writer speaks of "rich, deep, black land, moist but not wet," as if he could eat it.

Our conviction mounts. This is not "An American," nor yet Arthur Young or Dr. Mitchell masquerading. This is a personally interested underwriter for the Ohio Company, or whatever name the bright new scheme was then called, in which so many of our Virginia friends and Benjamin Franklin were interested, and which gleamed bright in the eye of many a rich and lordly potential proprietor in England. It was to prevent this dream falling into "wrong" hands that Benjamin Franklin went to England. Washington had seen the country and taken up lands in it. But it was many years after this before its settlement could be got under weigh. It was the subsequent wave westward after the Revolution that impoverished Virginia landholders who had kept faith entirely in Virginia lands, like Thomas Jefferson.

After this, with the glory of Virginia and the Ohio lands behind us, the book dispenses with North Carolina rather flatly. The products of North Carolina are rice, tobacco, indigo, cotton, wheat, pease and Indian corn and all sorts of roots, especially potatoes. Tobacco grows in the north but South Carolina cannot grow it. Indigo grows well, and rice, though not so well as in South Carolina. The writer notes, "In this part of the country swamps are to be found which when drained yield rice." Virginia has swamps also, but is not hot enough. Swamps in North Carolina remained undrained for want of people. He quotes Mr. John Lawson, whom we know, as published in 1718. As it is now 1775 Lawson has lasted well. Doctor Mitchell agrees with Lawson. Owing, says our editor, to the want of ports, new settlers have been driven into the back-country and into a "common husbandry" different from that of any other part of America.

North Carolina farmers enjoy two advantages: plenty of land, and vast herds of cattle, which run loose by day until they are summoned by horn into enclosures at night. In spite of the opportunity of "raising" manure for the indigo, the settlers rely upon moving on to fresh land when their cattle have worn out the forests. Their hogs fare well on mast (beech, oak and chestnut acorns and nuts) and fruit. The settlers export hides with barreled meat, corn, roots, pitch and tar. The writer inserts an estimate of what can be done by settling in the back of the province, exporting shingles, staves, pitch, tar, pease and pork, squared walnut and cedar and, of course, tobacco, although here tobacco represents only a quarter of the whole. Again, he recommends "easily transportable" crops like silk, indigo and cotton, "which would much advance the interests of Britain." Again, he speaks highly of fencing.

The account of South Carolina takes up more space than even Virginia and Maryland and begins with a report from Governor Glen, Royal Governor for nearly forty years.

Governor Glen admits to one of the drawbacks our writer sees — the climate of maritime South Carolina is "one of the most unhealthy climates in the world." But at eighty to a hundred miles from the seacoast, "the soil begins to rise into little hills and beautiful inequalities" and becomes healthful. The unhealthful swamps, however, are perfect for rice, and the back-country hills are "one continued forest." The trees are

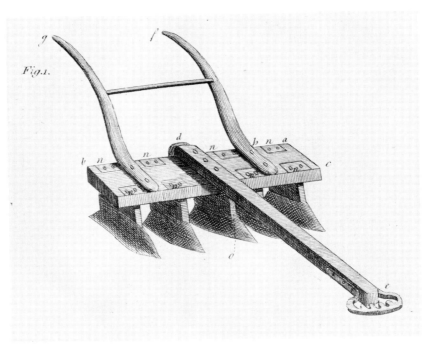

A drill plow from Arthur Young's *Letters*

enormous: chestnut oak, sixty feet to the first bough; scarlet oak, used in shipbuilding; red oak, for staves; Spanish oak, riving well into clapboards; black oak, durable under water; white iron oak, best of all for shipbuilding; live oak, most durable of all. And all affording mast for hogs. After this we have tulip trees so large a man lived for years in a hollow trunk; beech, hornbeam, sassafras, dogwood (for indoor building), red and white cedars, locust, hickories, walnut, chinquapin for building boats, birch, willows, laurel large enough for planks, sycamores, hollies, three sorts of mulberries, sumac and hazel.

As for fruit trees, they abound: the wild fig, the wild plum, currants (but not gooseberries), apples, pears, quinces, peaches, apricots, cherries, raspberries, strawberries and native vines. (European grapes ripen too early.) There are also oranges, sweet and sour, and lemons for export, limes, pomegranates, olives and all sorts of melons. Olives cannot be depended upon. All garden stuffs grow, although it is admitted that, due to the heat, those "more to the north" are preferable. Grains and pulse grow in the back-country. Pine lands occupy four fifths of the country and the only underwood in the dry white sand is the shortleberry and chinquapin, which Doctor Mitchell calls the "heath" of America. It is on these "pine barrens" that they grow indigo, in spite of that crop's needing rich, damp soil. Indigo and rice are the staple crops. He now devotes some time to describing rice culture, which is hard on the slaves, "decreasing" them considerably, although those on indigo increase in proportion. In fact, our writer is for discouraging rice culture, not for humanitarian reasons, but as hardly paying charges because the rice we sell to Spain and Portugal lessens their need for our wheat. Indigo and tobacco, he says, have all the same advantages as rice (for here rice is "all laid out in British commodities").

Doctor Mitchell considered indigo a "rank weed" like tobacco. On the other hand, Governor Glen was greatly in its favor. Again, our author advises silk, wine, oil, hemp and flax. He asserts (and proves with figures) great fortunes are to be made. With this fanfare ends Book I.

Starting Book II with Georgia, the author does not take long before he goes on to describe the lands in Florida and across the Gulf of Mexico, Louisiana and Illinois, full of current enemies and future promise. Georgia, he says, is in many respects the same country as Carolina. It was inconsiderable while settlers confined themselves to the coasts, but when, after the Proclamation of 1763, they found good land unpatented in the back-country, more settlers came in, and into the back-country of North Carolina as well. Vegetable growth and productions are the same as in South Carolina. There is a long letter from a settler who has lived there eight years and finds it intolerably hot near Augusta; impossible for him to do more than sit inside and do nothing for the greater part of the summer days, although the Negroes generally "delight in the most meridian beams." The rest of the year surpasses anything in England. He has six thousand acres. The forests have so little undergrowth one can ride, or even drive, through them. Wild mulberries support his silkworms.

Follows the usual lyrical description of the fruits, sporting (for a good man with a gun), fish, rich lands, cheap slaves and other labor. His cabbages weigh sixty pounds each; turnips twenty-five. He enumerates his slaves and their increase and goes on at great length for our editor, who wanted information before "settling a relation in Georgia" (now accomplished). Again, he knows of rich new land, purchased from the Cherokees — seven million acres, all now available, and, of course — we see it coming — desirable for indigo, hemp, flax, cotton, tobacco, vines and silk, those commodities for which Britain must now go to the Baltic, China, Holland, Spain and Turkey — all of which we "might produce generally as well in our colonies."

This sums up the conditions in the colonies on the very eve of their becoming states and explains as nothing else could the willingness of most of them to take to native manufactures, homespun robes of state and all. It also gives us a picture of the predicament of the southern states, expended beyond their natural inclinations to please the mother country and the entrepreneurs in London. We understand Washington's concern for composting, for turning away from tobacco, for escaping from indebtedness reckoned by strangers far away.

By the end of the eighteenth century, books on husbandry had proliferated at a pace. In England, even ancient writers of Roman times were reprinted, and officious farmers wrote their own books of directions. Several authors held forth at length upon matters of American husbandry, drawing upon their observations in England and Ireland. One such is Charles Varlo, who parlayed a long list of subscribers in Philadelphia, Boston and outlying rural areas to underwrite the publication of his book, *A New System of Husbandry,* which he says came "From Many Years Experience" and in which he promises to show the expense and profit of each crop on a hundred-and-fifty-acre farm, without manure and with cheap food for cattle, including a kitchen garden calendar, a newly invested thrashing floor and receipts in physic and surgery for all sorts of cattle. For good measure he throws in "a few Hints humbly offered for the perusal of the Legislators of America, shewing How to put a stop to runaway servants." "Printed for the Author in Philadelphia, 1785. Three dollars in boards, or three and a

half bound." Over five hundred of the most influential names among
"children of the mother country" subscribed and received pious wishes
of the author that "their land will flourish with milk and honey."

Mr. Varlo must have been a fast talker. His two unoriginal little
volumes are devoted to turnips, flaxseed for calves, a "pickle" for poi-
soning flies made of chamber-pot lees, the culture of madder and management in watering. His subscribers must have had to take comfort
from the impressive roster.

A livelier book of the same sort was written by Richard Parkinson,
who actually both traveled and farmed in this country in the years 1789,
1799 and 1800. His book, *A Tour in America, Exhibiting Sketches of
Society and Manners, and a Particular Account of the American System
of Agriculture,* was published in England in 1805. Mr. Parkinson had
already written one of those authoritative books on English farming,
called *Parkinson's Experienced Farmer Embracing the Whole System of
Agriculture, Breeding, etc.,* in two volumes. He hoped to negotiate the
sale of this book in America with a fine list of English gentlemen
subscribers rivaling those in Charles Varlo's *New System.* His "cause,"
however, in going to America, he explains in his preface, was to avail
himself of an introduction to George Washington from Sir John Sin-
clair, then President of the Board of Agriculture, to whom Washington
had written proposals for letting his farms to English or Scottish farmers. Parkinson had "speculated to make a rapid fortune" from Washington's farms of twelve hundred acres, to be rented at two shillings the

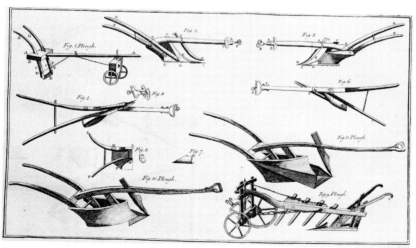

A page of ploughs from Arthur Young's *Letters*

acre or as much in produce delivered to him. Parkinson, wishing to view the farm first, hit upon a splendid scheme. He would go to America with a load of horses, cattle and hogs, chartering his own ship. This, with a view to printing his book in America, seemed "a most favorable prospect." The ship cost him eight hundred and fifty pounds and into it he put two blood stallions, Phenomenon and Cardinal Puff; ten blood mares; four lesser stallions; paired cattle of four kinds, Roolrights, North Devons, Yorkshires and Holderns; five boar and seven sows of four kinds. *And* his family, seven members in all, with two servants to care for the livestock.

Once all were on board, it was discovered ballast was wanting, and they were held up for two weeks while the livestock consumed the stores and the servants left. Rough weather, with Mr. Parkinson in sole charge of the livestock for a twelve-week voyage, lost him eleven horses, including Phenomenon. Still, he says, his speculations in both livestock and his book would have paid off, except for the shocking barrenness of the land. Had Washington, he says, offered him the twelve hundred acres as a gift, he would have refused it. He was compelled, he says, to treat the General with a great frankness, so that Washington "seemed at first to be not well pleased with my conversation." The general, says Parkinson, had been corresponding with Arthur Young and others and had been "not a little flattered" by different gentlemen from England, so Parkinson soon put him right, "giving him strong proofs" by showing him how inferior to anything in England were, one, his sheep, and two, his wheat yield. About Washington's mules Parkinson could say nothing — they were "very fine." Upon Washington's leaving the room (and no wonder), Colonel Lear said to Mr. Parkinson that indeed he had never seen any other man "so frank with the General." Parkinson felt complimented. He was also able, he thought, to chalk one up for himself against Mrs. Washington. That good lady, presumably provoked beyond manners by the conceit of her guest, who was keeping the dinner table conversation concentrated upon "the horses and cattle I have brought from England," said, "I am afraid, Mr. Parkinson, you have brought your fine horses and cattle to a bad market. I am of the opinion that our horses and cattle are good enough for our land," with which the unshakable Parkinson, "in sentiment, perfectly agreed."

Parkinson, therefore, free, as he is, "from all unfounded prejudices," takes up his pen to warn everyone *not* to go to America. He recounts his misfortunes. Parkinson had thought that, as he was in America and had got a large subscription to his intended treatise, a farm would "employ" his family and "improve" his own ideas. Washington had said Baltimore was the "risingest" town in America. However, Parkinson had to travel about a great deal first, meeting important people, among these "Mr. Bordley," who had written *Sketches on Rotation of Crops and Other Rural Matters* in 1797, some of which Parkinson handily inserted into his "present work." He "omitted waiting on Mr. Adams, the President," being told by Mr. Pickering that he never subscribed to books. He was offered four hundred acres near Baltimore, and was warned against accepting an offer of land near Pittsburgh by one who proceeded to tell him a very long tale of Indian atrocities, which he also "inserts." Finally he gets back to Orange Hill, near Baltimore, his final choice, three hundred acres for three hundred pounds a year, where he sets up a dairy. The trouble is that, with no servants, the work seems to have fallen on his wife and sons, as he is busy writing his book to tell how awful it all is. He includes many stories of the sad fates of those who lost all and were afraid to say so and go "home."

The book ends with excerpts from the innocent Mr. Bordley's *Sketches,* which Parkinson then tears to bits. Dickens and Thackeray need only to have read Mrs. Behn at the end of the seventeenth century, Byrd at the beginning and Parkinson at the end of the eighteenth century to feel confirmed in their prejudices.

To give a fair picture of American husbandry in the eighteenth century we may turn to the fairest of all observers, howbeit the most deeply concerned. George Washington had entered upon a correspondence with Arthur Young, English agriculturist and author, who asked leave to publish what Washington had written to him. Washington, obviously surprised, had replied that he cannot imagine his words will be of interest, but if they can be of help to anyone, of course, he is willing. And they are of the greatest interest, especially to us today.

Quoting a bit of animal husbandry first, to explain the background for some of Parkinson's quips at table, here is Washington on his sheep.

I would willingly have sent you a lock of the wool of my sheep, agreeably to your desire, but it is all wrought into cloth, and I must therefore defer it until after the next shearing. You may expect it by some future conveyance.

I cannot help thinking that increasing and improving our breed of Sheep would be one of the most profitable speculations we could undertake; especially in this part of the Continent, where we have so little winter that they require either no dry fodder, or next to none; and where we are sufficiently distant from the frontiers not to be troubled with Wolves or other wild vermen which prevent the Inhabitants there from keeping flocks. Though we do not feed our sheep upon leaves, as you mention they do in some parts of France; yet we cannot want for pastures enough suitable for them.

And on his mules:

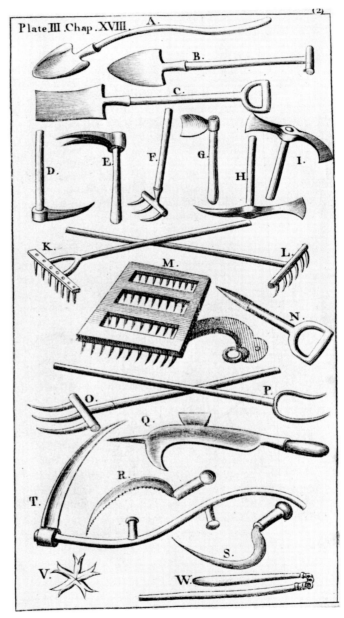

Bradley's illustration of the necessary hand tools for farming

For the multiplication of useful animals is a common blessing to mankind. I have a prospect of introducing into this Country a very excellent race of animals also, by means of the liberality of the King of Spain. One of the Jacks which he was pleased to present to me (the other perished at Sea) is about 15 hands high, his body and limbs very large in proportion to his height; and the Mules which I have had from him appear to be extremely well formed for Service. I have likewise a Jack and two Jennets from Malta, of a very good size, which the Marquis de la Fayette sent me. The Spanish Jack seems calculated to breed for heavy slow draught; and the others for the Saddle or lighter carriages. From these, altogether, I hope to secure a race of extraordinary goodness, which will stock the Country. Their longevity and cheap keep will be circumstances much in their favor. I am convinced, from the little experiments I have made with the ordinary Mules (which perform as much labour, with vastly less feeding than horses) that those of a superior quality will be the best cattle we can employ for the harness. And indeed, in a few years, I intend to drive no other in my carriage; having appropriated for the sole purpose of breeding them upwards of 20 of my best Mares.

He writes very fairly about the state of American farming:

Our farms are, in general, too large to admit of much nicety, and, I believe, it would be unhappy for us to have any great desire to be so, with our black labourers, and the more worthless wretches we employ to overlook them. The manner too, in which our attention has been engrossed by the cultivation of tobacco, and large quantities of Indian corn, has, no doubt, had some share in rendering us slovenly farmers. Having had, hitherto, plenty of fresh land for these articles, we have disregarded every means of improving our opened grounds, either by manure, or laying them down in grasses — but as we begin not to set some store by our woods, and tobacco has declined so much in value, that people are generally exchanging tobacco for wheat, I flatter myself, the face of our country will assume an appearance, that will not only do honor to our climate, but ourselves — indeed it has long been evident to me, that our sagacious northern brethren not only considered our climate as superior to their own, but our lands too as capable of being made so, from their constant annual emigrations among us. As we may be said to be entirely indebted to these for the best farms among us, it is very desirable that they should happen in a tenfold ratio.

Till very lately, the practice of fallowing grounds for wheat was seldom followed, and even now, it is by no means so general as could be wished. The usual mode of sowing it has been, and is now, too generally, in our own corn-fields, when the Indian corn is laid by, and which are cultivated every second or third year, without receiving any manure, or being laid down in clover after the crop is taken off. Those who are considered as the best farmers, and fallow most, trust entirely to their ploughing. Their fields are too extensive for the manure raised from their stock, and we have as yet no other in use. I thought it necessary to premise thus much, generally, respecting our mode of agriculture, to prevent our climate and soil being unjustly blamed for what we alone are chargeable.

A small meadow is a common object with every farmer; it is of Timothy, or natural grass; the Timothy is mowed but once a year, the natural grass twice; either, that is esteemed good, produces, in the year, from a ton and a half to two tons an acre; but many, from unfavourable situation or neglect, turn out much less. We also often have clover patches; they are commonly cut and fed green, and seldom made into hay. Some few farmers, in the spring, sprinkle clover seed on wheat, for pasturage, but it is rare, though every body approves it.

Washington's own practical experiments are recorded with care. Spanning thirty years, we quote an account of a composting experiment of April 1760.

Got several composts and laid them to dry in order to mix with earth bro't from the field below, to try their several virtues.
Mixed my composts in a box with ten apartments . . .
 1. 3 pecks of earth from below hill, no mixture
 2. 2 pecks above and 1 marle
 3. 2 pecks of above earth and 1 riversand
 4. 2 pecks of above and 1 peck horse dung
 5. 2 pecks of above and mud taken from creek
 6. has horse dung
 7. purer marle than other
  (Others inclined to sand this pure clay)
 8. sheep dung
 9. black mould
 10. clay below garden
All mixed with same quantity of same earth.
Planted each with three grains of wheat, oats and barley in rows, equal depths, done by a machine.

A letter to "John Beale Bordley of Wye, Maryland," in 1788 shows the methodical procedures Washington followed in crop rotation and land improvement. He begins by thanking Bordley for "the Wheat, Barley and Madder" and goes on to say:

Agriculture being my favourite amusement I am always pleased with communications that relate to it. To these the great improvements in Husbandry, of late years, in England, may be attributed; and to a liberal communication of experiments must this Country be indebted . . . Experiments must be made, and the practice of such of them as are useful must be introduced by Gentlemen who have leisure and abilities to devise and wherewithal to hazard something. The common farmer will not depart from the *old* road 'till the *new* one is made so plain and easy that he is sure it cannot be mistaken . . .

He seems happy to explain at some length to another farmer what his intended procedure in crop rotation and land improvement will be. He writes in 1788 and his plan carries him to 1794.

The plan he is "endeavouring" can best be explained by his example of "three fields . . . one in corn, one in wheat, and one in hay." In 1788 one is planted with corn in rows eight feet apart, the corn in "single stalks" two feet apart. Irish potatoes or carrots or both are grown in between. "Corn planted in this manner will yield as much to the acre as in any other . . . The quantity of Potatoes will at least quadruple the quantity of Corn." An added factor is that potatoes "do not exhaust the Soil." In 1789 he will sow "Buckwheat for manure," which will be ploughed in "when the seed begins to ripen and there is sufficiency of it to seed the ground a second time." In July it is ploughed again to give two dressings to the land, and in August wheat is sown to be harvested in 1790. In 1791 Indian pease are sown to be mowed when ripe, and this process may be modified to suit different areas for "preparatives." In 1792 barley and oats will be sown with red clover. In 1793 the field is in clover or hay for grazing. And in 1794 it is put into corn again. And so it goes on, one "field" after the other.

For a summary of the eighteenth-century American farmer's attitude we return to the correspondence with Arthur Young.

The more I am acquainted with agricultural affairs the better I am pleased with them. Insomuch that I can nowhere find so great satisfaction, as in those innocent and useful pursuits. In indulging these feelings, I am led to reflect how much more delightful to an undebauched mind is the task of making improvements on the earth, than all the vain glory which can be acquired from ravaging it, by the most uninterrupted career of conquests. The design of this observation is only to shew how much, as a member of human Society, I feel myself obliged by your labours to render respectable and advantageous an employment, which is more congenial to the natural dispositions of mankind than any other.

Furber's Flowers for the Month of July

1. Double Nasturtium G
2. Double white Maudlin B
3. Prince Picote July flower P
4. True Caper G
5. Virginian yellow Jasmine B T
6. Painted Lady Carnation P
7. Double blue Throatwort B
8. Scarlet Martagon B
9. White Lilly striped with purple B
10. Spanish Broom B T
11. Carolina Kidney Bean Tree C T
12. Double striped female Balsom P
13. True Olive Tree G
14. Red Oleander G
15. Painted Lady Pink B
16. White Lupin B
17. Princess Picote July flower P
18. Geranium noctu olens G
19. White Valerian B
20. Hop Hornbeam L T
21. Indian or China Pink F E
22. Double Pomegranate G
23. Double Mouse Ear B
24. Virginian Scarlet Honeysuckle G
25. Double blue Throatwort
26. French Marigold B
27. Double Scarlet Lychnis B
28. Double blue Larkspur B
29. Hungarian Climber G
30. Double Stock P
31. Bean Caper G
32. White Oleander G

7 *"Every Man His Own Doctor"*

THE BASIC DIFFERENCES between American medical practice in New England in the seventeenth century and that farther south in the eighteenth lay in the shift of responsibility for cures from the shoulders of the average housewife, minister or governor to those of large landowners and farmers, whose word was law in all matters, including medicine. Landholdings were bigger than in early New England; workers, slave or free, more numerous. There were larger groups of semi-ignorant people in charge of others. There was also, apparently, greater willingness to learn from the Indians. And books on home medicine abounded.

Where the seventeenth century had depended upon the herbals of Gerard, Parkinson and Culpeper, all reverently convinced that the world had been ordered by God for man's convenience, would man but discover the clues, the eighteenth century was full of authors quite willing to take the place of the Almighty. Or, at least, to aggrandize themselves and put each householder in an authoritative position, their books upon his shelves.

Another difference — the world had expanded and so had the attitudes of the healers. Realizing their importance, they ceased to be the modest ever-grateful seventeenth-century compilers of God-given simples and became arrogant individuals elbowing their way into homes with volumes attesting to their own vainglorious accomplishments.

All this is literally a world apart from John Parkinson's earnest effort to benefit mankind by handing on the known blessings of an ever-attentive Creator. And yet, some of the more primitive beliefs were still valid. For instance, even the great Sir Hans Sloane, buyer-up of the collections of other "curious" gentlemen to make, eventually, the basis of the British Museum, remained convinced that God invariably placed nearby the remedy for every type of disease prevalent in out-of-the-way places. "Cupping," the gentler method of bloodletting, as well as the more drastic method with lancets, was still universally practiced. When Washington ordered eight lancets from his London agents, they were undoubtedly for him to use in treating his slaves and perhaps even his family if a doctor was hard to come by. As doctors were. When Martha had the measles and the doctor was awaited for hours, Washington could not forbear, after noting in his diary the doctor's arrival at ten at night, to append, "I may add, drunk." Let us remember also that when Washington lay dying, his end was hastened by his being bled, at his own request, a remedy in which he had probably placed faith through his own practice.

There was another great difference between the centuries. Where the seventeenth century had approved of "portmanteau" concoctions, full of so many different ingredients that at least some of them must prove successful, the eighteenth century was bemused by the idea of one over-all remedy. Whether this was partly derived from the old alchemists' search for the Philosopher's Stone, or a universal panacea, it would be hard to say. Perhaps it was due to the sensational discovery by Jesuits of a Peruvian tree, named by Linnaeus for the Countess of Cinchon, who introduced the remedy to Spain in mid-seventeenth century. This was the source of quinine and must stand as the greatest single medical prize from the vegetable world.

After the cinchona bark had surpassed all human hopes in its efficacy in "intermittent" fevers — or those that, once incurred, seemed never to leave the victim — there was constant expectation of yet more vegetable miracles, could man but find the clues. Besides the wasting fevers, which carried off so many young men in the tropics and filled West Indian graveyards with tombstones to those in their late teens and early twenties, there were the other great scourges not confined to tropical swamps, chief among them venereal disease. While it is popular to accept the early writers' theory that Columbus brought infected crews back from the West Indies and inflicted the "pox" upon, first, southern Europeans and then the world, there are those who dare say it was a worldwide curse before this. Like "Baghdad boils" in Aleppo and "Aleppo boils" in Baghdad, any affliction is the more bearable if one blames it on someone else.

Early on in the seventeenth century, two American plants of great prevalence were seized upon hopefully as remedies for this curse: sarsaparilla and sassafras.

American sarsaparilla was first sent from Quebec to Tournefort as "Aralie" by a French physician, Sarrasin. The name of *Aralia* was given by Linnaeus to the genus, which is North American, and its familiar names show the reverence in which it was held: angelica tree, spikenard, life-of-man. The name sarsaparilla is derived from two Spanish words, *zarza parilla,* meaning "thorny vine." Used by Spaniards in the West Indies in the sixteenth century, it fell into disrepute — or at least into no repute — until it was resurrected as of possible benefit when used with mercury in syphiloid diseases as an alterative, and for the treatment of chronic rheumatism and "scrofulous affections." It can be made into a beer with molasses, can be smoked for asthma and has finally descended to the company of soft drinks. Perhaps it has not yet come into its own. Humanity seems reluctant to give up all hope for it.

Sassafras had an even greater vogue. Here was a handsome tree with easily recognizable mittenlike leaves, growing all over the coastal regions from New England through Virginia. Two shiploads of it went back with Martin Pring. The Indians had used it as a tonic and, like our native hickory nuts crushed, for thickening broths. When John Winthrop's ship was leaving England, a ship loaded with sassafras from the New World was coming into the harbor. Again, expectations had been raised too high, but loads were still being shipped abroad in the eighteenth century.

And we have evidence that for specific ills its reputation was still good. Dr. John Fothergill, for whom Linnaeus names a North American shrub belonging to the witch hazel family, *Fothergilla,* wrote in 1767 to Humphry Marshall:

If thou knows of any plant possessed of particular virtues and that is known by experience to be useful in the cure of diseases this I should be glad to have in particular, both the parts and the seeds of the same.

Humphry Marshall was engaged in sending seeds and plants abroad, in common with his cousin John Bartram, and was assisted by his son Moses Marshall, then studying medicine. He had sent some medicinal plants to Dr. Fothergill when he received a letter in 1771 referring to the benefits of "Sassafras Bark," which was agreed by Fothergill to be "a good medicine in various complaints; and especially in all such as seem to arise from a thin, sharp, scorbutic humour, especially in cold constitutions or aged people. From its sensible qualities it seems likely to expel wind, correct sharpness of the blood, and, if given properly, to increase urine and sweat. Attend to its effects and give a strong infusion

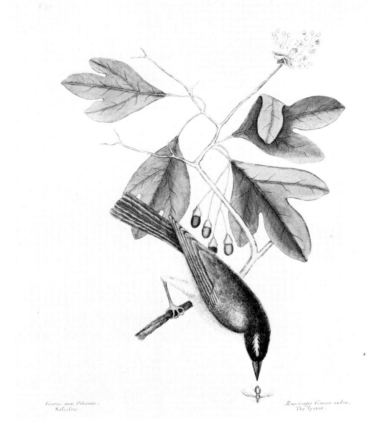

Catesby's Sassafras, Plate 55, Vol I

of it, in such of the complaints as may seem to proceed from these causes."

Another plant good for wholesale exporting was the American ginseng, William Byrd II's standby. (He always kept a bit in his mouth when exploring.) It resembled the Chinese ginseng, ancient promoter of virility in the aging or aged, especially when combined with powdered rhinoceros horn. Our ginseng looks rather like the Chinese, in that each has a very tortuous root that, like the mandrake root, when a little doctored, can remind one graphically of parts of the human body — its surest recommendation to the ignorant. The ginseng does

Catesby's Ginseng, Plate A-16

not seem to possess any particular medicinal properties, if, indeed, does its Chinese counterpart, but this was no deterrent to its sale. Vast areas of the New World were denuded of this vegetable gold. Today, so enduring is world opinion, it is being cultivated for the still-ready market. Catesby made much of finding American ginseng flourishing in the Carolinas.

An American plant with a good Indian reputation was the beautiful bright orange "butterfly weed," or *Asclepia tuberosa* L., called "pleurisy root" by the Indians' friends, who seem to have taken to it very early on. In Virginia, the dose was given to follow a strong emetic by one day, and the root pounded fine was given in warm water every two hours, for days if necessary, until the patient recovered. Rated at the beginning of this century, depending upon the quantity used, as diuretic, carminative, emetic, cathartic and expectorant, its diaphoretic properties also made it useful in the preliminary stages of pneumonia. It has even been considered for flatulence. Obviously, the Indians had something *there.*

To give each cure-all herb its day throughout the eighteenth century in America would be to plant ourselves an apothecary's garden to rival the Jardin des Plantes in Paris and the Physic Gardens in Chelsea and Oxford, the only difference being that, with the American plants, their reputations preceded and out-trumpeted their careful study. And, during the century, there was a subtle change in the public attitude toward the discovery of American medicinal plants. Where, at the beginning of the century, much was demanded of us from abroad — instant remedies for all the world's ills — toward the end of the century, as we grew toward independence, there was a great questioning among ourselves as to whether or not we might become truly free of Old World domination, even in the matter of "drugs and simples."

There are two more American plants to be considered individually before we try to survey the overall picture of eighteenth-century American medicine relating to horticulture. Both of these century-shaking remedies were of Indian origin and stemmed from the acceptance of the theory that where there was the greatest need would be found the sovereign cure.

The first of these plants is the Seneca snakeroot, now *Polygala senega* L. The need for a remedy for snakebite was apparent enough all up and down the coast, in the swampy morasses of the Great Dismal and on the rocky wastes of the Allegheny uplands. Indians of various tribes made much of their own remedies and, for a drink or a more substantial reward, would smear themselves with a juicy root or chew upon some leafy plant and allow themselves to be bitten. Names of "snakeroot" and "rattlesnake root" were applied to quite different plants, but the one that led all the rest was the one that bore the name of its first promoters, the Seneca Indians, and that owed its early prominence upon the printed page to no less a good American and astute publisher than Benjamin Franklin. As did the second sensational eighteenth-century remedy, *Lobelia syphilitica.* Marshall considered both of these plants individually later.

Franklin, personally, placed his faith medically in water, fresh air and electricity. His membership in the Royal Society hinged upon his experiments with all three, in relation to health. A strong swimmer himself, Franklin advocated a good, long swim as a prime antidote for many ills. For those without access to water, or what there was being too cold, Franklin advised what he also practiced — sitting naked for an hour or two in the early morning. For those with troubles with limbs and joints, "obstructions," epilepsy and even madness, he favored treatment by electric shock. He claimed success for many of his electrical treatments and harm from none, even when, seeking to treat a "Paralytic Patient" in Passy, Franklin made the patient and his friends join hands to receive the shock and "charged two jars to give it." Franklin "inadvertently" placed himself under an iron hook in the ceiling, connected by wire with the jars, and the charge went through him. "I neither saw the Flash, heard the Report, nor felt the Stroke. When my Senses returned I found myself on the Floor. I got up, not knowing how that happened. I then again attempted to discharge the jars, but . . . they were already discharged . . . On recollecting myself and examining my Situation, I found the Case clear . . ."

His general opinion of home medicine may be surmised from his comments on mesmerism, the latest craze in French medical circles in the 1780's.

Benefit from mesmerism, Franklin feared, in Passy in 1784, might prove, "like so many other cry'd-up cures, a Delusion. That Delusion may however in some cases be of use while it lasts. There are in every City a Number of Persons who are never in health because they are fond of medicines and always taking them, whereby they derange the natural functions and hurt their Constitutions. If these people can be persuaded to forbear their drugs in Expectation of being cured by only the Physician's Finger or an Iron Rod pointing at them, they may possibly find good Effects tho' they mistake the Cause."

In spite of his views, even upon those who overdose themselves and "derange the natural functions," Franklin as a young publisher had recognized the need for medically instructive books and had published at least three of fairly diverse interests and merits. He printed an American edition of the English *Quincy's Medical Lexicon,* without, I think, changing or adding to it in any way to adapt it for American use. He published two books for American home medicine, however, that are so extraordinary as to warrant individual consideration.

The first of these, published in 1734, the third edition of which I have seen, is a famous publication attributed to an eccentric character, a "Dr." John Tennent, self-appointed champion of "Senega Snake Root." His first book is entitled *Every Man His Own Doctor, or The Poor Planters Physician.*

Prescribing Plain and Easy Means for Persons to cure themselves of all or

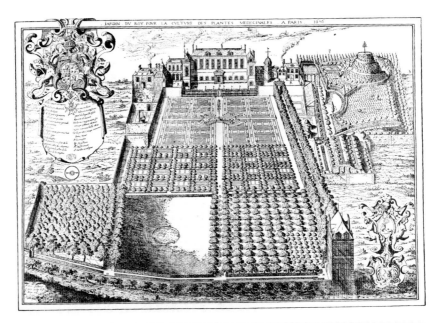

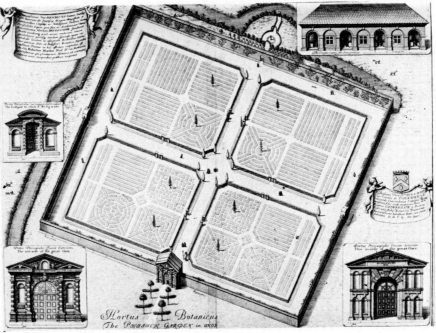

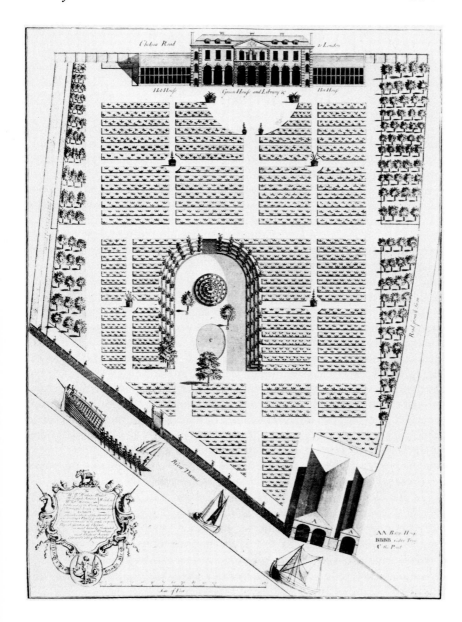

Three great "physic gardens" to which American plants were sent to be tried.
Paris. Oxford. Chelsea

most of the Distempers incident to this Climate and with very little Charge, the medicines being chiefly of the Growth and Production of this Country.

This is followed on the title page by a grim quotation on the "many shapes of death" from Milton's *Paradise Lost.* A note tells us it is a third edition, and then "Philadelphia. Re-printed and sold by B. Franklin, near the Market." And the year, 1734.

John Tennent settled in Spotsylvania County, Virginia, in 1725, married, bought land and interested himself in medicine. He left for England in 1739 for good, "not enjoying Health in America, and meeting with Ingratitude in the Colony . . ." In these fourteen years he had published, as well as many editions of *Every Man His Own Doctor,* a signed *Essay on Pleurisy* in 1736, crying up the value of his Senega, Snakeroot, and had gone to England in 1737 — we might think a little belatedly — to acquire a medical degree in Edinburgh. With letters of recommendation for his degree from several worthy doctors in London (he already had the recommendations of Governor Gooch of Virginia and William Byrd II), he failed to receive the degree and came, disgruntled, back to Virginia.

He felt he had caused enough of a sensation with his one-plant remedy to appear before the House of Burgesses and demand one thousand pounds. He received one hundred for his magnanimity in making public the efficacy of this plant. He returned to England and tried to get an award from Parliament for his services in treating the colonies, but Parliament was not impressed. He even tried bigamy to get himself out of debt, but failed there too, and was sued. Having quarreled with everyone, he took to the West Indies, where he published a treatise in 1742 decrying the use of vinegar in the epidemic fevers there so frequently fatal to Britons, and advocated his own three-step cure: copious bleeding; forty grains of Senega Snakeroot the next night; and a vomit to every person after the seventh dose of the powder.

In *An Epistle to Dr. Richard Mead, Concerning the Epidemical Diseases of Virginia, Particularly a Pleurisy and Peripneumony,* published in Edinburgh in 1738, Tennent had described "the surprising efficacy of the Senega Rattle-Snake Root" in the diseases "epidemic and very mortal in Virginia." Tennent feels sure that since this root will cure "Gout, Rheumatism, Dropsy, and many nervous Disorders" he can foresee "the highest probability that this root will be of more extensive use than any medicine in the whole Materia Medica."

Tennent's expectations would appear to have been well founded, based upon human requirements rather than medical fulfillments, as witness a note to Jefferson when he was President, in 1801. An impassioned request came to him from Elizabeth Town, New Jersey, asking for the seeds of Seneca root, from one who claimed himself as "being witness to its Efficacy in various deseases." Jefferson responded that he would endeavor to collect seed at Monticello, although the plant was becoming "extremely rare" and he suggested that, if his efforts should fail, both plants and seeds could be obtained from Bartram.

For the second great American remedy of the eighteenth century, after Seneca snakeroot, we go again to Benjamin Franklin, as Philadelphia publisher extraordinary.

Franklin's third medical publication (there may have been others but these three give us the scope of eighteenth-century medical practice by both doctors and laymen) was an American edition of the English Dr. Short's *Medicina Britannica or a Treatise on such physical Plants as are generally to be found in the Fields or Gardens in Great Britain, containing a particular account of their nature, virtues and uses*. Dr. Short feels this book is "adapted more especially to the occasions of those whose condition or situation in life deprives them in great measure of the help of the learned." He gives an appendix containing "the true Preparation, Preservation, Uses and Doses of most Forms of Remedies necessary for Private Families."

Franklin's "re-printing" is dated 1751 — the date of the only copy I can find. He, in his turn to reprint, provides also another preface and another appendix, both by his friend John Bartram. For good measure Franklin has requested Bartram to go through the plants mentioned by Dr. Short and to indicate which ones are to be found in our own fields and gardens.

We know from William Bartram's sketch of his father that "he had a very early inclination to the study of physic and surgery . . . In many instances he gave great relief to his poor neighbors . . ." William felt that "as most of his medicines were derived from the vegetable kingdom" this alone "might point out to him the necessity of, and excite a desire for, the study of Botany."

Since this little book is very hard to come by, I am including in full both Bartram's preface and his appendix. As for his notes throughout the book, they are so scanty as to serve no useful purpose for us, and must have been something of a disappointment to Franklin. Bartram has frequent negative comments: "I have not observed it grow in Pennsylvania or the adjacent colonies," "Not observed to grow with us" and "Never could find in any of our colonies." His positive comments will appear where the plants are mentioned in the Appendix to this book, as see this one on the foxglove: "grows only in curious gardens with us in America."

Medicina Britannica:

OR A

TREATISE

ON SUCH

PHYSICAL PLANTS,

AS ARE

Generally to be found in the *Fields* or *Gardens*
in *GREAT-BRITAIN:*

CONTAINING

A particular Account of their NATURE, VIR-
TUES, and USES.

Together with the Observations of the most learned Physicians,
as well ancient as modern, communicated to the late ingenious Mr. *RAY*, and the learned Dr. *SIM. PAULI.*

Adapted more especially to the Occasions of those, whose Condition or Situation
of Life deprives them, in a great Measure, of the Helps of the Learned.

By THO. SHORT, of *Sheffield*, M. D.

To which is added,

An APPENDIX:

CONTAINING

The true *Preparation*, *Preservation*, *Uses* and *Doses* of most
Forms of *Remedies* necessary for *private Families*.

The THIRD EDITION.

With a PREFACE by Mr. *JOHN BARTRAM*, Botanist of
Pennsylvania, and his Notes throughout the Work, shewing the Places
where many of the described Plants are to be found in these Parts of
America, their Differences in Name, Appearance and Virtue, from those
of the same Kind in *Europe*; and an Appendix, containing a Description
of a Number of Plants peculiar to *America*, their Uses, Virtues, &c.

LONDON Printed:

Philadelphia Re-printed, and Sold by B FRANKLIN, and
D. HALL, at the *Post-Office*, in *Market-street*. MDCCLI.

Title page from *Medicina Britannica* by Thomas Short, which was edited by John
Bartram for Benjamin Franklin

Here is Bartram's preface:

THE first Man that was famous for the Practice of Physick in the *Grecian* History was *Aesculapius,* the son of Apollo, who practiced an Age before the *Trojan* War, and, as they say, was so skilful in his Applications, as to cure Diseases, and raise the Dead; whereby he gained so great a Fame, as to have a Temple built to him, where those People that were ever afterwards cured of their Infirmities, either by his former Directions, or their own Discoveries, Wrote their Method of Cure, particularly, and reposed it in that Temple; from when, after Six Hundred Years, and about the Time of the Captivity of Jews, the famous *Hippocrates,* who was born and lived near the Temple, in the Island of *Coos,* searched the medicinal Receipts, and by those Informations, and his own Ingenuity, so enlarged his Knowledge in Practice of Physick, as to be to this Day called, *The Divine* HIPPOCRATES; but the Christians say, that he learned his wonderful Knowledge from the Writings of *Solomon,* and his Treatise of Plants, which was procured from the captive *Jews,* or the *Chaldeans,* after they had burnt the Temples: However, it is certain that most Nations, tho' never so barbarous, have made use chiefly of Vegetables for the cure of their Diseases, and doubtless with good Success; and certainly we have in our Country a great variety of good medicinal Plants, which may be administered to the People with great Advantage, if properly adapted to the Season, Age and Constitution of the Patient; the nature, Time and Progress of the Disease: Without which Caution it is not likely that the Practice should succeed generally. But it is very common with our People, when a Root or Herb has been given with good Success several Times in a particular Disease, and the Patient recovered soon after the taking of the Medicine, to applaud that Medicine exceedingly; then many that are sick of the same disease, or any other, that hath near the like Symptoms, apply directly to this famed Specifick, expecting immediate Relief; which often failing, by reason of its improper Application, as to Time, Constitution, or nature of the Disease, many choice Medicines grow out of Repute again, are disregarded, and little Use made of them, especially if they are common and easy to come at; whereas if their Virtues were well known, and a skilful person had the Administering of them, who knew how to properly correct and fit them to the Constitution of the Patients, and join suitable Vehicles or Companions with them, to lead them to the parts of the Body, where the Distemper lies, then those very Herbs or Roots, I suppose, might continue to increase in their Reputation.

So much for ancient history anent present custom.

John Bartram's appendix to Dr. Short's *Medicina* was the source for so many requests made subsequently upon him by and for English physicians and "curious" gardeners, we give it in full. I am sorry not to know the exact date of its first writing. This is the "third edition," 1751, though a tentative date of "1746 or earlier" was mentioned in the medical library where I found it. *Collinsonia* is named for Bartram's

Quaker patron in England; Dr. Colden is quoted as one living; and Kalm had just extracted the secret of "Colonel Johnson's" remedy in his visits of 1749 and 1750. Evidence to date Bartram's listing of his own remedies seems to make the 1740's a good blanket date. It is enough for us now to read his thorough, honest account of American medicinal plants in the first half of the eighteenth century.

MR. BARTRAM'S

APPENDIX:

CONTAINING

Descriptions, Virtues and *Uses* of sundry PLANTS of these Northern Parts of *America;* and particularly of the newly discovered *Indian* Cure for the *Venereal Disease.*

Aralia, called by some *Spikenard,* by others *Wild Licorice;* this bears large Clusters of Berries, ripe in *September,* which are pleasant and wholesome to eat: The Roots are of Balsamick Nature; the back Inhabitants use them to cure fresh Wounds; they bruise the Roots, then pour a little Spring Water to them, mixing them together, which brings the Mass to a mucilaginous Balsam, which they apply with good Success; the Roots chewed, and the Juice swallowed, help the Pains of the Loins.

Aralia Caule Nudo, commonly called *Sarsaparilla,* hath a long creeping Root, something like the *Spanish,* but is really a very different Plant, yet of great Virtue. The decoction daily drunk as Diet-drink, is much commended for cleansing the Blood, and curing a Dropsy; and outwardly applied is extoll'd for curing of the Shingles and cleaning and healing of Ulcers.

Erigeron, used by some for the Bite of Snake: it bears a white Flower in the Spring, something like a large Daisy, about a Foot high, the Roots run under the Surface of the Ground in small Fibres or Threads, of a hot Taste: The *Indians* pound this Root, and apply it to cold hard Tumours to dissolve them.

Saururus. Some of the Dutch call it *Aristolochia,* I suppose, because the Shape of Leaf hath some Resemblance to that Plant. It grows in wet Places and produceth a long Spike of white flowers; the Root is spongy like a Rush, and runs near the Surface of the Mud.

It is of excellent Virtue; being made into a Poultice, and applied to sore and impostumated Breasts, it ripens and heals them. The dried Leaves made into a Tea and drank, is commended for the pains of the Breast and Back.

Collinsonia. This Plant grows five Feet high; hath, in the Fall, after Harvest, a Smell, something like Hops, the Seed is much like Sage Seed. This, in some parts of the Country, is called *Horse Weed,* not only because Horses are very greedy of it, but it also is good for sore gall'd Backs. The Root is hard and knobby, and is much commended for Womens After-pains, being pounded, boiled and the Decoction drank.

Chelidonium, or *Sanguinaria,* called by the Country People, *Red Root,* or *Tumerick.* The Leaves broken yield a yellow Juice like the Garden Celandine; the Flower is white, and opens early in the Spring, the root dried and powdered is commended by *Dr. Colden,* as a Cure for the Jaundice, the Powder being given to the Weight of a Drachm in Small Beer; and by others, for the Bite of Rattle-Snake.

Virga-aurea, or that Species of *Golden Rod,* that is so famous for the Bite of a Rattle-Snake. This elegant Species hath slender purple Stalks, rising a Foot high, with a Spike of fine yellow Flowers for near one third Part of the Length of the Plant; the flowers grow out of the Bosom of the Leaves, three or four in little Tufts. This is extolled as a very effectual Cure for the Bite of a Rattle-Snake; the Herb boiled, and the Decoction drank, and the warm Herb applied to the Wound. It is used with good Success to cure the Swelling of the Throat and Neck, and the Pains of the Breast, it being a powerful Dissolver of viscid Humours.

Jacea, called by some *Throat-Wort,* because of its Virtue for the Cure of Sore-Throats. The Roots are as big as a Hiccory Nut, with some small Fibres; the Stalk is about four or five Feet high, without any Branches, with long narrow Leaves growing alternately thereon; the Flowers put forth toward the Top, surrounding the Stalk in a long Spike of purple Flowers.

The Root is bruised and boiled in Water, and the Decoction drank and gargled in the Mouth, and the Root applied, with warm Cloths dipped in the hot Decoction, to the Throat, gives Relief, it being of a warm discussing Nature.

Uvulary. It was formerly taken for a Species of *Solomon's Seal,* having smooth Leaves like it; but the Stalk grows through the Leaf and the little yellow Flowers something resemble a Lilly; it grows like a Crow's Foot; some People call it by that Name for that Reason; it is a good Root for gathering and breaking a Boil, and makes a fine Salve for Healing Wounds and Ulcers; it makes a fine maturating Poultice.

Triosteospermum, called in our Northern Colonies Dr. Tinker's Weed; in *Pennsylvania, Gentian;* and to the Southward *Fever Root,* where it is used for the Fever Ague; With us it was used with good Success for the Pleurisy, and in *New England* for a Vomit. It is a powerful Worker, a little churlish, yet may be a noble Medicine in skilful Hands.

Blazing-Star, as it is called by the back Inhabitants, by others, *Devil's-bit,* both fanciful Names; the Leaves spread on the Ground, four or five from one Root, and are three or four Inches long; with a fine Spike of white Flowers six inches long; it grows plentifully in the back Parts of the Country, on dry rich Soil; the Root is white, and about as thick as a Pipe-shank, and extremely bitter.

This precious Root is a great Resister of fermenting Poisons, and the previous Pains of Bowels, taken in Powder, or the Root bruised and steeped in Rum, of which take a spoonful at once, and as often as Need requires until the Pains remit.

Star-Grass. This hath some Resemblance to the Last, but the Leaves are narrower, and more pointed, and in Winter more yellow, and this grows in moist Places, amongst Hurtle-berries very plentiful in *Jersey,* and some low grounds in *Pennsylvania* and *Maryland.*

The Decoction of this Root drank, easeth the Pains of the Stomach and Bowels.

Liriodendrum, commonly called Poplar. The bark of the Root steeped in Rum, and the Rum drank, is much commended for the Cure of the Fever and Ague; and to the *Northward,* for Gout and Rheumatism.

Apocinum. From the Roots that run deep in the Ground, arise several hairy Stalks about two feet high, with narrow long Leaves set alternately round thereon; at the Top grow large tufts of orange-coloured Flowers, which are succeeded by long Pods, containing the Seeds, joined to white Down, which is by the Wind carried away when the Seed is ripe and bursts open; the Root must be powdered and given in a Spoonful of Rum, or rather as the *Indians* give it, bruise the Root and boil it in Water and drink the Decoction: Peter Kalm saith it is excellent for the hysteric Passion.

Orchis. It hath a Root as big as an Onion, it hath one or two leaves green all Winter, which are six or seven Inches long, and two broad, striped with white Lines from one End to the other. This Root is bruised and applied to the Ears, easeth the Pains thereof, and helps to break boils.

Centuarium Luteum, commonly called *Ground Pine.* It grows about a Span high, its slender Branches spread all round from one small fibrous Root, like our Penny-Royal, but as small as Wire, or the Leaves of Pine, from which it had its Name; the little Flowers are yellow, succeeded by little red Pods on the Tops of the Branches; it smells as strong as the Leaves of *Pine;* it commonly grows on old poor Clay Ground; it is of excellent Virtue, being made into an Ointment with Penny-Royal, Hemlock and Henbane (or it may do alone made into an Ointment) for Bruises and Strains, if it be green, for it loses much of its Virtue when dry, it being of an active penetrating Nature.

Elichrysum, called also *Cotton-weed,* or *Life-everlasting,* is very good for Baths or Fomentations for cold Tumors, Bruises or Strains; it may be mixed with Ground Pine.

Lobelia. This curious Plant rises from a fibrous Root to three or four Feet high, with a Spike of blue Flowers surrounding the Stalk for near a Foot in Length: It grows in rich shady Ground, it is a fearce Plant in many Parts of the Country.

The learned *Peter Kalm* (who gained the Knowledge of it from Colonel *Johnson,* who learned it of the *Indians,* who, after great Rewards bestowed on several of them, revealed the Secret to him) saith That the Roots of the Plant cureth the *Pox* much more perfectly and easily than any mercurial Preparations, and is generally used by the *Canada Indians,* for the Cure of themselves, and the *French* that trade amongst them, tho' deeply infected with it. They take a Handful of the Roots, and boil them in a Quart of

Water, and drink the Decoction beginning with a Half a Pint at first, if the Patient be weak, then increase the Dose every Day as he can bear its purging; but if he can't bear it every day let him omit it a day or Two, then take to it again, as he find Occasion, until he is cured: They wash with the Decoction; but if it be deep and rotton, they put some Powder of the inner bark of the Spruce-tree into it, which helps to dry it up; but if the Disease is inveterate, they drink the Decoction of *Ranunculus Folio Renisormus.* An old *Sachem* told Colonel *Johnson* of another Shrub, with a red Root, from which proceeds several slender Branches, eighteen Inches or two Feet long, on which grow Spikes of white Flowers which produce three-square black Seed-Pods; the Leaves some of our people drink as Tea, and some smoke it with Tobacco; the Roots of this, bruised and boiled and the Decoction drank, the *Sachem* said, he rather preferred to the *Lobelia;* but the *Lobelia* seems to be of the most general Use, and with extraordinary Success.

More particular Directions how to use the Lobelia-Root for the Venereal Disorder, obtained from the Indians by Col. J.

"AFTER making a Decoction of it, the Patient is
"to drink about two Gills of it very early in
"the Morning, fasting, the same before Dinner,
"and Bed-time, Add or diminish as you find it
"agree with the Patient's Constitution: The
"third Day begin Bathing, and continue it twice
"a Day until the Sores are well cleansed, and
"partly healed, then use the Lotion but once
"a Day till quite well; observing all the time
"to use a slender Diet (vegetable Food, and
"small Drink) as in other courses of Physick,
"Salivation excepted. These are the Direc-
"tions I have had from the Person who gave me
"the Secret."

Veronica Spicata. This Plant, from a fibrous Root, raiseth two or three Stalks from three to five Feet high, with three or four Leaves set at one joint (if they are set across) with a long Spike of white Flowers on the Top of each Stalk.

One Handful of the Roots of this Plant, boiled in a Pint of Milk, and drank, is used by the back Inhabitants for a powerful Vomit.

Eupatorium Folium Perfoliatum. This Plant grows in moist Places; the Stalks grow (through the Leaves, which are rough and pointed) two or three Feet high, branching out towards the Top, producing a large bunch of white Flowers, which are succeeded by fine Down, which bloweth away with the Seed.

This Herb boiled in Water, and the Decoction drank, is commended for a Vomit in intermitting Fevers, and used as a Fomentation for Pains in the Limbs.

FINIS

Here, then, we have the second most touted American cure for the world's ills. A floral tribute in reverse, as may be, to our greatest Indian negotiator.

Colonel William Johnson was one of the great pre–Revolutionary War characters in American history, considered the most powerful American of his day in England next to Benjamin Franklin. He had arrived from Ireland in 1738 to join his uncle in Boston and to set up a trading business with the Indians in the back-country on the Mohawk above Albany. From his commercial beginnings and friendly relations with Indian tribes, whose languages he learned, Johnson rose to a very respectable eminence as a soldier, statesman and commissioner. He built himself a baronial estate called Fort Johnson or Johnson Hall, having failed in his ambition to be granted a "manor" like the older New York Dutch land-holding families. (He was refused by Cadwallader Colden on the grounds that feudal tenures were abrogated.) Johnson, however, achieving distinction in many ways and quarters, bought up vast territories from the Indians, sent to his brother Warren for a coat of arms and was created a baronet for his victory at Lake George, which Horace Walpole referred to as "the only circumstance in our favour that has happened yet . . ." Johnson referred to Washington's misfortune at Fort Necessity as an "unlucky defeat," but there is no doubt that Braddock's failure made Johnson's success shine the brighter. A letter to this point is in Peter Collinson's letter book in the Linnaean Society in London where Breintnall in Philadelphia describes the Braddock defeat as due to overconfidence, contributing, by contrast, to Johnson's victory.

It is curious how stock characters run through our early history — the dishonest overseer, the well-connected governor sent to recoup his fortunes, the scientifically inclined near-genius stranded in the wilderness and lacking everything needed to bring his ideas to useful fruition . . . New York had its full complement.

Governor Clinton was one of those well-connected young men, younger son of the Earl of Lincoln, who was headed for debtors' prison when he was given the governorship of New York to restore his fortunes. Cadwallader Colden was one of the brilliant dabblers in the various infant sciences of electricity, botany, medicine . . . regretting, when in correspondence with his peers abroad, to have lost fluency in Latin for want of practice, rejoicing that in his daughter, Jane, he had bred a power in the wilderness to unravel some of the mysteries of the vegetable world within the framework of the Linnaean system. William Johnson is one of the powers of this wilderness, asserting himself against worthies like Governor Shirley of Massachusetts, who had sacrificed two sons in the wars but refused to recognize Washington's pleas for equal status for himself and his men with British regulars. In the end even Shirley fell victim to the relentless enmity of Johnson.

The one thing all these ambitious men have in common is their persistence in seeing themselves and each other in an English context, assessing their failures and successes in this wild land among wild people, by rules of a provincial motherland. Except for buying up vast tracts to the west, not one of them sees himself as part of the American fabric, in the way that Franklin and, later, Washington, saw themselves. Washington had made one last try to be a Britisher when he asked for equal standing and pay for himself and his soldiers. Refused, he became part and parcel of the American scene, buying up his men's shares in western lands, prospecting those lands for his own developments and dreams.

William Johnson had no doubts as to which world he wished to succeed in. Clever as he had proved himself in getting on well with the savages, the acclaims of London were sweetest in his ears even if he had to receive them theatrically dressed as a savage. Johnson had written, "There are many simples in this country which are, I believe, unknown to the learned, notwithstanding the surprising success with which they are administered by the Indians." As one who was always among the Indians, Johnson accepted their hospitality, which, as with many primitive peoples, included their wives. Johnson, who lived for years with his favorite Indian maiden, Molly, never married to legitimize any of his innumerable offspring, even his first two gently reared white daughters. Having begun rather early to suffer the results of his promiscuity, he was an obvious recipient of the Indian cure for his complaint. Toward the end of his life he settled down to retire in magnificent self-indulgence in yet another great manorial holding named Castle Cumberland. He boasted an English gardener, "a garden of two acres and a half without root or stump," a summerhouse (he was a great fancier of summerhouses to catch the breezes and the views) and guards of wild geese to hiss at intruders. He was still able, even carried about in a litter, to maintain his reputation for political power upon the frontier. One of the triumphs of his career was the assembling of the various Indian nations to a congress in Albany in 1754 to work out a policy to maintain peace and loyalty. This was the occasion that led Franklin to remark that if such a plan for strength in union could be worked out among simple savages, why should not all the British North American colonies be able to manage something of the same. A pity the memorial to the "Mohawk baronet" should lie with *Lobelia syphilitica* L.

A postscript to the episode of the blue lobelia lies in a pathetic letter written by Benjamin Gale of Killingworth in October, 1767, to the

Reverend Samuel Johnson of King's College in New York. Gale was still another of the natural geniuses surviving in the wilderness with few books and a vast longing for information. He had been reading Dr. Haller's *Medical Cases and Experiments* as communicated to the Royal Academy of Sciences at Stockholm and had come upon a cure for the venereal disease discovered by Peter Kalm from Sir William Johnson. Gale is inspired by the thought that this remedy is said by Dr. Haller to be better than mercury. If this be true, Dr. Gale is inclined to think it may also be of great service in the curing of "leprosy . . . Elephantiasis, the Canker . . . and old obstinate Scorbutic Cases . . ." He asks for seeds and instructions. Samuel Johnson forwards the letter to Sir William, saying Gale is "the most considerable physician in these parts." The world was wide and so was the wilderness.

A splendid illustration of the rapidly expanding world of the eighteenth century is the engraved title frontispiece to John Hill's *British Herbal,* published in 1756, purportedly of "Plants and Trees, Natives of Britain, Cultivated for Use or Raised for Beauty." The first illustration is of classically dressed figures representing "Aesculapius and Flora gathering, from the Lap of Nature, Health and Pleasure," an encouraging introduction to the delights awaiting the reader. The second large illustration is even more reassuring: "The Genius of Health receiving the tributes of Europe, Asia, Africa and America and delivering them to the British Reader." Here we can see one of the engaging inclinations of eighteenth-century illustrators: to depict an American Indian as a beautiful half-naked maiden sporting an Indian chief's ceremonial feather headdress. While this could have been quite possibly a capital offense in Indian circles, it glamorized the simple savage. So encouraged, the gentle reader could proceed with confidence.

Sir John Hill, who lived from 1716 to 1775, and certainly to be counted, seems to have won his way to some sort of top in spite of the opinions of his more learned contemporaries in medicine and natural history. Peter Ascanius wrote to Linnaeus in 1755, a year before the publication of the impressive herbal that gathered the tributes of "Europe, Asia, Africa and America," that "Dr. Hill, the too famous naturalist of England, is the lowest possible condition. I do not think any mortal has ever written with more impudence or more ignorance. His only excuse is that he must write in order to exist." A bit of doggerel about him may sum up the opinion of his peers:

> Essense of dock, valerian and sage
> At once the disgrace and pest of his age

and perhaps sum up also what his public was willing to adopt as home

The Genius of Health Receiving the Tributes of Europe, Asia, Africa and America

medical practice. We know Hill was having trouble with Linnaeus for being critical of him and for not, at least in this volume, using the Linnaean binominal system throughout. Later, in his *Flora Britannica,* published in 1760, and his monumental twenty-six-volume *The Vegetable System,* finished just before he died, Hill used the Linnaean system, but perhaps not soon enough to placate the great Linnaeus, who vengefully named a plant *Hillis parasitica.*

Hill's letter to John Bartram, dated 1766, lends life and credence to the Indian maiden's offerings and also gives us the nature of the man his fellows found hard to love. Written from London, December, 1766, he begins:

Sir: —

There is wanted here, on a very particular occasion four pounds of the root of *Lobelia Syphilitica,* or the Blue Cardinal dry'd to be used in medicine. My Lord Bute has given me permission to desire you to gather and send it over.

The same occasion wants, also two ounces of the root of *Actaea racemosa,* and eight ounces of *Collinsonia* root. If you will take the trouble of adding these, it will also be very acceptable.

I believe the name of Dr. Hill is known to you, although we never corresponded. I always have, and always shall, espouse your interest.

I am your faithful, humble servant,

                                            John Hill

One wonders what the "very particular occasion" may have been, but the three remedies requested really bring the Indian maiden to the forefront. Besides *Lobelia syphilitica,* the Indians' remedy for syphilis, the other two roots requested by Dr. Hill, *Actaea racemosa* (now *Cimicifuga racemosa* L. black snakeroot or black cohosh) and *Collinsonia* (now *Collinsonia canadensis* L. or richweed, stoneroot, or citronella) are both, also obviously, "tributes" from the Indian maiden to the "genius of Health." All three plants are still listed today in pharmacopoeias but with such varied uses that one hesitates to define the "occasion" Dr. Hill had in mind.

With slow mails and difficult communications there was still in the eighteenth century a brisk exchange of medical requests and information heading both ways across the Atlantic. In April, 1741, John Custis in Virginia wrote to his friend-in-horticulture, Peter Collinson in London, acknowledging the latter's wishes for his good health. Custis says, however, that his "rules to preserve it" by a "regular life" of sobriety, temperance and regularity have availed him little and he has fallen under "as severe an affliction as ever poor mortal did." Paralyzed by pain, he broke out with dry, red, fiery sores, which he believed saved his life because his pains eased, but he expects to be crippled the rest of his life. He has little taste for anything except his garden, his "chiefest pleasure . . . besides reading which if I did not delight in should have run mad."

In October, Collinson writes he "read your deplorable case to a very learned physician and my intimate friend," probably Dr. John Fothergill, lately settled near Collinson on Gracechurch Street to practice medicine. "He said he never met with the like to such a degree . . . [In] his opinion . . . [the] attack was something of a gouty humour which invaded every part . . . Owing to your sober regular life . . . you was all alike proof so no weak side to your whole man was invaded . . ." He sends a "medicine very safe and proper for you to take."

In May, 1742, Custis acknowledges "your dear and tender care" and the receipt of the "phiall of Tincture for my ailment," which he takes to be "Wilson's Rheumatic Tincture . . . a good medicine . . . when designed well." But he says, with "submission" to the "able Physician . . . He has quite mistook my case," which, he says, is no wonder . . . "like asking an expert limner to paint a face without seeing the original."

Here we have a picture of a plantation owner as his own doctor. "I have," writes John Custis to Peter Collinson, in 1742, "diligently studied Physick more than forty years." (His library of five hundred volumes contained nearly thirty on medical subjects.) He cites also his "large experience, having not less than two hundred young and old in my several families which I daily assist and all poor people that have not money to employ a doctor," which he says, "has been my constant practice a great many years, so that I must know something of the matter." His attack, he states, "was nothing of a gouty humour." He diagnoses his trouble as "a Negro distemper, endemical to Africa and other places where Negroes come from." Some years ago he bought from a ship a quantity of Negroes "who had this distemper on them" and they "gave it to more than fifty of my slaves; several have it at this time, the symptoms as I have." He believes he got it "endeavoring to cure them and getting cold sitting on a tedious Assembly in very severe weather." Those that are young, he says, get over it, but it takes two or three years. The old are crippled so they can hardly hobble. It kills no one. Pains seem most severe when the sufferer is in perfect health. Custis is sixty-four and expects to remain a cripple all his life, although he can now walk with a cane and ride a horse as well as ever, once he has "got up" from a block or chair. (He feels riding on horseback is better than traveling about in a chair because it "shakes the whole machine.") The "Tincture" has done no good. He has personally found only purges help those he has treated. One young man was cured by two purges of mountain flax and Custis will be grateful for "some of the Herb and some of the seed to propagate." By God's leave, he then goes on at length to describe his garden.

Small wonder that in 1745 Collinson rejoices his friend is still alive, and had benefited from the use of tar water, special cure-all of Bishop Berkeley, to whom also Collinson had sent Custis' letter.

Custis' affliction was the yaws, a disease, as he said, contracted from Negroes, syphilislike, but unrelated to sexual intercourse.

Meanwhile, throughout the eighteenth century, on the Atlantic seaboard, wherever settlements had been made with water highways as the prime means of communication, and where ships rode supreme, allegiance to the Old World apothecaries was very strong. In fact, it is to the apothecaries of the Old World that much of the encouragement for exploring the New is due: early financing, friendly reception of reports, treasuring, storing and growing specimens obtained and, finally, subsidizing publication of findings. The list of patrons and underwriters of such monumental undertakings as Catesby's *Natural History,* usually a nice selection of wealthy gardening noblemen, astute Quaker merchants horticulturally inclined, princes of the church with great gardens to be "stored," include also apothecaries with city establishments bordered by their physic gardens. Doctors were also apothecaries. Apothecaries inclined also to be botanists. All the great herbalists were trained apothecaries, Gerard and Parkinson among them. Linnaeus had run the usual course to be a doctor and had even been engaged in medical practice before he reverted to his earlier training and became a botanist for life. One of his books has a frontispiece illustrating a prettily proportioned storeroom for the apothecary's wares, all the labels conveniently readable, and a few symbols thrown in for ornament. (Incidentally, just such an elaborate eighteenth-century apothecary's storeroom as this is on view today for visitors to the great Spanish monastery of San Silos, where a still, an oven, a boiler, bellows, pestles, mortars and scales occupy the corners, and the walls are lined with carefully labeled and decorated drawers of dried herbs or shelves of neatly labeled bottles and jars.)

That to be an apothecary was a proud calling is witnessed by a tombstone in Blandon Parish churchyard to flamboyantly armigerous George Herbert, who wishes to do honor to his family as well as himself by including mention upon his tombstone of his father, an apothecary, and his grandfather, a "grocer of London." When William the Conqueror invaded England he was outfitted by the guild of grocers, a powerful guild that then included apothecaries. Later, the apothecaries, beginning to feel their oats, broke away and formed a guild of their own.

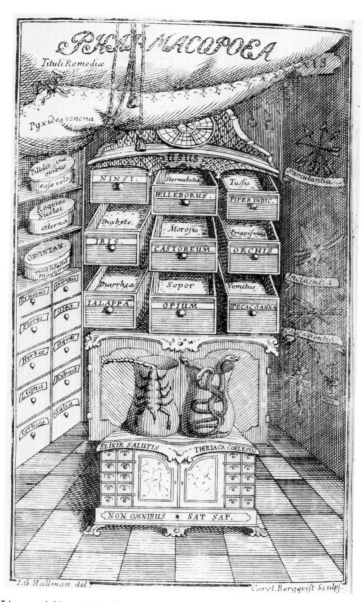

Linnaeus' *Materia Medica.* Frontispiece of Apothecary Shop

CAROLI LINNÆI

Archiat. Reg. & Med. ac Botan. Prof. Upsal.

Naturæ Curiosorum DIOSCORIDIS secundi,

MATERIA MEDICA,

LIBER I. DE PLANTIS.

Secundum

Genera,	Differentias,	Synonyma,
Loca,	Durationes,	Culturas,
Nomina,	Simplicia,	Præparata,
Qualitates,	Modos,	Potentias,
Vires,	Usus,	Composita,

Digestus.

Cum Privilegio S. R. Mtis Suec. & S. R. Mtis Polon. ac Electoris Saxon.

HOLMIÆ,
Typis ac sumptibus LAURENTII SALVII,
Anno 1749.

Linnaeus' *Materia Medica.* Title page

When Dr. John Mitchell of that mellifluous Virginia address "Ur-banna on the Rappahannock" had to retire to England because of ill health in 1746, he offered his place and properties for sale. His listings show him to have conducted an apothecary's shop with his practice. We know him also as a mapmaker and a writer on matters agricultural and economic to be edited and used later in the book we quote in our chapter on American husbandry. Friends with our friends, both American and English, he was seen off to England by John Bartram, who feared for his survival in Virginia, and welcomed into the society of medical and botanical patrons in England, many of whom we also know. We can hope they comforted him for the loss of a thousand botanical specimens he was taking to England when he was overhauled by a Spanish privateer. He was honored by Linnaeus by having the *Mitchella,* a little American partridge berry, named for him.

So it is not to be wondered at that, with all the new remedies being sought and processed, tried and reported upon, there were some very old and odd staples still being carried by American apothecary shops and in ships' medicine chests. In 1767 George Washington sent to his agents in London for some medical supplies. At about the same time a ship arrived in Williamsburg with such a cargo of drugs and medicines that two apothecary shops were able to run advertisements to announce fresh stock. Considered together and as a whole, the lists give us a very good idea of what was considered essential to the health of settlers far from the marts of medical commerce, and what was unobtainable in the wilds.

Washington's order consists of fifteen items, beginning with a pair of lancets in one case and six common ones, each in its own case. Then, in varying amounts: antimony (emetic and expectorant); flour of sulphur (laxative, diaphoretic, used in diseases of the skin); honey water (for combining ingredients in pill-making); spirits of turpentine (disinfectant, liniment, and remedy for tapeworm); the best Jesuit's bark powdered (for recurrent fevers); rhubarb powdered (the imported Chinese tonic, *Rheum officinale,* not to be confused with "pie rhubarb," *Rheum rhaponticum* L.); spirits of hartshorn (stimulant, sudorific, which, sniffed at, rouses the system); spirit of lavender (feminine restorative); spirit of nitre (diuretic, antispasmodic, diaphoretic); blistering plaster (probably "Burgundy pitch"); tincture of Castor (from glands under the tails of beavers of either sex. Russian beavers are supposed to have the best. Useful in hysteria, epilepsy and fevers with "nervous manifestations"); *Balsam capivi* (a diuretic, cathartic, useful in diseases of the mucous membranes); "Termerick" (to color medicines and treat jaundice).

The advertisements by apothecaries for "choice" assortments of drugs

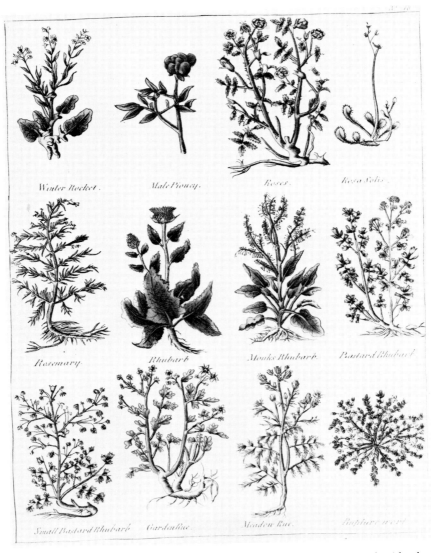

A page from an eighteenth-century edition of the longlasting home medical book, Culpeper's *Herbal*

and medicines duplicate most of Washington's needs and add time-honored ancient remedies like "Spanish flies" (to blister the skin); "manna" (the juice of the European flowering ash, *Fraximus ornus* L., a gentle physic); both Epsom and Glauber's salts; jalap (a Mexican root used as a cathartic); juice of buckthorn (from a European tree, *Rhamnus catharticus* L.); *Alkermes minerale* (a diuretic, emetic and alterative); and ipecacuanha.

Jefferson was one who, like Franklin, had great faith in the restorative powers of cold water. He maintained that getting wet never hurt anyone (although we know to our sorrow that Washington was thought to have brought on his own fatal illness by getting wet while out riding, and sitting down to dinner without changing). Jefferson was never concerned with severe personal illness or injury, but he took good care of his slaves and was very hospitable to, and interested in, requests for help with medicinal remedies. He wrote a "Memorandum" full of advice to one Jeremiah A. Goodman about the running of "the Tomahawk plantation," where Jefferson had designed an octagonal brick house, to be the "handsomest house in the state next to Monticello." His advice on doctoring the slaves was fairly simple.

In pleurisies, or other highly inflammatory fevers, intermitting fevers, dysenteries and venereal cases, the doctors can give certain relief; and the sooner called . . . the easier and more certain the cure, but in most other cases they oftener do harm than good. A dose of salts as soon as they are taken is salutary in almost all cases and hurtful in none. I have generally found this, with a lighter diet and kind attention restore them soonest. The lancet should never be used without the advice of a physician but in sudden accidents. A supply of sugar molasses and salts should be . . . kept in the house for the sick.

Jefferson became interested in cultivating benne seed, a plant of which much was hoped as a source of oil equal to olive oil. Grown by the Negroes in the south for their own use, it was taken up by their white owners, like other African plants (such as Guinea corn) the slaves had brought with them. Jefferson reports that the seed is eaten parched for dessert and used in soups, but its chief use was as an esculent oil. "It is the *Sesamum trifoliatum* of Miller's Dictionary where a good account of it may be seen." Jefferson adds, "for dysenteries and other visceral complaints . . . two or three leaves in a pint of cold water . . . yield a mucilage the consistency of white of egg . . . Dose is five or six pints in the course of one day . . ."

In his *Notes on the State of Virginia,* compiled in 1781 in answer to the request of the French legation in Philadelphia for some statistical accounts of Virginia, Jefferson replied in answer to "Query IV, A Notice of the Mines and other Subterranean Riches; its Trees, Plants, Fruits, etc." with, in part, a list of the "trees, plants, fruits, etc. . . . which would principally attract notice as being (1) Medicinal, (2) Esculent, (3) Ornamental, (4) Useful for Fabrication," adding the Linnaean to the popular names as the latter might not convey precise information to a foreigner. He adds that he will "confine myself, too, to native plants."

Jefferson lists and identifies twenty-one plants, wisely including no uses, a course followed today by the United States Government's booklet on *American Medicinal Plants of Commercial Importance,* put out by our Department of Agriculture to assist "many people in rural sections of this country" in the "collection of medicinal plants for the crude-drug market."

In 1771 Dr. Fothergill wrote to Humphry Marshall thanking him for reporting upon "the medicinal effects of some of your native simples . . . It is quite proper to record all useful observations . . . It requires a long time and much experience to know the use of any one medicine. We are apt sometimes to ascribe effects to wrong causes, and if a disorder wears off, after the use of any medicine, it is usual to place the recovery to the account of the medicine."

In this same letter he considers the use of sassafras bark.

We are so well pleased with our Ipecacuanha . . . we shall scarcely be soon prevailed on to admit of any substitute. I wish, however, your Ipecac may be attended to. Gather it when the leaves are decaying, wash it clean, dry it in the shade, and powder it fine. In case of sickness, where a vomit is required, give ten grains; wait half an hour, give a second dose, and try to such means how small a quantity will answer the purpose.

And then, almost as if he were ordering up something from his grocer:

I should be exceedingly glad to hear that you had any indigenous medicine, or simple, that would operate pretty freely and certainly by urine. We want such a remedy much. We can promote all the natural discharges with some degree of certainty, but this. We can vomit, purge, sweat to what degree we please; but we have no certain diuretic. This is much wanted in the cure of dropsies and other complaints. Listen carefully after such a remedy.

As an illustration of the pressures put upon Bartram as our earliest botanist explorer, this letter from one of Bartram's friends and neighbors will suffice. It is dated January 3, 1768, from Dr. Gale in Kinningworth. Dr. Benjamin Gale, graduated from Yale College in 1733 and credited with inventing his own superior drill-plough, wrote to John Bartram, then sixty-nine and on his way to explorations southward, to ask eagerly for traces of the Deluge; any appearance of the tree from which Peruvian bark was taken; any chance that the fabled stones used to extract poisons from vipers are "natural" or only "Factitious"; if Bartram has found any Cicuta (now *Conium* L., our water hemlock or spotted cowbane, names for the poisonous Old World hemlock that killed Socrates); if he has met with the meadow saffron (*Colchicum officinale* L.); and if either of these is found in America, he prays for seeds of each. And he asks Bartram for the botanical name of "the American Bloodroot whose virtues are great and many. Particularly, I look upon it as a specific in the nervous headache, or sick head-ache, as it is commonly called today." (For Bartram, this is *Sanguinaria canadensis* L.)

Gale suggests that he would be "infinitely delighted to spend one evening . . . I mean a winter evening . . ." with Bartram, to hear all he has to report. As would we all.

The Reverend Manasseh Cutler, born in Killingly, Connecticut, in 1742, was one of those men Oliver Wendell Holmes would consider as having "shared the passions of his time." Farmer boy, graduate of Yale with an aptitude for natural science and astronomy, familiar with Franklin's experiments with electricity, his early diaries are full of descriptions of natural phenomena. He taught school, studied the treatment of smallpox, read law and became an attorney, went into business as a merchant, read theology under his father-in-law and was licensed to preach. In 1771 he became pastor of the church in Ipswich Hamlet and participated in the early stages of the Revolution, witnessing the battles near Boston. In 1776 he became chaplain of the Eleventh Massachusetts Regiment, going with it to Rhode Island. Finding it hard to support a family on preaching alone, he took up the study of medicine, "rode out" with Dr. Elisha Whitney and soon, in his own words, became a practitioner. "In 1777 money had depreciated as much, at least, as five for one, but in 1779 it was nearer twenty to one. I have spent considerable of an estate in the support of my family and am now driven to the practice of physic."

He also found time to climb Mount Washington and write about it and to study botany with a growing desire to write a natural history of New England.

In keeping with his involvement with his times, in 1786 Cutler set out to drive to Ohio in a sulky, covering the distance of seven hundred and fifty miles in twenty-nine days. He was interested in the settlement of the western lands and helped form the Ohio Company, in which Washington and Franklin had long had hopes and expectations and for which Jefferson helped draw up the legislative ordinance of 1787.

His interest for us is that he, so immediately in touch with all the authorities busy fabricating the texture of the new United States, still found time to write on our plants from personal observation. He knows Franklin's letters on electricity written to Collinson and published by him. He has studied Catesby's *Natural History,* which he had to borrow from Harvard. He longs to procure Sir John Hill's *Natural History,* cannot, and asks to borrow it from Harvard to "determine . . . the botanical characters of Trees and Plants, but especially for ascertaining those which have already been discovered and described." He proposed to make a "catalogue" of the trees and plants that are "indigenous to this part of America and have not been described by botanists; those which are found growing here as well as in other parts of the world . . . and those which have been propagated here but are not the spontaneous production of the country."

Cutler also borrowed the Reverend Stephen Hales' *Statical Essays* to study his experiments in "vegetable statics." Dr. Hales was the English clergyman, physiologist and inventor who performed one of the first experiments to measure blood pressure. While he preached a sermon one Sunday, he left his white mare thrown and tied to a gate. Her blood, transferred through a goose's windpipe into a glass tube, rose to a height of eight feet, three inches. Linnaeus immortalized him by naming one of Washington's favorite native shrubs, "the silver-bell tree," *Halesia* for him.

"An Account of Some of the Vegetable Productions, Naturally Growing in the Part of America, Botanically Arranged by the Rev. Manasseh Cutler, F.A.A. and M.S. and Member of the Philosophical Society at Philadelphia" was presented as a paper before the Committee of the American Academy of Arts and Sciences in Boston in 1785 and published in the transactions of that body. Cutler had been elected a member of the Academy in 1781. This modest effort is credited with being the first treatise on New England botany. Cutler's is a firsthand account of plants he has personally seen and collected, arranged according to the Linnaean system, with suggestions as to their uses from his observations and from what he has been able to glean from a book on British plants by William Withering, M.D., known for his study of the foxglove and his correspondence about it with the Portsmouth, New Hampshire, physician, Dr. Hall Jackson.

Cutler's treatise antedated by two years Dr. Schoepf's *Materia Medica Americana,* an ambitious work published by the Erlangen Library in 1787 with over three hundred plates and deferential references to John Bartram's *Observations,* Clayton's *Flora Virginica,* Colden's *Flora Novae Borealis,* Kalm's *Travels,* Catesby's *Natural History* and Linnaeus' *Materia Medica.* This points up the growing importance of North

American plants in circles medical as well as horticultural, but Cutler's impact was more immediate. He identified the plant said to have caused the death of two child patients of Dr. Samuel Thomson as marsh rosemary and not lobelia. Why being sweated to death by one instead of the other should make all the difference we are sorry not to know.

Cutler's "Account" begins with a lament that Canada and the southern states have been visited by "eminent botanists from Europe" while the part in between "seems still to remain unexplored." He blames this on the fact that botany is not taught in our colleges due to "the mistaken opinion of its inutility in common life."

He thinks well of the Indians.

Feverbark or *Pinckneya pubens,* a southern remedy.
Sketched by P. J. Redouté

William Bartram's sketch of *Phytolacca decandra* used by Benjamin Schultz to illustrate his thesis

The native Indians were acquainted with the peculiar properties of certain vegetable productions which if thoroughly understood by the present inhabitants, might be made extensively useful, both in physic, arts and manufactures, and new branches of commerce. Their *materia medica* seems to have consisted of few articles . . . certain plants powerful in their operation, and sometimes producing sudden and surprising effects upon the human body. These savages seem to have had better ideas of the medical virtues of plants than some who have imagined that vegetables fit only for food were the most proper for medicine, and that combining a great number of the common plants might be a remedy for almost every disease. Vegetables called poisonous are capable of producing great and sudden alterations in the human body. May not many of them be found upon accurate and well-judged experiments, like some chemical poisons, to be the best medicines? The Indians . . . discovered effectual antidotes against the venom of rattlesnakes . . . possibly their greatest improvement in the knowledge of medicine.

(He quotes Catesby's story of the Indian smeared with purple bindweed safely handling a rattlesnake. Which gives us yet one more snakebite remedy to add to an already suspiciously long list.)

Yet another example of the promotion of a single American plant for many medicinal uses is the "Inaugural Bottanic-Medical Dissertation" of young Benjamin Schultz of Philadelphia in 1795. His subject is the "Phytolacca Decandra of Linnaeus" and he is submitting his study of our native poke, or pokeweed, for his doctor of medicine thesis at the University of Pennsylvania Medical School. Dr. Benjamin Smith Barton, Professor of Natural History and Botany, and Dr. Caspar Wistar, Professor of Anatomy, Surgery and Midwifery, are invoked. Peter Kalm and Cadwallader Colden, John Parkinson and Dr. Rush are quoted. All the specialists have been consulted and the future Dr. Benjamin Schultz had himself experimented with this possible wonder of the future upon dogs, upon himself and upon his friends. No less eminent an artist than William Bartram has drawn a picture to illustrate his paper. The plant itself is considered from every possible angle and for every possible use, as a dye plant, a poison, a spring vegetable and as a cure for each and all of the usual ills, from "yellow water" in horses, to cancers and ulcers in men, corns, scabies, herpes, rheumatic affections, dysentery, syphilis, phthisis, pulmonalis, mania, epilepsy and sundry eruptions.

For a definitive list of the most acceptable American plants for medicinal use we have Dr. Jacob Bigelow's *American Medical Botany,* published in the years 1817, 1818 and 1820. It would seem that few changes had taken place in the very early nineteenth century except the discovery of a new virtue in the foxglove, heretofore used for dropsy and now observed to have extraordinary effects upon the heart. And Dr. Bigelow hints of hopes for a vegetable that will cure gout, and declares part of his incentive in making this study is "that our own country people should have the benefit of collecting such articles than that we should pay for them to the Moors of Africa or the Indians of Brazil." Dr. Bigelow admits that while "we could not well dispense with opium and ipecacuanha" we may have indigenous substitutes for many other foreign drugs. Although we "abound in bitters, astringents and demulcents," he does not feel we have "discovered our anodynes and emetics."

To leave seventeenth-century worthies as Parkinson and Evelyn still in the running for eighteenth-century honors and not to mention Cotton Mather in a chapter on American medicine would be a terrible oversight if his *Angel of Bethesda,* the first book on medicine to be written in America, had ever been published until lately. While Cotton Mather, so irritating to some, like Oldmixon, trying to write on New England without having been there, made his place in medical history by learning of the African system of inoculation against smallpox from his slave and by advocating it with his friend, Dr. Zabdiel Boylston, this *Essay Upon the Common Maladies of Mankind* has only just (1972) seen the light of print. Perhaps it is as well Oldmixon was spared this added aggravation, as the book deals with all the medical facts known to the human race up to that time and many of the fancies, in several languages with countless witticisms, religious philosophizing, assorted plants and a great deal of sound common sense about human nature. Indeed, it is the only seventeenth- or eighteenth-century medical book concerning itself with the state of the patient's mind and soul. Perhaps we are even now not ready for it.

If it seems strange today to include in a book purportedly on gardens, wild American plants used in medicine, let us remember that much-used plants brought in from the wilds and cultivated included many of our most ornamental trees and shrubs of today as well as some of our prettiest garden flowers.

Furber's Flowers for the Month of August

1. Purple Althea Frutex B T
2. Ivy leaved Jasmine G
3. Iris Uvaria B
4. Purple Sultan B
5. Purple Toad Flax G
6. Purple Amaranthoides P
7. Double Arabian Jasmine X
8. Yellow Ketmia G
9. Purple Coxcomb Amaranth P
10. Shrubs St. Johns-wort B T
11. Pona's blue Throatwort G
12. Palma Christi B
13. Purple Convolvulus B
14. Polyanthos B
15. Indian yellow Jasmine G
16. Double flowering Myrtle G
17. Egyptian Scarlet Hollyhock B
18. Yellow striped Marvel of Peru B
19. Striped Monthly Rose B T
20. Double Feather few B
21. Semper Augusta Auricula P
22. Dwarf Convoluvulus B
23. Willow leaved Apocynum G
24. Apios of America G T
25. Virginian flowering Raspberry B T
26. Zisole from Genoa B T
27. Double Spanish Jasmine G
28. White Eternal B
29. Fruit-bearing Passion Flower C T
30. Scarlet Althea S
31. Canary Shrub Fox Glove S
32. Long blowing Honeysuckle B T
33. Double purple Virgins-Bower C T
34. Virginian Scarlet Martagon G

8 Eighteenth-Century American Vegetables

To CALL the vegetable gardens of the settlers on the Atlantic seaboard in the eighteenth century "colonial" is to name them fairly. While there were some innovations in their vegetables and their field crops, such as peanuts and sweet potatoes, "Guinea corn" or sorghum, Jerusalem artichokes, melons, gourds and Indian corn and beans, the staple crops in garden and field were much the same as those depended upon in England and the Low Countries, in France and in Spain. In fact, they were the staple crops of Roman times, carried by the Roman invaders to become the national standbys of a civilized European economy.

The cabbage family conquered more territory than the Romans and remained longer, in all its various forms: round heads, loose head, green curled, red and white, with its related cauliflowers and "Brussels" sprouts. Onions were as long-lasting: white, red and sweet. Peas, a favored fancy dish for centuries, were called, for the table, charming names like "Rounceval" and "Hotspur." For fodder the names were "chick" and "field." Beans, called "kidney" or "Windsor" or "speckled French," would seem to have been used shelled, like those the Indians showed the settlers. "Snap" beans sound like their being eaten young and green, although one of the names for peas, "Marrowfat" or "Dutch Admiral," imply that a full-grown quality was admired. Beets, radishes, carrots and turnips were allowed to grow to enormous size. With epicures the globe artichoke superseded the Indian, or Jerusalem, artichoke, which was, of course, not an artichoke nor from Jerusalem, but grew wild in quantities and was deemed by many to be coarse and

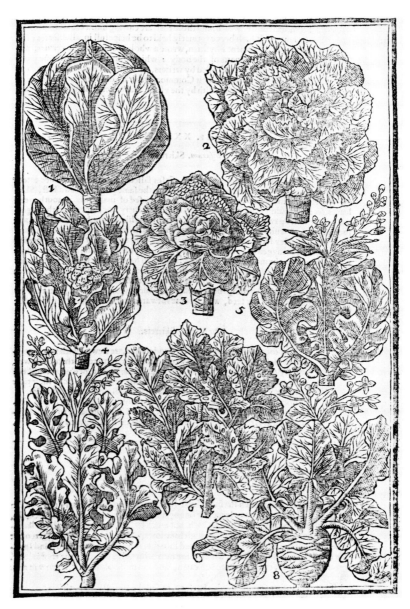

Parkinson's 1629 illustration of cabbages for "The Kitchen Garden"

"windy." A variety of beet, huge and coarse, called "mangel-wurzel," as it still is in parts of England today, was called "scarcity root" when it was sent to Martha Washington. Spinach was considered a necessity, as was anything green-leaved and early-growing in a country where non-productive winters could prove as conducive to scurvy as a long sea voyage. Delicate vegetables and salad plants were important to those who maintained the sort of table acceptable to their inquiring or perhaps nostalgic palates, like garden cresses, asparagus, endive, parsley, mustard, salsify, nasturtiums and an assortment of lettuces. Cucumbers were fancied either long with less space for seeds, which were held not to be healthful, or very short for pickling. Celery was for those who had root cellars, more important to the average householder than ice-houses, carefully planned architecturally and requiring care to keep filled.

In fact, when one considers the people to be fed on even a small plantation or in a large Philadelphia household or on a farm tucked away on the border or in a little village on the shores of Chesapeake Bay, served by small ships, one realizes the precedence given the seeds of the lowliest vegetables, the importance of their harvesting and preservation of seeds for resowing. Seed-selling nurseries were few and far away. Sometimes their function was taken over by ships docking with a fresh load of seeds to be sold from their stores after notices in local papers. Sometimes widows with green thumbs would set up shop and take orders, advertising themselves modestly. The more generous and also the more "curious" of the great landowners, with their extensive plantings, would save their seeds and send them out to those taking up land in the wilderness, or exchange them with each other. Consider, then, the excitement of news of a shipment of fresh seeds just in from the Old World, not of rare exotics, but of good reliable peas and beans and cabbages, "for ready money."

In the middle Atlantic states and to the south, cultivation never rested. There was no merciful covering of snow to allow gardeners a change of pace. In New England, by the time of the first snow flurry, roots and bulbs would have been gathered into the cellar, fruit arranged on shelves or, in the case of long-keeping apples, stored in barrels often inspected. The cider apples would have been made into cider and put into barrels with bungs, to facilitate "drawing" when ready or stored with a "mother" to make vinegar. Potatoes would be in bins, celery earthed up in a corner of the barn cellar, and all the other produce candied, salted, jellied, pickled, buried in sand, wrapped in paper or dried and hung from the beams. In the more southern settlements the gardeners were still outside working, experimenting on what could be sowed in the autumn, composting new shoots with the "haulms," or stalks of the old plants.

As we can see from their records, their diaries, calendars and seed bills, they all sowed the same sorts of seeds over and over again, either those they had saved, or those that they had been able to buy "fresh," in an eternal cycling.

From planting records and plans denoting the names and positions of the vegetables and fruits, we can form an idea of plants and design. Crop rotation engaged aspiring experts: how long to grow what crop where, and when to change to another. Broadcast or drill sowing was always a moot point. Special beds for each vegetable or an association of vegetables was the rule south of New England. In northern town gardens the layout was rows straight across between side paths with shrubby borders of currants or other small fruits. In the south, formal "squares" and "borders" were the rule. Jefferson speaks of his gooseberry and currant "squares." Washington refers to his artichoke, mint and other "beds" and to the "borders" in the kitchen garden. Sir Peyton, like Jefferson, has his "beds" numbered when he notes what he has sowed where. The selection of plants to be grown in kitchen gardens was more or less the same up and down the coast, except, of course, that melons and globe artichokes could be more easily grown in the south and vegetables improved by frost or long blanching in cold cellars would be more popular in the north. One let the best specimens of each plant go to seed to be collected and saved for the next planting, or ordered seeds from England or, if one was fortunate enough to see the advertisement and near enough to get to the ship, one could buy from captains who had brought garden seeds for sale. There were also those middlemen and middlewomen who sold seeds from their own stores. And at the end of the eighteenth century, there were competent nurserymen, though few and far between, who would sell not only seeds but also scions and young trees or shrubs already started and ready for transplanting.

From records early in the century, one sees warnings about the "farina" of different species of the same genus being kept from "mixing" to the deterioration of the seeds — no melons near cucumbers, for instance. No one had yet grasped the idea of improving strains. Shaddocks, ancestor of our grapefruit, were still grown as they had been brought from the East Indies by Captain Shaddock, although oranges and lemons were being grafted upon them as a curiosity. Bartram had noted that he could get a variety of colors by leaving some plants to grow close together, and he had experimented with cross-fertilizing lychnis, but on the whole, no one asked more of seeds than that they be as good as the original plant.

So the varieties of different vegetables available to the American gardener were not very great — in fact they were not much greater than those available a hundred years before, offered by Parkinson and Gerard. Philip Miller, authority on horticultural matters in the eighteenth century, was sedulously copied by John Randolph, a Williamsburg gardener and a connection of Jefferson's, who wrote a *Treatise* to adapt Miller to local conditions. Lists of peas and beans, both so vital to eighteenth-century American gardens, are very little longer than Parkinson's. The best pictures of the vegetables Washington and Jefferson and Sir Peyton Skipwith were growing can be seen in the illustrations in Parkinson and Gerard.

Washington and Jefferson between them covered nearly the entire range of materials available to, and popular with, eighteenth-century American gardeners. Field-crop rotation and innovations in the time-honored English-style plough constantly concerned them both. And they were always experimenting with fruits and vegetables for man or beast. Washington was primarily attracted to trees and shrubs, to what he called "clever" trees, by which he meant blooming sub-shrubs or small trees with which he could plant his foregrounds under what he hoped would be giant pines and tulip trees and coffee-bean trees and magnolias. Flowers he seems to have delegated to the distaff side. It was only "botanick" seeds from abroad that demanded his own sowing and watching, or those he experimented with in his composted soils. Jefferson, on the other hand, fancied all blooming plants, bulbs and annuals and perennials. He welcomed new sorts. He had infinite curiosity about all vegetables and any varieties of the sorts he already had. He liked to grow such remotely named varieties of ordinary vegetables as the "French broccoli from Pisa" as well as "Roman broccoli," pretty certainly the same.

There were many duplications. Indeed, Bradley on "Pease" is a case in point. In his *New Improvements of Planting and Gardening,* Bradley remarks:

The Kinds of Pease which I shall mention, are the Hotspurs for winter sowing, the Dwarfs and the Rouncival or Dutch Admiral, to be sown in the Spring. These sorts may well enough suffice for any garden without enumerating at least fifty other kinds that I have heard of which perhaps are so near akin to these that the difference can hardly be distinguished but in Names only. I have often wondered at the Indiscretion of some People who take a delight in giving cramp names to plants and make it their business to multiply Species without Reason, as if a Fruit would be the better for a Name that could not be understood, or that the works of Nature were not already numerous enough for us to contemplate.

We can see the careful arrangement of Mount Vernon, with the

Marjoram, thyme, hyssop, pennyroyal and sage. From Parkinson's 1629 "The Kitchen Garden"

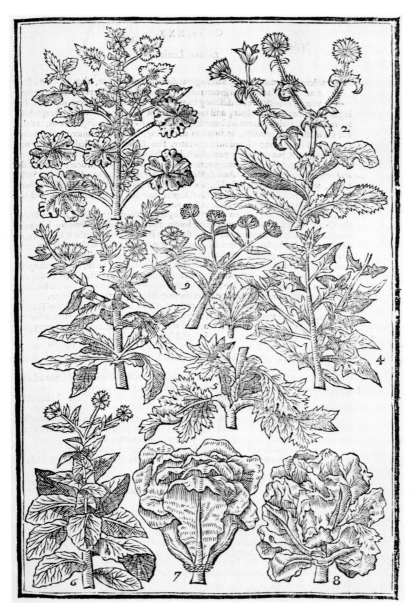

Mallows, endive, savory and lettuces. From Parkinson's 1629 "The Kitchen Garden"

Skirrets, parsnips, carrots, turnips and radishes. From Parkinson's "The Kitchen Garden" in his *Paradisus,* 1629

kitchen garden and the flower garden separate but equal. Since walking in gardens was a habit, for pleasure and health, the paths were wide and of either closely mown turf or of gravel — by which, of course, was meant pebbles and not our cut gravel of today. Gardens were kept in good order since they were often visited. Field crops were exactly that; anything grown in great quantities was sown broadcast in the fields or in long rows, for easy ploughing. Vegetables and fruits and herbs for home consumption were arranged in an area easily accessible from the house. Let us admit, however, that if we use the gardens of Mount Vernon as one of our models now, with references to what was grown at Monticello and at Prestwould, speaking of "wall" fruits and "espaliered" trees, this does not negate the same sorts of vegetables and fruits grown in humbler gardens both north and south. The point is to see what vegetables were considered desirable for a domestic garden. One obvious conclusion is that the culinary and other useful herbs were included with vegetables. The day of the "herb garden" had not arrived.

For basic lists of eighteenth-century vegetables, we have two English guides: first Philip Miller's *Gardeners Kalendar,* dedicated to the Worshipful Society of Apothecaries, which ran though many editions of the eighteenth century, and, second, *The Universal Gardener and Botanist* by Thomas Mawe and John Abercrombie, also an eighteenth-century textbook for gardeners. These two books were in many libraries besides those of Washington and Jefferson. For American lists we have a mid-century *Treatise on Gardening* by John Randolph, Jr., full of Virginia experience but leaning upon Philip Miller's *Gardener's Dictionary,* sixth edition, of 1752. We have also all the records of the vegetables actually planted by Washington, Jefferson and the Skipwiths of Prestwould.

These are vegetables "for the table" although some household vegetables were grown also in quantity to feed livestock, especially cabbages and turnips. Several vegetables common then, such as the skirret, are rare today, but we see the slow emergence of others, like the tomato, toward general acceptance. Salads were more varied than ours, selections of cucumbers more interesting, dependence upon the cabbage family more complete.

For good measure we shall later include two garden calendars, one for Virginia, the other for South Carolina.

A Treatise on Gardening, by a Citizen of Virginia is generally supposed to have been written by John Randolph of Williamsburg (1727 –1784). In Jefferson's library, it is listed as *Randolph's Treatise.* It is indeed a treatise rather than a complete set of instructions. It reads like a succession of familiar essays upon a list of vegetables that the author has chosen because they are those he especially recommends and about which the ordinary gardener would welcome instruction from a native of the Virginia climate. It leans heavily, as all studious gardeners did, upon Miller, but there is an air of friendly informality to the whole, which shows the author has learned from experience.

We list each of the entries but omit careful instructions as to planting times and conditions, and include only some of the personal comments that give a spark to the whole. Scholarly explanations of the names are nearly entirely from Miller.

ARTICHOKES, known to botanical writers by the name of Cynara
. . . Long dung is an enemy to them . . . The best way to preserve them is by laying straw on the surface of the ground over their roots . . . The leaves . . . I have been informed, clean pewter the best of anything . . . There are different sorts . . .

Cynara spinosa . . . to be cultivated and eaten like celery. The common name is Chardoon or Cardoon.

The Jerusalem Artichoke (*Helianthus*) is only a species of the Sunflowers, with a tuberous root, not unlike a Potatoe. Some admire them, but they are of a flatulent nature, and are apt to cause commotions in the belly.

ASPARAGUS Growth, a young shoot
. . . Butchers dung is what it delights in . . . The seeds are contained in those things which look like red berries.

BEANS, Vide *Faba,* gr. to eat
. . . The Windsor sort . . . are the best.

KIDNEY BEAN, *Phaseolus,* a long swift ship which the husk resembles
. . . The Dutch sort . . . the common kind . . . not so apt to be stringy . . . French beans and snaps are the same.

BUSHEL OR SUGAR BEANS
. . . Will grow around the stake to a great height . . . bear profusely . . . continue till destroyed by frost . . . esteemed very delicate . . . of various colours, as white, marbled, green etc.

CABBAGE ETC. Under *Brassica*
Is included in all the several species of the Cabbage, among which Cauliflowers and Broccoli are classes . . . Roman Broccoli is the proper sort to cultivate . . . When you cut the flowers or head, cut to five or six inches of the stem . . . strip off the skin . . . boil them in a clean cloth and serve them up with butter as Cauliflowers are. The stems will eat like Asparagus and the heads like cauliflowers.

The common White Cabbage is the proper sort for winter . . .

Savoy Cabbages . . . esteemed best when touched by the frost.

Battersea Cabbage is the earliest . . .

Sugar loaf is the finest.

Borecole . . . tough until the frost has made them tender.

Russian kind . . . small and soon degenerate.

Turnip Cabbage . . . fit only for soup.

Musk Cabbage . . . I have met these in Virginia, Miller says . . . the most delicious.

CAULIFLOWERS

. . . Must be sown critically to a day . . . The experience of this country as well as England, verifies the proposition . . . In Virginia the twelfth day of September is the proper time. In order to have cauliflowers in the fall you should sow your seed on the twelfth day of April . . . Col. Turner of King George who was eminent in cauliflowers . . . dug trenches a foot and a half wide quite down to clay . . . mixed with a spade some long dung into which he put his plants about five feet asunder . . . as they grew hilled them up with the most mould . . . Radishes or Spinach sown amongst the Cauliflowers . . . will preserve them from the fly; being a more agreeable food to that destructive animal.

CARROTS *Daucus*

. . . Two sorts, the orange and white . . . the former being generally used though the latter is much the sweetest . . . Sow them in drills about two feet distance . . . for weeding . . . Dung the ground the year before, for when they touch dung or meet with obstruction they fork. The seed should be rubbed before sown to get rid of the husk . . . and sown on a calm day as the seed is light and easily blown away.

CELERY, *Apium*. From Apex because the ancients made crowns of it

. . . One of the species of parsley . . . The sun is a great enemy to Celery . . . Recommend covering of your plants with brush at all seasons of their growth while the weather is hot from nine in the morning until six in the evening.

CELERIAC, *Apium dulce degener, radice rapacea*. Turnip rooted

. . . In the summer water your plants if the season is dry and in winter cover them with haum . . . to protect them from frosts.

PARSLEY, *Apium hortense*

. . . If intended for the table should be sown in drills pretty thick in light rich land . . . If for medicinal use (the roots being prescribed on many occasions) the seed should be sown thin and the plants drawn and treated as directed in the culture of carrots.

CUCUMBER, *Cucumis*

. . . Most refreshing and delicate of all vegetables . . . Three sorts . . . First *Cucumis sativus vulgaris* . . . the common sort, most in use, amongst which there is a difference in size, length, etc. Second, *Cucumis fructu albo* the white cucumber . . . cultivated in Holland chiefly . . . Third, *Cucumis oblongus* . . . cultivated only in curious gardens . . . remarkable for their length and fewness of seed.

CURRANTS, or Corinths, so called from a near resemblance to the Corinthian Grape (*Ribes* by the botanists.)

. . . Have many species, but the two principal are the red and white, of which the Dutch sorts are chiefly propagated in England.

CHAMOMILE, *Chamomelum* (from Melon, gr. an Apple, because it has the scent of one, or *Anthemis* as it is called by Dr. Linnaeus

. . . There are different species but the *Chamomelum odoratissimum repens flore simplici* is the sort chiefly propagated. It is used medicinally, and in making green walks and edgings . . .

CELANDINE, *Majus chelidonium*

. . . A medical herb often cultivated in gardens . . . It is an annual Celandine; the lesser is a Ranunculus. [This entry shows the "greater common Celandine" of Miller was cultivated in Virginia gardens; although Miller says it is seldom in gardens in England because if its seeds are permitted to scatter "the ground will be plentifully stored with Plants to a considerable Distance." Miller says "used in Medicine . . . aperitive and cleansing; opening obstructions of the Spleen and Liver, and of great Use in Curing Jaundice and Scurvy." The second "lesser Celandine or Pilewort," escaped to become a pretty little Virginia wild-flower, today defined as *Ranunculus ficaria.*]

CLARY, *Sclarea*

. . . Will last many years.

COMFREY, *Symphytum*

. . . Good for healing wounds . . . A great vulnerary . . . hardy, will grow anywhere and will last long.

CRESSES, WATER *Sisymbrium nasturtium*

. . . May be propagated by throwing the seed in standing water and not cutting it the first year . . . Agreeable warm taste . . . very good eating in Scorbutic cases, and is a great diarrhetic.

CRESS, INDIAN *Nasturtium inducum nasis tormentum,* because the seed when bruised is apt to cause sneezing, known to the botanists by the name of *Acriviola,* a sharp violet

. . . The flower is superior to a radish in flavour and is eaten in salads or without. My method is to plant the seeds in hills, three in a hill, leaving space in the middle to put the stick on which they are to grow . . .

[Miller has *Nasturtium indicum* under *Tropaeloum Lin.* in his eighth edition of 1768. This may help to date the publication or at least the writing of the *Treatise* as before that time, since anyone so devoted to Miller would want to check the latest edition before committing himself. Miller says the two sorts, the smaller "Indian nasturtium" and the larger-leaved and larger-flowered "Indian Cress" are both from Peru. The flowers are wholesome and the seeds much used pickled, in sauces.]

ELECAMPANE *Helenium*

. . . is a medicinal plant, the root . . . much used by Apothecaries . . .

ENDIVE *Endiva cichorium,* Succory

[From Randolph's meticulous directions for the cultivation of Succory in a country subject to frost, we may assume this was one of his standby vegetables. Miller gives four sorts of Cichorium: the wild, with its bright blue flowers, "escaped" today; the prickly; the broad-leaved, which is the common endive; and the curly-leaved, which he finds more palatable. He says all sorts are esteemed as aperitive and diuretic, opening obstructions of the liver, good for jaundice and provoking urine.]

ESCHALOT, vide Cives, under title Onion

FEATHERFEW, *Matricaria,* from *Matrix,* being good against diseases of the womb, or *Parthenium,* from *Parthenes,* gr. a virgin

The Greater Indian Cress or Nasturtium, *Tropaeolum majus.* From Curtis *Botanical Magazine*

. . . To be propagated from seed or roots . . . If you do not want the seeds, cut off the stems when the flowers are past as they often decay the roots.

FENNEL, *Foenieulum*
. . . May be propagated from seed or the plants, as Featherfew . . . Keep it from seedling as it will overrun the garden . . .

GARLICK, *Allium,* vide Onion

GOOSEBERRY, *Grossularia,* by some *Uva,* and by others *Crispa,* because villose and hairy
. . . but two sorts principally cultivated, the hairy Gooseberry and the large white Dutch . . . There is a small gooseberry, very leafy, not worth cultivation . . . Advise banishing them from the garden.

GROUND IVY, *Hedera Terrestris,* or *Glechoma*
. . . will grow in any shady place . . . overspread the ground if not restrained.
[One wonders why Randolph saw fit to include it at all — perhaps because it was already growing abundantly, which may, in turn, be due to its having had a reputation as a medicinal herb.]

HORSE RADISH, *Cochlearia,* because the leaves are hollow like a spoon
. . . is a species of the Scurvey grass . . . When you have cut from the root and separated as much as you have occasion for, put it into the ground again with the head just above the earth and it will restore itself . . . in very rich ground.

HONEY-SUCKLES, *Caprifolium,* because the Goats eat the tender plants
. . . The red is the Italian, the pale English; roots or cuttings will produce it. They may be removed in bloom for the sake of a prospect, and replaced when out of bloom.

LAVENDER, *Lavendule a lavendo;* because good in washings and bathing as it scents the water and beautifies the flesh
. . . A poor gravelly soil suits it best . . . will give it a more aromatic smell . . . Resists the winters here better . . .

LETTUCES, *Lactuca,* from *lac,* milk, they being of a milky substance which is emitted when the stalk is broken
. . . There is a common garden lettuce . . . sown for cutting young and mixing with other small salads . . . the worst of all the kinds in my opinion . . . most watery and flashy . . . very soon runs to seed.

I give . . . Imperial the preference for three reasons . . . it washes by far the easiest . . . it will remain longer before it goes to seed than any except the Dutch Brown . . . and lastly it is the crispest and most delicious of them all. The Dutch Brown and green Capuchin the soonest . . .

MARJORAM, winter, pot and wild *Origanum*
. . . Will stand a number of years.

MARSH MALLOW, *althaea*, gr. from *Althos* gr. medicament
. . . Transplanted into pots or elsewhere . . .

MINT, *Mentha* from *mens,* the mind, because it strengthens the mind
. . . Roots or cuttings . . . six inches asunder.

MELON, from *Maelon,* Apple, because of its fragrancy
. . . The green fleshed Melon and the netted wrought Melon . . . I have found very delicious in this country. There is a rough, knotty Melon called the Diarbekr . . . reckoned the most exquisite of all melons, which have been brought to great perfection here . . . The Portugal Melon has been called by the name of King Charles' Melon because he used to carry one in his pocket . . . The Cantaleupe originally came from Armenia . . . agrees with all stomach and palates. The Zatta Melon is greatly esteemed in Italy . . . Melons should never grow near one another if of different sorts . . . or by any means near Gourds, Cucumbers etc. because the farina of one will impregnate the other, spoil the relish of the fruit . . . The culture . . . is the same with cucumbers . . .

MILLET, from *Mille,* a thousand, from the multitude of seed it bears
. . . Four sorts, white, yellow, black and the Sorgo or Guinea Corn. It originally came from the western countries and is much esteemed in making puddings . . . The seed is good for poultry. The black sort, so called from its black seeds, is of no use or value.

MULLEIN, *Verbascum*
[Randolph gives only planting instructions. Of Miller's thirteen sorts the first is medicinal, "the Great White Mullein, Hig Taper, or Cow's-lung-wort."]

MUGWORT . . . *Artemisia,* wife of Mausolus, king of Caria who first brought it into use; for Parthenis, as it was before called, because supposed that a virgin goddess gave name to it; or Artemis gr. Diana because good for the disorders of women.
[Randolph says that the Moxa, used in treating gout, is the downy substance under the leaf of the common variety.]

ONION, *Cepa*
. . . Three sorts for winter use; the Strasbourg, the red Spanish onion, and the White Spanish Onion . . . Sorts which suit the spring and summer . . . the Scallion or Escallion . . . Cives the young Onion . . . The Welsh Onion . . . the Ciboule.

GARLICK . . . *Allium*
[Here has long directions for planting.]

PARSLEY, vide Celery

PARSNIPS, *Pastinaca sativa*
[Randolph gives us only Miller's directions for sowing.]

PEAS, *Pisum sativum*
. . . There are several sorts of peas . . . which have different properties, some being early and others late . . . There are the Charlton Hotspur,

Reading Hotspur and Master Hotspur . . . very little differing from one another . . . earliest and reckoned preferable in flavour . . . There are likewise the rouncivals, the Spanish marotto Peas, and the marrowfat or Dutch Admiral . . . These are of a later sort. There is a pea which came from Holland with an esculent husk . . . The Ormonds are the Hotspur . . . Pease may be preserved as kidney beans are by laying them in different layers of salt, in their pods, and being kept quite close.

POTATOES, *Solanum*
. . . Potatoes seems only a corruption of the Indian Patatas, it coming originally from America in 1623. There are more raised near London than any other part of Europe . . . generally propagated by the roots, small potatoes or offsets entire . . . Others cut the large ones in pieces observing to plant what they call the eye . . . Miller thinks the best method is to plant the fairest roots . . . in rows . . . a light sandy loam . . . The Irish method . . . to lay them on the sward and cover then six inches with mold and so hill them up as they grow . . . Let them be planted in any manner you think proper.

PEPPER, *Capsicum*
. . . Should be gathered before the pods grow hard for pickles.

RADISH, *Raphanus sativus*
. . . There are radishes known in this country by the name of Scarlet or Salmon, London short-topped, etc., but Miller says, no more than little varieties of the common sort arising from culture.

RASPBERRY, *Rubus,* being red
. . . Two sorts only that are propagated for the sake of their fruit, the white and red . . . by layers or suckers . . .

ROSEMARY, *Rosemarinus,* Sea-dew
. . . Delights in a poor gravelly soil . . .

RUE, *Ruta,* from *Ruo* gr. to preserve viz. health
. . . Not good for edging . . . Made use of only for medicinal purposes.

SPINACH, *Spinacia*
. . . A male and female plant . . . If the males are pulled up, the seed will not be worth anything . . . It delights in the best soil.

STRAWBERRY, *Fragaria,* from its aromatic scent
. . . Three sorts chiefly propagated, the wood, the scarlet or Virginian, and the hautboy . . . All strawberries should be at least a foot distant, but I recommend two feet . . . They ought to be planted in beds with alleys two feet wide . . . The scarlet strawberry will come a fortnight sooner than any other. The Chili strawberry will grow to the size of a hen's egg. The best dung if any, is that of cows, sheep and pigeons . . .

SAGE, *Salvia, salus vitae*
. . . Fifteen sorts, but the common or green and the red are principally cultivated. The broad-leaved sage is preferable for tea.

SALSIFY, or Goat's beard, *Tragopogon*
   [Miller says the third of his six sorts of Tragopogon is Salsify . . . The roots are dressed in different ways and served up to the table. Of late years there are some people who cultivate it for the stalks . . . like asparagus . . .]

TANSY, *Tanacetum*
   . . . The paths round the bed should be often dug in order to keep the roots within bounds.

THYME, *Thymus*
   . . . Impoverishes the ground much for nothing will succeed where thyme has grown the preceding year.

TURNEP, *Rapa*
   . . . White and purple rooted turnep . . . a great improvement to barren land . . . Of late years the turneps have been sown in fields for cattle, and yet it was practiced by the ancients . . . Recommends sowing Rape for cattle . . . The proper method of sowing Turneps in the field is with the drill plough . . . Lord Townshend sowed an acre in drills and worked it with a plough and another acre in broadcast and hoed by hand, and the Turneps sown in drills yielded a ton and a half in weight more . . . Sow a little soot along the drills which will keep the fly off . . .

Miller has another helpful hint it is strange Randolph, did not pick up — tobacco dust on the young shoots has been found as "serviceable as soot against the fly." Randolph ends his little book with a gardener's "work calendar," which we include at the end of this chapter.

Sir Peyton Skipwith of Prestwould in Mecklenburg County, Virginia, whose wife was the great recording gardener of flowers, grew many vegetables in his long life of gardening, all represented now on a scrap of paper or two and his order from Minton Collins of Richmond, in 1793, whose advertisements we were fortunate to turn up elsewhere.

For peas Sir Peyton ordered: early Charlton, Frame, Nonpareil, Golden Hotspur and Marrowfat. His beans are: Mazagan, Windsor, Long Podded. Cabbages are many: early Sugar, early Batt, green curled Savoy, yellow curled Savoy, red Dutch, Madeira, Drumhead, early York, large Winter, and Crouder. He also has cauliflower and coleworths but without special names. His onions are Portugal, red Spanish and white Spanish. Turnips are listed by color: yellow, green and red, and there is one called William Row. He grows two kinds of broccoli, early purple and white; two kinds of spinach; three kinds of cucumbers; short, long and prickly; celery, celeriac and artichokes.

He buys his seed in large quantities, by the quart, as in "6 quarts Marrowfat pease," or by weight, as "4 oz. Portugal onion." And he sows them all in individual beds: "2 beds red Dutch cabbage," "4 beds coleworts," with each bed carefully numbered on a plan. There is one exception, he "promiscuously scattered" onion, radish and lettuce in "all the other beds" in what was a popular method of space-saving, some vegetables being ready earlier than the others, which then had room to develop.

Because Virginia gardeners have left us the best records of what vegetables they grew, we must not assume that New England was still wrapped in the seventeenth century and growing "skirrets." An enterprising seed merchant of Salem, Massachusetts, advertised in the Essex *Gazette* of April, 1775, a splendid list of seeds just imported in the *Venus* from London. There are ten sorts of peas, both double and single parsley, cucumbers, turnips, four sorts of onions, "best swelling parsnip," four radishes, "true tennisball lettuce" as well as three other sorts — coss, marble and head, "upright celery" as well as "solid celery," three carrots — lemon, orange and purple, some beets, several beans and the usual cabbages. At the end he includes double pot marigold, sweet marjoram, summer and winter savory and thyme.

For the list of Washington's vegetables, I gratefully present the work already done by the Mount Vernon authorities. From Washington's diaries and his papers, they have collected every reference to every growing plant and arranged them all in both alphabetical and chronological order. While Washington was a great fancier of trees and shrubs and an expert in the field crops of the day, hemp, indigo, "spelts" (the grain that is easily husked for domestic use), lucerne, field turnips, carrots, peas and all the grasses for fodder, his listing of the vegetables for his kitchen is modest.

Artichokes . . . asparagus . . . kidney, lima and homony beans . . . beets . . . brocoli . . . burnet . . . cabbage . . . cale or cole . . . carrots . . . celery . . . chicory . . . colley flower . . . corn . . . horse radish . . . leeks . . . lettuce . . . mangel-wurzel . . . marjoram . . . mint . . . onions . . . parsley . . . parsnips . . . peas, Madzays, (Italian) field, black-eyed . . . Pepper, cayan . . . potatoes . . . pumpkin . . . radishes . . . rhubarb . . . savory . . . Savoy colley . . . spinach . . . strawberries . . . turnips . . . water melon.

One suspects that, as in the case with flowers, varieties and other sorts of vegetables may have been grown without his recording it. After all, why would a root of the "scarcity plant" be sent to Martha Washington and the donor thanked for her by her husband, unless she was known to be an interested home gardener?

Jefferson's vegetable list would seem at one time or other to include every available vegetable of his time, either ordered by him, regularly grown by him, sent home by him from abroad or given to him by friends and admirers. He began as a very young man to list what he sowed, when it came up and what was in bloom or "brought to table," using familiar names. In 1774 when he had a new neighbor, an Italian, Mazzei, from whom much was expected in grape-growing and silk manufacture, Jefferson began sowing vegetables under Italian names. Later he was to insist upon botanical names whenever possible, and sometimes did not use familiar names at all. When he was in France in 1784 he sent seeds home with French descriptions attached. And often he described seeds by the name of the places from which they came or where they were best grown. There are names copied from his gardeners who had saved seeds and labeled them for him, and also names denoting the donors. Obviously there must be duplications and overlays.

For Jefferson's vegetables with his own wording, herbs included, we are totally indebted to the magnificent piece of research done by Edwin Morris Betts in 1944 in editing all Thomas Jefferson's gardening records in his *Garden Book* and in his letters and papers relating to his garden at Monticello.

Before we give the list in its entirety, as nearly as we are able to judge its duplications, it may make it more interesting to identify some of the snags before we come to them. Some of the vegetables that were popular then are no longer much grown, like salsify and skirrets. Rape is turnips grown for their seed, which was crushed to make an oil or cakes fed to cattle. Orach is *Atriplex hortensis,* used like spinach. Tomatoes appear in the list, but were not actually grown by Jefferson until 1809.

The tomato arrived late in American gardens because of its relationship to the deadly nightshade family, to which the potato also belongs. While it was reputed to be eaten cooked in soups in England and raw in Spain with salad oil and vinegar, Miller's name for it in his 1768 edition, *"Lycopersicon,* Love Apple or Wolf's Peach," was not much of an inducement for cultivation. Under *Lycopersicon* Miller gives seven sorts, the first being "the Wolf's Peach of Galen" used in medicine. The second sort is "the Love Apple, or Apple-bearing Nightshade, commonly called Tomatoes by the Spaniards." It is like the first, he says, but with furrowed fruit, and is the sort the Spaniards and Portuguese put in their soups and sauces and eat like cucumbers with oil and vinegar. The seventh sort of *Lycopersicon* is the potato "introduced from America about the year 1623." That is Miller's picture of the family.

And beans. Jefferson has recorded planting over forty differently named beans, but it is apparent that a dozen sorts served him well for both table and field, and that the rest were duplicates or perhaps merely odd curiosities.

Beans, Garden and French, with Pease, Garden, Scottish, Sugar, Spotted and Ram's Ciches. From Parkinson's "The Kitchen Garden"

Under the broad bean, *Vicia faba,* the forage bean, come Jefferson's "horse beans," "Mazagan," "Windsor" and "English."

Under *Phaseolus vulgaris* come, I think, all those Italian beans of the mid-seventies and the French beans of the mid-eighties, as well, of course, as those listed as "snaps" or "green" at Monticello.

When friends thank Jefferson for their scarlet flowering bean and say their caracalla beans are doing well, we can tell that the first is an ornamental bean grown by Jefferson under four or five similar names, and the second is probably one of those beans given Jefferson by the Italian friend Mazzei, and like the others called Italian, Roman, Tuscan and even "Mazzei's."

Typically, under cabbage, Jefferson grows all the usual kinds: Battersea, Sugarloaf, York and Winter, which we have seen in the books and for sale, and then a good many others described by the use, like "cattle"; or by their looks, like "curled," "puckered," "red," "purple"; or from their provenance, like "Neapolitan," "Milan," "Roman," "Scotch," "Spanish," "French" and "Aberdeen." And a last category is those described by the donors' names.

Peas are, of course, legion, from the old favorites like the Charlton and Rouncival, Dutch Admiral and Spanish Morotto, to more Mazzei's and other donors' names, and various descriptive names like bush, bunch, cluster, long pod soup, hog and cow. Pearl and Nonesuch are the same. Garavance is the Spanish "Ciche" or "Ram's Ciches" (in Parkinson, *Cicer arietinum*), now called chickpea. Jefferson has it under Garavance and chick. And there are also more "early," "earliest of all," "forward" and "forwardest."

Borecole is a name for a loose-leaved cabbage . . . Capsicum was our cayenne pepper or something very like it . . . Cardoons are a sort of thistle, eaten like artichokes . . . Eschallots are shallots . . . Finnochia is a kind of giant fennel, growing wild in Italy and Spain . . . Orach was eaten like spinach although it looks like basil . . . Rocambole was a name for a sort of perennial onion that has garlic-tasting bulbets at the top of a long stalk, which does not die when they are harvested . . . Salsify is the "oyster plant," whose roots still please country palates today . . . Savoys are a sort of cabbage . . . Scorzonera is viper's grass, and must have been a scurvy remedy, coming up early in the spring . . . Skirrets have a skinny carrot root . . . Smallage is a sort of parsley.

To see the range of the vegetables and herbs grown at Monticello, we give a running list, with occasional comments in brackets, and in parentheses, when it is possible giving the varieties Jefferson noted.

Angelica . . . artichokes . . . asparagus . . . balm . . . basil . . . beans [over forty names] . . . beets (red, scarlet, white) . . . broccoli . . . cabbage [over thirty names] . . . caper . . . capsicum . . . carrots (early, large, orange, yellow) . . . cauliflower (Dutch, English) . . . celery (red, solid) . . . chickpeas . . . chicory . . . chives . . . cole . . . colewort . . . collards . . . corn [fifteen sorts, including "guinea," which is sorghum, introduced with the slaves] . . . corn salad . . . cress (English, garden, Italian, mountain, upland) . . . cucumber (early, forward, frame, green serpentine) . . . cymling (soft, warted). [This is *cucurbita verrucosa,* says Jefferson. It tastes like chicory roots.] . . . eggplant . . . endive (broad-leaved, smooth, winter, wild or succory) . . . Jerusalem artichoke . . . gherkin . . . gourd (long, orange) . . . horse radish. . . hyssop . . . kale [or borecole] . . . lavender . . . leeks . . . lentils . . . lettuce [fifteen names, including Dutch brown, cos, cabbage, ice and tennis-ball] . . . maize [name used in writing to foreigners; Indian corn at home] . . . mangel-wurzel . . . melons (cantaloupe, citron, musk, Persian, pineapple, green Venice, water) . . . mint . . . mustard (white, red) . . . nasturtium . . . okra . . . onions (hanging, Madeira, Spanish, white). [Perhaps "hanging" refers to the *allium,* called "rocambole," with bulbets at the top of the stalks, a sort of perennial onion.] . . . orach . . . oyster plant . . . parsley . . . pease [over fifty different names with many overlays like chick and Garavance, Dutch Admiral and Marrowfat, Pearl and Nonesuch, as well as the familiar names] . . . peendars [peanuts]. [Jefferson tried a small crop in the garden.] . . . pepper, cayenne . . . Pepper grass [*Lepidium sativum*] . . . pimpernell [Salvashella in Italian, so we know who gave it to Jefferson.] . . . potatoes (Indian, Irish, long, round, seed and sweet) . . . potato pumpkin . . . pumpkin . . . pumpion [Pumpion or pompion was the early name for pumpkins.] . . . white pumpkins [called "Zucche blanche" — our zucchini squash?] . . . radish (black, common, English scarlet, salmon, scarlet, summer, violet, white) . . . rape . . . rhubarb, esculent [Jefferson means not the medicinal kind.] . . . rosemary . . . rue . . . sage . . . salsify . . . savory . . . scallion . . . scarcity root [See also mangel-wurzel.] . . . sea kale [See cole and kale.] . . . shallots . . . sorrel . . . spinach (smooth, summer, winter) . . . succory . . . tansey . . . tarragon . . . thyme . . . tomatoes [after 1809] . . . turnip (early, early Dutch, English forward, Frasers' new, Hanover, long French, lopped, rose, summer, Swedish)

While listing even the most banal names may seem tedious, remember the old lady who objected to omitting any of the verses when singing hymns, since, if the poor man took the trouble to write them, the least we can do is sing them. The value of Jefferson's lists is that they indicate the wide range of his tastes, the willingness to grow anything that might prove of benefit to his fellows and the patience of his meticulous recordings. And it gives us the full scope of the American eighteenth-century vegetable garden.

Two garden calendars compared will sum up the accounts of vegetable-growing in the eighteenth century along the Atlantic seaboard. The one by "A Citizen of Virginia" is from the publication of our friend Randolph, who rather confusingly includes the part of the month — "latter end," "middle" and so on — with the vegetables. The other, from Carolina, is what has long been reputed to be the "first horticultural book published in America," written by Martha Logan of Charleston, South Carolina, friend to John Bartram. It has been referred to so often and so proudly that its size, if not its importance, has become greatly overestimated. Perhaps the fact that it was "Done by a lady" has made it burgeon in the minds of horticultural historians. One can wonder if any of them ever really saw it, for at the end of a long search, the only copy I have found turns out to fill both sides of two pages in *Tobler's South Carolina Almanack* of 1756. In the files in the New York Public Library it is described as the "earliest American treatise on the subject known to be extant."

Quite apart from her calendar, Martha Logan was a remarkable woman and deserves our admiration for her contributions to the eighteenth-century gardening world. Daughter of a proprietary governor of South Carolina, Robert Daniel, she was born in 1702 and had a long life of managing a plantation about ten miles from Charleston while boarding and teaching children in her home, selling garden seeds and plants and making a name for herself among American gardeners. We have seen her sending seeds to John Bartram, and filling Collinson with wistful envy. Her only published work, curiously enough, is entirely for the kitchen garden, although we know she excelled in the cultivation of all sorts of flowers.

VIRGINIA
From a treatice on gardening by a Citizen of Virginia

January
Prepare hot-beds for Cucumbers: as little as can be done this month in a garden; I would advise the preparing of your dung; and carrying it to your beds, that it may be ready to spread on in February.

SOUTH CAROLINA
Directions for Managing a Kitchen Garden every month of the year Done by a Lady

January
Plant peas and Beans: Sow Spinage for Use and for Seed: that which is preserved for Seed must never be cut: a small Quantity will yield plentifully in rich ground. Sow Cabbage for Summer Use, when they are fit transplant them into rich Earth. Sow Parsley. Transplant Artichokes into very rich mellow Ground and they will bear in the Fall. This month all kinds of Fruit-Trees may be Transplanted.

February

Sow Asparagus, make your beds and fork up the old ones, sow Leaf Cabbages: latter end transplant Cauliflowers, sow Carrots, and transplant for seed; prick out endive for seed, sow Lettuce, Melons in hot-beds, sow Parsnips, take up the old roots and prick out for seed, sow Peas and prick them into your hot-beds, sow Radishes twice, plant Strawberries, plant out Turneps for seed, spade deep and make it fine, plant Beans.

February

Sow Celery, Cucumbers, Melons, Kidney-Beans, Spinage, Asparagus, Radish, Parsley, Lettice, to be transplanted in shady Places: they must be moved young and watered every Morning: Pond or Rain Water is the best. If the season does not prove too wet, this Month is best for planting all Sorts of Trees, except the Fig, which should not be moved 'til March, when the suckers may be taken from the Roots of old Trees. The Fig will not bear pruning. The middle of this Month is the best for Grafting in the Cleft. If Fruit-Trees have not been pruned last Month, they must not be delayed longer. About the Middle of this Month, sow Spinage, Radish, Parsley and Lettice for the last time. Plant Dwarf and Hotspur Pease. Sow Onions, Carrots and Parsnips; and plant out Carrots, Parsnips, Cabbages and Onions, for Seed the next Year. Plant Hops, Strawberries, and all kinds of aromatic Herbs

March

Slip your Artichokes, if fit, plant Kidney Beans, Cabbages, Celery, Parsley, Cucumbers, Currants, Chamomile, Celandine, Nasturtium, Featherfew, Fennel, Ivy, Horse Radish, Hyssop, Lavender, Lettuce, Radishes twice, Marjoram, Marsh Mallow, Mint, Melons, Millet, Mugwort, Onions, and for seed, Peas twice, Potatoes, Raspberry, Rosemary, Rue, Spinach, Tansy, Thyme, Turneps. You may begin to mow your grass walks, and continue so to do every morning, and roll them; turf this month; plant Box.

March

Whatever was neglected last Month, may be done in this, with good Success, if it is not too dry; if it be, you must water more frequently. Now plant Rounceval Pease and all manner of Kidney Beans.

April

If Artichokes were not slipped last month, do it this, plant bushel and garden Beans, sow Cabbages the twelfth, sow Cauliflowers, Celery, Cresses, Nasturtium, Lettuce, Pease, Radishes twice, Sage will grow in this or any other month; Turneps, sow Salsify early Pepper; turf this month.

April

Continue to plant aromatic Herbs, Rosemary, Thyme, Lavender etc. and be careful to weed and water what was formerly planted. Lettice, Spinage and all kinds of Salading may be planted to use all the Summer but they must be frequently watered and shaded from the Sun.

May

Latter end sow Brocoli, Celery, Cucumbers for pickles, Endive, Featherfew, Hyssop, cuttings of Marsh Mallow, Melons, Peas, sow Radishes twice, Kidney Beans, turf this month.

June

Cabbages should be sown, sow Radishes twice, transplant Cabbages, prick out Cauliflowers, prick out Brocoli, draw up by roots all your weeds.

July

Transplant Brocoli, sow Cabbages, Coleworts, transplant Cauliflowers to stand, Endive, gather Millet seed, take up Onions, sow Radishes twice, sow Turneps, plant Kidney-Beans to preserve.

August

Sow Cabbages, latter end, Carrots, get your Cucumber seed, sow Cresses, prick out Endive, early sow Lettice, Mullein, gather Onion seed, plant Garlick, get Parsnep seed; twelfth, sow Peas for the fall, sow Radishes; middle, sow Spinach, though some say not until after the twentieth, sow Turneps.

September

Sow Cabbages tenth, sow Cauliflowers, plant cuttings of Currants, Clary, Comfrey, plant cuttings of Gooseberries, sow Radishes, plant layers of suckers of Raspberries, Rosemary, plant out Strawberries, string your Strawberries, and dress your beds, plant Tansy.

May

This month is chiefly for weeding and watering: Nothing sown or planted does well.

June

Clip Evergreens, and Herbs for drying, Thyme, Sage, Carduus, Rosemary, Lavender, etc. Sow Carrots, Parsnips and Cabbage. If the Weather is dry and hot the Ground must be well watered, after being dug deep and made mellow. Straw or Stable Litter well wetted and laid pretty thick upon the Beds where Seeds are sown, in the Heat of the Day, and taken off at Night is a good expedient to forward the Growth.

July

What was done last Month may also be done this. Continue to water, in the evening only. The latter end of this Month sow Pease for the Fall. Water such things as are going to seed, it being very needful to preserve good Seed. Turnips and Onions may be sown; Leeks, scallions and all of this Tribe planted.

August

Sow Turneps and another crop of Hotspur or Dwarf Pease. Still Continue to weed and water as before.

September

Showers of Rain will be frequent. Now prepare the ground for the following Seeds viz. Spinage, Dutch brown Lettice, Endive, and other crop of Pease and Beans. Now you may inoculate with Buds.

October

Latter end cut down your Asparagus, and cover your beds with dung, plant Beans for spring, sow Cabbages twentieth; transplant Cauliflowers, plant Horse Radish, prick Lettice into boxes, sow Peas for the hot-bed, Radishes; turf this month.

October

Dress your Artichokes, take all suckers from the Roots, leave no more than three in a Hill, put fresh Dung, well rotted, to the Roots; a Mixture of Dung thoroughly rotted, with what the Gardeners call untry'd Earth, is much the best. Untry'd Earth is rich and mellow, taken about half a Foot beneath the Surface of good new Land; this I would advise in Cases where Manure is wanting; indeed it is much better than any other and will amply reward the Labour; plant the suckers of Artichokes in Holes about a Foot square and two Feet deep, filled with the aforesaid Earth. Continue to inoculate. Sow large crops of Windsor and Garden Beans, Lettice, Radish, Endive. Set out Celery (for blanching) that was grown in the Spring before. Trim and dress your asparagus beds in the following Manner, the beginning of the month cut down the Haulm or Stalks, lay them over the bed and burn them; then dig the Earth about the Roots and make the Bed level; then cover about three Fingers deep with rotted Stable Dung and untry'd Earth. This may likewise be done the Beginning of November as the present Month.

November

Take up your Cabbages, sow Cabbages, take up your Cauliflowers, such as are flowered, and house them, take up your Carrots, trench all your vacant land, prune your trees and vines, plant out everything of the tree or shrub kind, that has a root to it; if any thing is done to your Artichokes, this is a good month; plant Box; turf early.

November

Earth up Celery and tie up Endive for blanching. Continue to sow Seeds, as Parsley, Spinage, Radish, and Lettice of all kinds. The latter end of this Month begin to prune Fruit-Trees, especially Vines which may now be done safely.

December

Cover your Endive with brush, cover Celery, and every thing else that needs shelter; if the weather will admit, turn

December

The Month being chiefly for the Management of the Orchard, plant and prune all manner of Fruit Trees and

December

over the ground that is trenched, in order to mellow and pulverize it. Whatever will prevent delay, and enable you to begin spading in February, should be done this month.

December

the like, and prepare Ground for transplanting in the Spring.

Furber's Fruits for the Month of September

9 Fruits

THE CELEBRATION of native American fruits began with the lyric and glowing accounts by the first explorers. Settlers and hopefully botanical voyagers added to the early discoveries. And "curious" gardeners of the seventeenth and eighteenth centuries secured the legend of excellence. We have many lists of fruits found growing by those who saw their futures made easier by the horticultural wealth available. We can follow the use made of native fruits and the attempts to grow Old World fruits in the New World. It is when we come forward, even if ever so little, into accounts of the nineteenth and twentieth centuries that we are astounded by the success of the early orchardists in producing fruits, now considered wholly American, of exceptional quality.

No wonder early observers waxed lyrical. The ground, the woods, the fields, the riverbanks were full of edible fruit. Vines loaded with grapes hung from the trees and ran on the ground. "Indian" peaches, *Prunus persica,* broke the trees and so covered the ground with fruit that walking became slippery until wild pigs would devour the harvest. There was a variety of small fruits to be preserved in sugar or dried. Plums and cherries abounded, all edible although not quite what the settlers hoped to make of them in time.

Wherever the settlers had come from in the Old World, they had seen wild fruits brought into gardens and coddled into bearing better fruit than they had produced in the wild. We have William Wood's seventeenth-century hopeful comment on the chokecherries, which "English ordering" might bring to be a good cherry, though they were then "as wild as the Indians." Still, they and the peaches made good brandies.

And the grapes! Surely much could be hoped from them when they had been moved and pruned and fed. All that seemed required after that was vintners, so vintners were sent for. That then all *they* required was their own sorts of wine grapes did not discourage anyone. Wine grapes were brought over. Hope for good wines ran high for a century.

And mulberry trees, growing in the forests in great plenty. Surely a good silk trade was in sight? Silks and wines! All that was needed was industry.

This excited hopefulness lasted throughout the eighteenth century in spite of repeated failures to grow European grapes well and to raise silkworms in quantity. It was not until the end of the century that even Washington and Jefferson began to feel that, as with olives and figs, pomegranates and tea, there were some Old World amenities that could not successfully be duplicated in the New.

Careful husbandmen had always made it a practice to "move in" the native fruits. Some writers have assumed that any housewife who could go out and pick berries in season in the wilderness would not consider making room for them near her house and garden, but there must have been many ingenious female souls who reckoned it more convenient to start their own "berry patches" near home than annually to risk bears and briers in the wilds. Even today we see luxuriant growths of black-berries and blackcap raspberries and red raspberries, each kind in its own area, near cellar holes or behind old barns.

Early accounts of small New England villages show us houses in rows on either side of long, wide streets, each house spaced from the next by a garden and an orchard, also fronting on the highway. More grandly, William Penn planned each "plat" in his ideal city to have a house in the middle with space for an orchard and garden on either side. This pattern for survival lasted in American life for over a hundred years, as we see in "requirements" made for settling Ohio lands in 1787–1788. The agents of the Ohio Company fostered a resolution to offer a limited number of one-hundred-acre lots free with the following conditions: within three years the settler must have set out at least fifty apple or pear trees and twenty peach trees; within five years he must have erected a dwelling house at least twenty-four by eighteen feet with eight feet between floors, a cellar ten feet square and six and a half feet deep and a brick or stone chimney. At the end of five years he must have fifteen acres fit for pasture and five acres ready for corn or other grains. With these conditions met, the settler would receive a deed, at the end of five years, to his "Donation lot."

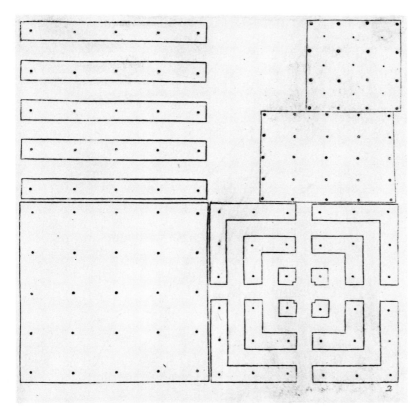

Several plans for laying out an orchard. From William Lawson's *New Orchard and Garden,* 1648. The upper right shows the space-saving quincunx

A cultivated orchard for each family was as much a necessity as a hearth or a roof. Everywhere in the American colonies encouragement was given for private ventures in fruit-growing and fruit 'improvement." Here was a universal American enterprise that did not need slave labor and could eventually profit even the smallest landholder. The rewards for all the clearing and planting, tending and experimenting, were apparent at the end of the century, when imported English and French fruits on their own stocks had so intermingled with plantings of treasured seeds from earlier tastings, munchings and hoardings, that a quantity of "American" fruit sprang up to rival fruits in England and France.

To provide any household the year round with both vegetables and fruit was a basic need. For vegetables, storing underground in cellars, burying in earth and straw, salting and drying were common ways to get them usefully through the winters. Fruit was a different proposition. Except for drying apples in rings behind the kitchen stove, fruit had to be preserved in sugar, or kept ranged on shelves in a dark cellar, frequently inspected. The quality of "keeping" was of first importance, except with the most delicate "dessert" fruits. "Summer" fruits were transient. "Winter" fruits could be kept in storage and, better still, if they were "long keeping," sent abroad to the West Indies and to England.

Fresh fruit for the table was the fancy of the well-to-do, who entertained literally "from soup to nuts" and served their especially cultivated fruit for "dessert," often accompanied by their own nuts. Puddings and pies came after the meat course but the dessert course was devoted to whatever fruit the host had reserved for his guests, to be followed by nuts and wine or, perhaps, combined with them. In any case, fruit was the crowning feature of an elegant dinner. Requirements for a good "dessert" fruit were its flavor, taste, texture and general appearance, qualities insisted upon in a fruit to come to the table to be eaten raw and discussed by rival growers — as connoisseurs felt free to criticize their hosts' wines.

English, French and "low German" settlers, already expert with fruits in their native lands, prudently brought scions of home fruits with them, as well as quantities of seeds. But it was early observed that the results of planting seeds of the most treasured varieties of apples and pears seldom produced the original sort. Grafting was understood and much practiced but chance was the arbiter of the quality of any new apple or pear orchard. And chance served them well. One especially good apple tree would spring up among hundreds, be recognized, popularized and nearly killed by removal of scions. Named for the vicinity in which it was discovered or for its owner, it would remain one of the popular American fruits for many years.

Pears required much the same system: planting as many as possible to get a few good new varieties. There were some outstanding successes, such as the Seckel pear, which was a chance seedling. There were also old favorites preserved by grafting, as, for example, the "oldest pear in the world, the Bon Chrétien" from France, being popularized here as the Bartlett and still reigning supreme.

Stone fruits were more likely to come true, or at least Jefferson thought they were. In 1786 he wrote from Paris of the French fruits and compared them with ours, summing up the case for stone fruits:

Of fruits, the pears and apricots alone are better than ours and we have not the apricot-peche at all . . . The fruits of the peach class do not degenerate from the stone so much as is imagined here. We have so much experience of this in America that tho' we graft all other kinds of fruits, we rarely graft the peach, the nectarine, the apricot or the almond. The tree proceeding from the stone yields a faithful copy of its fruit and the tree is always healthier.

It was a case of every orchardist for himself. He had to become his own authority. The only obtainable recognized expert on fruit-growing, in print, in the early eighteenth century was, oddly enough, our old

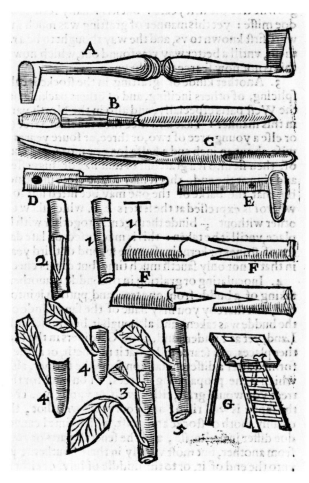

Parkinson's demonstration of the tools for and
methods of grafting. From his *Paradisus*

seventeenth-century friend, John Parkinson, and his *Paradisus in Sole, Paradisus Terrestris.* The whole third part of his book is devoted to "The Orchard" with full instructions on planning and planting. Each fruit is discussed and all the known "sortes" are enumerated. Illustrations accompany the text, beginning with an orchard plan (preferably a quincunx, a layout like the five on a dice) and a page of tools, with instructions on grafting and budding, or "inoculating." He favors dwarfing apples by grafting on the stock of the Paradise apple, which is otherwise not good for much. He recommends budding, or the insertion of the bud of one sort of apple into the bark of another, as better than grafting, or setting scions of one apple onto the root stock of a strong-growing sort. Scions, if carefully packed and stored, would last through a winter or a long voyage.

Parkinson's friendship with John Tradescant and other New World visitors as well as the head gardeners of the Jardin du Roi in Paris, began to pay off even as early as 1629, when this great book on gardening was published. Parkinson mentions several New World fruits and says how they are growing with him or with his friends in London. It must have inspired the settlers with confidence to read how their local blessings were faring in the land they had left.

For eighteenth-century fruits we have another authority available in Philip Miller, whose *Gardener's Dictionary* was known and used in its various editions throughout the country, owned by Jefferson, Washington and the Skipwiths.

As samples of the careful documentation of the sorts of fruits grown or ordered for delivery, here are three modest lists.

The first is the list of fruits grown at Prestwould at the end of the century as recorded by Lady Skipwith and her friends. The fruit records of the Skipwiths give us a fair idea of the popular and proved fruits suitable to be grown for home consumption far from markets, their sources duly noted and dittoed.

Fruit trees of different kinds grafted or planted at Prestwould 16 March, 1792.

Large Mayduke cherry from Prince's Garden; Black Pear and Cherries from Do.; Carnation Cherries, Do.; White Heart Cherrys. Do.; Cluster cherry ripe in May from Mr. Eppes; Quinces from Do.; Green gage plumbs from St. G. Tucker; Cloptons hangfast from Benedict; Esopus Spitzenburg, a very large red apple reckoned the finest eating apple in Am. next to the Newton Pippin. S.G.T.; Doctor Apple. A fine eating apple. S.G.T.; A very fine white clingstone peach S.G.T.; Candia peach, a very large yellow peach; A large clingstone peach; Newington Peach; Newington Nectarines; G. Clingstone Nectarines.

A list of pears noted at Prestwould:

Bengalime pear; a large roughlooking pear but when ripe the finest in the orchard called "Lady Skipwith's favorite;" Bell Pear; Twelve of Mrs. Watkins early sugar pear raised from the scion; only one "Lady Skipwith will find a name for them."

Scattered notes mention "Peach stones buried at Prestwould October; the Bary or Roi pear, the finest pear in the world S.G.T.; Newington Peach; Large Red Roman Nectarines; Large Red Pineapple Peach; White Heart Cherry; Bergamot Pear; Golden Pippin."

We have a memo of the seasons when the Prestwould fruits are "ripe or fit to gather."

May. Duke cherries, and strawberries of different kinds from early in May to the middle of June.

June. Black, white and English raspberries from the beginning of June to the middle of July. Red and Black currants and Morello cherries from the middle of June to the middle of July.

July. Red and white and blue plumbs from the first of July to the first of August.
Lockets Pear, first of July. Hone Pear from the Island about the middle of July. Catherine Pear from the kitchen garden between the middle of July and the first of August.

An end-of-century list of fruit trees imported from England is the list of fruit trees and bushes sent by George Washington's secretary, Tobias Lear, from England to Mount Vernon in 1794 aboard the ship *Peggy*. He writes that they are to be put in at Mount Vernon since he has yet no place of his own, and he states that he can later get scions. In the meantime he wishes George Washington to do the same and to give scions to his friends.

Fruit trees and bushes put on board the ship Peggy.
Capt. Lunt bound to Georgetown

Twenty-four Gooseberries;
 Large round Green Gooseberries;
 4 Larger long red;
 4 Long Iron Coloured;
 4 Fine round White;
 4 Long Smooth black;
 4 Round hairy red.
Twenty-four Currants:
 12 Large red Currants;
 8 Large white;

4 Large black
Six Apples:
   3 Stand Golden Pippin Apples;
   3 Stand Nonpareil
Twelve Pears:
   3 Stand Jorgoriell Pears;
   3 Stand Brown Bury;
   3 Stand Burgemot de Chantery;
   3 Stand Autumn Burgamot
Twelve Plums:
   4 Stand Green Gage plumb;
   4 Stand Orlean;
   4 Stand Seasomma
Twelve Cherries:
   6 Stand Duke Cherries;
   6 Stand Morello
   4 Amber heart
Two Almonds
Three Apricots
   1 Stand Elruge Apricot;
   1 Stand Orange;
   1 Stand Turkey
Three Nectarines
   1 Stand Elruge Nectarine
   1 Stand Newington;
   1 Stand Roman

("Stand" indicates it is to be grown free-standing, not against a wall.)

We have a modest check on what was being grown in New England, that cold but industrious northern neighbor. James Winthrop, librarian and jurist with horticultural interests and pursuits, annotated his copy of Samuel Deane's *New England Farmer or Geological Dictionary,* published in Worcester by Isaiah Thomas in 1790, with careful recordings of when his fruits in Cambridge and Milton, Massachusetts, blossomed, opened leaves and bore ripe fruit. These "Tables" were later published as *Observations of the Progress of Vegetation made at Cambridge, from 1793 to 1796, inclusive, by James Winthrop, Esq., F.A.A. and P.H.S. and of the Agricultural Society.* The fruit trees he grew are recorded in order of blossoming: apple, apricot, currant, cherry, gooseberry, grape, nectarine, peach, pear, plum, quince, raspberry, strawberry. His currants are white, red and black. His fig put out leaves but little else. And he grows both white and black mulberries.

For fruits generally available to American fruit growers of the eighteenth century, there is the 1790 list from the Prince Nurseries in which William Prince in Flushing, Long Island, is offering for sale "inoculated and grafted fruit trees," at one shilling and six pence each, that will bear well "upon the Mountains and highlands of the West Indies," can be shipped overseas and may be called for daily by "persons in New York having a mind for" them.

The Prince sales sheet lists, in all, sixteen English cherries, twenty-six "plumbs," ten apricots, eleven nectarines, thirty-five peaches, thirty-five pears, thirty-one apples, three mulberries, "fig trees," three kinds of currants, "quince trees" (like the figs, unnamed), three gooseberries, four raspberries and four strawberries.

A note of triumph for American fruit growers in the eighteenth century is sounded in a letter from Sir John Menzies in Scotland, who wished to "improve his grounds by mixing such of the American forest trees with the native pines of Great Britain as are likely to agree with the soil and climate." He requested seeds be sent and he also wished for "a small assortment of apples, pears, and peaches, of the best grafted or inoculated kinds, in trees two or three years old."

We shall consider seventeen sorts of fruit, in alphabetical order: apples, apricots, cherries, currants, figs, gooseberries, grapes, mulberries, nectarines, nuts, peaches, pears, plums, pomegranates, quinces, raspberries, strawberries.

APPLES

Since the beginning of printing in English, the apple has been named the symbol for the most desirable of fruits, the prize beyond price. Although apples are actually fruits of the temperate zones, they stood for whatever was the tastiest of Oriental, Biblical, mythical and classical fruits, supreme temptation in the gardens of Eden and the Hesperides, comfort in the Song of Solomon and handy reference for common people — like the apple of one's eye and what keeps the doctor away. While France always fancied pears and plums, Persia had sent peaches and apricots and nectarines, and grapes had been pictured upon Middle Eastern and Egyptian walls since art began, England's fruit had been the apple.

Small wonder, then, that the discovery in the eighteenth century that apples would grow better in the New World than ever they had in the Old, and that all the old sorts would combine and multiply into new sorts, was heralded in the English-speaking world. That new sorts could be fixed by grafting their scions upon others and the results named for their discoverers or places of origin made the fruit-growing world look to the central Atlantic states and New England for what was flourishing in apple culture.

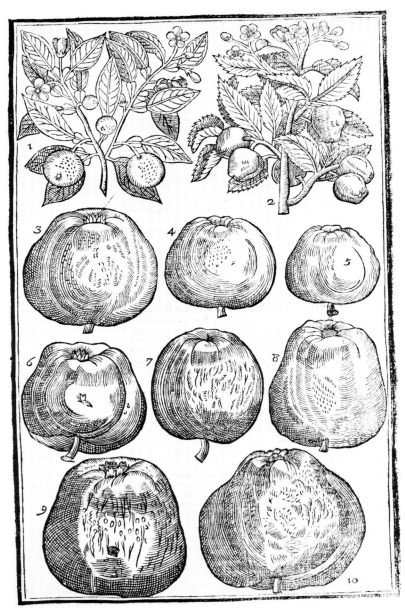

After showing the orange tree, Parkinson illustrates a typical apple tree and then shows the Pomewater, Golden Pippin, Pearmaine, Queen, Genneting, Pound Royal, Kentish Codlin, and an oddity, the Bardfield Quining

It was the good fortune of the newcomers to America that apples grown from seeds and scions brought from England, France and Germany grew swiftly, bore early and multiplied so fast, especially in the regions of southern New England, New York, Pennsylvania and New Jersey, that there was soon a collection of American apples to be sorted out, cultivated separately, increased by grafting and finally introduced as whole new sorts of apples. Sometimes a large orchard of seedling apples in a particularly propitious area would produce as many as three new apples, quite different from each other and much acclaimed. Obviously there were duplications, and the same variety in different places acquired different names.

John Lawson's list of apples growing in Carolina, in his history published in 1709, follows roughly the order of Parkinson's list, as if he may have had that in mind.

The Golden Russet thrives well . . . The Pearmains, of both sorts, are apt to speck and rot on the trees . . . Harvey apple (I cannot tell whether the same as in England) . . . is esteemed very good to make cider of . . . Winter Queening is a durable apple and makes good cider . . . Leathercoat, both apple and tree stand well . . . The Junating is early ripe and soon gone in these warm countries . . . Codlin no better and fairer fruit in the world . . . The Redstreak thrives very well . . . Long-stalk . . . makes good summer cider . . . Lady finger . . .

He comments upon the Pearmain and Codlin that the trees are prone to disease and do not live long and adds, "We beat the first of our codlin cider against reaping our wheat, which is from the tenth of June to the five and twentieth."

The Prince list of apples for sale at their nurseries in 1790 is as follows, with their spelling:

Newton pippins; Aesopus Spitzenberg; Pearmains; Vandevils; Large pippins, weigh a pound or more; Large red and green sweet apple, ripe at Midsummer, weighs a pound or more; Large early apple, two or three weeks earlier than either Junating or bow apple; English codlin; Red streaks; Early bow; Early Junating; Newton Spitzenberg; Jersey greening; Golden pippins; Russettings; Golden rennets; Lady-apple; Non pareil; Yellow bell flowers; Swaar; Rhode-Island greenings; Large white sweeting; Bell flowers; White pippins; Late bow; Seek no farther; Virginia crab; Holland pippin; Quince apple; Everlasting; Newark pippin.

That we know who grew many of these apples, and how and where, attests to the careful records kept by our good and great gardeners.

The first universally recognized New England apple, after Blaxton's Yellow Sweeting, was the Rhode Island Greening, named for the tavern keeper near Newport in whose orchard it originated. The tree finally died from overcutting of scions, but there was an ample supply of offspring and it is still on sale today.

Another centuries-old favorite is the Newton Pippin, sold in London's Covent Garden market well into the nineteenth century. Fancied by Governor Belcher, eighteenth-century governor of Massachusetts and of New Jersey. This was the apple Franklin took to London, which so intrigued Collinson he sent to John Bartram for grafts. Called Albemarle in our south. James Blair of Williamsburg grew it, as did George Mason, Washington and Jefferson.

Aesopus Spitzenburg, an apple that originated with the "Low Dutch on the Hudson," comes into season after the Rhode Island Greening and before the Baldwin, which originated in 1740 and was popular in Boston. Jefferson ordered "Spitzenburg apples" from Prince's and continued to grow them all his life. We have seen it fancied as "a large red apple" by the Skipwiths.

Pearmain was one of the few named varieties of apple cultivated by Henry Wolcott of Connecticut before 1653, and by the Pilgrims. Oblong, soft and mealy, red on the sunny side, it fell into neglect. Jefferson discovered he had some.

Washington grew Vandeviers, a winter apple, native of Delaware. Yellow streaked with red.

Codlins, or English Codlins, were yellow cooking apples, much grafted by Jefferson.

Red Streaks were a very popular cider apple, "revived" by cultivation by English settlers. Washington fancied his Maryland Red Streaks.

Golden Pippins were grown by the Skipwiths and Washington.

Russettings or Leathercoats were grown by Jefferson and Washington. The Roxbury Russet was originated near Boston, was taken to Connecticut and from there to Ohio by Israel Putnam.

Jefferson had, besides the well-known apples, a great number of others named after the friends or places they derived from, like his Taliaferro apple, for cider. The Doctor apple was named for Dr. Witt, Collinson's Philadelphia friend. Jefferson's Detroit apple was the White Belle Fleur and his Pumbray was Pomme Grise, both French apples that had come almost full circle to the East Coast after being brought to the St. Lawrence by the French.

APRICOTS

The apricot was a delicate and ornamental fruit tempting to the fruit collectors of the eighteenth century in American gardens. Not easily grown in the north except by James Winthrop near Boston, it was popular in the south, where gardeners like Washington and Jefferson made much of it. Directions were always given to crack the stone before planting. In Carolina John Lawson had seen "the biggest Apricock-tree I ever saw" in 1709. In 1785 Washington had apricot trees bordering his "grass plats" and moved an apricot, from the front lawn, that was twenty-one inches in circumference. In March, 1786, he noted the apricot trees beginning to blossom "and the grass to show its verdure."

Jefferson records planting many apricots, always breaking the stone first, before 1791, when he ordered from the Prince list "four large Earlys." In 1807 Jefferson planted Moor Park apricots. Moor Park was the English seat of Sir William Temple with a famous fruit orchard.

CHERRIES

Cherries had ranked high among favorite fruits in English gardens, and the excitement of finding a country "stored" with wild cherries was high until the cherries were put to the test. The initial disappointment was almost total. William Wood had warned of the wild chokecherry "furring" the throat and being "as wild as the Indians." Wines and preserves were made but it was obvious garden cherries from England were needed. The only form in which American cherries surpassed all others was the use by cabinetmakers of the very large *Prunus serotina* L., whose wood looks like mahogany when made up and waxed. It was from this cherry, "a lofty forest tree," according to Downing, that "cherry bounce" was made. "A favourite liqueur in many parts of the country," it was concocted by "putting the fruit along with sugar in a demijohn or cask of the best old rum."

John Lawson had the "common red and black cherry," given to suckering at a distance from the tree . . . ripe a month sooner than in Virginia.

Gardeners were pleased to find cherries grown against walls in England could survive here as standard trees. Those with carefully designed kitchen gardens, like Washington, liked to espalier them against a wall as well as to line them up in orchards.

By mid-nineteenth century our cherries were divided into four classes: Heart, of which the Mazzard and Black Heart are types; Bigarreau, from the French word meaning spotted, but now signifying hard sweet cherries; Duke, good for both dessert and cooking; Morello, said to be a cross between sour and sweet, with dark juice like the mulberry.

Washington, Jefferson and the Skipwiths were all partial to May Dukes, Carnations, Black Hearts, White Hearts and Morellos. George Mason had a double avenue of Morello cherry trees.

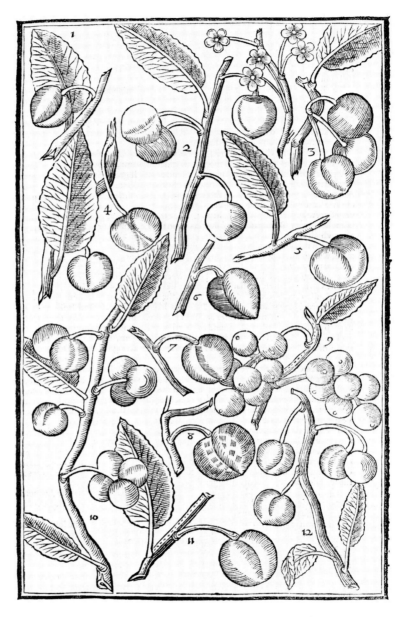

Parkinson's cherries are: May, Flanders, White, Great-leafed, Luke
Wards, Naples, Heart, Spotted, Wild Cluster, Flanders Cluster, Arch-
duke's (lower center) and Dwarf

CURRANTS

Miller lists four species: the common sour currant, from northern Europe but long cultivated and improved; the sweet Alpine currant, small and not cultivated; the common black currant, naturally from Sweden and other northern countries, from which Rob is made, greatly esteemed for sore throats; and the American black currant, sent to Mr. Peter Collinson from Pennsylvania "several years past . . . and dispersed to most parts of England . . . only kept by way of curiosity . . ." Miller says that of these sorts the red and white currants, developed from the common sort, are esteemed at table and for allaying fevers.

Prince's list is very brief: Large red currants; large black currants; large white currants.

In 1770 Jefferson listed as "work to be done at Monticello . . . Plant raspberries, gooseberries, strawberries and currants." In 1782 he notes that a quart of currant juice "makes 2 blue teacups of jelly, 1 quart of juice to 4 of purée." In 1794 he lists as "objects for the garden this year" his usual association of "strawberries, gooseberries, currants . . ." In 1798 he is informed by Martha that "Monticello shines with a transcendent luxury of vegetation . . ." and that of "strawberries, raspberries, currants, etc., there will be more than common."

Both John Custis and Sir William Johnson had white currants.

Tobias Lear ordered red, white and black for Mount Vernon.

FIGS

The Prince 1790 list offers "Fig Trees 2s each."

William Hamilton, Esq., is credited with bringing figs to this country, about 1790, to the Woodlands, near Philadelphia, where he collected both indigenous and exotic plants and trees into a spectacularly landscaped estate and nursery. Hamilton was a friend to, and customer of, the most accomplished growers of his time, but to attribute the introduction of the fig to him in 1790 is gilding an already much gilded lily. The Princes must have had figs growing for some time before they offered trees for sale. Jefferson planted a row of figs at Monticello in 1769. In 1787 he wrote from Paris to his friend William Drayton, President of the Society of Agriculture in Charleston, that the fig was so well known in America, like the mulberry, that "nothing need be said."

GOOSEBERRIES

Gooseberries are almost the earliest of Jefferson's fruit fancies. In 1767 he planted twelve cuttings of gooseberries, with his almonds and "muscle plumbs." Jefferson would seem to have cultivated exclusively and continually the English green gooseberry, sold by Prince in 1790 as "Green gooseberry, 9d each." Prince offers only two other kinds, the "Great Amber" and the "Large Yellow Oval."

Tobias Lear ordered some for Mount Vernon.

GRAPES

Considering the enthusiasm for wild grapes greeting the early settlers, the accounts of their efforts to domesticate them and start a wine industry, and the attempts to introduce the European wine grape and experienced wine growers and makers, the Prince list of grapes for sale in 1790 seems oddly modest. Especially when entered, as in our copy, under "Quince Trees." In fairness, however, we must state that at this very time the Prince family, fathers and sons, were engaged in trying to make a success of grape culture, culminating in 1830 with William Prince's book, *Treatise on the Vine.*

It was not until the nineteenth century that the lines became clear and American grapes came into their own for both wine and table. Horticultural historians have expressed surprise at the long struggle to grow the European grape while little effort was put into cultivating the native sorts, a sad insult when we remember the seventeenth-century governmental coercion of the settlers in Virginia to grow vines to make wine. And it has been superciliously surmised that the interest in grapes was for wine in Europe and for the table in America. The situation is explained by the nature of the grapes. No one tried to eat wine grapes, but everyone tried to make any stray American native grape into wine.

By mid-eighteenth century, government help was invited, even begged for.

A letter from Lord Stirling in America in 1763 to Lord Shelburne in England makes this plea. Lord Stirling was a member of the Provincial Council of New Jersey and had an estate at Basking Ridge. Governor Franklin, Benjamin Franklin's illegitimate son, William, who was later to disappoint his father and remain loyal, risking no wealth and position to join his father's cause, was also keenly interested in agriculture. With Governor Belcher, lately come from Massachusetts, and Charles Read, distinguished citizen and patriot who left copious notes on his farming practices, they made an energetic group of agricultural experimentors in the rich, rolling lands of the New Jersey countryside.

Stirling has reported on the growing of hemp and is adding a request for assistance with grape culture:

The making of wine, also, is worth the attention of the Government. Without its aid, the cultivation of the vine will be very slow; for of all the variety of vines in Europe, we do not yet know which of them will suit this climate; and until that is ascertained by experiment, our people will not plant vineyards — few of us are able, and a much less number willing, to make the experiment. I have lately imported about twenty different sorts, and have planted two vineyards, one in the Province [New York] and one in New Jersey; but I find the experiments tedious, expensive, and uncertain; for after eight or ten years' cultivation, I shall perhaps be obliged to reject nine tenths of them as unfit for the climate, and then begin new vineyards from the remainder. But, however, tedious, I am determined to go through with it. Yet I could wish to be assisted in it. I would then try it to a greater extent, and would the sooner be able to bring the cultivation of grape into general use.

Both Washington and Jefferson began as enthusiastic planters of wild grapes, growing them from seeds or cuttings. Later Washington abandoned his vineyard near the vegetable garden, but Jefferson continued undaunted and planted all sorts of foreign grapes, some from France, some even from the Cape of Good Hope. In 1810 he planted on the eleven uppermost terraces of his vineyard one hundred and sixty-five cuttings of a native grape grown by Major Adlum of Maryland from a grape discovered by the gardener of William Penn. Full circle, indeed. Jefferson had tasted the wine from it and declared it resembled "Comartin Burgundy."

MULBERRIES

The earliest settlers in the seventeenth century, cheered by the sight of wild mulberry trees, had foreseen a flourishing silk industry, but it was not until the eighteenth century that organized attempts were made to plant the mulberry most suitable for silkworm cultivation. In the seventeenth century King James I, hopeful of raising silkworms in England and opposed to the raising of tobacco anywhere, had not succeeded in either direction. In fact, his diverse causes were confounded by the offer of Sir William Berkeley, when governor of Virginia, to give a "Reward of fifty Pounds of Tobacco for each Pound of Silk." The planting of mulberry trees was greatly encouraged, but, as with so many enterprises undertaken to diversify industries in the Crown Colonies, all was drowned in the sea of tobacco.

The fruit of the wild American mulberry (*Morus rubra* L.) was not luscious enough to warrant domestic cultivation, although botanists like Michaux thought cultivated groves would improve the quality of the fruit. John Custis sent "White Mulberry seeds" to Peter Collinson in

London in 1736. "It is a hardy tree and will grow anywhere." He probably meant our red mulberry.

The English mulberry (*Morus nigra* L.) had delicious berries like our most improved blackberries today, and a juice so richly colored and lasting as to rival the best dyes. The true silkworm mulberry (*Morus alba* L., from China and eastern Russia) was imported rather late in the attempts to develop a silk trade in the United States.

Reputedly Jared Eliot first introduced the white mulberry "and with it the silk worm." His sixth essay in his *Essays upon Field Husbandry*, published in 1747, begins "with the Mulberry Tree . . . as we have but few of this kind . . ." He advises "the planting great numbers of them . . . a Part of Husbandry that will be much to our Honour and Advantage . . . render us more serviceable to our Mother Country . . ." He refers to "the Transactions of The Society established in London for the Encouragement of Arts, Manufactures and Commerce," and quotes from the Society's proposal to give "for every Pound Weight of Cocoons produced in the Province of Connecticut in the year 1759, of a hard, weighty and good Substance wherein one Worm only has spun, *Three Pence* . . . for every Pound Weight of Cocoons produced the same Year wherein two Worms are interwoven *One Penny* . . ." All this was to be determined by a "publick Filature" under the direction of Reverend Thomas Clap and Dr. Jared Eliot. In effect, the cocoons were to be unwound in their presence before the "generous offer" could be paid by "said Gentlemen." The very last note in Eliot's essay, labeled *"Nota Bene,"* has to do with the worms: when saving the worms found in the balls it is well to save both the oval and the round, since one is male and one female, and "the Female only produce the Eggs, and Male are necessary to impregnate the Female, in order to continue the Breed."

It is a pity that Connecticut and Pennsylvania, because of the cost of labor, never lived up to their fair promise. Georgia, in spite of warehouse fires and being "so new and small," did better.

According to one historian, the founding of Georgia was undertaken with three laudable goals in mind, one of which was to develop a silk, wine and drug-growing colony. The trustees calculated to save the mother country an estimated annual expenditure in the years of the 1730's of five hundred thousand pounds spent on silk from France, Italy and China.

Twenty thousand people in Georgia working for four months of every year would mean twenty thousand people in England working all the year round preparing the silk and things to be traded for it. Sir Thomas Lombe, a silk manufacturer in England, was sanguine. Oglethorpe was convinced. Italian silk growers accompanied the colonists.

By 1735 Georgia silk was presented to the Queen, who had it made into a fabric and the fabric into a gown, which she wore at court on her birthday. In mid-century a gentleman educated by observing silk manufacture in France was sent to take charge of the silk industry in Georgia. But the industry declined and gave way to rice and cotton, which were to prove Georgia's staple crops. Only the trees live on, some for over one hundred years.

In 1765 Washington grafted English mulberries on wild mulberry stock. In 1785 he planted mulberries in his serpentine walks.

In 1771 Jefferson planted "The Mulberry Row." In 1789 he ordered trees from France, "the best for the silkworm."

In 1790 the Prince Nurseries offer mulberries: Large Black English, Black American and White.

NECTARINES

The smooth peach, or nectarine, grows where the peach grows and does better on peach stocks or plum stocks than on its own. It is a native of North India. Tradescant was growing them for Lord Cecil in Hatfield House in the early seventeenth century.

Prince's list: Fairchild's Early Nectarine, Large Green Clingstone, Yellow, Red Roman, Yellow Roman, Temple's, Italian or Brugnon, Newington, Genoa, and Brinyon Nectarine.

In 1769 Jefferson planted half a row of peach stocks for inoculating nectarines. He was also planting peach stocks for inoculating almonds and apricots upon them. At the same time he put in a row of pomegranates, twelve and a half feet apart, twelve in a row, the same of figs, and the same of walnuts. All this is in the first planting plan for Monticello.

James Winthrop chronicles the dates his nectarines bloomed and fruited in Cambridge and Lexington from 1793 on.

NUTS

American nut trees offered prodigious crops for the early settlers. The woods were full of chestnuts (one sort a tree and the other a shrub, smaller but sweeter than the European), hickories of several sorts, some to be identified by their chief devourers as "pignuts" and some, because of their bark, which could be used to seat chairs, as "shagbarks." There were walnuts, black and not as good as the English walnut, but edible if eaten when the shell had softened, when it could also be used for dyeing; and so-called "white walnuts," or butternuts, rich and oily.

Then there was the delicious "Illinois nut" or "paccan," surpassing all but the English walnut in flavor and favor.

Early accounts made much of the hickory nuts — how the Indians served them cracked to be eaten by the handful and the shells spat out, and how they thickened their broths with the nuts cracked and cooked so that the shells sank to the bottom of the brew. Mrs. Grant, in her *Memoirs of an American Lady*, tells of elaborate teas served to honored guests in mid-century Albany, which included nuts as well as fancy pastries. Nuts were served at the end of good dinners, with fruit or with wine, as we see in accounts of dining at Mount Vernon. And Washington served them at his camp table in the field to end a meal that, otherwise, pie-less and fruit-less, he admitted, lacked amenities.

In eighteenth-century gardens, both in England and the American colonies, nuts were in demand. Parkinson had considered nut trees as orchard trees, especially "The Filberd," which is "Very like unto the Hasell nut tree that groweth wilde in the woods with long catkins instead of flowers and a somewhat hard shell though not as hard as the woodnut." He received "from Virginia Hasell nuts, smaller, rounder, browner, thinner-shelled."

The Prince Nurseries offered Madeira nut, Long Black Walnuts, White Walnuts of many sorts, American Hazelnut, Barcelona nuts; Fill buds, Hard-shelled Almonds, Sweet Almonds.

Madeira nuts were English walnuts with some fancied superiority. Originally from Persia, they became the most English of nuts, *Juglans regia* L. These probably included the "French walnuts" planted by Washington in 1770. By 1786 he had a border in the North Garden of "the English Walnut trees."

Jefferson, as usual, grew a profusion of experimental nuts, budding English walnuts upon our own black walnuts, sending from Paris for gallons of hickory nuts, "scaly bark . . . Hiccory . . . Pignut." White walnuts were the *Juglans cinerea* L., our butternut, and the black walnut was *Juglans nigra* L., justly popular today for its wood.

The hickory family was large, nearly all of it planted by Jefferson. Washington had a row of shellbark hickory, Miller's *Carya ovata*. They both planted quantities of the pecan nut, *Carya illinoensis*, which Washington called Mississippi nuts. The "Mockernut," *Carya tomentosa*, got its name from the Dutch word meaning "heavy hammer," an intimation of its hardness.

"Fill buds" were planted by both Washington and Jefferson, as were both Spanish and American chestnuts and almonds. Jefferson even tried pistachio nuts, and Washington planted a "physic nut," *Jatropha curcas*, from the West Indies.

PEACHES

In the eighteenth-century American colonies, and later in the states, peaches were in great plenty. Everyone grew them, especially the Indians. Everyone wanted them. As the settlers arrived, European peaches were welcomed and "ingrafted." "Stones" of good peaches remained a friendly currency throughout the century. Collinson sent stones of the "best peaches" in England to Custis in Williamsburg, in 1737. Peach brandy became a staple, like cider. Peaches, like our apples, came down the rivers and lakes with new names attached.

Parkinson in 1629 gives us twenty-one named peaches. Miller in 1768 gives us thirty-one. By 1850, Downing could list over two hundred and fifty named peaches.

Prince offers thirty-five peaches, many of them sounding like duplicates, playing on the names nutmeg, clingstone, stone and malagatune. Prince's Peaches, 1790, included the Scarlet nutmeg peach; White nutmeg; Green nutmeg or Early Ann; Rare ripe peach; Old Newington; New Newington; Large early clingstone; Large early peach; Large red clingstone, weighs from 11 to 12 ounces; Yellow clingstone, called the Carolina Canada, weighs a pound; the white blossom peach; Fine large French peach called Murgetong; Fine red clingstone, equal to a pineapple for goodness; English swalch peach; Large red stone peach, weighs from 10 to 15 ounces; Large Yellow clingstone, weighs 10 or 12 ounces, ripe October 15th; Large white clingstone, weighs 14 ounces; Large lemon clingstone; Lemon peach; English double blossom peach; Large winter clingstone peach; Large yellow malagatune peach; Large yellow clingstone peach; Large white stone peach; White winter clingstone peach; Blood peach; Carolina clingstone peach; Western Newington peach; Barcelona yellow clingstone; Elizabeth peach; Yellow Catherine peach; Red cheek malagatune peach; Large blood clingstone peach; Large heath peach; Green Catherine peach.

Jefferson and Washington and Lady Skipwith, our key growers and buyers, were peach fanciers, especially Jefferson. The Catherine Peach was sent to Custis by Collinson, who heard it was good from the governor's lady.

PEARS

While the apple was the standby fruit of old England, and endowed with sturdy English names, the pear was peculiarly French, and the names of the old varieties all relate to their origins or fancied likenesses;

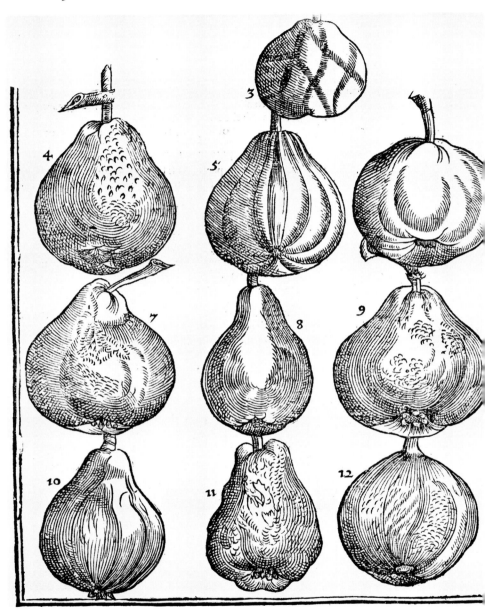

Parkinson's Pears. The upper left pear is the famous Bon Chrétien, still popular as our Bartlett, Washington's Bergamot is at the upper right. The six lower pears are: Summer Bon Chrétien, Best Warden, Pound, Windsor, Gratiala and Gilloflower.

one discovered in the parish of St. Germain; one found by a gate in Poicteau and preserving the old spelling; one resembling a lady's thigh.

Pears are a "pome fruit," like apples, and, unlike the stone fruits that a homesick Jefferson in Paris remembered as always coming true to seed in America, they can result in many varieties. Perhaps it is because pears are such an old fruit, so long and so carefully cultivated, that they seem to have remained identifiable to a degree beyond the apples running wild in the American colonies. A few new pears did appear, like the Seckel, but in the main the names of the pears seem fairly constant. Prince's thirty-six sorts in his 1790 catalogue are almost all precisely named, unlike his apples and peaches.

Let us give John Lawson's account of the pears grown in Carolina before 1709:

The Warden Pear here proves a very good eating pear and is not so long ripening as in England . . . Katherine excellent . . . Sugar-pear . . . and several others without name. The Bergamot we have not, nor either of the Bonne Chreitiennes, though I hear they are all three in Virginia.

A remarkable specimen of the "Sugar pear" is the pear planted by Governor John Endecott in what is now Danvers, near Salem in Massachusetts. It has survived as a single living tree since 1630, still sending out new shoots. Our first description is by the Reverend William Bentley of the First Church, Salem, written in his diary after one of his exploratory walks. On September 21, 1796, he visited Orchard Farm, so called by the Governor after he converted it from a wilderness called Birches. Only one tree left bears the Sugar Pear. "It is in front of the site of the house; rises in three trunks from the ground and is considerable high . . . I brought away some of the pears . . ." Several later entries refer to the pear tree, especially one in 1802 to say the old pear tree "hung still full of pears." In 1809 and 1810 Dr. Bentley sent scions to President John Adams in Quincy, at his request after he heard of the tree from Bentley, and Adams reported that he had "engrafted a number of stocks which have taken well according to their present appearances . . ."

As can be seen and guessed from Prince's list, pear names were even more easily misspelled and also duplicated than apple names.

In 1764 Washington was planting a great quantity of "Bergamy" pears, from Colonel Mason, in long rows interspersed with "Spanish pears," Early June and the Black Pear of Worcester (part of the coat of arms of the city of Worcester in England today. Said by Washington to be large and coarse but good for baking). In 1785 Washington planted "Bury" and St. Germain and some Orange Bergamots. His Spanish pear may have been the Bon Chrétien, one of the oldest and most honored of French pears, taken to England and brought to America early on to be popularized as the Bartlett.

Jefferson's pears are less specifically named but no less generally planted upon his terraces. He had the Seckel (called "Sickle") in 1807.

In the 1790's forty-nine pear seeds were planted in the Western Reserve as received from "Uncle Stone" in Rutland, Massachusetts. In 1850 they were bearing well and were called "the old Stone pears."

PLUMS

Parkinson says there are "many more varieties of Plummes than of Cherries" and implies this richness is due in part to his "very good friend Master John Tradescante, who has wonderfully laboured to obtaine all the rarest fruits he can heare of in any place in Christendome, Turkey, yea or the whole world . . ." Parkinson names over sixty sorts of plums, ending with the "Pishamin or Virginia plum."

Under the "Use of Plums," Parkinson mentions their efficacy in choleric agues since they "coole." The tart plums are "thought to bind . . . the others, being sweet, to loosen the body."

The woods and beaches of the New World offered a variety of wild plums to the settlers: chiefly the beach plum, the sloe or Allegheny plum

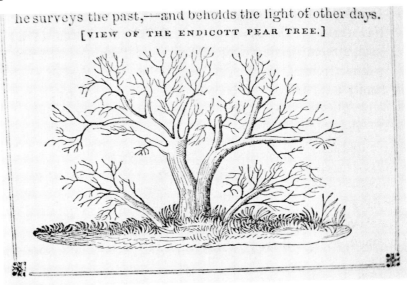

he surveys the past,—and beholds the light of other days.

[VIEW OF THE ENDICOTT PEAR TREE.]

An eighteenth-century sketch of the Endicott Sugar Pear

and the Chickasaw plum. But John Custis in Williamsburg in 1736 commented that the climate there was too hot for plums or grapes to do well.

As with other fruits, the seeds planted in the fertile soil and heavy loams of the Hudson Valley resulted in new sorts. While the English propagated by layers of common plums, like Muscle and Brussels, the Americans thought, Downing says, more highly of seedlings raised from common plums, like Blue Gage and the Horse plum. For dwarfing, seedlings of Mirabelle were employed.

The Prince list is extensive:

Green Gage; Yellow Egg; White sweet; Orleans; Red Imperial; Wild Allegheny; Catherine; Cherry; Matchless; Large pear plum; Drab d'Or; Apricot Plum; White Bonum Magnum; Whitton; Jeanhative; Precious detour; Fotheringham; Red Perdigron; Brignole; White Damson; Large red sweet; Large Holland; early sweet Damson; Red Bonum Magnum; Winter Damson Frost.

Washington and Jefferson both grew Greengage. The Yellow Egg and White Bonum Magnum were the same plum, as is the Mogul, grown by Washington and Jefferson. The Orleans plum went to Mount Vernon from Lear's list. Red Imperial and Red Magnum Bonum are the same. All Damson plums are credited to John Tradescant's tour of the Mediterranean as a volunteer against Barbary pirates early in the seventeenth century. Washington planted a dozen Damson plums in 1786 and at the same time one hundred and seventy-seven wild Cherokee plums. So Prince was wise to include our wild plums. Jefferson sent from Paris for quantities of our wild plum stones. He ordered the French plum "Brugnol" to be sent to Monticello as the plum most used for drying.

POMEGRANATES

The coat of arms of the city of Granada features a pomegranate, quite simply the "apple of Granada," (*Punica granatum* L.), brought to England for the first time by John Tradescant. It may have been this early introduction, the novelty of the fruit and then the disappointment of its not being able to ripen in England, even in "his Lords Garden at Canterbury," that led to its repeatedly being sent to the New World to be tried out there. Even to New England in the seventeenth century. It seems to have been one of the exotics for which much was hoped in a milder climate.

In 1762 Peter Collinson wrote to John Bartram that he was "ready to burst with desire for root, seed or specimen of the waggish Tipitiwitchet

Sensitive," (*Dionaea muscipulum* Ellis), and warned him about a plant Collinson has sent to him:

Don't use the pomegranate inhospitably, a stranger that has come so far to pay his respects to thee . . . Plant it against the side of thy house, nail it close to the wall. In this manner it thrives wonderfully with us, and flowers beautifully and bears fruit this hot year. I have twenty-four on one tree . . . Doctor Fothergill says, of all trees this is the most salutiferous to mankind.

In 1764 Mrs. Lamboll sent from Charleston to John Bartram, who had sent the Lambolls some angelica and dried apples, his own barrel, containing pomegranates and oranges.

Jefferson planted pomegranates from George Wythe in 1771 and replanted some, so he achieved some success, but not enough, as he "wanted" some in 1754.

QUINCE

While the Prince Nurseries' catalogue of 1790 boldly headlines "Quince Trees," the items under the heading are grapes, and one is left to order quince trees at the overall price of one shilling sixpence each for

Parkinson's two quinces, the Common and the Portugal

an unnamed variety. As the quince tree had been popular for well over
a hundred years in the New World, we may assume that the quince in
eighteenth-century America was much the same quince as "set the dames
awork" in Josselyn's time in the seventeenth century, *Cydonia oblonga*
Mill.

John Lawson commented upon the quinces growing in Carolina before 1709: "I am not a fair judge of the different sorts of Quinces which
they call Brunswick, Portugal and Barbary . . . but as to the fruit, no
place has fairer and better relish . . . Pleasant eaten raw . . . Of this
fruit they make a wine or liquor which they call Quince-Drink and
which I approve of beyond any drink which that country affords, though
a great deal of cider and perry is there made. The Quince-Drink most
commonly purges . . . cleanses the body very well . . . The least slip
of this tree stuck in the ground comes to bear in three years."

Washington and Jefferson both planted rows of quinces. In eighteenth-century New England gardens there was always a quince at the
lower corner of the vegetable garden — at least in Portsmouth and
Newburyport — not quite an orchard tree but an inevitable finish to a
well planned, useful garden.

RASPBERRIES

Of raspberries there seems to have been the same assortment, with the
same rules for cultivation as for currants. Prince Nurseries offer four
sorts: White raspberries; English red raspberries; American raspberries;
Large Canada raspberries.

Lawson reported that in North Carolina "Our raspberries are of a
purple colour and agreeable relish, almost like the English, but I reckon
them not quite so rich. When once planted, 'tis hard to root them out.
They run wild all over the country, and will bear the same year you
transplant them, as I have found by experience." This is reporting on
raspberries brought into gardens before 1709, common practice with
thrifty and good gardeners.

Wild American raspberries, brought into gardens for cultivation,
were one of those garden fruits that proved superior to imports. Our
native sorts were (1) The American red, *Rubus strigosus,* similar to the
European *Rubus Idaeus* L., and (2) the American "black-cap raspberry," *Rubus occidentalis* L. Both of these American species have
yellow-fruited varieties. Jefferson's references to cultivated raspberries
are legion.

STRAWBERRIES

Strawberries there were in plenty when explorers arrived and settlers followed. In New England they stained the ground red. The Indians made "bread" of them. The English settlers made preserves and tarts just as they had in old England, where their garden strawberries had been brought in from the woods.

Thomas Tusser, in his book *Five Hundred Points of Good Husbandry,* first published in 1557 and reprinted many times thereafter, puts it neatly.

> Wife, into thy garden, and set me a plot,
> With strawberry roots, of the best to be got,
> Such growing abroad, among thorns in the wood,
> Well chosen and picked, prove excellent good.

After she has planted them in September, she must look to them again in December.

> Hide strawberries, wife,
> To save their life.
> If frost do continue, take this for a law
> The strawberries look to be covered with straw.

There is an indication of how her small fruits were arranged. We are back again in September.

> The barberry, respies, and gooseberry too,
> Look now to be planted as other things do.
> The gooseberries, respies and roses all three,
> With strawberries under them trimly agree.

William Rogers claimed in 1645, of the strawberry found growing in New England, that "one of the chiefest doctors in England was wont to say that God could have made, but God never did make, a better berry."

In Virginia there was the same richness. Thomas Hariot's account, *To the Adventurers, Favorers and Welwillers of the Enterprise for the Inhabiting and Planting in Virginia,"* written after his voyage undertaken for Sir Walter Raleigh in 1587, reports that "strawberries there are as good and great as these which we have in our English gardens."

Prince's list of four strawberries is very clear: large hautboy strawberries; Chili strawberries; red wood strawberries; Hudson strawberry, very large, very fine.

The eighteenth-century sorts from which our strawberries have come were our own Wild or Virginia Scarlet, the Pine or Surinam (it seemed to have a pineapple fragrance), the Wood and Alpines of Europe, the Hautbois from Bohemia, the Chili from South America. This last was especially fancied by Collinson, Custis and Jefferson.

Furber's Fruits for the Month of October

10 "Rid to All My Plantations"

E VER SINCE, early in the seventeenth century, John Parkinson, in his witty and comprehensive *Paradisus,* had admitted the existence of a pleasure garden as apart from a garden entirely for "Meate or Medicine," the English-speaking world had been toying with the idea and elaborating upon it. The French had never been deluded by the Protestant suspicion that anything undertaken for personal pleasure deserved less of the Almighty's blessings than something undertaken, declaredly, for the public good. While the happiness of the royal and noble had never seemed to the English sole reason for designing away great areas of the landscape in purely frivolous designs, and though the enclosure of heretofore open lands wreaked havoc on the economy of the rural laborer, the landed English remained aware of an obligation to grow, process and administer useful and medicinal plants. In no other society did *noblesse oblige* include dosing to the extent it did in rural England. The lady of the manor, the wife of the parson, were expected to take care of quite extraordinary needs in the hamlets and villages, all from their own gardens.

On the continent great books on gardens and gardening were dedicated to the pleasure of those of noble rank. In England books of the same sort — often the same books in translation — were dedicated to a noble patron but designated as help for the "young gardener," which is to say, the beginner in the art. Assiduous cultivation of the practicing gardener by book publishers reached such an extreme that even noble writers hid behind names borrowed from gardeners to dukes, paying for the privilege.

So it is fair to say that when the splendid *Paradisus* appeared, dedicated to Her Majesty but aimed at every gardener in the kingdom, to dignify both his profession and the idea of pursuing pleasure through planting, the whole of English gardening was catalyzed into the mold we now recognize as particularly English.

This democratizing of the art of garden design, freeing the human conscience to take delight in nature for its own sake, was, strangely, a good deal helped along by the classics. Where every gentleman had been reared with the greatest respect for Virgil and Horace and the Grand Tour was premised upon the study of classical ruins wherever they might be found, where all medicine and much of the activity of religious orders were bound up with growing ancient and honorable remedies for the human frame, the entire reversal of the pyramid was not difficult. Plants and gardens became of the highest intellectual importance. What Vitruvius had recommended in house-siting, what Virgil had designated as the "Genius of the Place," always to be consulted in garden design, the pleasures Horace had taken in his own purely ornamental retreat, were resurrected and followed meticulously. No one was in the least intimidated by what French royalty had wrought, or even Persian kings. The idea of being able to repeat lines of Virgil as one paced in one's garden (obviously having to be laid out by oneself with one's stride and elocutionary abilities in mind), and then to come upon a feature or folly representing exactly what Virgil was describing, became an enviable achievement. And as, at the same time fresh air and exercise had suddenly achieved importance as health measures, somewhat superseding pill-taking and bloodletting, the idea of the garden's being useful as an aid to good health became popular, verifying the last half of Parkinson's four purposes in creating a garden as envisaged by the Almighty — "for Meate or Medicine: for Use or for Delight."

It certainly represented a freeing of the human spirit, especially of the English human spirit. No longer was it only monks who cultivated exotic foreign plants on the chance that they might prove beneficial. No longer was it only to royalty that adventurers from distant parts brought back strange and beautiful trees and flowers. English bishops and Quaker merchants created gardens as holding-rooms for these introductions. A camaraderie of growers sprang up that knew no bounds of dress or manner, birth or wealth. A sailor with a new tulip bulb needed no other introduction. A nobleman of great resources could be commandeered to grow things of whose future value or beauty he could have no inkling. Nurserymen for the general public sprang up where they had existed before mainly to furnish royal parks. They wrote books and persuaded gardeners working for royalty to pose as the authors. There was a great yeasting of books on how-to-grow-it. As a sign of changing times, the most telling title among all these publications was that of a book on day-to-day gardening called *A Clergyman's Recreation.* A spate of "Garden Kalendars" told what to do each month of the year. And, inevitably, there was a great and heavy laying on of hands, by those who felt they knew more about the subject than anyone else, in books on "Taste."

How this wave of gardenese writing crossed the Atlantic and what were the results of its breaking upon our shores is all there, clear as day, in the libraries of affluent eighteenth-century Americans. The fact is that, though all these authors were read, the owners of their books in the new land went right ahead and did what they wanted to do anyway.

That Washington had never received more than a rudimentary rural Virginia education is not probed by biographers searching for spurs to later greatness. By some, his passion for land and its management is attributed to early frustrations seeing his mother manage his patrimony at Ferry Farm. But for his talent for the laying out of pleasure grounds, like his estate at Mount Vernon, there are no early clues. Perhaps he saw something that pleased him at Belvoir, the Fairfax estate next to Mount Vernon, later totally destroyed by fire. Perhaps he had listened to his neighbors' stories of English gardens. We know the books he read and find nothing he took wholesale from them.

Not to be behindhand in explaining why and how the great are great, I confess I find only one explanation for Washington's quiet assumption of responsibility for land use and his obvious pleasure in land layout.

Search as I may, I find no original for the design of the gardens of Mount Vernon beyond the steady progress of the owner in developing his own obviously long-considered plan. For all this and his always open-ended interest and practice in agricultural procedures and animal husbandry, my clue is that they were inborn traits, inherited from generations of landed gentry all so inclined.

Washington was not an aristocrat, although his aristocratic manners occasionally bothered those with democratic insistencies. His family was armigerous, but not ostentatiously so, like the Byrds whose William Byrd II had taken pains to approach the College of Heralds in London to secure his family's coat of arms for himself. The Washington family had long used its stars and stripes as useful signs of ownership and relationship, a convenient advantage to which the country was welcome when the time came to give it, too, a distinctive symbol. As a matter of fact, the Washington family, settled on the shores of Virginia for three generations of farming, was exactly what Captain John Smith meant when he begged future settlers of the new land to send no more non-

Washington's map of the different farms making up his property of Mount Vernon. The Mansion House farm is lower center and from here he kept watch over all the rest, often bringing back attractive shrubs and trees he had noticed on his rides

working aristocrats and profligates like those he had saved at Jamestown, but to get the landed gentry to send their "spare kindred." The Washingtons came to carry on in the New World exactly as they had in the Old. Land management and improvement, responsible care of inferiors, interest in new systems to improve their labors, a dedication toward service for the state, a deep sense of public and personal justice — it was in the blood.

George Washington's father sent the sons of his first marriage "home" for their education, but there was no outward resentment on the part of his elder son by the second marriage when circumstances denied him similar advantages. George's older half brother, Lawrence, appointed his guardian, obviously tried to make it up to the younger boy and generously handed on all he could of his own social advantages, even, one can see, his ideal of bravery in combat and admiration for military heroes. It was under this brother's wing that the young George met the Fairfaxes, at Belvoir. These were the real aristocrats, nearest neighbors to the family home the older brother had inherited and had named Mount Vernon for the British admiral under whom he had served. It was through the Fairfax friendship that George acquired skills in surveying and, quite possibly, fox-hunting. It was certainly at Belvoir that he acquired his drawing room and ballroom manners, which proved as useful in his career as many of his other skills.

Washington's plans for developing both house and grounds, when he came in his turn to inherit Mount Vernon, would seem to have been in his mind for some time, so orderly was their accomplishment. First the house, which, incidentally, was in exactly the sort of situation most advised and approved by all the classical writers, had to be enlarged, both upward and outward. High columns across the east front on the river side made the wide sweep of the view more tolerable in hot weather, less bare in cold. Curved colonnaded walks, which stretched out from the west front to the kitchens and stables on one side and the servants' quarters and workrooms on the other, formed an arc half-framing the oval around which ran the carriage drive.

The plan made by Washington for Mount Vernon, drawn by Samuel Vaughan from a paced survey in 1787 and much copied and verified by visitors, looks rather like an ornate bell hung from a beam represented by the Potomac and the long expanse of lawn running between the house and the river. The drive for carriages around the oval or circular lawn directly back of the house forms the ring from which the "bell" hangs. This lawn, fenced by posts and iron chains, centers on a sundial. Looked at from the house, with one's back to the river, the sides of the "bell" begin at two little buildings for house servants and services exactly complemented by the buildings at the ends of the colonnades, the one on the left the kitchen, the one on the right the gardener's quarters. There is a wide way between these pairs of buildings to allow carriages to go to the stables and, presumably, to allow carts to be brought up to the house door. The lines of the bell are sketched in two long symmetrical serpentine drives, tree-bordered, graveled and wide enough for carriages or for people to walk in groups. These enclose a lawn of enormous dimensions, sometimes called the bowling green, but large enough for several simultaneous games of bowls. Against the outer sides of the bell are two great oblongs with peaked ends, not unlike church windows. These are the vegetable garden on the left and the flower garden on the right. Back of the vegetable garden, where the land slopes away and is terraced into a "fall," are the stables and an intended vineyard.

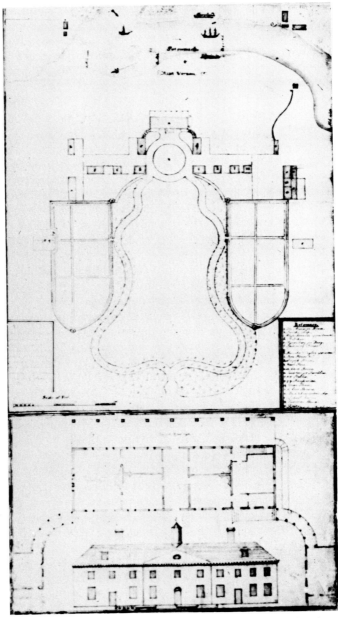

A contemporary sketch of Washington's Mount Vernon, showing
his original design

Beside and back of the flower garden is a greenhouse, against the rear walls of which are the servants' quarters.

Tying the church-window gardens and the serpentine drives into the design are four small pepper-pot garden houses, forming a rectangle with two each on the inside walls of the vegetable and flower gardens, and with the garden entrances from the serpentine drives between them. The little corner houses nearest the mansion are reached by shrub-planted walks of their own and are referred to by Washington as the "new necessaries." The two farther pepper pots in each of the two big gardens are referred to as "seed-houses." Later the one in the flower garden would be used as a schoolhouse. These four small houses firm up the elaborately curved sides of the bell design and build it into a masterly piece of symmetrical landscape planning.

When this extremely efficient and beautifully balanced design for the house and grounds of a busy Virginia plantation are understood, one can go on to enumerate other features and arrangements, all carefully worked into the plan. Where the clapper might hang from the bell is the inner entrance gate, flanked by two mounts, from which the carriage drive, having entered from a main entrance gate on the highroad, barely to be seen from the mansion, turns and approaches the house on that side.

In front of the house on the river side are wharves for loading and unloading and for mooring the plantation's boats for fishing and travel-ing and freight. The family tomb is halfway up the hill from here. Toward the front of the mansion's eastern slope a summerhouse will be cleverly set on the top of a dry well by Washington's heir, Judge Bush-rod Washington. In the expanse before the house are "clumps" of ornamental trees and the place where Washington will have a deer park when he has given up his fox hounds. Within the design for the garden proper the two "mounds" flanking the inner entrance each support a weeping willow. This is a new idea for planting: the ancient concept of a mount as a place for viewing, with sides concealed in greenery to make it seem natural. Stretching out toward the sides of the design and west toward the main entrance from the highway, hardly visible from the mansion, are other conventional features, two "wildernesses" and two "groves," both carefully planned and planted. Inside the design are the various "shrubberies," about whose planting Washington was particu-larly concerned for several years, as can be seen in his directions to be quoted later.

When one considers the amount of plant material to be used in the serpentine drives and shrubberies, the shrub-bordered walks to the "necessaries," the groves and the artificial wildernesses, one can see why

An early nineteenth-century sketch of one of the little
pepper-pot garden houses, necessaries, toolhouses or schoolhouse.

Washington, as he rode about his plantations, or hunted or rode out to
call upon friends, was always on the alert for trees or shrubs to be
moved in.

The total competence of the design for the gardens of Mount Vernon
surprised foreign visitors of the time and encouraged the usual foreign
visitor's kindly comments upon the unexpected excellence of anything
found in the New World not copied exactly from the Old. It added to
the wonder that Washington had never even traveled abroad except for
his visit to Barbados when he was taking care of his ailing brother.

Comments are made even by modern garden enthusiasts that, besides
Washington's library lacking the in-depth culture of Jefferson's, he possibly rarely read in it. Evidence is that he made careful study of books
like Miller's *Dictionary* and applied what he had learned every day of
his life at Mount Vernon. One directly quoted bit of book use in his
diaries is his account of trying to set a horse's leg from Gervase Markham's *The Horse.* (It would have succeeded if the horse had not
thrashed about in his sling the next day, undoing the work and making
another try impossible.)

The elements of the design of the Mount Vernon gardens show that

G Washington

THE

UNIVERSAL GARDENER
And BOTANIST;

OR, A

GENERAL DICTIONARY

OF

GARDENING and BOTANY,

Exhibiting in Botanical Arrangement, according to the Linnæan Syſtem,

Every TREE, SHRUB, and Herbaceous PLANT, that merit Culture, either for USE, ORNAMENT, or CURIOSITY, in every Department of GARDENING.

Compriſing accurate Directions, according to real Practice, for the Management of the

KITCHEN-GARDEN,	NURSERY,	HOT-BEDS,
FRUIT-GARDEN,	PLANTATIONS,	FORCING-FRAMES,
PLEASURE-GROUND,	GREEN-HOUSE,	HOT-WALLS, and
FLOWER-GARDEN,	HOT-HOUSE, or STOVE,	FORCING in general.

Deſcribing the proper Situations, Expoſures, Soils, Manures, and every Material and Utenſil requiſite in the different Garden Departments ;

Together with

PRACTICAL DIRECTIONS

FOR

Performing the various Mechanical Operations of GARDENING in general.

By THOMAS MAWE,
Gardener to his Grace the Duke of Leeds.

And JOHN ABERCROMBIE,
Authors of Every Man his Own Gardener, &c.

LONDON,
Printed for G. ROBINSON, in Pater-noſter Row ; and T. CADELL, in the Strand.
MDCCLXXVIII.

Washington's copy of a popular practical book on gardening by John Abercrombie, author of *Every Man his own Gardener,* and Thomas Mawe, gardener to the Duke of Leeds

Washington had read widely in his gardening books, mastered the subject as laid out in them for the use of English and French landholders of means and resources, and had proceeded to lay out his own garden of exactly the appropriate size and style for his manor house. It seems to have pleased him to use all the usual features of an English garden of the period except for water effects, where he seems to have felt the Potomac water enough for even the most ambitious garden designer.

And here let us remember the visitor to Monticello who remarked to Thomas Jefferson that all his garden lacked in excellence of design was a river close by in the valley below. One cannot please foreigners and it is better not to try. Both Washington and Jefferson stuck to their own lasts through blizzards of foreign visitors, coming to see and staying to realize that both were truly great. Neither of them ever added one least suggested feature to his own, each so original, design.

The placing of the buildings and gardens at Mount Vernon and their relations to each other are worthy of any garden-designing noble striving to outpass a neighboring duke. The approach in serpentine curves, the walks, shrubbery-bordered even to the outbuildings, the selection of various trees for the "shrubberies" and the "groves" and "clumps" and the "wildernesses," the hidden boundaries, the use of a ha-ha, the symmetry of the two gardens, one for vegetables and one for flowers, the poignancy of a "botanick" garden for exotic plants sent him from east and west, all tucked in for convenience between one of his new "necessaries" and the house where the weaving was done for the entire plantation's clothing — all these carefully planned and executed elements of the overall plan are worthy of any English poet-turned-gardener.

Without the literary and classical pretensions, Washington felt no need for a temple dedicated to a muse, for a grove named for Virgil, for seats inscribed with inspiring thoughts, for vistas to ready-made ruins. His bowling green, far from being tucked away on the side of the house, as it is at Middleton, for instance, is in the heart and center of his design. The vast expanse of mown grass can both set off the house to those arriving by carriage and serve the convenience of those who wish to step out and have a game after their two o'clock dinner.

His pepper pots for gardenhouses and "necessaries" are attractive individually. The summerhouse and the covers for his icehouse and wells, if built after his time, are in dignified keeping with his domestic architecture. Nowhere did he overstep, overdo, overdesign or overbuild. The whole concept is a tribute to beautiful practicality.

Except for his initial error as a very young man in placing Fort Necessity where it would have been ideal for a farm but not for a fort, and his failure (perhaps because of this) to achieve, also as a very young man, a much-desired regular commission in the British Army, it would seem that everything to which Washington turned his mind and his hand succeeded.

Of his especial talents for land and soil, agricultural and animal management, landscape design and maintenance, and all the arts of a

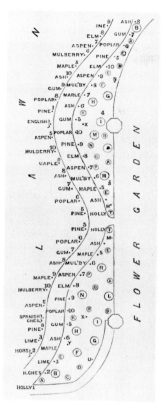

An early nineteenth-century interpretation
of the planting of the shaded carriageway
between the flower garden and the lawn at
Mount Vernon

rural economy, we are constantly aware as we read his papers, which scholarly hands have collected and edited over the years. One would think there was nothing left even to be commented upon by a newcomer. And yet the reading of the original words leaves one with a sense of fresh enthusiasm. Confining oneself only to words about gardening, about laying out grounds and harvesting crops, about sowing seeds and grafting fruit and protecting delicate shrubs and digging up handsome local trees and experimenting with soils and manures and sending and receiving all sorts of useful or unusual plants and seeds, one is swept into a steady progression of wise management.

This is the evolution of an ideal middle Atlantic seaboard estate in a world still new and unsettled, in a society in ferment, in a state of horticultural uncertainties, where even the cross-fertilization of plants was only beginning to be understood and practiced. It is interesting to see the premium put upon animal-breeding and the lack of any conception that the same practices could be applied to the plant world. Selective breeding of animals had long been popular with those who loved hunting and racing, who raised sheep for wool, cattle and goats for meat and milk, pigs for their flesh and poultry for eggs and food and occasionally even for fighting. And yet, when it came to carrots and cabbages, for instance, even Washington was experimenting with the soil, with exposures, with methods of sowing — close together in drills, scattered, in hills.

With animals, however, methods were more direct. He had two famous jackasses, one from Lafayette and Malta, and one sent him by the King of Spain. The Spanish one he planned to use to breed a race of mules suitable for drawing coaches. The jack from Malta was to be used to create a superior breed of mules for working in the fields. (Mules were stronger than horses and ate less.) In the heavy soil of Virginia, on the muddy troughs that served for roads, a new race of draft animals was needed. Similarly hounds for fox-hunting, horses for racing or hunting, or for riding into battle as officers' chargers, sheep that would yield more than five pounds of wool each — all these were being carefully considered, with records on covering and crossing carefully kept. And all the time the fruit trees and the cornfields and the vegetables were left to divine providence.

The wonders of the western plains were still to burst upon farmers hungry for new and better lands. In rural Virginia in the eighteenth century, land that would take the plough, and water that would save the crops in times of drought were all that could be hoped for. If by combining textures, importing sand or "marl," ditching, draining, leveling, digging-in woods soil, or seaweed, or animal ordure and guts, redesigning ploughs and studying the times for planting and harvesting, the farmers noted improvements in the results of their very considerable labors, that was the best they could do.

When Washington made his tour of the country, what with all the royal welcomes at every crossroad, he never failed to take note of the soil and the condition of the agriculture. His conclusions had a very personal note. If, he said, he could have settled where the best land was available, he would have chosen New York, Pennsylvania or New Jersey. There was also, he noted, some good land in New England, but it was under snow half the year and he gave full credit for the superiority in some matters there to the industry of the inhabitants.

The chronology of Washington's life as it relates to Mount Vernon makes his successes as farmer-gardener-landscape-designer all the more astounding. In the beginning he had rented Mount Vernon for six years after Lawrence's death and he managed it for his brother's estate, but he was not free to do more than dream of what he would do if he were its master. With the death of Lawrence's only child in 1754, the estate became truly his, but there again, what with his duties in the French and Indian War, he was not able to undertake his ownership seriously until he had returned from the wars to marry Martha Dandridge Custis and take her there as his bride.

He settled in, in 1759, to learn a great deal, both from his own lands, other lands he had come into through marriage and those he was managing for his stepchildren. Those first three years were not good for Mount Vernon's tobacco, although the Custis lands fared better. Washington began to realize and to resent the system of a one-crop economy, which destroyed the land and was financed from a great distance, and a year late, by English brokers. He was never a believer in the wisdom of slavery but he was at a loss as to how to proceed without it. However, he did see his way out of tobacco and into wheat, and the Mount Vernon flour began to be famous. Besides reorganizing his mill, he introduced a new still, which turned out quantities of marketable cider and peach brandy — beyond the needs of his own plantations. Rotation of crops and a design for a better plough occupied him, as they did Jefferson. By 1767, the change from tobacco was assured. The mill was flourishing and he was involved also in hemp and flax. His flour was celebrated. He was no longer beholden to the whims of London tobacco brokers. But the determined improvement never ceased. Whether he was at Mount Vernon or not, Washington watched over it, survived its failures and corrected them. His devotion shows in his letters to his various overseers, some good, some poor, none as good as the owner could wish.

Here are George Washington's instructions for planting the two very considerable orders he had given the Bartram Nurseries, appended to the *November 1792 Catalogue of Trees, Shrubs and Plants* of John Bartram, son of the first John. This succeeded the March, 1792, list from which Washington had ordered and of which the November list is to reorder what had failed.

Directions for disposing of the Trees, Shrubs etc. mentioned in the aforegoing list.

The intention of giving the heights to which they may grow is, that except in the centre of the six ovals in the west lawn, and at each end of the two large ovals, none of the tall or lofty growing trees (evergreens) are to be planted. But this I would have done of them, whether anything occupied these particular spots or not — removing them as they do, to some other parts of the aforesaid ovals. At each end of the four smaller ovals, trees of middling growth (for instance those which are to 15, 20 or even to 30 feet) may be planted. My meaning is, that in the centre of every oval (if it is not already there) one of the lofty growing trees should be planted, and the same done at each end of the two large ovals; and at the ends of the four smaller ones, trees of lesser size to be planted. The other parts of all of them to receive the shrubs, putting the tallest always nearest the middle, letting them decline more into dwarfs toward the outer parts. This was my intention when they were planted in the ovals last spring, but I either did not express myself clearly, or the directions were not attended to. I now hope they will be understood and attended to, both. The two trees marked thus (*) in the margin [43 Pinus larix 40 to 60 and "Scotch Fir"] I would have planted by the garden gates opposite to the Spruce Pines. I believe common pines are now in the places where I intended these, but they may be moved, being placed there merely to fill up the space. If any of these tall growing trees are now in any other part of the ovals except those here mentioned (and that you may be enabled better to ascertain this, I send you a list of what went from Bartram's Garden last spring), I would have them removed so as to conform to these directions, and if there be more with what are now sent, than are sufficient to comply with these directions then there may be one on each side of the two largest, making five in each. You will observe that the Pinus Strobus (or white pines) are the loftiest of all the tall trees which now are or have been sent, and that it is these which are to form your centres and the end trees of the two large ovals.

I must request also, that except the large trees, for the centre and sides, no regularity may be observed in the planting of the others in the ovals. This I particularly desired last spring, but found when I got home it was not attended to.

When you have disposed of all the trees agreeably to these directions, return this Paper and the general list which accompanies it, back again to me, as I may have occasion for them in procuring plants in future.

Note:

If there are now growing in the ovals as many as four of the Hemlock Spruce (sent last spring) let them be taken up when the ground is hard and deep frozen in the winter and placed on the sides of the two large ovals instead of the white pines which you might have put in them in consequence of the aforegoing directions.

One can feel for both the absentee planner and the, literally, on-the-spot gardener.

In a carefully selected and chronologically arranged collection of Washington's garden accounts, diary entries and horticulturally oriented correspondence, the editing of which explains the perfection and authenticity of today's Mount Vernon, it is possible to follow Washington's development of Mount Vernon, tree by shrub and brick by brick. With his characteristic deliberation, combined with his ability to carry far-distant goals constantly in mind, we see him proceeding with the building of the garden walls and the removal of the little gardenhouses from the middle of the inside walls of the two great gardens, to be set at their ends. To balance these he sets two similar structures in the near corners of each of the gardens, designs them to be used as "necessaries" and creates curved, well-planted brick walks to each. The inner walls of the gardens are palisaded or covered with structures against which trees can be espaliered. A "botanick" garden is created, between the house for weaving and sewing and the "necessary," where all the rare plants constantly arriving, desired or not, are carefully put for observation and especial care. The greenhouse is begun and proves to be beyond the powers involved to make it practical and easy to maintain, so Mrs. Carroll in Maryland is appealed to for information as to how hers has been constituted — the proportion of glass to wall heights and so on. English landowners are known to depend upon hedging for barriers against livestock, so a large quantity of hedging plants is ordered, "white thorn" especially. European grapes, tried in an area below the vegetable garden and behind the stables, seem to have proved disappointing, either for the table or for wine, so the area is to be turned into a "vineyard nursery." Great quantities of apples are ordered to make an orchard at one of the farms, presumably, considering their sort ("red strick"), for cider. Dessert fruits — apples, apricots, cherries, "pairs" — are trained against the garden walls, or, in the case of apples and pears, cordoned beside the paths and the center beds of vegetables.

The flower beds are well "boxed in," presumably with the dwarf box, which has been given by Mr. Lee and has been "sprouting" successfully. The "tree box" from the same source, also sprouting, must have been used for larger accents. An elegant fleur-de-lis design has been laid out on a parterre, and earns only a moan from an English visitor who admits its perfection but hopes it represents "a dying groan from the excesses of our ancestors." An enlightened soul.

There are so many roses that "Old Sall" takes two days to "pick" them. A palmetto from South Carolina needs special attention against the Virginia winter, but is such a feature that Washington himself sees to its covering with brush. The weeping willows set high upon the mounts, one on either side of the entrance from the long drive from the main lodge gates before the serpentine gravel ways take over, have been girdled by rabbits. The extensive plantings of local trees — elms, pines, ashes — are all failing for want of watering and proper care. They will have to be replaced. And, of course, this is only within the confines of the garden proper. The manor house grounds and outbuildings are all to be surrounded in their turn by a bank planted with trees.

There is almost no reference to flowers or the flower garden in all these accounts and entries. There is one charge for "dressing the flower beds." One notes that the accomplished tutor, secretary and companion, Tobias Lear, has taken Mrs. Washington to see a flower garden. And yet a visitor exclaims at the color and luxuriance of the flowers.

In a letter to the Reverend William Gordon of Boston, dated December 5, 1785, General Washington writes: "I have too Mrs. Washington's particular thanks to offer you for the flower roots and seeds which she will preserve in the manner directed."

In 1799 the Reverend John E. Latta of Pennsylvania describes his visit to Mount Vernon, noted by Washington in his diary on July 3. "Upon entering the garden I am met by the gardener who very politely shows me all the most curious plants and trees. The garden is very handsomely laid out in squares and flower knots and contains a great variety of trees, flowers and plants of foreign growth collected from

Lathyrus odoratus, Sweet Pea. One of the few garden flowers Washington records planting. Curtis *Botanical Magazine*

almost every part of the world. I saw there English grapes, oranges, limes and lemons in great perfection as well as a great variety of plants and flowers, wonderful in their appearance, exquisite in their perfume, and delightful to the eye."

The inference is, I think, that the flower garden and the flowers were Mrs. Washington's domain. We know she did not enjoy writing and that Washington generally sent messages for her with letters he was already writing. We know that she was a superb housekeeper, hostess, manager of a large plantation in the Virginia tradition, one who saw her household clothed and fed in the best possible style. She trained and supervised all the spinners and weavers and tailors and dressmakers. She made the guests' punch with her own hands. She reserved time for herself to meditate. She took careful notice of the whole household procedure. Coming from a large household, where she had borne four children before she was twenty-six, in a countryside more richly reward- ing agriculturally and horticulturally than the comparatively poor Mount Vernon soil, endowed with a father-in-law who was one of the best and keenest gardeners on the whole coast, she may very easily have wanted to take over the flower-growing at Mount Vernon. As we know, she came with her own slaves, which made it unwise for the dying Washington to set his own slaves free until Mrs. Washington should die herself and be able to release them all. We may suppose that the lack of accounts of caretaking among the flowers beds was because Mrs. Washington pre- ferred to turn her own people on to do what she wished them to do and kept no account of it herself, being, seemingly, quite independent of written recording, which must have seemed to her to require so much of her husband's time. This is my only explanation of why foxgloves, larkspurs and other flowers, sent to "brighten the garden," are never seen again in records.

Which is a pity, because, in reading Washington's correspondence and diary entries, we see minor dramas unfold, and are left hanging upon their resolutions. One of the most dramatic of these is the se- quence following Washington's polite letter to Mrs. Carroll. Another is the adventure of the *Peggy,* freighted with fruit trees from England. And there are others, like the relationship with Michaux, the trouble with the Reverend Mr. Gordon's gifts, the worry over plants for the relatives of the Marquis de Lafayette and the disappointment of Wash- ington, recorded in his visits to the two leading nurseries of the time, John Bartram's near Philadelphia and the Prince Nurseries on Long Island.

With reference to these last, it is possible to quote both comments in full. They show clearly Washington's predilection for good design and a fine show of bloom.

In June, 1787, he "rid to see the Botannical Garden of Mr. Bartram, which though stored with many curious plants, shrubs and trees, many of which are exotics, was not laid off with much taste nor was it large."

In October, 1789, he visited "Mr. Prince's fruit gardens and shrubberies at Flushing on Long Island." He found that "these gardens, except in the number of young fruit trees, did not answer my expectations. The shrubs were trifling, and the flowers not numerous."

The episode of Mrs. Carroll and her greenhouse began innocently, with Washington writing from Mount Vernon to Mr. Tench Tilghman in August, 1784, to say he hopes to finish his greenhouse "this fall" but he finds that neither he nor any person about him is "so well skilled in the internal construction as to proceed without a possibility of at least running into errors." He therefore asks the favor of a short description of the "greenhouse at Mrs. Carroll's." Washington is afraid he has planned his "upon too contracted a scale" . . . "forty feet by twenty-four in the outer dimensions and half the width disposed of for two rooms back of the part designed for the green house, leaving the latter in the clear not more than about thirty-seven by ten." However, as there is no cover on the walls yet, he can raise them to any height. The information he needs is: the dimensions of Mrs. Carroll's greenhouse, what kind of floor it has, how high above the floor are the bottoms of the window frames, how high the windows and the distance from their tops to the ceiling. Is the ceiling flat or what other, and how is it all heated, by a stove and flues, of whose disposition, size and construction he wishes full details. As, he says, he is to leave home the first of the next month and wishes to give the workmen instructions before he goes, he will be glad to hear from Mr. Tilghman on this subject.

Obviously he did hear and was able to proceed, because five years later, from New York, he is writing to Mrs. Carroll, of Mount Clare, Maryland, direct. As he has been lately sent from Europe a gardener who professes to understand the culture of rare plants and a greenhouse, Washington is desirous of profiting by the "very obliging offer" Mrs. Carroll was pleased to make him "some time ago." What he asks of Mrs. Carroll now is that, "reconciling your disposition to oblige with your convenience" she will spare him "such 'aids' as will not 'impair your collection.'" Trusting that this will be the "rule of your bounty," Washington says he has requested General Williams to notify her when "an opportunity offers to transport the trees or plants in the freshest state to Mount Vernon." He will "pay any expense which may be incurred in fitting them for transportation and to receive them from your gardener for that purpose." He has the honor, etc.

The response was immediate. Mrs. Carroll is obviously overcome with desire to oblige the President. The trees will be put in order and await only the General's procuring "a proper vessel" to convey them. A shaddock tree, on which she has endeavored to graft other fruits, will be sent with a lemon tree and some plants of the aloe and a geranium. She is flattered by his remembrance and sends her compliments to Mrs. Washington.

Then General Williams sounds an alarm. He has called upon Mrs. Carroll. The trees will be ready in about two weeks but are of such size and weight and so heavily fruited that, what with them and their "boxes of considerable weight," it will be necessary to procure a "commodious vessel and a husky navigator." Washington, however, may rely upon his "giving every attention and employing every care that the peculiarity of this little commission requires."

In New York, far from Mount Vernon and his gardener, Washington hears the alarm. He writes that "from the purport" of General Williams' letter, he (Washington) has reason to fear that his request to General Williams to forward the plants from Mrs. Carroll was "so incautiously expressed" as to lead General Williams into a mistake. And Washington, consequently, into "an expense I had no intention to incur." Washington had never intended more than to "embrace the opportunity of the Packet from Baltimore to Alexandria or any other casual conveyance . . . by which plants could easily be sent. If a large vessel be employed for this purpose the cost would far exceed the value of the things." He had "no expectation of large trees or of any plants beyond their infant growth." The first would be "a robbery of the good lady" without answering his purposes so well as things of smaller growth. If it is not too late . . . He begs General Williams to receive his sincere thanks for the pains taken.

General Williams answers within the week from Baltimore, regretting his "error." He has been twice to Mrs. Carroll and will be going again. He finds the visits "agreeable," but hastens to explain the reason for Mrs. Carroll's extreme indecisiveness. As these trees are all to be complimentary gifts, Mrs. Carroll is in a state, trying to decide which will be "most suitable . . . most fortunate . . . most acceptable." She feels she really must send her tree that bears both lemons and oranges, her only one. Williams assures her she must not make the sacrifice, as the tree, burdened with fruit, might arrive damaged. Washington's intent, he persuades her, is to cultivate young trees . . . Mrs. Carroll insists on sending the unique tree and Williams "soothes" her by promising to send at least the small trees immediately. So two careful boatmen have been engaged, each to take some of the smaller plants. The larger ones can go later by "some ship that may go from here to lode with tobacco in Potomac."

Within a few days Williams writes that Mrs. Carroll called upon him before he could call on her and they have agreed that it is "most eligible, at present, to send only the small trees." How small these were can be guessed by Williams' shipping only a half dozen. This letter apparently crossed one from Washington to Mrs. Carroll, entreating her not to rob her greenhouse of any "grown or bearing plants." If it is not too late, he begs this may not happen. His greenhouse, he repeats, is "by no means in perfect order." He writes again to Williams, begging him to send no large trees, especially not the "one of which she has not a second." In no time there is a letter from Mrs. Carroll at Mount Clare to Washington in New York to say she insists on giving him fruiting trees so that he and Mrs. Washington may gather their own fruit on their return, and it only remains for General Williams to inform her when the greenhouse *is* in order. This is enclosed in a letter from General Williams, who says that Mrs. Carroll has now housed the large trees against early frosts, but that she has sent five boxes and twenty pots of trees and young plants, among which are two shaddocks, one lemon and one orange, three to five feet in length, nine small orange trees, nine lemon, one fine balm-scented shrub, two pots of aloes and some tufts of knotted marjoram — all now safely stored upon the schooner *Surprise.*

But even then, Mrs. Carroll had not finished. Reference in the account book of 1797 shows monies paid boatmen for bringing "two lemon trees" from Mrs. Carroll. As all good gardeners know, Mrs. Carroll's was the greater pleasure.

The crisis over the ship *Peggy* was more real and, perhaps, more happily resolved. When Tobias Lear was in England he ordered a handsome list of ninety-eight fruit trees for himself to be sent to Mount Vernon and planted in there until he could find a place to put them for himself. The list gives us a very good idea of the best fruits for a gentleman's orchard.

Washington and his friends are to use them for scions or grafts. Indeed, that may be all Lear himself will take at a later date. By the same ship are five thousand plants of the white thorn for Washington. There are also furze seeds, for another possible hedge plant. The whole lot will leave for Georgetown on February 19, 1794.

When nothing has arrived by mid-May, Washington (in Philadelphia) is justifiably anxious that the ground be prepared for such as may survive the long voyage and can be nursed to life.

"A mild and placid March and pleasant April has caused a most luxuriant vegetation . . . The white thorn and the fruit trees must have perished and, if not, the season is very late for them. But by the end of May the *Peggy* has arrived. Good news in June says the plants are all in the ground at Mount Vernon and doing well.

The affair of the plants Moultrie caused anxiety. General William

Moultrie, in December, 1791, wrote that he was sending from Charleston by the Baltimore packet, under the care of Governor Howard, the plants that he had promised. They are two boxes with palmetto royal, one box with two apopynaxes and one box with two oleanders. A note says that they all stand "our winters" (presumably those of Charleston) very well except the apopynaxes, which must be housed. "The seed of the Indian creeper" will be sent direct. By February, Washington wrote to the same General Williams who had dealt for him with Mrs. Carroll, listing the plants and stating his "apprehension that some accident has befallen them." He says that if they have reached Baltimore and have escaped destruction from the severity of the weather and are found to be in such preservation as to be worth sending to Mount Vernon, he would have them sent direct to Mount Vernon by the first vessel that may be bound that way. The charges from Charleston and to Mount Vernon will be paid as soon as they are ascertained. The assiduous Williams discovers that the packet bearing the Moultrie plants was to have stopped at Norfolk on the way to Baltimore. It struck, however, on Willowby Bar and, the ship being in great danger, a part of the cargo had to be thrown overboard. By the first of March Williams learns that the Moultrie plants had been saved and given to a Colonel Newton to preserve. Since, however, Williams is not acquainted with Colonel Newton, he hesitates . . . Whether or not Williams dared, like plants were later growing at Mount Vernon.

Washington also had orders to fill.

In December, 1784, Washington is importuned in a letter, of which the last sentence and the signature only is in Lafayette's own hand, for seeds to be planted in the King's Garden in Paris. They are to be procured from "Kentucke" and are as follows:

The seeds of the Coffee Tree which resembles the Black Oak.
> Do. of the Pappa Tree
> Do. of the Cucumber Tree
> Do. of the Blackberry Tree
> Do. of the Wild Cherry Tree
> Do. Buck-eye Tree
> Do. of Wild Rye, Buffalo Grass, Shawnee Salade, Wild Lettuce, Crown Imperial, Cardinal flower, the Tulip-bearing laurel tree, and the seeds of everything else curious which that famed country produces.

"His Excellency" can have the whole order "carefully sent to the Director of the French Pacquets at New York that it might be transmitted to Paris." And then Lafayette's message: "God bless you, my dear General. I am requested by Mr. St. John to sign this and do it with the greater pleasure as these seeds and trees will be very welcome in France. Lafayette"

In May of 1785, from Fauquier, "T. Marshall" writes his "Dear General" that he will with the greatest pleasure execute the small commission by collecting "the different seeds agreeable to the list." The crown imperial, the tulip-bearing laurel and the cardinal flower, however, he is not acquainted with, but does not doubt he will find them out by inquiry.

In July, Washington writes to Lafayette that he has commissioned three or four persons, of whom Colonel Marshall is one, to procure "in Kentucke" the seeds mentioned in the list from New York, "and such

Cardinal flower, requested of Washington by Lafayette. Curtis *Botanical Magazine*

others as are curious." He will forward them as soon as they come to him, "which cannot be until after the growing crop has given its seeds." (Here the good gardener cannot forbear pointing up a natural difficulty.)

For Washington's own summation we have his letter to J. Anderson.

Mount Vernon, April 7, 1797.

I am once more seated under my own vine and fig-tree . . . and hope to spend the remainder of my days . . . which in the ordinary course of things (being now in my sixty-sixth year) cannot be many, in peaceful retirement; making political pursuits yield to the more rational amusement of cultivating the earth.

Freed, as I now am, from the toils, the cares, and responsibility of public occupations, and engaged in rural and agricultural pursuits, I hope (aided by the recollection of having contributed my best endeavours to promote the happiness of that country which gave me and my ancestors birth) to glide peaceably and gently on in the shades of retirement, and with good will to all men, until *my time* shall be no more. In doing this I promise myself more real enjoyment than in all the bustling with which I have been occupied for upwards of forty years of my life, which, as the wise man says, has been little more than *vanity and vexation*.

We cannot do better than close our account of Mount Vernon with that of a Polish visitor.

June, 1798

In the evening [General] Washington showed us round his garden. It is well cultivated, perfectly kept, and is quite in English style. All the vegetables indispensable for the kitchen were found there. Different kinds of berries, currants, raspberries, strawberries, gooseberries — a great quantity of peaches and cherries, but much inferior to ours; they are destroyed by robins, blackbirds, and negroes before they are ripe. There were very many beautiful trees: the tulip-tree with flowers like the tulips, white with an orange touch at the base; magnolias with flowers whose scent is almost as strong as the smell of an orange-tree, but not so pleasant; the sweeter scent — the small violet flowers have the pleasantest smell I have ever noticed, a mixture of strawberries and pineapple; the splendid catalpa is not yet in flower; the New Scotland spruce of beautiful dark green, and many other trees and shrubs, covered with flowers of different hues, planted so as to produce the best of color-effects. The weeping-willows were deprived of their best decoration: the amount of snow was so great last winter that their boughs were broken under its weight.

The whole plantation, the garden, and the rest prove well that a man born with natural taste may guess a beauty without having ever seen its model. The General has never left America; but when one sees his house and his home and his garden it seems as if he had copied the best samples of the grand old homesteads of England.

Furber's Flowers for the Month of September

1. Red Sow-Bread F E
2. White Sow-Bread F E
3. White Corn-Marygold G
4. New Tree Primrose B
5. Sour leaved Geranium G
6. Quilled African Marigold B
7. Hearts Ease B
8. Shrub Cotton G
9. Shefford's Hester Auricula P
10. Virginian Birthwort G
11. Virginian upright Bramble B T

12. Scarlet Indian Cane G
13. White Colchicum B
14. Bean Caper G
15. All-red Amaranthus B
16. Double white Soapwort B
17. Yellow Indian Cane G
18. Virginian Poke B
19. Gentianella F E
20. White Monthly Rose B T
21. Yellow Amaranthus P
22. Oriental Arsmart B
23. Broad leaved Cardinal P
24. Yellow Colchicum B
25. Hardy golden Rod B

26. White Althea Frutex B T
27. Chequered Colchicum B
28. Yellow Colutea G
29. Dwarf Pomegranate G
30. Striped single female Balsam B
31. African Marigold B
32. Honour & Glory Auricula P
33. White Flower Moth Mullein B
34. Double Cochicum B
35. Three-leaved Passion-Flower

11 "To Be Got When I Can"

THE wide and rolling countryside of Mecklenburg County, Virginia, has only a few eminences where bluffs rise above river bends. Little creeks run through to join a wide and shallow river flowing slowly from falls in the higher country. A huge reservoir now obscures small islands once carefully noted on early surveys. Names like Buffalo and Bluewing commemorate a land teeming with game. Sugartree and Bluestone recall natural advantages noted long ago. This was once a wild forest where men lived by shooting game and died from snakebite, especially in the hot months from March to September, when snakes were most active.

In the late seventeenth century and the early eighteenth, a tide of tobacco-growing rose from depleted fields in the lowlands to richer soil inland and on to the foothills of the "endless mountains." The land was cleared, to be submerged by the one great paying crop of this part of an increasingly trade-minded world. Tobacco engulfed all, with its concomitant, slave labor. The small self-contained farms, the mills and mines and trading posts that had formerly set the pattern for developing the water-laced wilderness, gave way before the unstoppable new business of raising a questionable crop by questionable methods.

Many people sensed the drawbacks of a tobacco economy: the speedy impoverishment of the land, forcing moves to ever-fresher fields; the ever-increasing need for slaves able to sow, weed, harvest and cure the crop; the pressures for shipments by avaricious landholders to even more greedy merchants in London. Doubts and protests were recorded, but drowned in the fortunes made by a few. At its peak the economy founded on tobacco became only that, with tobacco leaves for money, credit and barter.

Polite society generally could ignore the production of this "golden leaf" or "sotweed," the name depending upon the sentiments of the observer, but not the system. Slaves received careful attention, whatever lapses have been recorded, because they were the source of energy upon which all depended. When fears were voiced for the future of a countryside and way of life that tolerated slavery, even the most receptive hearers realized that to ask these planters to give up slavery would be asking people to give up all the power they had and all they knew. Slaves were of ever-preesnt interest, valuable necessities. Their food and shelter, nursing and clothing, came first among plantation requirements. The master went regularly to see them. The mistress took care of their emergencies, supervised their cures and educated the likely ones for indoor service.

So it should not surprise us to find that at the end of the eighteenth century the treasured garden records of a large plantation house should include no mention of this crop even as it floated on the tobacco sea, while the names of trusted slaves sound like those of the family.

Washington noted this land as poor as he rode through on his tour in 1791 and observed that the small town of Clarksville, near this plantation, handled nearly one third of the tobacco crop for the entire countryside. It is worth remembering that at this time Washington had converted the economy of Mount Vernon away from tobacco and into a varied crop system, though still slave dependent.

Every researcher has had rewarding plums drop, plop! upon a field that was about to be abandoned. After hunting for mention of garden matters where people had such heavy business on hand it is a wonder if they stopped to consider gardening in this tobacco-ridden country, one comes upon the lovingly kept records of a lady to whom gardening was the delight and resource of her life.

Over and over again Lady Skipwith tells us what she grows and where and how and whether or not she is successful. She identifies her plants from her garden reference books, chiefly from her carefully acknowledged authority, Philip Miller in his enormous *Gardener's Dictionary.* And she is not alone. Her husband, a great gardener of vegetables, includes, with his orders for vegetable seeds, many bulbs and roots also carefully listed. These may be plants in which he, perhaps, is especially interested, but it is likely that she has asked him to get them for her, for relatives and friends and neighbors, from all of whom she has eagerly acquired some of her treasures. And she has given away and suggested for others a wealth of plants, again all duly listed. Her lists are a paper

Bust of Lady Skipwith

treasure trove over which we can pore, seeing as we go, no doubt as she did, everything in full and delightful bloom. And fruit. For Lady Skipwith is also a fruit fancier, meticulous, critical of the quality to be found in each fruit. Generous with her observations, just in her judgment. A perfect gardener.

Jean, Lady Skipwith, was the second wife of Sir Peyton Skipwith, seventh baronet, who had first married her older sister, Anne. That he must have been a remarkable man in his own right can be, however remotely, deduced from his being able to keep his title throughout the American Revolution, and to have succeeded in marrying his deceased wife's sister. That he was able to perform both these rather ticklish feats in Virginia, the boiling pot of American freedom from British restraints and prerogatives, and the one colony in which the Church of England had undisputed authority, attests to rather especial ability. Called up once during the Revolution on charges of treason, he quickly cleared himself and returned unscathed to plant his vegetables in raised beds by methods he also recorded. One other remarkable fact remains to be noted: he is said to have won the entire plantation on which he settled himself and his second family, building a beautiful new house by his own plans and with his own slaves, from the profligate William Byrd III in a gambling game.

The family of Skipwith was a distinguished one whose history is recorded on a tombstone of ample proportions brought from another site and laid on top of another's grave at the entrance to the parish church of Blandford, south of Petersburg.

We know it was ordered from England by the man whose grave it was to cover, to be carved in England with an inscription he wrote and left sealed in his will.

Sir William Skipwith, the father of Sir Peyton, wrote what appears today on the white marble recumbent stone, as follows:

Sir William Skipwith, Baronet who deceased the 25th of February, 1764, aged 56 years. He descended from Sir Henry Skipwith of Prestwould in Leicestershire, created Baronet by King James the First — Was honoured with King Charles the First's Commission for raising men against the usurping powers and proved loyal to his King, so that he was deprived of his estate by the usurper who occasioned his and his sons' deaths. Except Sir Grey Skipwith, grandfather of the abovesaid Sir William Skipwith, who was obliged to come to Virginia for refuge where the family hath since continued.

In his will, Sir William leaves a picture of a just and careful man, dividing large properties among his wife and children with forethought, naming the slaves who shall be given to each one and keeping them in families already established with their "future increase." Each of his three sons receives a whole family or more. His daughters had each been given a "girl slave," with "her increase," when she married or turned twenty-one, gifts confirmed when he gives each son-in-law title to the "Negro woman" (named in the will as "Fanny," "Venus") now in his possession. There is much disposing of large properties to his three sons and arranging for his wife's support. He concludes by saying he wishes to be buried "in a proper part of the Church Yard" and asks that "a single plain marble" be sent from England and put on his grave, with "this inscription on it wrote on a paper and sealed up in my will." He desired "none of my friends or children put themselves in mourning except my wife as to herself or not as she pleases. I also desire that my funeral may not be expensive as I don't approve of feasting at funerals . . ."

This is the man who, as one of the trustees of Blandford when Petersburg and Blandford became towns in 1748, ruled against wooden chimneys and swine running at large. Previously there had been three little tobacco towns, called Peter's Point, Pocahontas and Ravenscroft, sited at the falls of the Appomattox. Farther down the river was Blandford, where the wealthier planters lived with gardens running down to the river's edge.

This had seemed rich country to William Byrd II when he laid out the dividing line between Virginia and North Carolina in 1727 and 1728. Although it seemed relatively poor to Washington on his tour through this part of his country in 1791, he remarked that "nearly a third of the tobacco exported from the whole state besides a considerable quantity of wheat and flour, much . . . manufactured by the mills of the town." William Byrd II, however, had been attracted by the area and had taken up land thereabouts in parcels of varying dimensions.

The early settlers there in the first part of the eighteenth century had mainly been Scots, come to build solid fortunes in trade and milling. The first Skipwith place had been called Greencroft. A small creek near the site perpetuates their name in its own — Skippers. Hugh Miller, a Scottish merchant and vestryman of Blandford church, lived nearby at Elm Hill. Births of his three children are recorded in the Bristol parish register: Anne, 1742; Robert, 1746; and Jane, 1748. Births of seven slave children are recorded in 1760. Hugh Miller moved his family "home" to Scotland and it was there, in Edinburgh, that young Peyton Skipwith, sent abroad to receive a gloss to his education and undoubtedly also to learn how to run the family business, courted Anne. They were married in 1765 and came back to Virginia to settle on the plantation left Anne by her father. After bearing his children, one of whom would go back to England to inherit the family title, Anne died in childbirth in 1779. One daughter had married a Carter of Corotoman and another St. George Tucker of Bermuda. We shall see these families furnishing plants for the garden at the new home of their father and their aunt, now their stepmother.

For Sir Peyton, in 1788, married the second Miller sister, who had changed her name from Jane to Jean. He courted her when she was a forty-two-year-old daughter living in England with her widowed mother. Sir Peyton had begged his "dearest Miss Miller" that, on his way to Corotoman, he be allowed to tell his daughter there was the probability of his being accompanied by "Lady Skipwith and not Miss Miller . . . in fact, by their mother and not their aunt." Some planning as to where they could be married was necessary, but, that difficulty surmounted, the newly married couple settled into Elm Hill and immediately began to build a new house for themselves named Prestwould in honor of the Skipwith family seat in England. We shall hear of plants brought from Elm Hill for the new garden at Prestwould. We may imagine that by this time in her life Lady Skipwith was a proficient

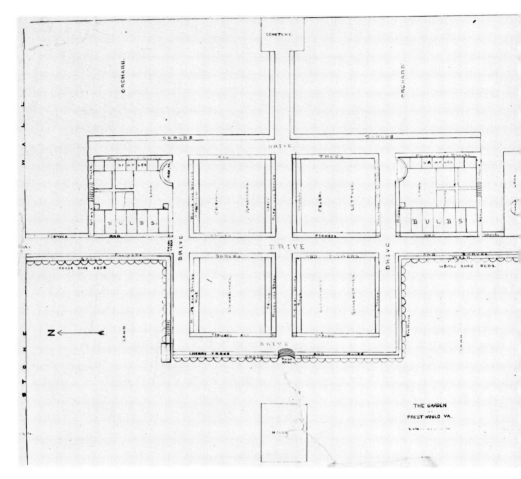

Plan of the garden at Prestwould. The house lower center, river on the right and the family cemetery upper center

gardener, in the tradition of those times in England, where there was little else in which an intelligent spinster could excel.

Prestwould as it stands today is a handsome four-square Georgian house of proportions suitable for very hot weather, with high ceilings and side doors and windows. Walls are thick against both heat and cold. A huge fireplace of simple but handsome design dominates every room. All materials were local: stone blocks of a mellow color, floors of the heartwood of loblolly pine, paneling and stairs of oak. A variation of the usual plantation house pattern has the huge central hall cut in two by a paneled wall, making a handsome front room of the entrance toward the land — and a much larger room of the back half toward the river entrance. Here a wide staircase takes off and turns at a square landing to rise to the upstairs hall where the bedrooms are reached. In the upstairs hall on the side toward the river are three large windows with wide sills. Lady Skipwith was said to have kept her potted plants here in winter so that the whole house was fragrant with the scent of orange and lemon blossoms. From these windows the family ferry was in full view, far below on the banks of the river with the islands, on one of which she had a garden of wildflowers and on another, an orchard. A third island was the place where Sir Peyton could leave his young cattle for the summer. (William Byrd II had made note of three islands.)

One approaches the house by a short avenue between well-built walls of "tabby," an innovation where the usual adornment for the sides of the avenue was a double row of "Virginia cedars," as at Tuckahoe. A gate leads into a wide enclosure and the drive continues to the house, which commands a knoll facing the river. To the right the wall shuts off "the street" of slave quarters, running at right angles to the approach to the house. Several small clapboard houses with huge chimneypieces still stand. Presumably the vegetable gardens, farm and animals were on this side. A "schoolhouse" and "office" of white clapboard, smartly styled, are on the house side of the wall and the house has a side verandah overlooking this part of the estate. There is a basement entrance here, and back stairs for servicing the house. Toward the river the land slopes away, sometimes steeply, and directly in front of the house, but far from it, stands a gate, which would seem to indicate a river entrance of some pretension. Old and large cedars, formally planted between the river wall and the remains of a small gardenhouse on this left side of the house as one faces the river, indicate the possible site of a drive and a garden. The family graveyard is far down at the foot of a slope on this side. Large magnolias, oaks and a huge mulberry tree seem part of an original parklike planting. The place has a peaceful and self-contained air, as of living for itself alone in the midst of a great "silent country."

Myths blow about. Someone has said somewhere that Sir Peyton knew Brandon well and that the garden at Prestwould was laid out to be like that at Brandon. Both places have the same serene air. At Brandon the garden lies flat between the house and the river, spaciously divided into large square beds with wide grass paths between. Trees and shrubs are included, as they are at Westover, where the garden has much the same proportions. A garden at Prestwould would have had to drop in terraces or "falls" toward the river if it was sited between the river and the house. It was the custom to leave "falls" clear, as at Westover, and

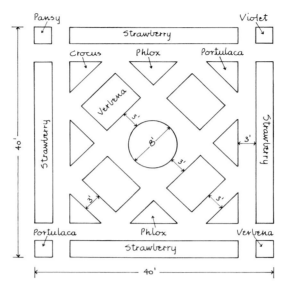

Two plans for garden beds found in the Skipwith papers

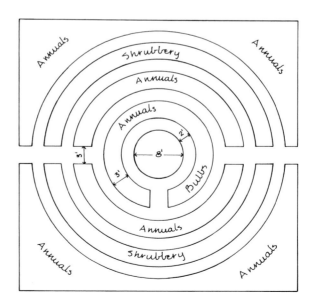

locate the garden, walled on its own, inside the walls of the park. At Prestwould it lay on the slope on the left side just forward of the corner of the house, a simple but ample arrangement of walks and squares where a keen and "curious" garden mistress could direct its maintenance. One wonders how much she did herself, brought back to the land of her birthplace and many black helping hands. In England, even in affluent households, the temptation to work in the garden overcame many ladies' scruples. It was this ability that so impressed Andrew Downing fifty years later when he saw a duchess exclaim at a weed and pull it out with no to-do whatever. Would, he wished, that American women realized these joys.

We may guess where the garden was, but we do not have to guess what was in it. Lady Skipwith speaks to us today, as she did to her friends. And we have contemporary pictures of nearly all of her plants from the books we know she used.

In the Archives of the College of William and Mary at Williamsburg is a Skipwith collection of bits and pieces: lists of plants on the backs of old bills, a freshly copied list or two, some bills for seeds and planting, a list of wildflowers and another locating the same, a notice of an extensive modern auction, a photograph of a marble bust, two plans for geometrically designed garden beds, a note as to where vegetable seeds have been sown, another identifying fruit trees now bearing, a list of the consecutive fruit crops for one season and some notes on how to raise trees from cuttings. These all fall between the years 1785 and 1805. The auction is 1946, with a picture of the house and grounds, the slave quarters and gardenhouse and driveway and home pastures from the air, the lists of the furniture, all very fine, in the house, and of the stock, horses, ponies and cattle, also very fine, from the barns. On the back of the photograph of the marble bust is written "Jean Lady Skipwith 1748–1826, 2nd wife of Sir Peyton Skipwith 1749–1805 of Prestwould, Mecklenberg Co., Va., daughter of Hugh Miller of Scotland and Virginia." These are the records we have for replanting Lady Skipwith's garden and the vegetables and fruits at Prestwould at the end of the eighteenth century.

The last Skipwith owner of Prestwould found these papers in a box when clearing out the house before the auction, and deposited them with the college. There are several obscurely written words, and some lists use the old way of writing the first *s* of two, so Cassia appears to be Cafsia. When the list has "See . . ." in parentheses and then "1 sort" or "2 sort," Lady Skipwith means us to look up the name given after "See" in Philip Miller's *Dictionary* and find what he lists as the first sort, or second, or whatever. The eighth edition, of 1768, seems to suit her references exactly, and this is also the edition used by Thomas Jefferson.

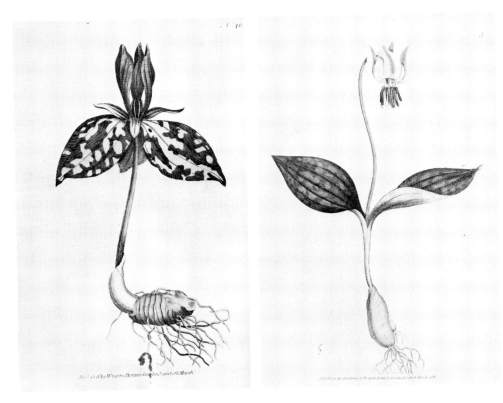

The lists sometimes run without separations between the individual flowers listed, as if she knows them so well she tells them off by rote. There are also endearing categories: "Shrubs to be got when I can"; "Bulbous roots to get when in my power." Enough to warm the heart of any gardener anywhere. She keeps her wildflowers separate, probably proud of their number, although she grows many of them in her garden as well as on the island in quantity, as noted on "the Island map list."

The fruits and vegetables are interesting to compare with what Lady Skipwith's contemporaries, Jefferson and Washington, were growing. They all used the great Prince Nurseries on Long Island. Some lists follow the Prince advertisements verbatim, order, prices and all. We see what fruit trees were the most popular, when the fruits ripened and their qualities. And we can surmise from the quantities of vegetable seeds ordered what a plantation had to grow to feed its family, slaves and livestock. (Cabbage for instance. Cattle were fed cabbages in nonpasture country.) We have also the very list of a Richmond nurseryman

Three of Lady Skipwith's
wildflowers: *Trillium sessile, Erythronium dens canis*
and *Viola pedata.* From
Curtis *Botanical Magazine*

from whom Sir Peyton ordered, and again, there is a similarity between
his vegetable requirements and those of Mount Vernon and Monticello.

"Shrubs to be got when I can" and "Bulbous roots to get when in my
power" are short lists of only three or four items each. One feels sure
they eventually grew at Prestwould. A very long list notes "Wild flowers in the garden," and more wildflowers, some of these over again, are
on the "Island map list." Perhaps written for someone who asked her,
is "My house plants are — " because it ends, "I once had a tolerable
collection of annual and other flowers but the neglect of a few years had
lost the greatest part of them and only the most hardy and such as would
sow themselves now remain."

And there is a running list of the more familiar garden flowers called
"List of flowers for Mrs. Boyd," ending "with a very few annual and a
good many wild flowers, amongst the latter the spotted Canada martagon lily is much admired." A list of "Flowering shrubs," begins with
"A tolerable collection of roses . . ."

One cannot read Lady Skipwith's lists without realizing that here was a remarkable woman, full of intellectual curiosity and determination, creating a garden in what must have been something of a wilderness with plants from the wilderness itself. Beside the garden flowers she had known in England are the flowers and shrubs and trees of the countryside. Discovered by earlier travelers and settlers, they had been sent to England for identification often by no less an authority than the great Linnaeus, and recorded by no less knowledgeable a person than Philip Miller. As she finds them growing upon her island or has them brought to her from the uplands, she notes each one from her *Gardener's Dictionary,* how it grows and how it is best propagated. Sometimes she has a plant that is "not in Miller," and what a joy that must have been. And yet she is so far from and out of the orbit of botanists eager to hear of new plants, that all she can do is grow the plant and call it a "Blue Star flower, not described by Miller."

In some cases she uses earlier names than the ones used by Miller, so when she writes "Ketmia" we are glad to find it under *Hibiscus* in

 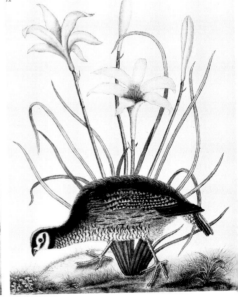

Catesby's Canada Martagon, Plate A-11.   Catesby's "Attamusco Lily," Plate A-12.

Two of Lady Skipwith's American native garden favorites

Miller because *H. Syriacus* was formerly referred to as *Ketmia syriacus.* Sometimes she says "what I call" and gives the familiar name, as in "blue funnel flower," which is the name also used by Jefferson for the plant we now call Virginia cowslip, Virginia bluebells or Roanokebells, in fact *Mertensia virginica.*

It is important as well as interesting to know what the various flowers looked like at the time. Many have since been "improved" out of all recognition. Sweet peas, for instance, and roses and violets have been brought a long way, often losing their scent while acquiring such attributes as size and long-blooming habits. Even Sir Peyton's vegetables have changed so much that he, and even his cattle, might hardly know their cabbages.

To see what the eighteenth-century garden looked like, we have two invaluable sources. The first is the earliest of illustrated seed catalogues, Robert Furber's gorgeous commercial venture, *Twelve Months of Flowers.* A gardener himself, like Philip Miller, Furber got out a plant catalogue showing what was available from his nursery and how any one resident in England could expect to have blooming flowers in every month of the year. Published in 1730, the catalogue consists of twelve handsome plates, which show the available flowers with all the dash and style of Dutch flower paintings. Under these enormous bouquets, arranged in very elaborate urns and bowls, is a numbered list of the familiar names of each flower with a corresponding number discreetly attached to each bloom. We can see what Lady Skipwith and Sir Peyton meant when they wrote of hyacinths, pinks and pansies, and ordered as "Prince Picoti, or July Flower."

The second source for illustrated reference lies in Curtis' *Botanical Magazine,* the first six volumes of which seem to have been generally known and easily available. Lady Skipwith may have had her own copies, as Washington and Jefferson had theirs. Internal evidence puts them in Lady Skipwith's hands, as many of her familiar names follow Curtis when she departs from Miller, and there are direct quotes from Curtis, such as "ornamental for a mantelpiece in winter."

We brief Lady Skipwith's collection of lists, using her categories:

MY HOUSE PLANTS . . . Oranges * Lemons * Limes * Oleander * Dwarf Myrtle * Rose Geranium * *Chrysanthemum Indicum* (the latter hardy enough to live in the garden through the winter though the first frost destroy the flower).

*

BULBOUS ROOTS TO GET WHEN IN MY POWER . . . Meadow saf-

Lady Skipwith's Corn flag. From Curtis *Botanical Magazine*

fron (see Colchicum) a bulbous root about the size of a tulip, flowers in autumn and the leaves continue green all winter. Called by the common people Naked Ladies, great varieties may be obtained from seed * Mariana (see Watsonia), a bulbous root shaped like a kidney, a red flower, many on a stalk. They rise well from seed * Cyclamen raised from seed from which a great variety may be obtained, is four years before it flowers from seed. Blooms in December and continues its beauty till late in the spring.

*

SHRUBS TO BE GOT WHEN I CAN . . . Widow wail (see Cneorum) a low evergreen shrub with a small yellow flower, easily raised from seed

Chrysanthemum indicum. One of Lady Skipwith's
house plants

sown in the fall * Early shrub Anonis (see Ononis) raised from seeds in
the open ground, very beautiful and when once established gives no trouble,
the seeds should be sown in September commonly called Rest Harrow *
Spotted Cistus (see Cistus) Hardy, can be raised from seeds or cuttings
but best from seeds, sown in the spring which will come up in five or six
weeks. It exudes a balsamic gum or species of opium and is a most
desirable shrub continuing two or three months in flower. * Double
blossomed Cherry raised by budding upon the common wild cherry, very
handsome (see Cerasus).

*

LIST OF FLOWERS FOR MRS. BOYD . . . Double blue and blush-

coloured hyacinths, grape and feathered Do. * Double, single and polyanthus Narcissus * Large Snow Drop * Yellow Autumnal Amaryllis *
Daffodil * Corn Flag * Double Jonquil * Common Starflower * Lily of
the Valley * Bulbous Iris * Persian Iris * Florentine White Iris * Common
Blue * Yellow and Tawny Day Lily * Large White Lily * Bermudian Ixia
* Columbines * Blue and white sweet violets * English cowslip * Wallflower * Sweet William. With a very few Annual and a good many wild
flowers — amongst the latter the Spotted Canada Martagon Lily is much
admired.

*

WILD FLOWERS IN THE GARDEN . . . Dog's Tooth Violet (see Erythronium) * Puccoon, or Bloodroot (see Sanguinaria) * Greater Celandine having no stalk * Tuberous insipid Fumatory (see Fumaria) *
Monkshood, Wolfsbane * (see Cypripedium) and Moccasin flower * Claytonia * Solomon's Seal (see Polygonatum 1, 3, 5, 8th sorts) * Sessile Trillium * Atamasco Lily (see Amaryllis 2nd sort) * Hounds Tongue (see
Cynoglossum 4 sort) * Commelina (see Miller) 1 sort * Virginia Spiderwort (see Tradescantia) * Asters of various kinds * Cultivated Violets
(see Viola) some with a pansy flower * Lychnis (see Phlox) six sorts all
Handsome * Dwarf Cassia. An annual. Seed from the Forest or Cool
Spring. * Carolina Kidney-bean (see Glycine) Winged leaves and blue
flowers growing in whorls — 2nd sort. Got the seeds from G. Skipwith *
Carolina Coral-tree (see Erythrina) 1st sort — got the seeds from Mrs.
Miller * Limodorum Tuberosum — South Carolina — by Jim * Tway
blade (see Ophrys) I have I suppose 2 sorts * Blue Star flower — not
described by Miller * American cowslip (see Meadia) * Dodecatheon
Bears Ear of Virginia * Bermudiana (see Sizranchium) the blue flower
with grasslooking stalks and leaves, plenty in the orchard * Canada columbine (see Aquilegia) * Starflower (see Ornithagalum 7th sort * Liverwort (see Hepatica) single blue. By sowing the seeds some varieties may
be obtained. To be sown in August soon after they are ripe * Cassia or
Wild Senna (see Cassia 6th sort).

*

FLOWERING SHRUBS . . . A tolerable collection of Roses, amongst
which are a double and single Yellow Rose * Marble and Cabbage Rose *
Purple, White, and Persian Lilac * Scorpion and Bladder Senna * White
and Yellow Jasmine * English and Red-trumpet Honeysuckle * Syringa or
Mock orange * Double white and Common Althea * Calicanthus and
Mountain Pea tree * Georgia cluster pea * Everlasting pea and Convolvulus (of different colours) *

*

PLANTS . . . White Dittany (see Dictamnus) easily raised from seed
sown in the fall — very ornamental with little trouble * Cudweed Goldi-

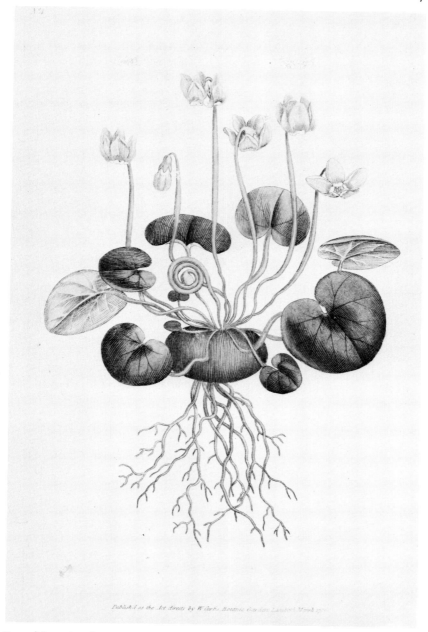

Round-leaved cyclamen, "easily raised from seed." From Curtis *Botanical Magazine*

locks, or Eternal flower — raised from seeds sown in April. It doesn't bear removing and flowers best the first and second year * Spotted and striped flowered Alstroemeria — Native of Peru — the latter very sweet-scented — here they would be house plants. * Prickly Lantana (house plant) very brilliant, seldom without flowers. * Purple cupped statice or thrift, dried — it retains its colour which renders it ornamental for a Mantel-piece in Winter — a biennial yet often increased by parting its roots, but more advantageously from seeds * Candytuft * Anemone * Cortusa — or Bear's Ear Sanicle — can be raised from seed or roots — the purple is the finest * Egg Plant (Brown Jolly) see Melangena * Ice Plant (see Mesembryanthemum) should be raised in pots — I must get some seed if I can * Balsam Apple (see Momordica) * Loranthus (per-haps the seed I got from Mrs. S. like dried cherry has a bright scarlet flower. * Fraxinella (see Dictamnus M.) raised from seed, sown soon after they are ripe, very ornamental with little trouble — valuable * Early shrub Anonis. Raised from seed in open ground very beautiful and when once established gives no trouble. The seeds should be sown in September. (See Ononis Miller) 5th sort. Purple shrubby Rest Harrow grows natu-rally on the Alps * Cudweed Goldilocks, or Eternal flower raised from seeds which should be sown in April — It doesn't bear removing — and ought to be sown every year as it flowers best the 1st and 2nd year — * Cyclamen raised from seed from which a great variety may be obtained — is four years from the seed before they flower which is in December and will continue in beauty until late in the Spring (write to Mrs. S. for seeds) * Erythronium, Dog's Tooth Violet — What we call Island Martagon * Commelina (see Miller 1st sort) * American cowslip (see Miller) * Lychnidea, or Bastard Lychnis (see Phlox). What we called Woods Pink, Trestle flower, small blue flower in April * Ixia Bermudiana * Black-berry Lily * Hibiscus. American Ketmia, what was sent me by the name of Holy Oak, 4th sort. The 6th sort Indian Ketmia I expect is the flower Helen found at the spring. 19th sort is what we call Okra. In the En-cyclopaedia tis the 7th sort which is there called Esculent Syrian Mallow * Coral-tree (see Erythrina) Mrs. Miller's Scarlet Bean very handsome * Medeola the Lilly or Little Martagon — perhaps what we got by the Branch at Elm Hill with the whorled leaves * Dwarf Cassia * Cowslip * Double Rocket * Columbines * Bloody wall flower * Widowed Wall Flower * Musk Scabious * Sweet William * Pinks of various kinds, very fine * Chinese Pink, double and single * Woods Pink * Variety of Holly-hocks * Crimson Mallow * Holy Oak * Caper Bush * Apocynum * Spider-wort * Sun Flower * Monkshood * Everlasting Pea * Ladies Slipper * Trestle Flower.

Two scraps of lists add or repeat:

White Dittany (see Dictamnus) easily raised from seeds sown in the fall — very ornamental with little trouble * Cudweed Goldilocks, or eternal flower — raised from seeds sown in April. It don't bear removing and flowers best the first and second year * Spotted and striped flowered Alstroemeria, native of Peru, the latter very sweet and scented. Here they would be house plants. * Prickly Lantana (house plant) very brilliant. Seldom without flowers * Purple cupped statice or Thrift. Dried, it retains its colour which renders it ornamental for a mantel-piece in winter. A biennial yet often increased by parting its roots, but more advantageously from seeds * Candy-tuft * Anemony.

Hibiscus, China Rose. From Curtis *Botanical Maga-zine*

ISLAND MAP LIST [seems to suggest where plants on an earlier list are located]:

Erythronium. Dog's Tooth Violet. What we call Island Martagon. * Convallaria. Polygonatum. Solomon's Seal (our Jacobs Ladder). Two sorts, one with the red, the other purple berries and I believe a third sort in the point of the island * Cut-leaved violet (see other list). * Sessile Trillium * Tuberous-rooted Limodorum * Pulmonaria virginica. Lungwort. What I call blue funnel flower * Cyclamen * Sanguinaria * Fumaria — insipid Fumitory etc. * Stinking Black Hellebore — Bears-foot or Setterwort * Campanula pyramidalis. What we here call Bear grass * Claytonia, the little narrow-leafed black-rooted flower from the foot of the garden * Ixia Bermudiana, perhaps the blackberry lily in the garden * Bastard Lychnis (see Phlox). What we here call Woods Pink * Trestle flower, small blue flower in April * Coral tree Mrs. Miller's scarlet bean, very handsome.

To round out our knowledge of Lady Skipwith's plants, we add a list of flower seeds bought from Minton Collins, nurseryman of Richmond in 1793.

3 double variegated fall Hyacinths * 3 double variegated narcissus * 3 tuberose * 6 tulips * 12 ranunculus * 3 Polianthus narcissus * 3 Persian Iris * 2 doz. yellow and blue crocus * Sweet peas 2 sorts * Sweet scabious * Yellow lupins * Mignonette * Prince Picoti or July flower * Indian Pink * Double Charlotte Pink * Queens Stock * Red 10 week stock * Widow wall flower * Sweet Sultan * Double Balsam * Sweet William * Ice Plant * Striped French Marigold * French honeysuckle.

Except for a memo on raising trees — poplar, mulberry, cedar and holly — this sums up our Skipwith garden records.

That the Skipwiths made successful and happy lives with their gardening and farming may be deduced from their wills and from a deposition made by their only son, Humberton. Lady Skipwith's will is of greatest interest to us today as it shows she had an extensive library. To her two daughters and her daughter-in-law she wills two hundred volumes each, "to be selected alternately from my library." To her son-in-law Tucker Coles she wills her twenty-volume *Encyclopaedia Britannica.* What a boon it would be if these would come back to the house and again form the base of reference for gardening.

Humberton Skipwith, now successor to Sir Peyton Skipwith's "seat in Virginia," says of himself in 1829 (three years after the death of his mother) that he has been educated to no profession, his pursuits having been agricultural exclusively. With "about 10,000 acres of land in the County of Mecklenburg and two adjoining counties, chiefly on the Dan and Stanton Rivers . . . about four hundred slaves . . . money . . . and other property" he had been "left by my parents in the enjoyment of most of the comforts collected around them in the course of a long life of industry and care."

"Industry and care" sums up the essence of Prestwould and its gardens, and of our most generously recording American lady gardener.

Furber's Flowers for the Month of October

1. Tuberose Flower P
2. Single Nasturtium B
3. Yellow Perennial Poppy B
4. Purple Polyanthos B
5. Saffron Flower B
6. Striped double Colchicum B
7. Single blue Periwinkle C T
8. Trumpet flower C T
9. Camomile double S E
10. Semper Augustus Auricula P

11. IndianTobacco B
12. Arbutus double B T
13. Best flowering Geranium G
14. Guernsey Lilly G
15. Autumn Carnation B
16. Agnus Castus B T
17. Long blowing Honeysuckle G T
18. Spiked Aster B
19. Belladona Lilly G
20. Ever green Honeysuckle B T
21. Leonurus or Arch-

angel Tree G
22. Black Crane's Bill B
23. Scarlet Crane's Bill G
24. Marigold tree G
25. Musk Scabious B
26. Double white Musk Rose B T
27. Box leaved Myrtle G
28. Michaelmas Daisie B
29. Yellow Passion flower C T
30. Hollyhock always double B
31. Virginia Shrub Acre S

12 *Catalogues and Lists*

WE HAVE SEEN a cordial fraternity developed among botanists in eighteenth-century America and an immediately profitable one among gardeners and collectors. In England there was a close and cooperative relationship among nurserymen who accepted new acquistions to grow with a view toward marketing those adaptable to the English climate. These are impressively able men: amateur botanists, friends with and to prominent and "curious" collectors, authors of books upon gardening. Professional nurserymen were highly regarded throughout the eighteenth century — indeed, their trade had been greatly respected and resorted to in the century before when Gerard and Parkinson mentioned them in their herbals.

While, in the American colonies at the beginning of the eighteenth century, selling plants and seeds was chiefly on a humble level, there were several ambitious enterprises. John Bartram, encouraged by Peter Collinson to collect American rarities, started his botanical garden at Kingsessing near Philadelphia in 1725, and eventually made it a business. Later in the century, from a commercial origin, the Prince family's nursery on Long Island grew into a great nineteenth-century horticultural business. There were also, as we know from Jefferson's and Peyton Skipwith's accounts, nurseries around Washington and probably around most other large centers, where some unusual fruits and vegetables, plants, vines and seeds were obtainable. But it was not until the arrival of Bernard M'Mahon at the end of the century to set up his nursery in Philadelphia and to write his book about it under the patronage of gardeners like Thomas Jefferson (who made M'Mahon chief recipient of materials brought back by the Lewis and Clark Expedition) that American gardeners could enjoy all the advantages available early in the century to gardeners in England.

As there is comfort in numbers, so there is assurance in repetitions of garden favorites in lists made by both experts and amateurs in the sources to which we have ready reference: publications of London nurserymen we know were read by our gardeners; catalogues of our best nurseries, Bartram's, Prince's and, later, M'Mahon's; garden diaries of Jefferson and Washington; Lady Skipwith's notes; the correspondence of Collinson and Bartram and their friends; Philip Miller's *Gardener's Dictionary,* known to all; and the equally popular *Botanical Magazine,* edited by William Curtis and in the libraries of Jefferson, Washington and Lady Skipwith; letters of advice and request from and to both sides of the Atlantic; and lesser but no less authentic bits of information from literally here, there and everywhere. There is no need to make "inspired guesses" as to what was grown.

A group of London nurserymen in the eighteenth century combined to form the Society of Gardeners, and published a book to encourage the growing of "exotic" or new plants with which they were experimenting. In 1730 appeared *A Catalogue of Trees, Shrubs, Plants and Flowers, both Exotic and Domestic which are propagated for Sale in the Gardens near London . . . By a Society of Gardeners.* Two of these men were Robert Furber of the early illustrated garden catalogue *Twelve Months of Flowers* and Christopher Gray, who bought up the plants from Bishop Compton's garden in Fulham when the bishop who succeeded that benefactor of horticulture decided not to keep the garden. We know Gray as an expert gardener from the letters of Peter Collinson, and Furber's fame is still with us in print and picture.

"Robert Furber, Gardener . . . over against Hyde Park, Kensington" produced a comprehensive *Catalogue* of the "Curious Trees, Plants, Etc. . . . For the satisfaction of such Gentlemen that are curious in collecting of foreign Trees and Shrubs, and are not willing to be at the expense of building Stoves and Greenhouses." These plants, "both Domestic and Exotic," will prosper in the English climate in open ground, and may be obtained from the above Mr. Furber at reasonable rates. He furnishes the botanic names "opposite to the English, that it may be useful to Everybody, the Gardeners understanding what Gentlemen mean when they write for any of the following Plants, and that Gentlemen may understand what the Gardeners mean when they call any of the following Plants by the Names used amongst them." Among the sections devoted to fruits, trees and shrubs, the section entitled "A Catalogue of Flowers for the open Borders" is of most use to us, because it lists the plants most likely to be useful in American gardens in the eighteenth century. It is a relatively short list.

Hyacinths, double and single, many sorts; Snow-drops, double and single; Narcissus, several Sorts; Iris with bulbous Roots, several Sorts; Colchicums, double and single, many Sorts; Crocus's, several Sorts; Tulips double and single, many Sorts; Fritillarias, several Sorts; Dens canis, two Sorts; Jonquils, double and single; Martagons, several Sorts; Crown Imperials, several Sorts; Winter Aconites; Ranunculus's several Sorts; Mountain Ranunculus; Double Saxifrage; Anemonies, several Sorts; Lilies of the Valley, two Sorts; Asphodils, two Sorts; Yellow Day lily; Geraniums, several Sorts with knobbed Roots; Cyclamens, two Sorts; Iris with tuberose Roots, several Sorts; Spiderwort, three Sorts; Fraxinella, two Sorts; Bachelors Buttons, two Sorts; Thrift, three Sorts; Double and Single Sweet Williams; Fairchild's Mule; Campanula's several Sorts; Carnations, several Sorts that blow without breaking the Pod; Wall Flowers, many Sorts; Perennial Poppy; Rose Campions, double and single; Lychnis's, three Sorts, single and double; Double ragged Robin; Double Lychnis, a sort of Catch-Fly; Gentianella's; Daisies, several Sorts; Auricula's, several Sorts; Polyanthos, several Sorts; Pinks, single and double, several Sorts; Violets, several Sorts; Hepatica's, single and double; Flammulla Jovis; Hollyhocks or Garden Mallows, several Sorts.

The importance and interest of this list to us is that almost all the flowers mentioned in it we have seen growing in our eighteenth-century American gardens.

Robert Furber's original and gorgeous commercial venture in his printing of twelve large plates to show how gardeners in England could have flowers blooming in every month of the year is invaluable in showing us what eighteenth-century American gardeners meant when they mentioned tulips, irises and honey-suckle, and other plants since "improved" out of recognition. Twenty-five American plants and trees are shown and many of the spring buds and blooms of our trees make charming additions to the great swirls of flowers.

Robert Furber did the same thing for fruits through the year and found both schemes so successful that he followed them with a small book "explaining" both sets.

Furber's list of "explained" flowers is helpful to us as showing the characters and placements of the flowers and shrubs, marked with letters for their proper places in the gardens: "Flowers for Open Borders, marked B. Flowers for Borders to be Covered, marked B.C. Flowers that are proper for edging, marked F.E. Flowers for Spreading Edging, marked S.E. Flowers for Pots, marked P. Flowers for Green-House,

overleaf: Catalogue of the Society of Gardeners

Exiguus spatio, variis sed fertilis herbis.

Catalogus Plantarum,

Tum Exoticarum tum Domesticarum, quæ in Hortis haud procul a Londino Sitis in Venditionem propagantur.

A

CATALOGUE

OF

Trees, Shrubs, Plants, and Flowers,

BOTH

EXOTIC *and* DOMESTIC,

Which are propagated for SALE,

In the GARDENS near *LONDON*.

Divided, according to their different Degrees of Hardinefs, into particular BOOKS, or PARTS; in each of which the Plants are Ranged in an Alphabetical Order.

To which are added,

The Characters of the *Genus*, and an Enumeration of all the particular *Species* which are at prefent to be found in the feveral Nurferies near *London*, with Directions for the proper Soil and Situation, in which each particular Kind is found to Thrive.

By a SOCIETY of GARDENERS.

Et nunc omnis ager, nunc omnis parturit arbos;
Nunc frondent Silvæ, nunc formofiffimus annus.   Virg. Ecl. 3.

LONDON:

Printed in the YEAR M. DCC. XXX.

marked G. Flowering-Tree-Kinds proper for a Green-House, marked G. Flowers and Flowering-Border Trees, marked B.T. Flowering Climbing-Plants, marked C.T. Large Flowering-Trees, marked L.T."

We are interested to see he places roses in open borders. The rose garden, as such, was to come later.

The second quarter of the eighteenth century marked a great increase in the interest on both sides of the Atlantic in American plants suitable for cultivation in gardens. There was also a demand for all sorts of trees suitable for planting in parks and beside streets, for blooming and fruiting shrubs to add to the increasingly popular ornamental "shrubberies" and for varieties of "curious" plants for collectors. John Bartram, encouraged by Peter Collinson, was developing his "botanical garden," the first in North America, to make a holding place for interesting plants that could be sent across the Atlantic as soon as they appeared worthy of, and hardy enough for, the journey. Started by Bartram to please himself, the garden soon became a place to be visited, and eventually it turned into a family business, continued after his death by his sons. Our catalogue is a late one, published after his death but obviously still his. His son John kept the name, but the notes on our copy are in the hand of William Bartram. This will be seen to be mainly trees and shrubs, with the botanical names carefully noted.

The Bartram catalogue lists the botanical names in the first column with the familiar names opposite. I have changed these about, as we are giving all other lists by the familiar names. I have left the spelling uncorrected and filled in the torn parts only where the missing name was only half-destroyed. William Bartram's corrections are given in parentheses. At the end of the catalogue there is an "Explanation of Letters of Reference"; I have here placed the appropriate letter before each familiar name whenever it is included. These letters are a help to modern identification insofar as they indicate the sort of soil in which the plants were originally found. They are as follows:

a   A good moist mould or Soil on Clay and Gravel
b   A good loose Soil on Clay
c   A moist rich soil in rocky Mountains (or Low Bottoms)
d   A wet sandy Soil on Clay and Gravel
e   Richest deep moist Soil
f   Light dry Sandy Ridges
g   Dry rocky Ridges
o   Any soil and Situation.

This is the list from which Washington ordered trees and shrubs for Mount Vernon:

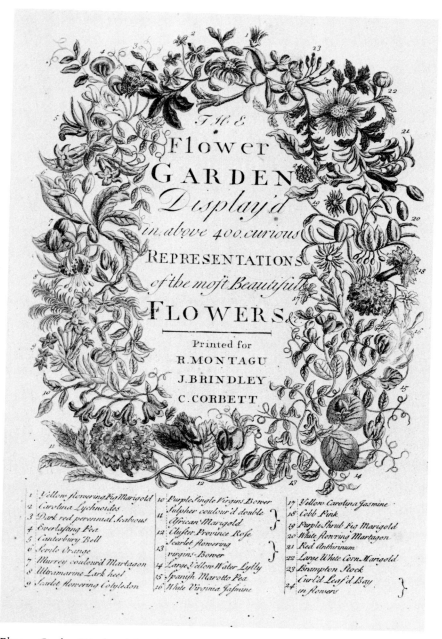

Flower Garden Displayed, in which Furber and his friends "explain" their flowers

CATALOGUE OF AMERICAN TREES, SHRUBS AND
HERBACIOUS PLANTS,
most of which are now growing,
and produce ripe Seed in
JOHN BARTRAM'S Garden, near Philadelphia.
The Seed and growing Plants of which are disposed of
on the most reasonable Terms.

a Tulip Tree — Liriodendron
Sweet Gum — Liquid Ambar styraci flua (W.B.)
f Sweet Fern — Aspleni F
b White Pine — Pinus *Strobilus* (Strobus W.B.)
a Swamp Pine — _____ Palustris
c Pinaster or Mountain Pine — _____ Sylvestris
b Frankinsense Pine — _____ *Toda*
Long leaved Pine — _____ Phoenix
Dwarf Pine — _____ Pumila
Pennsylvania Pine — _____ Echinatus
a Larch Tree, White and Red — _____ Larix
Balm of Gilead Fir — _____ Abies Canadensis
c Hemlock Spruce — _____ Abies Virginiana

Bartram's house, in the middle of his botanical garden. A carved stone on one side has: "John : Ann : Bartram : 1731." Over the front window of his study has been added "TIS GOD ALONE, ALMIGHTY LORD. THE HOLY ONE BY ME ADORED JOHN BARTRAM 1770"

a Newfoundland Spruce, black red and Dwarf	—— *Abies* (*Picaea foliis brevoribus* W.B.)
Bald Cyprus	Cupressus Disticha
White Cedar	—— Thyoides
o Red Cedar	Juniperus Virginiana
o Sasafras Tree	Laurus Sasafras
Red Bay	—— Nobilis
a Benjamin or Spice Wood	—— Benzoin
Carolina Spice Wood	—— Geniculata
a Rose Laurel	Magnolia Glauca
o Florida Laurel Tree	—— Grandiflora
a Cucumber Tree	—— Acuminata
Umbrella Tree	—— Umbrella
o Great Yellow Sweet Plumb	Prunus Americana
Crimson Plumb	—— Missisippe
b Chicasaw Plumb	—— Chicasaw
a Beach or Sea-side-Plumb	—— Maritima
Dwarf Plumb	—— Declinatus
o Bird or Cluster Cherry	—— Padus Sylvatica (virginiana W.B.)
a Evergreen Bay of Carolina	—— Serratifolia
Dwarf Bird Cherry	—— Racemosa
Crab Apple	Malus Coronaria
c Quickbeam	Sorbus Americana
	Mespilus Nivea
	—— Pumila
a Great Hawthorn	—— Axarol
Cockspur Hawthorn	—— Spinoza (*coccinea* W.B.)
b Dwarf Hawthorn	—— Humilis
Carolina Hawthorn	—— Apiisolia
d Swamp Service, 2 varieties with red and black fruit	
————	Crategus Prunifolia
	—— Canadensis
a Dwarf Swamp Service 2 varieties red and black fruit	
Arbor Vitae	————
e Dogwood	Thuya Odorifera (*odorata* W.B.)
	Cornus Florida
a Red Willow	—— Sylvestris
White berried Swamp Dogwood	—— Sanguinea
e Mountain Dwarf Cornus	—— Perlata
a Great Black Haw	—— Venosa
Small black Haw	Viburnum Prunifolia
d Water Elder	—— Spinosum
c Mountain Viburnum	—— Tini folia
a Tough Viburnum	—— Triloba
	—— Lanceolata

CATALOGUE of American TREES, SHRUBS and HERBACIOUS PLANTS, most of which are now growing, and produce ripe Seed in John Bartram's Garden, near Philadelphia. The Seed and growing Plants of which are disposed of on the most reasonable Terms.

Bartram's Catalogue, with corrections made in the writing of William Bartram

c Arrow wood

a Elder   —— Dentatum
  Fringe Tree   —— Alnifolium

c Arrow wood	
	—— Dentatum
	—— Alnifolium
a Elder	Sambucus
Fringe Tree	Chionanthus
	Itea Virginia
Button Wood	Cephalanthus Capitalis pendulis
Horn Beam	Carpinus Ostrya
b Hophornbeam	—— Betula
a Bermudas Mulberry	Calicarpa
Upright Honeysuckle	Azalea Rosea
d Swamp Azalea	—— Viscosa
a Sweet Azalea	—— Caroliniana
e Bladder Nut	Staphyleea Trifol . . .
b Jupiter's Beard	Amorpha Bar . . .
Shrubby Indigo (W.B.)	—— Indigopher (*indigo fera* W.B.)
a	Stewartia Malachodendron
d Winter berry	Prinos Glabra
Ink berry	—— Verticillata
a Burning Bush of Virginia	Eyonimus Semper Virens
———	—— Latifolia
b Tree Whortleberry	Vaccinium Arboreum
Indian Goosberry	—— Pendulum
d Swamp Whortleberry	—— Evonimifolium
Whortleberry with a large	
black Fruit	
———	—— Pusillum
	—— Racemosum
Whortleberry	—— Nigrum
	—— Pavifolium
d or Cranberry	—— Palustre
c Mountain Laurel	Rhododendron maximum
Common Laurel	Kalmia latifolia
d Dwarf Laurel	—— Glauca
Thyme leav'd Kalmia	—— Angustifolia
Dwarf Laurel of Florida	—— Ciliata
b Sorrel Tree	Andromeda Arborea
d Iron wood of Carolina	—— Plumata
———	—— Spicata
b Male Whortleberry	—— Latifolia
a Virginia red Buds	—— Lanceolata
d Carolina red Bud	—— Nitida
Boggy Andromeda	—— Globulifera
a Evergreen Andromeda	—— Crassifolia
c Canady Honey Suckle red	
and Yellow	Lonicera Canadensis
e Virginia scarlet Honeysuckle	—— Periclyminium
c Dwarf Cherry	—— Chamaecerassus

b	Indian Currants	_____ Symphoricarpos
	Diarvilla	Diarvilla Canadensis
d	Spiked Willow Herb	Lythrum
a	Tooth ache Tree	Xanthoxilum Virginianum
	Kidney Bean Tree	Glycine Frutescens
	Indian Patatoes	_____ Apios
	Canada Barberry	Oxijacantha Canadensis
e	White Birch of Canada	Betula Papyrifera
a	Red Birch	_____ Lenta
c	Sweet Birch	_____ Nigra
a	Dwarf Birch	———— Nana
c	Aspen Birch	_____ lifolia
d	Common Alder	Alnus Rubra, Betula
a	Sea side Alder	_____ Maritima
	Silver leaved Alder	_____ Glauca
e	Sugar Maple	Acer Sachariflua
a	Scarlet Maple	_____ Rubra
c	Silver leav'd Maple	_____ Glauca
	Ash leav'd Maple	_____ Nigundo
c	Dwarf Mountain Maple	_____ Arbustiva
	Striped Bark Maple	_____ Ornata
c	Dwarf Yew	Taxus Canadensis
	Creeping Syringa (Shade)	Mitchelia Repens
	(Clammy Birthworth W.B.)	Artistalochia Frutescens
e	Linden	Tilia
a	Great White Ash Tree	Fraxinum Excelsior
c	Black Ash	_____ Nigra
o	. . . . White Oak	Quercus Alba
b	. . . . Black Oak	_____ Nigra
	. . . . Red Oak	_____ Rubra
	. . . . Spanish Oak	_____ Hispanica
	. . . . Dwarf Oak	_____ Nana
a	Willow leaved Oak	_____ Phyllos
	Water Oak	_____ Deltoide
f	Barren black Oak	_____ Folio Amplissima
a	Live Oak	_____ Aegilops
g	Chestnut Oak	_____ Castania
	Willow Oak with broad leaves	_____ Dentata
b	Dwarf Chinquapin Oak	_____ Chinquapin
	. . . . Oak	_____ Lobata
	. . . . Oak	_____ Campana
	. . . . White Oak	_____ Palustris
f	Scarlet Oak of Florida	_____ Flammula
	Gall bearing Oak	_____ Gallifera
a	Halesia or Silver Bells	Halesia Letrantera
	2 varieties	(Tetragorotheea W.B.)

Trefoil Tree	Ptelea
e Black Walnut	Juglans Nigra
White Walnut or Butter Nut	_____ Alba
b Thick shell Hycory	_____ Hycory
c Pignut Hycory	Juglans Cinerea
a Shelbark Hycory	_____ _____
e Great Shelbark Hickory	_____ _____
b Balsam Hicory	_____ Odorifera
a Hazelnut	Corylus Nucleo Rotundiori & Duriori
c Dwarf Filbert or cuccold nut	_____ Cornata
b Witch Hazel	Hamamelis
Red Root (Jersey Tea W.B.)	Ceanothus Foliis Trinerviis
(Staff Trees W.B.)	Celastrus Scandens
a Nine Bark	Spirea Opulifolia
Ipecacuanha	_____ Foliis Ternatis
Spiraea (Indian Pipe-stem)	_____ Aruncus
d Poison Ash	Rhus Vernix
c Buck's Horn Shumach	_____ Cervina
a Beech or Sea-side Shumach	_____ Lentisci Folia
o Scarlet Shumach	_____ Glabra
a - - - -	_____ Canadensis
Poison Vine	_____ Radicans
b Poison Oak	_____ Triphyllon
c Sweet flowering Locust	Robinia Pseudacacia
b Peach Blossom Acacia	_____ Villosa
a Honey Locust	Gleditsia Triacanthus
Catalpa	Bignonia Catalpa
Cross Vine	_____ Crucigera
Yellow Jasmin	_____ Semper Virens
Trumpet Flower	_____ Radicans
Water Tupilo	Nissa Tupilo
Ogeche Lime	_____ Ogeche
Sower Gum	_____ Sylvatica
a Prickly Ash	Aralia Spinosa
c Spiknard False	_____ Nudicaulis
e Spiknard	_____ Racemosa
a Cotton Tree	Populus Deltoidea (Deltoide W.B.)
Black Poplar	_____ Foliis Cordatis
Aspen	_____ Tremula
d Bog gale	Myrica Gale
Candleberry	_____ Caerifera
a Dwarf Sweet Candlebury	_____ Angustifolia
e Button wood or water beach	Platanus Occidentalis
Prickly Goosberry	Grossularia Canadensis
o Beach Tree	Fagus Sylvatica
Chestnut	_____ Castenea

	Chinquapin	_____ Castenea Pumila
a	Sweet Shrub of Carolina	Calicanthus
o	Holley Tree	Ilex Aquifolium
a	Yapon or Cassena	_____ Yapon
		_____ Augustifolium
	Dahun Holly	_____ Dahun
	Jersey Tea (Mountain Tea	
	W.B.)	Gaultheria
		Epigea Procumbens
o	Bunch Grape	Vitis Vinefera
	Small blue Grape	_____ Librusca
a	Fox Grape red black & white	_____ Vulpina
a	Bull Briar	Smilax Aspera
	Black Briony — many more	
	species	_____ Annua
o	Persemmon	Diosperos Guajacaina
c	New River Horse Chestnut	Aesculus Octandra
o	Scarlet flowering horse	
	chestnut	_____ Caroliniana
a	Leather Bark	Dirca
	Clethra	Clethra Alnifolia
	Rasberry	Rubus Idaeus
	Mulberry	Morus Nigra
a or e	Papaw Apple	Anona Nuda
b	Shrub St John'swort	
	2 species	Hypericon Kalmianum
e	Judas Tree	Cercis Siliquastrum
b	Purple berried Bay	Olea Americana
e	Carolina Pepper Tree	Vitis Petroselenefolia
	Lote or Nettle Tree	Celtis (Celtis orientalis W.B.)
	Three Undescript Shrubs	(Philadelphua
	lately from Florida	(Alatamaha
		(Gardenia

The 1790 Prince list, after the enumerations of all the fruits, which we have dealt with elsewhere, is titled

To Be Sold
By WILLIAM PRINCE
At Flushing Landing, on LONG-ISLAND, near New-York
A large Collection, as follows, of
FRUIT TREES AND SHRUBS

and begins, after the fruits, with:

ROSES
Moss Provence rose, 3s.
Yellow rose, 1s. 6d.
Rosa Mundi, 2s.
Large Provence rose, 1s. 6d.
The monthly rose, 2s.
The red damask rose, 1s.
The white damask rose, 1s.
Primrose, 1s.
Musk rose, 2s.
Cinnamon rose, 1s.
Thornless rose, 1s.
American wild rose, many sorts, 6d.

EVERGREEN TREES AND SHRUBS
Red Virginia Cedar, 1s. 6d.
Weymouth's pine, 1s. 6d.
Black spruce fir, 1s. 6d.
Hemlock spruce fir, 1s. 6d.
The Kingsbridge laurel, 2s.
Large silver fir, 1s. 6d.
The balm of Gilead fir, 2s.
Pitch pine, 1s. 6d.
Jersey pine, 1s. 6d.
Virginia pine, 1s. 6d. each.

TIMBER TREES AND FLOWERING SHRUBS
American white oak, 1s.
American black oak, 1s.
Large New-England white oak, 1s.
Pin oak, 1s.
Scarlet oak, 1s.
English passion flower, 2s.
American passion flower, 1s. 6d.
Oleander, with red flowers, 2s.
American white thorn, 6d.
Scarlet maple, 1s.
Sugar maple, 1s. 6d.
Fringe tree, or Venetian sumach, 2s.
Snow-drop tree, 2s. 6d.
Pride of China, 2s.
Benjamin tree, 1s. 6d.
Scarlet flowering horse chestnut tree, 2s.
Andromeda, 1s. 6d.
Dwarf cypress, 2s.

William Prince Catalogue, 1790. Courtesy Library of Congress

Lombardy or Italian poplar,
Bladder Sena,
Monthly honey-suckle, 6d.
Late white American honey-suckle, 1s. 6d.
Dwarf acacia, with red flowers, 2s.
Carolina kidney bean tree, with purple flowers, 2s.
Threethorn'd acacia, with white flowers, 1s.
Leburnum, with yellow flowers, 1s. 6d.
The lender bome, or lime tree, 1s. 6d.
Liquid amber tree, 1s. 6d.
American medler, 1s. 6d.
Weeping willow, 1s. 6d.
The sweet-scented shrub from Carolina, 2s. 6d.
The aspe tree, 1s. 6d.
Catalpa flower tree, 1s. 6d.
Broad leav'd dog-wood, 1s. 6d.
White dog-wood, 1s. 6d.
Hard shell almonds, 1s. 6d.
Sweet almonds, 1s. 6d. each
Magnolia, 4s.
Tulip tree, 2s.
Snow-ball tree, 1s.
Bastard tamarind tree, 1s.
Locust tree, 9d.
Button tree of Virginia, 1s.
Blue lilac, 1s.
The Balsam Peru, 1s. 6d.
White lilac, 1s. 6d.
Syringas, 1s. 6d.
Standing American honey-suckle, 1s. 6d.
Candle-berry myrtle, 9d.
Sugar birch, 1s.
Sassafrass, 1s.
Poplar, 1s.
Carolina bird cherry, 1s.
Yellow willow, 9d.
Double flowering almond, 2s.
Carolina allspice, 1s. 6d.
Rhododendrun, 2s.
The balsam willow, 1s. 6d.
Madeira nut, 2s.
Long black walnuts, 1s.
Round black walnuts, 1s.
White walnuts, many sorts, 1s. 6d.
American hazle-nut trees, 1s.
Barcelona nuts, 1s. 6d.
Fill buds, 1s. 6d.

White althea frutex, 1s.
Purple althea frutex, 1s.
Double tube rose roots, 1s.

It is worth noting here that when the British took possession of the area during the Revolution, Howe set guards at the gates to protect this first nursery for trees and plants in the colonies.

Quite possibly stimulated by such lists as Bartram's and Prince's, John Bartram's somewhat younger cousin, Humphry Marshall, started a notable collection of native American trees and shrubs near Philadelphia. Marshall, also a Quaker, began his collection of plants with the high purpose of applying himself to the study of horticulture and botany to further the "introduction and cultivation of foreign useful and valuable plants" and "the discovering the qualities and uses of our own native vegetable productions and applying them to the most useful purposes." This experiment came to a successful conclusion with the collection of native trees and shrubs and the publication in 1785 of the first really American book on American plants, Arbustum Americanum: *The American Grove, or an Alphabetical Catalogue of Forest Trees and Shrubs, Natives of the American United States, Arranged according to the Linnaean System.* This is an impressive small volume written in English and translated into a French edition. The descriptions are succinct, fresh and make good reading today.

The interest in American trees and shrubs seemed to grow by what it fed upon. In *A Catalogue of Seeds from Canada of growth 1765, imported by a Society of Gentlemen at Edinburgh,* over seventy trees and shrubs are listed as well as over forty "useful" plants.

In 1772 Benjamin Franklin wrote to John Bartram that he was at last able to send him "your medal," which would arrive through Benjamin Franklin's son Bache, with some seeds from Franklin of the cabbage turnip and the Scotch cabbage. The medal weighed 487 grains and is inscribed:

To
Mr. John Bartram
from
a Society of Gentlemen
at
Edinburgh
1772

On the reverse is the simple word *Merenti,* enclosed in a laurel wreath.

One last tribute to the Bartram Nurseries comes as a letter from Jefferson to John Bartram, Jr.

*

By Mr. Bingham who left Paris about a fortnight ago I took the liberty of asking your acceptance of a copy of Linnaeus's *Systema vegetabilium* translated into English and enlarged with many new plants furnished by Linnaeus, the son, and which have never before been published.

Inclosed is a list of plants and seeds which I should be very glad to obtain from America for a friend here whom I wish much to oblige. I have stated the Linnaean name to every one except those which are mentioned otherwise. I will pray you to send me these plants and seeds, packed in that careful manner with which you are so perfectly acquainted. For the time of the year proper to send them, I leave it to yourself, only hoping it will be as soon as the proper season will admit. Mr. F. Hopkinson will have the goodness to pay your demand for these things, and the expense attending them. Mr. Robt. Morris will have occasion to send many vessels to France. Some of these will probably come to Havre. This would be the best port to send them to because they would come from thence by water. But if no opportunity occurs to that port, let them come to Nantes or L'Orient. In every case address them to the care of the American Consul at the port. Your favor herein will greatly oblige Sir your most obedient humble servant.

While Miller was the ultimate authority, there was another great horticulturist in England with a very direct influence upon American gardens. He was a successor to Philip Miller at the Chelsea Physic Garden. William Curtis, great London botanist and nurseryman, was commemorated in a "Sketch" written by Dr. Robert John Thornton, known to us for his great book, *The Temple of Flora,* in which a series of pictures dramatically places plants in what were supposed to be appropriate settings, which often outdid nature. Our little shooting star, *Dodecatheon media* L., for instance, is pictured on the brink of a rocky coast by a vast sea where a sailing ship rounds a promontory. Our Turk's-cap lily, *Lilium superbum* L., towers in the foreground of a stupendously high-peaked mountain range. Moods are induced to a degree never seen before or since in botanical paintings. Dr. Thornton's declared intention may have resulted in too much competition among his illustrators. The rest of his accomplishments would seem to be less theatrical. A note to explain the author of the "Sketch of the Life and Writings of the Late Mr. William Curtis" says: "This gentleman is a Lecturer of Botany at Guy's Hospital; Author of the Philosophy of Botany; the Temple of Flora; the Genera of British Plants; the Genera of Foreign Plants; the Grammar of Botany; the Philosophy of Medicine; and The Philosophy of Politics." For our purposes this excerpt illustrates the interinvolvement of botany, medicine and gardening, so much the way of thought and practice in the eighteenth century.

According to Dr. Thornton, young Curtis showed the same inclination toward botany as the young Linnaeus and, like him, filled his portion of his father's garden with wildflowers and their accompanying

River entrance to the Chelsea Physic Garden. Watercolor. Courtesy of the Chelsea Public Library

insects, which soon overran the whole. Curtis had a Quaker grand-father, an apothecary at Alton, who was called into conference and tried to start young Curtis on his way in medicine. Again like Linnaeus, Curtis preferred the earlier botanical studies, took to his pen and produced a scientific study of the browntail moth, which was ravaging the English countryside in 1783. His exploration of the fields in pursuit of insects was to bear fruit later with his monumental *Flora Londonensis,* with illustrations of all the plants that grew naturally around London. Curtis soon attracted the attention of the Company of Apothecaries and became their "demonstrator of plants" at Chelsea, an appointment once held by Philip Miller. The duties of the holder of this office were that he point out the medicinal plants in the Chelsea Garden, recently bequeathed to the Company of Apothecaries by Sir Hans Sloane; that he present annually fifty new specimens of plants before the Royal Society, until two thousand different plants should be growing in the garden; and that he herbarize constantly in the London countryside, demonstrating "names and virtues" of plants collected in a public lecture before the Company.

The Chelsea Garden plan called for an arrangement of plants in the classes considered most useful and "necessary to be known," such as medicinal, culinary, poisonous and agricultural, all grown as "living examples" of the classes and orders of the Linnaean system. There was also the intention to grow "hardy, ornamental flowers and shrubs, chiefly exotic and cultivated in the gardens of the curious," and to make a collection of "British Plants." This last inspired Curtis to undertake an illustrated study of the plants in the London area, for which he, like Catesby, needed financial assistance. As in the case of Catesby, it was forthcoming from generous and interested individuals, this time Dr. Lettsom. At the same time Curtis was bent upon founding his botanical magazine, to come out in numbers at one shilling each, containing three plates and three descriptions. Twelve numbers would make an octavo volume. Cautiously he promised that, due to the "earnest entreaties of many of his subscribers," he would deviate from his original intention of publishing "only plants contained in the highly esteemed works of . . . luminaries of Botany and Gardening," would occasionally produce new ones as they flowered in his own garden at Lambeth and would "enter on the province of the florist" to give one figure at least of "double or improved flowers." Begun in 1787, this project was continued until Curtis' death in 1799, when he left two hundred "figures" to be published by his successor, Dr. John Sims.

The scorn of botanists for florists' successes is obvious in Dr. Thornton's comment upon Curtis' yielding to the "earnest entreaties." Dr. Thornton laments that every botanist "must feel the degradation Mr. Curtis submitted to . . . to give double flowers . . . knowing they are esteemed monsters by botanists," but he praises the illustrations by several different artists, which "rise superior to those of Miller or Catesby for accuracy."

Knowing that the first volumes of *The Botanical Magazine: or Flower Garden Displayed* were in the hands of our leading end-of-the-eighteenth-century American gardeners, we give a list of the familiar names of the plants contained in the first ten issues, including "the most ornamental FOREIGN PLANTS cultivated in the Open Ground, the Greenhouse and stove." We may not be surprised to see many American importations. We are fortunate to be able to reproduce the original illustrations of many of these plants. The last one listed, the zinnia, has to be shown in all its original ugliness to explain the "entreaties" for "improved" specimens.

Except for the removal of the long *s*'s, the spellings are his.

A Adonis, spring*** Aitonia, cape*** Allamanda, willow-leaved*** Almond, Dwarf*** Alstroemeria, striped-flowered and spotted-flowered*** Alyssum, bladder-podded, purple, sweet, and yellow*** Anemone, Snow-drop and star*** Anthericum, Savoy*** Antholyza, scarlet-flowered*** Apple-tree, Chinese*** Archangel, balm-leav'd***

Alstroemaria pelegrina. Curtis *Botanical Magazine*

Arum, three-lobed*** Aspalathus, small-leaved*** Aster, alpine and bristly-leaved*** Azalea, scarlet***

B   Balm, great-flowered*** Bell-flower, Carpatian and great-flowered*** Bindweed, purple*** Bladder-Senna, scarlet and common*** Blite, strawberry*** Blue-bottle, greater*** Borbonia, heart-leaved*** Bramble, dwarf*** Broom, Spanish*** Browallia, tall*** Bucherna, clammy*** Buddlea, round-headed*** Bulbocodium, vernal***

C   Camellia, rose*** Candy-tuft, Gibraltar and purple*** Caper, Shrub*** Cassia, dwarf*** Catananche, blue*** Catchfly, pendulous*** Catesbaea, thorny*** Celsia, linear-leaved*** Centaurea, wood-leaved*** Cereus, creeping*** Chironia, berry-bearing and shrubby*** Chrysanthemum, indian*** Cineraria, blue-flowered and wooly*** Cistus, beautiful, gum, hoary or rose*** Clematis, or Virgin's-bower, entire-leaved*** Cockle, rose and smooth-leaved*** Coltsfoot, alpine*** Columbine, canadian*** Convolvulus, azure,

Cistus formosus. Curtis *Botanical Magazine*

narrow-leaved, small, silky-leaved*** Coreopsis, whorled*** Corn-flag, common, square-leaved, superb*** Coronilla, purple, rue-leaved, sea-green*** Crane's-bill, angular-stalked, birch-leaved, clammy, flesh-coloured, heart-leaved, horn-leaved, sorrel, two coloured, three coloured*** Crepis, bearded*** Crocus, spring*** Crow-foot, grass-leaved, mountain, plantain-leaved, upright double*** Crown imperial*** Cudweed, giant*** Cyclamen, round-leaved and Persian*** Cyrtanthus, narrow-leaved*** Cytisus, common***

D Daffodil, great, lesser, peerless, reflexed*** Daisy, cotinus-leaved*** Daisy, great double*** Daphne, trailing*** Day-lily, tawny, yellow*** Diosina, one-flowered*** Disandra, trailing*** Dittany of Crete*** Dodecatheon, Mead's*** Dog's tooth*** Dog's bane, tutsan-leav'd*** Draba, sengreen*** Dragon's-head, toothed***

E Epidendrum, two-leaved*** Erinus, alpine***

F Fagonia, cretan*** Fennel flower, garden*** Ferraria, curled*** Fig-

Dianthus chinensis (China or India Pink). Curtis
Botanical Magazine

marigold, bearded, golden, green-flowered, hatch-leaved, jagged leaved,
two-coloured*** Flax, tree, yellow*** Franklin's Tarter*** Fuchsia,
scarlet*** Fumitory, glaucous, hollow-rooted, solid-rooted***

G Garlick, purple-headed*** Genista, triangular-stalked*** Gentian,
large-flowered*** Geranium, anemone-leaved, dwarf, ivy-leaved,
prickly-stalked, rasp-leaved, striped, spear-leaved, square-stalked***
Germander, broad-leaved shrubby*** Globe-flower, Asiatic*** Glycine, dingy-flowered, purple, scarlet*** Goodenia, smooth*** Gorteria,
rigid-leaved***

H Heath, Arbutus-leaved, blush-flowered, stalk, great-flowered, herbaceous,
honeywort-flowered, Masson's porcelain*** Hedysarum, creeping-
rooted*** Hellebore, black, livid or purple, winter*** Henbane,
golden-flowered*** Hepatica*** Hermannia, alder-leaved, marsh-
mallow-leaved*** Hibiscus, bladder, China rose, Syrian, superb***
Honey-wort, great*** House-leek, cobweb, dwarf, gouty*** Hyacinth,
grape, starch, two-coloured*** Jasmine, common, sweet*** Indian-

Oenothera fruticosa, Shrubby Oenothera. Curtis *Botanical Magazine*

cress, greater, small*** Indigo, white-leaved*** Jonquil, common, great*** Ipomoea, scarlet, winged-leaved*** Iris, Chalcedonian, dwarf, elder-scented, persian, particoloured, peacock, Siberian, spurious, tall, variegated***

I   Ixia, bending-stalked, Chinese, crocus-leaved, long-flowered, saffron-coloured,*** Ixora, scarlet***

J   Justicia dichotomous***

K Kalmia, broad-leaved, glaucous, hairy, narrow-leaved***

L Laburnum, common*** Lachenalia, three-coloured*** Ladies-finger, four-leaved*** Ladies-slipper, two-leaved, white-petal'd*** Lantana, prickly*** Lathyrus, blue-flowered, jointed-podded, tuberous*** Lavatera, annual*** Laurustinus, common*** Lead-wort, rose-coloured*** Lilac, common*** Lily, Atamasco, Catesby's chalcedonian, orange, white*** Limodorum, tuberous-rooted*** Lobelia, shrubby, scarlet*** Lopezia, Mexican*** Loosestrife, bulb-bearing*** Lotus, black-flowered, winged, hairy*** Lungwort, Virginian*** Lupine, Perennial, yellow*** Lychnidea, early-flowering*** Lychnis, Chinese, scarlet***

M Mahernia, cut-leaved, winged*** Manulea, wooly*** Marigold, French*** Melianthus, small*** Metrosideros, harsh-leaved*** Michauxia, rough-leaved*** Mignonet*** Milk-wort, box-leaved, heath-leaved, spear-leaved*** Mimosa, myrtle-leaved, whorled-leaved*** Monarda, crimson*** Monkey-flower, narr. leaved, orange*** Monsonia, large-flowered*** Mullein, borage-leaved*** Myrtle, woolly-leaved***

N Narcissus, hoop-petticoat, narrow-leaved, two-flowered*** Navel-wort, blue, round-leaved*** Nightshade, cut-leaved***

O Oenothera, dwarf, purple, rose-coloured, shrubby*** Ornithogalum, golden*** Orpine, evergreen*** Othonna, wormwood-leaved***

P Passerina, great-flowered*** Passion-flower, common, fringed-leaved, winged*** Pea, sweet, Tangier*** Periwinkle, Madagascar*** Persicaria, tall*** Phylica, heath-leaved*** Pimpernel, Italian*** Pink, China or Indian, superb*** Plumeria, red*** Poppy, eastern, prickly*** Portlandia, great-flowered*** Potentilla, large-flowered*** Primrose, lilac double*** Primula, mountain, silver-edged*** Protea, honey-bearing, Puccoon, Canada***

Q Quaking-grass, great***

R Rag-wort, purple*** Raspberry, flowering*** Rest-harrow, round-leaved, shrubby, yellow-flowered*** Reseda, sweet scented**** Rose, ever-blowing, moss*** Robinia, rough-stalked*** Rudbeckia, purple***

S Sage, golden*** Saxifrage, oval-leaved, saffron-coloured, strawberry*** Scabious, sweet*** Scorzonera, Tangier*** Selago, oval-headed*** Self-heal, great-flowered*** Sida, crested*** Sisyrinchium, Iris-leaved*** St. John's-wort, Chinese, heath leaved, large-flowered, warty*** Slipper-worth, Fothergill's, pinnated*** Snowflake, spring*** Soap-wort, basil*** Soldanella, alpine*** Sophora, winged-podded*** Speedwell, cross-leaved*** Spigelia, Maryland*** Squill, bell-flowered, Byzantine*** Stapelia, variegated*** Star of Bethlehem, Neapolitan*** Stock, Mediterranean*** Stone-crop, poplar-leaved*** Strawberry, one-leaved*** Strelitzia, Canna-leaved*** Struthiola, smooth*** Sun-flower, perennial*** Sweet William***

T Tansey, fan-leaved*** Thrift purple-cup'd*** Toad-flax, alpine, branching, black-flowered, purple, three-leaved*** Tradescantia, virginian*** Trefoil, crimson*** Trillium sessile*** Tulip-tree, common*** Turnera, narrow-leaved*** Turnsole, peruvian***

V Vervain, rose*** Violet, cut-leaved***

W Wall-cress, alpine*** Wall-flower, changeable*** Willow-herb, narrowest-leav'd*** Wood-sorrel, striped-flowered, goat's-foot*** Zinnia, many-flowered***

Within this list any American gardener along the Atlantic Coast could find much to suit his soil and climate. We can recognize many of Lady Skipwith's and Jefferson's favorite flowers.

In all fairness to accomplished gardeners, we must mention the greatest of American nurserymen at the turn of the century. Bernard M'Mahon, for whom our "Oregon-grape" was named *Mahonia,* was an Irishman who arrived in Philadelphia in 1796 and started a career as seedsman and nurseryman extraordinary. It is said that the Lewis and Clark Expedition up the Missouri and to the Pacific was planned at his house. It is certain that many of the horticultural finds of that great journey across North America, for which Jefferson obtained the funds from Congress, found their way to M'Mahon's nursery beds. The Prince Nurseries also benefited and were able to introduce *Mahonia nervosa* at twenty dollars a plant. Bernard M'Mahon was an expert gardener honestly outspoken. He was one of the first to expose some of the true flaws in the American character, instead of prolonging the old stereotypes, when he said that Americans admire size, that they will buy a plant because of its "bigness" rather than its horticultural excellence. We can hear him say this today at flower shows as we admire some of the results of "improving" old favorites. In 1806 M'Mahon published his *The American Gardener's Calendar,* which held sway for fifty years as the definitive American gardening book. The "advertisement" for his nursery, with which the book opens, announces his intention to establish a much-needed "repository of seeds of Garden Vegetables, of the Grasses, Grains and Roots used in Rural Economy; of plants used in dyeing and other arts, and of useful Trees, ornamental Shrubs etc. . . ." He modestly solicits "lovers of improvement in every part of the United States . . ." to send him indigenous plants from their various vicinities "with or without names," which he will exchange for seeds of "culinary vegetables, grasses, fruits or such other kinds as they may desire . . ."

Besides his "seed establishment," he has a "Botanical Agricultural and Horticultural Book Store, where every valuable work, ancient or modern, on those subjects may be had on moderate terms."

And he has recently published "an *extensive* treatise on Gardening entitled 'The American Gardener's Calendar,' adapted to the seasons and climates of the United States (Price $3.50) containing a complete account of all the work necessary to be done in the

Kitchen Garden	Pleasure Grounds
Fruit Garden	Flower Garden
Orchard	Green House
Vineyard	Hot House and
Nursery	Forcing Frames

For every month of the year."

Besides all this he gives instructions for laying out all the above "according to modern taste and the most approved plans," and the ornamental planting of pleasure ground "in the ancient and modern stile." There is a catalogue of thirty-seven hundred plants divided into their separate departments for use or ornament, with their "true Linnaean or Botanical, as well as English names . . ."

His lists begin with "Seeds of Esculent Vegetables." He lists sixty-seven, including old favorites like coriander, corn-salad, orach, rampion, rocambole and skirret. He does not include sweet corn. His "Select List of Fruit Trees" is much what we are used to, all the usual varieties we have considered, with almonds, filberts, barberries, mulberries, nectarines and two sorbuses. He offers five strawberries, which we recognize, and five currants. Native American blueberries, cranberries, blackberries, and raspberries are commercially still in the future. He offers under "hardy Deciduous Trees and Shrubs" over four hundred species, half of them American from east of the Mississippi. Under "Hardy Evergreen Trees and Shrubs" he has about one hundred, again half of them American. His hothouse and greenhouse plants number fifteen hundred listed, probably to attract the "curious" in warmer climates. For our purposes, it will be enough to quote the lists of herbs and medicinal plants, giving the English names and the Linnaean according to M'Mahon. The spelling and capitalizations are his. His very tempting perennial flowers, biennial flowers, hardy annuals, tender annuals and hardy bulbous and tuberous "flower-roots" are not so far advanced beyond Curtis' as to need listing here.

AROMATIC, POT AND SWEET HERBS

Anise	*Pimpinella Anisum*
Sweet Basil	*Ocynum Basilicum*
Bush Basil	*Ocynum minimum*
Caraway	*Carum Carui*
Clary	*Salvia Sclarea*
Coriander	*Coriandrum sativum*
Chamomile	*Anthemis nobilis*
Dill	*Anethum graveolens*
Common Fennel	*Anethum Foeniculum*
Sweet Fennel	*Anethum v. dulce*
Hyssop	*Hyssopus officinalis*
Lavender	*Lavendula Spica*
Pot Marigold	*Calendula officinalis*
Sweet Marjoram	*Origanum Majorana*
Pot Marjoram	*Origanum Onites*
Winter Sweet Marjoram	*Origanum heracleoticum*
Spear Mint	*Mentha viridis*

Pepper Mint	*Mentha piperita*
Pennyroyal Mint	*Mentha pulegium*
Rosemary	*Rosmarinum officinalis*
Common Sage	*Salvia officinalis*
Summer Savory	*Satureia hortensis*
Winter Savory	*Satureia montana*
Smallage	*Apium graveolens*
Tarragon	*Artemisia Dracunculus*
Common Thyme	*Thymus vulgaris*
Lemon-scented Thyme	*Thymus Serpyllum*

SEEDS OF MEDICINAL PLANTS

Garden Angelica	*Angelica Archangelica*
Large Balsam Apple	*Monardica Charantia*
Small Balsam Apple	*Monardica Balsamina*
Bugloss	*Anchusa officinalis*
Carduus Benedictus	*Centaurea Benedicta*
Celandine	*Chelidonium majus*
Comfrey	*Symphytum officinale*
Bitter Cucumber	*Cucumis Colicinthus*
Elecampane	*Inula Helenium*
Fenugreek	*Trigonella Faenum-Graecum*
Feverfew	*Matricaria Parthenium*
Foxglove	*Digitalis purpurea*
Gromwell	*Lithospermum officinale*
Ground Ivy	*Glecoma hederacea*
Hemlock	*Comium maculatum*
Horehound	*Marrubium vulgare*
Hound's-Tongue	*Cynoglossum officinale*
Indian Physic	*Spirea trifoliata*
Blue Lobelia	*Lobelia siphilitica*
Liquorice (roots)	*Glycyrrhiza glabra*
Lovage	*Ligusticum Levisticum*
Dyer's Madder	*Rubia tinctorum*
Marsh Mallow	*Althaea officinalis*
Sweet Milfoil	*Achillea Argeratum*
Horse Mint	*Monarda punctata*
Mugwort	*Artemisia vulgaris*
Nep, or Cat-mint	*Nepeta Cataria*
Palma Christi	*Ricinum communis*
Red Chick-weed	*Anagallis arvensis*
Carolina Pink-root	*Spigelia marilandica*
Poppy	*Papaver somnifera*
Rattlesnake-root	*Polygala Senega*
Garden Rue	*Ruta graveolens*

True Turkey Rhubarb	*Rheum palmatum*
Common English do	*Rheum Rhaponicum*
Monk's Rhubarb	*Rumex alpinus*
Officinal Scurvy-grass	*Cochlearia officinalis*
Virginian Snake-root	*Aristolochia Serpentaria*
Southernwood	*Artemisia Abrotanum*
Virginian Speedwell	*Veronica virginica*
Tansey	*Tanacetum vulgare*
Thoroughwort	*Eupatorium perfoliatum*
Virginian Tobacco	*Nicotiana Tabacum*
English Tobacco	*Nicotiana rustica*
Holy Thistle	*Carduus marianum*
Winter Cherry	*Physalia Aikekengi*
Wormwood	*Artemisia Absinthum*
Worm-seed, etc. etc.	*Chenopodium anthelminiscuta*

With which beneficial list we close our conglomerate catalogue of plants for eighteenth-century American gardens.

Since we have decided to snip off our research with the end of the century, we do so, but we have to admit a certain sadness in forgoing great riches waiting in the lap of Flora: the Lewis and Clark Expedition, Dr. Hosack's botanical garden on Manhattan, the introduction of exotic plants from South Africa — much is about to happen. It is gratifying, however, to find a contemporary summing-up of the range we have explored and to have the encouragement of knowing that what we now feel was important and significant appeared exactly that to a researcher of the time.

When Frederick Pursh left England in 1799 to begin his masterwork, *Flora Americae Septentrionalis, or A systematic Arrangement and Description of the Plants of North America,* he was prepared to remain in the United States as long as his project should require. He returned to England in 1811 to escape a threatening war, to avail himself of extensive libraries and to study the collections and herbariums of Morison, Clayton, Catesby, Walter and the Michaux. In 1816 his great work was published.

The preface is a tribute to our friends and their works and gardens, a compliment to our great men in the flesh where we can meet them only in their words and records.

Pursh was becoming an authority, to be commemorated in plant names himself as he laboriously gave credit to Linnaeus and Plukenet, Lamarck, Ellis, the Michaux, father and son, and Willdenow, names already incorporated into those of many plants he seeks and sees. He meets Dr. Barton and goes to the Bartram gardens (which he credits largely to Dr. Fothergill, without mentioning Collinson). He visits Hamilton's Woodlands, rich in rare American species. He becomes friends with Merriwether Lewis; Bernard M'Mahon; Dr. Muhlenberg; with Dr. Hosack, who is starting his botanic garden on Manhattan Island; with Aloysius Enslen, back from his travels in the southern states and on his way home to Austria and his patron, Prince Lichtenstein. Many of these men were working toward writing a *Flora* of the United States themselves, using their own collections. They seem to have generously handed material over to him.

Furber's Flowers for the Month of November

1. Ficoides or fig Mari-
   gold G
2. White Periwinkle C T
3. Earliest flowering
   Laurustinus B T
4. Blue Periwinkle C T
5. Tree Candytuft G
6. Embroidered Crane's
   Bill B
7. Yellow spiked Eternal
   G
8. Striped single Anemone
   B
9. Borage G
10. Thyme-leaved myrtle
    G
11. French Marigold B
12. Colchicum Agripina
    Major B
13. Ilex-leaved Jasmines S
14. Great purple Crane's
    Bill B
15. Arbutus, or Strawberry
    tree B T
16. Double Nasturtium G
17. Broad leaved red
    Valerian B
18. Myrto-Cistus G
19. Virginian Aster B
20. Campanula Canariensis
    G
21. Pheasants Eye B
22. Perennial dwarf Sun
    Flower G
23. Double Featherfew B
24. Carolina Star Flower G
25. Scarlet Althea S
26. Spanish white Jasmine
    G
27. Lavender, with divided
    leaves G
28. Golden Rod B
29. American Viburnum S
30. Yellow Dwarf Aloe G
31. Single Blue Anemone
    B
32. Purple Ficoides G
33. Groundsell tree B T
34. Pellitory with Daisy
    flowers S
35. Scarlet single Anemone
    B
36. White Egyptian Holly-
    hock B
37. Caper Bush
38. Dwarf Colutea G

13 *Landskip and Offskip*

AFTER THE BREAKTHROUGH in botanical communication achieved by the adoption of the Linnaean binomial system, the second revolutionary revelation among gardeners was the emergence of the idea in England of landscape gardening as an art. The first innovation may have contributed directly to the second. The whole gardening world was beginning to be compressed within book covers. While the Linnaean system required identifications of plants to be made in Latin, it could be explained in English for the understanding of all. And the revolution in English garden design, from the purely formal to the seemingly informal and natural, was primarily an intellectual concept, exhaustively set forth by all and sundry in English print.

The adoption of the old English words of *landskip* and *offskip* into gardening language signaled the beginning of the emergence of something new in the philosophy of gardening, in a country where everything horticultural seemed possible because of the climate and the sophistication of the gardeners. While the word *landskip* soon gave way to *landscape,* the term *offskip,* or a distant view, lingered.

The landscape school in painting had been rapidly developing from the early conventions of religious and classical subjects. The Italian landscape apparent over the shoulders of the seated Virgin had become a main inspiration of paintings, although titles were still related to tiny figures in the lower corners, fleeing into Egypt or stopping to nurse the Christ Child. A distant village, or ruined castle, could be tucked in to lend interest. Or a hermit and a cave, like a leftover St. Jerome. Classical subjects were also minutely incorporated and a distant Aeneas could be seen struggling up a rugged mountain path bearing the aged Anchises on his shoulders. The import of the paintings was a poetic portrayal of a natural scene attuned to a mood, usually one of gentle melancholy.

While the English gentlemen's Grand Tour brought many of these paintings back to be hung, frame over frame beside frame, on the walls of country houses, the painter who most pleased the English taste was one who showed nearly English landscape features of trees and small groves and streams in a manageably proportioned countryside. That Claude Lorraine painted with his mirror in hand, reducing the view over his shoulder to intimate and comprehensible detail, added to the inspiration of gardeners seeking to frame their own landscapes. Various moods depicted in painted landscapes, still depending upon grandiose titles, began to influence those converted to tearing up old formalities to create their own natural masterpieces. Much was written about the "picturesque" in gardening, and of how to induce moods in the spectator — of awe, anticipation or melancholy. Compounded with the classical revival in architecture, quotes from Virgil and Horace were added to the pleasures of wandering about a garden. The intellectual thrust of the new gardening art struck deep and wide.

Other forces were at work besides the study of landscape painting and the revival of classical forms. The early eighteenth century was full of crisp criticism and barbed satire. Nothing and no one could escape being eviscerated in print, even gardens and gardeners. The rigors of conformation to geometrical design must have long irked the English spirit to have the sudden turning upon the old style of gardening involve the great minds of the age. Never before or since has such a company of poets, priests, essayists, philosophers and novelists held forth upon the subject of gardens.

Pope found authority for a change in garden design among the ancients, and loosed thunderbolts of his own. Hogarth wrote upon "Beauty," cautioning moderation in curves, then totally replacing straight lines. He established the "Hogarth line," an ideally modest curve now constantly referred to in flower-arranging although somewhat exaggerated in execution. Edmund Burke, great if unsuccessful emancipator of the tax-ridden colonies, wrote tellingly about his own ideas of beauty. Horace Walpole devoted his attention to gardening and applied himself to a Gothic interpretation. Samuel Johnson realized that in the lives of the poets their gardens were reflections of their personalities, and threw in shrewd comments of his own. Defoe had his opinions of English gardens and gardening although *Robinson Crusoe* was not made their vehicle. Magazines welcomed letters from gardening readers, irate

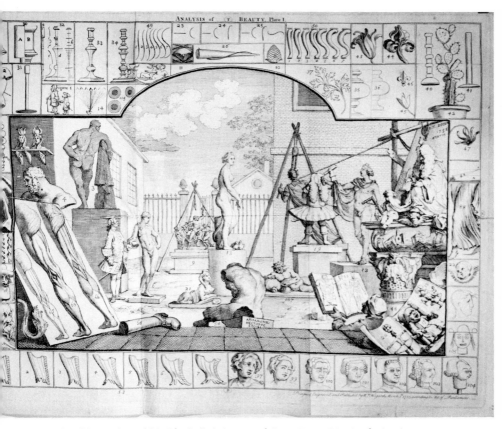

Hogarth's illustration of his ideal slightly curved line. From his *Analysis of Beauty*

or creative, and entered the lists themselves. A coup de grâce was given topiary in the pages of the *Spectator*. Sir Uvedale Price wrote ponderously upon "Taste" and "The Picturesque." And these outlets were few among many.

Evolution of garden design in England from the frankly formal to the seemingly natural was a carefully studied procedure. The great professional landscape gardener, William Kent, urged forward by his friend Pope, was immortalized by Walpole's report of his well-known sprightly leap over the garden wall to declare all England a garden. He knew it well before he leapt. And he was only confirming the ideas of a large group of scholarly landowners who had wearied of the two sides of a garden mirroring each other.

At the beginning of the seventeenth century Francis Bacon, called by Pope "the wisest, brightest, meanest of mankind," had written wistfully of his ideal garden, with jibes at formal flower beds like inferior jam tarts. At the end of the seventeenth century Sir William Temple had also written upon ideal gardens and had introduced the first suggestion of the influence of Chinese taste, of which much was to be heard later. Temple said *sharadwadgi* — a word never heard before or since in any language — was a term used by the Chinese to indicate a naturalness in garden design, where "beauty shall be great and strike the eye, but without any order or disposition of parts that shall be commonly or easily observed." Whoever, he said, has observed the work on "the best India gowns, or the paintings on their best screens or porcelains, will find their beauty is all of this kind, that is, without order." But he does not advise "any of these attempts in the figure of gardens among us; they are adventures of too hard achievement for any common hands . . . whereas in regular figures it is hard to make any great and remarkable faults." Earnest students examining the word *sharadwadgi* suggested it came from a somewhat similar Japanese word meaning "not being symmetrical," and that Sir William Temple may have heard it in Holland. In these days of "calculated leaks," one may wonder.

Sir William Temple has left us the classic historical description of a garden, which stands as an example of all the next century was seeking to erase. Moor Park in Herefordshire was described by him in 1685 as "the perfectest figure of a garden I ever saw, either at home or abroad." He knew it well because he had spent his honeymoon there in 1655 after marrying Dorothy Osborne, cousin to the then owner, Sir Richard Franklin. Temple describes the garden in all its symmetrical glory as a "model to those that meet with such a situation, and are above the regards of common expense."

It lies on the side of a hill (upon which the house stands) but not very steep. The length of the house, where are the best rooms of most use or pleasure, lies upon the breadth of the garden, the great walk that lies even with it, and which may be as I remember about three hundred paces along, and broad in proportion, the border set with standard laurels at large distances, which have the beauty of orange trees out of flower and fruit; from the walks are three descents of many stone steps in the middle and at each end, into a very large parterre. This is divided into quarters by gravel walks, and adorned with two fountains and eight statues in the several quarters; at the end of the terrace walk are two summer houses, and the sides of the parterre are ranged with two large cloisters, which are paved with stone and designed for walks or shade, there being none other in the whole parterre. Over these two cloisters are two terraces covered with lead and fenced with balusters, and the passage into these airy walks is out of the two summer houses at the end of the first terrace walk. The cloister facing the south is covered with vines, and would have been proper for an orange house, and the other for myrtles, or other more common greens, and had, I doubt not, been cast for that purpose, if this piece of gardening had been then in as much vogue as it is now.

From the middle of this parterre is a descent by many steps flying on each side of a grotto that lies between them, covered with lead and flat into the lower garden, which is all fruit trees ranged about the several quarters of a wilderness which is very shady; the walks here are all green, the grotto embellished with figures of shell rock-work, fountains, and waterworks. If the hill had not ended with the lower garden, and the wall were not bounded by a common way that goes through the park, they might have added a third quarter of all greens; but this want is supplied by a garden on the other side of the house which is all of the sort, very wild, shady, and adorned rough rock-work and fountains.

So we know what the new wave was to dash against.

Before we participate in the dismemberment of all this formal beauty, we must seek the sources from which the destructive wave arose. In justice to the Chinese, upon whom, with Virgil, much of the burden has been placed, we may wonder how much of this revolutionary reaction against medieval symmetry was in the Chinese text and how much in the imagination of inspired English prophets of change. With them, all things, including reported Chinese taste, followed ideas touted previous to, and independently of, the Chinese antisymmetry bombshell. Similarly, search as one may the pictures of Chinese gardens at this time, there are no graphic portrayals of any natural asymmetrical fancies at the Chinese court. Judging by both Chinese and European pictures, the idea of Chinese pleasure gardens would seem to have been very architectural and right-angled indeed, up to the very smallest pagoda roof atop however many others, in the midst of many-gated, high-walled, paved enclosures and balustraded lakes.

Gardening had long been called "The Clergyman's Recreation," as a charming small book asserted, and everyone knew that some of the best plants and plantings were due to the labors of gentlemen of the church, from bishops to country rectors. The emergence of French priests in China as authorities in garden design should have come as no surprise. Sources that seemed authentic allowed for the new passion for artful naturalness to be attributed to the Chinese. Father Attiret, resident Jesuit painter at the Imperial Court in Peking, had written a letter published in an anthology of French belles-lettres, *Lettres Edifiantes,* in 1749, which was translated and published in English by one of those clergymen madly addicted to gardening, the Reverend Joseph Spence.

Père Attiret's letter, to be much quoted and little read for years to come, was addressed to one Monsieur d'Assaut, who had asked what Jesuits did in China. As the reply deals mainly with a description of the Imperial Garden, great pleasure park of the Manchu rulers, his inquirer may have been left still wondering about the Jesuits. Père Attiret, as painter to the court, had access to this garden, little known or visited even by Chinese. The letter abounds with long descriptions. The conclusion, that the Chinese use art to imitate nature, is one of which any artist would approve.

Père Attiret notes the preponderance of flowering trees in China, where they cover whole mountains. He describes a canal that winds — *"ici il serpente"* — with flowery banks in all seasons upon edges of rough stones instead of being laid out in a straight line with paved sides. Describing a group of buildings on a hill with gilded columns, varnished timbers and roofs of blue, red, yellow and green tiles, he comments approvingly upon the stone-paved approach to this fairy palace because it, too, winds. The Chinese here aim, he says, to represent a rustic retreat, however palatial, and use *"une anti-symétrie"* to attain *"un beau désordre."* A thicket of flowering trees seems quite wild and natural. In short, Attiret says the Chinese make Europeans seem sterile and lacking in imagination, and he concludes that in the Imperial Garden the Chinese have *"réuni la tout ce que l'art et le bon goût peuvent ajouter aux richesse de la nature."*

The translator of this letter, the Reverend Joseph Spence, who is also Sir Harry Beaumont, will later summarize for us what English gardeners should strive toward. We turn here to see what this seemingly rather unfertile seed became when nurtured by that great exponent of all things Chinese, Sir William Chambers.

Born in Sweden of English trader parents, Chambers had had the unique experience, among those who cried up the perfection of Chinese taste, of having set foot in China. As a young man he had been employed in the Swedish East India Company. Obviously, while his visits to China in the second quarter of the eighteenth century must have been confined to ports open to foreign traders, where visitors were scarcely allowed ashore, he was nevertheless able to cash in on his Chinese experience by writing two extremely influential books, one on Chinese architecture and one on Chinese gardens. His title to knighthood was Swedish but he retained it throughout his career in England, where, after studying at the Ecole des Beaux Arts in Paris, he became a distinguished classical architect. Lord Bute, whom we know as friend to Peter Collinson and a keen gardener himself, appointed Chambers to tutor the young Prince of Wales in architecture and later to become architectural adviser to his widow, Princess Augusta. For her, Chambers designed several Chinese buildings among the classical garden temples at Kew, one of them the pagoda standing today. His book about laying out these gardens, published in 1763, was in the library of Thomas Jefferson. In 1772 he published a book on Oriental gardening, mentioning Father Attiret only once. In 1775 he published a book upon Chinese buildings.

Just as Parkinson had complained in his *Paradisus* in 1629 that a plant had only to be said to come from America to win instant acceptance, rather over one hundred years later the Chinese hallmark was popular on any idea, and chinoiserie bloomed in both France and England, swept along by the authoritative Chambers. In his *Dissertation on Oriental Gardening,* Chambers, by then Comptroller of His Majesty's Works, is not above sneering at his detested rival, landscapist "Capability" Brown, for his "poverty of imagination," to correct which Chambers undertakes his account of the "Chinese manner of gardening."

The Chinese, Chambers says, regard gardening as an art, to be ranked with the great productions of the human understanding, and claim that its efficacy in moving the passions yields to that of few other arts whatever. "Their Gardeners are not only botanists, but also Painters and Philosophers, having a thorough knowledge of the human mind, and of the arts by which its strongest feelings are excited." From here on the Chinese speak as one with Sir William Chambers. They "take nature for their pattern and their aim is to imitate all her beautiful irregularities." They are given to vistas, relating them all to one central point. As for color — the Chinese prefer subtle color combinations. (This last idea lay dormant until Gertrude Jekyll and William Robinson reintroduced it at the end of the nineteenth century. The English eye has not yet entirely caught the message.) The Chinese, according to Chambers, have ha-has, or fences concealed in wide ditches; statues of nymphs in groves; grottoes cut in rocks and encrusted with shells; gloomy woods to excite terror; arbors; clipped yew hedges; artificial lakes, cascades, fountains; groves of familiar fruit trees; woods of the usual timber trees; gardens of familiar English flowers arranged by size. In fact, except for some fancy bridges and for some hedges allowed to grow free at the top though clipped below, the Chinese would seem to have much the same ideas in gardening as many English gentlemen of Chambers' time, except, of course, that they never never have paths or roads or streams in straight lines. The embellishment of nature by art, or "the improvements of art," became a rule without which nature was as nothing in the judgment of critics both greater and lesser than, for instance, Abigail Adams.

Water and rocks and changes in the level of the land, free-standing
unclipped trees, paths that wander instead of paths that walk straight
and turn right-angled corners, the necessity for surprises around screen-
ing shrubbery, the affectations of ruins or caves or Greek and Roman
temples or thatched-roofed villages miles away, the charm of walking a
guided tour past obelisks and urns and bowers and grottoes with frequent benches to sit upon to command the vistas cut for that particular
setting — all these new fashions swept away the old formalities, however grand. Every man became his own landscape gardener, even the
very wealthy who could afford to have Kent and Brown and Repton
come to tear up the old for them.

Alexander Pope is given credit for introducing the Virgilian phrase
"genius of the place" into the language of gardens. The term "landscape gardening" is credited to the poet William Shenstone, busy in his
turn with developing his own property, the Leasowes (luckily for his
rhyming friends, pronounced Lezzos).

Born in 1714 at the Leasowes in Shropshire, Shenstone was orphaned
at an early age and, after a succession of guardians, he came, in 1745,
into the care of his own fortune and into charge of his own place.
He thereupon "took the whole estate into his own hands, more to the
improvement of its beauty than the increase of its produce," according to
Samuel Johnson in his *Lives of the Poets.* We cannot but be impressed
by this great scholar's command of the jargon of the art of landscape
gardening in England in mid-century.

Now was excited his delight in rural pleasures, and his ambition of rural
elegance; he began from this time to point his prospects, to diversify his
surface, to entangle his walks, and to wind his waters; which he did
with such judgement and such fancy as made his little domain the envy of
the great and the admiration of the skilful; a place to be visited by travellers,
and copied by designers. Whether to plant a walk in undulating curves, and
to place a bench at every turn where there is an object to catch the view, to
make water run where it will be heard, and to stagnate where it will be
seen, to leave intervals where the eye will be pleased, and to thicken the
plantation where there is something to be hidden, demands any great powers
of mind, I will not inquire; perhaps a sullen and surly speculator may think
such performances rather the sport than the business of human reason. But
it must at least be confessed that to embellish the form of nature is an
innocent amusement; and some praise must be allowed by the most super-
cilious observer, to him who does best what such multitudes are contending
to do well.

This praise was the praise of Shenstone; but like all other modes of
felicity, it was not enjoyed without its abatements. Lyttleton was his
neighbour and his rival, whose empire, spacious and opulent, looked with

disdain on the *petty state* that *appeared behind it*. For a while the inhabitants of Hagley affected to tell their acquaintance of the little fellow
that was trying to make himself admired; but when by degrees the Leasowes
forced themselves to notice, they took care to defeat the curiosity which
they could not suppress, by conducting their visitants perversely to incon-
venient points of view, and introducing them at the wrong end of a walk
to detect a deception; injuries of which Shenstone would heavily complain.
Where there is emulation there is vanity; and where there is vanity there will
be folly.

The pleasure of Shenstone was all in his eye; he valued what he valued
merely for its looks; nothing raised his indignation more than to ask if
there were any fishes in his water.

His house was mean . . . his care was of his grounds . . . In time his
expenses brought clamours about him . . . His groves were haunted by
beings very different from fauns and fairies. He spent his estate in adorning
it, and his death was probably hastened by his anxieties.

We shall see this garden reported upon later by Thomas Jefferson. In
the meantime, since we are about to introduce the Reverend Joseph
Spence into his rightful place at last, we include here Johnson's description of the garden belonging to Spence's idol, the man whose witticisms
Spence devoted himself to reporting, Alexander Pope.

Johnson describes the move made when Pope was twenty-seven:

This year (1715) being, by the subscription, enabled to live more by
choice, having persuaded his father to sell their estate at Binfield, he purchased, I think only for his life, that house at Twickenham to which his
residence afterwards procured so much celebration, and removed thither with
his father and mother.

Here he planted the vines and the quincunx which his verses mention;
and being under the necessity of making a subterraneous passage to a garden
on the other side of the road, he adorned it with fossil bodies, and dignified
it with the title of a grotto; a place of silence and retreat, from which he
endeavoured to persuade his friends and himself that cares and passions
could be excluded.

A grotto is not often the wish or pleasure of an Englishman, who has
more frequent need to solicit than exclude the sun, but Pope's excavation
was requisite as an entrance to his garden, and, as some men try to be proud
of their defects, he extracted an ornament from an inconvenience, and vanity
produced a grotto where necessity enforced a passage.

The Reverend Joseph Spence, friend of Pope, translator of Attiret,
was generous with his ideas for redoing the gardens of his friends and
hosts. Sometimes, as when he sweepingly advised cutting down many
trees at Knole, one wonders if his advice was asked, let alone taken. He
left behind him many little sketches, some sent after he had dined, with

Pope's villa at Twickenham

diagrams and lists of plant material. He could lay out a city garden at one sitting, so to speak, or devote himself to large and elaborate plans, carefully annotated and with plant lists on the reverse side, rather like those Jefferson made for himself at Monticello. His plant lists include many American importations. Surprisingly, his plans contain a good deal more geometric design than appears in his theories on gardens.

There is a letter from him to a Mr. Wheeler in 1751, of which several copies with various changes indicate Spence's intentions to make it his final statement on the principles of garden design. As he devotes the last half of the letter to a description of his own estate, on which he has been working for three years, he may have wanted to hold up publication until he was quite satisfied with his accomplishments. The first half of the letter is devoted to "general rules."

Of these rules there are sixteen and they are worth quoting however briefly and in part only, since they comprehend the basic ideas of landscape gardening in England in mid-century.

1. Consult the "genius of the place" . . .

2. Fix the principal point of view and all secondary points of consequence in the disposition of the parts.
3. Follow Nature. Gardening is an imitation of "Beautiful Nature" and not works of art.
4. Assist or correct the general character of the ground.
5. Conceal any disagreeable object.
6. Open a view to whatever is agreeable.

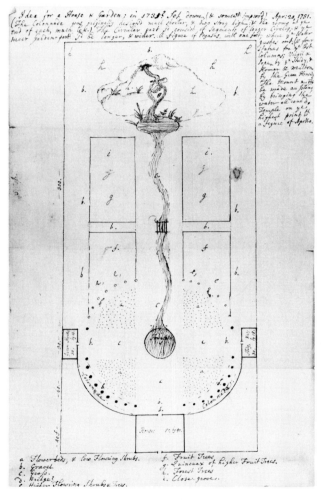

A little sketch of an ideal garden by the Reverend
Joseph Spence

7. Manage your plantations so you may be led to some striking object to change, in such a manner that the surprise itself is pleasing.
8. Conceal the bounds of your grounds everywhere.
9. Unite the different parts of your garden gently together.
10. Contrive the outer parts to unite well with the country around them.
11. Mix useful things in the ornamental parts, and ornamental in the useful.
12. Make objects that are near seem farther off by showing more of the intermediate ground, increasingly narrowing the view towards them.
13. Draw distant objects nearer by planting what will fall in and unite, to the eye, with distant objects.
14. Study variety in all things, inequality of ground, mixture of land and water, opposition of light and dark shades, breaking lines of trees, putting different kinds of trees in grovettes, no more than three or four of the same sort of tree together and none in a line. Kent staked out his groves with sticks first.
15. Observe the enmities and friendships of different colours and place only the most friendly next each other.
16. In mixing lights and shades, let the former have prevalence. The Chinese exceed our pleasure-ground makers, flinging their thick groves on hills at a distance.

And then he quotes from Pope:

> He gains all ends who pleasingly confounds,
> Surprises, varies and conceals the bounds.

This, he says included all he has said, and adds that he has heard Pope often include it all in one word, "Variety."

Spence is of particular interest to us because he uses so many American trees, shrubs and flowers in his recommendations to his hosts or patrons. We could leave his list of rules as the *obiter dicta* on eighteenth-century English gardens if we did not have a still closer connection with American gardeners in another, much published, summing up of all that was desirable in eighteenth-century English garden design.

Besides the books in Jefferson's own library, a framework of American eighteenth-century thought in even so small an area as gardening and agriculture can be constructed from a list he made, now famous, of books advisable for every man's library.

Dated August 3, 1771, from Monticello, and written at the request of young Robert Skipwith, soon to marry Tabitha, younger sister of Jefferson's wife, Martha, the list contains about one hundred and fifty titles. Broken into categories by Jefferson, the headings are, in order: Fine Arts; Politics; Trade; Religion; Law; History, Ancient and Modern; Natural Philosophy; Natural History; Miscellaneous. Fine Arts occupies nearly half of the total and, interestingly for us, begins with a book on gardening: "Observations on Gardening, Payne. 5/." Jefferson includes prices after each entry as those quoted by "Thomas Waller, bookseller, Fleet Street, London" and says the "whole catalogue as rated here comes to £107 s10." For our purposes, besides the gratification of seeing a book on gardening lead all the rest, it is pertinent to note that the authorities responsible for the changes in English styles of gardening are well represented: Dryden's *Aeneid*, Pope's *Iliad* and *Odyssey* and his *Collected Works*, Shenstone's *Works*, bound copies of the *Spectator*, *Tatler* and the *Guardian*, Percy's *Miscellaneous Chinese Pieces*, Burke on the *Sublime and Beautiful*, Hogarth's *Analysis of Beauty*, translations of Cicero, Addison's *Travels*, and Miller's *Gardener's Dictionary*.

In Jefferson's library, though not recommended to young Skipwith, we know there was a copy of Sir William Chambers' *View of Kew Gardens*, 1763, and one called *James on Gardening*, printed in 1728, an English translation of a fascinating work written in French by a young nobleman, Antoine Joseph Dezallier D'Argentville, but attributed by his publishers to his professor of architecture and landscaping, the authoritative Alexander Le Blond. There was also a copy of Joseph Spence's *Polymetis*, a ten-volume treatise on classical mythology as illustrated by ancient works of art.

In an age when to write and be published seems to have superseded desire for any credits for authorship, it is still surprising to see that Thomas Whately's little book, *Observations on Modern Gardening*, in mid-eighteenth-century England went through many editions with no author's name affixed to the title page. It is surprising even when one discovers he had written a lively account of injustices in taxing the colonies, which also appeared with no name and which he acknowledged as his own only very late in his life. It must, however, have given him pleasure, even in his active political life, to see the popularity of his book laying down the principles to be observed in the "new style" of gardening, with examples of the places where they had best been carried out. That our two most distinguished American garden visitors, Thomas Jefferson and John Adams, carried Whately on their tour of English gardens makes it necessary to report, however briefly, his views as the leading arbiter of the "new style" in landscaping.

My copy of Whately is the third edition, 1771, between Jefferson's of 1770 and Adams' of 1772. No author is mentioned, only the printer, T. Payne, who must have rejoiced at this runaway best seller. *Observations on Modern Gardening, illustrated by Descriptions* is the title and it is followed by a poem signed *"F,"* which, for one mistaking the F for a P, could give the authorship to that originator of much of the English garden revolution, Alexander Pope.

Where wealth, enthroned in Nature's pride,
With Taste and Bounty by her side,
And holding Plenty's horn,
Sends Labour to pursue the toil,
Art to improve the happy soil,
And Beauty to adorn.

The table of contents consists of sixty-seven "Observations" grouped under sixteen subject-headings between the introduction and conclusion. The introduction declares the materials of the art of gardening to be

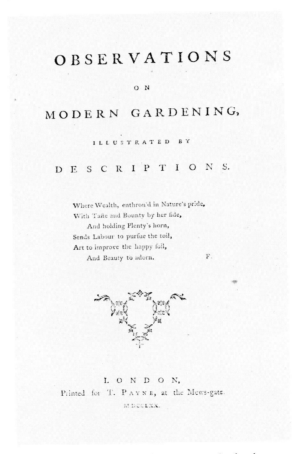

Title page from Thomas Whately's popular book *Observations on Modern Gardening,* used by both Jefferson and Adams

chiefly ground, wood, water and rocks. Cultivation of nature has introduced a fifth — buildings. Every "landskip" is composed entirely of these five parts. Beauty depends upon "the application of their several varieties." The first subject, "Of Ground," includes twelve short chapters and especially describes the thirty-acre lawn at Moor Park and the hill at Ilam. "Of Wood" follows, with thirteen chapters and descriptions of the groves at Claremont and Esher Place. "Clumps" of trees are discussed and the necessity of variety in trees and shrubs. "Of Water" needs nine chapters and is illustrated by the vast expanse of water at Blenheim and the cleverly contrived water views at Wotton. "Of Rocks" takes four chapters, with descriptions of romantic Middleton Dale, dignified Matlock Bath, terrifying New Weir on the Wye and fanciful Dove Dale. "Of Buildings" takes five chapters and features a Temple of Pan at Enfield Chase and the ruins of Tintern Abbey. So much for the materials available for creating gardens. "Of Art" follows and Whately adds three more chapters to discuss effects near the house and on the approach to it, as exemplified at Caversham. "Of Picturesque Beauty" points out the pitfalls when care is not taken. "Of Character" deplores the overdoing of "frivolous attempts" to achieve it . . . with heathen deities and heroes in the woods, revelry in summer-houses, melancholy under cypresses and the "environs of buildings . . . crowded with puerilities." Whately then presents, under "General Subject," the differences between a farm, a garden, a park and a riding. Farms can be pastoral, as at the Leasowes, or ancient, simple and ornamental, as at Woburn. Parks can be bordered by a garden, as at Pains Hill, or blended with a garden, as at Hagley. Gardens can surround an enclosure, or occupy the whole, as at Stowe. Ridings differ from gardens in extent, yet agree with it in many particulars, as exemplified by Persfield. With a brief poetic tribute to the Seasons, Whately sums up:

Whatever contributes to render the scenes of nature delightful is amongst the subjects of gardening . . . The whole range of nature is open . . . from the parterre to the forest . . . whatever is agreeable to the senses or the imagination . . . but . . . the genius of the place must always be particularly considered . . .

We are now ready for a tour of English gardens with Adams and Jefferson.

The art of politics, like necessity, makes strange bedfellows, as John Adams and Benjamin Franklin had realized when, early in the years of treaty-making after the Revolution, they had to share a bed and room in a French inn. Adams was the first into the room and instantly shut the window. Franklin followed and as instantly opened it. Adams said he was an invalid and found the night air deadly. Franklin pointed out his own good health, due, he said, to his passion for fresh air, even to his habit of walking around his room naked every morning to let his pores breathe. If the two of them spent the night in a room of that area with no fresh air, Franklin said, all the oxygen would be used up early in the morning, all the air would have been breathed at least once. Adams sprang into bed and pulled the bedclothes over his head. Franklin lectured and, by Adams' account, continued to lecture after he got into bed, but, Adams noted with satisfaction, he was soon "seized by sleep."

Love of gardening combined with politics can also ring odd changes. It was still more treaty-making that allowed Adams and Jefferson to take a brief holiday together to visit English gardens. Adams as first American minister to London had sent for Jefferson, in a like ministerial capacity in Paris, to come to London to confer on matters still pending about shipping and fisheries and boundaries. Jefferson, who had long wished to visit Europe and England but had been unwilling to leave an ailing wife, had arrived in Paris and was pleased to have the chance to visit England.

One writer, describing their tour, emphasized the social discrepancy between Jefferson the aristocrat and Adams the Yankee farmer. Actually Adams considered himself the more aristocratic of the two, and they were both dedicated farmers. Adams and Jefferson were contrasting American prototypes. The deepest difference lay in their attitudes to anything foreign. Adams had been fixed from birth to his own Yankee star. Nothing anywhere in the world was to be compared to his own country and his particular part of it. The whole political scene abroad was for him an opportunity to set the world right about the innate superiority of all things American. Jefferson, on the other hand, felt no urge to prove anything from his past except, perhaps, the natural and horticultural contributions of Virginia. Like Adams' Puritan ancestors, he wished the world to see that man was capable of creating a perfect state. But he was eager, also, to learn from the greatnesses of observable history.

That Americans' spirits were understandably high when dealing with their late enemies is evident in diaries and letters. A symbol of the times lies in a small canvas made by Benjamin West in Paris preparatory to recording the preliminary peace negotiations in 1782. To the left of a velvet-draped background stand and sit the Americans: Jay; Franklin; Franklin's illegitimate son, William Temple Franklin, whom Franklin was hoping to make into an American patriot and had taken on as his secretary; Laurens and John Adams. Before them lies the treaty upon a red-velvet-covered table. From the other side of the canvas appears to come a cloud of steam threatening them all. In reality it represents the space reserved for the British, who never turned up to be painted, to Adams' astonishment. Indeed, when he, still astonished, asked the artist many years later how this could have ever happened, or not happened, he had to be satisfied with the reply that perhaps it was due to Mr. Oswald, the British representative, being rather ugly with only one eye.

One thing our two heroes did have in common when they set out together to see the great gardens of England was a guidebook. Jefferson's copy of Thomas Whately's *Observations on Modern Gardening* he had bought in Paris from the library of an old friend and loyalist, the Reverend Samuel Hanley, pre-Revolution Professor of Moral Philosophy at the College of William and Mary. As we know, Jefferson had long before recommended this book as the first for a Virginia gentleman's library. Adams' copy of Whately is a later one, 1772, still unattributed to the author on the title page, where Adams has written, "By Thomas Whately, Esq." In the margins of the index and again in the margins of the text, Adams has repeated the name of each place he visited opposite Whately's reference to it. In all, Adams visited nineteen places. An extra notation on six of these has "Visited with Mr. Jefferson, April, 1786." A visit Adams later made with Mrs. Adams is checked as "Pains Hill, June, 1786" but we can compare his comments with those of Jefferson, who visited Pains Hill earlier and alone.

As Jefferson made a thorough "Memorandum" of his visits to English gardens in April, 1786, and kept an account of expenses, we follow his order, prefacing his comments with a brief account of Whately's views or, if the place is not given by Whately as an example, with a description from another contemporary account. Tips given to the servants are recorded from Jefferson's account book. Adams' comments, from his letters or his diaries or from those of his wife, Abigail, will be given after Jefferson's. Each man's summing-up of the excursion will end the account.

CHISWICK

Chiswick was one of the earliest gardens designed by William Kent, protégé of Pope and of the young Lord Burlington and the third Earl of Shaftesbury. With Pope's works, both Adams and Jefferson were familiar. With Burlington's enthusiasm for Palladian architecture and Shaftesbury's philosophy of "Platonic idealism," Jefferson would have been acquainted. The idea that harmony, balance and proportion are the foundations of both morality and beauty, for which "right models" can

Chiswick House. From *Seats of the Nobility*

be found in antiquity, was Shaftesbury's idea, which Kent was always trying to embody in landscape gardening.

The place was, soon after Jefferson's visit, to be rented to the new Horticultural Society and to be the scene of John Paxton's first English assignment.

Jefferson commented:

Chiswick. Belongs to the Duke of Devonshire. A garden of about six acres; the octagonal dome has an ill effect, both within and without; the garden still shows too much of art. An obelisk of very ill effect; another in the middle of the pond useless.

April 2. Gave servants at Chiswick 4/6.

HAMPTON COURT

Laid out by Cardinal Wolsey in a flowerless formal design of knots and alleys, later embellished by Henry VIII with a mount and heraldic beasts and flowers behind palings or box borders, still later bereft of the box borders by Queen Anne, Hampton Court may well have produced an "ill effect" to one come to study English gardening.

Jefferson commented:

Hampton Court. Old fashioned. Clipt yews grown wild.

April 2. Gave servants at Hampton Court 4/6.

TWICKENHAM

Jefferson commented:

Twickenham. Pope's original garden, three and a half acres. This is a long, narrow strip, grass and trees in the middle, walk all around. Now Sir Well-bore Ellis's. Obelisk at the bottom of Pope's garden, as monument to his mother. Inscription: "Ah, Edita, marrum optima, mulierum amatissima, Vale." The house about thirty yards from the Thames; the ground shelves gently to the waterside; on the back of the house passes the street, and beyond that the garden. The grotto is under the street, and goes out level to the water. In the centre of the garden a mound with a spiral walk around it. A rookery.

April 2, gave servants at Twickenham, Pope's garden 2/.

ESHER PLACE

The groves at Claremont and Esher occupy a lengthy "Observation" under Whately's "Of Wood." In both cases he says trees were planted too close together and will have to be thinned out. At Esher Place, however, due to varieties in the situation, where the grove winds along the banks of the river on the side and at the foot of a steep ascent, "many happy circumstances" concur and render this "little spot more agreeable than any at Claremont." He quotes, "In Esher's peaceful grove, When Kent and nature vie for Pelham's love." Jefferson, using his Whately on both "Ground" and "Wood," makes several original observations.

Esher. From a later edition of Whately's *Observations*

Jefferson commented:

Esher Place. The house in a bottom near the river; on the other side the ground rises pretty much. The road by which we come to the house forms a dividing line in the middle of the front; on the right are heights rising one beyond and above another, with clumps of trees; on the farthest a temple. A hollow filled with a clump of trees, the tallest in the bottom, so that the top is quite flat, On the left the ground descends. Clumps of trees, the clumps on each hand balance finely — a most lively mixture of concave and convex. The garden is of about forty-five acres, besides the park which joins. Belongs to Lady Frances Pelham.

April 2, gave servants at Esher Place 6/.

CLAREMONT

"Claremont. Lord Clive's. Nothing remarkable" follows immediately, with no tip to anyone.

PAINS HILL

Whately uses Pains Hill as the essence of a park. Jefferson and Adams visited Pains Hill. Parks and gardens, Whately says, are much

Claremont. From *Seats of the Nobility*

alike except in proportions. Each with the same species of ornament and scenery must maintain a state of high cultivation. But a park should seem to be reclaimed from a forest, with wildness kept in bounds. Pains Hill is situated at moor's edge above a fertile plain and the river Mole. Large gardens lie between the river and the park, which fills up the cavity of a crescent between hills. The prospects, according to Whately, are "only pretty, not fine," so Pains Hill's beauties lie in the scenes within, which are both grand and beautiful, "with a boldness of design and a happiness of execution . . . to rival nature." A Gothic building overhanging a height, a hermitage in a thicket, groves, lawns and a lake, three bridges, a ruined arch, a grotto, a gloomy path, a wild wood, a tower, a Temple of Bacchus and a hanging wood are among the features.

Jefferson commented:

Paynshill. Mr. Hopkins. Three hundred and twenty-three acres, garden and park all in one. Well described by Whately. Grotto said to have cost £7000. Whately says one of the bridges is of stone, but both now are of wood, the lower sixty feet high; there is too much evergreen. The dwelling-house built by Hopkins, ill situated; he has not been there in five years. He lived there four years while building the present house. It is not finished; its architecture is incorrect. A Doric temple, beautiful.

April 2, gave servants at Paynshill 7/.

Later Abigail and John Adams were to visit Pains Hill on their way to Portsmouth and Windsor. June 26, 1786, Adams describes "Paines Hill, Surry" as "the most striking piece of art that I have yet seen. The soil is a heap of sand, and the situation is nothing extraordinary. It is a new creation of Mr. Hamilton. All made within 35 years. It belongs to Mr. Hopkins who rides by it but never stops. The owners of these enchanting seats are very indifferent to their beauties."

WOBURN

Whately considers that opportunities to bring some degree of polish and ornament to the surroundings of a farm, pastoral or ancient, have resulted in the idea of an "ornamental farm," nowhere better executed than at Woburn. Here, of the one hundred and fifty acres, thirty-five are "adorned to the highest degree." Of the rest, two-thirds are in pasture, one-third in tillage. But the decorations are communicated to every part, disposed along the sides of a walk that forms a broad belt about the grazing grounds and arable lands and on to the brow of the hill, where the two lawns are each encompassed by a garden. One lawn commands a ruined chapel, the other an octagonal structure. Little seats and alcoves and bridges occur at intervals. The house and the lodge and a neat Gothic building with a small menagerie attached command far views. Flowers abound, many brought in from the fields. Whately admits, however, that the simplicity of a farm is wanting.

Jefferson seems to have felt so, too. He commented:

Woburn. Belongs to Lord Peters. Lord Loughborough is the present tenent for two lives. Four people to the farm, four to the pleasure garden, four to the kitchen garden. All are intermixed, the pleasure garden being merely a highly ornamented walk through and around the divisions of the farm and kitchen garden.

April 3, gave servants at Woburn's farm 6/6.

Adams commented that Woburn was "beautiful."

CAVERSHAM

Under the heading "Of Art" Whately deals with Caversham as a place in which the approach to the house excels in all principles of good design applied to modern gardening. A mile in length and not once in sight of the house, the entrance drive can never be mistaken for any other way. From an elegant lodge on either side of the entrance, it crosses the breadth of a lovely valley, in winding, easy sweeps. Presenting ever-new scenes to the view, it slants at last up a gentle rise to the mansion. Great trees are thickened by the perspective; a clump hangs over a bold ascent; a fine grove crowns an opposite brow; another beautiful grove spreads perfect gloom. Maples, hawthorns, oaks, beeches of enormous size are combined in this beautiful approach, which is actually confined within a narrow valley without views, buildings or water.

Jefferson, however, saw more than the approach. He commented:

Caversham. Sold by Lord Cadogan to Major Marsac. Twenty-five acres of garden, four hundred acres of park, six acres of kitchen garden. A large lawn separated by a sunk fence from the garden, appears to be part of it. A straight, broad gravel walk passes before the front and is parallel to it, terminated on the right by a Doric temple, and opening at the other end on a fine prospect. This straight walk has an ill effect. The lawn in front, which is pasture, well disposed with clumps of trees.

April 4, Caversham, gave servants 3/6.

Adams saw Caversham with Jefferson, commented that it was "beautiful" and continued with him on the fifth of April, the sixth and the seventh, to see the next five places commented upon by Jefferson.

WOTTON

Whately makes much of Wotton under his heading "Of Water." If, he says, the water at Wotton were all exposed, a walk of two miles along the banks would be tedious without those changes of scene that now supply perpetual variety. Divided into four parts, each one is different in character and situation. The first is a reach of river flowing through a mead with clumps of trees. The second was a formal basin from which now issue two broad streams that can be supposed to join a large river. That river makes the third division and a lake into which it falls is the fourth. An island, which is the "point of view," is topped by an Ionic portico commanding a scene that includes a lawn of at least one hundred acres. A Tuscan portico is next the basin. An elegant bridge with a colonnade upon it makes a picturesque object from an octagon building across the lake. A Chinese room on a nearby island is an object from the bridge. All are parts of a related whole and in one part, where the connection may seem lost, the arches of a stone bridge partially seen in a wood preserve the connection.

Jefferson commented:

Wotton. Now belongs to the Marquis of Buckingham, son of George Grenville. The lake covers fifty acres, the river five acres, the basin fifteen acres, the little river two acres — equal to seventy-two acres of water. The lake and great river are on a level; they fall into the basin five feet lower. These waters lie in the form of [and he makes an L] the house is in the middle of the open side, fronting the angle. A walk goes around the whole, three miles in circumference, and containing within it about three hundred acres; sometimes it passes close to the water, sometime so far off as to leave large pasture grounds between it and the water. But two hands to keep the pleasure grounds in order, much neglected. The water affords two thousand brace of carp a year. There is a Palladian bridge, of which, I think, Whately does not speak.

April 5, Wotton (Marquis of Buckingham's) servants 3/.

Adams commented, "Wotton is both great and elegant, though neglected."

STOWE

Whately devotes most of his whole heading "Of Gardens" to Stowe after he has dealt briefly with "a garden surrounding an enclosure," which may be composed simply of a walk about a field. The field may be a lawn; the walk, for pleasure, may be planted on the sides with a profusion of ornament and exhibit a variety of scenes. This "species of garden, therefore, seems proper only for a place of very moderate extent . . ."

On the other hand, where, as at Stowe, the whole enclosure is a garden, hidden gravel walks to every part are indispensable during bad weather, and wide grass walks, slowly curving, conduct the visitor in fine weather to "elegant, picturesque and various scenes." The house stands on the brow of a gentle ascent. Part of the garden in the declivity spreads toward a winding valley, which separates the eminence on which the house stands from a higher one across the valley. Begun "when regularity was in fashion," the gardens are still bounded by a gravel walk of between three and four miles, planted with trees and bordered by a "deep-sunk fence" enclosing a space of "near four hundred acres." Inside this evidence of the original plan, "every symptom of formality is obliterated." A former octagon basin is now an irregular piece of water receiving two streams and falling down a cascade into a lake. The lawn in front of the house is open to the water, with two elegant Doric pavilions placed opposite each other on the boundaries. A noble Corinthian arch stands against the hills. From here all the gardens are seen, including the queen's amphitheater with an Ionic rotunda, a pyramid upon the brow of the hill and the king's pillar on the descent, "not gay but grave," encompassed by a wood.

At the king's pillar scenes are unconfined: one to the lake and a wood behind three pavilions joined by Ionic arcades, which is known as Kent's Building. This fronts the rotunda, though from a considerable distance. It is also to be seen from the Temple of Bacchus, from which point the scene is a "most animated landskip."

The distant country does not just "glimmer in the offskip, but is close and eminent above the wood and connected by clumps with the garden." Whately describes the view from Kent's Building back toward all the others, and finds the character of the whole "sober and temperate." In contrast, another feature, "the Elysian fields," lying in the valley below the other side of the house, is "very lightsome and very airy." One enters this from under a Doric arch that forms a vista toward a Pembroke bridge and a lodge built like a castle in a park. A Temple of Friendship is also in sight, as are temples of Ancient Virtue and one for British Worthies decorated with effigies of those distinguished by military, civil or literary merit. A column is sacred to a Captain Grenville who fell in action at sea. The whole of the Elysian fields is filled with "representations of those who have deserved best of mankind . . . solitude never having been reckoned one of the charms of Elysium." A dark alder grove contrasts with this scene of joy and above this upon a pinnacle is "a large Gothic building," from which a path leads to the Grecian valley commanded by a Temple of Victory and Concord with six Ionic columns supporting a pediment, spreading "awe over the whole."

Whately concludes by saying that "magnificence and splendor" are the characteristics of Stowe, "pomp blended with beauty, amenity with grandeur." He cannot forbear to add, however, in his final paragraph, that "in the midst of so much embellishment as may be introduced into this species of garden a plain field or a sheep walk is sometimes an agreeable relief, and even wilder scenes may occasionally be admitted."

Jefferson commented:

Stowe. Belongs to the Marquis of Buckingham, son of George Grenville, and who takes it from Lord Temple. Fifteen men and eighteen boys employed in keeping pleasure grounds. Within the walk are considerable portions separated by enclosures and used for pasture. The Egyptian pyramid is almost entirely taken down by the late Lord Temple to erect a building there in commemoration of Mr. Pitt, but he died before beginning it and nothing is done yet. The grotto and two rotundas are taken away. There are four levels of water, receiving it one from the other. The basin contains seven acres, the lake below that ten acres. Kent's building is called the temple of Venus. The enclosure is entirely surrounded by ha-ha. At each end of the front line there is a recess like the bastion of a fort. In one of these is the temple of Friendship, in the other the temple of Venus. They are seen, the one from the other, the line of sight passing, not through the garden, but through the country parallel to the line of the garden. This has a good effect. In the approach to Stowe, you are brought a mile through a straight avenue pointing to the Corinthian arch, then you turn short to the right. The straight approach is very ill. The Corinthian arch has a very useless appearance, inasmuch as it has no pretension to any destination. Instead of being an object from the house, it is an obstacle to a very pleasing distant prospect. The Grecian valley being clear of trees while the hill on each side is covered with them, is much deepened in appearance.

April 6, Stowe (Marquis of Buckingham's) servants 8/.

Adams commented upon Stowe in his general summary:

. . . Temples of Bacchus and Venus are quite unnecessary as mankind have no need of artificial incitements to such amusements. The temples of ancient Virtue, of the British Worthies, of Friendship, of Concord and Victory are on a higher taste . . . I mounted Lord Cobham's Pillar. One hundred and twenty feet high, with pleasure as his name was familiar to me from Pope's Works.

LEASOWES

Whately considers Leasowes first under "Of A Farm," as exemplifying the improvements to be desired to "blend the useful with the agreeable." Opening the garden to the country and "by force of refinement" returning to simplicity is embodied in the "ideas of pastoral poetry." So "a place conformable to them is deemed a farm in utmost purity."

Whately described the Leasowes, paternal home of Shenstone the poet, as a place with many natural advantages and beauties surrounded by a walk that reveals them all in turn.

From many accounts the Leasowes, when the poet lived and worked there, was one of the most visited English gardens of its time. Shenstone was observant of, and eager to outdo, his neighbor, Lord Lyttleton, busy improving *his* paternal acres of Hagley, next door. The poet wrote to Lady Luxborough about one of the "features" at Hagley: "Mr. Lyttleton has near finished one side of his castle. It consists of one entire tower and three stumps of towers . . . The situation gives it a charming effect . . ." Jealous of attention paid to Hagley, Shenstone felt free to incorporate some of its features into his views. He is pleased to report that an artist engaged in painting scenes at Hagley has visited him to sketch what "I call Virgil's Grove, here." Fond of his friends and given to commemorating their visits, he dedicated conceits about his garden to them, inscribing their names upon rustic benches and urns with appropriate quotations, or erecting busts and obelisks set in suitable groves.

A poem to Shenstone from a lady admirer begins: "Health to the bard, in Lezzo's happy groves . . ." goes on at some length about fairies, and ends "Let order, peace and housewif'ry be mine. Shenstone, be Genius, taste, and glory, thine."

Leasowes as a *"ferme ornée"* became one of the showpieces of England.

Jefferson commented:

Leasowes in Shropshire. Now the property of Mr. Horne by purchase. One hundred and fifty acres within the walk. The waters small. This is not even an ornamented farm — it is only a grazing farm with a path around it, here and there a seat of board, rarely anything better. Architecture has contributed nothing. The obelisk is of brick. Shenstone had but three hundred pounds a year and ruined himself by what he did to this farm. It is said he died of the heart-aches which his debts occasioned him. The part next the road is of red earth, that on the further part grey. The first and second cascade are beautiful. The landscape at number eighteen and prospect at thirty-two are fine. The walk through the wood is umbrageous and pleasing. The whole arch of prospect may be on ninety degrees. Many of the inscriptions are lost. April 7, Leasowe's (Shenstone's now Horne's) servants 5/.

Adams commented:

Shenstone's Leasowes is the simplest and plainest, but the most rural of all. I saw no spot so small that exhibited such a variety of beauties.

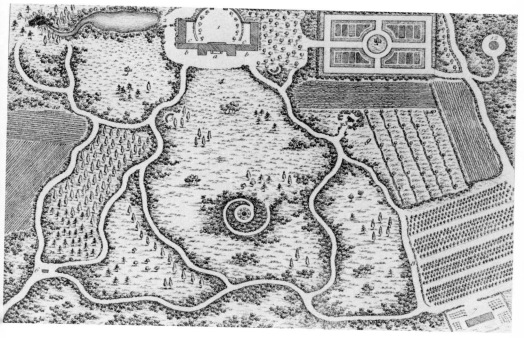

The idea of a *ferme ornée* was especially attractive to those who both farmed and gardened. One can see traces of the idea at Monticello. This is from a French book of drawings

HAGLEY

Whately devotes pages to Hagley under "Of A Park" because it exemplified the "happy blending" of both park and garden. Situated in lovely country between the Clent and Witchberry hills, both of which belong to it. The latter rise in three swells, one wood-covered, the next topped by a sheepwalk surmounted by an obelisk, the third ornamented with a portico after the Temple of Theseus in Athens and nearly as large. The house is seen from all of these hills. Distant views from the Clent Hills are particularly fine. The house, set low in the park, commands the adjacent grounds, which are wooded and interspersed with lawns of various sizes and shapes. An octagon seat, sacred to the memory of James Thomson, stands on his favorite spot, the brow of a steep slope above a meadow, beyond which the country "becomes the offskip." An antique tower stands in a dusky wood in the midst of which is a Doric portico, called Pope's Building. Progressing to a knoll crowned by a rotunda, one perceives a bridge with a portico upon it set to terminate a piece of water. Behind this is a wild grove and a Gothic seat from which one sees the tower, which appears to be part of a ruined castle commanding an extensive prospect and visible from afar. Below it in a thicket is a hermitage, and, after a succession of groves and glades, the Tinian lawn, ringed by stately trees and a grove in which an urn, placed there by Pope, establishes an effect of composure and thoughtfulness "to which the mind is insensibly led by the rest of this elegant scene." Careful planting of trees for various effects on both the eye and the mind, gravel paths to each important site, frequent benches and varied arrangements of water . . . all combine to blend the two characters of park and garden.

Jefferson comments:

Hagley, now Westcot's. One thousand acres; no distinction between park and garden — both blended but more of the character of a garden. Eight or nine labourers keep it in order. Between two and three hundred deer in it, some of them red deer. They breed sometimes with the fallow. This garden occupying a descending hollow between the Clent and Witchbury hills with the spurs from those hills, there is no level in it for spacious water. There are, therefore, only some small ponds. From one of these there is a fine cascade, but it can only be occasionally by opening the sluice. This is in a small deep hollow with recesses of stone in the banks on every side. In one of these there is a Venus pudique, turned half around as if inviting you with her into the recess. There is another cascade seen from the portico on the bridge. The castle is triangular, with a round tower at each angle, one only entire; it seems to be between forty and fifty feet high. The ponds yield a great deal of trout. The walks are scarcely gravelled.

April 8. Hagley (Lord Westcot's) servants 5/ -ent in the village 2/6. ["-ent" may represent refreshment of tea for two after all this.]

Adams commented:

Lord Lyttleton's seat interested me, from a recollection of his works as well as the grandeur and beauty of the scenes. Pope's Pavilion and Thomson's Seat made the excursion poetical.

BLENHEIM

Whately, under "Of Water," makes much of the solution to the original water problem at Blenheim. Originally, he tells us, there was a deep valley between the house site at Blenheim and the opposite "plantations"; it was such an interruption it had to be bridged, "but the forced communication was only a subject of railery." Whereupon they flooded the valley to make it seem a broad river with bold shore. The bridge remained unaltered, but the water gives it propriety. The site on the far bank of "Fair Rosamund's Bower," where a spring of water is called Rosamund's Well, is marked by a single willow. Whately has no reproaches for Sarah, Duchess of Marlborough, who allowed the old house at Woodstock to be torn down to improve the general sweep of the view from her castle, "a prodigious pile of a building which, with all the faults of its architecture, will never seem less than a princely habitation . . ." In the middle of the extensive lawn commanded by the house stands a column, "a stately trophy," between which and the house is the original bridge, "established in all the importance due its greatness." The water runs off into rivers, cascades, lakes, pools — everywhere a fine expanse with "undetermined extremities . . ."

Jefferson commented:

Blenheim. Twenty-five hundred acres of which two hundred is garden, one hundred and fifty water, twelve kitchen garden, and the rest park. Two hundred people employed to keep it in order, and to make alterations and additions. About fifty of these employed in pleasure grounds. The turf is mowed once in ten days. In summer about a thousand fallow deer in the park and two or three thousand sheep. The palace of Henry II was remaining until taken down by Sarah, widow of the first Duke of Marlborough. It was a round spot levelled by art, near what is now water and but a little above it. The island was part of the high road leading to the palace. The well is near where the bower was. The water here is very beautiful and very grand. The cascade from the lake, a fine one, except this garden has no great beauties. It is not laid out in fine lawns and woods, but the trees are scattered thickly over the ground, and every here and there small thickets of shrubs, in oval raised beds, cultivated, and flowers among the shrubs. The gravelled walks are broad — art appears too much. There are but a few seats in it, and nothing of architecture more dignified. There is no one striking position in it. There has been a great addition to the length of the river since Whately wrote.

April 9, Blenheim (D. of Marlborough's) servants 7/.

John Adams commented:

Stowe, Hagley and Blenheim are superb.

A year later, from London in 1787, Abigail Adams wrote about *her* visit to Blenheim.

She is writing to her niece.

London, October 3, 1787.
. . . We returned home through Bristol, and took Oxford in our way, from when we went to Woodstock and visited Blenheim, the seat of the Duke of Marlborough, which was built at the public expense, and granted by the Crown to the Duke, for the services he had rendered his country. This

castle is upon the grandest scale of anything I have ever yet seen. We enter the park through a spacious and elegant portal, of the Corinthian order, from whence a noble prospect is opened to the palace, the bridge, the lake, with its valley, and other beautiful scenes. The front of this noble edifice, which is of stone, is three hundred and forty-eight feet from wing to wing. On the pediment of the south front, towards the garden, is a noble bust of Louis the Fourteenth, taken by the Duke from the gates of Tournai. This, the gardener told us, he never failed pointing out to the French gentlemen who visited the place, and that they shrugged their shoulders and *mon-Dieu'd*. But, before I describe to you the gardens, I will attempt to give you a short, though imperfect account of the palace.

This follows and, after a glimpse of the garden from the library, she moves out.

[162]

Leasowes.
visited, with all
afternoon in April
1786.

The ideas of *pastoral poetry* seem now to be the standard of that simplicity; and a place conformable to them is deemed a farm in its utmost purity. An allusion to them evidently enters into the design of * the Leasowes, where they appear so lovely as to endear the memory of their author; and justify the reputation of Mr. Shenstone, who inhabited, made, and celebrated the place; it is a perfect picture of his mind, simple, elegant, and amiable, and will always suggest a doubt, whether the spot inspired his verse, or whether, in the scenes which he formed, he only realized the pastoral images which abound in his songs. The whole is in the same taste, yet full of variety; and except in two or three trifles, every part is rural and natural. It is literally a grazing farm lying round the house; and a walk as unaffected and as unadorned as a common field path, is conducted through the several inclosures.

Near the entrance into the grounds, this walk plunges suddenly into a dark narrow dell, filled with small trees, which grow upon abrupt and broken steeps, and watered by a brook,

* In Shropshire, between Birmingham and Stourbridge. The late Mr. Dodsley published a more particular description than is here given of the Leasowes; and to that the reader is referred for the detail of those scenes of which he will here find only a general idea.

which

Inscribed page from Adams' copy of Whately's
Observations

From two bow windows in this noble gallery, the eye is delighted with a view of the declivity, descending to the water, and the gradual ascent of the venerable grove, which covers the opposite hill.

From the house, we visited the gardens; and here I am lost, not in confusion, but amidst scenes of grandeur, magnificence, and beauty. They are spacious, and include a great variety of ground. The plain, or as artists term it, the lawn, before the palace, is kept in the most perfect order: not a single spire of grass rises above another. It is mowed and swept every other day, and is as smooth as the surface of a looking-glass. The gardener, who have lived twenty-five years upon the place, told us that he employed about sixty-three hands during the summer, in mowing, sweeping, pruning, lopping, and in ornamenting the grounds. From this lawn is a gradual descent to the water, and you pass through spacious gravel walks, not in straight lines, as Pope expresses it,

> "where each alley has a brother
> And half the platform just reflects the other";

but pleasing intricacies intervene. Through the winding paths, and every step, open new objects of beauty, which diversified nature affords of hill, valley, water, and woods; the gardens finally are lost in the park, amidst a profusion of venerable oaks, some of which are said to have stood nine hundred years. The gardens are four miles round, which I walked; the park is eleven. There is a magnificent bridge consisting of three arches; the water which it covers is formed into a spacious lake, which flows the whole extent of a capacious valley. This was built at the expense of Sarah, Duchess of Marborough, as well as a column which I shall mention in turn. The gardener, who was very loquacious and swelled with importance, told us, that since his residence there, the present Duke has greatly enlarged and improved the grounds; that he had beautified them by the addition of some well-placed ornaments, particularly the temple of Diana, and a noble cascade, round which are four river gods, represented as the guardian genii of the water.

This celebrated park was first enclosed in the reign of Henry the First. His successor, Henry the Second, resided at this seat, and erected in this park a palace, and encompassed it with a labyrinth, which was fair Rosamond's bower, celebrated by Addison. There are now no remains of it, except a spring at the foot of the hill, which still bears the name of Rosamond's Well . . . There are now two sycamores planted as a memorial upon the spot where the old palace stood. The column will close my narrative. This is in front of the palace of Blenheim at about half a mile distance, and is one hundred and thirty feet high; on the top of which is John, Duke of Marlborough . . ."

Two more entries are in Jefferson's accounts of visiting English gardens with Whately as his guide. These are not dated, nor does money seem to have changed hands.

ENFIELD CHASE

Whately has included Enfield Chase under his heading "Of Building" because of the happy situation of the Temple of Pan, which he could wish to be brought forward out of its thickets.

Jefferson commented:

Enfield Chase. One of the four lodges. Garden about sixty acres. Originally of Lord Chatham, now in the tenure of Dr. Beaver, who married the daughter of Mr. Sharpe. The lease lately renewed — not in good repair. The water very fine; would admit of great improvement by extending walks, etc. to the principal water at the bottom of the lawn.

MOOR PARK

Whately mentions Moor Park first among his examples of modern garening under "Of Grounds" because of the thirty-acre lawn "on the back front of the house."

Jefferson sees more.

Moor Park. The lawn about thirty acres. A piece of ground up the hill of six acres. A small lake. Clumps of spruce first. Surrounded by a walk — separately enclosed — destroys unity. The property of Mr. Rous, who bought of Sir Thomas Dundas. The building superb; the principal front a Corinthian portico of four columns; in front of the wings a colonnade, Ionic, subordinate. Back front a terrace, four Corinthian pilasters. Pulling down wings of building; removing deer; wants water.

This is the second Moor Park, named by its creator, Sir William Temple, for the first Moor Park in Herefordshire, where he had spent his honeymoon and written his immortal account of the garden there, which we have quoted. This Moor Park, which Jefferson visited, in Surrey was reputedly so firmly in the formal style as to attract visits from William III. Here Sir William Temple spent his declining years, growing superior fruits of many sorts. This is probably the origin of the Moor Park Roman apricot offered for sale by the Prince brothers on Long Island in 1791.

KEW

Jefferson had his own single purpose in mind when he visited Kew on April 14. He describes only the "Archimedes screw for raising water" and draws a diagram of it. He gave the servants five shillings and spent sixpence on lemonade.

And we have Adams' recording of a visit on April 20, 1786, "with

Mr. Jefferson and my family" to Osterly "to view the Seat of the late Banker Child," a large house fronting three ways, with an inner court, a greenhouse and a hothouse.

. . . Blowing roses, ripe strawberries, cherries, plumbs etc. in the hot house. The Pleasure Grounds were only an undulating gravel walk between two borders of trees and shrubs. All the evergreens, trees and shrubs were here. There is a water for fish ponds and for farm uses, collected from the springs and wet places in the farm and neighbourhood. Fine flocks of deer and sheep, wood doves, guinea hens, peacocks, etc. The verdure is charming, the music of the birds pleasant. But the ground is too level . . . Mrs. Child is gone to New Market it seems to the races. The beauty, convenience and utility of these country seats is not enjoyed by the owners. They are mere ostentations of vanity. Races, cocking, gambling, draw away their attentions.

On the same day they "called to see Sion House belonging to the Duke of Northumberland." This farm is watered by a rivulet drawn by an artificial canal from the Thames. Adams found it a

. . . repetition of winding walks, gloomy evergreens, sheets of water, clumps of trees, green houses, hot houses, etc. The gate which lets you into this farm from the Brentford Road is a beautiful thing and lays open to the view of the traveller a very beautiful green lawn interspersed with clumps and scattered trees.

Descriptions of her visit to two more gardens by Abigail Adams show how well she has learned her lessons.

From Exeter we went to Plymouth . . . and crossed over the water to Mount Edgcombe, a seat belonging to Lord Edgcombe. The natural advantages of this place are superior to any I have before seen, commanding a wide and extensive view of the ocean, the whole town of Plymouth, and the adjacent country, with the mountains of Cornwall. I have not much to say with respect to the improvements of art. There is a large park, well stocked with deer, and some shady walks, but there are no grottos, statuary, sculpture or temples.

Her account of stopping at Windsor on her way back from Portsmouth shows she, too, enjoys literary references as background for viewing the English landscape.

. . . Windsor . . . I was charmed and delighted with it. The most luxuriant fancy cannot exceed the beauties of this place. I do not wonder that Pope styles it in the seat of the Muses. Read his "Windsor Forest" and give full credit to his most poetic flights. The road by which we entered the town was from the top of a very steep hill; from this hill a lawn presents itself on each side. Before you, a broad straight road, three miles in length; upon each side a double plantation of lofty elms lift their majestic heads, which is exceeded only by a view of the still grander forests at a distance, which is thirty miles in circumference. From this hill you have a view of the Castle and the town.

In summarizing his visits to English gardens, Jefferson wrote to John Page:

The gardening in that country is the article in which it surpasses all the earth. I mean their pleasure gardening. This, indeed, went far beyond my ideas.

Adams' summary seems so much in character, it lends a piquancy to the entire excursion.

Mr. Jefferson and myself went in a Post Chaise to Woburn Farm, Caversham, Wotton, Stowe, Edgehill, Stratford upon Avon, Birmingham, the Leasowes, Hagley, Stourbridge, Worcester, Woodstock, Blenheim, Oxford, High Wycomb, and back to Grosvenor Square.

But in mid-tour he recounts an incident not mentioned by Jefferson. When they arrived at Edgehill and Worcester, Stowe gardens behind them, Leasowes ahead, they were interested in the scenes where "Freemen had fought for their Rights." At Worcester the people appeared so "ignorant and careless" that Adams was, as he was so often, "provoked" to say, "And do Englishmen so soon forget the Ground where Liberty was fought for? Tell your neighbours and your Children that this is holy Ground, much holier than that on which your Churches stand. All England should come in Pilgrimage to this Hill, once a Year." He said they seemed much pleased.

The Gentlemen's Seats were the highest Entertainment we met with. Stowe, Hagley and Blenheim, are superb. Woburn, Caversham and the Leasowes are beautiful. Wotton is both great and elegant tho neglected. Architecture, Painting, Statuary, Poetry are all employed in the Embellishment of these Residences of Greatness and Luxury. A national Debt of 274 millions sterling accumulated by Jobs, Contracts, Salaries and Pensions in the Course of a Century might easily produce all this Magnificence. The Pillars, Obelisks etc. erected in the honour of Kings, Queens and Princesses, might procure the means.

Lord Lyttletons Seat interested me, from a recollection of his Works, as well as the Grandeur and Beauty of the Scenes. Pope's Pavilion and Thomson's Seat made the Excursion poetical. Shenstone's Leasowes is the simplest and plainest, but the most rural of all. I saw no spot so small that exhibited such a Variety of Beauties.

Adams then sweeps into his final pronouncement:

It will be long, I hope, before Ridings, Parks, Pleasure Grounds, Gardens and ornamented Farms grow so much in fashion in America. But Nature has done greater Things and furnished nobler Materials there. The Oceans, Islands, Rivers, Mountains, Valleys, are all laid out upon a larger Scale. If any Man should hereafter arise, to embellish the rugged Grandeur of Pens Hill, he might make something to boast of, although there are many Situations capable of better improvement.

That about does it for Adams' observations upon modern gardening in England, except for one final loyal comment. In July of 1786, he confided to his diary:

In one of my common walks, along the Edgeware Road, there are fine Meadows of Squares of grassland belonging to a noted Cow keeper. These plots are plentifully manured. There are on the side of the Way, several heaps of manure, an hundred loads perhaps in each heap. I have carefully examined them and find them composed of straw, and dung from the stables and streets of London, mud, clay or marl, dug out of the ditch, along the hedge, and turf sward cut up with spades, hoes and shovels in the Road. This is laid in vast heaps to mix. With narrow hoes they cut it down at each end, and with shovels throw it into a new heap, in order to divide it and mix it more effectually. I have attended to the operation as I walked, for some time. This may be good manure, but is not equal to mine, which I composed in heaps on my own farm, of horse dung from Bracketts stable in Boston, marsh mud from the sea shore and street dust from the plain at the foot of Pens Hill in which is a mixture of marl.

Furber's Flowers for the Month of December

1. Royal purple Auricula P
2. African white Flowered Heath S
3. Pansies, or Hearts ease B
4. White Corn Marigold G
5. Strawberry Daisie F E
6. Cape Marigold S
7. Shining-leaved Laurustinus B T
8. Marvel du Monde Auricula P
9. Red Spring Cyclamen G
10. White Cyclamen G
11. Yellow Ficoides G

12. Yellow round Eternal G
13. Christmas Flower B
14. White Winter Primrose
15. Gentianella F E
16. Yellow Corn Marigold G
17. Scarlet Geranium S
18. Canary Pellitory S
19. Valerianella G
20. Winter double Crowfoot B
21. Striped leaved Geranium G
22. Cape Marigold, white Within S
23. St. Peters Shrub B T
24. Mountain Avens B

25. Single Purple Anemone B
26. Sage & Rosemary tree G
27. Winter Wall Flower B
28. Winter Flowering Pear L T
29. Lavender-leaved Groundsel Tree G
30. Scarlet African Aloe with Pineapple Leaves G
31. Spanish Virgin's Bower C T
32. Glastenbury Thorn L T
33. Humble Plant S
34. Basella S
35. Monthly Rose B T
36. Trifid African S

14 The American Way

IN THE American colonies, the seventeenth-century gardens had been almost totally what it is now fashionable to call "relevant." They existed to feed, clothe, clean, cure and comfort the settlers. Grace notes were rare, like the walk from his house to the creek, where Governor John Endecott kept his shallop, being planted so thickly with damson trees and grapevines that a person might pass unobserved. The gardens of the eighteenth-century colonies and states expanded as the manner of life expanded, and began to acquire the interest and style, the variety and charm, that can come with a relaxed society, one that feels sure of holding its own and more, too.

One essential in English landscape design was space. Although French landscapists had thought of painted backdrops for town gardens, depicting miles of campagna complete with ruins and clouds, this could not equal being able to see into the next county. After space came groves of trees asymmetrically placed. And water. In England these three requirements could involve ambitious landowners in extensive operations. In the American colonies on the Atlantic seaboard, south of the rockbound New England coast, whose taste had jelled with its inception, these three requirements were easily met. Space was there and in plenty. Trees were huge and needed only selecting and thinning, and water was the way of life.

An original introduction by the English landscape school was attention to mood. Le Nôtre had intended to inspire only admiration. The English landscape school wished to inspire such uncontrolled emotions

Tulip Tree. One of our most popular American forest trees, brought
into American gardens and sent abroad. Catesby Plate 48, Vol. I.
Catesby made two pictures of this tree with the "Baltimore bird," perhaps because the coloring of the two seemed somewhat complementary

as awe and terror. The most sublime landscape feature was supposed to
strike fear into the observer's marrow.

As anyone might have predicted, all of this fell on relatively infertile
soil across the Atlantic. Classical studies had early been insisted upon.
Virgil and Horace were bedside reading in the wilderness for those
striving to cling to their education. Pope was in every library. Addison
and Steele were enjoyed and quoted. Yet nobody in America tried to
create a landscape calculated to awe anyone else. The Natural Bridge
did for visiting foreigners in search of that sort of sensation. American

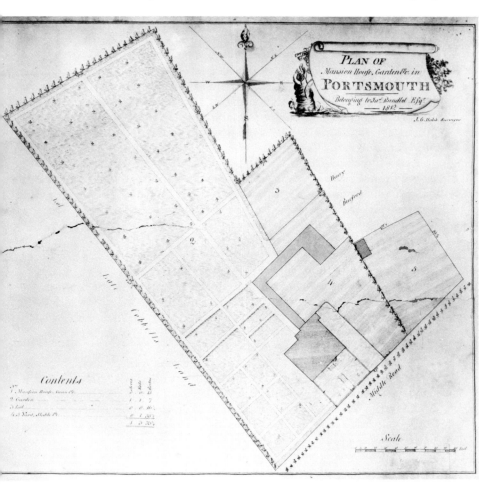

Plan of the Rundlett-May house and garden in Portsmouth, New Hampshire

gardens were for domestic enjoyment, with collections of shrubs and flowers. Views were upstream and downstream, with shipping moving upon the water. Trees were kept for shade or fruit or bloom or beauty. The summerhouse was to catch the breezes, not to recall Apollo, and the vines and the hummingbirds were a reminder, not of ancient Rome, but of today and now, if we may but sustain it. The only aspect of the new wave in English gardening was the emergence of that pretty excuse for combining utility and pleasure, the *ferme ornée*. It was from this that the "roundabout" walk derived, very early one of Jefferson's adoptions for Monticello and later for Senator Gore for Gore Place.

But interest in the changing ideas of gardening in England was stimulating. While we did not aim to create emotions in the hearts of the beholders of our pleasure grounds, we were pleased to have our trees required, our shrubs ordered, our flower seeds sent for.

Only a few influential landowners who returned from abroad were torn between the long-accepted symmetrical plans, handed down by the early English, French and Dutch settlers, and the new free style. The standard American middle-of-the-road garden layout was fairly predictable, from New England to the Carolinas.

A two- or three-story house with a central hall and two or four chimneys would stand clear on its foundations with no embellishments other than, often, some terracing, which lent dignity and increased a sense of privacy when the house stood high on a town street. On one side or on both, generous lawns would be broken by large ornamental trees, framed by square paths, bordered, perhaps, by roses in narrow beds, centered, possibly, by a raised bed on which seasonal features were displayed — tulips in the spring, gay-leaved plants in the summer and fall. Behind the house, beyond a modestly proportioned lawn or on one side, with terracing to supplement the front "falls," would be a formally patterned flower garden in oblongs or squares, with a wide path, often bordered by flower beds, which led down through a small orchard to the vegetable and small fruits gardens.

Arbors, trellises, places to sit in vine-encased privacy could be encountered at well-spaced intervals. A stable with carriage houses and a paddock or cow yard would be behind the house and to one side with its own access. Various paths would lead to it from the garden and the house where ells attached, sometimes one after the other and at different dates, housed a summer kitchen, and a "cool room," a well, a woodshed, and an ample earth-closet with assorted-sized holes and another similar closet next door for servants and workers. These appurtenances called for a quantity of flowering vines.

The orchard trees were more convenient to pick and prune if they were grafted on dwarf stock. The vegetable garden was laid out in its own formal style with borders of currants and with grass or gravel walks down past the squared-off onion and asparagus beds to the inevitable quince in one of the far corners. There would be a garden seat there, too, as a well-cared-for vegetable garden was something for the owner to show to friends aspiring to rival or excel him in new varieties of peas or beans or salad stuffs.

That this type of garden was general among the well-to-do professional or successful trader home-owners can still be seen in small seacoast ports and inland towns. Wholly American, it exudes a sense of individual orderly independence, even among neighbors with similar ideas in similar houses on either side.

In the hills of Virginia one sees this same modest plan, although the actual garden area may be farther separated from the house, as are the stables and other outbuildings. The formal pattern of the flower garden becomes a definite design afloat upon a lawn or field but clearly a fancy to be enjoyed on the way to orchard and vegetables, fields and pastures.

Larger American establishments, with access to rivers or inlets from the sea to serve as highways, necessarily depended upon straight ways to the wharves and, across the main axis, to buildings placed along the sides in order of their functions. Some of the big river plantations that stood high above the river used a splendid succession of "falls" to set them off from the river or bay. These would be kept shaved by scythes and not cut up by flower beds, as they were a feature in themselves, like the bowling green, sunken and with slightly sloped edges to keep in the balls and give spectators an advantage. Ornamental ponds helped with drainage in low-lying areas, but they were clearly cut and not blurred by planting at the edges or encouraged to look wild or even natural.

If the land on which the house stood was not on a bluff, the garden, instead of being tucked away on one side and walled so as not to interfere with the clear grandeur of open space, was laid out between the river and the house. Here a vast and wild expanse could be rendered a pleasure ground of intersecting paths, matching borders and beds, paired-off effects in small trees or shrubs surrounded by ever-increasing circles of bright flowers, with covered ways on the extreme sides or at the ends for sitting and viewing all through lattices and climbing vines. High walls and iron gates flanked by posts topped with birds or urns or seated hounds would enhance the privacy and dignity. In the center of the whole might be a monument, a memorial urn, with the founder of the family or the planner of the garden immortalized, probably in his own words, in carved marble.

Both in the north and the south, if there was sufficient land, only a very distant church and churchyard and, a particular attachment to the land by those who had found, tilled and tended it, there would be a family burying ground with various styles of monuments bespeaking the generations of tastes through which the holding had survived. It would be walled as securely as the garden, with a stray climbing rose or two escaping over the wall, a weeping willow by the gate to veil the entrance, cypresses and yews to mark the corners. The whole would seem like another, smaller garden of a sort, tucked away, yet present in every consciousness.

Gardens on the large, working plantations, where the family remained

A typical riverside plantation with the mansion house presiding over the well-arranged outbuildings, including a mill and a warehouse

in residence throughout the working year, were very large to afford space for daily walks, side by side, by the owner and his farthingaled lady, especially on wet days when only the gravel or brick walks would be dry. Teahouses; "necessaries" for convenience when the distance to the facilities provided in connection with the house would be too distant; little gardenhouses for tools, roots or schooling the young; towers for doves or pigeons to provide squabs for the table or sport for the guns; neatly designed little houses for the well, some like Chinese temples, as were some of the birdhouses high on their poles — all these elaborations added grace and interest.

Some of the prettiest features of these large plantation houses were the covered ways that led from the family rooms to the various working areas that supported the household, curved and open colonnades through which food or clean laundry or fresh hot or cold water was brought from the outside kitchen and washhouses or through which the family waste was removed to a well-planned distance. On the side of a steep site some of these activities could take place underground and not interfere with the views from the house, as at Monticello. Similarly, the outbuildings could be planned to look attractive and set off the whole establishment, depending mainly upon the climate as to how near or far they were sited. Planting around them could be one of the major features of the estate. To look charming at a distance or to ensure privacy for those in transit, the ways to the "necessaries" near the house were screened by flowering shrubs. The main drive to the house as well as the way from it to the stables would be well shaded and protected by rows of trees. Some great houses had deer parks where the deer could be seen from the house over what seemed an unbroken expanse of green, since the fences to keep them in their enclosures were sunken in a wide ditch not detectable from the house. Hedges of native wild shrubs, the thornier the better, would hide outlying fields planted with varied crops, leaving the utilitarian harvests to "working farms," sometimes at a stout riding distance from the "home plantation."

On a river bluff a summerhouse would command the view and the breezes, sometimes thriftily constructed on top of an icehouse or root cellar. In a wide and open expanse such a conceit as a "mount" from which to view the countryside over the garden wall, or the garden itself from a vantage point, would be a rare fancy. Occasionally, a pair of mounts would add architectural significance to an entrance or the sides of a building, as at Mount Vernon, in the first instance topped with weeping willows, and the White House in Washington, where Jefferson had them on either side of the White House façade as he had added matching heights on either side at Monticello.

Here we present, though regrettably briefly, Jefferson's lifelong consistent design for Monticello. That we have not described it before is not due to neglect but to its having been well documented many times.

Quite simply, the plan evolves from the leveling of the top of a hill commanding a wide view of the valley below and the distant site of the University of Virginia. The level top is oval in shape and allows for a house site on the valley side and an extensive lawn toward other hilltops behind. A drive is designed to wind slowly up and around the site. Terraces on the sides and front are arranged to take care of a vineyard, beds of fruits and vegetables, and a slope of ornamental trees and shrubs over whose flowering tops the wide views may be surveyed. Cultivated fields spread across the valley where the officious foreign visitor lamented the absence of a river. At the back of the house on the lawn side, near the house and cut into the lawn, is an arrangement of oval beds, lying parallel with the house, into which Jefferson liked to put flowers in showy quantities. The lawn, in fact the whole design, is shaped rather like the sole of a shoe with the house for a heel. It forms an elongated

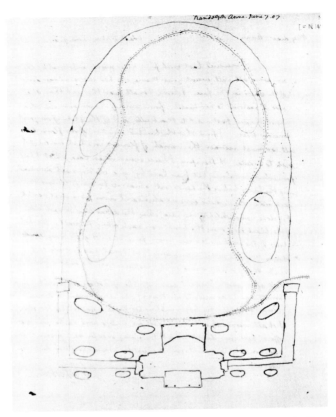

Jefferson's sketch of his long-lasting ideal plan for Monticello. This is in an 1807 letter to his niece. Another similar plan, but with six "shrubberies" instead of these four, was made a generation before this one

loop, within which Jefferson wandered his "roundabout" walk, among sometimes six, sometimes four, large ovals of shrubberies. In his sketched plans these ovals are ranged in an even number opposite each other. Around these his walk made long moderate curves. His ideal plan called for the walk to be bordered on each side by all the flowers sent him or grown by him. It is a handsome plan, reminiscent of a *ferme ornée,* and a pleasant and informal way of enjoying a garden dispersed about a lawn. I have seen a similar walk in a French country mansion of about the same date. Strangely, it seems to be unique in American gardens, even today.

There is a family burying ground, as at Mount Vernon, halfway up the slope at the back of the hill, planned to be planted with melancholy trees and shrubs. There were plans for a deer park or a sort of small wild animal preserve nearby, where some of our native wild animals could be coaxed to show themselves for visitors.

Interestingly, Jefferson arranged for sitting places and viewing places to be, not at strategic intervals about his garden or terraces, but provided for on the top of his outlying mounts on either side of his house, which are not designed as mounts *per se* but to disguise underground accommodations. A little office building commands the level on the side of the entrance drive. The top of the other level is equipped with seats for commanding the view.

For an intimate sketch of gardens in and about Albany before the American Revolution, we have an American classic comparable in some ways to William Bartram's *Travels,* though considerably diluted by being remembered in the tranquillity of a Scottish parsonage a generation after the event. Mrs. Anne Grant had spent a brief part of her enviably adventurous childhood as Anne MacVicar, the daughter of a British Army officer in a Highland Regiment stationed on the then frontier above Albany. A small child when she arrived at Claverack on the Hudson, she learned Dutch, and at age five accompanied her father through the wilderness to his post at Oswego. A clever child, self-reportedly well read in the Bible and *Paradise Lost,* she attracted the attention of Madame Schuyler in Albany, who took her in, when she was seven, to live with her.

The *Memoirs of an American Lady* take the form of a biography of Madame Schuyler and her family, with vivid accounts of local phenomena, which give the book its style of historic immediacy. The account of the annual spring scene when the ice began to break up in the Hudson River is worthy of comparison with William Bartram's description of fighting bull alligators in the Georgia swamps.

Anne's father, after the conquest of Canada, decided to take up land and settle in Vermont, but he abandoned his scheme and his land in 1768 and took his wife and thirteen-year-old daughter home to Inverness-shire. He later forfeited his holdings to the new republican government, leaving his daughter dowerless. That she was able to retrieve her American fortunes by turning her scarce ten years in the American wilderness into a classic account of life up the Hudson before the Revolution seems only just.

Her description of gardens and gardening have been quoted often, but inadvertent hints given by her, which may have escaped too-frequent quoting, lend useful suggestions as to home-landscaping in the upper Hudson Valley in mid-eighteenth century.

The first of these is her descriptions of the houses and the social gatherings out-of-doors in the late afternoons. The houses are arranged in "modest dignity" side by side, though at some distance from each other and from the street. Albany, as she describes it, "in proportion to its population, occupied a great space of ground." Stretched along the bank of the Hudson, one very wide and long street lay parallel to the river, the space between it and the shore being occupied by gardens. A small but steep hill in the center of the town was crowned by a fort. From the foot of this hill a street sloped down to join the other street, much wider than the other, paved on each side, the middle occupied by public edifices: the marketplace, a guardhouse, the town hall and the English and Dutch churches. Two irregular streets, not so broad but equally long, ran parallel and were crossed by others.

The city, in short, was a kind of semi-rural establishment; every house had its garden, well and a little green behind; before every door a tree was planted, rendered interesting by being coeval with some beloved member of the family. Many of their trees were of a prodigious size and extraordinary beauty, but without regularity, everyone planting the kind that best pleased him, or which he thought would afford the most agreeable shade to the open portico at his door which was surrounded by seats and ascended by a few steps. It was in these that each domestic group was seated in summer evenings . . . grouped according to similarity of years and inclinations . . . Servants were housed above the town, where early settlers had cleared and built neat cottages "for their slaves surrounded with little gardens and orchards . . . wildly picturesque and richly productive."

Mrs. Grant remembers, as a "singular coincidence," that not only the training of children

but of plants . . . was the female province . . . Everyone in town and country had a garden, but all the more hardy plants grew in the field in rows, amidst the hills, as they were called, of Indian corn. These lofty plants sheltered them from the sun, while the same hoeing served for both; there cabbages, potatoes, and other esculent roots, with a variety of gourds grew to a great size and were of excellent quality . . . Kidney-beans, asparagus, celery, great variety of salads and sweet herbs, cucumbers, etc. were only admitted into the garden into which no foot of man intruded after it was dug in spring. Here were no trees, those grew in the orchard in high perfection . . . Strawberries and many high flavoured wild fruits of the shrub kind abounded so much in the wood that they did not think of cultivating them in their gardens which were extremely neat but small, and not by any means calculated for walking in . . .

The fondly remembered picture of the American housewife going to

tend her garden would seem to prohibit any cultivation beyond that of
the prettiest necessities.

Mrs. Grant, a generation later and in another land, can

yet see . . . a respectable mistress of a family going out to her garden in an
April morning, with her great calash, her little painted basket of seeds, and
her rake over her shoulder, to her garden labours . . . A woman in very easy
circumstances, and abundantly gentle in form and manners, would sow and
plant, and rake incessantly. These fair gardeners, too, were great florists;

The Yellow Day Lily. Possibly the longest-lasting
garden flower we have. *Hemerocallis flava* came over
in the seventeenth century and is still an indispensable corner-filler in even the most modern garden.
Curtis *Botanical Magazine*

their emulation and solicitude in this pleasing employment did, indeed, produce "flowers worthy of Paradise." These, though not set in "curious knots," were ranged in beds, the varieties of each kind by themselves; that, if not varied and elegant, was at least rich and gay.

While this pretty picture may seem to some a willfully idealized portrait of a lady gardener never stooping below rake-level to work wonders in her little plot, the author does almost demolish the picture herself by adding tersely, right after "rich and gay," "To the Schuylers this description did not apply; they had gardeners and their gardens were laid out in the European manner."

Besides mentioning the "regular assembling together on porches every fine evening," Mrs. Grant has something to say of the entertainment offered guests, invited or not. She maintains that by Scottish standards the reception may have seemed a little cold — with no apologies.

Dinner, which was very early, was served exactly in the same manner as if it were only the family . . . After sharing this plain and unceremonious dinner which might, by the bye, chance to be very good one . . . tea was served at an early hour. And here it was that the distinction shown to strangers commenced. Tea here was a perfect regale, accompanied by various sorts of cakes unknown to us, cold pastry . . . great quantities of sweetmeats and preserved fruits . . . plates of hickory and other nuts ready cracked.

If, Mrs. Grant says, "you stayed supper," here again the hosts departed from their "usual simplicity." Having dined between twelve and one and having had tea at a time she does not indicate, she says you would be ready "for either game or poultry roasted . . . shellfish in the season . . . fruit in abundance . . ."

Mrs. Grant's description of the house she knew and loved best gives us a tempting breakdown of rooms replete with "valuable furniture . . . the favourite luxury," all carefully shut up to keep out the flies, "which in that country are an absolute nuisance." About the outside of the houses she is less enthusiastic, except for the open portico by the front door, floored like a room and furnished with chairs and sofas, roofed with a "slight wooden roof painted like an awning," latticed, shaded by a grapevine in which innumerable nearly domesticated little birds made their home, nesting upon an inner shelf especially provided them for this purpose.

The house was a two- or three-story brick house with a wide center hall, fronting the river, with a smaller house attached to the rear where the family lived in winter. This had a basement kitchen. In the summer the Negroes "dressed" the food for the family in outer kitchens. On the brink of the river ran the great road to Saratoga and the northern lakes. The house stood three hundred yards from the road, with a "simple avenue of morella cherry trees, enclosed with a white rail" between it and the road. On the south side, that is to say, on the other side of the road and between it and the river, was laid out an enclosure divided into three parts — a hayfield, a garden, an orchard — all surrounded by simple deal fences. And here Mrs. Grant introduces her little horror picture, which has superseded all other descriptions of eighteenth-century American gardens — the posts to which the deal boards are fixed "are surmounted, every one, with an animal skull for yet more little birds than those accommodated on the portico to nest in . . . a hospitable arrangement for the accommodation of the small familiar birds before described." This must, indeed, have been a bird-loving family, as the Negroes, not content with the portico shelf and all the skulls, were allowed to nail up any quantity of old hats with holes in them, to the "end of the kitchen." Another innovation to attract birds to these early settlements was a dead tree left standing "in the middle of the back yard for their emolument."

Mrs. Grant has an anecdote of a British major whose troops on the frontier looked likely to run wild and deteriorate for lack of proper sports (no horses) and any occupation beyond shooting all the game in the wilderness. He determined upon gardening as the solution, and set one hundred men to work the wild woods into "a large garden, bowling green, and enclosed field." The predestined spot for the major's garden was partially cleared, and "if a mulberry, a wild plum or cherry tree was particularly well-shaped or large . . . as well as some lofty planes and chestnuts . . . they were marked to remain . . . When shrubs were grubbed up . . . he left many beautiful ones peculiar to the country. To see the sudden creation of this garden, one would think the genius of the place [ah Virgil, ah Pope!] obeyed the wand of an enchanter . . . A summer house in a tree, a fish pond and a gravel walk were finished . . ." The example, Mrs. Grant says, spread to all the forts.

So, thank you, Mrs. Grant.

A description of the van Rensselaer manor house, built in 1765 in the north section of Albany and recollected a century later, serves to confirm the change in the style of living brought about by land investment and industrial and agricultural prosperity after the opening up, and securing of, the frontier. It would seem to belong to the nineteenth century except that the age of the trees and the general style and layout conform to the houses and gardens of affluent Philadelphians of the mid-eighteenth century.

The recollection is that of one who as a boy played with children visiting old Mrs. van Rensselaer and her brother, and coping with an elderly butler named Pfink and a gardener very jealous of his green-

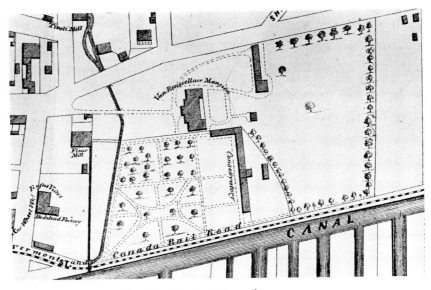

Plan of the van Rensselaer Mansion, built in 1765

houses and grapery. The grounds were large, by his account, fenced all about with a high picket fence except on the canal side, where the fence was solid and had no gate. Inside the fence was a thick planting of trees and shrubs. The manor house faced south, sideways to the canal, with a wide lawn at the back and a road leading through a gate to stables and offices, a laundry, tool house and the gardeners' houses, all hidden by planting. Another service road ran east to the canal by the greenhouses and grapery, also hidden from the house by planting. The entrance road passed a brownstone gate house and divided to sweep about the house, front and back, in an ellipse. The main drive crossed a little brownstone bridge over a creek and approached the house past the lawn planted with great elms. The creek was dammed to create a succession of small ponds with waterfalls, and there were walks planted with native shrubs and ornamental trees.

The formal garden lay between the house and the canal, with the long conservatory flanking it on one side. The main layout of the garden was two broad walks, one from the east side of the house and on a line with the front of it, nearly to the canal. The other walk was shorter and ran north and south. At their intersection was a brown sandstone basin about twenty feet across with a single jet of water capable of being thrown as high as the roof of the house. The flower beds were along the paths and scattered through the grass on either side. The path from the house, after passing the fountain, was covered with an arbor of vines and roses and ended in an open space by the canal, where there were two larger-than-life busts, one of Washington and the other of Lafayette, facing the arbor toward the house.

There are elements in this description that place the general aspect of the grounds as later than the style of those originally planned — the flower beds sprinkled about the grass in the garden, for instance, and, obviously, the subjects of the ornamental busts. But the surrounding shrubberies, the geometrical layout of the garden, within easy access of the house and with the conservatory on one side, the use of native material in the plantings, are all in keeping with the end of the eighteenth century.

In Loudon's *Encyclopaedia of Gardening,* published in England in 1834, the "mansion of General van Rensselaer" is described as having "more of the accompaniments of shrubbery, conservatory etc. than is often seen in America . . ." By the 1850 edition Loudon has dropped it from reference, but by then he was relying upon Mrs. Trollope for his descriptions. With reference to our autumn coloring, he quotes only her, "not that her description is the best, but because, as she shows in her work an evident dislike to both the people and the country, she cannot be suspected of exaggeration."

The descriptions of American gardens, even as seen by Mrs. Trollope and quoted in Loudon's *Encyclopaedia,* give us a sense of eighteenth-century American garden history encapsulated that would be hard for us to rival in any summation of our own. The whole eighteenth-century foundation is still solidly visible, now grown to maturity. And our native trees still excite praise.

To a stranger, Mr. Loudon reports, as to one James McNab, coming into New York in 1834, the preponderance of evergreens on outlying prominences gave a "gloomy" appearance, but when he landed, the trees and shrubs made everything seem like one great garden. Indigenous trees and those brought up from the south were remarkable for "diversity of form and variety of foliage." The *Platanus occidentalis, Lirodendron, Liquidambar, Gleditschia triacanthos* and the catalpa were pre-eminent. The only imported trees appeared to be fruit trees, Lombardy poplars and weeping willows. And he gave special praise later to the groves of arbor vitae up the Hudson.

Mrs. Trollope's description of sailing past the mansions of New York and Philadelphia, whose lawns are washed by the "silvery waters" on which she swiftly floats, is as lyric as it is possible for it to be, "presenting a picture of wealth and enjoyment." Her description of the region of the Allegheny mountains as a garden entire with all the famous and sought-after shrubs "in equal profusion" would warm the heart of even the most slurred inhabitant. Especially of those who lived in the narrow valleys, where "little gardens or fields are hedged round with sumachs, rhododendrons and azaleas and the cottages were covered with roses."

It seems to be universally acknowledged in books about eighteenth-century American gardens, unless they are all relying on one source, that the Philadelphians alone espoused gardening in the formal, European style almost to a man, or, let us say, almost to a rich man. Good gardeners were, apparently, obtainable, and they, also to a man, were from abroad and equally addicted to the formal style. This is interesting as, by all eighteenth-century accounts, Philadelphia abounded with growers of native plants, enthusiasts for planting parks of American trees, scientists interested in medicinal plants and passionate orchardists. One of the writers on this "rage" for European formal style in Philadelphia ascribes it to sudden wealth. Another thinks it is due in part to the popularity of "prospective views of gentlemen's seats" being engraved

Azalea nudiflora var *coccinea,* Scarlet Azalea. The shrub that so pleased Jefferson

and published early in eighteenth-century England and snapped up in the print shops of early-eighteenth-century Philadelphia. There was also, according to this last apologist, the influence of the "Philosophical Optical Machine," which became very popular as evening entertainment in mid-eighteenth-century Philadelphia when its operator advertised it as a safe, cheap and easy way to travel. In any case, the "newest taste" in Philadelphia just before the Revolution comprised box-bordered walks, terraced levels, statues, temples, obelisks and plaster-of-Paris figures in "full stature or busts . . . Birds and many other Sorts . . . for Ornamenting Garden Walks."

Fairhill, considered one of the "show places of colonial America," Josiah Quincy found superior to anything he had seen even in the south. He felt John Dickinson, who had inherited it in 1770, should be the happiest of men with "the antique look of his house, his gardens, Greenhouse, bathing house, grotto, study, fish-pond, fields, meadows, vista through which is a distant prospect of Delaware River . . ."

A wealthy Scot, Captain Charles Cruickshank, bought Clifton Hall, laid it out in terraces and box borders and a hothouse and had *his* bath in a private garden.

Ezra Stiles, who visited Bush Hill near Philadelphia in 1754, admired the "very elegant garden in which are seven statues in fine Italian marble . . ." Another visitor was taken with the fishing house, which stood "romantically in a wood over the Schuylkill on a projecting rock."

Penn's Springettsbury was still a place to be visited in mid-eighteenth century, with its two-mile vista, "pretty pleasure garden," graveled walks planted with shrubs and evergreens, "small wilderness," groves, a "neat little park though without deer," spruce hedges cut into figures; in fact, as Stiles approvingly remarked, "the most agreeable variety."

Abigail Adams has left us descriptions of two of the best gardens of the time, one in New York, one in Philadelphia. From Richmond Hill, "near the city of New York," she writes in 1789:

Richmond Hill (N.Y.)
27 September, 1789

I write to you, my dear sister, not from the disputed banks of the Potomac, the Susquehanna, or the Delaware, but from the peaceful borders of the Hudson; a situation where the hand of nature has so lavishly displayed her beauties, that she has left scarcely any thing for her handmaid, art, to perform.

The house in which we reside is situated upon a hill, the avenue to which is interspersed with forest trees, under which a shrubbery rather too luxuriant and wild has taken shelter, owing to its having been deprived by death, some years since, of its original proprietor, who kept it in perfect order. In front of the house, the noble Hudson rolls his majestic waves, bearing upon his bosom innumerable small vessels, which are constantly forwarding the rich products of the neighbouring soil to the busy hand of a more extensive commerce. Beyond the Hudson rises to our view the fertile country of the Jerseys, covered with a golden harvest, and pouring forth plenty like the cornucopia of Ceres. On the right hand, an extensive plain presents us with a view of fields covered with verdure, and pastures full of cattle. On the left, the city opens upon us, intercepted only by clumps of trees, and some rising ground, which serves to heighten the beauty of the scene, by appearing to conceal the part. In the back ground, is a large flower-garden, enclosed with a hedge and some very handsome trees. On one side of it, a grove of pines and oaks fit for contemplation.

"In this path

How long soe'er the wanderer roves, each step
Shall wake fresh beauties; each last point present
A different picture, new, and yet the same."

A year later from the same place to an English friend:

I have a situation here, which, for natural beauty may vie with the most delicious spot I ever saw. It is a mile and half distant from the city of New York. The house is situated upon an eminence; at an agreeable distance flows the noble Hudson, bearing upon its bosom the fruitful productions of the adjacent country. On my right hand, are fields beautifully variegated with grass and grain, to a great extent, like the valley of Honiton in Devonshire. Upon my left, the city opens to view, intercepted, here and there, by a rising ground, and an ancient oak. In front, beyond the Hudson, the Jersey shores present the exuberance of a rich, well-cultivated soil. The venerable oaks and broken ground, covered with wild shrubs, which surround me, give a natural beauty to the spot, which is truly enchanting. A lovely variety of birds serenade me morning and evening, rejoicing in their liberty and security; for I have, as much as possible, prohibited the grounds from invasion, and sometimes almost wished for game laws, when my orders have not been sufficiently regarded. The partridge, the woodcock, and the pigeon are too great temptations to the sportsmen to withstand. How greatly would it add to my happiness to welcome here my much esteemed friend.

Within the same year, 1790, she has moved to Bush Hill.

Philadelphia
21 November, 1790

. . . amusement and pleasures from a flock of sheep, which are daily pastured by a shepherd and his dog upon the lawn in front of our house. Bush Hill, as it is called, though by the way there remains neither bush or shrub upon it, and a very few trees, except the pine grove behind it — yet Bush

Hill is a very beautiful place. But the grand and sublime I left at Richmond Hill. The cultivation in sight and prospect are superior, but the Schuylkill is no more like the Hudson, than I to Hercules . . .

From which she is to move a year later in 1791.

. . . We have had a very severe winter in this State, as you may judge when I tell you that we have consumed forty cords of wood in four months. It has been as cold as any winter we have at the northward. The 17th and 18th of this month I dined with all my windows open, put out the fires, and ate ice to cool me; the glasses at 80. This is the 20th. Yesterday it snowed nearly the whole day, and to-day it is a keen northwester; and I presume it will freeze hard tonight. Yet the verdure is beautiful; full as much as I shall find by the middle of May in Massachusetts, where I hope then to be. Yet I shall have some regrets at leaving this place, just as the season begins to open all its beauties upon me. I am told that this spot is very delightful as a summer residence. The house is spacious. The views from it are rather beautiful than sublime; the country round has too much of the level to be in my style. The appearance of uniformity wearies the eye, and confines the imagination. We have a fine view of the whole city from our windows; a beautiful grove behind the house, through which there is a spacious gravel walk, guarded by a number of marble statues, whose genealogy I have not yet studied, as the last week is the first time I have visited them. A variety of fine fields of wheat and grass are in front of the house, and, on the right hand, a pretty view of the Schuylkill presents itself. But now for the reverse of the picture. We are only two miles from town, yet have I been more of a prisoner this winter than I ever was in my life. The road from hence to the pavement is one mile and a half, the soil a brick clay, so that, when there has been a heavy rain, or a thaw, you must wallow to the city through a bed of mortar without a bottom, the horses sinking to their knees. If it becomes cold, then the holes and the roughness are intolerable. From the inhabitants of this place I have received every mark of politeness and civility. The ladies here are well-educated, well-bred, and well-dressed. There is much more society than in New York, and I am much better pleased and satisfied than I expected to be when I was destined to remove here. Adieu.

Your sister

In Charleston, South Carolina, gardens had always been a prime consideration, but it is a rewarding and pleasurable confirmation to find that in the record books of property transfers of the eighteenth century, the "Plat Books" trace out garden plans as well as boundaries and house sites. In almost every case the garden is shown to be laid out in a pattern of square or rectangular beds, with a central feature in a little circle and perhaps quarter circles in the corners. Sometimes an orchard or vegetable garden is included in an overall formal design, taking up the entire space. Sometimes a bordered walk runs down one side to a bordered series of beds far from the house. Occasionally there is a long arborway crossing at right angles, a longer shrub-bordered way among a number of square beds, two deep on either side of the main path. These are all town gardens, though, as Loudon reports, "At Charleston the houses of the suburbs are for the most part surrounded by gardens . . . orange trees, monthly roses . . . piazzas and spacious balconies . . . Upon the walls and columns are creeping vines and a great number of passion-flowers." Captain Basil Hall, touring the estates of his American friends after helping them put down the pirates in Tripoli, noted the quantity of Pride of India trees, *Melia azedarach,* planted throughout southern towns in gardens and as street trees.

In the early 1740's Eliza Lucas, later to be Eliza Pinckney, wrote effusively girlish, but wisely observant, letters to her friend "Miss Bartlett," who had returned to London from visiting in Charleston. It is one of these letters that gives us an account of one of the great southern garden layouts. Eliza Lucas was on a tour of "several very handsome Gentlemen's seats, at all of which we were entertained with the most friendly politeness. The first we arrived at was Mr. William Middleton's 'Crowfield,' where we spent a most agreeable week." Her description follows in full:

The house stands a mile from but in sight of the road and makes a very handsome appearance; as you draw near it new beauties discover themselves; first the fruitful vine manteling the wall loaded with delicious clusters. Next a spacious Basin in the midst of a large Green presents itself as you enter the gate that leads to the House which is neatly finished, the rooms well contrived and elegantly furnished.

From the back door is a spacious walk a thousand feet long, each side of which nearest the house is a grass plat ornamented in a Serpentine manner with Flowers; next to that on the right hand is what immediately struck my rural taste, a thicket of young, tall live oaks where a variety of airey choristers pour forth their melody, and my darling the mocking bird joyn'd in the artless Concert and inchanted me with his harmony. Opposite on the left hand is a large square bowling green, sunk a little below the level of the rest of the garden, with a walk quite around composed of a double row of fine, large flowering Laurel and Catalpas which afford both shade and beauty.

My letter will be of unreasonable length if I don't pass over the Mounts, Wilderness, etc., and come to the bottom of this charming spot where is a large fish pond with a mount rising out of the middle the top of which is level with the dwelling house and upon it a Roman temple; on each side of this are other large fish ponds properly disposed which form a fine prospect of water from the house.

Beyond this are the smiling fields dressed in vivid green; here Ceres and Pomona joyn in hand to crown the hospitable board . . . I am quite tired of writing as I suppose you are of reading and can't say a word of the other seats I saw in this ramble except the Counts large double row of oaks on each side the avenue which leads to the house and seems designed by Nature for pious meditation and friendly converse.

It is fitting for us to end with Loudon describing Mount Vernon and Monticello as still among the foremost examples of landscape gardening in the United States. Mount Vernon, though "in a very poor order," is unchanged from the time when Washington died. "The narrow path at the top of the bank above the river which was begun by him just before he was carried off by sudden illness remains in its unfinished state." Monticello seems also to have retained Jefferson's stamp undisturbed: "ascended by a spiral approach, laid out by the proprietor himself, and passing through fruit and ornamental trees, many of which were planted by his own hands. The southern declivity of the hill is covered with vineyards, the east and west by orchards, the north side by a forest, and the champaign lands below are devoted to the culture of corn and tobacco."

In the preface to his *American Calendar,* in which Bernard M'Mahon felt free to comment upon Americans and their gardens as he had come to do so much for both, he says, "America has not yet made that rapid progress in gardening, ornamental planting, and fanciful rural designs which might naturally be expected from an intelligent, happy and independent people possessed so universally of landed property, unoppressed by taxation or tithes, and blessed with consequent comfort and affluence."

Perhaps we may even now continue to tell ourselves, like John Adams, that our ways, diverse though they be, were right for us.

The garden historian's viewpoint is both a worm's- and a bird's-eye view. If one believes that an understanding of a time and a people can be attained through finding out what they grew and why, these natural approaches are as rewarding as any. Living materials make good witnesses. They also make a lively connection with past treasures that have faded or turned to dust. The gardens of an era, the flowers, trees and vegetables most fancied and depended on, the methods and manpower, designs, influences, tastes, needs and exigencies, even the successes and errors can bring us in the end to an understanding of the Americans living and working in gardens, orchards, fields and swamps, and help us to understand finally the country they so carefully founded.

*An Appendix of the Plants
Most Frequently Cultivated
in Eighteenth-Century American Gardens*

An Appendix of the Plants
Most Frequently Cultivated
in Eighteenth-Century American Gardens

To produce an appendix of the plants most commonly planted in American gardens of the eighteenth century, both native and introduced, and those sent to be planted in English gardens, requires a degree of hard-hearted selection that exasperates scholars and comforts only the hard-working gardener. Obviously there is a world of horticultural discoveries and triumphs barely touched upon by even the most ardent seekers for new things to grow in their own gardens and parks. The object of making this list at all is to lend a spark to the restoration of gardens of the period, with enough references to the trees, shrubs and flowers, fruits and vegetables mentioned by their discoverers and users to give the growers a sense of their background.

Authority for these plants has come from the accounts of the early eighteenth-century surveyors, botanists, colonizers, historians and horticultural enthusiasts; from the letters of "curious" gardeners; and from books of medicine, used, written or published locally. The list of plants grown toward the end of the century has been fortified with particular information derived from the catalogues of such popular nurserymen as the Bartrams, the Princes and Bernard M'Mahon, and from overseas publications of English horticultural experts, such as Robert Furber, the Society of Gardeners and William Curtis, whose books were in our gardeners' libraries.

Identification by modern botanical names has been arrived at by reference to Asa Gray's *Manual of Botany,* eighth edition, as edited by M. L. Fernald; Alfred Rehder's *Manual of Cultivated Trees and Shrubs,* second edition; and

Liberty Hyde Bailey's *Standard Cyclopedia of Horticulture* as my final authorities. However, on the way from the earliest botanical definitions given, I have enjoyed checking Philip Miller's *Gardener's Dictionary,* eighth edition, with Thomas Jefferson's *State of Virginia,* Humphry Marshall's *Arbustum Americanum,* Curtis' *Botanical Magazine,* Bernard M'Mahon's *American Gardener's Calendar,* and with mid-nineteenth-century references such as Johnson's *Gardeners' Dictionary,* J. C. Loudon's *Encyclopaedia of Trees and Shrubs* and his *Encyclopaedia of Gardening,* with John Darby's *Botany of the Southern States,* and M. A. Curtis' *Botany of North Carolina.* And least and last of all as a guide to familiar names used in the eighteenth century, with a little book, *A Synopsis of the Genera of American Plants,* printed by J. M. Carter of Georgetown, D.C., in 1814.

As always, my execution is limited to that of a working gardener seeking to reconstruct the past. From an age when everyone spelled to please himself, to an age when even expert botanists do not always agree, the paths are frequently tortuous. Capitilization was a way of life in the eighteenth century and lends extra charm to plant names, but today's style is regrettably lower case and without fanfare. I ask my readers to bear with me and remember the words of William Cole, simpler extraordinary, who said, "What a pleasant thing it is for a man (whom the ignorant think to be alone) to have plants speaking Greek and Latin to him and putting him in mind of stories which otherwise he would never think of." Our object is to give pleasure and leave final rule-making to the experts.

References to the users, growers, senders and receivers must necessarily be only token recognition, not all or the earliest or even the most important — only enough to serve, as with people at a large party, as a pleasant introduction.

The principal references are to:

John Evelyn	Henry Laurens
Bishop Compton	Mr. and Mrs. Thomas Lamboll
John Banister	Dr. John Fothergill
Mark Catesby	Dr. Alexander Garden
Robert Beverly	Dr. Cadwallader Colden
John Lawson	Jane Colden
William Byrd II	Dr. Joseph Bigelow
John Clayton	Dr. Manasseh Cutler
John Custis	Sir Peyton and Lady Skipwith
Peter Collinson	George Washington
William Bartram	Thomas Jefferson
John Bartram	The Prince Nurseries' 1791 Catalogue
William Johnson	John Bartram Nurseries' 1792 Catalogue
Joseph Chew	M'Mahon Nurseries' 1805 Calendar
Martha Logan	

A

Abies Fir. In the eighteenth century "fir" stood for most needled ever-greens not noticeably pines. From the long list of "firs" ordered and grown, the only true fir was the balsam, "Balm of Gilead Fir," *Abies balsamea* (L.) Mill. Bartram's. Prince's.

Abutilon Indian mallow. Flowering maple. Naturalized from India. Es-caped to roadsides. Collinson grew a plant he received from Bartram as *"Abutilon carolinianum."* It was probably *Hibiscus palustris* L., mallow rose, or *H. moscheutos* L., also mallow rose, swamp rose.

Acacia *Acacia* in the eighteenth century was applied to acacias, mimosas, locusts, pseudo-acacias, honey locusts, robinias and gleditsias. Marshall has the "Triple-thorned Acacia or Honey Locust" under *Gleditsia,* and the "False Acacia" under *Robinia.*

Under *Gleditsia,* he gives:

"Gleditsia spinosa. Triple-thorned Acacia or Honey Locust." Now *Gleditsia triacanthos* L. Washington. Jefferson. Collinson. Bartram's. Prince's.

"Gleditsia aquatica. Water Acacia." Now *Gleditsia aquatica* Marsh. Catesby. Collinson.

Under *Robinia* Marshall lists:

"Robinia Pseud-Acacia. White-flowering Robinia or Locust Tree." Now *Robinia pseudo-acacia* L., black locust, the "fragrant white-flowering locust." Collinson. Bishop Compton. Kew. Jardin des Plantes (named for the overseer, Monsieur Robin, friend to Tradescants.) Some of these trees still stand.

"Robinia rosea. Rose-coloured Robinia." Now *Robinia hispida* L. Jef-ferson. Collinson reported to Bartram, 1762, "made a glorious show as well as the white." Catesby. The Lambolls to Bartram. Prince's and Bar-tram's offered all four.

Jefferson's "Egyptian Acacias," from Green Spring, near Williamsburg, defined as *"Mimosa nilotica* or *farnesiana,"* was *Acacia farnesiana* Willd.

Acacia arabica Willd., gum arabic, was sent to Jefferson.

Acer Maple. American maples were in demand for wood, sap, blossoms and autumn coloring. Evelyn requested "the peacock tail tree," our bird's-eye maple.

Marshall lists:

1) *"Acer pensylvanicum.* Pennsylvania dwarf, mountain maple." Now *A. spicatum* Lam. Bartram to Collinson, 1751. Bartram's to Wash-ington. Requested from Paris by Jefferson.

2) *"A. glaucum.* The silver-leaved Maple." Now *A. saccharinum* L. Linnaeus thought it the sugar maple. Probably that of Lawson and Bev-erly. Bartram to Washington.

3) "*A. negundo.* The ash-leaved Maple." Now *Acer negundo* L., Bartram's "Box Elder."

4) "*A. canadense.* American striped maple." Now *A. pennsylvanicum* L. Bartram to Collinson, 1758. Bartram's "Striped Bark Maple."

5) "*A. rubrum.* The scarlet flowering Maple." Now *A. rubrum* L. Bartram to Collinson, 1756. Popular for brilliant blooms, or "keys." Catesby's "Red-flowered Maple of Virginia." Bartram's. Jefferson to the Countess de Tesse, 1790.

6) "*A. saccharum.* The Sugar Maple." Now *A. saccharum* Marsh. After his visit to Vermont, Jefferson ordered "all you have." Washington from Bartram's, 1792.

Bartram's Nurseries carried silver-leaved, scarlet, sugar, ash-leaved, dwarf and striped maples. Prince Nurseries, 1790, carried sugar and scarlet maples. Other maples mentioned:

The "southern sugar maple," *A. barbatum* Michx., used by upcountry Indians for sugar.

The Norway maple, *A. platanoides* L., requested of Philip Miller by Bartram, 1756. Washington ordered two from Bartram's, 1792.

Jefferson grew *A. tataricum* L., a *"jolie petit arbre propre au bosquets."* Every eighth tree on Washington's serpentine drives was a maple. Undefined.

Achillea *Achillea santolina.* Now *Santolina chamaecyparissus* L. Lavender-cotton-leaved milfoil. M'Mahon. *A. ptarmica flore plena* L., double sneezewort. M'Mahon. *A. millefolium* L. M'Mahon. The cult of dried-flower arrangements was strong. Skipwith.

Acnida *Acnida cannabina* L. Now *Cannabis sativa* L., Hemp. Jefferson, 1781, "useful for fabrications."

Aconitum Aconite.

1) *A. alba.* Variety of *A. napellus* L. M'Mahon.

2) *A. lycoctonum* L. Yellow, from Siberia, June blooming. M'Mahon.

3) *A. napellus* L. Medicinal monkshood, popular since seventeenth century. M'Mahon.

4) *A. uncinatum* L. Our wild monkshood. Clayton to Bartram, 1761. Bartram to Collinson, 1762. Lady Skipwith grew "Wolfsbane, see *Aconitum,* both vernal and autumnal." *A. autumnale* Reichb., from North China, is nineteenth century. I do not know which one flowered late for Lady Skipwith. "Winter aconite" is now *Eranthis hyemalis* Salisb. Linnaeus and Curtis have *Helleborus hyemalis.* Miller's fifth *Helleborus* is "Winter Aconite," recommended to be planted alternately with snowdrops. Furber's "January."

Actaea *A. racemosa.* One of Jefferson's medicinal Virginia plants. Now *Cimifuga racemosa* (L.) Nutt. Black snakeroot. Black cohosh. Probably what Dr. Hills requested of Bartram, 1766.

A. spicata L. var. *rubra.* White baneberry. White cohosh. Doll's-eyes. Necklace-weed. Called *Christophoriana* by Bartram and Collinson.

A. rubra Ait. Red baneberry. Snakeberry. Formerly called Herbe Christopher. Collinson reported "a new Christopheriana in flower," 1745. In 1746 Bartram is "glad the white-berried Christopheriana grows with thee."

Adiantum *A. pedatum* L. Common maidenhair. Perhaps the "most curious *Adiantum*," for which Dr. Fothergill thanked Humphry Marshall in 1771, urging him to "look carefully after your ferns. You have a great variety." Fothergill had more American ferns than any of his acquaintances.

Kalm reported that in Albany tea is made of it for coughs, learned from the Indians. It is ". . . reckoned preferable in surgery to that which we have in Europe . . . A great quantity to France every year."

Adonis *A. autumnnalis* L. Flos Adonis. M'Mahon.

A. vernalis L. M'Mahon. Now *A. aestivalis* L. Summer Adonis. Pheasant's-eye.

Aesculus *A. hippocastanum* L. Horse chestnut. From Constantinople to England, sixteenth century; its nuts reputedly good for short-winded horses. By eighteenth century much planted. Collinson sent nuts to Custis, 1734, and suggested if "planted before your houses next the street at Williamsburg . . . would have a fine effect . . . a specious show . . . a noble, beautiful, large spike of flowers." Custis, 1737, had some started but they were "so slow . . . a man need have the patience of Job and the life of Methusala to wait upon them . . ."

Collinson sent horse chestnuts to Bartram, 1753; delighted to hear, 1763, they had flowered.

A. octandra Marsh. "The New River Horsechestnut, a pretty large tree with pale yellowish flowers," listed by Marshall, as was also the *A. pavia* L. "The scarlet flowering horse chestnut." A shrub.

Washington brought nuts of *A. octandra* from the Cheet River, planted 1785. Ordered all three from Bartram's, 1792, as did Jefferson, who ordered *"Aesculus virginica,* yellow horse chestnut," to be planted at Monticello on the slope leading to the shops, with Pride of China, catalpas and crabs. There also *"Aesculus virginica"* variegated, and *"Pavia."*

Agave *A. americana* L. Century plant. Washington.

A. virginica L. False aloe. Rattlesnake master. Thick-leaved snakeroot. Listed by Jefferson as ornamental, 1781.

Ailanthus *A. altissima* L. Tree of heaven. Peter Collinson received from his Chinese correspondents and raised "a stately tree," 1751.

Albizzia *Albizza julibrissin* Duraz. "Mimosa or silk tree." "Silk tree of Constantinople." Jefferson received seeds from William Hamilton, who, 1805, had trees twenty feet high. Jefferson's was flourishing in 1806. William Bartram told Jefferson, 1808, the "Mimosa julibrissin" was brought to this country by Michaux the elder.

Alcea Old name for mallow. John Bartram's "Loblolly Bay or Alcea."

Alder *Alnus serrulata* (Ait) Willd. Smooth alder. Jefferson planted at

Monticello, 1771. Bartram sent "silver-leaved alder" to Collinson, 1758. Black alder is *Ilex verticillata* L. Gray. Witch alder is *Fothergilla gardeni* Murr.

Alnifolia, alder-leaved, described several shrubs. Catesby gave name *Alnifolia* to our sweet pepper bush, or white alder. Now *Clethra alnifolia* L.

Alligator Wood   (Because no good for boats. Kalm.)
Liquidambar styraciflua L. Sweet gum.

Allium   See chapter on vegetables. *Allium sativum* L. Garlic. Jefferson.

Allspice   *Calycanthus floridus* L. Jefferson. Bartram's. Prince's. Washington.

Almond   *Prunus amygdalus* Batsch. Collinson to Custis. To Bartram. Flowering almond, *Prunus amygdalus albo-plena* L. Jefferson grafted double-blossomed almonds, 1794. Skipwith.

Alfalfa   Lucerne. *Medicago sativa* L. Introduced as fodder crop and to improve land. Washington. Jefferson.

Aloe   Agave, American aloe. See Yucca.

Alstroemeria   Lady Skipwith's houseplant. *A. pulchella* L. was a garden favorite for summer planting.

Alatamaha   Offered by Bartram's as "an unidentified shrub," probably *Franklinia alatamaha* Marsh. Now *Gordonia alatamaha* Sarg.

Althaea   (Greek, a cure, in reference to the medicinal properties of some species.) Includes hollyhocks, mallows and hibiscus. Also called *Alcea* and *Ketmia,* early names for Hisbiscus. See also *Malva, Hibiscus, Lavatera.*

A. rosea Cav. Our common garden hollyhock. Jefferson. Lady Skipwith. M'Mahon. From China in sixteenth century.

A. officinalis L. Marshmallow. British native. Jefferson.

A. frutex Jefferson's, Lady Skipwith's and Prince's name for *Hibiscus syriacus* L. Shrubby althaea, "Rose of Sharon." (The English "Rose of Sharon" is *Hypericum calycinum* L.)

A. ficifolia, Cav. Antwerp hollyhock, orange yellow. M'Mahon.

Scarlet althaea, Furber's "China Rose," is *Hibiscus rosa-sinensis* L.

Alyssum maritimum   Lam. *A. saxatile* L. Sweet alyssum. Skipwith.

Amarantus   Gerard's "Floramor . . . many-colored leaves like the feathers of a parrot."

Miller's "Flower Gentle." *Amaranthus tricolor* from Jefferson in Paris. Miller's *Amaranthus cristatus* is now *Celosia cristata* L. Cockscomb. Jefferson.

A. hypochondriacus L. Prince's feather. Jefferson.

A. caudatus L. Love-lies-bleeding. Called "Nun's-whip" in France and Boston. Globe amaranth, Collinson to Custis, is *Gomphrena globosa* L. As "Amaranthoides," Collinson sent to Custis "a charming flower . . . gathered ripe and hung up in the shade will keep its color for many years."

Amaryllis   Miller's "lily-daffodil." His first *Amaryllis*, "commonly called the yellow autumnal narcissus," is now *Sternbergia lutea* L. Lady Skipwith.
  Miller's second, "a Virginia and Carolina sort," is the Atamasco lily, now *Zephyranthes atamasco* L. Herb. Lady Skipwith. Jefferson
  Miller's third, the Jacobaea lily, is now *Sprekelia formosissima* Herb. M'Mahon's "Scarlet amaryllis."
  Miller's fourth, "the Guernsey lily" is now *Nerine sarniensis* Herb. M'Mahon.
  Miller's fifth, the belladonna lily, from Portugal, is *Amaryllis belladonna* L. M'Mahon to Jefferson.

Amaryllis lutea. Yellow Amaryllis.
Curtis *Botanical Magazine*

Amelanchier   Provençal name of a European species, adopted for Juneberry, sugarplum, shadbush, serviceberry, etc. We have nineteen native amelanchiers. The botanical name came too late to help early settlers sort out this shrub from our native hawthorns (some under *Mespilus,* some under *Crataegus*), medlars, service trees and various berries.

American Bloodroot   *Sanguinaria canadensis* L. Dr. Benjamin Gale requested the botanical name from Bartram.

American Columbo   *Swertia caroliniensis* (Walt.) Ktze. Jefferson planted a bedfull.

American Cowslip   *Dodecatheon meadia* L. Skipwith.

Amorpha fruticosa L.   Bastard indigo. Indigo bush. Jefferson listed as a desirable shrub, 1771, "naturally in Carolina." Bartram sold Washington *A. fruticosa* and *A. cerulia.* "Foliage light and delicately pennated, garnished with flowers."

Amsonia tabernaemontana Walt.   Clayton to Bartram, 1761, who had seen it in Clayton's garden. "New southern Virginia plant named after a doctor here."

Amygdalus   Collinson sent Custis *"Amygdalus nana flore simplici et duplici."* Bartram's *"Amygdalus pumila flore plena,"* the dwarf double-flowering almond, "a most elegant flowering shrub, ornamental in vases, for courtyard, etc." Prince's.

Bartram's also offered *"Amygdalus persica flore plena,"* the double-flowered peach.

Now both under *Prunus.*

Ampelopsis arborea **(L.) Koehne**   Pepper vine. Skipwith. Jefferson. Prince's.

Andromeda   Several handsome, usually evergreen, blooming shrubs native to Pennsylvania, Virginia and the Carolinas, were referred to as "Andromedas." Miller lists four North American; Marshall, seven; Bartram's, eight. Today we have one true *Andromeda,* bog rosemary. *A. glaucophylla* Link. The others are now under *Chamaedaphne, Cyrilla, Leucothoe, Lyonia, Oxydendrum, Pieris* and *Zenobia.*

From Marshall we list:

1) *"Andromeda arborea.* The Sorrel Tree." Now *Oxydendrum arboreum* L. Catesby. Collinson. Jefferson to the Countess de Tesse. Collinson asked Custis for seed of "a very pretty plant that he [Catesby] calls Sorrel Tree that grows between Williamsburg and York."

2) *Andromeda plumata,* the "Ironwood of Carolina." Marshall wrote to Dr. Lettsom, "The plumed Andromeda of Bartram is the *Cyrilla."* Now *Cyrilla racemiflora* L. Requested for the Countess de Tesse by Jefferson.

3) *"Andromeda spicata."* Collinson, "received from J. Bartram, from Pennsylvania, 1758, a spiked Andromeda."

4) *"Andromeda latifolia.* Male Whortleberry." Now *Lyonia ligustrina* (L.) D.C. Maleberry. Male blueberry.

5) *"Andromeda lanceolata.* Virginia Red Bud."

6) *"Andromeda nitida.* Carolina Red Bud." Now *Lyonia lucida* (Lam) K. Koch. Tetterbush.

7) *"Andromeda globulifera.* Boggy Andromeda." Now *A. glaucophylla* Link.

8) *"Andromeda crassifolia.* Evergreen Andromeda." Bartram sent a "sod of Evergreen Andromeda" to Collinson in 1761. Now *Chamaedaphne calyculata* (L.) Moench.

Bartram's listed:

Andromeda pulverulenta	now *Zenobia pulverulenta* Pollard.
Andromeda axillaris	now *Leucothoe axillaris* Don.
Andromeda acuminata	now *Leucothoe populifolia* Dipp.
Andromeda paniculata	now *Lyonia lugustrina* Muhl.
Andromeda ferruginea	now *Lyonia ferruginea* Nutt.
Andromeda floribunda	now *Pieris floribunda* Benth. and Hook.
Andromeda mariana	now *Pieris mariana* Benth. and Hook.
Andromeda racemosa	now *Leucothoe racemosa* Gray.

Anemone   M'Mahon in 1805 lists:

"Anemone hepatica"   American hepatica, now *H. triloba* Choix and *H. acutiloba* D.C.

"Anemone pulsatilla"   Pasqueflower, *A. pulsatilla* L.

"Anemone" probably includes also:

Anemone hortensis L.   Garden anemone

Anemone coronaria L.   The Mediterranean anemone,

especially when M'Mahon lists "double anemone" from France. "Dr. Witt's daisy or double mountain ranunculus . . . a pretty thing," which Collinson requested from Bartram in 1737, was probably *Anemonella thalictroides* L., rue anemone, once called the "small mountain ranunculus."

A. quinquefolia L. is our wood anemone. Lady Skipwith, like Jefferson, grew several "anemones."

Anemone sylvestris. Snowdrop Anemone. Curtis *Botanical Magazine*

Anemone Hortensis. Star Anemone. Curtis *Botanical Magazine*

Angelica   The Lambolls requested of Bartram, 1761, and thanked Mrs. Bartram for it, 1765, when it arrived with a barrel of dried apples.

A. sylvestris L., listed as medicinal by Jefferson, 1781.

A. atropurpurea L. Alexanders. Early settlers rejoiced to find it.

Angelica archangelica or *Archangelica officinalis* is the cultivated kitchen-garden plant. Universal.

Angelica Tree   *Aralia spinosa* L.

Annona   Papaw. Dr. John Mitchell to Bartram, 1747: "The Duke of Argyle wants the Papaw Tree or Anona."

Annona reticulata L. The custard apple.

Asimina triloba (L.) Dunal. Papaw is the American custard apple.

Anonis   See *Ononis.* Lady Skipwith's shrubby rest harrow. Miller's fifth "Alpine purple shrubby rest harrow with red blossoms." His fifteenth "grows naturally in Carolina," from where Catesby sent seeds to England. Seeds for Miller's thirteenth came from Virginia.

Anthemis nobilis L.   "Camomile." Jefferson.

Antholyza aethiopica L.   "A green-house bulb" from the Cape. M'Mahon to Jefferson.

Anthoxanthum odoratum L.   "Sweet-scented grass." Jefferson.

Antirrhinum majus L.   "Snapdragon blooming." Jefferson, 1767.

Apium graveolens var. *dulce* D.C.   Celery. See chapter on vegetables. Jefferson.

Apocynum   The illustration for Cornut's *Canadensium plantarum,* 1635, shows a picture of *Aesclepias tubersoa* as "Apocynon Minus."
     Lady Skipwith's *Apocynum* among her wildflowers is likely to be *Aesclepias tuberosa* L. Butterfly weed. Pleurisy root. And also what Collinson requested in 1734 of Bartram — "Root of the Swallow-wort or *Apocinon* with narrow leaves and orange-coloured flowers" — remarking upon the Creator's omniscience in giving each seed a "silken thrum" to float it in the air.
     A. androsaemilifolium L. is dogbane, moderately ornamental. Collinson.
     A. cannabium L. is Indian hemp.

Apple   See chapter on fruit.

Apples of Love   Tomatoes. *Lycopersicum esculentum* Mill. Collinson wrote Custis, 1742, "Apples of Love are very much used in Italy to put when ripe into broths and soup giving it a pretty tart taste . . . They call it Tamiata." Tomatoes came slowly to the American kitchen garden. Jefferson began to plant them in 1809.

Apricot   See chapter on fruits.

Aquilegia   *Aquilegia canadensis* L. Taken to France from Canada by early Jesuits, pictured in Cornut's *Canadensium plantarum,* 1635. Tradescant introduced it to England too late for Parkinson's *Paradisus.* Collinson, 1747, had "Virginian columbine" in flower. Jefferson had it blooming, 1791.
     Lady Skipwith's "Columbines," with border flowers like rockets and wallflowers, probably meant *Aquilegia vulgaris* L., the common European columbine, or *A. alpina* L. All three columbines were listed by M'Mahon, 1805.

Arachnis hypogaea L.   Peanuts. Jefferson's "groundnuts" or "peendars."

Aralia   *A. nudicaulis* L. Wild sarsaparilla. Small spikenard.
     A. spinsoa L. Angelica tree. Hercules'-club. Devil's walking stick. Prickly ash. Marshall's *"Aralia spinosa,* Virginian Angelica Tree." To Collinson, 1760.

A. racemosa L. Spikenard, to Collinson, 1723. Collinson noted that the roots dried and pounded and drunk in wine are "exceedingly good to expel wind" and the berries make a good syrup.

A. hispida L. Bristly sarsaparilla. Wild elder. Requested of Marshall by W. Hamilton, 1796.

Arbor vitae *Thuja occidentalis* L.

Arbutus unedo L. Strawberry tree. Collinson reported this, as *Arbutus Andrachne,* flowered first in Dr. Fothergill's garden, 1765. Jefferson, 1778.

Arbutus uva-ursi See *Arctostaphylos.*

Arctostaphylos *Arctostaphylos uva-ursi* (L.) Spreng. Bearberry. Marshall reports a successful medicine in "calculous complaints."

Arenaria Bartram wrote Gronovius he had found an "odd, pretty kind of Lychnis" growing in the snow on the "Jersey Barrens." Probably *Arenaria groenlandica* Spreng.

Argemone grandiflora Sweet Jefferson's prickly poppy, 1767.

Arisaema "Arum or Cuckoo pint," Collinson to Custis. Lords-and-ladies. Collinson says he has several "Arums": one sent as skunk cabbage; a variegated arum; another sent as Indian turnip; a "green dragon"; and a dwarf Indian turnip from Bartram. Indian turnip, or Jack-in-the-pulpit, is now *Arisaema atrorubens* (Ait.) Blume. Small Jack-in-the-pulpit is now *Arisaema triphyllum* Torr., sent Collinson by Bartram. M'Mahon.

Dragonroot. Green dragon. Now *Arisaema draconitum* (L.) Schott.

Aristolochia Birthwort. *"Aristolochia serpentaria.* Virginia Snake-root" listed by Jefferson as medicinal. *Aristolochia* has aromatic roots and ensures women easy delivery because of the shape of the bloom, otherwise reminding one of a Dutchman's pipe. *Aristolochia macrophylla* Lem., the Dutchman's-pipe vine, was much used for shading porches and summerhouses. Marshall's "Shrubby Pennsylvania Birthwort, fine for arbors." Bartram's "Clammy American Birthwort."

Arrow-wood See *Viburnum.* Collinson requested, 1735.

Artichoke George Washington grew "French artichokes," *Cynara scolymus* L., and had a field of Jerusalem artichokes, *Helianthus tuberosus* L., in 1787.

Arsmart See *Polygonum.*

Arum See *Arisaema.*

Arundo Donax Now *Phragmites communis* Trin. Collinson, 1762. Jefferson listed as "useful for fabrication."

Asarum *A. virginicum* L. Wild ginger. Collinson.

Ascyrum *A. stans* Michx., St. Peterswort. *A. hypericoides* L., St. Andrew's Cross.

Marshall's two species of this "small shrubby plant . . . resembling St. Johnswort, *Ascyrum hypericoides* and *Ascyrum villisum,"* were requested by Sir Joseph Banks, 1789, for William Aiton, "Gardener to His Majesty."

Collinson grew "a St. Andrew's Cross from Virginia as noted by Clayton."

Ash   See *Fraxinus.*

Ash, Mountain   See *Sorbus.*

Ash, Prickly   See *Aralia.*

Ash, Poison   See *Rhus toxicodendron,* poison oak.

***Asimina trioba* (L.) Dunal**   The North American papaw. Occasioned more trans-Atlantic correspondence than any other American plant except the "Colocasia" (*Nelumbium luteum*). The pulp, sweet and edible in autumn, made its mark with early settlers and historians. Catesby recorded the papaw, Collinson grew it and both importuned Bartram for fruit. "His Lordship" had a tree but wanted to see the fruit, 1736. In 1737, Collinson requested fruit and blossoms in rum, to be painted by Catesby and for Linnaeus. In 1756, Collinson wants a potted plant.

Asp. Aspen   See *Populus.*

Asphodel   Asphodel, a beautiful name, like andromeda, attached to a variety of flowers. Our native yellow asphodel is *Narthecium americanum* Ker. Bog asphodel.

Miller's *Asphodelus luteus.* King's spear, used in medicine, from Sicily. Now *Asphodeline lutea* Reichb. M'Mahon. Skipwith.

Aster   Never had the world seen so many asters as we produced in North America. Tradescant introduced "Aster virginiana." Catesby had one named for him. Furber featured several in *Months of Flowers.* Lady Skipwith had "asters of various kinds." Bartram complained of *Aster ericoides* L. as a weed. At first the American asters fell roughly into two groups: the New England asters with rough leaves, tall and dark purple, *A. novae angliae* L., and the New York asters, with paler, bluer blossoms and smoother leaves, *A. novae belgii* L. "Sure your country is inexhaustible in asters," wrote Collinson.

The "China aster" *Callistephus hortensis,* was sent to Bartram by Collinson, 1735. "The noblest and finest plant thee ever saw, of that tribe . . . per the Jesuits from China to France, from thence to us . . ."

The Lambolls sent "double blue China asters, red and white" to Bartram. Miller had blue, white and red China asters, single and double, by 1753.

Atamasco Lily   *Zephyranthes atamasco* (L.) Herb. Skipwith.

Auricula *Primula auricula* L. One of the earliest plants to be hybridized. Richard Bradley's *New Improvement of Planting* quotes a complaint that the new auriculas were increasing so rapidly, and wise and great men decreasing so fast, that there would soon be auriculas with no great men to take names from. Furber's *Months of Flowers* are full of varieties. 1767 Jefferson was sowing auriculas. In 1807 he complained to M'Mahon that there was none "worth a cent" until he could get good ones from London. Collinson to Custis. The Lambolls to Bartram.

Azalea   "Azalea. Upright Honeysuckle." Marshall's three were *"Azalea nudiflora,* Red-flowered azalea"; *"Azalea viscosa,* White Sweet Azalea"; and *"Azalea viscosa palustris,* Swamp Azalea, a variety of the white."

   Collinson was growing *"A. nudiflora viscosa."* Catesby had seen *"A. viscosa palustris"* at Peckham. Jefferson, greatly taken with an azalea in Vermont, "the richest shrub I have ever seen," requested *A. nudiflora* and *A. viscosa* to be sent to France. Bartram's offered three azaleas: *A. rosea,* Upright Honeysuckle; *A. viscosa,* the Swamp Azalea; and the Sweet Azalea, *A. carolininiana.* Today these are all classed as rhododendrons.

B

Baccharis halimifolia **L.**   Groundsel tree, consumption weed. Marshall's "Plowman's Spikenard." Bartram to Lord Petre, 1741.

Balm   *Melissa officinalis* L. Jefferson.

Balm, Bee   *Monarda didyma* L. Oswego tea. Bartram to Collinson.

Balm, Horse   *Collinsonia canadensis* L. Richweed, stoneroot. Named for Peter Collinson by Linnaeus. (See *Bartramia.*)

Balm of Gilead   *Abies balsamea* L. Fir.

Balm of Gilead   *Populus candicans* Ait. Poplar.

Balsam   *Impatiens balsamina* L. In mixed colors, by Collinson. Double-blossomed, by Skipwith, Jefferson. Sir Peyton ordered white, purple and red, single and double.

Balsam Apple   *Momordica balsamina* L. Skipwith.

Balsam Cucumber   Miller's "Male Balsam Apple," "Pomme de Merveille." He considered *Impatiens* the "Female Balsam." Skipwith, Jefferson.

Balsam Poplar   *Populus balsamifera* L. Collinson grew both poplars, *P. candicans* Ait. (lately *P. tacamahaca* Mill.), and *P. balsamifera* L.

Balsam of Peru   *Myroxylon pereirae.* Jefferson ordered three from Prince, 1791.

Balsam Willow   *Salix pyrifolia* Anderss. Prince's.

Barbados Nuts   Physic nuts. *Jatropha curcas* L. Washington, Jefferson.

Barberry   See *Berberis.*

Bartramia   Collinson wrote Bartram in 1740 that Bartram's name should have been given to *Collinsonia,* as Bartram had sent Collinson the seeds in his very first lot. Gronovius wrote Bartram in 1746 that "with the assistance of Linnaeus" new genera had been discovered, one named *Bartramia* and another *Coldenia. Bartramia* now belongs to another genus. *Coldenia* is now a "railroad weed." Collinson in 1758 had a *Bartramia* in flower in his stove house, the flowers so small as to need a magnifying glass. He will send one, dried, to Bartram.

Sweet Flowering Bay. Catesby's
Plate 39, Vol. I

Basteria   The name under which Lamboll send *Calycanthus floridus* to Collinson. Used also by Bartram, 1763.

Bay, Loblolly   "Your loblolly bay or Alcea," 1761, John Bartram to William Bartram. Now *Gordonia lasianthus* (L.) Ellis.

Bay, Bull   *Magnolia grandiflora* L.

Bay, Laurel   *Kalmia latifolia* L.

Bay, Purple-Berried   *Ligustrum vulgare* L.

Bay, Red   *Persea borbonia* (L.) Spreng.

Bay, Rose   *Rhododendron maximum* L. Collinson asks of Bartram.

Bay, Swamp   *Persea palustris* (Rap.) Sarg.

Bay, Tree   *Lindera benzoin* (L.) Blume.

Bay, White-Flowering   *Magnolia glauca* L.

Bearberry   *Arctostaphylos uva-ursi* (L.) Spreng. (Formerly *Arbutus uva-
ursi.*)

Bear Grass   *Yucca filamentosa* L. Skipwith. Also silkgrass.

Bear's-Ear Sanicle   *Cortusa matthioli* L. Skipwith.

Bearsfoot   *Veratrum viride* Ait. Hellebore. "Stinking black Hellebore."
Skipwith.

Beech   See *Fagus.*

Belamcanda chinensis (L.) D.C.   Blackberry lily. Skipwith.

Benjamin Bush   *Lindera benzoin* (L.) Blume. Now *Benzoin aestivale* Nees.

Benzoin aestivale Nees.   Benjamin bush. See above.

Bermudiana   *Sisyrinchium angustifolium* Mill. Skipwith.

Betony   *Stachys officinalis.* Franch.

Betula   Marshall lists five birches:

Betula nigra. Black or sweet birch. Now *Betula lenta* L.

Betula lenta. Red birch. Tough. Good for canoes. Now *Betula nigra* L.

Betula papyrifera. White paper birch. Now *Betula payrifera* Marsh.

Betula populifolia. Aspen-leaved birch. Gray birch. Now *Betula populifolia* Marsh.

Betula humilis. Dwarf birch. Now *Betula minor* Tuckerm., dwarf white birch; or *Betula pumila* L., low swamp birch; or *Betula Michauxii* Spach.

Both black and white birches were listed as "useful" by Jefferson. He admired paper birches near Lake Champlain. Collinson grew all of Marshall's five; Bartram sent him three red birches in 1756 and seeds of the paper birch in 1751; and he received the *"Betula nana"* from Canada, a new species, in 1751, reported in the *Gentleman's Magazine.*

Bilberry   See *Vaccinium.*

Bignonia capreolata L.   Cross vine. Quarter vine. Bartram's *"Bignonia foliis conjugatis"* ran twenty feet up the corner of his house in 1763. Offering *Bignonia crucigera,* 1782, Bartram's catalogue said, "Mounting to tops of buildings." Catesby wrote, "This elegant plant is a native of both Virginia and Carolina and blooms there in May . . . in England not before August." Flowers orange red.

Jefferson's *"Bignonia sempervirens,"* or yellow jasmine, is *Gelsemium sempervirens* (L.) Ait. "Trumpet vine," "trumpet creeper" and "trumpet honeysuckle" are all now *Campsis radicans* L.

Bignonia Americana. Catesby's Plate 82, Vol. II

Birch   See *Betula.*

Birdcherry   *Prunus cerasus* L.

Birthwort   *Aristolochia macrophylla* Lam. Favored for arbors.

Blackberry Lily   *Belamcanda chinensis* D.C.

Black Briony   *Smilax tamnoides* L.

Black Gum or Black Haw   *Viburnum prunifolium* L.

Bladder Senna   *Colutea arborescens* L. Skipwith.

Bladder Ketmia   *Hibiscus trionum* L. Skipwith.

Bladdernut Tree   *Staphylea trifolia* L.

Blazing Star   *Liatris spicata* Willd. Collinson.

Bloodroot   *Sanguinaria canadensis* L. Red puccoon. Jefferson.

Bloody Wallflower   *Cheiranthus.* Skipwith.

Blue-Eyed Grass   *Sisyrinchium.* Skipwith.

Blue Funnel Flower   *Mertensia virginiana* D.C. Jefferson. Skipwith.

Bonduc   Kentucky coffee tree. *Gymnocladus dioica* (L.) K. Koch. Requested of Washington.

Box Elder   *Acer negundo* L.

Box   *Buxus.*

Brier, Green   *Smilax.*

Brier, Sensitive   *Schrankia.*

Brompton Stock   *Matthiola incana* var. *annua* Voss.

Broom, Scotch   *Cytisus.*

Broom, Spanish   *Spartium.*

Bubbyflower Bush   *Calycanthus floridus* L. Jefferson.

Buckthorn, Sea   *Rhamnus caroliniana* Walt. Evergreen. Given Washington by Michaux, 1786. Bartram to Collinson.

Burning Bush   *Euonymus atropurpurea* Jacq.

Buttonbush   *Cephalanthus occidentalis* L.

Buttonwood   *Platanus occidentalis* L.

Buxus sempervirens **L.**   Common box. Tree box. Washington.

Buxus sempervirens suffruticosa **L.**   Edging box. Earliest references to box in American eighteenth-century gardens come from John Custis writing to Collinson about his "dutch box edgings" in 1737. He fancied evergreens and was delighted with a variegated box from Collinson in 1738. Washington was cultivating boxwood trees before 1788. As Jefferson does not refer to box in his garden book, it may be that the use of box was not as prevalent in the eighteenth century as it later became.

Buxus aureus   Variegated box. Fancied by Custis. Offered in 1792. Bartram's.

C

Cabbage   See chapter on vegetables.

Cabbage Rose   See *Rosa centifolia* L.

Cajanus indicus **Spreng.**   Pigeon pea brought from Africa by slaves. Custis to Collinson.

Calceolus   Latin name for a slipper by which North American lady's-slippers were first known. See *Cyprepedium*.

Calceolus. The Yellow Lady's-Slipper. Catesby's Plate 73, Vol. II

Callicarpa americana **L.**   Marshall's "Carolina shrubby Callicarpa." Bartram's catalogue says "very showy and pleasing . . . flowers of a delicate incarnate hue, and soft clusters of purple berries." Washington. Jefferson planted, 1771, at Monticello; ordered sent to France, 1788.

Calistephus hortensis **Cassini**   The China aster. In 1735 Collinson sent Bartram seeds of white and purple China asters, "the noblest and finest plant thee ever saw, of that tribe. It was sent per the Jesuits from China to France; from thence to us . . ." The Lambolls sent double blue, double red and double white China asters to Bartram.

"Calocasia"   Supposed name of an American water lily, in much demand. See *Nelumbium.*

Calopogon pulchellus **L.**   Lady Skipwith.

Calycanthus floridus **L.**   Carolina allspice. Sweet Betsy. Strawberry bush. Sweet shrub. Pictured by Catesby. Planted by Jefferson as "the bubbyflower bush." Extolled by Marshall. Believed to produce medicinal oil. Sent to Collinson by the Lambolls. In bloom in Collinson's garden in 1760 with the white lady's-slipper, the mountain laurel, red acacia and the fringe tree. Requested of Marshall by William Hamilton. Washington ordered five from Bartram's. Prince's "Sweet Scented Shrub from Carolina," highest priced at 2s.6d.

Camomile　*Anthemis nobilis* L. The Lambolls requested from Bartram a "camomile that would bloom." Jefferson.

Campanula　Bellflower. Jefferson sowed bellflower with African marigolds and white poppies. Probably *C. medium* L., Canterbury bell. The Lambolls sent Bartram Canterbury bells, 1761.

　　1763, Collinson to Bartram, "I have thy charming Campanella in flower — six feet high . . . Pray where was the identical spot where it was found?" Probably *Campanula americana* L., which Collinson introduced to England in 1763.

　　M'Mahon offered nine *Campanulas: C. medium, C. grandiflora, C. persicifolia, C. carpatica, C. pyramidalis, C. lilifolia, C. rapunculoides, C. trachelium* and *C. glomerata.*

Canada Columbine　*Aquilegia canadensis.* Lady Skipwith.

Candleberry　*Myrica cerifera* L.

Candleberry Myrtle, narrow-leaved.
Catesby's Plate 69, Vol. I

Candleberry, Pennsylvania.　*Myrica pensylvanica* Loisel.

Candytuft　*Iberis sempervirens* L. Perennial.
　　Iberis umbellata L. Annual. Both at M'Mahon's. Lady Skipwith grew "Candytuft." See *Iberis.*

Canewood *Physocarpus opulifolius* Maxim. Ninebark. "Pray send me a walking cane of the Cane-wood"; Collinson to Bartram, 1734. ". . . Pretty common in our gardens. It goes here by the name of the Virginia Guelder-Rose"; 1735.

Miller's *"Spiraea opulifolio,* Spirea with a Marsh Elder leaf, commonly called Virginia Guelder Rose."

Marshall's *"Spiraea opulifolia.* Guelder Rose-leaved *Spiraea,* or Nine-bark."

Canna indica L. Indian shot. Custis 1735 called it "Indian frill." Collinson calls it *"Cana indica* or Wild Plantain or Bonana."

Canterbury Bells. *Campanula medium* L. The Lambolls to Bartram, 1761.

Cape Jasmine Cape jessamine. *Jasminum officinale* L. Jefferson.

Caper Bush *Capparis spinosa* L. Lady Skipwith. Jefferson's import from France and Italy.

Capsicum Red pepper. Lady Skipwith had "Miller's sixth sort," from Barbados, with oval-shaped fruit. Probably *Capsicum frutescens* var. *baccatum* Frish. Jefferson planted "Cayenne pepper" in 1768. Washington.

Cardinal Flower *Lobelia cardinalis* L. Washington was importuned by Lafayette's friend to send seeds, 1784. Jefferson. Skipwith.

Carnations *Dianthus caryophyllus* L. Jefferson at Shadwell, 1767. Bartram reported to Collinson, 1761, "a glorious appearance of carnations from thy seed."

Carolina Coral Tree *Erythrina corallodendron* L. Skipwith.

Carolina Kidney-Bean Tree Our native wisteria, but called *Glycine frutescans* until the importation of the Chinese and Japanese wisteria. Lady Skipwith. Prince's "Carolina Kidney Bean Tree with purple flowers." Prince's to Jefferson 1791.

Carolina Pepper Tree See *Ampelopsis arborea* (L.) Koehne. Marshall's *"Vitis arborea,* Carolina Vine, Pepper vine or Pepper Tree."

Carolina Rhamnus *Rhamnus caroliniana* Walt. Buckthorn.

Carpinus caroliniana Walt. American hornbeam. Hop hornbeam is *Ostrya virginiana* (Mill.) K. Koch.

Carya See Hickory.

Cassena *Ilex vomitoria* Ait. Yaupon. Collinson requested of Custis. Bartram's.

Cassia fasciculata Michx. Partridge pea, Lady Skipwith's "Georgia Cluster Pea."

Cassia marilandica L. Wild senna. Introduced into England by Collinson. Lady Skipwith has dwarf cassia, "an annual seed from the forest."

Castanea dentata (Marsh.) Borkh. American chestnut.

Castanea pumila (L.) Mill. American dwarf chestnut. Chinquapin. Collinson requested it frequently from Custis and Bartram and finally grew it. Custis described the "chicopine" to him, 1734, as "a pretty small nut of a

Cassia chamaecrista. Dwarf Cassia.
Curtis *Botanical Magazine*

pyramid shape . . ." Custis was sent some by Robert Cary. Collinson listed his as "Catesby 9."

Jefferson grew three edible chestnuts, these two and the Spanish *C. sativa* L.

Catalpa bignonioides Walt. Catesby wrote, "This tree was unknown to the inhabited parts of Carolina until I brought the seeds from the remote parts of the country. And though the inhabitants are little curious in gardening, yet the uncommon beauty of this tree had induced them to propagate it and 'tis become an ornament to many of their gardens and probably will be the same to ours in England."

Dr. Garden and Dr. Witt sent it to Bartram. Collinson listed his as "Catesby 49." Prince's. Bartram's. Washington, 1785, "planted . . . two catalpas West of the Garden House."

Ceanothus americanus L. Collinson, 1762, from Maryland. Good for coughs, "a pretty tea from dried leaves." Bartram's red root.

Cedar, Red *Juniperus virginiana* L.

Cedar, White *Chamaecyparis thyoides* (L.) B.S.P. Cypress. Both valuable timber. Confusion surrounding "cedars" was resolved by Kalm, who wrote that "white cedar" grows in swamps, has wood resembling cedar and looks like a Swedish juniper tree. Called a "red cedar." For "cedar" wood: the American white cedar grows as far north as to meet the American red cedar, which then takes over furnishing cedar wood.

Cedar of Lebanon *Cedrus libani* Loud. Collinson sent two cones to Bartram, 1753. Collinson had several trees. He considered the first in England to be the two by the gate of the Chelsea Physic Garden. (See sketch page 312.)

Celandine *Chelidonium majus* L. Lady Skipwith.

Celastrus scandens L. False bittersweet. Waxwork. Collinson's *"Euonymus scandens."* William Bartram's "Staff Tree." Grown by Collinson for his "curious" nobles.

Celery See chapter on vegetables.

Celosia cristata L. Cockscomb. Fancied by Jefferson, 1767. The Lambolls to Bartram: "Holds color when dried."

Centaurea M'Mahon offered:

C. *alpina*	Alpine centaury
C. *glastifolia*	Woad-leaved centaury
C. *aurea*	Golden centaury
C. *alba*	White-flowered centaury
C. *cineraria* L.	Dusty miller
C. *cyanus* L.	Cornflower, bachelor's-button, blue bottle
C. *american* Nutt	Basket flower
C. *nigra* L.	Knapweed
C. *moschata* L.	Sweet Sultan. Lady Skipwith. The Lambolls to Bartram.

M'Mahon gave Jefferson C. *macrocephala* Puschk, 1807.

Centaury, American Red William Bartram painted a "fine red Centaury," which Collinson said was admired by Ehret and was a "most elegant plant if we can but get it in our gardens." See *Sabatia brachiata* Ell. and *Sabatia lanceolata* Torr. and Gray.

Cerasus For domesticated cherries, see chapter on fruits. Many fruits called *Cerasus* are now under *Prunus. Cerasus pumila* (Michx.) L. In 1760 Collinson records, "received from Bartram . . . a dwarf plum, new species." Collinson noted it as *"Prunus virginana sylvestris angustifolia: from Fl. Virg."*

Philip Miller wrote Bartram in 1759 that he had received the stones from Canada via Paris and figured it "now common in our gardens."

Cercis canadensis L. Redbud. Judas tree. Requested of Custis by Collinson, 1735. Collinson has a "large tree" in his own garden, but "more friends to oblige" and it does not seed with him. In 1739 he thanks Custis for seeds. Jefferson's "ornamental." Washington. M'Mahon.

Bartram's listed both it and the European variety.

Chamaecyparis thyoides (L.) B.S.P. White cedar. Bartram. Lady Skipwith. Kalm observed it in shingles, fence posts and joiners' work, and discussed the tree with Bartram.

Chamaedaphne Two ornamental shrubs "figured" by Catesby: *Chamaedaphne calyculata nana* Rehd. and *Chamaedaphne calyculata angustifolia* Rehd. Collinson.

Chamaelirium luteum (L.) Gray. Blazing star. Devil's bit. Bartram to Collinson.

"Chamaerhododendron or Great Laurel" Collinson from Bartram. To be figured by Catesby if fresh blossoms can be sent by Bartram (blossoms were sent in alcohol). Catesby noted several young plants sent from Pennsyl-

Chamaedaphne, Catesby's Plate 98, Vol. II

Chamaerhododendron, Catesby's Plate A-17, showing both Bartram's Great Laurel, now *Rhododendron maximum,* and the mountain laurel, now *Kalmis angustifolia*

vania, and pictured on the same plate *Rhododendron maximum* L., first discovered by Bartram, and *Kalmia angustifolia* L.

***Cheiranthus cheiri* L.**   Wallflower. Lady Skipwith's "Bloody Wallflower," listed by M'Mahon as variety of *C. cheiri.*

***Chelidonium majus* L.**   Grown by Lady Skipwith with pride. European "Swallow-wort," now a nuisance.

***Chelone glabra* L.**   Red and white. Turtle head. Balmony.
    Bartram received seeds of the red from John Clayton, 1765, "under cover . . . to Mr. Franklin." Collinson had received the red from Virginia in 1750, and in 1751 he received the white from Bartram. Clayton to Miller, 1752.

***Chenopodium botrys* L.**   Oak of Jerusalem. Used for dosing young slaves.

Cherry   Domesticated. See chapter on fruits. Wild. Often planted for ornaments or curiosity.

Cherries   For the table. See chapter on fruits.
    Wild cherries planted for ornament or curiosity:
    Dwarf cherry (*Cerasus pumila* Michx.) Now *Prunus pumila* L.
    Chokecherry (*Cerasus virginiana* D.C.) Now *Prunus virginiana* L. Ehrh.
    Wild or Black cherry (*Cerasus serotina* D.C.) Now *Prunus serotina* Ehrh.

Evergreen, Ornamental cherry (*Cerasus caroliniana* Michx.) Now *Prunus caroliniana* Ait. Found on the Congaree River in mid-Georgia where Bartram never forgot coming upon it "in full bloom." Collinson's "Evergreen Bird Cherry."

Bartram's "Sea-Beach Cherry." *Prunus maritima* Wang.

European Bird Cherry. *Prunus padus* L.

European Cherry laurel. *Prunus laurocerasus* L.

Cherry laurel American. *Prunus caroliniana* Ait.

Portuguese laurel. *Prunus lusitanica* L. Introduced into England in 1719 by Mr. Fairchild.

American Bird Cherry (*Cerasus serotina*) now *Prunus serotina* Ehrh., was known to Parkinson but lost to English gardeners until it was reintroduced by Bartram, who sent it to Collinson. Flowered in 1741 in gardens of Lord Petre.

Chestnut   See *Castanea, Pavia* and *Aesculus*.

Chestnut, European	*Castanea sativa* Mill. Jefferson. Washington.
Chestnut, American	*Castanea dentata* Borkh. Jefferson. Washington.
Chestnut, Chinquapin	*Castanea pumila* Mill. Collinson.
Chestnut, Horse	*Aesculus hippocastanum* L. Collinson to Custis.
Buck-eye, Ohio	*Aesculus glabra* Willd. Bartram.
Buck-eye, Sweet	*Aesculus octandra* Willd. Bartram.
Buck-eye, Red	*Aesculus pavia* L. Collinson. Washington.
Horse Chestnut, Yellow	*Aesculus glabra* Willd. Jefferson.

Chimaphila maculata   "Pyrola with variegated leaves." Bartram to Collinson, who asks for "another sod" in 1759.

China aster   *Callistephus hortensis* Cassini. Collinson to Bartram.

Chinaberry Tree   *Melia azedarach* L. Jefferson.

Chinaroot   *Smilax*. Catesby reported inhabitants of Carolina make a diet drink, which cleanses the blood . . . In spring the roots are eaten like asparagus. "Called there China-Root." See Sassafras.

China Rose   See *Hibiscus*

China Tree   Pride of India. Golden rain tree. Varnish tree. Offered by Prince's, 1790. See *Koelreuteria paniculata* Laxm. Washington planted six, 1786. Jefferson, 1811, from the Countess de Tesse.

Chinquapin   *Castanea pumila* Mill. Banister. Catesby. Custis sent it to Collinson, as did Bartram.

Chionanthus virginica L.   Fringe tree. Collinson asked of Custis in 1735. Wrote to Bartram in 1760 of its blooming with his other American shrubs, mountain laurel, red acacia and Carolina allspice. Washington came upon it while riding and brought it home. Jefferson, 1791.

"Christopheriana"   Herb Christopher. See *Actaea*.

Chrysanthemum indicum L.   Lady Skipwith's pride, "hardy enough to live in the garden though the first frost destroy the flower." First of the

Chinese chrysanthemums, from which our modern hybrids are descended. (Curtis Plate No. 327, 1796.)

"Chrysanthemum americanum"   Catesby found growing beside the Savannah River a scaly cone surrounded by drooping peach-colored petals. Appears to have been a *Rudbeckia*.

Chrysanthemum leucanthemum **L.**   Our field daisy, declared a nuisance by Bartram, who was reproached by Collinson for considering it a weed.

Chrysanthemum parthenium **Pers.**   Feverfew.

Cinquefoil   *Potentilla fruticosa* L. Marshall's "American Shrubby Cinquefoil."

Cistus   Collinson asked Bartram for more of Bartram's "Rock Blood-wort," which Collinson took to be a *Cistus*. Catesby reported in 1740 that his "Rock Cistus from Carolina" had flowered and was beautiful. The first in Europe. Probably *Helianthemum canadense* (L.) Michx. Darby gives two: *H. corymbosum* Michx. and H. *carolinianum* Michx. (perhaps Catesby's) and laments they are not more often cultivated in gardens.

Marsh cistus or wild rosemary, from Bartram to Collinson, is *Andromeda polifolia* L.

Spotted cistus. Lady Skipwith. Probably *Cistus ladaniferus* L. var. *maculatus*. "To be got when I can." "It exudes a balsamic gum . . . continues two or three months in flower."

Cistus landaniferus. Gum Cistus.
Curtis *Botanical Magazine*

Cladrastis lutea **Koch.**   Yellow-wood. Michaux's *"Virgilia lutea."*

Clary   The Lambolls asked Bartram for the "common sort." Bartram sent *Salvia sclarea* L., 1761.

Claytonia caroliniana **Michx** and similar *C. virginica* **L.**   Collinson, 1746, reported to Linnaeus his claytonia nearly in flower. Bartram reported his in bloom to Collinson, 1756. Collinson wrote of his blooming, 1767. Dr Fothergill thanked Humphry Marshall for one, 1772, fondly believing not another in England.

Lady Skipwith grew claytonias in her wild flower garden: "The little narrow-leaved black-rooted flower from the foot of the garden."

Clematis viorna **L.** Leather flower. Perhaps the red, reticulated clematis sent by Bartram, raised by Lord Petre and stolen from Collinson.

Clematis virginiana **L.** Virgin's bower.

Clethra alnifolia **L.** Sweet pepperbush. Introduced by Catesby. Listed by Jefferson. Bartram's. Washington. Bartram to Collinson by 1751.

Clinopodium Savory or calamint. Bartram to Collinson, 1735, with "tricolor leaves." To Dillenius by Bartram, 1742, as "the variegated Clinopodium." Collinson from Dr. Witt, "a fine plant." Now under *Satureja* L.

Cneorum triococcum Widow wail. Lady Skipwith's "low evergreen shrub with small yellow flower." In Furber's *Months*.

"Cobb nuts." *Corylus avellana* L. To Washington in 1785 from "Sister Lewis."

Cockscomb *Celosia cristata* L. Grown by Jefferson, 1767, "like Prince's Feather."

Cockspur Thorn *Crataegus crus-galli* L. Jefferson.

Coffee Tree, Kentucky *Gymnocladus dioica* Koch. (*Gymnocladus canadensis* Lam.) Canada bonduc or nickar tree. Washington, 1785. John Clayton asked seeds of Bartram. Washington was importuned for seeds from France (with crown imperial and cardinal flower).

Colchicum autumnale **L.** So-called autumn crocus.

Colchicum luteum **Baker** Old name, *Amaryllis lutea*. The only yellow *colchicum*. Lady Skipwith's "autumnal yellow Amaryllis." The Lambolls requested from Bartram.

Coldenia nuttallii **Hook** Slender annual "railway weed" named for Dr. Cadwallader Colden.

Collinsonia Horse balm. *C. canadensis* L. var. *punctata* (Ell.) Gray. Strong-scented North American perennials named for Peter Collinson, first introduced to English gardens in 1741.

"Colocasia" "The great water lily . . . it grows in the Jerseys." Collinson asked of Bartram. See *Nelumbium luteum* Pers.

Columbine *Aquilegia*.

Columbo See *Swertia*.

Coltsfoot *Tusilago farfara* L.

Colutea arborescens **L.** Bladder senna. Lady Skipwith. Collinson from Bartram. Furber's "January," "Yellow Colutea." Jefferson received from Edinburgh. Bartram's listed "large papillonaceous flowers."

Commelina virginica L. Day flower. Lady Skipwith. "Annual trailing Commelina with a sopewort leaf." Collinson. Bartram.

Comptonia asplenifolia Gaertn. Sweet fern . . . named for Bishop Compton. Requested of Bartram by Philip Miller.

Convallaria majalis L. Lily of the valley. Lady Skipwith. Collinson to Custis 1738.

Convolvulus Bindweed. Catesby described "Purple Bindweed of Carolina" and how Indians daub themselves with the juice and handle rattlesnakes. Lady Skipwith had "many colors."

Coralberry Indian currant. *Symphoricarpus vulgaris* Michx. Now *S. orbiculatus* Moench.

Coral Honeysuckle *Lonicera sempervirens* L. Jefferson's trumpet honey-·suckle.

Coral Tree *Erythrina corrallodendron* L. West Indies. Lady Skipwith.

Coreopsis A family of American natives that became garden flowers.

Corallodendron humile. Coral Tree. Catesby's Plate 49, Vol. II

Coreopsis verticillata. Curtis Botanical Magazine

Corn See chapter on vegetables.

Corn Flag See *Gladiolus.*

Corn Salad *Valerianella olitoria* Poll. Lamb's lettuce.

Cornel Tree Cornelian cherry. *Cornus mas.*

Cornus Dogwood. Bunchberry.
    Cornus alba Bartram's "White berried Swamp Dogwood," 1792. Washington.

C. alternifolia L. Marshall's "Female Virginian Dogwood," pictured by William Bartram. Collinson.

C. canadensis L. Dwarf cornel bunchberry. Pudding berry.

C. racemosa Lam. Marshall's "Swamp American Dogwood."

C. florida L. Miller's "Male Dogwood." Dr. Fothergill requested of Humphry Marshall. Marshall's "Male Virginian Dogwood, whose calyx is its greatest beauty." Grown by Custis, sent to Collinson, who requested, 1734. Collinson grew but saw only one bloom in England. Pictured by Catesby. A pink variety possible? Custis thinks he has one. Jefferson sent to France.

C. mas L. Cornelian cherry. Washington. Bartram.

C. sanguinea L. Marshall's "American Red-Rod Cornus."

Corona solis Sunflower. Collinson's grew from a sod with *Calceolus*. See *Helianthus*.

Coronilla emerus L.   Scorpion senna. Lady Skipwith. Jefferson.

Cortusa matthioli L.   Purple coronilla. Bear's-ear sanicle of Lady Skipwith. "Purple is best."

Corylus American hazelnut.

From the time William Wood, in 1640, wrote of the "Snake murthering hazel," presumably with a switch in mind, the American hazelnut, *Corylus americana* Walt., and the *Corylus cornuta* Marsh., dwarf filbert or cuckold nut, both listed by Marshall, were fancied. Jefferson had both the Americans and the European *C. avellana* L., 1774.

Cotton *Gossypium*. Byrd reported "grows kindly" east of the Dismal, and observed that the good women mix cotton with their wool for outer garments.

Jefferson tried to improve the sorts.

Cotton Tree Cottonwood. *Populus deltoides* Marsh.

"Cottonweed or Life Everlasting" Requested by Collinson of Bartram. In Bartram's medical appendix, called "Elichrysum." See *Helichrysum*.

Cowslip Lady Skipwith's "Cowslips" and "American Cowslips" may mean she had both *Caltha palustris* L. and *Dodecatheon meadia* L. She had the "Virginia Cowslip," *Mertensia virginica* L., called "Blue Fennel Flower," as did Jefferson. Custis asked Collinson for the "Jerusalem Cowslip," or *Pulmonaria officinalis* L. Lungwort. Collinson said it was "in very little request in our gardens." Collinson and Custis referred to *Mertensia virginica* L. as the "Mountain Cowslip," which Custis sent to Collinson (bloomed 1736). Perhaps also the cowslip sent to the Lambolls by Bartram.

Crab Apple *Pyrus coronaria* L. (*Malus coronaria* Mill.).

Cranberry, American *Vaccinium oxycoccos* L. and *Vaccinium macrocarpon* Ait. Only recently cultivated.

Cranberry, High-Bush *Viburnum trilobum* Marsh. Jefferson ordered "all you have" from Prince, 1791.

Cranberry, Mountain *Vaccinium vitis-idaea* L.

Crape Myrtle *Lagerstroemia indica* L. Brought from East Indies. Washington.

Crataegus **American hawthorn.**

   C. *crus-galli* L. Cockspur thorn. Bartram's "Cockspur," Prince's "American White Thorne. Bartram to Collinson, 1734, who already had it. Jefferson at Monticello, 1791.

   C. *phaenopyrum* (L.) Medic. Washington thorn. The sort Washington and Jefferson used for hedging, as it grew all around Washington, D.C. Hence its name.

   C. *monogyna* Jacq. English hawthorn. Ordered from England in quantity by Washington for hedging.

   C. *marshallii* Eggleston. For Humphry Marshall, who first described it as "the Wild Service Tree" (his only entry under *Crataegus* in *The American Grove*).

Creeper, Virginia "American Ivy," *Parthenocissus quinquefolia* (L.) Planch. Mentioned by Parkinson. Noted growing over all walls and houses by Kalm.

Cress *Lepidium sativum* L. is garden cress. "Great Garden Cresses" are our nasturtiums. *"Nasturtium indicum"* is now *Tropaeolum majus* L. and *Tropaeolum minus* L. Grown in the seventeenth century for salad; in the eighteenth, chiefly for ornament. The Lambolls to Bartram.

Crocus, Autumn Commonly used for *Colchicum autumnale* L. Blue.

Crocus vernus **L.** Common garden crocus, blue and white. Collinson to Custis. Sir Peyton Skipwith ordered two dozen from the Richmond seedsman, "mixed blue and yellow." Collinson sent Bartram "twenty sorts."

Cross Vine See *Bignonia capreolata* L.

Crown Imperial Lily *Fritillaria imperialis* L. Custis to Collinson, 1739, "I had this spring a lemon-coloured crown imperiall you were kind to send me . . . looked on as a great rarity. I have two roots of the orange-coloured . . ." Jefferson. Lady Skipwith. Requested of Washington.

Cucumber See chapter on vegetables. "Turkey cucumber" seeds sent to Custis by Collinson, 1737. Custis grew cucumbers three feet long and fourteen inches around. The Lambolls sent cucumbers to Bartram "for pickling."

Cucumber Tree *Magnolia acuminata* L. Bartram. Collinson.

"Cudweed Goldylocks or Eternal Flower" Also "cottonweed." Called *Elychrisum* by Bartram. Everlastings and live-forevers applied to several dryable flowers.

   Helichrysum arenarium D.C. Yellow everlasting.

   Helichrysum orientale Gaert. (Formerly *Gnaphalium orientale* L.) Also yellow.

Gnaphalium sylvaticum is wood cudweed with small yellowish flower heads. A perennial. Lady Skipwith.

Cunila origanoides (L). Britt. Common dittany. W. Byrd reported used against horseflies.

Cupressus Linnaeus's name for the white cedar. Now *Chamaecyparis thyoides* (L.) B.S.P.

Cupressus sempervirens L. The "pyramidical cypress" given Washington by Michaux, 1706.

Currants See chapter on fruits.

Custard Apple, American *Asimina triloba* (L.) Dunal. Papaw. Marshall's "Pennsylvanian Triple-fruited Papaw." *Asimina parviflora* (Michx.) Dunal. Marshall's "Carolinian Smooth-barked Annona."

Cyclamen Lady Skipwith raised many from seed, "great variety," blooming after four years. "Blooms from December to spring in great beauty." Probably *Cyclamen europaeum* L.

Cymnel Early American name for squashes. Also cymlings.

Cynoglossum virginianum Wild comfrey. Hound's tongue. *C. officinale* L. Lady Skipwith.

Cypress See *Chamaecyparis* and also *Cupressus* and *Taxodium*.

Cypress, Bald *Taxodium distichum* Rich. These are the "kneed cypresses" Byrd saw in the Dismal "shooting their tops very high." Marshall's "Virginia deciduous Cypress tree." Much in vogue among the "curious" in England. Collinson's at Mill Hill is still alive. Many specimens of great size survive in England with the cedars of Lebanon, popular at the same time. Catesby described the cypress "except the tulip tree, tallest in this part of the world."

Cyrilla racemiflora L. Leatherwood. Bartram to Collinson, 1736. Described by Humphry Marshall to Dr. Lettsom as "the Plumed Andromeda of Bartram."

Cyprepedium acaule Ait. Catesby said, "This plant produces the most elegant flower of all the Helleborine tribe and is in great esteem with the North American Indians for decking their hair, etc. They call it the Moccasin Flower which also signifies in their language a shoe or slipper." In 1740 Collinson wrote Bartram that in the last "cargo" he had received a *calceolus,* "a fine red one, a very curious flower indeed. M. Catesby painted it." Our common pink lady's-slipper. Skipwith.

Cyprepedium spectabile Salis The showy lady's-slipper. Collinson's bloomed in 1760.

Cyprepedium pubescens The yellow lady's-slipper Catesby saw in Collinson's garden at Peckham in 1738. Jefferson, 1791. Beverly reported this wildflower so shocked "a grave gentleman" that he dropped the flower indignantly as "a Waggery of Nature."

"Cytisus anagyroides laburnum" Now *Laburnum anagyroides.* Golden chain. Bartram's "Citisus laburnum, foliage delicate embellished with pendant clusters of splendid yellow papillonaceous flowers." Washington planted "Cytire," given him by Michaux, "a tree of quick growth in a cold climate," 1786. Jefferson from Thouin. Prince's "Leburnum with yellow flowers."

Cytisus scoparius **Link.**   Scotch broom. Recommended for hedges in Virginia and feeding pigs. Tops used medicinally in Europe. Jefferson.

D

Daffodil   See *Narcissus.*

Daffodil, Sea   Spider lily, American *Hymenocallis occidentalis* (LeConte.) Kunth. Also in the Old World, *Pancratium maritimum.* Lambolls.

Dahoon Holly   *Ilex cassine* L. Sometimes confused with *Ilex vomitoria* Ait. Both by Bartram's.

Daisy   Our field daisy *Chrysanthemum leucanthemum* L. Marguerite. Bartram's reported inspiration to study botany after he had thoughtlessly ploughed it up.

Damson Plum   See chapter on fruits.

Dandelion   *Taraxacum officinale* Weber. Kalm observed that eating them, as the French did, in salads, was "not usual here."

Daphne mesereum **L.**   Bartram's "early sweet flowering little shrub."

Datura stramonium **L.**   Jamestown weed. Jefferson said the French invented a preparation from this "most elegant among poison plants," which "every man of firmness" carried in his pocket in the time of Robespierre "to anticipate the guillotine." He refused, on account of his grandchildren, to grow it in his garden, but he listed it among Virginia's medicinal plants.

The Lambolls sent purple *Stramonium* to Bartram. Kalm considered it one of our worst weeds.

Day Flower   *Commelina nudiflora* L. Skipwith. Bartram. Collinson.

Day Lily   *Hemerocallis flava* L. and *H. fulva* L. Universal.

Delphinium   Larkspur. *D. ajacis* L. and *D. consolida* L. Jefferson, 1767. The Lambolls sent "Double rose larkspur" to Bartram, 1762. Annuals. The great hybrid perennials are yet to come.

Dens canis   *Erythronium dens canis* L. Skipwith. *E. americanum* Ker. Skipwith.

Devil's Bit   *Chamaelirium luteum* (L.) Gray. Blazing star.

Dewberry   *Rubus trivialis* Michx. One of our native fruits.

Dayflower. Catesby's Plate 62, Vol. II

Dianthus   D. *barbatus* L. Sweet William. Jefferson. Skipwith.

D. *caryophylus* L. Clove pink. Clove gillyflower. Carnation. Jefferson. Skipwith.

D. *chinensis* L. (Or *sinensis*.) Indian pink. Jefferson. Skipwith. Collinson to Bartram and Dr. Witt.

D. *deltoides* L. Maiden pink. M'Mahon's.

D. *plumarius* L. Grass pink. Pheasant's-eye. Scotch. Jefferson. M'Ma'hon's.

D. *superbus* L. M'Ma'hon's.

Curtis features only four: *D. barbatus, D. caryophyllus, D. chinensis, D. superbus.*

Custis requested "cornation seed" of Collinson, 1725. Bartram wrote Col-

Dianthus superbus. Curtis *Botanical Magazine*

linson, 1762, "I have now a glorious appearance of Carnations from thy seed — the brightest colours that ever eyes beheld."

Dictamnus albus L.   Fraxinella. Gas plant. Skipwith, both white and purple.

Digitalis purpurea L.   Foxglove. A "sovereign" eighteenth-century remedy for dropsy. Custis's "white flower" identified for him by Collinson as foxglove, 1737. Collinson had sent Custis the seeds as "a rare flower with us." Custis sowed "rose-coloured" foxglove," 1738. Kalm saw it, 1748. Bartram noted, in his editing of Short's *Materia Medica,* "This species of digitalis grows only in curious gardens." Dr. William Withering, English author of a medical treatise on the foxglove, sent the seeds (and, presumably, the treatise) to Dr. Hall Jackson in Portsmouth, New Hampshire, who sent seeds, 1789, to Dr. James Thacher, in Boston, "to try of its efficacy" and to cultivate it as "a beautiful flower in the garden."

Dr. Wistar, for whom wisteria is named, wrote to Humphry Marshall and his son, Dr. Moses Marshall, 1797, sending them Dr. Withering's *Treatise,* saying they must be pleased to have such a plant and asking for one back, with the book. He could not "omit mentioning" that one of Dr. Withering's patients in the Edinburgh Infirmary had vomited to death, which determined Dr. Wistar to have nothing to do with the medicine, although "dropsies are so often fatal that we must try everything."

Dionaea muscipula Ellis   Venus' flytrap. Governor Dobb's "Fly Trap Sensitive." Bartram's "Tipitiwitchet." Acclaimed by Collinson as "a new species, a new genus." A plant curiosity from the Carolina swamps, much in demand. Collinson, in 1763, sent a specimen to Linnaeus, who "will be in raptures at the sight of it." Collinson requested William Bartram to draw it.

Dioscorea alata L.   (Once also *Batatas Decne.*) Yam. Kalm ate some at "Dr. Franklin's" that had come by ship from the West Indies.

Diospyros virginiana L.   Persimmon. Indian plum. Captain John Smith et al. Catesby. Parkinson. Washington. Custis to Collinson, who remarked it sounded like the medlar — better eaten after touched by frost. Jefferson to the Countess de Tesse.

Dirca palustris L.   Virginian marsh leatherwood. Striped maple. Moosewood. Collinson asked Bartram, "Send more seeds." Kalm observed it used for cord, as a purge and for switching children.

Dittany *Cunila origanoides* (L.) Britt. Our common dittany. William Byrd II stuck it in the bridle as a remedy against horseflies. Bartram to Collinson, 1757.

Dodecatheon meadia L.   Lady Skipwith's "Bear's Ear of Virginia." American cowslip. Shooting star. Named *Meadia* by Catesby for his patron, Dr. Mead. Renamed by Linnaeus for a plant described by Dioscorides. Banister to Bishop Compton. Bartram found it on the banks of the Shenandoah and sent it to Collinson.

Dodecatheon meadis L. Here shown in Catesby's Plate A-1 by his name, *Meadia*

Dogbane   *Apocynum androsaemifolium* L. Skipwith.

Dogberry   *Cornus floridus* L.

Dog's-Tooth Violet.   See *Erythronium.*

Dogwood   *Cornus floridus* L. Custis.

Draba verna **L.**   Whitlow grass. Naturalized. Observed by Kalm.

Dracocephalum parviflorum **Nutt.**   Dragonhead. Bartram to Collinson. Lord Petre had great luck with it.

Draconitum foetidum   Observed by Kalm as skunk cabbage. Now *Symplocarpus foetidus* (L.) Nutt.

Dragon   Dragon Arum. Dragonroot *Arisaema draconitum* Schott.
Dragon Plant. *Dracunculus vulgaris* Schott.
Dragonhead, False. *Physostegia virginiana* Benth.
   I suspect this was Lord Petre's success. Collinson also grew it.

Dutchman's-Pipe.   *Aristolochia macrophylla* Lam. Bartram sent Collinson seeds from the Ohio River, 1761. Bartram referred to is as "clammy birthwort."

E

Echinops ritro **L.**   Globe thistle. Custis 1738 from Collinson.

Eggplant   *Solanum melongena* L. Lady Skipwith's "Brown Jolly. See Melangea," 1791. Jefferson after 1810.

Eglantine   *Rosa eglanteria* L. Naturalized.

Elm   See *Ulmus*.

Elder   *Sambucus canadensis* L. One of Bartram's weed complaints.

Elecampane   *Inula helenium* L. The Lambolls requested of Bartram, 1761.

***Empetrum nigrum* L.**   Black crowberry and *Empetrum atropurpureum* Fern. Purple crowberry. Collinson's "Berry-bearing heath," stolen in 1762. Bartram to Collinson, 1764.

***Epigaea repens* L.**   Trailing arbutus. Mayflower. "Some call it Creeping Ground Laurel," Bartram to Collinson.

***Eranthis hyemalis* Salisb.**   Miller. Curtis. Linnaeus' *Helleborus hyemalis*.

***Erythrina corallodendron* L**   Carolina coral tree. Lady Skipwith's "Mrs. Miller's Scarlet Bean, very handsome." Philip Miller's first sort "grows naturally in South Carolina from whence Mr. Catesby sent the seeds in the year 1724." Catesby 49. Collinson.

Euonymus   Spindle Tree. Marshall lists three:
  1) *E. atropurpureus* Jacq. Burning bush. Wahoo. Washington ordered three from Bartram's.
  2) *E. americanus* L. Strawberry bush. Bursting heart. Washington ordered one from Bartram's. To Collinson. Jefferson.
  3) *E. obvatus* Nutt. Running strawberry bush. Only now coming into its own as a ground cover.
  Note: Our evergreen climbing shrub *E. radicans* Sieb. is nineteenth-century, from Asia.

Eupatorium   Ancient herbs, useful in medicine, which graduated to flower borders:
E. perfoliatum L. Boneset.
E. purpureum L. Joe-pye weed.

Evergreen   With few natural evergreens in England, the many sorts in the New World took on added attractions. See Cedars, Firs, Junipers, Laurels, Magnolias, Pines, Rhododendrons, Spruces, Yews.

Everlastings   Similarly, with the barren seasons of cold in the New World, flowers that could be dried and retain their color seemed especially desirable. From France: the immortelles, *Helichrysum arenarium* L. and *H. bracteatum* L. From England: the globe amaranth, *Gomphrena globosa* L. From our roadsides: several sorts of *Antennaria*, pussy toes; *Anaphalis margaritacea* L., pearly everlasting; and *Gnaphalium obtusifolium* L., cudweed.

Everlasting Pea, however, was not for drying; it was merely indestructible. *Lathyrus grandiflorus* Sibth. and Smith. One of the few flowers Washington recorded planting himself.

Evonymus   See Euonymus.

F

Faba aegyptica   Supposedly the name for our *Nelumbium lutea* Pers., seen by Kalm in West Jersey, desired of Bartram by Collinson, described by Bartram in 1751 and immediately sought after for Gronovius and "curious botanical friends." The name *Faba,* an early name for broad beans, derives from the fact that our Indians ate it. The "curious" were right, as this is one of two strong-growing aquatics; one North American and yellow, the other Asiatic and white. Collinson chides Bartram for our apathy in not growing it in our "garden pools." Calling it "the Colocasia," Bartram recounts several attempts to get seed. By 1765, Collinson is planting the seeds and sending some to the Queen, without results on either count. However, in 1768 the Duchess of Portland commissions William to draw the *"Faba Aegyptica"* for her. And in 1769 Dr. Fothergill, who is to become William's patron for drawings, writings and travel, "expects the Colocasia when convenient." Today, the "Sacred Bean," *Nelumbo lutea* (Willd.) Pers., also called water chinquapin or pond nuts, still rises high from the water. Not to be confused with our yellow pond lily, or spatter-dock, a *Nuphar,* or with our fragrant pond lily, *Nymphaea odorata* Ait.

Fagus   Beech. Marshall had "one Species of this Genus," besides the chestnut and chinquapin, "somewhat improperly joined with it." His *Fagus sylvatica atro-punicea* is now *Fagus grandiflora* Ehrh. [*F. sylvatica* L. is the European beech.] Marshall appended *Fagus-Castanea dentata,* the American chestnut tree, which is now *Castanea dentata* (Marsh.) Borkh. and *Fagus-Castenea pumila,* the dwarf chestnut tree or chinquapin, which is now *Castanea pumila* (L.) Mill. All these trees, beeches and otherwise, were observed by Kalm, planted by Washington and Jefferson and offered by Prince's, Bartram's and M'Mahon's.

Fair Maids of France.   *Ranunculus aconitifolius* L. Skipwith.

Fern   Fothergill had the "greatest collection of American ferns in England."

Fern, Sweet   *Comptonia asplenifolia* Gaertn. Named for Bishop Compton.

Ficus carica L   Fig. Delight of southern gardeners, source of seasonal correspondence and envy. Wythe. Jefferson. Washington.

Filipendula   Meadowsweet. Dropwort. Also, according to Kalm, called tea bushes. *F. hexapetala* Gilib. (formerly *Spiraea filipendula* L.) is an introduced and escaped garden flower. *Spiraea alba* Du Roi, also called meadowsweet, is the one likely to have been called tea bush.

Fir   The Scotch fir was a pine; the silver fir a spruce; the hemlock fir a hemlock; the balsam fir a fir. See *Abies, Picea, Tsuga* and *Pinus.*

As noted under *Abies,* in the eighteenth century "firs" stood for most needled evergreen trees not noticeably pines. Collinson wrote Bartram, 1736, pines had "leaves set by pairs" and firs "leaves set singly on the branches," and requested "all the Pines and Firs your part affords."

Miller listed:
1) "Silver Fir or Yew-leaved Fir Tree."
Now *Picea abies* L. Mill. Jefferson. Collinson.
2) "Common Fir or Pitch Tree, Norway or Spruce Fir." Now *Picea abies* L. Collinson. It did not take the United States by storm until the early nineteenth century.
3) "Virginia Fir Tree . . . Hemlock Fir." Now *Tsuga canadensis* (L.) Carr. Canadian hemlock. The Carolina hemlock is *Tsuga caroliniana* Engel. Bartram's. Washington.
4) "Pitch-leaved Fir Tree. Newfoundland Black Spruce Fir." Now *Picea mariana* (Mill.) B.S.P. Prince's. Bartram's. Collinson.
5) "Pitch-leaved Fir Tree with loose cones. The Newfoundland White Spruce Fir." Now *Picea glauca* Moench. Voss. Bartram's. Collinson.
6) "Balm of Gilead Fir." Now *Abies balsamea* Mill. Bartram's. Prince's.

Fire Pink   *Silene virginica* L. Banister's drawing sent to Compton.

Flag

Blue Flag	*Iris versicolor* L.
Corn Flag	*Gladiolus communis* L.
Cat-tail Flag	*Typha latifolia* L.
Crested Dwarf Flag	*Iris cristata* Ait.
Poison Flag	*Iris versicolor* L.
Slender Blue Flag	*Iris prismatica* Pursh.
Southern Blue Flag	*Iris virginica* L.
Sweet Flag	*Acorus calamus* L.
Yellow Flag	*Iris pseudocorus* L.
Dwarf Violet Flag	*Iris verna* L.
Red Flag	*Iris fulva* Ker.

Flax   See *Linum*. Toad-flax. See *Linaria*.

Flower de Luce   Fleur-de-lis. *Iris pseudacorus* L. original of the French symbol, since by growing in a river it indicated a ford to the beleaguered Clovis and was adopted by Louis VII as the Fleur de Louis. Jefferson reported "Flower de Luces just opening," May, 1767.

Flower Fence   *Poinciana pulcherrima* from Barbados. Now *caesalpinia pulcherrima Swartz*. Washington obtained it to set out at Mount Vernon.

Flos Adonis   *Adonis autumnalis* L.

Fothergilla   Witch alder. Dr. Fothergill, Quaker physician in London, friend, neighbor and rival gardener to Peter Collinson, patron of desperately frustrated young William Bartram, was early honored by Linnaeus by having this ornamental American shrub named for him. 1788, Jefferson ordered it for the Countess de Tesse. 1793, Dr. Moses Marshall regrets to some London nurserymen that his plants are too large to ship abroad. Marshall lists *"Fothergilla gardeni*, Carolina Fothergilla," and says it was first sent to Collinson by Bartram as "Gardenia." Bartram wished to honor Dr. Garden of Charleston, whom Linnaeus preferred to honor with "Cape Jasmine." Washington ordered *"Fothergilla gardeni"* from Bartram's, 1792.

Foxglove *Digitalis purpurea* L.

Fragaria Strawberries. See chapter on fruits.

"Franklinia alatamaha" in Marshall's *Grove,* was first observed by John Bartram in 1760 but not collected until fifteen years later when William Bartram revisited the spot and collected seeds. He named it for "that Patron of sciences and truly great and distinguished character, Dr. Benjamin Franklin." It was never again seen in the wild. Now *Gordonia alatamaha* Sarg.

Frasera caroliniensis Walt "American Colombo." Jefferson 1810.

Fraxinella *Dictamnus albus* L. Gas plant. Lady Skipwith.

Fraxinus Ash. Marshall lists four:

"Fraxinum americana. Carolina or Red Ash." Now *F. pensylvanica* Marsh.

"Fraxinus alba. American White Ash." Now *F. americana* L.

"Fraxinus nigra. Black Ash." Now *F. nigra* Marsh.

"Fraxinum pennsylvanica. Pennsylvanian sharp-keyed Ash."

Collinson, in 1735, asked Bartram for "all the sorts of Ash." White Ash seeds requested from France by Jefferson. Ash trees were one of Washington's repeats in his serpentine drives. Several very old whites ashes were observed at Mount Vernon by Sargent, 1917.

French Honeysuckle *Hedysarum coronarium* L. Lady Skipwith.

Fringe Tree *Chionanthus virginica* L. Catesby, for Plate 68, called it an "Amelanchier," as did Collinson, who had it 1760. Jefferson lists it as

"Funnel flower" to Jefferson and Lady Skipwith *Pulmonaria virginica.* Curtis *Botanical Magazine.* Now *Mertensia virginica*

Virginia ornamental "Fringe or Snowdrop Tree." Catesby describes
"bunches of white flowers hanging on branched foot-stalks." Marshall's
"Virginian Snow-Drop Tree." One of the native shrubs Washington
brought in from his rides. The time of blooming of the fringe tree was
an indicator to Jefferson of the advance of spring.

Fumaria officinalis **L.**   Common fumitory of Europe. Escaped. Lady Skipwith grows "Tuberous insipid Fumatory, the ninth sort in Miller." Cornut
called it *Fumaria tuberosa insipida,* growing naturally in North America.
Now *Adlumia fungosa* (Ait.) Greene.

Fumitory, Climbing   Mountain fringe. *Adlumia fungosa* (Ait.) Greene.

Funnel Flower, Blue   Lady Skipwith's and Jefferson's name for *Mertensia
virginica* L.

G

Gaillardia   Blanket flower. Showy American herbs welcomed into English
borders. Named in 1788 for a French botanist.

Galanthus nivalis **L.**   Common snowdrop. Randolph to Jefferson. Skipwith.

Gale   American bog gale is *Myrica gale* L. "Spleen-wort-leaved Gale or
Shrubby Sweetfern," whose "infusion is good in diarrhea," became *Comptonia peregrina* var. *asplenifolia* (L.) Fern.

Galega officinalis **L.**   Goat's rue. Collinson had both blue and white. Collinson thanked Bartram for *Galega,* probably our *Tephrosia virginia* (L.)
Pers.

Galingale   A name that includes several edible and ornamental grasses.

Gallberry   Gall bush. *Ilex.* William Byrd II's dashing account of struggling
through the Great Dismal includes a description of the gallbush as "a
beautiful evergreen" that "may be cut into any shape." Its berries turn
water black, like oak galls.

   Byrd said its leaves "bespeak it to be of the 'alaternus family,' " which
reveals it to us as "Black Alder. Winterberry." *Ilex verticillata* (L.) Gray.

Gall of the Earth   *Prenanthes serpentaria.* Pursh. "Dr. Witt's Snakeroot,"
according to Collinson.

Garavances and Garbanzo   Chickpeas. *Cicer aretinum* L. Jefferson.

Gardenia   The Countess de Noailles. Lafayette's gardening aunt, thought this
was the name for *Fothergilla.* Instead, it is the name of a very fragrant
South African shrub most inappropriately named by Linnaeus for Dr.
Alexander Garden of Charleston, South Carolina, who had a beautiful
garden and took a great interest in plants. He had visited Bartram's garden
and declared it "a perfect portraiture of himself." He assisted both Bartrams, corresponded with Collinson and finally had to return in poor health
to England, seen off by an anxious John Bartram.

Gaultheria procumbens L. Mountain tea. Wintergreen. Marshall's check-erberry. Named for a Quebec doctor by Kalm.

Gelder Rose Guelder rose; also Guilder. Anciently *Viburnum opulus* var. *roseum* L. The inevitable shrub by the cottage door in England and across much of Europe. The name may come from its being first cultivated at Guelders, between Germany and Holland. Today we call it *V. opulus* var. *sterile* D.C., but it is the same long-loved shrub. Jefferson. M'Mahon's.

Gelsimium sempervirens Ait. Carolina yellow jessamine. "Jessamine" to Jefferson and Skipwith. Jefferson called *Bignonia capreolata* L., also ever-green, "Virginia Yellow Jasmine."

Gentian Ague weed. Catesby's 70, *Gentiana virginiana* became *G. Cates-baei* Walt. and is now *G. saponaria* L., soapwort gentian. To Collinson from Bartram, 1765. Considered medicinal by Jefferson. *Gentiana crinata* Froel. was welcomed from Bartram by Collinson as "that charming autumn blue gentian."

Gentiana virginiana. Catesby's Plate 70, Vol. I

G. lutea L. Popular European gentian. Collinson. Observed by Kalm in "Mr. Bartram's Herbarium."

Geranium Crane's bill. Kalm observed the skunk has an odor like *Geranium robertianum* L. Collinson grew *Geranium maculatum* as Virginian and one identified by Dillwyn as *G. carolinianum* L. from "Flora Virginica." Jefferson asked that *Geranium maculatum* be sent to Paris with *Geranium gibbosum*. *Gibbosum* means "swollen on one side." Sorry, no clue.

Georgia Cluster Pea *Cassia fasciculata* Michx. Partridge pea, Golden cassia. Prairie senna. Lady Skipwith.

Georgia Fever Bark *Pinckneyana pubens* Michx.

Gerardia flava L. Yellow foxglove. Collinson thanks Bartram for the

"Yellow Foxglove," 1756. Collinson has it growing as *"Digitalis lutea magno flore"* and as Dillwyn's *Gerardia flava.* "Received from J. Bartram 1756 one sod of great yellow perennial Digitalis."

Gilead, Balm of Fir.   *Abies Balsamea* (L.) Mill.

Gilead, Balm of Poplar.   *Populus balsamifera* L.

Gillenia   Indian physic. American ipecac. *Gillenia trifoliata* (L.) Moench. Bowman's root. Found near Williamsburg. American ipecac is *Gillenia stipulata* (Muhl.) Bail. Collinson thanked Custis for "Ipecacuana." A ship to London 1738 carried four hogsheads of "ipecacuana." Fothergill wrote to Humphry Marshall in 1771 to use "your ipecac" to find out how small a dose works.

Gilliflower   Means "blooming in July." See *Dianthus* and July flower.

Clove Gilliflower   *Dianthus caryophyllus* L.

Stock Gilliflower   *Matthiola incarna* R. Br.

After his stay in France, Jefferson referred to "Giroffle."

Ginger, Wild   *Asarum canadense* L. and *Asarum virginicum* L.

Ginseng   *Panax quinquefolius* L. Dwarf ginseng is *Panax trifolius* L., called groundnut.

Gladiolus communis **L.**   Corn flag. Lady Skipwith.

Gleditsia triacanthos **L.**   Honey locust. *G. aquatica* Marsh is water locust. See Acacia.

Globe Amaranth   *Gomphrena globosa* L. Collinson to Custis.

Globe Thistle   See *Echinops.* Custis from Collinson, 1738.

Glycine max.   Soybean

Gnaphalium   See now *Helichrysum petiolatum* D.C. and also *Leontopodium alpinum* Cass.

Goat's Rue   See *Galega officinalis* L. and *Tephrosia virginiana* Pers.

Goldenrod   See *Solidago.*

Gomphrena globosa **L.**   "Perennial Globe Amaranthus with radiated straw-coloured flowers." Miller's third. Lady Skipwith. Jefferson. One of the dried-flower circle. Custis received it as "Aramanthoides" from Collinson.

Gooseberry   See chapter on fruits. To Custis from Collinson.

Goldilocks   Lady Skipwith grew "Cudweed Goldilocks"
Helichrysum arenarium D.C. is yellow everlasting.
Helichrysum orientale is "Golden Mothwort or Cudweed," Parkinson's "Golden Flower Gentle."

Goodyera pubenscens   Collinson received roots of "striped-leaved orchis" from Bartram, January, 1758. Flowered in August.

Gordonia alatamaha **Sarg. (***Franklinia alatamaha***)**   Identified by Sir Joseph Banks as a species of *Gordonia.* The famous tree discovered by Bartram, found again by his son, grown by him and never seen again in the wild. Loblolly bay. Bartram reported his killed by the frost, 1763. The original

Gordonia was named for James Gordon, London nurseryman who received and grew many North American specialties. Collinson, 1765.

Gossypium   Cotton exercised Jefferson and Washington for many years, as they tried for new and better sorts. One from Peter Collinson.
   G. *hirsutum* L. was American upland cotton.
   G. *herbaceum* L. was from India, Africa, Syria.
   G. *barbadense* L. was Sea Island cotton.

Grapes   See chapter on fruits.

Grape Hyacinth   *Muscari botryoides* L. Jefferson. Skipwith.

Gratiola aurea Muhl.   Hedge hyssop. "A very pretty Gratiola," Bartram to Collinson.

Greek Valerian   *Polemonium reptans* L. Jacob's-ladder. Collinson. Bartram. Each to the other. Collinson agreed the American is "pretty and different from ours . . ."

Ground Cypress   *Lycopodium complanatum* L. "A singular pretty plant," Collinson to Bartram, 1734.

Groundsel   *Senecio vulgaris* L.

Groundsel Tree   *Baccharis halmifolia* L.   Sea myrtle, consumption weed, plowman's spikenard. Collinson from Bartram, 1741, for Lord Petre, who considered it to be the male *Senecio arborescens* because it was downier than the groundsel tree.

Guelder Rose, English   *Viburnum opulus* var. *sterile* L. Mason sent plants to Washington when he returned Washington's carriage, 1785. Guilder and Gelder also.

Guelder Rose, Virginian   *Spiraea opulifolia* L. or *Physocarpus opulifolius* (L.) Maxim. Bartram to Collinson.

Guernsey Lily   See *Nerine sarniensis* Herb. Collinson to Custis.

Guinea Corn   *Panicum maximum* Jacq. Requested by Collinson.

Gum, Black   *Nyssa sylvatica* Marsh. Collinson requested from Custis, 1742.

Gum, Sour   Marshall's upland Tupelo, *Nyssa sylvatica* Marsh. Collinson to Bartram on the gum trees: "each a distinct genus. Consult *Flora Virginica*." 1742.

Gum, Sweet   *Liquidambar styraciflua* L.

Gymnocladus dioica Koch.   Formerly G. *canadensis* L. and M. Marshall's "Guilandina dioica or Bonduc or Nickar," Kentucky coffee or Kentucky mahogany tree. Collinson requested seeds of the bonduc tree from Bartram, 1762, "which thou picked up on thy rambles on the Ohio."
   Clayton requested seed of the Canada bonduc of Bartram, 1763. Washington was asked for seeds. A large Kentucky coffee tree stands today near Bartram's house in Kingsessing.

H

Halesia carolina **L.** Silverbell tree. Named for Reverend Stephen Hales (1677–1761), expert on "vegetable statisticks," who tied his prostrate mare to a gate, while he preached, a goose's windpipe attached to one of her arteries to test blood pressure. Catesby's "Frutex," 69. Collinson to Bartram, 1766: "Nature seems to have exhausted her stores in the Carolinas: in the variety of the *Magnolia,* Loblolly Bays, Allspice, *Stuarties,* Red Acacias, *Halesias,* etc."

Marshall lists two *Halesias;* one with two-winged fruit and one with four-winged. Bishop Compton's "Snow-drop Tree," reintroduced by Collinson from seeds raised by Gordon, 1762.

Offered as snow-drop tree by Prince's. As *Halesia tetraptera* by Bartram's. One ordered by Washington.

Halesia carolina L. Catesby's *Frutex,*
Plate 64, Vol. I, and very likely
Banister's *Frutex,* Silverbell Tree

Hamamelis virginiana **L.** Witch hazel. Marshall says, "remarkable for being in bloom late in the fall." Kalm, 1748, noted it in blossom in October. John Clayton sent it, 1743, to Catesby "in a case of earth from Virginia. It arrived at Christmas and was then in full blossom." Catesby Appendix Plate 2.

"Harebell or English Hyacinth" Formerly *Hyacinthus nonscriptus* L. Now *Scilla nonscripta* Hoff. and Link. Skipwith.

Haw, Black *Viburnum prunifolium* L. "And a specimen of the Black Haw in flower and leaf, for this we know not," Collinson asked Bartram, 1738.

Haw, Red Jefferson wrote from Paris for a "cupful each of the red and and black haws . . ." Marshall's hawthorns are under *Mespilus,* beginning with the cockspur hawthorn as *Mespilus coccinea.* Jefferson considered the cockspur hawthorn "our common one." Now *Crataegus crus-galli* L.

Haw, Possum Possums were allowed two haws: *Ilex decidua* Walt. and *Viburnum nudum* L.

Hawthorn See *Crataegus,* and good luck.

Hazel See *Corylus.* American hazelnut is *Corylus americana* Walt. Dwarf filbert or cuckold nut is *Corylus cornuta* Marsh. Collinson asks Bartram if he has a hazel nut of "the odd kind . . . found in the forks of the Schuylkill beyond the Blue Mountains . . . different from the Cuckold's Nut, which I take to be your common sort?" Bartram says not so and sends nuts of the other.

Hedeoma pulegioides **L.** Pennyroyal. Kalm was advised to drink it as tea for a cold and to rub it on limbs for pain.

Hedera helix **L.** English ivy. Kalm, 1748, noted it little used; other wall-coverings preferred. *Hedera quinquefolia,* Kalm's name for Virginia creeper, which he observed in quantity, is now *Parthenocissus quinquefolia* Planch. Kalm's *Hedera arborea* is now *Ampelopsis arborea* (L.) Koehne. Greater use of English ivy was planned from abroad by William Hamilton, 1785.

Hedges A never-failing project with eighteenth-century American landowners. Where stone walls offered a God-sent solution for clearing fields, hedges could be ornamental: lilacs, clipped hemlock, "Virginia cedar," eglantine roses combined with juniper, etc. Where stumps were in plenty, they could be used as fences in long frantic snarls across the fields. Logs or split-rail fences were used, but a cheaper and more natural barrier was desirable. English thorn was imported by Washington; Virginia thorn planted by Jefferson. Thorny locust was considered, especially the "red Acacia." Virginia cedars were closely ranked. Thorny vines were sought. The ha-ha, a fence sunk in a ditch, was used near the house by Washington to keep cattle and deer away without seeming to. Box was used for edging, never so large as to make a hedge. Collinson advised Custis to consider protective hedging for young plants of "your cedar . . . Phileria or Yaupon Bays or Laurell . . ."

Hedysarum coronarium **L.** French honeysuckle. Requested by Aiton of Humphry Marshall for the King's Garden, 1789. The Lambolls to Bartram. Washington's "Scarlet or French Honeysuckle as my gardener calls it and which he says blows all summer" was planted at each column of the covered ways and "against the circular walls between the store house etc. and the two new Necessaries."

Helenium Sneezeweed. *H. autumnale* L.

Helianthemum Rock rose. Custis. Bartram to Collinson.

Helianthus annus **L.** Sunflower. Kalm says Indians put seeds in corn soup.

Helianthus multiflorus. Curtis
Botanical Magazine

Helianthus tuberosus L.   Jerusalem artichoke.

Helichrysum arenarium D.C.   Yellow everlasting. Bartram's "Elychrisum," as in " 'erbs." Lady Skipwith's "Goldilocks." Custis from Collinson.

Heliotrope *Heliotropium peruvianum* L. From Paris by Jefferson, 1786: "The smell rewards the care."

Helonias bullata L.   Swamp pink. Requested of Marshall, 1789, for the King's Garden by Aiton through Sir Joseph Banks. Bartram sent it to Linnaeus, 1753, and inquired, "Pray, how doth our friend Kalm go on with his history of our country's plants?"

Hellebore, Black *Helleborus niger* L. Christmas rose.

Hellebore, Stinking Black   Bearsfoot. *Helleborus feotidus* L. Skipwith.

Helleborus viridis L.   From England to New England and naturalized. Hellebore is an ancient name for a plant supposed to cure madness. A powerful cathartic and vermifuge, and a remedy for coughing cattle, it exerted a fascination in household medicine. Catesby's "Lily-leaved Hellebore or *Helleborine lilifolio*" takes us to the orchids. The "Red Helleborine," pictured by William Bartram, Collinson received from Bartram, 1756.
Arethusa bulbosa L. and *Calopogon pulchellus* (Salisb.) R. Br. may be the "great and small hellebores" requested by Collinson, 1734.

Herbs   From about 1730, when Americans continued to ignore the initial *h* in "herb" and the rest of the English-speaking world began to pronounce it, nearly two hundred years passed before formally artistic small gardens were devoted entirely to herbs for their aesthetic and aromatic qualities, while their use in cooking was popularized. Please see under Kitchen Garden.

Herb Twopence *Lysimachia nummularia* L. In a sod from Bartram to Collinson, "very acceptable."

Hesperis matronalis L. Rocket. Sweet rocket. Dames' violets. 1738, Skipwith. The Lambolls to Bartram, 1762.

Hibiscus Rose mallow

Using M'Mahon's list as our guide, we find him offering, under "plants": *Hibiscus palustris, H. moscheutos, H. speciosus, H. virginicus, H. militaris.* Under "shrubs": *Althaea frutex,* Hort., Syrian ketmia, "many varieties double and single."

H. palustris L. is swamp rose. "Marsh-mallow," mallow rose, sea hollyhock.

H. syriacus L. is shrubby althaea. Rose-of-Sharon in America.

H. militaris L. is halberd-leaved hibiscus.

H. moscheutos L. Swamp rose, mallow rose, wild cotton. The Duke of Argyle, through Dr. Mitchell to Bartram, would like "the large Ketmia with flowers like Cotton."

H. trionum L. Flower of an hour, bladder ketmia. The Lambolls to Bartram. Skipwith.

H. esculentus L. Okra. Noted by Kalm: "reckoned a dainty . . . especially by the negroes." From the West Indies. Mentioned by Lady Skipwith.

H. coccineus Walt. Bartram's "a most elegant flowering plant. Flowers large of a spendid crimson colour." Washington ordered one, 1792. Lady Skipwith's "Crimson Mallow."

Hibiscus speciosus. Superb Hibiscus. Curtis *Botanical Magazine*

Hibiscus syriacus. Shrubby Althaea. Jefferson's Althaea. Curtis *Botanical Magazine*

Collinson compliments William Bartram on his painting of the "crimson Hibiscus." Asks for seeds from Charleston where they *"must* ripen."

H. rosa-sinensis L. Collinson saw Miller's *"Ketmia sinensis,"* the double China rose, in flower in 1767. Collinson explains that a plant looking like a mallow but with a seed vessel like a pod is "Ketmia."

H. manigot L. Reckoned the same as *H. coccineus* Walt.

H. speciosus Ait. Curtis Vol. V, Plate 360: "native of Carolina." Dr. Fothergill, 1778. William Hamilton had it from Humphry Marshall, 1799. Dr. Fothergill is obliged to Bartram for the "orange coloured Hibiscus," 1774.

Hickory *Carya*

C. illinoensis (Wang.) K. Koch. Pecan.

C. aquatica Michx. f. Bitter pecan.

C. cordiformis (Wang.) K. Koch. Bitter pignut.

C. ovata (Mill.) K. Koch. Shagbark.

C. lacinosa (Michx.) Loud. Big shell bark.

C. tomentose Nutt. Mockernut. White-heart hickory.

C. glabra (Mill.) Smooth pignut.

C. ovalis (Wang.) Sarg. Sweet pignut.

Washington planted in 1785 "a row of the Shellbark Hickory Nutt" and wrote, "Planted in that square of my Botanical Garden . . . 95 of the Gloucester hiccory nut . . . also 21 of the Illinois Nuts . . ." 1786. Jefferson asked for "Illinois nuts" to be planted, 1786. Collinson received "Hickerys" from Custis, 1735. Jefferson asked that "Gloster hiccory" be sent from Bartram to Paris, 1786. He seems to have planted all known hickories at Monticello. Catesby was much taken with the "hiccory Tree," which had appeared in Parkinson's *Theatrum Botanicum* and was universally popular. Indians "draw oil from the kernels . . ." Hogs and wild animals benefit. Wood is of much use for tools for agriculture: saplings make the best barrel hoops for tobacco, rice and tar.

Holly See *Ilex.*

Hollyhock *Althaea rosea* L. Lady Skipwith had "a variety," as did Jefferson.

Holly, Sea *Eryngium maritimum* L. "Eringo or Sea Holly is what you call Rattlesnake Root"; Collinson to Custis.

"Holy Oke" Lady Skipwith's "American Ketmia," Miller's fourth sort, was sent her by the "name of Holy Oke." "American Ketmia with a Papaw leaf and a large yellow flower having a purple bottom, a pyramidal six-cornered fruit and round seeds of a flat taste."

Honesty *Lunaria annua* L. The Lambolls to Bartram.

Honey Locust *Gleditsia triacanthos* L. Washington planted one by the South Garden House.

Honeysuckle Blanket word covering *Lonicera, Azalea,* even *Glycine.* Marshall lists seven American *"Lonicers,* Honeysuckle or Woodbine":

"Lonicera caroliniana Carolina scarlet trumpet-flowered Honeysuckle."

"*Lonicera virginiana* Virginian scarlet Honeysuckle."
"*Lonicera sempervirens* Evergreen Honeysuckle."
"*Lonicera canadensis* Canadian dwarf-cherry Honeysuckle."
"*Lonicera Diervilla* Yellow flowering *Diervilla.*"
"*Lonicera marylandica* Maryland scarlet *Lonicera.*"
"*Lonicera symphoricarpos* Indian Currants. St. Peter's Wort."
Under "*Azalea,* Upright Honeysuckle" Marshall has three:
"*Azalea nudiflora* Red-flowered azalea."
"*Azalea viscosa* White Sweet Azalea."
"*Azalea viscosa palustris* Swamp Azalea."

Catesby's Plate 57 is of the "upright honeysuckle," which "rises with two or three straight stiff stems, with white, red or purplish pleasantly scented flowers." He has seen it in London at Mr. Collinson's in Peckham and Mr. Bacon's at Hoxton. Lady Skipwith has red trumpet honeysuckle, English honeysuckle and French honeysuckle. Washington has "Scarlet or French." Jefferson has "Wild Honeysuckle," 1766, at Shadwell. He ordered six "monthly honeysuckle" from Prince, 1791. Sowed *L. alpigena* L., 1810. He listed "*Azalea nudiflora,* Upright Honeysuckle," among Virginia ornamentals.

Prince's, 1771, offers "Standing American Honeysuckle;" in 1790 also the "Late White American Honeysuckle."

Bartram's offers:
"*Lonicera canadensis* Canada Honeysuckle, red and yellow."
"*Lonicera periclymenium* Virginia Scarlet Honeysuckle."
"*Lonicera chamaecerasus* Dwarf Cherry Honeysuckle."
"*Lonicera indora* 'Twines around and ascends trees.' "
"*Lonicera symphoricarpos,* in winter garnished with clusters of red berries."
M'Mahon's offer four *Lonicera:*
"The Common English Honeysuckle *L. Periclymenum*";
"The Yellow Upright *L. Diervilla*";
"St. Peter's Wort *L. symphoricarpa*";
"Italian *L. caprifolium.*"

Hop *Humulus lupinus* L.

Hop Hornbeam *Ostrya virginiana* (Mill.) K. Koch. Ironwood.

Hop Trefoil *Trifolium agrarium* L. Used to improve the soil. Thomas Jefferson. George Washington.

Hornbeam *Carpinus caroliniana* Walt.

Horse Chestnut *Aesculus hippocastanum* L.

Horseradish *Amoracia rusticana* L. Washington. Jefferson.

Horseweed *Collinsonia.* Bartram says "horses are very greedy of it" and it is good for galled backs. The root is commended for women's afterpains, boiled and drunk in a concoction. *Collinsonia canadensis* L. is citronella.

House Leek *Sempervivum tectorum* L.

Hound's-Tongue *Cynoglossum officinalis* L.

Houseplants   When few had greenhouses, hothouses, glass houses or even, like Jefferson, a glassed-in porch, "houseplants" were treasured.   Lady Skipwith kept hers in the southern windows of a large upstairs hall: "Oranges, Lemons, Limes, Oleanders, Dwarf Myrtle, Rose Geranium, *Chrysanthemum indicum* . . . Alstroemerias, Prickly Lantanas."

Houstonia serpyllifolia Michx.   Painted by W. Bartram for Fothergill, 1766.

Hyacinths   Eighteenth-century hyacinths were not yet "florists' " flowers. They came from the fields of their native areas or from years of cultivation without improving.   Pictures of hyacinths in Furber's *Months of Flowers* are more like what we associate today with English bluebells.

Lady Skipwith lists four sorts of hyacinths: double blue and blush-colored hyacinths; grape hyacinths and feathered hyacinths.   Sir Peyton ordered from Richmond three "double variegated fall hyacinths."   Jefferson's *Hyacinthus comosus* bloomed 1791, his purple hyacinths in 1766, his feathered hyacinths in 1782.

M'Mahon's lists:

"*H. orientalis* Garden hyacinth common."

"*H. monstrosus* Feathered garden hyacinth."   Sent to Jefferson. See below.

"*H. comosus* Two coloured garden hyacinth."

"*H. non scriptus* European harebells."

"*H. cernuus* Bending hyacinth."

H. serotinus Late flowering hyacinth."

"*H. amethystinus* Amethyst-coloured hyacinth."

"*H. romanus* Roman Grape hyacinth."

"*H. muscari* Musk Grape hyacinth." See below.

"*H. botryoides* Blue Grape hyacinth."

"*H. racemosus* Clustered Grape hyacinth."

As we know now, *Muscari botryoides* Mill. is the common grape hyacinth. *Muscari comosum var. monstrosum* Hort. is the feathered hyacinth.

Hydrangea arborescens L.   Our handsome native hydrangea.   Bartram's, as "ornamental in shrubberies, flowers white in large corymbs."   Washington, 1792.   A monument at Mill Hill marks where it first bloomed in England.

Hydrastis canadensis L.   Yellow root.   "Billy sent me a delightful drawing of what is called with you the 'Yellow Root' . . . It seems a new genus . . ."   Collinson, 1763.   Miller wrote to Bartram, 1755, that he had the yellow root and was calling it *Warneria.*

Hymenocallis occidentalis (Le Conte) Kunth.   American spider lily.

Hypericum angustifolium   Evergreen "adorned with fine yellow flowers." Bartram's.   Washington.

Collinson grew fifteen kinds of *Hypericum,* one with pale red fruit that Dillwyn calls *H. canadense.*

H. aureum Bartram.   Bartram's.   Ordered by Washington.

H. calcinum L.   Rose-of-Sharon in England.

Hypericum calycinum. Curtis *Botanical Magazine*

H. Kalmianum L. Collinson's *"H. angustifolium pensylvanicum.* Smells like *Reseda."* Sent by Bartram, 1757.

H. perforatum L. Bartram found the "common English Hypericum a pernicious weed."

H. prolificum L. Collinson's *"H. frutescens pensylvanicum."*

H. virginicum L. Marsh St. Johnswort. Kalm observed it in a bog. Collinson lists "two shrub St. John's-Worts from Virginia." Marshall's "Virginia shrubby hypericum."

Hyssopus officinalis L. Jefferson.

I

Iberis *I. amara* L. Annual candytuft. M'Mahon's.

I. unbellata L. Common annual candytuft. M'Mahon's.

I. odorata L. "Purple sweet scented." M'Mahon's.

I. linifolis Flax-leaved. M'Mahon's. Collinson.

I. sempervirens L. Perennial candytuft. Collinson. "A new candytuft."

I. semperflorens L. Perennial, evergreen. M'Mahon's *I. rotundifolis* (his only perennial *Iberis*). Collinson. Lady Skipwith grew "Candytuft." Curtis had purple candytuft and Gibralter candytuft.

Iceplant *Mesembryanthemum.* Skipwith. Jefferson: "Should be raised in pots." Curtis has six "Fig Marigolds."

Ilex Holly.

I. aquifolium L. English holly. Listed as Virginian by Jefferson.

I. opaca Ait. American holly, with duller leaves but evergreen and spiny.

I. vomitoria Ait. Cassine.

I. montana T. and G. Mountain winterberry.

I. decidua Walt. Possum haw.

I. verticillata L. Gray. Winter berry. Black alder.

I. glabra L. Gray. Inkberry. Bitter gallberry.

I. coriacea (Pursh.) Chapm. Sweet gallberry.

Marshall lists under "Ilex. Holly-Tree" three species:

"Ilex aquifolium. American Common Holly," which he says grows in moist ground in Maryland and New Jersey;

"Ilex Cassine. Dahoon or Carolina Holly," with spiny leaves;

"Ilex canadensis. Canadian or Hedge Hog Holly," some with variegated leaves.

Collinson has *"Ilex cassine.* Dahoon Holly," which Catesby sent "over." Also "Hedgehog Holly," sent to Custis. Kalm reported *Ilex aquifolium,* growing in wet places, evergreen and rare, was dried, boiled in beer and taken for pleurisy.

The Lambolls sent "holly berries" to Bartram. Washington planted holly in "clumps" in his shrubberies. He was constantly sowing and moving holly trees.

Ilex vomitoria L. Catesby for Plate 57 says a strong decoction of dried leaves in a pot, drunk and disgorged many times, is used by the American Indians for a clean-out every spring. The ritual is accompanied by burning all bedding at the same time.

Ilex verticillata Gray. Black alder. Winterberry. Probably the "Red Berry" Washington looked for when riding out to look for movable shrubs and trees. The inner bark was supposed to be good as poultices on ripening tumors.

Iceplant. *Mesembryanthemum aureum.* Fig Marigold. Curtis *Botanical Magazine*

Illinois Nut   Pecan. *Carya illinoensis* (Wang.) K. Koch. Jefferson. Washington.

Indian   Used to describe a plant's origin or its uses, "Indian" does not seem to have confused anyone in the eighteenth century when applied to plants from either the East or West Indies, from China, South America, or as used by the American Indians. The list is long:

Indian Arrow-wood *Viburnum dentatum* L.

Indian Bean *Catalpa bignonioides* Walt.

Indian Cherry *Rhamnus caroliniana* Walt.

Indian Corn *Zea mays.*

Indian Cress *Tropaeolum majus* L.⎤ Our garden Nasturtium, from
                 Tropaeolum minus L.⎦ Peru to England, 1569

Indian Cucumber-root *Medeola virginiana* L.

Indian Cup or Jug *Sarracenia purpurea* L.

Indian Currant *Symphoricarpos vulgaris* or *S. orbiculatus* Moench. Coralberry.

Indian Fig *Opuntia vulgaris* Mill.

Indian Frills *Canna indica* L.

Indian Hemp *Apocynum cannabinum* L.

Indian Mallow *Abutilon theophrasti* Medic. Natzd. from India.

Indian Paint *Lithospermum canescens* (Michx.) Lehm. One of the puccoons.

Indian Physic *Gillenia trifoliata* L. Moench. Bowman's root.

Indian Physic *Gillenia stipulata* (Muhl.) Baill. American ipecac. Indian physic in Jefferson's State of Virginia is *Spiraea trifoliata.*

Indian Pink *Dianthus sinensis* L. Jefferson. Lady Skipwith.

Indian Pink. Catesby's Plate 78, Vol. II. Now *Silene virginica* L.

Indian Pink *Spigelia marilandica* L.
Indian Pink *Silene virginica* L.
Indian Pipe *Monotropa uniflora* L.
Indian Plum *Diospyros virginiana* L.
Indian Poke *Veratrum viride* Ait. False Hellebore.
Indian Rice *Zizania palustris* L.
Indian Sweetmeat. Black Haw. *Viburnum prunifolium* L.
Indian Shot *Canna indica* L.
Indian Strawberry *Duchesnia indica* (Andr.) Focke. Natzd. from Asia.
Indian Tea *Ilex vomitoria* Ait.
Indian Tobacco *Lobelia inflata* L.
Indian Turnip *Arisaema tryphylla* or *A. atrorubens* (Ait.) Blume.
Indian Wheat *Fagopyrum tataricum* Gaertn.
Indian Paintbrush *Castilleja coccinea* (L.) Spreng.

***Impatiens balsamina* L.** Garden balsam.

***Impatiens biflora* Walt** Jewelweed. Noted by Kalm, 1748, as attractive to hummingbirds.

Indigo *Indogofera leptosepala* Nutt. Bartram sent a hollow stick filled with "indigo seed" to Jared Eliot as from his son William.
Indigo, Bastard *Lotus corniculatus* L. Horned bastard indigo.
Indigo, Shrubby bastard. Indigo bush. *Amphora fruticosa* L.
Indigo, False *Baptisia tinctoria* (L.) R. Br. wild indigo.

Ipecac, American Ipecacuanha *Gillenia stipulata* (Muhl.) Baill. Collinson received "ipecacuanha" from Bartram and reserved it for himself, with a plant of lady's-slipper, giving the remaining contents of two boxes to Lord Petre and to Catesby. Ewan thinks this was *Gillenia stipulata.*

Ipecac, Wild Virginia, Carolina. *Euphorbia ipecacuanhae* L.
Byrd's remedy. "We saw abundance of ipecacuanha in the woods . . . I persuaded Meanswell to take vomit of it . . ."

Ipomoea
I. coccinea Scarlet ipomoea. Red morning glory (Natzd. from S.A.).
I. quamoclit L. (Introduced from Trop. Am.) Cypress Vine.
I. purpurea L. Our common morning glory from tropical America.

Iris M'Mahon listed:
I. pumila Dwarf flag iris. Jefferson "Dwarf Flag."
I. susiana Chalcedonian iris. Jefferson's. "Dwarf Persian." Sir Peyton's "Three Persian iris."
I. florentina Florentine (a variety of *I. germanica*). The Lambolls to Bartram. Logan to Bartram.
I. cristata Ait. Crested iris. Dwarf. Collinson.
I. germanica L. German iris.
I. pseud-acorus L. Yellow iris. Lady Skipwith's "Large Flag or Flower de Luce." Jefferson.
I. siberica L. Siberian iris.

Iris versicolor. Particolored Iris.
Curtis *Botanical Magazine*

I. versicolor L. Various-colored "Blue Flag." Gray. Custis to Collinson.

I. virginica Muhl. Virginia iris. "Southern Blue Flag." Gray. Lady Skipwith's evergreen purple flag? *I. prismatica Pursh.*

I. fulva Ker. Red iris. Lady Skipwith's "Bulbous flag, red flower."

I. verna L. Dwarf or violet iris. Jefferson's violet flag. Banister's discovery. Collinson.

Itea virginica L. Tassel-white. Sweet spires. Virginia willow. Collinson from Bartram, 1758. Jefferson listed it as a Virginia ornamental and requested seeds sent to him in Paris, 1786.

Ironwood *Ostrya virginiana* (Mill.) K. Koch.

"Ivy" *Kalmia latifolia* L. "Ignorantly called ivy" by Jefferson, Washington and others.

Ivy, American *Pathenocissus quinquefolia* (L.) Planch.

Ivy, English *Hedera helix* L.

Ivy, Kenilworth *Cymbalaria muralis* Gaertn.

Ivy, Poison *Rhus radicans* L.

Ixia Seems to have been another of those blanket names in the eighteenth century.

Ixia Bermudiana Lady Skipwith's name for her blackberry lily, *Belamcanda chinensis* D.C. Blackberry lily was once called *Pardanthus chinensis* Ker. or "Leopard Lily."

Ixia caelestina "Bartram's Celestial Lily," painted by William Bartram for Collinson, 1768. Now *Salpingostylis caelestina* (Bartr.) Small. William Bartram wrote, 1767, about "Purple flowered Ixia of St. John's River, East Florida." Sent to Benjamin Rush.

J

Jacea Throatwort. Recommended medically by Bartram. Over four feet tall, with roots like hickory nuts, long, narrow, alternate leaves and a long spike of purple flowers. Collinson received three from Dr. Witt: "Early Jacea, Elegant Jacea, and Gigantic Jacea." Asked Bartram for specimens "as they grow in your country." In 1749 he has "a new Jacea with hoary rough leaves" from some mixed seeds from Virginia. Miller's *Jacea* are under *Centaurea,* which gets us across the Atlantic and into an assortment of centaurys, like sweet sultan, bachelor's-button, knapweed and scabiosa, all now "escaped" or "introduced" to our fields and roadsides. *Centaurea jacea* L., however, was here, with a sketch made of it, in 1766. And there is a *Centaurea americana* Nutt., which might have made it with Dr. Witt. Which illustrates the difficulties of the eager early gardeners.

Jack-in-the-Pulpit *Arisaema atrorubens* (Ait.) Blume is the large one. *Arisaema triphyllum* L. Schott. is the small one. *Arisaema draconitum* (L.) Schott. is Dragonroot. Dragonarum.

Jacob's-Ladder See *Polemonium.*

Jacobaea *Senecio jacobaea* L. Stinking Willie. From Bartram to Collinson: "We have four or five beautiful species of Jacobaea . . . valued by the Indians and back inhabitants for the cure of the same diseases that the ancients used their Jacobaea for, though none of them knew the name of the plant."

Jalap Jalap is the cathartic species of *Convolvulus.* Wild jalap is a name for the May apple,. *Podophyllum peltatum* L. Now used against skin cancer.

Jalapa *Mirabilia jalapa* L. Four o'clock. Marvel of Peru.

Jamestown Weed *Datura stramonium* L.

Jasmine, Arabian *Jasminum sambac* Soland. White turning purple. Collinson to Custis. Jefferson.

Jasmine Jessamine. *Jasminum officinale* L. White. The jasmine of India.

Jasmine, Cape *Gardenia jasminoides* Ellis. Formerly Linnaeus' *Gardenia florida.*

Jasmine, Italian and Spanish *Jasminum grandiflorum* L. Collinson. The Lambolls to Bartram.

Jasmine, Yellow Or jessamine. *Gelsemium sempervirens* Ait. Carolina yellow jessamine. *Bignonia sempervirens* in Jefferson's "Notes." Yellow jessamy in Catesby, Plate 53, who said it lost its leaves in winter, although Parkinson listed it as evergreen. Scarce in Virginia. Carolina full of it. Catesby called it *"Gelseminum sive Jasminum luteum odoratum virginianum scandens sempervirens."*

Jasmine. The Yellow Jasmine.
Catesby's Plate 53, Vol. I

Jeffersonia diphylla **(L.) Pers.** Once *Podophyllum dyphyllum,* reported, 1791, by Dr. Moses Marshall to Sir Joseph Banks as growing in great plenty 250 miles west of Philadelphia. William Hamilton, 1796, thanks Humphry Marshall for "Podophyllum or Jeffersonia."

Jersey Tea *Ceanothus americanus* L. Red root. Marshall's *Grove* says used to cure "slight Gonorrhaeas" and as substitute for Bohea tea, "from which it acquired its name."

Jerusalem

Jerusalem Artichoke	*Helianthus tuberosus* L.
Jerusalem Cowslip	*Pulmonaria officinalis* L.
Jerusalem Cherry	*Solanum pseudo-capsicum* L.
Jerusalem Cross	*Lychnis chalcedonica* L.
Jerusalem Oak	*Chenopodium bothrys* L.
Jerusalem Sage	*Phlomis fruticosa* L.

"Jerusalem" was a name like "Turkey," which could have been applied as assuming an origin, or a stopover trading place in a long route. Or it may have implied an especial praise for a "sovereign" remedy. As, for instance, Jerusalem oak was recommended by Colonel Corbin in 1759 for use in the care of slave children. "To be well looked after and give them every spring and fall the Jerusalem Oak seed for a week together." A plantation remedy for worms.

Jonquil *Narcissus jonquilla* L.

Judas Tree *Cercis canadensis* L.

Juglans

Juglans cinerea L. Butternut. White walnut. Kalm. Bartram. Washington. Jefferson. Collinson.

Juglans nigra L. Black walnut. Kalm. Bartram to Collinson. Jefferson. Washington.

Juglans regia L. Persian or English walnut. Washington. Jefferson.

July Flower Gilliflower, which see also. The Lambolls, 1762, to John Bartram, a collection of "July Flowers, or stock gillyflowers," as follows: "dwarf stock July flower; striped stock July flower; queen stock July flower; purple stock July flower." All *Matthiola* varieties, as is "Brumpton Stock," which arrived in the same package.

Matthiola incana R.Br. is the common stock.

Matthiola incana var. *annua* is ten-weeks stock.

Matthiola incana var. *autumnalis* is Brompton stock.

Matthiola bicorna D.C. is purplish, fragrant at night, closed by day.

Parkinson had "Double and Single Garden Stock Gilliflowers" of several colors, some striped.

Juniper *Juniperus virginiana* L. Red cedar. Savin. Collinson wrote Bartram, 1735, "Our curious botanists are sadly perplexed about the difference between Red and White Cedars." No wonder, since our white cedar is not a juniper but a cypress. Kalm, who saw avenues to houses of considerable size made with double rows of "Virginia Cedar" trimmed to "leave a fine crown," finally solved it geographically. The Virginia cedar is a juniper and takes over for the north the function the white cedar, *Chamaecyparis thyoides* (L.) B.S.P., performs for the south.

K

Kalmia In 1734 Collinson asked Custis for "a sort of Laurel or Bay that bears bunches of flowers not much unlike the Laurus Tinus . . . by some improperly called Ivy and if the sheep eat it it kills them . . ." Custis sent a "tub of laurel plants."

"Please to remember," Collinson wrote Bartram, 1736, "to get some strong plants of your Ivy or Bay . . . and plant in a box to stand a year or two . . . till it flowers in the box . . ." For, "as to the Bay Laurel called Ivy . . . the seed is so small and chaffy . . . none grows." In 1743 Collinson was bemoaning the loss on shipboard, due to rats, of "the Great Rhododendron and lesser Kalmias."

Kalm arrived in America, September 17, 1748, to find a shrub already named in his honor. In 1761 Collinson reported his broad-leaved kalmia (*K. latifolia* L.) in flower. In 1766 Collinson thanks Bartram for the "pretty thyme leaved Kalmia," (*K. angustifolia* L.). Washington planted "Ivy" ("Ivy vulgo" to Collinson). Jefferson in 1786 asked for *Kalmia latifolia* and *Kalmia angustifolia* to be sent to France. In 1781 he bracketed them as "Dwarf laurel, called Ivy with us."

Kentucky Coffee Tree   Bonduc. *Gymnocladus dioica* Koch. Bartram. Washington.

Ketmia   Old name for hibiscus and mallow. Collinson said a plant looking like a mallow but with pods is a ketmia.

King's Cure-All.   A back-country name for *Oenothera biennis* L. Virginia tree primrose, made much of by Parkinson. Requested of Custis by Collinson.

Kitchen Garden   The kitchen garden *per se* did not originate with Parkinson's *Paradisus* but it was certainly defined by it. Separate from the "garden of pleasant flowers" and from the orchard proper, but with its own fruit-bearing trees, shrubs and bushes," it contained "all sortes of herbes as rootes and fruits that are usually planted in gardens to serve for the use of the table." And, "as many take pleasure in the sight and knowledge of other herbes that are Physicall, and much more in their property and virtues . . . I should add a Physicke Garden or Garden of Simples . . ." This, Parkinson says, would result in a "quadripart complement of whatsoever arte or nature, necessitie or delight could affect." Whereupon into the kitchen garden he puts all vegetables including "pot-herbes," "sweet-herbes" and "such herbes as are of most necessary uses for the Country Gentlewomen's houses."

Koelreuteria paniculata Laxm.   China tree. Pride of India. Golden rain. Introduced 1763. Washington. Jefferson. Prince's. Madame de Tessé sent seeds to Jefferson, 1809.

L

Laburnum   One of those general names for a shrub or tree with dangling yellow blooms.

Laburnum anagyroides Medikus. Golden chain tree, formerly *Cytisus laburnum* L. Scotch laburnum is now *Laburnum alpinum* Griesb., formerly Miller's *Cytisus alpinus*. Important, because our familiar laburnum was grown under several names. Prince's, 1790, offered "Leburnum with yellow flowers." Laburnum sent to Custis by Collinson in 1735, and thought lost, "came up well" in 1736 and grew to four or five feet. Collinson advises proper distances to let them grow to "pretty large trees." Jefferson grew it as "Cytisus laburnum." He sowed laburnum in 1807 "in the six circular beds of shrubs with one or two seeds of the honeysuckle of Lewis's river." Washington ordered in 1792 from Bartram's "*Citisus laburnum*. Foliage delicate, embellished with pendant clusters of splendid yellow papillonaeous flowers."

Lactuca sativa L.   Lettuce. See chapter on vegetables.

Lady Pease   *Lathyrus odorata* L. Skipwith. Jefferson.

Lady's-Slipper   *Cyprepedium,* which see for the several sorts. Skipwith. Bartram. Collinson. Lawson.

Lantana, Prickly   Lantana grown by Lady Skipwith as a house plant, is *Lantana camara* L., the South American name for these shrubs and Linnaeus' name for the prickly sort. There were many varieties, hers probably West Indian, as she had friends there. "Very brilliant, seldom without flowers." Sounds like what was called *L. sanguinea* Medikus.

Lantana aculeata. Prickly Lantana.
Curtis *Botanical Magazine*

Larch   *Larix.*

    L. laricina (Du Roi) K. Koch. American or black larch. Tamarack, hackmatack.

    L. decidua Mill. European Larch. Kalm, in 1748, united all our friends in one comment: "Having read in Mr. Miller's *Botanical Dictionary* that Mr. Peter Collinson had a particular larch tree from America in his garden, I asked Mr. Bartram . . . he himself had sent it to Mr. Collinson. He found the cones in New Jersey. I afterwards saw it in great numbers in Canada."

    Marshall puts larches under pines, *Pinus-Larix,* and gives three sorts — the red American larch, the white and the black, differing only in the color of their cones.

    Collinson asked Bartram, 1742, if he had found "no old trees that yielded turpentine?" The Venetians, he said, made the best turpentine from this tree, called "the Venice Turpentine."

    Bartram writes, 1753, that he and his "little botanist," Billy, will journey to visit Dr. Colden and collect on the way the seed of Balm of Gilead and *Larix.*

    Jefferson did not plant "Larix seeds" until 1812. As an ornamental, the larch came slowly into its own in American parks. It would seem to have appealed chiefly to those planting "clumps" for varying foliages. Washington ordered larches from Bartram's, 1792.

Larks' Heels   Parkinson's garden delphiniums.

Larks' Spurs   Yellow. Parkinson's Indian cresses. Our nasturtiums.

Larkspurs *Delphinium*

Custis sent our wild larkspurs to Collinson. Either *D. exaltatum* Ait. or *D. carolinianum* Walt.

D. ajacis L. is the annual English garden delphinium. The gigantic hybrids of Oriental imports were still to come.

Lathyrus latifolius L.   The perennial common everlasting pea. Jefferson. Washington.

Lathyrus odoratus L.   The annual common garden sweet pea. Lady peas. Painted lady peas. Skipwith. Washington. Jefferson. M'Mahon's.

Laurel   Blanket word in the eighteenth century covering a variety of ever-green-leaved trees, shrubs, creepers and vines. See *Epigaea, Kalmia, Laurus, Rhododendron.*

Laurus   Marshall lists four under "*Laurus,* The Bay Tree."

  "*L. Benzoin* The Benjamin Tree or Spice-Wood." (Today *Lindera benzoin* (L.) Blume.)

  "*L. Borbonia* Red-stalked Carolina Bay-Tree." (Today *Persea borbonia* (L.) Spreng.)

  "*L. geniculata* Carolina Spice-wood Tree." (Today *L. geniculata* Walt.)

  "*L. sassafras* The Sassafras Tree." (Today *L. sassafras* L. The *S. officinale* of Nees.)

In 1736 the Duke of Richmond would like some *Laurus sassafras* and Lord Petre would like more. In 1743 Dr. Fothergill proposes to make a distilled water from the flowers, some with water, some, perhaps, with rum. Later, in 1771, he writes to Humphry Marshall that he thinks sassafras bark "a good medicine in various complaints . . . such as seems to arise from a thin, sharp, scorbutic humour . . . cold constitutions or aged people . . . It seems likely to expel wind, correct sharpness of the blood . . . to increase urine and sweat. Attend to it effects . . ."

"Laurus Nova 9"   Requested from France for "Laurus nova 9," Jefferson confessed himself at a loss. Faced with the same request, Lady Skipwith would have resorted at once to Miller to find his ninth *Laurus* is the camphor tree, *Camphora officinarum,* now *Cinnamomum camphora,* which the French lady may, indeed, have intended. Especially as she suggested plants "De Caroline" only if Mr. Jefferson finds himself having to write to Charleston, exactly where this "new" medicinal shrub from the Orient could be expected to be grown.

"*Laurus Borbonia.*"   Ordered from Marshall by William Hamilton, 1796.

Laurustinus   *Viburnum tinus* L. Mediterranean. Collinson to Custis, recommended for a hedge. Collinson clipped his in April.

Lavender *Lavendula vera* D.C. Collinson had *L. vera, L. spica* Cav. (smaller than *L. vera*) and the Spanish *L. stoechas*. New England concerned itself with lavender earlier than elsewhere, although Jefferson planned to grow it.

Lavatera trimestris L. Annual Lavatera. Curtis *Botanical Magazine*

Lavatera Annuals, perennials, shrubs and "tree mallows."
  L. trimestris L. Easy to grow. Effective.
  L. olbia L. A perennial shrub. Jefferson.

Leatherbark, Leatherwood *Dirca palustris* L. Moosewood. Virginia marsh leatherwood. Marshall. Kalm observed moosewood or leatherwood used as cord for binding. Told that root, boiled in water and drunk, becomes a purgative.
  Grown by Collinson as "Thymelea virginica."
  Bartram wrote to Collinson, 1743, of "Leatherbark or Mezereon seen on Captain Isham Randolph's land." Yellowish flowers "abundant enough to be attractive."

Ledum palustre Wild rosemary. Marsh cistus. (Marshall's only *Ledum*.) Requested of Humphry Marshall by William Hamilton, 1796. Collinson 1763.
  (*Ledum groenlandicum* Oeder is Labrador tea. Confusing, as *Ledum palustre* grows in New Jersey. There New Jersey tea is *Ceanothus*.)

Leeks See chapter on vegetables.

Lemon *Citrus limonia* Osbeck. House plants for Lady Skipwith. Greenhouse plants for Washington from Mrs. Carroll.

Leonurus villosus **Desf.** Motherwort.

Lettuce *Lactua sativa* L. See chapter on vegetables.

Leucojum vernum L. and *L. autumnale* L. Spring and Autumn snowflake. Custis. Skipwith.

Leucothoe *L. axillaris* Don. was *Andromeda axillaris* Lam. Marshall. Bartram.
L. catesbaei Gray was *L. axillaris* Michx.
L. populifolia Dipp. was *Andromeda accuminata* Ait.
L. racemosa Gray was *Andromeda racemosa* L.
Just to clear things up.

Liatris spicata L. Willd. Button snakeroot. Blazing star.
Chamaelirium luteum (L.) Gray is also blazing star and rattlesnake root.
In 1735 Dr. Witt sent Collinson "the large Jacea or Blazing Star." (Dr. Ewan says *Liatris spicata.*) Blazing star was sent by the Lambolls to Bartram.

Ligustrum vulgare L. Common privet. Prim.
Kalm saw it everywhere and wondered if it was one of the shrubs "the English have introduced," which it is.

Lilacs *Syringa vulgaris* L. Our dooryard lilacs. Purple and white.
Syringa persica L. Persian lilac. With finer and smaller blossoms and leaves..
   Both sorts introduced into England from Persia, sixteenth century. Collinson wrote Bartram, proposing to send him some, and said Custis had a fine "collection." As these two lilacs, in both purple and white, were the entire range of lilacs possible, Custis must have had them in some quantity. Jefferson had both kinds. Washington moved "two large lilacs" in 1785 to either side of "the North Garden gate" and took up a "clump" beside a grass plat to move it to a shrubbery.

Lilies, American
   "Please to remember all your sorts of lilies as they happen in thy way," Collinson wrote to Bartram, 1734, and added, "Your Spotted Martagons will be very acceptable." "Martagon" was the style of turban worn by Sultan Muhammed I. Applied now to lilies with revolute petals rather than bell-shaped blooms. Collinson, 1736: "The noble Marsh Martagon flowered with me this spring." In 1739 he reported, "the stately Martagon thee . . . found on a bank near Schuylkill . . . six feet high with fifteen flowers."
Dr. Fothergill requested American martagons of Marshall, 1768, saying he has "very few" — hard confession from one with the largest collection of American ferns in England.
Lady Skipwith said her martagons, especially the "Spotted Canada Martagon Lily," were much admired.

Lilium, American
   L. superbum L. American Turk's-cap lily. Pictured handsomely in Thornton's *Temple of Flora,* theatrically but incorrectly set against towering

mountain peaks. This is probably the lily most often requested.

L. canadense L. The wild yellow or Canada lily. Has nodding flowers only slightly reflected, and is probably Collinson's "new yellow Martagon . . . a little between that and a lily . . ." Shown in Catesby.

L. philadelphicum L. Wild red lily. Wood lily. Also much in demand. Catesby's 8. Sent Collinson by Bartram, 1730.

L. catesbaei Walt. Southern red lily. Catesby 58.

L. Michauxii Poir. Southern swamp lily. Carolina Turk's-cap lily. Now *L. carolinianum* Michx. Collinson seems to have grown them all. Jefferson grew *L. canadense* and *L. superbum*.

Lilium, Imported

L. candidum L. Belladonna. Madonna. One of the oldest of garden lilies, first to arrive as Governor Bradford's "fair white lily" at Plymouth. Jefferson. Lady Skipwith. The Lambolls to Bartram.

L. chalcedonicum L. Scarlet Turk's-cap. Called "Fiery Lily" by Jefferson and by Collinson, who sent it to Custis, 1742.

L. pomponium L. The little Turk's-cap. Like *Lilium superbum* but smaller and with disagreeable odor. M'Mahon's.

L. tigrinum L. Tiger lily and *Lilium bulbiferum* L. Both old favorites brought by the settlers and still able to take care of themselves.

Lily Another of the generous blanket names for a wide assortment of eighteenth-century garden flowers. All popular.

Lilium bulbiferum. Orange Lily.
Curtis *Botanical Magazine*

Lillio-Narcissus. Catesby's Plate
A-5. Now *Hymenocallis occidentalis*

Lily, Zephyr, or Atamasco *Zephyranthes atamasco* Herb. Catesby 12.
Lily, Blackberry *Belamcanda chinensis* (L.) D.C. Skipwith. Jefferson.
Canadian Lily of the Valley *Maianthemum canadense* Desf.
Lily, Crown Imperial *Fritillaria imperialis* L.
Lily, Day *Hemerocallis flava* L. and *H. fulva* L.
Lily of the Valley *Convallaria majalis* L.
Lily, Ragged *Pancratium occidentalis* (LeConte) Kunth.
Lily, Spider *Hymenocallis occidentalis* (LeConte) Kunth.
Lily, Trout *Erythronium americanum* Ker.
Lily, Zephyr See Atamasco, above.

Lime *Citrus aurantifolia* Swingle. Grown by Washington from Mrs. Carroll.

Lime Tree See *Tilia* (also called Line-tree).

Lime Tree, Ogeche *Nyssa.* The tupelo. Bartram's.

Limodorum A name for *Calopogon*, "Red Helleborine" to Collinson. Lady Skipwith grew *"limodorum tuberosum* from South Carolina by Jim." Curtis received it in a sod with *Dionaea muscipula* Ellis.

Linaria cymbalaria Mill. Kenilworth ivy.

Linaria vulgaris Mill. Butter-and-eggs. To the reproaches of Collinson, Bartram considered it a nuisance.

Lindera benzoin Now *Benzoin aestivale* Nees.

Linum Flax Garden varieties and fiber-producing.

Liquidambar styraciflua L. Sweet gum. Bilsted. Alligator tree. Bishop Compton's *Styrax virginiana.* Ordered by Jefferson to be sent to Paris.

Liquidambar. Catesby's Plate 65, Vol. II

Listed by him as one of Virginia's useful trees. Collinson thanks Bartram
for sweet gum and wants black gum, too. In 1738 Collinson requests
Bartram to send sweet gum in blossom, "an extraordinary plant," to go to
"some curious botanists in Holland" who "beg this favour in order to settle its botanical character." In the same year Linnaeus also "wants them
much" in a "little bottle of spirits."

Liriodendrum tulipifera L. Tulip tree. Marshall's "Virginian Tulip
Tree," important as he referred to a family of magnolias as "Laurel-leaved
Tulip Tree." Collinson aked Custis for "ones" of the "Flowering Poplar
or Tulip Tree," 1737. Bartram filled several orders for the tulip tree for
Collinson, who liked to give away seeds. In his *Catalogue,* Collinson
writes, 1745, that the tulip tree at Waltham Abbey was ninety-six feet
high and nine feet around. Lord Peterborough's "famous" tree at Parson's
Green died, 1756. In the same year a tulip tree Collinson had given Sir
Charles Wager flowered in his garden just opposite Lord Peterborough's,
"so Parson's Green is not likely to be without a Tulip Tree." All this introduced by Catesby's sketch and seeds sent to Bishop Compton's garden.
Prince's and Bartram's.

Lithospermum canescens (Michx.) Lehm. Indian paint and puccoon.
Other "pucoons": *L. croceum* Fern. and *L. caroliniense* (Walt.) MacM.
Not fancied for gardens of the "curious," although Custis sent it to Collinson, who listed it as "a Bugloss with yellow flowers," a good description.

Liverwort *Hepatica triloba* Choix and *H. acutiloba* D.C. Lady Skipwith
had "single blue" and noted "by sowing the seeds some varieties may be
obtained."

Lobelia cardinalis L. Cardinal flower. One of the showiest contributions
to the English herbaceous border. Jefferson from M'Mahon's. Lafayette
requested from Washington.

Lobelia syphilitica L. Blue rival to the scarlet cardinal flower. Recommended to Colonel William Johnson, early Indian negotiator and admin-
istrator. Linnaeus first made money and reputation in Sweden prescribing
mercury for young dandies. One can see what hopes were aroused by this
Indian "secret." Sir John Hill ordered four pounds of the roots from
Bartram in 1766. Dr. Hope of Edinburgh asked Bartram for seeds at
about the same time. Collinson had "Blue Cardinal" from Bartram, 1751.

Loblolly Loblolly was a sixteenth-century English name for a simple
pudding, something usual and ordinary. Applied to two trees common
in the south, the loblolly bay of North Carolina, *Gordonia lasianthus* (L.)
Ellis, and the loblolly pine, *Pinus taeda* L.

Collinson reported his loblolly bays from Bartram had been stolen from
Mill Hill. The Lambolls sent loblolly bays to Bartram, as did Martha
Logan.

When Bartram's "Franklinia," discovered by John and collected by

Loblolly Bay. Catesby's Plate 44,
Vol. I. Also called by him *Althaea
Floridana*

William and never again seen in the wilds, was sent to Collinson, it was
announced as a new sort of *Gordonia.* L'Heritier, patron of Redouté,
named the new tree *"Gordonia pubescens."* It was later called *Gordonia
alatamaha* Sarg. to commemorate where the Bartrams first saw it.

The loblolly pine still holds its own. The floors of Prestwould, the
Skipwith mansion, are made of the heart of *Pinus taeda* L. Miller says
"Hibiscus with winged seeds Vervain Mallow of Florida with Bay Leaves
slightly crenated" is "commonly called Loblolly Bay in America."

Locust, Black *Robinia pseudo-acacia* L.

Locust, Bristly, Mossy *Robinia hispida* L. Rose acacia.

Locust, Clammy *Robinia viscosa* Vent.

Locust, Honey *Gleditsia triacanthos* L.

Locust, Water *Gleditsia aquatica* Marsh.

Lombardy Poplar *Populus nigra* var. *italica* Du Roi. A variety of the
black poplar, *Populus nigra,* introduced with obvious success, 1784, by
William Hamilton as *P. dilatata* Ait. Jefferson brought home a tree, 1789,
"somewhat different from the common tall and slim Lombardy, Mr. Jefferson's being a tree of some shade. (Told to General Cocke by Jefferson.)

Lonicera Among all the "honeysuckles" these seem to be the main ones
cultivated:

L. alpigena L. Jefferson's red-berried honeysuckle. Collinson.

L. sempervirens L. Trumpet honeysuckle. Jefferson. Washington. Lady
Skipwith.

L. tatarica L. Given to Collinson by Christopher Gray, London nursery-man, 1760. Grown by Miller, 1752, from seeds from Tartary via Petersburg.

L. canadensis Bartr. Fly honeysuckle. To Collinson from Bartram, 1759.

Lords-and-Ladies *Arisaema triphyllum* (L.) Schott. Custis. Collinson.

Lotus, American *Nelumbio lutea* (Willd.) Pers.

Lovage *Levisticum*

Love Apples *Lycopersicum esculentum* Mill. "Called by the Italian Tami-ata . . . much used by them in soups and broths." Collinson to Custis.

Love-in-a-Mist *Nigella damascena* L. Jefferson's nutmeg plant.

Love-Lies-Bleeding *Amaranthus caudatus* L. Custis.

Lucerne *Medicago sativa* L. Sent to J. Logan by Collinson, care of Bar-tram, as Burgundy trefoil.

Dillenius sent Bartram, 1738, as a perennial food for cattle. ("Sow thin.") Good where a country "wants pasture."

Humphry Marshall's paper on "Botany as applicable to Rural Economics" praised clover, saint-foin and lucerne, 1786.

Lunaria annua L. Honesty. Jefferson. Lady Skipwith. M'Mahon's.

Lungwort *Pulmonaria officinalis* L.

Lupin *Lupinus perennis* L. Wild lupin. Requested of Bartram by Col-linson.

Lupinus luteus L. Yellow lupin. Skipwith.

Lupinus perennis. Curtis *Botanical Magazine*

"**Lychnidea** or Bastard Lychnis (see Phlox) What we call Woods Pink, Trestle Flower, Small blue flower in April." Lady Skipwith's *Phlox divaricata* L.

Collinson refers to a "very pretty Lychnis with pale blue flowers and a sweet smell," 1740. Undoubtedly the above. Miller has "Phlox . . . familiarly Lychnidea or Bastard Lychnis." Seven sorts, all North American. This the first.

"Lychnis" Bartram to Gronovius speaks of an "odd pretty kind of Lychnis with leaves as narrow and short as our Red Cedar, of humble growth, perennial and so early to flower as to flower sometimes when snow is on the ground . . ." *Phlox subulata* L.

Lychnis Campion. Of the true lychnises there are many old garden favorites. Many were introduced into gardens and escaped to flourish in the wilds. Former under *Agrostemma silene*. The following are all European imports.

Bartram, 1739, produced a peach-colored lychnis by experimenting with artificial hybridization.

L. githago Scap. Corn cockle. Also *Agrostemma githago* L.
L. chalcedonica Fisch. Jerusalem cross. Maltese cross.

Lychnis chalcedonica. Scarlet Lychnis

L. coronaria Desr. Mullein pink. Rose campion.
L. Flos-Jovis. Desr. Flower of Jove.
L. Coeli-rosa Desr. Rose of heaven.
L. dioica L. Red or morning campion.
L. alba Mill. White or evening campion.
L. viscaria L. German catchfly.
L. flos-cuculi L. Ragged robin. Cuckoo flower.

"*Lychnis viscosa virginiana* . . . *coccinea* . . . flowers red with deep notches at end of each . . ." Catesby 54. *Silene virginica* L. is Indian pink, seen and called a Lychnis by Banister.

Lycopersicum esculentum **Mill.** Jefferson, who was growing "tomatoes" given him in 1809 and "Spanish tomatoes" in 1811, was one of the first to adventure with this now indispensable part of the American diet. While "love-apples" had been grown for ornament and amusement, their seemingly near relationship to supposedly poisonous nightshades made everyone afraid to eat them. Collinson wrote to Custis of a lady who had seen people in Spain using them in soups and salads. Realizing they were considered a delicacy abroad and had caused no violent deaths, people were persuaded to admit them to the kitchen garden in the nineteenth century.

M

Macock   Banister's name for a necked gourd.

Madder   *Rubis tinctorum* L. Roots sent from England, 1630. Washington thanked Bordley of Wye, Maryland, for madder.

Magnolia   Marshall listed four species of *"Magnolia.* The Laurel-leaved Tulip Tree."

"1) *Magnolia acuminata.* Long-leaved Mountain Magnolia, or Cucumber Tree."

Catesby's II A-15. Bartram, returning from his journey to the country of the Five Nations, reported to Collinson he had found "a great mountain Magnolia three feet in diameter and above a hundred feet high . . ."

Magnolia flore albo. Catesby's Plate A-15. (As this is in Catesby's Appendix, does this represent a fresh sketch from a Magnolia in England or sent on request?)

Bartram, 1744, describes another to John Mitchell. Collinson, 1746, recorded growing two. Mountain magnolia bloomed, 1762, the largest and highest in England. Michael Collinson, 1774, reported to Bartram that in his late father's garden — "almost all derived from your bounty" — the "Blue Mountain Magnolia" was blooming profusely.

"2) *Magnolia glauca* Small Magnolia or Swamp Sassafras . . . of an agreeable smell . . . Seeds and bark used in cure of rheumatism."

Catesby I 39. Sweet bay.

Rose laurel. Ordered by Washington from Bartram's. Riding in search of trees to move, 1785, Washington found "many small and thriving plants of the Magnolio" and transplanted them. A great year for Mount Vernon, 1786, Washington replaced ten "swamp magnolias."

"3) *Magnolia grandiflora* Evergreen Laurel-leaved Tulip Tree."

Catesby I 61. The laurel tree of Carolina.

Bartram's "Florida Laurel Tree." Bull bay.

Washington, 1786, transplanted forty-six of the "large Magnolia of South Carolina . . . six at the head of each serpentine walk next the circle . . ." the rest in the north and south shrubberies. At the same time he planted 140 seeds of the "large Magnolia or Laurel of Carolina."

Washington named his Arabian stud Magnolio and kept him in a special enclosure next the garden. Having bred all his best mares to him, Washington sold Magnolio to Colonel Henry Lee for a vast tract of "Kentucke Land" in December, 1788.

"4) *Magnolia tripetela.* The Umbrella Tree."

Catesby II 80.

Magnolia. The Umbrella Tree. Catesby's Plate 80, Vol. II

Ordered from Bartram's Nurseries by Washington.

Jefferson grew all four of these magnolias, as did Collinson.

Bartram listed all four, as did M'Mahon's.

Mahogany Tree *Swietenia mahagoni* Jacq.

Maiden Cane   "Arundo" to Washington and Collinson.
   Arundo phragmites. To Jefferson, a useful Virginia reed.
   Arundo donax L. Today *Phragmites communis* Trin. An ornamental grass
   from the Mediterranean. Our variety is *P. communis* var. *Berlandieri*
   (Fourn.) Fern.

Malcomia maritima **R. Br.**   Virginian stock. The Lambolls to Bartram.

Mallow   Another blanket name. The range of handsome, large-flowered
plants familiarly called "mallows" includes hollyhocks and hibiscus.

Mallow, Musk	*Malva moschata* L. A garden favorite.
Marshmallow	*Althaea officinalis* L.
Hollyhock	*Althaea rosea* Cav.
Mallow, Poppy	*Callirhoe* Nutt.
Mallow, Glade	*Napaea* L.
Mallow, Globe	*Sphaeralcea coccinea* Pursh.
Mallow, Carolina	*Modiola* Moench.
Mallow, Virginia	*Sida hermaphrodita* L. Rusby.
Mallow, Indian	*Abutilon* Mill.
Mallow, Rose	*Hibiscus* L.

Maltese Cross   *Lychnis chalcedonica* L.

Malva rotundifolia **L.**   Listed by Jefferson as "Mallow." Medicinal.

Mangel   Mangel-wurzel. Scarcity root. Washington thanked someone who
sent a "root of the Scarcity Plant" to Martha Washington, a complimentary
gesture to popularize this nutritive vegetable promoted by Dr. Lettsom,
1786, in England. Now a staple crop.

Maple   *Acer.* Under the various familiar names:

Maple, Ash-leaved	Box Elder. *A. negundo.* L.
Maple, Black	*A. nigrum* Michx f.
Maple, Mountain	*A. spicatum* Lam.
Maple, Norway	*A. platanoides* L.
Maple, Rock or Sugar	*A. saccharum* Marsh.
Maple, Scarlet	*A. rubrum* L.
Maple, Silver or White	*A. saccharinum* L.
Maple, Southern Sugar	*A. barbatum* Michx.
Maple, Striped	Moosewood. *A. pensylvanicum* L.
Maple, Sycamore	*A. pseudo-platanus* L.

Maracocs   Familiar name for the fruit of the native passion flower.

Marbled Rose   Lady Skipwith's "Rosa Marmorea" in Rea's *Flora.* M'Mahon's lists "Marble Rose" as a "variety of *R. gallica,*" after *R. gallica* var.
versicolor, the "Mundi Rose."

"Mariana see *Watsonia"*   Lady Skipwith's *Watsonia meriana* Mill. A
gladiolus-like ornamental from the Cape.

Marigold   "Marigold" until well into the eighteenth century was *Calendula
officinalis* L. With the discovery in Mexico of *Tagetes erecta* L., called
"French marigolds," calendulas became "pot marigolds."

Jefferson's marigolds sowed in 1764 are likely to have been calendulas. By 1808 he heard from Edgehill that they had plenty of "the two kinds of Marigolds you gave us." In 1812 Jefferson was sowing "African Marigolds." M'Mahon offered "Pot Marigolds" and double African and double French, also quilled African marigolds. Sir Peyton Skipwith ordered striped French marigolds, 1793.

Marjoram   *Origanum* An early Dutch traveler in Virginia visited a garden of two acres on the James where Dutch roses and fruits abounded with "sweet-smelling herbs . . . rosemary, sage, marjoram, thyme . . ."

Marjoram was one of Jefferson's "Objects for the garden," 1794.

Washington spoke of marjoram in 1789. "Knotted or Sweet" makes it sound as if it was to be clipped as well as used for flavoring. Under M'Mahon's "Aromatic, Pot and Sweet Herbs."

Sweet marjoram, *Origanum marjorana* L. An annual.

Perennial marjoram, *Origanum onites* L.

Marshmallow   *Althaea officinalis* L. Jefferson.

Martagon   The name for Sultan Muhammed I's style of turban. "Marsh Martagon," 1736, Bartram to Collinson, was *Lilium superbum* L. Turk's-cap lily. The Lambolls to Bartram. Skipwith. See Lilies.

Matthiola   Stock gilliflower. *Matthiola incana* R. Br. is the common stock, biennial or perennial.

M. incana var. *annua* Voss. is ten-weeks stock, annual, spring blooming.

M. incana var. *autumnalis* Voss. is the late-blooming queen or Brompton stock. The Lambolls sent "Brumpton Stock" to Bartram, also dwarf, striped and "Queen." The Virginia stock they sent is *Malcomia martima* R. Br.

Marvel of Peru   Four o'clock. False jalap. *Mirabilis jalapa* L. Jefferson, 1767.

May Apple   *Podophyllum peltatum* L. Catesby, for Plate I 24, says, "roots said to be excellent emetic . . . used as such in Carolina, which has given it there the name of Ipecacuana, the string roots of which it resembles." "A pretty plant," Collinson, 1734, "sent me by Dr. Witt."

Meadia   The name, in honor of his patron, Dr. Mead, Catesby gave to the "American cowslip," now *Dodecatheon meadia* L., because Linnaeus thought it similar to the plant described by Dioscorides.

Meadow Saffron   *Colchicum autumnale* L. Lady Skipwith says "called by the common people Naked Ladies."

Meally Tree   Pliant, or Way-Faring Tree. Marshall's name for *Viburnum*. (Pliant Meally Tree is his name.)

Medeola virginiana L.   Indian cucumber root. Lady Skipwith's "little Martagon" from the branch at Elm Hill.

Medlar, Neapolitan   Collinson to Custis, "which we always graft on white thorn and so must you." Bartram, 1738, reported "The medlar bone . . .

Believe it is the English kind . . . One of our persimmons is worth a dozen of them."

Melia azedarach L.   China tree. Pride of India. Chinaberry. Introduced by the Lambolls' son-in-law, Thomas, who corresponded with William Bartram. Enormously popular ornamental tree. Skipwith. Jefferson. Washington. Collinson's "Bead Tree."

Menziesia pilosa (Michx.) Juss.   Hamilton asks from Marshall. A small Alpine, cultivated like *Andromedas* and *Rhododendrons*.

Mertensia virginica D.C.   Virginia cowslip. Bluebells. Jefferson's and Lady Skipwith's "Blue Funnel flower." Custis' "Mountain Cowslip" to Collinson.

Mespilus   Medlar

Under "Medlar Tree" Marshall lists ten sorts: pear-leaved thorn, the cockspur hawthorn, wedge-leaved mespilus, great azarole or hawthorn and a smaller one, a yellow-berried hawthorn, a parsley-leaved mespilus, the wild service, a plum-leaved medlar and a dwarf red-fruited medlar. The imported medlar is *Mespilus germanica* L. Confusion is understandable, as this fruiting medlar can be grafted on to pear, quince or thorn (*Crataegus*), as see Collinson to Custis.

Mignonette   *Reseda odorata* L. Jefferson. Sir Peyton Skipwith.

Mignonette. Sweet-scented *Reseda* or Mignonette. Curtis *Botanical Magazine*

Mimosa pudica L.   Sensitive plant. Jefferson.
   M. julibrissim is now *Albizzia julibrissim* Duraz. Jefferson. *M. farnesiana* is now *Acacia farnesiana* Willd. Jefferson.

Mirabilis jalapa J.   Jefferson, 1767. Later his *"Jolie plante vivace d'ornement"* in ovals by the portico at Monticello. He also grew *M. longiflora* L.

Mitchella repens L. Partridge berry. Squaw berry. Named for Dr. Mitchell of Rappahannock, naturalist, plant collector, mapmaker and author.

Mitella "Has flowered strongly . . . a pretty odd thing . . ." Collinson to Bartram, 1741.

Moccasin Flower *Cypridedium acaule* Ait. Lawson. Bartram. Lady Skipwith. Collinson.

Mock Orange *Philadelphus coronarius* L. Skipwith. Jefferson, in circular beds at the corners of the house, 1807. Bartram's *Philadelphus inodorus* L., ordered by Washington, 1792.

Modesty Shrub Jefferson. Probably *Mimosa pudica* L.

Monkshood See *Acoritum napellus* L. Lady Skipwith.

Moon Seed Marshall lists three under *Menispermum:* Canadian, Virginian, Carolinian. Collinson.

Morus Mulberry. Much planted and sought after.
M. *alba* L. White mulberry, imported for silkworms.
M. *nigra* L. Black mulberry, with superior fruit.
M. *rubra* L. Our native red mulberry.
Prince's, 1790, offered all three. Washington, Jefferson, Skipwith, *et al.*

Mountain Cowslip *Mertensia virginica* (L.) Pers. Custis to Collinson.

Mountain Laurel *Kalmia latifolia* L. Bartram, Collinson, *et al.*

Mountain Rhododendron *R. maximum* L. Bartram, Collinson, *et al.*

Mountain Magnolia *M. acuminata* L. Bartram, Collinson, *et al.*

Mountain Tea *Gaultheria procumbens* L. Marshall.

Mulberry See *Morus.*

Myrtle A common name for *Vinca, major* and *minor.*

Myrtle, American Bog Gale *Myrica gale* L.

Myrtle, Candleberry *Myrica cerifera* L.

Myrtle, Dwarf *Myrtis communis* L. Houseplant. Lady Skipwith.

N

Napaea dioica L. Glade mallow. Virginia marshmallow. Miller advised having a few plants of this and *Napaea hermaphrodite* (now *Sida hermaphrodita* Rusby.) in every garden. Both white-flowered. Jefferson listed both as medicinal. Hamilton requested the first from Marshall.

Narcissus Daffodil. Jonquil. These ancient favorites are now divided into three main groups, judged by the length of the center cup or crown.
I. True daffodils or trumpet daffodils have crowns longer than the perianth segments.
Example: *N. pseudo-narcissus* L. Common daffodil and *N. bulbocodium* L. Hoop-petticoat daffodil.

Narcissus bulbocodium. Hoop-
petticoat Narcissus. Curtis *Botanical Magazine*

Narcissus triandrus. Reflexed Daffodil. Curtis *Botanical Magazine*

Narcissus angustifolius. Narrow-
leaved Narcissus. Curtis *Botanical
Magazine*

Narcissus major. Great Daffodil.
Curtis *Botanical Magazine*

II. Star narcissi or chalice flowers have crowns about half the length of the perianth segments.

Example: *N. triandrus* L. and *N. incomparabillis* Mill.

III. True *Narcissi* have the crown reduced to a rim.

Example: *N. poeticus* L. Pheasant's-eye. Poet's narcissus.

N. jonquilla L. Jonquil.

N. tazetta L. The polyanthus narcissus.

Under "Daffodils" Parkinson gives forty pages with sixty-four illustrations of "Daffodil, Jonquil, or Narcissus." Autumn crocuses were included. *Colchicum parkinsonii* is named for Parkinson today. Collinson sent Custis an "Autumn Narcissus with a yellow crocus-like flower." Perhaps this one.

Under *"Narcissus"* M'Mahon offers *N. poeticus, N. pseudo-narcissus, N. bicolor, N. triandrus, N. orientalis, N. odorata, N. tazetta, N. bulbocodium, N. jonquilla, N. serotinus* and *N. moschatus.*

Collinson sent Bartram "sweet white narcissus" and was told it was common in Pennsylvania, having spread from its early arrival with the original settlers. "I perceive what thou calls the 'Double Sweet Daffodil' we call the 'Sweet White Narcissus,'" Collinson wrote. The Skipwiths grew "Polianthus Narcissus," "double variegated Narcissus," "Autumnal Narcissus," "a fine double jonquil" and "daffodils."

One can see why the present divisions became necessary.

Nasturtium *Tropaeolum majus* L. Jefferson. "Indian Cress."

Nectarines Requested by Jefferson of George Whythe in Williamsburg, 1770. See chapter on fruits.

Nelumbio lutea **(Willd.) Pers.** American lotus. Water chinquapin.

Nerine sarniensis **Herb.** "Guernsey Lily," because it was washed ashore on that island on its way from South Africa. Collinson to Custis, 1736. Lady Skipwith, 1792.

Nettle Tree *Celtis occidentalis* L. American yellow-fruited nettle tree, the juice of which was said "to give ease in violent dysentries." Collinson.

Nickar Tree Bonduc. Kentucky coffee tree. Mahogany tree from Kentucky. Marshall's *Guilandica dioica.* Now *Gymnocladus dioica* Koch. Bartram, Washington, *et al.*

Nicotiana tabacum **L.** The long-disputed blessing or curse of our economic and social history. A book is not enough.

Nigella damascena **L.** Called fennel flower because of the shape of its leaves. Love-in-a-mist. The seeds of *N. sativa* L. are used in seasoning. Also called Roman coriander and nutmeg flower.

Jefferson's nutmeg plant, sowed in one of his oval beds. Probably the Lamboll's "nutmeg" to Bartram.

Nightshade *Phytolacca americana* L. American poke. Garget. Kalm's "American Nightshade." He declared it, along with the *Datura* or jimson weed, one of "the worst weeds here, no one knowing any particular use for them." A good definition of weed. Today our nightshade, with a prefix of "deadly," is *Atropa belladonna* L.

Enchanter's nightshade is *Circaecanadensis* Hill. The nightshade family is *Solanum,* which may be why tomatoes did not catch on here as edible until the early nineteenth century.

Ninebark   *Physocarpus opulifolius* Maxim. Marshall's *"Spirea opulifolia.* Guelder-Rose-leaved Spira or Ninebark." See Canewood.

"Norway Firs"   To Randolph in Philadelphia, 1798. Now *Picaea abies* (L.) Karst.

Norway Maple   *Acer platanoides* L. Bartram asked of Philip Miller, 1756, who sent seedlings from a large tree, adding, "cuttings grow like willows." In no time Bartram's is offering Norway maples.

Nut   See chapter on fruits.

Nut, Bladder   *Staphylaea trifoliata* L. American bladdernut. Skipwith.

Nutmeg Plant   *Nigella damascena* L. Jefferson. The Lambolls to Bartram.

Nymphaea   Water lilies. Collinson reproached Bartram for not cultivating our native water lilies. Americans did not take to water gardens for another century.

Nyssa   The tupelo tree. Catesby 4 and 60.
   Marshall lists three:
   1) *"Nyssa aquatica,* the Virginian Water Tupelo Tree."
   2) *"Nyssa ogeche.* The Ogeche Lime Tree," now included with the above. The fruit is the size of a "Damascene Plum" and agreeably acid — so "Lime Tree." Called "Olive Tree" by early French settlers on the Mississippi.
   3) *"Nyssa sylvatica* Upland Tupelo Tree or Sour Gum." Now *Nyssa sylvatica* Marsh. Pepperidge. Sour gum. Black gum. Requested of Bartram by Collinson.

O

Oak   *Quercus* Banister had ten American oaks in his catalogue. Quoted by Ray. Bartram, 1753, sent Collinson a quantity of different sorts of oaks, with a chilly reception. Collinson wrote, "Our ingenious friend, John Bartram, will be arraigned with want of judgement to distinguish things aright," though he conceded that even he, with two sorts of oaks in England, could have fancied there were more from the "different figure of their leaves and the shape and size of their acorns." Considering there are today over thirty fairly common American oaks, Bartram was not far off.

Bartram's offered fifteen oaks: white, black, red, Spanish, dwarf, willow-leaved, water, barren black, live, chestnut, willow oak with broad leaves, dwarf chinquapin, dwarf white, scarlet oak of Florida, gall-bearing and a few "dwarf oaks with unidentifiable names."

The most common American oaks are:

Oak, Basket	*Quercus prinus* L.
Oak, Black	*Quercus marilandica* Muench.
Oak, Chestnut	*Quercus montana* Willd.
Oak, Chinquapin	*Quercus prinoides* Willd.
Oak, Live	*Quercus virginiana* Mill.
Oak, Pin	*Quercus palustris* L.
Oak, Red	*Quercus rubra* L.
Oak, Scarlet	*Quercus coccinea* Munech.
Oak, Spanish	*Quercus falcata* Michx. (American "Spanish").
Oak, Water Oak, Possum	*Quercus nigra* L.
Oak, White	*Quercus alba* L. Catesby.
Oak, Willow	*Quercus phellos* L.

Washington planted live oaks in his shrubberies and on the sides of the grass plot in front of the house, 1785. *Q. nigra,* 1786. Jefferson was constantly involved with many sorts of oaks. He buried a great friend under a favorite oak, unnamed, at Monticello in 1771. Sent acorns of *Q. alba, Q. prinus* and *Q. phellos* to Madame de Tessé. Also sent to France the chestnut oak and our Spanish oak, which he considered "a variety of *Q. rubra.*" He sent acorns of the true Spanish cork oak to William Drayton to try in Charleston because it would not grow at Monticello. He planted English oaks, *Q. robur* L., at Monticello, and acorns of red, white and willow oak. He even planted the poison oak, which is not an oak at all, as see below.

The Italian evergreen holm oak, *Q. ilex* L., was sent to Custis by Collinson, who asked him for the willow-leaved oak. The Lambolls sent Bartram "Trees of Live Oaks, Water Oaks, Red Oaks . . ." Prince's confined themselves to four oaks: white, black, pin and scarlet.

Oak, Poison *Rhus toxicodendron* L. A small American tree or shrub that aroused interest abroad. Considered fit for a shrubbery by Jefferson. Collinson.

Oenothera biennis **L.** Virginia tree primrose. Custis to Collinson. Parkinson.

Okra *Hibiscus esculentus* in Miller. Wild in the West Indies. Kalm observed it planted here. Skipwith. Jefferson.

Oleander *Nerium oleander* L. One of Lady Skipwith's houseplants.

Ononis **L.** Collinson sent Bartram "the long purple-spiked Ononis" and said it "made a fine show."

Lady Skipwith grew "Purple Shrubby Rest-Harrow, Miller's fifth sort." M'Mahon's.

"Opopino, a beautiful flowering tree," from the Lambolls to Bartram eludes me unless they meant Opopanax, *Mimosa farnesiana* Mill. Jefferson's favorite.

Opuntia **Mill.** Prickly pear. Indian fig. Collinson wrote to Bartram he had heard that in "Augustine" the fruit was a great food of the inhabitants.

Oranges China oranges and sour oranges, with pomegranates, from the Lambolls to Bartram. Lady Skipwith had oranges as houseplants. Washington grew them, thanks to Mrs. Carroll, in his greenhouse.

"Orchis or *Satyrion."* Bartram to Collinson. "Thy sod of Orchis in full flower," wrote Collinson to Bartram, and again, "The pretty humble beautiful plant, with a spike of yellow flowers, I take to be a species of Orchis or Satyrion."

Ornithogalum umbellatum **L.** Seen by Bartram and not found again. Could be this old garden favorite "escaped." Lady Skipwith.

Ostrya virginiana **Koch.** Hop hornbeam, described to Collinson by Bartram.

Oxycoccus vitis-idaea "A species of Hurtleberry" in bloom, 1756, with Collinson. Now *Vaccinium vitis-idaea* L.

Oxydendrum arboreum **(L.) D.C.** Sorrel tree. Sourwood. Custis to Collinson.

P

Paeonia The Lambolls in Charleston requested peony roots of Bartram and were sent "several," 1761.
Paeonia officinalis, crimson, single or double, was the ancient European peony. The double white *P. albiflora* Pallas. arrived here shortly after mid-century from Siberia, as did *P. tenuifolia* L. Raised from seed from Siberia by Collinson. M'Mahon. Tree peonies and other peony species arrived in American gardens in the nineteenth century.

"**Padus** . . . the lovely tree growing in Governor Glenn's garden." To Bartram from the Lambolls. Probably *Prunus padus* L., the European bird cherry.

"**Painted Lady Pease** . . . in my Botanical Garden next the Necessary House," planted by Washington, 1788. A variety of *Lathyrus odoratus* L. The everlasting pea or perennial sweet pea, *Lathyrus latifolius* L., was also planted by Washington, Jefferson and Lady Skipwith.

Palmetto Royal *Sabal palmetto* Lodd. Sowed by Washington in his Botanical Garden 1786.

Panax quinquefolium **L.** Ginseng. An export of considerable value financially, if not medically, to China. As with sassafras, ships left our shores loaded with this one cargo. Catesby made much of ginseng, as did William Byrd II, who kept a piece in his mouth through all ordeals in the Great Dismal. By the end of the eighteenth century, Sir Joseph Banks was importuning Humphry Marshall for information and "one or two hundred weight of the fresh roots." Collinson reported ginseng, 1740, in his garden, from Dr. Witt, who told him ". . . Indians would travel three, four or five days without food by only keeping a bit of the root in their mouths . . ."

Pancratium maritimum **L.** Catesby. Grown by Collinson as "an Amaryllis or Narcissus from North Carolina sent me by Governor Dobbs." To Bartram by the Lambolls as "the ragged Lilly or Pancratium." Sea daffodil, spider lily and "Sea Pancratium," offered by M'Mahon's. American sort now under *Hymenocallis.*

Pansy *Viola tricolor* L. Skipwith.

Papaver orientale **L.** Oriental poppy.
Collinson sent Bartram "Tournefort's fine Armenian Perennial Poppy," 1741.

Papaver somniferum **L.** Opium poppy. Doctor Bond of Philadelphia, 1781, thanked Humphry Marshall for fine quality of opium sent him. Cautioned Marshall to take good care of the seed.

Papaw The North American papaw is *Asimina triloba* (L.) Dunal., and a dwarf, *A. parviflora* (Michx.) Dunal. Seeds of *A. triloba* begged of Custis by Collinson, 1747, and of Bartram many times; also the fruit, in rum, and a flower for Catesby to draw.

Pardanthus Leopard flower. Now *Belamcanda chinensis* (L.) D.C. Lady Skipwith's blackberry lily. Collinson's "Bermudiana from Persian seed."

Passiflora Passion flower. Custis sent Collinson two sorts. One was *P. incarnata* L., edible, the fruit called maracocks. The other was *P. lutea* L. Collinson played his cards wisely, never asking Bartram for southern plants until he knew he was near them.

Peaches See chapter on fruits.

Peach, Double-flowering, is *Prunus persica semiplena*

Peacock Tail Tree Early name for the American bird's-eye maple.

Peas, Edible See chapter on vegetables.

Peas, Ornamental
Pea, Everlasting *Lathyrus latifolia* L. Washington. Jefferson. Joseph Chew. Sir William Johnson. Skipwith.
Pea, Georgia Cluster *Cassia fasciculata* Michx. Skipwith.
Pea, Mountain Pea Tree Lady Skipwith's eludes me, unless she means *Thermopsis montana* Nutt., buffalo pea, or perhaps *Thermopsis carioliniana.* Curtis, from the North Carolina hills.
Pea, Partridge *Cassia chamaecrista* L. Skipwith.
Pea, Sweet *Lathyrus odorata* L. Washington. Jefferson. Joseph Chew. Sir William Johnson. Skipwith.

Pecan Illinois hickory. Illinois nut. *Carya pecan illinoensis* (Wang.) K. Koch. One of our great contributions. Jefferson. Washington.

Pelargonium Now familiarly called "geranium." From South Africa, late in the eighteenth century.

Pellitory, American   *Parientaria pennsylvanica* Muhl. Collinson.

Peony   "Does the peony flower grow with you? We have none of it here." Thomas Lamboll to Bartram, who sent roots. See *Paeonia.*

Persian Jasmine   Early name for Persian lilac. *Syringa persica* L.

Periploca graeca **L.**   Silk vine. An early introduction from Southern Europe, though Collinson says to Bartram, "the fine Periploca from the Ohio . . . is growing in my garden . . ." 1763. It attained the height of fifteen feet. Bartram had seen it, but failed to collect it, 1738.

Periwinkle   *Vinca minor* L. Sent by Joseph Chew to Sir William Johnson as "a fine creeper for borders and hedges."

Persicaria orientale **L.**   Collinson, in 1737, sent Bartram seeds. "A noble annual . . . six or seven feet high and makes a beautiful show with its long bunches of red flowers . . . Called the great Oriental *Persicaria."* The Lambolls sent it to Bartram.

Polygonum orientale. Tall Persicaria. Curtis *Botanical Magazine*

Philadelphus with Smilax. Catesby's
Plate 84, Vol. II

Persimmon   *Diospyros virginiana* L. Universally popular.

Petunia   Belongs to the next century.

Philadelphus   Catesby discovered *P. inodorus* L. "growing on the Bank of the Savana River." Catesby 84. Skipwith.

   P. coronarius L.   Mock orange. From southern Europe. M'Mahon's carried both.

Phillyrea latifolia **L.**   Given to Washington by M. Michaux. Collinson suggested a hedge of it to Custis.

Phlox   "It is wonderful to see the fertility of your country in *Phlox* . . ."
Collinson to Bartram, 1765. "Many of the King's specimens" set Collin-
son "alonging." *Phlox* was one of the unique American gifts to English
borders and rock gardens. Gathered up at first with *Lychnideas* and called
"Bastard lychnis."
Lady Skipwith grew what is now *Phlox divaricata* L., or Wild Sweet William, as "early-flowering Lychnidea. See *Phlox* . . . what we call woods
pink, trestle flower, small blue flower in April." She wishes us to refer to
Miller.
Bartram found *Phlox subulata* L., ground pink and moss pink, and described it to Collinson.
Kalm saw *Phlox glaberrima* L. and *P. maculata* L., both red, growing in
woods and meadows and concluded that, by adding to them *Bartisia
coccinea, Lobelia cardinalis* and *Monarda didyma,* "we must own the
land is undoubtedly adorned with the finest red imaginable."
Collinson grew *P. divaricata, P. maculata, P. paniculata, P. subulata.*

Phlox carolina L.   It looks like our modern hybrids. Was offered by
M'Mahon's as *P. paniculata, P. suaveolens* and *P. stolonifera,* and with
these other sorts brought the total to fourteen. But the west was still to be
opened up and Mr. Drummond was not to send his phlox from Texas
until 1835.

Phragmites communis Trin.   Common reed. Jefferson.

Physocarpus opulifolius Maxim.   Ninebark. See Canewood.

Physostegia virginiana Benth.   One of Collinson's "not in England before."

Phytolacca americana L.   Poke. Garget. The subject of an *Inaugural Botanico-Medical Dissertation* by Benjamin Schultz, pupil of Dr. Wistar,
Philadelphia, 1795. Collinson wrote Bartram, 1753, "Dr. Colden has
lately confirmed to me the success of the *Phytolacca* in cancers. As it is to
be applied outwardly, the danger is the less."

Picea   Spruce. Except for Jefferson's "Silver Fir," which was *Picea canadensis* B.S.P., the spruce tree did not catch on as an ornamental for another
century.

Pinckneya pubens Michx.   Gearbia bark. Feverbark.

Pine   *Pinus.* Once considered to be divided by sex, "Pines and Firs." Included trees now under *Abies, Tsuga, Picea* and *Pinus.* One understands
Bartram's task when asked, 1736, to make a "general collection" for
Collinson. "The difference between Pines and Firs," wrote Collinson
kindly, "is that all Pines have their leaves set by pairs, or fascicles, and in
all Firs the leaves are set singly on the branches." Bartram sent Collinson
a three-leaved pine, 1751.
Prince's listed Weymouth's, pitch, Virginia, Jersey.
Bartram's offered white, swamp, pinaster or mountain, long-leaved, dwarf,
Pennsylvania, frankincense.

M'Mahon, to all these, added foxtail, stone, mugho. Weymouth's name was attached to the white pine because it first grew well in England on Lord Weymouth's property. Used by Jefferson.

Washington planted twenty "young pines" at the head of his cherry walk. In 1785 he brought home three wagonloads of "young pines" and planted them in every other hole around the walks. Finding the walks around his wilderness too thin, he doubled the pines. In 1792 he ordered white pines from Bartrams and planned to have them make the high centers of his "shrubberies." Jefferson thanked F. A. Michaux for his account of the "pines and firs of our country." Jefferson used pine and hickory for firewood, pine for his carpenters, and he sowed white pine in special lots. He sent pitch pine and black pine to France. He did not, however, seem to use pines for landscaping, as did Washington, unless three Scotch pines from Philadelphia were solely ornamental. He listed white, pitch and yellow pine as Virginia assets.

American Pines, by their familiar names, are:

Pine, Jersey, Poverty, Scrub *P. virginiana* Mill. Marshall's No. 1

Pine, Loblolly, Oldfield *P. taeda* L. Marshall's No. 5 and his "Frankincence Pine"

Pine, Long-leaf, Yellow, Georgia *P. australis* Michx. or *P. palustris* Mill.

Pine, Pitch *P. rigida* Mill. Marshall's No. 3

Pine, Pond *P. serotina* Michx. f, Marshall's No. 2

Pine, Red or Norway *P. resinosa* Ait.

Pine, Table-mountain, Prickly *P. pungens* Lamb.

Pine, White Weymouth's *Pinus strobus* L. Marshall's No. 4

Pine, Yellow, Short-leaf *P. echinata* Mill. Marshall's No. 1.

Introduced Pines are:

Pine, Austrian *P. nigra* Arnold. 1759.

Pine, Cluster *P. pinaster* Ait. Very early.

Pine, Mugho *P. Mugho* Turra. 1779.

Red Pine, Norway *P. resinosa* Ait. 1756.

Pine, Scotch *P. sylvestris* L. Very early.

Pineapple Washington wrote from Barbados in 1751 of the many delicious fruits . . . "the Pine Apple, China Orange . . . the Avagado pair . . . though none pleases my taste as does the Pine . . ."

Pinks See *Dianthus*

Pinkroot The Lambolls sent Bartram "two sorts Pink-Root, of which the narrow leaf is the right sort for worms." This is Indian pink, *Spigelia marilandica* L. Carolina pink or pinkroot. Perhaps the Lambolls' other one was *Spigelia gentianoides* Chap. from Florida.

Pinus Please see Pine

Plane Tree *Platanus occidentalis* L. Catesby's 56. Buttonwood. The American plane, one of the first American trees to be sent to and grown in England. Parent of the hybrid plane.

Plumeria. Catesby's Plate 82, Vol. II

Pliant Meally Tree   Marshall's name for *Viburnum.*

Plumeria, Rose   Catesby 98. Introduced to Barbados from America. "Red Jasmine" in Jamaica.

Podophylum peltatum **L.**   May apple. Mandrake. Wild jalap. To Collinson from Bartram. Now used against skin cancer.

Podophyllum diphyllum **was renamed for Jefferson**   *Jeffersonia diphylla.* Bartram to Collinson. M'Mahon to Jefferson.

Poison Oak, Poison Wood   *Rhus toxicodendron* L. Catesby. Listed by Jefferson as ornamental.

Polemonium   Jacob's-ladder. Greek valerian.
   P. caeruleum L. is Jacob's-ladder.
   P. reptans L. is Greek valerian.
   Bartram sent our *P. reptans* to Collinson, who thought it the same as the English sort but admitted when it bloomed that it was different and "pretty." 1741.

Polyanthes tuberosa **L.**   Tuberose. Collinson to Custis, 1736. Bartram to the Lambolls, 1761. Clayton's destroyed by frost, 1765. Lady Skipwith grew both double and single tuberoses. Jefferson received some from M'Mahon.

Polygala senega **L.**   Seneca snakeroot. Mountain flax. This was Dr. Tennent's cure-all. Collinson had it from Bartram, 1751. See the chapter on medicine.

Polygonatum   Solomon's seal.
"Please to remember those Solomon's Seals," wrote Collinson, 1734. "The 'cluster-bearing Solomon's Seal' . . . is a very rare plant." *Smilacina racemosa* (L.) Desf.
The common European Solomon's seal is *P. multiflorum* All. American two-flowered Solomon's seal is *P. biflorum* (Walt.) Ell.

Polyanthus   A name applied to the hybrids of the *Primula eliator* Holl. Oxlip. Cowslip is *Primula officinalis* L. in England. Americans like to call the marsh marigold, *Caltha palustris* L., by that name. "American cowslip" is applied to *Dodecatheon meadia* L. and "Virginia Cowslip" to *Mertensia virginica* L. Just to sort out the overlaps. "*Polyanthus Narcissus,*" grown by Lady Skipwith, is *Narcissus tazetta* L.

Polygonum sagittatum L.   Arsmart. Apparently a popular remedy. One of Jefferson's medicinal Virginia plants.

Pomegranate   *Punica granatum* L. See chapter on fruits.

Poplar   *Populus.* Of Miller's seven sorts, the last two are American, and Lady Skipwith quotes him on their propagation by cuttings. Washington used poplars dug up in his fields to be combined with ash trees and elms to border his serpentine roads. He bought some "aspans" also. Jefferson, besides knowing those on his wife's inherited estate of Poplar Forest, was well aware of the wide selection of native poplars and had several sent to him in France. Prince in 1790 carried the Lombardy poplar, said to have been introduced by William Hamilton of Philadelphia, and the "aspe" tree, both ordered by Jefferson. Bartram's carried the "Cotton Tree," as *P. deltoides;* the Black poplar, as *P. foliis cordatis;* and the Aspen, as *P. tremula.*
Marshall lists six poplars: *P deltoides, P. heterophylla, P. nigra, P. tremula, P. balsamifera, P. balsamifera lanceolata.*
The commonest of the American poplars are:
P. balsamifera L. *P. tacamahaca* Mill. Balsam poplar.
P. candicans Ait. Balm of Gilead.
P. deltoides Marsh. Northern cottonwood. White poplar.
    A large tree. Bartram's. Miller. Jefferson.
P. heterophylla L. Swamp or black cottonwood.
P. tremuloides Michx. Quaking aspen.
European imports were the European aspen, *P. tremula* L. and the Lombardy poplar, *P. nigra* var. *italica* Du Roi. Our tulip tree was early referred to as the tulip-bearing poplar. It is *Liriodendron tulipifera* L.

Poppy   *Papaver.* The Oriental poppy was sent to Bartram by Collinson in 1741 as the Armenian poppy, *Papaver orientale* L. The Lambolls sent Bartram the "dwarf poppy," perhaps *P. nudicaule,* introduced to England, 1730, soon after the Oriental poppy and grown by Collinson and Jefferson. The opium poppy, considered a necessity in medicine, is *P. somniferum* L., and the prickly poppy, also grown by Jefferson, is *Argemone mexicana* L. While we are on the poppies, the horn poppy or sea poppy, which greeted Higginson on his voyage to the shores of Cape Ann in the early seventeenth century, was *Glaucium flavum* Crantz, one of our earliest and most successful "escapes."

Portulaca   Purslane. Skipwith.
   Portulaca oleracea L. Pusley. French salads. Indian weeds. Kalm observed it growing wild among the corn, as did Champlain.

Potatoes   See the chapter on vegetables. The Lambolls sent "Brimstone Potatoes" to Bartram. Washington grew quantities of different sorts, as did Jefferson.

Prickly Ash   See *Xanthoxylum.*

Pride of China   *Melia azedarach* L. Washington, Jefferson. Introduced by Thomas Lamboll as "Pride of India." Prince's Nurseries.

Prince's Feather   *Amaranthus hypochondriacus* L.

Prince Picoli   July flower. *Dianthus.* Sir Peyton's pink.

Privet   *Ligustrum.* "For a hedge in the garden," Jefferson.

Primrose, Tree   *Oenothera biennis* L. Perkinson's American tree primrose.

Prinos verticillatus   Pennsylvania winterberry. Bartram to Collinson. Now *Ilex laevigata* Gray.

Prunus   See chapter on fruits.
   For convenience:
   P. persica Sieb. and Zucc. Peach.
   P. persica var. *nucipersica* Schneid. Nectarine.
   P. communis Fritsch. Almond.
   P. armeniaca L. Apricot.
   P. domestica L. Garden plum.
   P. americana Marsh. Common wild plum.
   P. angustifolia Marsh. Chicksaw plum.
   P. maritima Marsh. Beach plum.
   P. triloba Lindl. Flowering almond.
   P. mahaleb L. Mahaleb cherry.
   P. pennsylvanica L. Common bird cherry.
   P. cerasus L . Sour, pie, morello cherry. Bartram's.
   P. avium L. Sweet cherry. Mazzard.
   P. serotina Ehrh. Wild black cherry.
   P. virginiana L. Chokecherry.
   P. padus L. European bird cherry.

P. lusitanica L.   Portuguese laurel.

Puccoon   *Lythospermum caroliniense* (Walt.) MacM.
   Lythospermum canescens (Michx.) Lehm. Indian paint.

Pulmonaria   *P. officinalis* L. Spotted lungwort. Jerusalem cowslip.
   P. saccharata Mill. Bethlehem sage.

Pumpkin   *Cucurbita.* See chapter on vegetables.

Punica granatum L.   Pomegranate. Jefferson. Washington. The Lambolls.

Purple Shade or Purple Weed Lady Skipwith. The Lambolls to Bartram. Probably purple shrubby rest-harrow *Ononis spinosa* L.

Ptelia trifoliata **L.** Hop tree. Wafer ash. Washington 1792.

Pyracantha coccinea **Roem.** Firethorn. Noted by Parkinson. Washington, 1792.

Pyramid of Eden. *Swertia caroliniensis* (Walt.) Ktze. Linnaeus said Dr. Gordon called it "the Glory of the Blue Mountains." Collinson begged for seed. An American gentian. Jefferson.

Pyramidical Cypress *Cupressus sempervirens* L. Given to Washington by Michaux and planted "each side of garden gates."

Pyrus communis **L.** Common pear. See chapter on fruits.

Pyrus malus **L.** Apple. See chapter on fruits.

Pyrus spectabilis **Ait.** The Chinese flowering apple. Dr. Fothergill introduced this Chinese native to England, 1780. First of a long line of ornamental crabs.

Pyrus coronaria **L.** Jefferson's fragrant wild crab.

Q

Quamoclit Mexican name for the cypress vine. Indian pink. Now *Ipomoea quamoclit* L.

Quercus Oak. Evelyn, in his *Sylva,* names two sorts of oaks in England: *Quercus urbana,* fittest for timber, and *Quercus sylvestris,* or robur, which needs space to spread its limbs. The variety of oaks in the New World took the Old by surprise.

We list here only the best-known American oaks:

Q. alba L. White oak. Marshall's first, most popular with the swine, except for the chestnut oak. Banister. Catesby. Jefferson. Prince's. Bartram's.

Q. nigra L. Black oak. Banister. Catesby's water oak. Marshall's fourth. Jefferson. Prince's. Bartram's.

Q. rubra L. Red oak. Banister. Marshall's ninth. Prince's. Bartram's. Jefferson.

Q. virginiana L. Live Oak. Marshall's evergreen oak. Jefferson. Washington.

Q. coccinea Muench. Scarlet oak. Banister said it was in Bishop Compton's garden. Prince's. Bartram's.

Q. falcata Michx. Spanish oak. (The early Spaniards saw a resemblance to their oak *Q. veluta.*) Banister. Bartram's.

Q. phellos L. Willow oak. Marshall's thirteenth. Jefferson. Requested of Custis by Collinson, 1736, and of Bartram, 1737.

Q. prinoides Willd. Chinquapin oak. Marshall's seventeenth.

Q. prinus L. Chestnut oak. Banister. Jefferson. Marshall's sixteenth.

Q. marilandica Muench. Black jack. Jefferson. Marshall's sixth.

Q. ilicifolia Wang. Scrub oak. Formerly *Q. Banisteri* Michx. since he discovered it.

Q. velutina Lam. Yellow-bark oak. Formerly Bartram's *Q. tinctoria.*

Q. palustris L. Pine oak. Prince's.

Quince *Cydonia oblonga* Mill. See chapter on fruits. The "Japanese Quince" is *Chaemomeles japonica* Lindl.

R

Radish *Raphanus sativus* L. See chapter on vegetables.

Rampion *Campanula rapunculus* L. A vegetable whose fleshy roots are edible. *C. rapunculoides* L. A garden ornamental turned weed.

Ranunculus Having explained that the name comes from liking to grow in damp places pleasant to frogs, Miller lists only the garden-cultivated sorts and gives us eleven.

R. aconitifolius L. Miller's fourth sort is the "Double Mountain Ranunculus," also called "Fair Maids of France," always white. Bartram. Collinson. Dr. Witt. Possibly the ranunculas sent to Bartram by the Lambolls and ordered by Sir Peyton by the dozen. Jefferson. M'Mahon's.

R. acris. var. *flore pleno* Hort. Yelow bachelor's-button. M'Mahon's. The "great double yellow Globe Crowfoote" was admired by Sir Thomas Hanmer, who grew both of these ranunculas as, I think, did Jefferson.

R. asiaticus L. in a variety of colors. May be the origin of Jefferson's "Red Ranunculus" sent home from France. See Furber.

Ranunculus aconitifolius. Mountain Crowfoot or Fair Maids of France. Curtis *Botanical Magazine*

"Rape," said Jared Eliot, is "Colewort or Cale gone to seed." Oil is made from seeds.

Rare as in rare ripe corn, means "early."

Raspberry *Rubus idaeus* L. See chapter on fruits.

Raspberry, Flowering *Rubus odoratus* L. Collinson thanks Bartram, says it "has been long in our Gardens." Called "Virginian Flowering Raspberry." Furber's August. Bartram's.

Rattlesnake Root *Polygala senega* L. Dr. Tennent again.

Red Berry Tree Washington, searching for trees to move, found "the red berry of the swamp." *Ilex verticillata* (L.) Gray. Bartram's.

Redbud *Cercis canadensis* Gray. In the same year as above, 1785, Washington moved "from the woods and the old field, Red Bud." Bartram's.

Redroot Bartram's name for *Ceanothus americanus* L. In 1734 Collinson requested "the pretty shrub called Red Root."

Reseda odorata **L.** Mignonette. Jefferson.

Rest Harrow, Purple Shrubby *Ononis fruticosa* L. or *Ononis rotundifolia* L. Skipwith.

Rest-harrow. *Ononis fruticosa.*
Curtis *Botanical Magazine*

"Retmic" is Ketmia, copied wrong from Lady Skipwith's lists.

Rhamnus Buckthorn. Hart's-horn. One of Washington's medicines. Also an ornamental.

  R. cathartica L. "Ramnus tree . . . each side of the garden gates." Washington, from Michaux.

  R. caroliniana Walt. Indian cherry. Hamilton requested of Marshall, 1796.

Rheum rhaponticum **L.** Rhubarb. A foregone conclusion in most gardens. Franklin told Bartram the Siberian was the best.

***Rhexia virginica* L.**   Meadow beauty.

Rhododendron

    R. calendulaceum Torr. Flame azalea. Requested of Marshall by Hamilton.

    R. canadense Zabel. Rhodora. Requested of Jefferson by friends in France.

    R. carolinianum Rehd. Sweet azalea. Bartram.

    R. catawbiense Pursh. Mountain rose bay. Bartram. Jefferson.

    R. maximum L. Great laurel. Rose bay. Bartram. Jefferson. Collinson. Washington.

    R. nudiflorum Torr. Pinxter flower. Jefferson.

    R. roseum (Loisel) Rehd. Upright honeysuckle. Bartram's.

    R. viscosum Torr. Swamp azalea. Swamp honeysuckle. Bartram.

Rhubarb   *Rheum rhaponticum* is our "Pie plant." The medicinal rhubarb came originally from China. The Berbers or Moors disclosed its cathartic properties and attached their name to the original "rha" to make the common name.

Rhus   Sumac.

    R. copallina L. Shining sumac. Jefferson to France, 1786.

    R. diversiloba Torr. and Gray. Poison oak. As above. Jefferson listed as shrubs.

    R. glabra. L. Smooth sumac. As above. Jefferson to France, 1786.

    R. toxicodendron L. Poison ivy. Fascinating to foreigners. Bartram to Collinson.

    R. typhina L. Staghorn. As above.

Robinia

    R. hispida L. Rose acacia. Bristly locust. Catesby. Collinson. Washington.

Robinia hispida (Roughstalked Robinia). Curtis *Botanical Magazine*

Rosa semperflorens (Ever-blowing   *Rubus odoratus.* Flowering Rasp-
Rose). Curtis *Botanical Magazine*   berry. Curtis *Botanical Magazine*

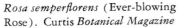

R. *pseudo-acacia* L. False acacia. Black locust. White fragrant locust.
Collinson from Bartram. Washington.

R. *viscosa* Vent. Clammy locust.

Rocambole Perennial onion. See chapter of vegetables.

Rocket Sweet rocket. Dames' violet. *Hesperis matronalis* L. The Lambolls to Bartram. Double variety. Skipwith. Collinson to Custis.

Rosa The Prince Nurseries listed the commonly grown roses as: moss
Provence; yellow rose; rosa mundi; large Provence; monthly; red damask;
white damask; primrose: musk rose; cinnamon rose; thornless rose; American wild rose and many other sorts.

R. *alba.* L. The white rose. Jefferson.

R. *carolina* L. Jefferson.

R. *centifolia* L. Cabbage rose. Jefferson.

R. *centifolia* var. *muscosa* Ser. Moss rose. Jefferson.

R. *centifolia* var. *parvifolia* Rehd. Burgundian rose.

R. *cinnamomea* L.

R. *damescena* Mill. Damask rose.

R. *foetida* var. *persiana* Rehd. Yellow rose. Jefferson.

R. *laevigata* Michx. Cherokee rose. Jefferson, 1804.

R. *gallica versicolor* Thorny. Rosa mundi. Jefferson.

R. *moschata* Mill. Musk rose. Jefferson.

R. *rubiginosa* L. Sweetbrier. Eglantine. Jefferson.

Rudbeckia purpurea. Purple Rudbeckia. Curtis *Botanical Magazine*

R. *spinosissima* L. Scotch rose.

R. *virginiana* Mill. and R. *palustris* Marsh. are the commonest sorts of
American wild roses.

Rose Bay   *Rhododendron maximum* L.

Rose, Guelder   *Viburnum opulus* var. *sterile* D.C.

Rose-of-Sharon   In America *Hibiscus syracus* L. Jefferson. Skipwith. In
England *Hypericum calycinum* L.

Rose Vervain   *Verbena canadensis.* Brit. Also rose verbena. To Collinson.

Rubia tinctorum **L.**   Requested of Marshall by Hamilton. Madder. In
demand since the earliest days.

Rubus odoratus **L.**   The rose-flowering raspberry. Bartram. Very popular
here and abroad.

Rudbeckia   One of our American species in great demand as garden flowers.
Collinson wrote, "I often reflect what a numerous train of yellow flowers
your continent abounds." Asks for seeds of the "two fine red-petalled
Rudbeckias." He grew several listed in *Flora virginica,* our R. *hirta* L.,
black-eyed Susan, among them, and also our R. *lacinata* L., golden glow.

Rue   *Ruta graveolens* L. Jefferson.

S

Saint Andrew's Cross   *Ascyrum hypericoides* L. Byrd II reported he saw it
"almost everywhere we went . . . At hand during the summer months

when the snakes have vigor enough to do mischief . . ." Yet another early remedy for snakebite.

Salix Willow. *S. babylonica* L. Weeping willow. Washington. Jefferson. *S. vitellina* L. Yellow willow. Jefferson. Washington.

Salvia *S. officinalis* L. Sage. Universal. *S. azurea* Lam. One of our better perennial border plants. Introduced to England, 1728.

Sanguinaria canadensis **L.** Bloodroot. Puccoon. Dr. Benjamin Gale to John Bartram: "I want to know the name of the American Bloodroot. Its virtues are great and many, particularly . . . as a specific in the nervous headache . . ." Jefferson. Skipwith. Used as a stimulant in small doses; an emetic in large. Popular with the Indians.

Sanicle Miller's *Sanicula officinarum* is *S. marilandica* L. Black snakeroot. Lady Skipwith's "Bear's-Ear Sanicle" is *Cortusa matthioli* L.

Saponaria officinalis **L.** Bouncing Bet. Soapwort. Universal.

Sarracenia purpurea **L.** Our common pitcher plant. Josselyn's "hollow-leaved lavender." Catesby's "side-saddle flower." Collinson's "surprising flowers of the red and yellow Sarracenia." One of our sensational discoveries.

Sarracenia. Pitcher Plant. Catesby's Plates 69 and 70, Vol. II

Sarsaparilla See *Smilax.* "Pray what is your Sarsaparilla?" Collinson to Bartram, 1734. *Aralia nudicaulis* L. is our "wild sarsaparilla" or "small spikenard."

Sassafras varifolium **Ktze.** is the former *S. officinale* and *Laurus sassafras* of Linnaeus. Catesby. Collinson. Lord Petre. Fothergill. Bigelow. Combined with sarsaparilla, it makes the "Lisbon diet drink." Jefferson rated it ornamental.

Saurus cernus **L.**   Water dragon, swamp lily, dragon's tail. Bartram's remedy for sore breasts, requested by Collinson and Fothergill.

Savin   *Juniperus sabina* L. The Lambolls to Bartram.

Savory   *Satureia horensis* L. Summer savory. Jefferson.
   S. montana L. Winter savory. The Lambolls to Bartram.

Saxifraga virginiensis **Michx.**   Noted by Josselyn.

Scabious   *Scabiosa atropurpurea* L. Sweet scabious. Skipwith.

Scarcity Root   Mangel-wurzel. Bailey says, "Often called *Beta vulgaris* var. *macrorhiza.*" Forage root sent Washington.

Schrankia uncinata **Willd.** Sensitive brier. Bartram to Collinson.

Scorpion, Bladder   *Colutea arborescens* L. Jefferson, Skipwith.

Scorpion Senna   *Coronilla emerus* L. Skipwith.

Scotch Pine   *Pinus sylvestris* L. Jefferson from Bartram's.

Scutellaria   Miller's fifth sort is North American. *S. montana* Daphm. Perhaps Lady Skipwith's, as she says, "see Miller."

Sedum   A large family in universal favor. *S. acre* L. Stone crop or wall pepper arrived early. *S. spectabile* Bor., showy sedum, has been with us a long time. *S. telephium* L., Orpine, live-forever, was popular for the border.

Self-Heal   *Prunella vulgaris* L. The Lambolls requested of Bartram.

Seneca   *Polygala senega* L. See chapter on medicine.

Senecio elegans **L.**   Purple ragwort. Curtis. Skipwith.

Senna   Partridge pea. *Cassia fasciculata* Michx. Skipwith. The Lambolls to Bartram.
   Bladder senna. *Colutea arborescens* L. Jefferson. Skipwith.
   Scorpion senna. *Coronilla emerus* L. Skipwith.

Sensitive Plants
   Schrankia uncinata Willd., sensitive brier. Bartram to Collinson, "Our thorny sensitive plant." Clayton to Bartram.
   Dionaea muscipula Ellis. Bartram's "Carolina Tipitiwichet." Venus's flytrap, much desired by Collinson. Jefferson requested it sent to him in Paris. *Mimosa pudica* L., Jefferson's sensitive plant, in one of his oval beds.

Serviceberry   *Amelanchier canadensis* L. Universally favored.

Service Tree   *Sorbus domestica* L. *Sorbus americana* in Marshall. Washington.

Setterwort   Stinking black hellebore. *Helleborus foetidus* L. Skipwith.

Silk Grass   *Yucca filamentosa* L. Adam's needle. Skipwith. Washington.

Silk Tree   *Albizzia julibrissin* Duraz.   Hamilton.   Bartram.   Washington. Jefferson.

Silphium laciniatum **L.**   Compass plant. Bartram to Collinson.

Silybum marianum **Gaertn.**   *Blessed thistle.* M'Mahon's.

Silverbell Tree   *Halesia carolina* L. Catesby's snowdrop tree.

Sisyrinchium angustifolium **Mill.**   Blue-eyed grass of Bermuda. Rush lily. Skipwith.

> *S. graminoides* Bicknell of Virginia. Requested by Collinson from Bartram as good against stoppage of the bowels.

Skunkweed   *Symplocarpus foetidus* L. Catesby. Bartram to Collinson.

 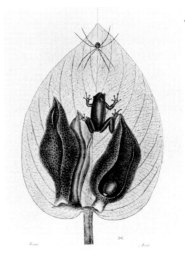

Sisyrinchium iridioides. Curtis *Bo-*   Skunkweed. Catesby's Plate 7 1,
tanical Magazine   Vol. II

Smilax   The bay-leaved smilax, *S. laurifolia* L., noted by Catesby. Called also false China brier. Marshall lists nine sorts of smilax. His first is *Smilax sarsaparilla,* our best source for the drug until more southern varieties were discovered. Wild American sarsaparilla in *Aralia nudicaulis* L.

Snakeroot   Every man appears to have his own. Tennent's was *Polygala senega* L. Breintnall's, requested from abroad, was *Sanicula marilandica* L. *Aristolochia serpentaria* L. was Virginia snakeroot, noted by Catesby. *Cimicifuga racemosa* Nutt. is black snakeroot and a lovely border plant. The Lambolls sent three sorts of snakeroot to Bartram.

Snapdragon   *Antirrhinum majus* L. Jefferson.

Snowdrops   *Galanthus nivalis* L. The common snowdrop. Miller says Linnaeus separated the "great Snowdrop" and called it *Leucojum.* Collinson grew *Leucojum vernum* L., which is now called snowflake. Lady Skipwith grew the large snowdrop. The Lambolls sent the double kind of snowdrop to Bartram. Your guess . . .

Solidage   Goldenrod. In great demand as a border plant in England. Collinson grew ten sorts, beginning with *S. odora* Ait., sweet goldenrod, 1736, which he claimed "made a fine tea."

Solomon's Seal   *Polygonatum multiflorum* All. is the great garden preference. European.

> *P. officinale* All. is smaller. *P. biflorum* (Walt.) Ell. is an American wild-flower, perhaps the sort the Lambolls requested of Bartram.

Sorbus   *S. americana* Marsh. is the American mountain ash or dogberry.
> *S. aucuparia* L. is the European mountain ash or rowan tree. Bartram had both, as did many others.

Sorrel   See Sourwood Tree.

Sorrel Tree. Catesby's Plate 71, Vol. I

Sourwood Tree   Sorrel tree. *Oxydendrum arboreum* D.C. Catesby. Collinson.

Spanish Broom   *Spartium junceum* L. Collinson to Custis. The Lambolls had the white variety, *S. junceum* var. *ochroleucum* Spreng.

Spider Lilly   See *Pancratium* and *Hymenocallis*.

Spigelia marilandica **L.**   Pinkroot. Carolina pink. Worm pink. Catesby. Collinson. Logan.

Spiderwort   *Tradescantia virginiana* L. Skipwith.

Spindle Tree   *Euonymus americana* L. Burning bush. Collinson thanks Bartram. Has.

Spiraea opulifolia **L.**   Virginia Guelder rose. Canewood. Collinson has.
> *S. alba* Dur. Meadowsweet. To Collinson.
> *S. alnifolia* Collinson's name for *Clethra alnifolia* L., sent by Bartram.
> *S. tomentosa* L. Hardhack. Steeplebush. Indian pipeshank. To Collinson, 1736.

Spigelia marilandica. Maryland
Spigelia or Worm-Grass. Curtis
Botanical Magazine

The Little Yellow Star Flower.
Catesby's Plate 33, Vol. I

Statice sinuata. Curtis *Botanical
Magazine*

Stewartia. Catesby's Plate A-13

S. trifoliata Jefferson's "Indian physic" eludes me. Perhaps *S. virginiana* Brit.

"Spruce Fir, Northern" Requested of Bartram by Clayton, 1761, is probably *Abies alba* Mill., the silver fir.

Squills Requested of Collinson by Bartram. *Scilla nonscripta* Hoff. and Link. Common blue squill. Harebell. Was Linnaeus' *Hyacinthus nonscriptus.*

Stachys officinalis **L.** Betony.

"Staggerweed" *Dicentra eximia* Torr. Bartram to Clayton, 1744.

Starflower, Little Yellow *Ornithogalum luteum* to Catesby 33. Skipwith. Miller's seventh. Probably *Hypoxis hirsuta* (formerly *H. erecta* L.) Coville.

Starflower, Blue Skipwith. "Not in Miller." An aster?

"Star-Root," which, according to Byrd, "infallibly cures the bite of a rattlesnake," escapes me.

"Statice, Purple-cupped or Thrift" *Limonium vulgare* Mill. Lady Skipwith's wished-for plant from Curtis' *Botanical Magazine.* "Dried it retains its colour." Another of the everlastings.

Stewartia malachodendron **L.** One of our most ornamental small trees, named by Catesby for the Earl of Bute, patron of botany. From Clayton in Virginia to Catesby in Fulham. Called *Malachodendron* by Mitchell. Collinson wrote, "Flowered for the first time at Kew in the Princess of Wales' garden, the Paradise of our world."

Stocks Stock gilliflowers, that is, July-blooming common stock, *Matthiola incana* R. Brd.
Ten-weeks stock, *M. incana* var. *annua* Voss. Virginia stock is *Malcomia maritima* R. Br. The Lambolls to Bartram. Ordered by Skipwith. Martha Logan sent seed of striped stock gilliflowers to Bartram.

Stoechas Now *Lavandula stoechas* L. Wild Spanish lavender. Bartram asks Clayton for seeds, 1761.

Storax Tree, Carolina *Styrax americana* Lam. Marshall. With an orange fragrance. *Liquidambar styraciflua* L., the sweet gum, produces the storax gum resin today, formerly produced by the *Styrax officinalis* L. *Halesia carolina* L. is related.

Stramonium Datura. Jimson weed. The Lambolls sent purple stramonium to Bartram.

Strawberries See chapter on fruits.

Strawbery Bush *Calycanthus floridus* L. and *Euonymus americana* L.

Strawberry Tree *Arbutus unedo* L. Jefferson. Custis.

Sugar Maple Sugar tree. *Acer saccharum* Marsh. Requested, 1736, Collinson of Bartram.

Sweet Fern *Comptonia asplenifolia* Gaertn.

Sweet Gum *Liquidambar styraciflua* L. Collinson asked Bartram for blossoms for Dutch botanists and seeds for Lord Petre and the Duke of Richmond. Catesby noted the Indians chewed the gum as a tooth preservative.

Sweet Pea *Lathyrus odoratus* L. Skipwith. The Lambolls to Bartram. Jefferson.

Everlasting pea. *Lathyrus latifolius* L. Collinson. Jefferson. Washington.

Sweet Scabious   Musk scabious. *Centaurea moschata* L. Skipwiths.

Sweet Shrub   *Calycanthus floridus* L. The Lambolls to Bartram. Collinson. Jefferson.

Sweet Sultan   *Centaurea moschata* L. The Lambolls to Bartram. Skipwith.

Sweet William   *Dianthus barbatus* L. Jefferson, 1767. Skipwith.

Sumac   *Rhus typhina* L. Staghorn sumac. Clayton to England. "Most lovely," Collinson. Bartram's.

Sunflowers   *Helianthus annus* L. Pre-Columbian. With varieties. Catesby. Skipwith.

"Swallow-wort or Apocinon"   *Asclepias tuberosa* L. Butterfly weed. Collinson asked for root. "Swallow-wort" is also celandine, *Chelidonium majus,* brought in as an eye remedy.

Swertia   Dr. Garden's "Glory of the Blue Mountains." Collinson's "Pyramid of Eden," identified as *Swertia* by Linnaeus. Collinson asked for seeds for Gordon to raise. *S. caroliniensis* (Walt.) Ktze. Columbo. Jefferson's oval bed.

Symphoricarpus vulgaris **Michx.**   Coralberry. Indian currant. Now *Symphoricarpus orbiculata* Moench.

S. albus Blake is the western shrub M'Mahon named snowberry when he sent it to Jefferson, 1812, with the fragrant shrub *Ribes odoratum* Wendlands. Two common garden shrubs today but late for the eighteenth century.

Symplocarpus foetidus **L.**   Skunk cabbage. Collinson's pride.

Syringa   Lady Skipwith's "or Mock Orange" is now *Philadelphus coronarius* L. Our wild Carolina shrub is *P. inodorus* L. *Syringa vulgaris* L. is our common lilac and *S. persica* L. the other lilac, introduced in time for Custis' "collection" and praised by Collinson.

T

Taxodium distichum **Rich.**   (*Cupressus disticha* L.) Bald cypress. Byrd II commented from the Dismal, "These trees . . . shooting their large tops very high."

Bartram's. Fancied in England.

Taxus   Yew. *Taxus canadensis* Marsh. is the shrub. Washington's "Yew or Hemlock" is likely hemlock. Except for Custis, the day of the yew had not arrived on the American seaboard. No Prince's. No Bartram's.

Tephrosia virginiana **Pers.**   American goat's rue. Bartram to Collinson.

Thalictrum   Meadow rue. Collinson grew *T. aquilegifolium* L. from Virginia; *T. flavum* L., the yellow one, from Europe; and *T. dioicum* L. from Virginia.

Thermopsis caroliniana **L.**   Figured by Curtis in the *Botanical Magazine*. Skipwith.

Thuja occidentalis **L.**   Common arbor vitae, commonly called white cedar. Kalm solved the dispute over red and white cedar. Arbor vitae or white cedar was much requested: Clayton of Bartram, Collinson of Custis, Bartram of Custis. Bartram's.

Tilia   Linden. Lime. Basswood. *Tilia americana* L. is our native linden or basswood. *T. vulgaris* Hayre, the common European linden, was planted by early settlers.

Tipitiwitchet   Bartram's name for Venus' flytrap. *Dionoea muscipula* Ellis. Governor Dobbs of North Carolina described it to Collinson after he described *Schrankia* in 1760 and called it "Fly Trap Sensitive." Bartram sent to Collinson and Linnaeus. Collinson gave it to Gordon to raise. Collinson's garden, 1768.

Tobacco   *Nicotiana rustica* L. was introduced into Spain by Monardes and popularized in Europe by Nicot. Choicer varieties were found later as its cultivation became a way of life for many and of death for some. From King James against and William Byrd II pro, the opposing sides have never agreed. Collinson's hint to Bartram has also lasted — a good insect killer for fruit trees is water that has had tobacco leaves soaked in it.

Toothache Tree   *Zanthoxylum americanum* Moll. Catesby 26. Prickly ash. Catesby says the seed and bark are aromatic, hot and astringent, used by people inhabiting the seacoasts of Virginia and Carolina for the toothache. Collinson. Bartram's.

Trestle Flower   Lake Skipwith's name for the pale blue *Phlox divaricata* L., called also woods pink and wild sweet William.

Trillium erectum **L.**   Collinson.

Trillium sessile **L.**   Catesby. Skipwith.

Trollius europaeus **L.**   Globe flower. Skipwith. Catesby.

Trumpet Creeper, Trumpet Flower, Trumpet Vine   *Campsis radicans* (L.) Seem.

Trumpet Flower, Evening   *Gelsemium sempervirens* (L.) Ait.

Trumpet Honeysuckle, Coral Honeysuckle   *Lonicera sempervirens* L.

Tsuga canadensis **Carr.**   Common hemlock. *T. caroliniana* Engelm. Carolina hemlock.

Tuberoses   *Polianthes tuberosa* L. Skipwith. Jefferson.

Tulip   Custis' portrait shows him holding a tulip with a book on *The Tulip*

Trumpet Flower. Catesby's Plate 65,
Vol. I
Trumpet Honeysuckle *Lonicera
sempervirens* L.
Trumpet Flower, Evening *Gel-
semium sempervirens* (L) Ait.

in his hand. Parkinson shows many sorts. The parrot tulip was fancied by
Jefferson. Collinson sent seeds and offsets of the best breeding tulips to
Bartram.

Tulip Tree   *Liriodendron tulipfera* L. Universally acclaimed. Catesby. Collinson. Bartram's. Prince's.

Tupelo   *Nyssa sylvatica* Marsh. Black gum. Catesby 41. Bartram's.

Tussilago farfara L.   Coltsfoot. Naturalized since the earliest settlements.
Byrd II noted it "formerly used . . . for coughs and colds."

U

Ulmaria Filipendula   "The red or purple Ulmaria has flowered — a sweet
pretty thing and quite new." Collinson to Bartram, 1763. *F. ulmaria*
Maxim. Queen of the meadows.

Ulmus

    U. americana L. American white elm. Easily the world's most beautiful
    tree. Washington, January, 1785, "Found about half a dozen young
    elms . . ."

    U. campestris L. English elm.

    U. glabra Huds. Scotch elm. Wych elm. *Ulmus glabra* var. *camperdownii*
    Rehd. is the "umbrella tree" of nineteenth-century American lawn plant-
    ings.

Umbrella Tree   The great umbrella tree was the *Magnolia tripetela* L.
(formerly *Magnolia umbrella* Lam.).   Referred to among his several magnolias as the "Umbrella" by Bartram, 1762. This in a letter to Collinson,

who, in 1760, first succeeded in flowering "the Umbrella" sent him from South Carolina in 1753.

V

Vaccinium   The so-called blueberries of the New World grew in such profusion as to defy classification by any but scholars and to resist transplanting to, and cultivation in, the fruit garden until very recently. The two sorts of cranberry were also left in the wilds. Odd, when one sees other wild small fruits, strawberries, blackberries and raspberries brought in near the houses.

Valerian, Greek   The pre-Linnaean name for the *Polemoniun caeruleum* L., Jacob's-ladder of Europe, and for the smaller American native *P. reptans* L. Sent Collinson by Bartram.

The "Great Valerian" sent Bartram by the Lambolls was probably garden heliotrope, *Valeriana officinalis* L., a fine border plant.

Venus' Flytrap   See *Dionaea muscipula* Ellis. Bartram's "Tipitiwitchet."

Viburnum   In the familiar names of viburnum, arrow-wood, laurestinus and viorne, one may see the wide circle of those interested in viburnums after the first early settler brought the old familiar guelder rose with him to grow beside his door. *Viburnum opulus* var. *sterile* L. is its name today, and its round balls of bloom have given it its particular familiar name of "snowball bush," formerly *V. opulus* var. *roseum* L.

With this European visitor secured, we may consider the American viburnums all for sale from Bartram's Nurseries:

"*V. prunifolia* Great Black Haw" (now *V. prunifolium* L.). Requested by Collinson. Sent by Bartram, 1738.

"*V. triloba* Mountain Viburnum" (now *V. trilobum* Marsh.). Highbush cranberry.

"*V. dentatum* Arrow-Wood" (now *V. dentatum* L.). Southern *arrow-wood*.

"*V. alnifolium*" Bartram gives no other name. (Now *V. alnifolium* Marsh.) Alder-leaved viburnum. Hobblebush. Moosewood.

"*V. tinifolia* Water Elder" (now *V. nudum* L.). Possum or swamp haw. Marshall's *Grove* has all these and:

V. lentago L. Sweet viburnum. Nannyberry. The berries have a sweet pulp. Marshall calls it "Canadian Viburnum."

V. acerifolium L. Maple-leaved viburnum. Arrow-wood. Jefferson grew *V. Opulus, V. acerifolium, V. nudum* and *V. prunifolium*. Collinson seems to have grown the entire collection.

Returning to the guelder rose. In 1785 George Mason, who had borrowed Washington's coach, returned it with some "Guelder Rose." In Virginia this could have been what Collinson said was called the Virginia guelder rose, *Spiraea opulifolia* L.

When Jefferson planted at Poplar Forest "Althaeas, Gelder Roses, Roses, Calycanthus," one can guess the second-named was the Virginia native, as he later purchased "Gelder Rose" from Maine's Nursery in 1807.

Viola   That two of the universal favorites of all flower gardens, — pansies and violets — should both be under *Viola* makes listing them confusing.

So we begin with the pansies and the little *Viola tricolor* L., Johnny-jump-up, ladies' delight, heartsease. Tricolor, when planted by Jefferson 1767. *Très colores* and *Pensées* when he sent them from France. The plant nearest to today's "improved" pansies was the *Viola cornuta* L., horned violet or bedding pansy, which we now speak of as violas.

Violets were the *V. odorata* L., sweet violets. Now, alas, hard to find with fragrance. Lady Skipwith had both blue and white and, as well, grew the wild violet, which she called "Cut-leaved," as did Curtis in his picture of the *Viola pedata* L., which we call birdfoot. When Lady Skipwith lists her "violets" she notes, "very handsome. Some with a pansy flower."

Virginia   Since to list the plants referred to as "Virginia" would be to recapitulate much of what has gone before, we enter here only Virginia spiderwort, or *Tradescantia virginiana* L., one of the earliest of Virginia discoveries to be named for the place of its finding by John Tradescant.

W

Wahoo   Indian arrowroot. Burning bush. Spindle tree. *Euonymus atropurpureus* Jacq. One of those home remedies whose efficacy is indicated by the wild cry of its familiar name. Where an overdose could be poisonous, potions of the root bark could range from tonic to laxative. Held beneficial in liver disorders. Also very ornamental. Collinson. Bartram.

Wallflower   *Cheiranthus cheiri* L. Skipwith.

Under *Cheiranthus,* Miller lists sixteen sorts — all our old favorites in one basket: dames' violets, the stock gilliflowers and leucojum. Confusion may be forgiven when Skipwiths grow double and single "Old Bloody Wallflower" and "Widow Wallflower," not to be confused again with their widow wail flower, which is *Cneorum triococcum.* M'Mahon's offers ten-weeks stocks as *Cheiranthus,* and Miller says "Stock Gilliflowers are distinguished from Wall Flowers by their heavy leaves." The Skipwiths listed all these Miller-mentioned flowers separately, so we know they had them all.

Water Lily   See *Nelumbio, Colocasia, Nymphaea.*

Watermelon   *Citrullus vulgaris* Schrad. Washington. Originally from Africa. Another staple we owe to the slaves?

***Watsonia meriana* Mill.**   Skipwith.

Willow   Marshall gives three American willows:

"*Salix nigra* Rough American Willow," which "rises often with a leaning or crooked trunk . . . twenty feet."

"*Salix fericea* Ozier or Silky-leaved Willow . . . eight or ten feet."

"*Salix humilis* Dwarf Willow . . . three or four feet." Which does not sound very exciting, considering the fifty-odd native willows of today. Bartram offers only the "Red Willow," which turns out to be his *Cornus sanguinea*. Prince's Nurseries, however, know the popular taste, and offer the balsam willow, *Salix balsamifera* (Barr.) Anderss. And, at last, the all-popular weeping willow, *Salix babylonica* L., which Washington and Jefferson both fancied, as they both did the yellow willow, *Salix vitellina* L. The story of the weeping willow's advent has many versions, all involving an abandoned basket. Mr. Thomas Willing of Philadelphia was remembered by General Cocke of Virginia as having received a basket of fruit from Madeira. He threw the basket into a sink in his yard, where part of it took root and became the first weeping willow ever known in America. "Mr. Jefferson saw it in 1775 when he supposed from its size that at that time it must have been four or five years old."

Wisteria   Our own wild wisteria, now called *Wisteria frutescens*, was grown by Lady Skipwith as *Glycine frutescens* L., or her "Carolina Kidney Bean Tree," straight from her Carolina forests. But with the introduction of far grander sorts from China and Japan in 1818, the beautiful climbers were named by Nuttall in honor of Dr. Wistar of Philadelphia (whom we know from the dedication of the treatise on pokeweed, illustrated by William Bartram) and our native wilding was renamed to go with its glamorous cousins.

X

Xanthoxylum   See *Zanthoxylum*.

Xeranthemum annum **L.**   Common immortelle. Oldest of the everlastings. The Lambolls to Bartram.

Y

Yarrow   *Achillea millefolium* L.   An early favorite. Good for dried arrangements.

Yapon   A name, like wahoo, that may signify expression of the medicine's success. "Yappon or Carolina Tea," says Byrd, "passes for tea in North Carolina but is nothing like it." Sometimes called yaupon and credited to both the Carolinas and Virginia. Catesby called this "an emetic broth," used as a spring clean-out by the Indians, the dose accompanied by the burning of their bedding and the insides of their houses.

Ilex vomitoria Ait.

Ilex cassena Michx. Cassene. Closely similar.

Yellow-Root   *Hydrastis canadensis* L. "Pray send": Collinson to Bartram. Miller wrote Bartram that it is new and flowered in his garden.

Yellow-Wood.   (*Cladrastis tinctoria* Raf.   The *Virgilia lutea* of Michaux.) Now *Cladrastis lutea* Koch.

Yew   English yew.   *Taxus baccata* L.   Custis.   Jefferson.   Canadian yew. *Taxus canadensis* Marsh.   Washington refers to planting "Yew or Hemlock."

Yucca   Adam's needle.   *Yucca filamentosa* L.   Washington.   Skipwith.   Jefferson.

The silk grass of early fame in Virginia.   Said to have been introduced to England by Sir Walter Raleigh.

Z

Zanthoxylum

Z. americanum Mill.   The American northern prickly ash.   Toothache tree.

Z. clava-Hercules L.   The southern prickly ash.   Hercules'-club.

Gray spells it with an X Bailey with a Z.   Only Gray retains reference to Hercules.   Collinson noted "Toothache Tree of Virginia *vide* Catesby." In 1762, he saw "Toothache or Zanthoxylum Tree No. 1 in flower." Bartram, 1744, calls it *Zanthocelum*.

Zinnia multiflora. Curtis *Botanical Magazine*

Zea Mays Indian corn. Source of many experiments in hybridization late in the century.

Zephyranthes atamasco Herb. (Formerly *Amaryllis atamasco* L.) Atamasco lily. Catesby's *"Lilionarcissus virginiensis."* "A native of Virginia and Carolina . . . where in particular places the pastures are as thick sprinkled with them and martagons as cowslips and orchises are with us in England." (The Indian name for them, "cullowhee," is now the name of a town.)
Collinson, before 1739. Skipwith.

Zinnia multiflora L. A Mexican contribution, which arrived just in time to get into the eighteenth-century flower garden, but in such inferior shape that it is one of the few American wildflowers whose "improvement" we applaud.

Peter Collinson's List of Seeds and Plants

Peter Collinson's listing of seeds and plants he had received from John and William Bartram. From the Linnaean Society, London.

A List of Seeds contained in Each Box

1. Weymouth Pine or White Pine or Mast Pine
2. Hemlock Spruce Fir
3. Tulip Tree
4. White Ash
5. Swamp Pine
6. 2 and 3 Leaved Pine
7. Jersey Pine
8. Small Magnolia
9. Red Flowering Mapple
10. Striped Bark Mapple
11. Silver Leaved Mapple
12. Sugar Mapple
13. Dwarfe Mountain Mapple
14. Chinquapin
15. Sweet Chestnut
16. Poplar Leaved Birch
17. Larkspur
18. Beech Mast
19. Dogwood
20. Black Mulberry
21. Red Cedar
22. Lime Tree
23. Mountain Chestnut Leaved Oake
24. White Oake
25. Swamp White Oake
26. Champain Oake
27. Spanish Oake
28. Black Champian Oake
29. Barren Black Oake
30. Scrubby White Oake
31. Bastard Champian Red Oake
32. Dwarfe Scarlet Oake
33. Scarlet Leaved Oake
34. Willow Leaved Oake
35. Tupelo or Nissa or Black Gum
36. Black Spruce Firr
37. Great Mountain Magnolia
38. Judas Tree
39. Shagged Bark Hickory
40. Balsamick—Hickory
41. Small Twiged Sweet Hickory
42. Common Rough Hickory
43. Red Cedar Berries
44. Ceonothus or Red Root
45. Great Mountain Kalmia or Rhododendron
46. Olive Leaved Kalmia
47. Thyme Leaved Kalmia
48. Candleberry Myrtle or Mirica
49. Evergreen Privet or Prinos
50. Pensilvania [illegible]
51. Great round leaved Viburnum
52. Red Berries Viburnum
53. Mountain Viburnum
54. Arbortifa
55. Sweet Black Birch
56. Benjamin or all spice of Pensilvania
57. Clethra or Sweet Spirea
58. Stones of the Papaya Tree
59. Lotus or Celtis with Yellow Fruit
60. Jersey Tea an Epigea
61. Fringe Tree
62. Beach or Sea Sumach with Lentiscus Leaf
63. Horn beam
64. Spiked Andromeda
65. Red bud Andromeda
66. Broad-leaved Andromeda
67. White Spirea
68. Prinos or Red Winter Berry
69. Hydrangea
70. Black Larch
71. Silver Leaved Alder
72. Common Pensilvania Alder
73. Padus or Cluster Cherry
74. Broad Leaved Evonymus
75. [missing]
76. Bleu Berried Cornus
77. Toxicodendron Triphyllon
78. Toxicodendron or Poison Oak
79. Johnsonia
80. Ptelea arbor Trifolia
81. Broad Leaved Swamp Viburnum
82. Black Berried Cratagus
83. Red Berried Cratagus
84. Dwarfe Birch
85. Aralia Spinosa or Angelica Tree
86. Ash leaved Mapple
87. Cephalanthus or Buttonwood
88. Large Beach Cherry
89. Hamamelis or Gold Fringe Tree
90. Sweet Gum or Liquid Amber Tree
91. Red Sumach
92. Swamp Spanish Oake
93. Black Walnut
94. White Walnut
95. Honey Locust or 3 Thorn'd Acacia
96. Rhamnus occidentatis
97. Evonymus Scandens
98. Narrow Leaved Thorn
99. Broad Leaved Thorn
100. Highland Roses
101. Swamp Roses
102. [illegible]
103. Spiny Viburnum
104. Tough Viburnum
105. Red Spirea

Bibliography

Bibliography

For the convenience of those who, like myself, turn to the Bibliography before reading the book, I have made a record of where each volume I used was found. The key to the abbreviations of the sources follows:

A.	Author's Library
A.A.S.	American Antiquarian Society
B.A.	Boston Athenaeum
B.M.B.L.	British Museum Botanical Library
B.M.L.	British Museum Library
Boston Pub. Lib.	Boston Public Library, Rare Books
Cong. Lib.	Congressional Library
Countway	Francis A. Countway Library of Medicine, Harvard Medical School
D.O.	Dumbarton Oaks Garden Library
H.	Harvard, Houghton Library
Ips. Pub. Lib.	Ipswich Public Library
Kew	Royal Botanic Gardens Library
L.H.	L. Hodgkins
Lin. Soc.	Linnaean Society, London
M.H.S.	Massachusetts Historical Society
Mass. Hort. Soc.	Massachusetts Horticultural Society
N.Y. Pub. Lib.	New York Public Library, Rare Books
V. and A.	Victoria and Albert Museum, London
W.D.E.	W. D. Edmunds
Y.	Yale, Beinecke Library

493

Adams, Abigail. *Letters of Mrs. Adams,* Edited by Charles
    Francis Adams (Boston 1840)   B.A.
————. *New Letters of Abigail Adams,* Edited by Stewart
    Mitchell (Boston: Houghton Mifflin Co., 1947)   B.A.
Adams, Abigail and John. *Familiar Letters* (New York:
    1876)   A.
————. *The Book of Abigail and John* (Cambridge: Har-
    vard University Press, 1975)   A.
Adams Family Correspondence, Adams Papers, Series II
    (New York: Atheneum 1965)   A.
Adams, John. *Diary and Autobiography* (Cambridge: Har-
    vard University Press, 1961)   B.A.
———— *Adams-Jefferson Letters,* Edited by Lester J. Capon
    (Chapel Hill: University of North Carolina Press,
    1959)   A.
Addison, Joseph. *Essay on Taste* (Spectator No. 409)   A.
————. *Essay on Nature and Art in the Pleasures of the
    Imagination* (Spectator 414)   A.
Aiton, William. *Hortus Kewensis* (London: 1789)   A.
Amherst, Hon. Alicia. *A History of Gardening in England*
    (London: Quaritch, 1895)   D.O.
Bartram, John. *Letters,* Manuscripts at the British Museum
    Botanical Library   B.M.B.L.
————. *Observations. Travels from Pensilvania to On-
    ondage, Oswego, and the Lake Ontario* (London:
    1751)   Cong. Lib.
————. *Preface, Notes and Appendix for Franklin's Edition
    of Thomas Short's Medicina Britannica* (Philadel-
    phia: Franklin, 1751)   Countway
————. *Letters,* Manuscripts of the Linnaean Society and   Lin. Soc.
    British Museum Botanical Library   B.M.B.L.
Bartram, William. *Travels in the Carolinas, Georgia and
    Florida* (1791), Edited by Mark Van Doren (Dover
    Reprint, 1928)   A.
————. *Travels,* Edited by Francis Harper (New Haven:
    Yale University Press, 1958)   A.
Beach, S. A. *The Apples of New York* (Albany: 1905)   A.
Beatty, Richmond Croom. *William Byrd of Westover* (Bos-
    ton: Houghton Mifflin Co., 1932)   A.
Behn, Aphra, Mrs. *The Widow Ranter or the History of
    Bacon in Virginia* (Reprint, New York: Phaeton
    Press, 1967)   D.O.
Betts, Edwin Morris. *Thomas Jefferson's Garden Book*
    (Philadelphia: American Philosophical Society,
    1944)   A.
———— with Hazlehurst B. Perkins. *Thomas Jefferson's
    Flower Garden at Monticello,* (Richmond: 1941)   A.
————. *Thomas Jefferson's Farm Book* (American Philo-
    sophical Society, 1944)   B.A.
Beverly, Robert. *The History and Present State of Virginia,*

Edited by Louis B. Wright (Chapel Hill: University of North Carolina Press, 1947) A.

Bigelow, Jacob, M.D. *American Medical Botany* (Boston: 1817) Countway

———. *Florula Bostoniensis Native Medicinal Plants of the United States* (Boston: 1824) A.

Birket, James. *Some Cursory Remarks made by James Birket in his Voyage to North America 1750–1751* (Reprint, Yale, 1916) Cong. Lib.

Blanton, Wyndham B. *Medicine in Virginia in the Seventeenth Century* (Richmond: William Byrd Press, 1930) D.O.

———. *Medicine in Virginia in the Eighteenth Century* (Richmond: Garrett and Massie, 1931) D.O.

Blunt, Wilfrid. *The Art of Botanical Illustration* (London: Collins, 1950) A.

———. *The Compleat Naturalist, A Life of Linnaeus,* (London: Collins 1971), Both with acknowledged assistance by William T. Stearn A.

Boitard, M. *L'Art de Composer et Décorer Les Jardins* (Paris: date torn. About 1800) A.

Bordley, John Beale. *Sketches on Rotation of Crops* (Philadelphia: 1797) Cong. Lib.

———. *Essays and Notes on Husbandry and Rural Affairs* (Philadelphia: 1799) Cong. Lib.

Bradley, Richard. *The Country Gentleman and Farmer's Monthly Directory* (London: 1736) A.

———. *New Improvements of Planting and Gardening, Both Philosophical and Practical* (London: 1710) A.

———. *A Complete Study of Husbandry* (London: 1727) Mass. Hort. Soc.

Brett-James, Norman G. *The Life of Peter Collinson* (London: privately printed 1935) Mass. Hort. Soc.

Bridenbaugh, Carl and Jessica. *Rebels and Gentlemen* (New York: Reynall and Hitchock, 1942) D.O.

Bridenbaugh, Carl, *Myths and Realities, Societies of the Colonial South* (Baton Rouge: Louisiana State University Press, 1952) Cong. Lib.

Bruce, Philip Alexander, *Social Life in Old Virginia* (New York, Capricorn, 1965) A.

Buchan, William, M.D. *Domestic Medicine of the Family Physician* (Philadelphia: Dunlap, 1772) A.A.S.

Budd, Thomas. *Good Order Established in Pennsylvania and New Jersey* (London: 1685) Cong. Lib.

Buchoz, Pierre-Joseph. *Collections des Fleurs de la Chine Peintes dans le Pays* (Paris: 1772) D.O.

Bunyard, Edward. *Old Garden Roses* (London: Country Life, 1957) A.

Burke, Edmund. *A Philosophical Enquiry Into the Origin of Our Ideas of the Sublime and Beautiful* (London: 1759, Facsimile reprint, Scolar Press, 1970) A.

Burnaby, Andrew. *Travels Through the Middle Atlantic
    Settlements in North America 1759–1760* (Lon-
    don: 1798)   Cong. Lib.
Byrd, William II. *Letter to Hans Sloane 1709* (William and
    Mary Quarterly, 2nd Series, VI p. 186)   Cong. Lib.
———. *Letter to Lord Egmont 1736* (American Historical
    Review, 1896–1898)   Cong. Lib.
———. *Prose Writings of William Byrd of Westover*
    (Cambridge: Harvard University Press, 1966)   A.
    Includes: *Secrets History of the Line*
             History of the Dividing Line
             A Progress to the Mines
             A Journey to the Land of Eden   A.
———. *Secret Diary 1709–1712,* Edited by Louis B.
    Wright and Marion Tinling (Richmond: 1941)   A.
———. *Secret Diary 1739–1741,* Including *Letters* and
    Literary Exercises 1696–1726, Edited by Maude
    Woodfin and Marion Tinling (Richmond: 1942)   A.
Carter, J. M., Printer of Georgetown, D.C., *A Synopsis of
    Genera of American Plants* (Georgetown: 1814)   A.
Carter, Robert. *Letters of Robert Carter 1720–1727* (San
    Marino: Huntington Library, 1940)   B.A.
Catesby, Mark. *The Natural History of Carolina, Florida and
    the Bahama Islands* (London: 1731)   D.O.
Chambers, Sir William. *Dissertation on Oriental Gardening*
    (London: 1772)   Mass. Hort. Soc.
——— *The Art of Laying Out Gardens Among the Chinese*
    (Gentleman's Magazine, May, 1757)   V. and A.
Chapman, A. W. *Flora of the Southern States,* 3rd Ed. (New
    York: American Book Company, 1897)   A.
Chase, Isabel Wakelin Urban. *Horace Walpole: Gardenist*
    (Princeton: Princeton University Press, 1943)   B.A.
Chastellux, Marquis de. *Travels in North America,* Vol. I
    (Dublin: 1787) Vol. II (London: 1787)   A.
Ch'En Shou-Yi. *The Chinese Garden in Eighteenth-Century
    England,* Tien Hsia Monthly Vol. II (Photostated
    from Victoria and Albert Museum, Kindness of Ver-
    onica Babington-Smith)   V. and A.
Cheston, Emily Read. *John Bartram, 1699–1777* (John
    Bartram Association, Philadelphia, 1938)   A.
———. *William Bartram 1739–1823* (John Bartram As-
    sociation, Philadelphia, 1938)   B.A.
Clayton, John. *Flora Virginica,* Edited by Gronovius (Hol-
    land: 1762) Photolithograph by Arnold Arboretum,
    1946)   A.
Clifford, Joan. *Capability Brown* (U.K.: Aylesbury Shire
    Publications, 1974)   A.
Coats, Alice M. *Flowers and Their Histories* (London, New
    York, Toronto: Pitman Press, 1956)   A.
Coats, Peter. *Flowers in History* (London: Weidenfeld and
    Nicolson, 1970)   A.

Cobbett, William. *A Year's Residence in the United States
of America* (Reprint, Carbondale: Southern Illinois
University, 1964)   B.A.
Colden, Jane. *Botanic Manuscript,* Edited by H. W. Rickett
(New York: Chanticleer Press, 1963)   A.
Coles, S. W. *American Fruit Book* (New York: 1949)   A.
Collinson, Peter. *Commonplace Books.*   Lin. Soc.
———. *Hortus Collinsonianus,* Edited by L. W. Dillwyn
(Pamphlet printed 1843)   A.
———. *Notes Relating to Botany* (Collected by Aylmer
Bourke Lambert)   Lin. Soc.
Cook, Eben Gent. *The Sotweed Factor or a Voyage to Mary-
land — A Satyr in Burlesque Verse* (London: 1708)   B.A.
de Crèvecoeur, Hector St. John. *Letters from an American
Farmer* (New York: Signet, 1963)   A.
Curtis, William. *The Botanical Magazine or Flower Garden
Displayed* (London: 1787–1800)   B.A., D.O.
                                                          Mass. Hort. Soc.
Cutler, Manasseh. *Journals and Correspondence* (Cincin-
nati: 1880)   Countway
———. *Plants of New England* (Boston: 1785)   Countway
Dabney, Virginius. *Virginia, The New Dominion* (New
York: Doubleday, 1971)   A.
Dallaway, The Reverend James. *Supplementary Anecdotes
of Gardening in England,* with additions to Horace
Walpole's *On Modern Gardening* (London: Chatto
& Windus, 1876)   A.
Darby, John. *Botany of the Southern States* (New York:
Barnes, 1860)   A.
D'Argenville, A. J. Dézallier. See under Le Blond.   A.
Darlington, William. *Memorials of John Bartram and
Humphry Marshall,* Introduction by Joseph Ewan
(New York: Hafner, 1967)   A.
Deane, Samuel. *New England Farmer or Georgical Diction-
ary* (Worcester: Thomas, 1797)   Mass. Hort. Soc.
Dispensatories, *The National Standard Dispensatory* (Phila-
delphia: Lippincott, 1891)   A.
Downing, A. J. *The Fruits and Fruit Trees of America*
(New York: 1846)   A.
Drayton, Governor John. *The Carolinian Florist 1807* (Co-
lumbia: University of South Carolina Press, 1943)   A.
Dunthorne, Gordon. *Flower and Fruit Prints of the 18th
and 19th Centuries* (Washington, D.C.: 1938)   D.O.
Eliot, Jared. *Essays Upon Field Husbandry in New England
and Other Papers 1748–1762* (New York: AMS
Press, 1967)   A.
Ellis, William. *The Practical Farmer* (London: 1732)   A.
Evelyn, John. *Sylva 1664* (Scolar Press Facsimile,
1973)   A.
———. *Sylva, or a Discourse of Forest Trees and The
Propagation of Timber in His Majesty's Domin-
iums* with notes by A. Hunter (York: 1776)   A.

————. *Kalendarium Hortense 1706* (Reprint, Herb
   Grower, Falls Village Press, 1963)   A.
————. *Diary and Correspondence,* Edited by William Bray
   (London: Henry G. Bohn, 1859)   A.
Ewan, Joseph. *William Bartram, Botanical and Zoological
   Drawings of* (Philadelphia: American Philosophical
   Society, 1968)   A.
Ewan, Joseph and Nesta. *John Banister and His Natural His-
   tory of Virginia* (Urbana: University of Illinois
   Press, 1970)   A.
Fagin, N. Bryllion. *William Bartram, Interpreter of the
   American Landscape* (Baltimore: Johns Hopkins,
   1933)   A.
Fisher, Joshua Francis. *A Discourse on the Private Life and
   Domestic Habits of William Penn* (Philadelphia:
   1836)   Cong. Lib.
Fitzherbert, Sir Anthony. *Husbandry and Surveying from An-
   cient Tracts Concerning the Management of Landed
   Property* (London: 1767)   A.
Fletcher, Stevenson W. *John Bartram, Farmer-Botanist*
   (Typescript: John Bartram Association)   A.
Flexner, James Thomas. *Sir William Johnson, Mohawk
   Baronet* (New York: Harper, 1959)   W.D.E.
Fothergill, John. *Some Account of the Late Peter Collinson*
   (London: 1770)   B.M.B.L.
Fraser, Charles. *A Charleston Sketchbook 1796–1806* (Caro-
   lina Art Association, 1959)   A.
Frick, George Frederick with Raymon Phineas Stearns. *Mark
   Catesby, The Colonial Audubon* (Urbana: University
   of Illinois Press, 1961)   A.
Furber, Robert. *Twelve Months of Fruits* (London: 1732) D.O.
————. *Twelve Months of Flowers* (London: 1732)   D.O.
————. *A Short Introduction to Gardening* (London:
   1733)   Kew
————. *The Flower Garden Displayed* (London: 1734)   Kew
Gilpin, William. *Practical Hints Upon Landscape Garden-
   ing,* 2nd ed. (Edinburgh: 1835)   A.
Grant, Mrs. Anne. *Memoirs of an American Lady with
   Sketches of Manners and Scenery in America as They
   Existed Previous to the Revolution* (Longmans,
   1809)   A.
Griffith, R. Egglesfield, M.D. *Medical Botany* (Philadelphia:
   Lea and Blanchard, 1847)   A.
Harvey, John. *Early Gardening Catalogues* (Chichester,
   U.K: Phillimore and Co., 1972)   A.
Hatch, Alden. *The Byrds of Virginia* (New York: Holt,
   Rinehart and Winston, 1969)   A.
Havighurst, Walter. *Alexander Spotswood, Portrait of a
   Governor* (New York: Holt, Rinehart and Winston,
   Colonial Williamsburg, 1967)   A.

Herbst, Josephine. *New Green World* (New York: Hastings House, 1954)   A.

Heydrick, U.P. *A History of Horticulture in America to 1860* (Oxford and New York: Oxford University Press, 1950)   A.

———. *Grapes of New York* (Albany: 1908)   A.

Hogarth, William. *The Analysis of Beauty* (London: 1753)   A.

Hollingsworth, Buckner. *Her Garden was Her Delight* (New York: MacMillan, 1962)   A.

Ives, John M. *New England Book of Fruits* (Salem: 1847) A.

James, John. *Translation of The Theory and Practice of Gardening* By Le Sieur Alexander Le Blond (London: 1725)   A.

Jefferson, Thomas. *Notes on the State of Virginia* (New York: Harper Torchbooks, 1964)   Cong. Lib.

———. *Catalogue of the Library of Thomas Jefferson 1815* by E. M. Sowerby (Library of Congress, 1952)   A.

———. *Writings,* Collected by P. L. Ford, 12 vols. (New York: Putnam, 1892)   Cong. Lib.

———. *Garden Book,* Edited by E. M. Betts (Philadelphia: 1953)   A.

———. *Farm Book,* Edited by E. M. Betts (Philadelphia: 1953)   B.A.

Johnson, Samuel. *William Shenstone, Alexander Pope,* from *The Lives of the English Poets, The Works of Samuel Johnson,* Vol. XI (London: 1809)   A.

Kaempfer, Engelbert. *Amoenitatum Exoticarum* (Amsterdam: 1712)   D.O.

Kalm, Peter. *Travels in North America,* Edited by Adolph B. Benson. *English Version,* 1770 (Dover Reprint)   A.

Kirk, J. W. C. *A British Garden Flora* (London: Edward A. Arnold, 1927)   A.

Langley, Batty. *New Principles of Gardening* (London: 1728)   A.

Lauder, Sir Thomas Dick. *Sir Uvedale Price on the Picturesque,* Edition, 1810 (London: 1842)   A.

Lawson, John. *A New Voyage to Carolina,* Edited by Hugh Talmadge Lefter (Chapel Hill: University of North Carolina Press, 1967)   A.

Lear, Tobias. *Accounts of Tobias Lear,* Edited by Stephen Decatur, 1933.   B.A.

Le Blond, Alexander (for A. J. Dézallier D'Argenville). *Theory and Practice of Gardening,* Translated by John James, 2nd ed. (London: 1728)   A.

Lemery, Nichols. *Dictionaire au Traite Universel Des Drogues Simples* (Amsterdam: 1714)   A.

Lettsom, J. C. *Natural History of the Tea Tree* (London: 1772).   D.O.

Lick, David E. with Thomas R. Brendle. *Plant Names and*

Plant Lore Among the Pennsylvania Germans (Penn. German Society, 1927)   Mass. Hort. Soc.

Lockwood, Alice G. B. *Gardens of Colony and of State* (New York: Scribner's, 1931)   A.

Lossing, Benson J. *The Home of Washington and its Associations* (New York: Townsend, 1865)   Ips. Pub. Lib.

Loudon, J. C. *Encyclopaedia of Gardening* (London: 1835)   A.

Marambaud, Pierre. *William Byrd of Westover* (Charlottesville: University Press of Virginia, 1971)   A.

Marie, Alfred. *Jardins Français Classique des XVIIᵉ et XVIIIᵉ Siècles* (Paris: 1949)   A.

Marshall, Humphry. *Arbustum Americanum, The American Grove* (Philadelphia: 1785), Facsimile (New York: Hafner, 1967), Introduction by Joseph Ewan   A.

Mason, Francis Norton. *The Papers of John Norton and Sons, Merchants of London and Virginia 1750–1795* (Richmond: Dietz, 1807)   Mass. Hort. Soc.

Massey, A. B. *Medicinal Plants of Virginia* (Blacksburg: Virginia Polytechnic Institute, 1942)   Mass. Hort. Soc.

Mawe, Thomas, and John Abercrombie. *Universal Gardener and Botanist* (London: 1778)   D.O.

———. *Every Man his Own Gardner* (London: 1797)   A.

M'Mahon, Bernard. *The American Gardener's Calendar* (Philadelphia: 1806)   A.

Mill Hill School (Site of Collinson's "Little Paradise"). *Book of Plants* (Pamphlet)   A.

Miller, Philip. *The Gardener's and Florist's Dictionary* (London: 1724)   Kew

———. *The Gardener's Dictionary,* Abridged by the Author (London: 1735)   A.

———. *The Gardener's Kalendar* (London: 1775), Facsimile by National Capitol Area, Federation of Garden Clubs, 1971   A.

———. *The Gardener's Dictionary,* Eighth Edition (London: 1768)   A.

———. *Figures of the Most Beautiful, Useful and Uncommon Plants Described In The Gardener's Dictionary* (London: 1790)   D.O.

Millspaugh, Charles F., M.D. *Medicinal Plants* (Philadelphia: 1892)   A.

du Monceau, Duhamel. *Practical Treatise of Husbandry* (London: 1762)   Mass. Hort. Soc.

Morel, J. M. *Theorie Des Jardins ou L'Art Des Jardins De La Nature* (Paris: 1802)   A.

Morgan, Edmund S. *Virginians at Home* (Williamsburg: 1952)   A.

Napheys, G. H., M.D. *The Prevention and Cure of Disease* (Chicago: 1871)   A.

Oldmixon, John. *The British Empire in America* (London: 1708)   Cong. Lib.

Osborn, James, M. *Joseph Spence: Anecdotes of Books and Men* (Oxford: Oxford University Press, 1966)   A.

Parkinson, John. *Paradisi in Sole, Paradisus Terrestris 1629* (Reprint, London: Methuen, 1904)   A.

Parkinson, Richard. *A Tour in America, 1798, 1799, and 1800.*   B.A.

Penn, William. *Correspondence Between William Penn and James Logan and Others* (Philadelphia: 1870)   B.A.

———. *A Brief Account of the Province of Pennsylvania 1681.*   Cong. Lib.

———. *Information and Directions — A Further Account, 1685.*   Cong. Lib.

———. *A Letter to the Free Society of Traders, 1683.*   Cong. Lib.

———. *Description of West New Jersey, 1676.*   Cong. Lib.

———. *Charter of Liberties for Pennsylvania, 1682.*   Cong. Lib.

———. *Letter to the Earl of Sunderland, 1683.*   Cong. Lib.

———. *Letter to Governor Winthrop, 1700*   Cong. Lib.

———. *Letter to Col. J. Winthrop, 1696*   Cong. Lib.

Pepper, William, M.D. *The Medicinal Side of Benjamin Franklin* (Philadelphia: Campbell, 1911)   Countway

Pinckney, Elise. *Thomas and Elizabeth Lamboll, Early Charleston Gardeners* (Charleston Museum, 1969)   A.

Pope, Alexander. *Complete Poetical Works* (Boston: Houghton Mifflin Co., Cambridge Edition, 1903)   A.

Porcher, Francis Peyre, M.D. *Resources of the Southern Fields and Forests* (Charleston: 1869)   A.

Prince, William. *A Short Treatise on Agriculture of the Linnaean Botanic Garden at Flushing, New York* (New York: 1828)   B.A.

Pursh, Frederic. *Flora of North America* (London: 1816)   A.

Quincy. *Medical Lexicon* (Philadelphia: Franklin, 1751)   Countway

de la Quintinye. *Instructions pour les Jardins Fruitiers et Potagers* (Amsterdam: 1697)   A.

Randolph, John. *A Treatise on Gardening* (Reprint Appeals Press, 1924)   A.

Randolph, Sarah. *The Domestic Life of Thomas Jefferson,* 3rd edition (Monticello: 1967)   A.

Ravenal, Harriott Horry Rutledge. *Eliza Pinckney* (From *Women of Colonial and Revolutionary Times*) (New York: Scribner's, 1896)   A.

Rehder, Alfred. *A Manual of Cultivated Trees and Shrubs,* Second Edition, Twelfth printing (New York: Macmillan, 1974)   A.

Repton, Humphry. *The Art of Landscape Gardening,* edited by John Nolen (Boston: Houghton Mifflin Co., 1907)   A.

Richardson, Emma B. *Charleston Garden Plats* (Charleston Museum, 1943)   A.

Rowland, Kate Mason. *The Life of George Mason* (New York: Putnam, 1892)   A.

Rutland, Robert Allen. *George Mason, Reluctant States-*
man (Williamsburg: 1961)   A.

Sachs, Julius. *History of Botany* (Reissued, New York: Russell and Russell, 1967)   A.

Sanecki, Kay N. *Humphry Repton* (U.K.: Aylesbury Shire
Publications, 1974)   A.

Short, Thomas. *Medicina Britannica* with Bartram's Appendix. (Philadelphia: Franklin Press, 1751)   Countway

Shultz, Benjamin. *An Inaugural Botanico-Medical Disserta-*
tion (Philadelphia: 1795)   A.A.S.

Sioussat, St. George Leakin. *Virginia and The English Com-*
mercial System, 1730–1733 (Washington: American
Historical Association, 1906)   B.A.

Small, J. K. *Flora of the Southeastern United States,* 2nd ed.
(New York: 1913)   Mass. Hort. Soc.

Smith, A. William. *A Gardener's Book of Plant Names*
(New York: Harper and Row, 1963)   A.

Spence, Joseph. *Letter to the Rev. Mr. Wheeler Sept. 19,*
1751, from *Anecdotes of Books and Men,* edited by
James M. Osborn   A.

———. *Lists* and a *Sketch* from Spence Manuscripts at
Beinecke Library, Courtesy of James M. Osborn   Y.

Stearn, William T. *Excerpts on Linnaeus from the Hunt*
Catalogue (London: Nelson, 1966)   D.O.

———. *Botanical Latin* (London: Nelson, 1966)   D.O.

Steen, Nancy. *The Charm of Old Roses* (New Zealand:
Reed, 1966)   A.

Steiner, Bernard C. *The First Lord Baltimore and his Colo-*
nial Projects (Annual Report of the American Historical Association, 1905)   B.A.

Swem, E. G. *Brothers of the Spade* (Barre, Mass.: Barre
Press, 1957)   A.

Tennent, John. *Every Man His Own Doctor,* 3rd edition
(Philadelphia: Franklin, 1734)   A.A.S.

———. *An Epistle to Dr. Richard Mead,* 1738   Cong. Lib.

Varlo, C. *A New System of Husbandry* (Philadelphia:
Printed for the Author, 1785)   A.

Walpole, Horace, Earl of Orford. *On Modern Gardening,*
Chapter XXIII in Vol. III, *Anecdotes of Painting in*
England (London: Chatto and Windus, 1876)   A.

———. *Notes to a New Edition of Thomas Whately* and
Observations on Modern Gardening, with plates by
Mr. Wollet (London: 1801)   A.

Warren, Ira., M.D. *Warren's Household Physician for Physi-*
cians Families, Mariners and Miners (Boston: 1883)   L.H.

Washington, George. *Correspondence with James Anderson*
(Charlestown: 1800)   Cong. Lib.

———. *Collected Writings and Papers,* Edited by W. C.
Ford, 12 Volumes (Boston: Athenaeum)   B.A.

————. *Diaries,* Edited by John C. Fitzpatrick (Boston: Houghton Mifflin Co., 1925)   B.A.

————. *Catalogue of Washington's Library in the Boston Athenaeum* (Boston: 1897)   A.

————. *Letters on Agriculture to Arthur Young* (London: 1801)   B.A.

Watson, John Fanning. *Annals of Philadelphia and Pennsylvania* (Philadelphia: 1779)   Cong. Lib.

Watts, William. *Seats of the Nobility and Gentry* (London: 1779–86)   B.A.

Whately, Thomas. *Observations on Modern Gardening,* 3rd edition (London: Payne, 1771)   A.

Woodward, Carl Raymond. *Ploughs and Politicks* (New Brunswick: Rutgers University Press, 1941)   A.

Wertenbacker, Thomas J. *The Planters of Colonial Virginia* (Princeton: Princeton University Press, 1922)   A.

Wesley, John. *Primative Physic, or an Easy and Natural Manner of Curing Most Diseases,* 16th edition (Trenton: 1788)   A.A.S.

Xenophon. *Treatise of Householde* from *Ancient Tracts Concerning the Management of Landed Property* (London: 1767)   A.

Index

Index

bold